W9-DDD-679

THE
ABC-CLIO
COMPANION TO

The Media
in
America

Founded in 1857, Harper's Weekly: A Journal of Civilization *used investigative reporting and editorial illustrations to become a major source of social and political commentary until its demise in 1916.*

THE
ABC-CLIO
COMPANION TO

The Media in America

Daniel Webster Hollis, III

ABC-CLIO

All illustrations were provided by the Library of Congress, except the following: AP/Wide World Photos, 95, 102, 194, 281; NASA, 252.

Library of Congress Cataloging-in-Publication Data

Hollis, Daniel Webster, 1942–
    The ABC-CLIO companion to media in America / Daniel Webster Hollis,
III.
    p. cm. — (ABC-CLIO companions to key issues in American history and
life)
Includes bibliographical references and index.
ISBN 0-87436-776-X (alk. paper)
    1. Mass media —United States—History—Handbooks, manuals, etc.
I. Title. II. Series.
P92.U5H58 1995 302.23'0973—dc20 95-13097

ABC-CLIO, Inc.
130 Cremona Drive, P.O. Box 1911
Santa Barbara, California 93116-1911

This book is printed on acid-free paper ∞.
Manufactured in the United States of America

For
Lynda, Heather, and Adam

Contents

Preface

A number of textbooks have been published on journalism and some specialized studies exist for subjects such as computers or high-tech telecommunications. Yet, there is a need for an encyclopedic media reference source that covers all areas related to multimedia history. The ABC-CLIO Companions series is meant to complement other resources, such as monographs, rather than to be comprehensive. The selection of entries focused upon (1) notable "firsts" in the history of the media in America, and (2) media organs and personalities of significant influence. Further, selections have been balanced chronologically from colonial times to the present and geographically across the nation. Finally, each media form represented in both print and broadcast as well as varying technology has been included, showing its historical development and importance.

The criteria for information in entries included conciseness blended with historical facts without much elaboration. Every effort has been considered to make the Companion's use by readers efficient. Space devoted to comment or interpretation has been limited to the need for basic understanding only. Besides the table of contents, alphabetical listing of entries, and index, careful consideration has been given to make the Companion's format user-friendly. Important subjects without their own entries have been included in related entries referenced with a "See" label, while "See also" items are cross-referenced after entries. For those interested in pursuing any topic further, individual entries feature sources that can be used as a starting point. The complete reference list includes some bibliographies as well as general works. The chronology which highlights the major events in the various media categories provides a perspective upon the relationship of various events to each other.

I am grateful to ABC-CLIO and especially editor Todd Hallman for their encouragement and guidance throughout the project. Jacksonville State University granted a leave of absence in 1994 which allowed me to complete the research and writing. The History Department provided support including use of a laptop computer. My colleague Professor David T. Childress graciously read and offered suggestions for some subjects. The interlibrary loan service at Jacksonville State University, especially Debra Thompson, proved invaluable. My family to whom this book is dedicated, showed patience and support throughout my labors.

Introduction

The American media have suffered the slings and arrows of government censorship and intimidation as well as occasional wrath of the American public. Yet, the story of the media, in both their business and service functions, reveals a profound influence upon the peculiar characteristics of America and its people. Media have operated through most of American history on two often distinct levels: locally and nationally. Such a division of labor offered greater not less opportunity for media voices. The media affect or reflect public attitudes about virtually every area of American life: government, society, culture, religion, the economy, literature, science, education. Moreover, the variety of media forms has grown immensely during the course of the twentieth century allowing the public/consumer so many different choices of access to news, entertainment, education, and opinion that it would boggle the minds of earlier generations.

Beginning in the colonial period and far into the nineteenth century, the modest costs of printing meant that the number of competing sources seemed boundless in local media markets. Newspapers dominated the early era but actually approached their opportunities for public appeal and influence reluctantly. The early nineteenth century witnessed the emergence of a new media genre, periodicals ranging from general to specialized subject matter and target audiences. Technology, whether in the printing process or telecommunications, rapidly transformed the speed and extent of coverage available to media outlets. Individual media moguls soon dominated each category of the industry and demonstrated the media's power of persuasion as well as their pattern of selective emphasis. By the middle of the nineteenth century, many media organizations and owners proved that considerable profits rewarded aggressive and innovative talents.

With the advent of broadcast media after World War I, competition with the print media began to take shape despite some early alliances due to joint ownership in certain markets. The motion picture industry instantly found itself a popular molder of public tastes, fashion, and the cult of celebrity, a power that was not lost on industry executives. Television brought even more dramatic changes than radio because it competed with many of the specialized popular magazines as well as newspapers. Despite the relatively short span of its life, the computer already has impacted every single area of media activity. Still, throughout the history of the American media the factor that most often decided success or failure was management skill rather than pure technology. Thus, ultimately the bottom line for all media became the financial statement. In the second half of the twentieth century, media ownership shifted from individuals to corporate to public ownership. Additionally, individual media businesses became part of larger multimedia conglomerates in which the board room further displaced the media professionals in decision making. All of the top ten media companies in 1994 were multimedia conglomerates. Media critic Ben Bagdikian estimated that by 1993 twenty-three conglomerates controlled more than half the media outlets in America.

The media as much as any other American business have proven the adage that fulfillment and success are not limited to social elites. Many entrepreneurial media persons from Benjamin Franklin to Walter Annenberg have proven that ability and ingenuity are rewarded financially in America. Moreover, many first- and second-generation immigrants made their impression upon American media, including Joseph Pulitzer and Rupert Murdoch. Although women and minorities participated to some extent from the very early days of American media history, it was not until the twentieth century that they have assumed singular important roles.

Toward the end of the twentieth century, the phenomenon of "alternative media" has both broadened the public access and diluted the influence of traditional media power brokers such as the broadcast networks, *Time, New York Times, Washington Post, Los Angeles Times.* The public today can communicate through computer electronic mail or on-line bulletin boards, receive direct video broadcasts from satellites, tune in to 1,200 talk media shows with listener/viewer interaction, or produce their own local access television program. Alternative media have become popular in part because established media are blamed for a variety of perceived ills: checkbook journalism, ideological bias, ethical lapses, sensationalism, superficial news coverage, celebrity status for highly paid media messengers. Recent opinion polls show that the media have fallen below highly unpopular institutions such as the presidency and the Congress in believability and trustworthiness.

Throughout the history of the American media, the role of government has been a central factor in their development. In the early colonial period as part of the British Empire, colonial printers answered directly to the government because of Parliament's Licensing Act (1662) which served as a weapon of censorship. After the lapse of the Licensing Act in 1694, freedom of the press gradually took root but only after government was forced to retreat from its attempt to muzzle the press through the threat of "seditious libel" prosecution.

The American Revolution proved the value and potency of the press in marshalling public opinion against unpopular government. As a result, the initial Congress under the Constitution proposed the First Amendment, which protected both freedom of the press and speech against unwarranted government intrusion or regulation. Thereafter, when self-restraint or cooperation failed, courts interpreted the extent of press freedom or free speech. In short, the media certainly did not have a license to print or broadcast anything so that the media themselves, through organizations such as the American Society of Newspaper Editors and the National Association of Broadcasters, became chief policemen of the industry's ethical standards. Yet, government attempts to impose prior restraint upon the media have occurred periodically throughout our history notwithstanding the First Amendment.

At the same time that government sometimes sought to limit press freedom or free speech, political leaders found that media coverage could be coordinated for their benefit. Indeed, due to the proven example of the advertising industry's successful use of media to shape favorable images of products to consumers, the media have become the chief vehicle for political campaigns to project politicians' images to the public. Thus, it is sometimes difficult to distinguish whether politicians manipulate the media or the media unduly shape the public's image of the government or its officials.

The philosophical question regarding the proper role of the media has increasingly become a choice between dealing with reality and truth or merely manufacturing superficial illusions for the sake of profits. British journalist Malcolm Muggeridge once lamented that the media too often succumbed to abuse of power because it was easy "to exploit the weaknesses and wretchedness of men." Because contemporary media are first and foremost business enterprises where profit margins rule decision making rather than an impartial public service motive, perhaps the public expects too much in terms of media fairness and balance. Moreover, there is much less competent reporting and too much commentary by media professionals today compared to earlier eras. The reason is obvious; it is easier to express an opinion than dig out the facts of a story. During much of the nineteenth century, the public understood that most media expressed a point of view reflecting management's opinions. Thus, readers selected their sources with no illusion that the purported product was in any sense free of bias. Yet, most of today's media proclaim that their product is objective and free of bias. Hence, a more sophisticated and enlightened public has grown cynical about the anomalous claim versus the reality.

THE
ABC-CLIO
COMPANION TO

The Media
in
America

Abolitionist Movement

The ability of media to influence public opinion on social issues emerged first in the abolitionist attack on slavery from the 1830s to the Civil War. The objective of the abolitionist press was to educate Northerners about the evils of slavery so that constitutional action would abolish it. Beginning as a small minority in the 1830s, the abolitionists gained majority support for their position across the Northern states by the election of 1860.

The organized movement to abolish slavery actually began tardily and grew slowly. Slavery had been sanctioned by the Constitution and accepted as an issue for regulation by the states rather than by the federal government. The first serious debates about the status of slavery occurred as additional territory was acquired in the West. Following the War of 1812, a tacit agreement between slaveholding and nonslaveholding states provided for the admission of one slave state for each free state. The slave states in the South wanted to maintain an equal number of votes in the Senate to block any attempts to regulate slavery, since the nonslaveholding majority grew larger each year in the House of Representatives. Thus, the dispute over the status of slavery in Missouri during 1819 and 1820 became a prelude to later sectional clashes over the issue.

Before William Lloyd Garrison founded *The Liberator* in 1831, abolitionists had depended on personal persuasion to advance their cause. Garrison's paper featured clippings from Southern newspapers about the repression of slave unrest as well as testimony about the evils of the slave trade and the hardships of life and work for slaves in the South. *The Liberator* stirred immediate hostile reaction from many Northern editors as well as Southern slave interests. It also provided a model for other abolitionist newspapers. The headquarters of James G. Birney's *Philanthropist*, published in Cincinnati, was attacked by angry mobs despite Birney's rather moderate tone. Elijah Lovejoy's *St. Louis Observer* caused such a reaction that the operation was moved across the Mississippi River to Illinois. Nevertheless, it was destroyed twice by mobs there, and a third attack led to Lovejoy's murder in 1837.

Black editors also joined the abolitionist cause pioneered by Garrison. In 1827, John B. Russwurm and Reverend Samuel Cornish launched the first black-owned newspaper, *Freedom's Journal*, in New York City. Although it lasted only a couple of years, *Freedom's Journal* provided news to the black community as well as voicing its opposition to slavery. David Walker first published his famous "Appeal" to abolish slavery in *Freedom's Journal*. Phillip Bell printed the *Weekly Advocate* (later the *Colored American*) from 1837 to 1842 in New York City, with Cornish serving as editor. Harvard graduate Dr. Martin Delaney started *The Mystery* from Pittsburgh in 1843 as an outspoken voice for blacks. In 1848, the paper was sold to the African Methodist Episcopal Church; it was renamed the *Christian Herald* (later the *Christian Recorder*) and is still published today, making it the oldest black weekly. Other black-owned papers were published in Cleveland, New Orleans, and San Francisco up to the Civil War.

Former slave Frederick Douglass's contributions to abolitionist publications gave authenticity and frankness to the antislavery campaign in the 1830s and 1840s. Douglass founded his *North Star* in 1847 and continued to publish the weekly from New York City until 1860 (later renamed *Frederick Douglass' Paper*). Circulation reached 3,000, and the *North Star* became a leading voice of influence in Northern cities clamoring for abolition.

The abolitionist campaign ultimately aimed for political action to complement the education process. The first major political effort was the petitioning campaign in the 1837 session of Congress. Sympathetic congressmen introduced petitions that they hoped would be debated, highlighting the issue before the nation. The House of Representatives adopted a "gag rule" that

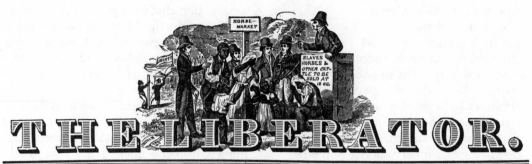

THE LIBERATOR.

VOL. I.]   WILLIAM LLOYD GARRISON AND ISAAC KNAPP, PUBLISHERS.   **[NO. 33.**

BOSTON, MASSACHUSETTS.]   OUR COUNTRY IS THE WORLD—OUR COUNTRYMEN ARE MANKIND.   [SATURDAY, AUGUST 13, 1831.

William Lloyd Garrison's abolitionist paper The Liberator *reported on the evils of slavery. The controversial publication became a model for other antislavery newspapers.*

prevented debate on the floor, but the Senate had a full airing of the petitions. The abolitionists organized third parties for presidential election years, beginning with the Liberty Party in 1840. The Free-Soil Party in 1848 supported the Wilmot Proviso, which would have prevented slavery in any western territory acquired from Mexico. The Republican Party, which was founded in 1854, was essentially an abolitionist party at first. The abolitionist press spoke loudly for the third-party efforts during the campaign years and succeeded in using elections as yet another platform to publicize their message.

The major Northern dailies divided over the slavery issue prior to the Civil War. The most powerful voice against slavery was Horace Greeley's *New York Tribune* after its founding in 1841. Greeley consistently and vigorously denounced slavery in his paper, first supporting Northern Whig antislavery efforts and then switching in 1854 to the new Republican Party. Yet Greeley did not obtain support from the other dailies, William Cullen Bryant's *Post* being a notable exception. James Gordon Bennett's *Herald* reflected the mainstream sentiment that abolitionists were too radical and unrealistic in their demands. In the Midwest, Joseph Medill's *Chicago Tribune* mirrored Greeley's sentiments about slavery. By the 1860 election, most of the mainline Northern newspapers had swung over to at least tacit sup-

port for the end of slavery, a testimony to the persuasion of abolitionist editors. The press strongly backed Republican Abraham Lincoln's election in 1860, which sealed the fate of slavery as well as the temporary union of the states.

See also Douglass, Frederick; *Freedom's Journal;* Garrison, William Lloyd; *New York Tribune* and *Herald Tribune.*

Reference Dillon, Merton L., *The Abolitionists: The Growth of a Dissenting Minority* (1974).

Advertising

The most important source of media income from the early newspaper days to the multimedia era of the late twentieth century has been advertising. The demonstrated success of advertising created an intense competition among industries to achieve innovative methods of marketing their products. By the mid-nineteenth century, an advertising industry began to burgeon, centered along Madison Avenue in New York City. The 1906 Pure Food and Drug Act brought about the first federal regulation of advertising, which led to debates about the First Amendment rights of advertisers.

Although advertising first appeared in the Boston News-Letter in its second issue of 1704, publishers did not solicit ads. However, papers that did not sell significant advertising found themselves in dire financial straits. By the middle of the eighteenth century, enterprising newspapers were actively selling ads for three to five shillings for ten lines or less, which took up half or more of their space. Early ads were essentially announcements of the availability of goods or services printed without artifice. Indeed, the physical appearance of the ads was more like that of a modern classified section. Prominent among early ads were requests for the return of runaway slaves or for help in discovering the identity of thieves or recovering deserters during wartime. Merchandise ads for clothing, foods, beverages, or books usually did not mention prices. Ads for medicinal products were notorious for their outrageous claims. Numerous lottery ads sought to raise money for various causes, including the financing of colleges. Ads announced ship sailings and theater schedules in papers of port cities.

During the Revolutionary War, advertising increased because of the many requests for material assistance for the military. The war caused advertising rates to double, but they fell back after the end of fighting to about 50 cents a square (12 lines) for the first ad. Legal notices generally sold at a higher rate than commercial ads. After independence, mercantile dailies could fill 12 of their 16 columns with advertising, since many of their readers bought the papers for the ads alone. Some ads covered two columns with large type and remained prominent on the front page. Even partisan political papers devoted as much as three-fourths of their space to advertising. By the 1820s, some newspapers offered advertisers an annual rate of $32 to $40, with a subscription included.

When major dailies converted to an eight-page format at midcentury, most advertising moved to the back three or four pages. Papers still had to economize space and kept ads in small type—the so-called agate rule—and usually within a single column. Ads remained concise and rarely covered an entire column. James Gordon Bennett's *New York Herald* stopped accepting annual ads and required ads to be placed daily after 1847, as a means of attracting readers. Advertisers in the 1850s designed the logotype format (using agate type to

form a large capital letter), spanning two or three columns, to avoid the agate rule. Others simply reprinted a short statement numerous times in a column to gain readers' attention. The "penny press" papers, such as Charles Dana's *New York Sun*, began reducing the square from 12 lines to six, for the same 50-cent charge. Advertisers began to negotiate rates with publishers but were required to make advance payments.

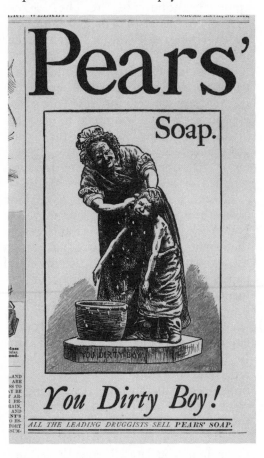

This Pears' soap advertisement appeared in Harper's Weekly *in 1883. The ad is typical of merchandise marketing in that the price is not mentioned.*

Several newspaper advertising salesmen established their own advertising agencies in the 1840s. Volney Palmer founded the first agency in Philadelphia in 1841 and sold ads for newspapers on a commission basis. Palmer's business also had offices in New York City and Baltimore. In the

1850s, S. M. Pettengill founded another major advertising company in New York City. Because of the fluctuation in rates at midcentury, advertising agents often obtained as much as a one-half return for their commissions. The most difficult ads to handle were those for patent medicines, which often smacked of quackery. Newspapers tended not to censor the ads at first, preferring to fall back on the principle of caveat emptor, let the buyer beware. The *New York Times* set the standard in the 1850s for honest advertising, which meant refusing patent medicine ads.

By the end of the Civil War, most newspapers routinely positioned advertising on the back pages, except for New York's *Herald* and *Sun*, which continued to place ads on the front pages. Although the federal government enacted a wartime 3 percent tax on advertising in 1862, the measure was repealed in 1867.

George Rowell founded an advertising agency in Boston in 1865; it later moved to New York City and became the largest in the nation. Rowell started the "advertising list," which offered to buy space in several papers for a set price and guaranteed payment to papers. In 1869, Rowell began publishing the *American Newspaper Directory*, which included advertising rates and circulation figures. Francis W. Ayer founded the N. W. Ayer & Son agency (named for his father) in 1869 and began publishing a newspaper annual in 1880. Advertising income doubled in the decade of the 1870s, totaling almost $40 million by 1880.

Advertising rates remained flexible throughout the late nineteenth century. The *New York Herald* had a reputation for having the highest rate at 36 cents per line in 1883. When Joseph Pulitzer bought the *New York World* in 1883, he offered ads at half the *Herald*'s rate. Rates in Boston were half of the New York average, and they were one-third lower in Philadelphia. The *World* allowed two- or three-column ads, thereby violating the traditional agate rule, and also allowed illustrations.

The advent of department stores such as Wanamaker's in Philadelphia, Stewart's in New York, and Field's in Chicago created the biggest boon to advertising sales in the 1880s. Still, patent medicines continued to lead advertisers overall, although some papers and magazines would not accept such ads. Soap manufacturers such as Cincinnati's Procter & Gamble developed some ingenious ads for products, including Ivory soap. Baking powders, baby food, and seed also emerged as new clients. The *Philadelphia Public Ledger* pioneered the format of classified advertising after the Civil War. By 1890, the Sunday edition of the *Chicago Tribune* contained about 15 pages of classified ads.

By the time of World War I, advertising income had reached $250 million, more than six times the 1880 total. Advertising agencies led by N. W. Ayer & Son entered new realms of copywriting, graphic design, and market research in the 1890s. Psychologists such as Walter D. Scott became consultants to ad agencies, which experimented with new forms of display and various jingles and slogans. Bicycles and cereals became the new advertising rage in the 1890s, followed by automobiles after 1910. Although national companies bought space chiefly in magazines, local department stores advertised mainly in newspapers.

When muckraking journals such as *Collier's* assailed patent medicine ads, Congress moved to require accurate advertising (but not labeling) as part of the 1906 Pure Food and Drug Act. After relying on caveat emptor for so long, many publishers tried to make a virtue of publishing only clean ads. The Associated Advertising Clubs of America, founded in 1905, adopted an ethical code for truth in advertising. By the early 1920s, 37 states had adopted statutes making false advertising a misdemeanor. The American Association of Advertising Agencies was founded in 1917, and its members eventually controlled three-fourths of all advertising.

Much of early radio advertising fostered sales of the parent newspaper. In 1922, commercial advertisers paid only $50 for ten minutes of advertising time. The Radio Act of 1927 stated only that advertising must be clearly identified as a paid announcement. Network program "sponsorship" by advertisers grew slowly, beginning at one-fourth and increasing to one-third by 1930 and to nearly 100 percent by the 1940s. Albert Lasker, owner of the Lord & Thomas agency, became the most successful advertising innovator of the postwar era, making Pepsodent toothpaste and Lucky Strike cigarettes known to all. Ads increasingly featured testimonials about the effectiveness of products as well as touting protection against the social dangers of things such as bad breath or body odor. Ford Motor Company spent $1 million promoting the new Model A car in 1927, and cigarette advertising employed contests as a sales gimmick.

Advertising revenues had reached a peak of $860 million when the stock market crashed in 1929. The Great Depression affected newspaper circulation less than it did advertising. Advertising income dropped each year after 1929 and hit a low point of $470 million in 1933. Recovery was gradual, with income back to $630 million in 1937, just below the 1920 total. Advertising losses caused some marginally financed papers to either fold or merge with others.

Organizations such as the Association of National Advertisers and the American Newspaper Publishers Association (Bureau of Advertising) sought to monitor false advertising, but in 1938, Congress gave the Federal Trade Commission oversight authority to prevent misleading ads. The post–World War II era saw advertising rates raised by 20 to 25 percent, and income increased from $2 billion in 1941 to $4 billion by 1948. Increased advertising for television—known as commercials—in the 1950s boosted total spending to $11 billion by 1959. Television advertising rates were pegged to audience ratings, determined by companies such as A. C. Nielsen. Advertising space increased to about 60 percent in most daily newspapers by the 1940s, up from an average of 40 percent earlier in the century. Market research using behavioral psychology became a driving force behind ads and commercials in the 1950s. Use of color in newspaper and especially magazine advertising was also notable in the 1950s.

Advertisers became concerned about increased government regulation and relied on the First Amendment to protect their industry's flexibility. During the 1970s, the Supreme Court ruled that although advertising must be given First Amendment protection, such a grant was not an absolute license. The government required tobacco products to carry hazardous health warning labels on packaging in the 1960s but only later required such disclaimers in advertising. The government prohibited advertising liquor on television but allowed beer and wine ads. By 1986, the most expensive television ads were those airing during the Super Bowl—at $1 million per minute. The largest advertisers in the late 1980s were Phillip Morris, Procter & Gamble, and General Motors. About 50 million television commercials were broadcast in 1988, and the average citizen was exposed to as many as 5,000 advertisements per day. Computer technology became essential to quantitative advertising market research in the 1970s.

Reference Fox, Stephen, *The Mirror Makers: A History of American Advertising and Its Creators* (1984).

American Broadcasting Company (ABC)

The American Broadcasting Company (ABC) was created in 1943 as part of a purchase of one of the National Broadcasting Company's (NBC's) radio networks. ABC followed the other two networks—NBC and the Columbia Broadcasting System (CBS)—into television broadcasting and competed well in the entertainment and news areas as one of the big three.

After the Federal Communications Commission (FCC) criticized NBC for its monopolistic practice of operating two radio networks—the red and the blue—NBC reluctantly agreed to sell its less profitable 168-station blue network to Edward J. Noble. The purchase was financed by Noble's candy fortune and loans from New York banks. Although the blue network had designed a discount advertising format to promote its daytime programs, it had yet to make a profit when ABC acquired it. Indeed, except for George Hicks's coverage of the Allies' 1944 D-day landings in Normandy, ABC was scooped by other networks in war coverage.

ABC's new programming director, Adrian Samish, moved away from the daytime soap operas flourishing on competing networks to a game-show format. The network also contracted with singing star Bing Crosby to produce prerecorded musical programs. Then in 1948, ABC launched its first television program, a documentary on New York City. A professional football game was televised to several stations in the Midwest later that year. The ABC network was able to make the transition from radio to television without losing more ground to its competition.

Recognizing that entertainment would become even more of a premium with television, some Hollywood studios such as Twentieth Century Fox offered to buy ABC as an outlet for televising their old films. ABC refused Fox's offer and instead agreed to merge with United Paramount Theaters in 1951, resulting in the first cooperative venture between Hollywood and broadcasting. Significantly, Leonard Goldenson of Paramount became president of ABC, a post he held for the next 30 years. Goldenson divided the company into five segments: radio, television, radio stations, television stations, and films. He cut deals with Walt Disney and Warner Brothers in 1954 for the production of innovative television programs such as the fantasy-filled "Disneyland" and the classic action-adventure "Cheyenne." Also in 1954, partly because it had little daytime programming, ABC was the only major network to provide extensive coverage of Senator Joseph McCarthy's hearings into supposed Communist infiltration into the U.S. Army. The ratings success of the McCarthy hearings allowed ABC to become serious about regular daytime programming.

Even though ABC became an industry leader in 1961, when it replaced the 30-second commercial break in prime-time programs with a 40-second break to allow more advertising, its financial base was shaky. Its decision to convert to all-color television programs in 1965 caused a severe financial strain. International Telephone and Telegraph (ITT) loaned ABC $25 million in 1966 in preparation for a merger that did not occur. Although the governing boards of ABC and ITT as well as the FCC approved of the merger, the Justice Department objected because of antitrust questions, and the deal was called off in 1968.

Despite winning respect from media professionals, ABC still remained in the shadow of NBC and CBS. One of the avenues to equality was the sports programming implemented by Roone Arledge: "Wide World of Sports" in the 1960s and "Monday Night Football" in the 1970s. These successes were complemented with Olympic Games coverage every four years, which made the events immensely popular for the first time in the United States. Arledge later became head of ABC news. ABC was able to attract talent from the other networks, including NBC's Barbara Walters, who became a news anchor, and CBS's chief programmer Fred Silverman. ABC's daytime soap operas began to compete well with NBC and CBS, and its news division began the innovative "Nightline" show with Ted Koppel in 1980.

ABC's evening news program, anchored by John Daly until 1960, provided competent presentations, but the ratings trailed those of NBC and CBS. ABC attempted to strengthen its ratings in 1968 by imitating the highly successful NBC anchor duo of Chet Huntley and David Brinkley. Howard K. Smith and Frank Reynolds teamed until 1970, when former CBS newsman Harry Reasoner joined Smith. Neither combination stirred audience movement, and ABC hired NBC's "Today" show host Barbara Walters to be coanchor with Reasoner in 1976. Yet the real anchor success story for ABC evening news was Peter Jennings. His first stint as anchor from 1965 to 1968 was unimpressive, but a more mature and experienced Jennings returned in 1983 to lead ABC evening news to the top of the ratings.

During the 1980s, merger mania struck U.S. business. Media conglomerate Capital Cities Communications, which owned newspapers in Kansas City and Fort Worth as well as several radio and television broadcasting stations, purchased ABC for $3.5 billion. ABC approved the sale in large part to avoid the possibility of a hostile takeover by an unwanted suitor such as media mogul Ted Turner, who would have dissolved ABC into his own companies. Goldenson stepped down as chief executive officer after the merger in favor of Thomas S. Murphy, a Capital Cities executive. In 1987, Capital Cities/ABC revenues were the largest in the industry at more than $3.2 billion.

Reference Quinlan, Sterling, *Inside ABC: American Broadcasting Company's Rise to Power* (1979).

American Newspaper Publishers Association (ANPA)

From its founding in 1887, the American Newspaper Publishers Association (ANPA) has fought to protect the interests of the nation's daily newspapers. The ANPA has tended to be conservative in its rivalries with other media, such as radio, and in its response to government regulatory efforts. Yet the ANPA has consistently supported technological improvements in publishing.

By 1880, 17 local and statewide newspaper trade associations existed to promote their business, but most of the papers represented were small dailies or weeklies. In 1885, these individual groups consolidated into the National Editorial Association, but the major dailies were still unorganized. William H. Brearly, advertising manager of the *Detroit Evening News*, convinced other business representatives of the major dailies that their papers needed access to national advertising. The result was the formation of the ANPA in 1887 with 46 charter members.

Although publishers such as James W. Scott of Chicago and Charles W. Knapp of St. Louis were early leaders, most of the presidents of the ANPA were managing editors or business managers. The ANPA tended to oppose labor unions and strikes, tried to moderate increases in newsprint prices and postage rates, and promoted technological improvements, but the primary concern was advertising. Many dailies depended on advertising agents to obtain sufficient ad revenue. Agents often forced rival publishers to bid against one another, driving ad rates higher—along with the agents' commissions. Advertising rates were pegged to circulation, which was often difficult to calculate. In order to assist its members' competition with magazines, the ANPA established a Bureau of Advertising in 1913. During the ANPA's early history, the percentage of newspaper revenues from advertising rose from about half in the 1880s to about two-thirds by the time of World War I.

Membership in the ANPA continued to grow in the twentieth century. By the 1930s, there were 850 members, and in 1960, there were 1,200 members. Its leadership since the 1940s has been more progressive than in the early decades. The ANPA did not oppose radio stations carrying news in the 1920s, partly because many newspapers owned radio stations and there was a belief that radio news reports would actually increase newspaper sales. With the appearance of offset printing, the ANPA established a research center in 1951 to aid members in making the transition from hot to cold typesetting. The Research Institute (since 1954) continued to assist publishers by maintaining a flow of information about expanding technology. In 1960, the ANPA founded the Newspaper Information Service to coordinate newspaper publishing with educational institutions as well as to serve the general public. The service promoted the study of journalism as a career, created awards for high school and college newspapers, and published a variety of brochures and newsletters. The ANPA was a strong supporter of accreditation of college journalism schools.

The opposition to government intrusion led the ANPA to occasional battles with the federal government. After many years of trying, it succeeded in 1913 in removing the import tariff on foreign newsprint. When Congress passed the National Recovery Act in 1933, calling for government supervision in the workplace, the ANPA opposed closed shops and favored exempting newsboys from child labor codes. At the same time, publishers accepted the requirement for a 40-hour workweek for medium-sized and large dailies. The National Recovery Administration (NRA) accepted the ANPA code, but the NRA labor codes were declared unconstitutional in 1935. Nonetheless, the National Labor Relations Act reinstated most of the provisions of the NRA, such as the right to collective bargaining.

During the 1960s, increased operating costs, competition, and television's popularity forced some city newspapers to enter into joint operating agreements to pool resources and services. In 1969, however, the Supreme Court scuttled the joint operating agreements, charging that they violated the antitrust laws by eliminating competition. The decision prevented competing dailies from sharing information and facilities. The ANPA lobbied for passage of the Newspaper Preservation Act of 1970, which allowed the revival of joint operating agreements under specified conditions. The ANPA has proved on more than one occasion that its lobbying clout with presidents and Congress is considerable.

See also Newspaper Preservation Act.

Reference Emery, Edwin, *History of the American Newspaper Publishers Association* (1949).

American Society of Newspaper Editors (ASNE)

A concern for self-regulation and ethics led the editors of major city dailies to establish the American Society of Newspaper Editors (ASNE) in 1922. The organization soon broadened to include medium-sized papers. Since its founding, the ASNE has been the conscience of editorial boards and provides specific guidelines in its canons.

The leader behind the organization of the ASNE in New York City was Casper S. Yost, editor of the *St. Louis Globe-Democrat*, who served as president for the first five years. Actually, given the absence of regulation or guidelines over the previous 200 years, editors had encountered few difficulties related to ethical behavior. Yet heightened competition, spurred by publishing's fixation on profitable balance sheets in the twentieth century, led many editors to question the direction of the profession.

Initially, as a professional organization, the ASNE limited its membership to editors in chief, editorial page editors, and managing editors of daily papers in cities of at least 100,000 population. Soon the population limit was lowered to 50,000, and the board of directors was allowed to invite notable editors from even smaller newspapers to join the ASNE. The group holds annual meetings in Washington, D.C., to discuss relevant professional issues. It publishes a monthly bulletin and the annual proceedings of its meetings.

At the first annual meeting in 1923, Henry John Wright of the *New York Globe* convinced the organization to approve a code of ethics known as the "Canons of Journalism." The preamble cited the necessary qualities of an editor—intelligence, knowledge, experience, reason—as well as the responsibilities of being a teacher to other journalists and an interpreter for readers. The categories of the canons included responsibility to the public, support for freedom of the press, independence from all influences, honesty, accuracy, impartiality, fair play, and decency.

The question of how the ASNE would respond to clear violations of its code occurred in the 1920s. Fred G. Bonfils, copublisher of the *Denver Post*, was charged with blackmailing Harry Sinclair over the infamous Teapot Dome oil scandal. Willis J. Abbot of the *Christian Science Monitor* and Tom Wallace of the *Louisville Times* wanted the ASNE to be a vigorous enforcer of its canons. They persuaded the membership to expel Bonfils, but president Yost argued that the ASNE should not become a police force, and the decision was overturned. Bonfils resigned voluntarily from the ASNE.

In a 1933 resolution approved by the ASNE, members agreed to allow interpretive reporting in their papers. The main reason for the clause was the growing tension on the international scene caused by totalitarian aggression. Under the new policy, reporters could not only reveal their subjective thoughts more readily but also become more specialized in their coverage. A new phenomenon known as "bylines" appeared, wherein writers who used facts with opinion signed their articles. Such bylines appeared more frequently in large dailies.

Henry R. Luce and Robert M. Hutchins created an uproar in the media with their Commission on Freedom of the Press in the 1940s. The commission's 1947 report decried the tendency toward monopolies, which it said endangered freedom of the press. In response to press criticism of the commission, in 1950, the ASNE named a ten-member committee of editors and educators to assess the state of the profession. Their report stressed the necessity for free competition but argued that media professionals rather than owners were the ultimate arbiters of freedom of the press.

As the role of reporters changed from gatherer of news to commentator, and as the function of editors and news anchors often became one of celebrity, the public's favorable view of the press declined sharply, beginning in the 1970s. Media professionals have revitalized ethical concerns from the boardroom to the classroom. The ASNE itself responded to the clamor when its standards for ethics were updated in 1975 with a "Statement of Principles" replacing the 1923 canons. The statement differed little from the earlier canons, except for an emphasis on the protection of freedom of the press and on the responsibility of editors to maintain integrity.

References Pitts, Alice Fox, *Read All About It— Fifty Years of the ASNE* (1974); Saalberg, Harvey, "The Canons of Journalism: A 50-Year Perspective," *Journalism Quarterly* (1973).

Animation

Although animated drawings existed before the age of motion pictures, the impact of animation on media paralleled the emergence of movies. Initially, animation required an artist to spend hours painstakingly drawing each frame for the camera. As an art form, animation reached a peak of influence at the Walt Disney studios in the 1930s through 1950s. Computerized images introduced in the 1970s made possible the sophisticated lifelike portrayals in movies such as the *Star Wars* trilogy and *Jurassic Park*.

Beginning in the 1820s, inventors sought a method to photograph objects in motion. Drawings were animated with lantern slides in children's toys as early as 1825, prior to the invention of the daguerreotype photographic system in 1838. After photography emerged, animation turned to the use of still photos shown in rapid succession. Coleman Sellers of Philadelphia built the first equipment for such a process. The roll film camera invented by George Eastman created an inexpensive method of photography. Thomas A. Edison used an Eastman "Kodak" camera in his first experiment with a motion picture machine in the 1890s. Edison marketed a machine built by Thomas Armat and Francis Jenkins in 1896 that projected motion pictures on a screen. A new era for media had begun.

There were many other experimental techniques tried between 1896 and the heyday of movies in the 1920s. One involved stop-motion trick photography in which objects before the camera would be altered in between camera shots, producing not only the effect of motion but also the appearance of real-life actions. Film producer Edwin S. Porter became an expert in stop-motion techniques, using them in films such as *The Great Train Robbery*. These methods were especially effective to place a variety of backgrounds behind the actors. Norman Dawn used painted glass held over the camera lens as another method of merging two dimensions on film.

In 1906, the celluloid overlays developed by Winsor McCay and others became the primary technique for animated cartoons such as Pat Sullivan's "Felix the Cat" series. McCay drew the entire scene, including characters and background, on one overlay. Each successive overlay would create the appearance of movement through the camera, because each picture frame consisted of one overlay drawing. McCay's first animated film, *Little Nemo*, appeared in 1911, based on his newspaper comic strip. Other comic strips also became the subject of animated films.

McCay's time-consuming production methods were improved by Raoul Barre's "slash system" after 1914. Barre eliminated redrawing the parts of scenes that did not move by placing stationary backgrounds on one overlay that could be used more than once and placing action sequences on separate overlays. John Bray developed the "in-betweening" concept, in which animators drew different parts of a subject's movement using transparent overlays while preserving the identical appearance of the subject. Bray also produced the first color cartoon in 1919. Max Fleischer's rotoscope projection machine allowed animators to merge their products with films. The production of animated films was made more efficient by the new technologies. Newsreels even resorted to animated editorial cartoons as part of their presentation of news events or personalities.

By the 1920s, the division of labor in the production of animated films became regularized. Photographic advances such as freeze-frame, reverse action, zoom shots, and time-lapse all affected animated productions as well as feature films. Yet until the end of the 1920s, the producers of animation were captives of their techniques and lacked development of their stories and characters. Walt Disney changed all that after he learned the craft in the 1920s and launched his own production company.

Walt Disney Productions, founded in Los Angeles in 1923, began with no technical deviations. The first Disney productions, such as the "Alice" series in the mid-1920s, were typical of the times, lacking any particular style or story development. Disney's initial innovation was the application of sound to animation, which led to the first synchronized sound animation feature, *Steamboat Willie*, in 1928. Disney used the "storyboard" to allow his animators to create a story line with animated objects. The *Three Little Pigs* in 1933 made popular the song "Who's Afraid of the Big Bad Wolf," which resonated with depression-era audiences. The addition of Technicolor made animated films all the more attractive. The well-known Disney characters made their appearances gradually—Mickey Mouse in 1928, Goofy in 1932, and Donald Duck in 1934. In 1937, Disney daringly produced a full-length animated film, *Snow White and the Seven Dwarfs*, at the height of feature film popularity. It was a box-office winner in part because the production costs were so low. *Snow White* was followed by the equally successful *Dumbo* (1941) and *Bambi* (1942). Disney's animated films proved timeless in their appeal to children and have played to larger audiences in each succeeding generation.

Other animators took their cue from Disney's success. Fleischer's studios produced the "Betty Boop," "Popeye," and "Superman" cartoon series and the feature-length *Gulliver's Travels*. Paul Terry created the popular "Mighty Mouse" and "Heckel and Jeckel" series in the 1940s. Walter Lantz brought his "Woody Woodpecker" series to major studios such as Universal. Other major production houses entered the animated field: Metro-Goldwyn-Mayer's "Tom and Jerry" and Warner Brothers' "Porky Pig," "Bugs Bunny," and "Roadrunner and Coyote."

Film producers began to use animated objects from models or puppets in regular feature films. David O. Selznick's 1933 *King Kong* demonstrated the possibilities. Special-effects photography made possible the application of animation illusions used in *King Kong* and *The Invisible Man*. By the 1950s, Madison Avenue became attracted to animations for their advertising, mainly on television; "Mr. Magoo" became the spokesman for General Electric. Bill Hanna and Joe Barbera began producing animated features for Saturday morning television and commercials in the 1950s. Their biggest hit, "The Flintstones," became a prime-time ABC television show in 1960 and the subject of a motion picture in 1994.

George Pal began using special-effects animation techniques for science fiction features such as *War of the Worlds* (1953).

The emergence of computer graphics in the late 1950s led to further technological sophistication, such as blending live action with animation in Disney's *Mary Poppins* (1964). The Disney techniques were copied in the *Pink Panther* movies. Live-action animations made possible hit television series such as Jim Henson's "Muppets" in the late 1970s. Henson's puppetlike creations possessed uncanny human qualities. George Lucas brought the computerized possibilities to a peak of development with his variety of humanlike creatures dominating the *Star Wars* trilogy beginning in 1977. Steven Spielberg's 1994 *Jurassic Park* re-created the historically extinct dinosaur figures in amazing confluence with the live-action humans.

See also Motion Pictures.

Reference Hoffer, Thomas W., *Animation: A Reference Guide* (1981).

Associated Press

Begun in 1848 as a local New York organization, the Associated Press has become the most significant press association for U.S. news media, as its subscribers expanded from large dailies to smaller papers and radio and television. The Associated Press has consistently promoted the development of new communication technologies.

During the Mexican War (1846–1848), several New York dailies pooled their newsgathering resources. Toward the end of the war, editors and publishers—including Horace Greeley, Henry Raymond, David Hale, and James Gordon Bennett—met in the offices of the *New York Sun* to discuss continuing the cooperative venture permanently. In 1849, the six New York papers founded the Harbor News Association, which was transformed in 1856 into the General News Association of the City of New York. This was later shortened to the New York Associated Press, with the additional membership of the *New York Times*.

Obtaining rebates from Western Union,

the association relied on the telegraph to obtain a virtual monopoly on the distribution of news to other major city dailies. With the opening of the Atlantic cable in 1858, Associated Press made agreements with European news agencies to obtain foreign accounts. Newspapers in the interior found that the only way to obtain international news was through an Associated Press franchise. Several midwestern newspapers formed the Western Associated Press in 1862, headquartered in Chicago, which established a cooperative arrangement with the New York association in 1867.

During the 1870s, Congress investigated numerous complaints of monopolistic practices against the Associated Press, but the association successfully defended its selling of franchises as a business function. Responding to criticism of the high use charges, the Associated Press allowed major cities to lease access to wires beginning in 1875. By 1900, cities as distant as New Orleans and Denver received leased-wire news from New York. The lease service was less expensive, so small dailies could afford to subscribe. The Associated Press relied on local reporters and even Western Union operators to transmit news for the service.

Competition soon appeared with the creation of United Press in 1882. Quickly, the two rivals met secretly and agreed to share news accounts. When the arrangement was made public in 1891, several subscriber papers revolted and forced a reorganization of Associated Press in 1893 as the Associated Press of Illinois. Melville Stone, publisher of the *Chicago Daily News*, became general manager and contracted with European news agencies to cut off United Press's foreign access. By 1897, the New York dailies, except for the *Sun* and Hearst's *Journal*, joined the new Associated Press, and United Press became defunct. After an adverse Illinois court ruling, the Associated Press was rechartered in New York in 1900 as a non-profit association whose members would contribute without charge to a news pool. Associated Press began operating foreign bureaus before World War I and founded the World Service in 1946. After 1915, member papers could use press reports other than those provided by Associated Press. In 1945, the Supreme Court forced Associated Press to allow more than one daily in a city to be a member of the service.

Beginning in 1913, Associated Press installed automatic teletype machines in subscriber offices, and a news photo service was established in 1927. The Associated Press reluctantly agreed in 1940 to allow radio stations to become members, but the Radio-Television Association was not formed until 1954. During World War II, Associated Press began a leased cable arrangement and an overseas radiophoto service.

Kent Cooper served as general manager from 1925 to 1948. Cooper's employment with Associated Press started in 1910, when he convinced Stone to use the telephone as well as the telegraph to distribute news to members. Cooper expanded the number of bureaus and started covering tabloid-type human-interest stories. In 1931, the association organized the Managing Editors Association, which critiqued news coverage to enhance quality. Frank J. Starzel, a staff member since 1929, was general manager from 1948 to 1962. Serving as general manager from 1962 to 1976, Wes Gallagher began the technique of task force reporting on major news subjects. Gallagher also aggressively recruited women reporters. Technology innovations pioneered by Associated Press included filmless cameras, electronic darkrooms that permit computerized photo development, and electronic editing on computer terminals. Associated Press even publishes its own magazine, *AP Log*, featuring essays by its reporters.

An Associated Press reporter won a Pulitzer Prize in 1922 for an account about the burial of the unknown soldier at Arlington Cemetery. Three Associated Press reporters won Pulitzer Prizes in the 1930s, and three more won for their World War II reporting. Associated Press reporters and photographers also won Pulitzers during the Korean and Vietnam Wars. Only the *New York Times* has garnered more Pulitzers than the Associated Press.

By the end of the 1980s, Associated Press's 308 bureaus in 71 nations served almost 90 percent of U.S. newspapers, 8,500 foreign subscribers, 6,000 television stations, and 1,000 radio stations.

References Gramling, Oliver, *AP: The Story of News* (1940); Schwarzlose, Richard A., "Early Telegraphic News Dispatches: Forerunner of the AP," *Journalism Quarterly* (1974).

Atlanta Constitution

Within a few years of the founding of the *Atlanta Constitution* in 1868, editor Henry Grady established the paper as a leading daily in the post–Civil War South. The Howell family owned the *Constitution* from 1876 until 1950, when the paper became part of the Cox chain. Ralph McGill made the *Constitution* a voice of moderation during the civil rights era in the 1950s and 1960s. The morning *Constitution* joined the Cox-owned evening *Journal* to provide a window on the economic and political changes in Atlanta and the South after World War II.

The *Atlanta Constitution* was founded in 1868 by Carey Styles, a former Confederate colonel who was uneasy about the absence of a strong anti–Radical Republican newspaper in Atlanta during Reconstruction. Within a year, he sold it to G. H. Anderson and his son-in-law William A. Hemphill. The *Constitution* alienated many Democrats in 1872 by backing Horace Greeley and the Liberal Republicans against President Grant. The *Constitution* acquired the competing *Sun* in 1873, but its real dynamic leadership began when lawyer-businessman Evan P. Howell became the half owner and editor in 1876.

Meanwhile, Henry W. Grady had begun to establish a solid reputation as an editor and newsman. Grady began his career at age 19 editing the *Rome (Georgia) Courier* but quit after the owners would not allow an attack on local political corruption. In 1872, Grady seized an opportunity to become one-third owner and managing editor of the new *Atlanta Herald*. In a short time, Grady made the *Herald* the sprightliest paper in

Georgia, but the depression of the mid-1870s forced its sale to the *Constitution* after only four years. Grady worked part-time as a reporter for the *Constitution* and a correspondent for James Gordon Bennett's *New York Herald* over the next four years. Finally, in 1880, Howell and Hemphill offered Grady an ownership stake and editorship of the *Constitution.*

Grady's chief efforts at the *Constitution* during the decade of his editorship were to urge the South to leave behind the hobgoblins of its checkered history and embrace the industrialism thriving in the Northeast. The so-called New South image painted by Grady was touted by a few within the South and by fellow journalists in other parts of the nation. The theme gained national currency after Grady's much-publicized speech to the New England Society in New York City. Grady also sought to make the *Constitution*'s style reflect a literary sophistication not often associated with the region. He recruited fellow Georgian Joel Chandler Harris as a frequent contributor to the paper. Harris, of "Uncle Remus" fame, established one of the first syndicated columns by a southern journalist and also served as associate editor for 24 years. Even with his editorial duties, Grady retained his reporting skills, most notably in a detailed account of the Charleston earthquake of 1886. The *Constitution* introduced elements of "new journalism" such as features writing. By the time of Grady's death in 1889, the *Constitution*'s weekly edition had the largest sales in the South at 140,000.

Grady was succeeded by Clark Howell, son of the publisher. Howell kept alive the *Constitution*'s reputation for solid reporting and editorial sharpness over the following decades. Competition increased with the founding of the evening *Atlanta Journal* in 1883 (edited by Hoke Smith from 1887 to 1898) and the *Atlanta Georgian* in 1903, a crusading paper that helped end the convict-lease system and became part of the Hearst chain in 1912. The *Constitution* became caught up in the yellow press rage of the 1890s and clamored for U.S. intervention in Cuba, which led to the Spanish-American War. The *Constitution* won a public service Pulitzer award in 1931. Clark Howell continued as editor and publisher until his death in 1936.

After serving as business manager and general manager since 1920, Clark Howell Jr. became publisher of the *Constitution* in 1936 and named Ralph McGill, formerly of the *Nashville Banner*, editor in 1938. McGill launched assaults on the Ku Klux Klan and the Talmadge political machine in Georgia. He spoke out early for moderation in the civil rights campaign of the 1950s and won a Pulitzer Prize for his editorials on the subject in 1959. The *Constitution* was sold to Cox Newspapers in 1950 by the Howell family. Although Cox also owned the *Atlanta Journal*, the two papers maintained separate editorial operations. McGill became a nationally syndicated columnist and stepped down as editor in 1960. Eugene Patterson succeeded McGill as editor and won a 1967 Pulitzer Prize for his editorials denouncing race hatred, but he resigned shortly thereafter. Reporter Jack Nelson won a 1960 Pulitzer for reports on the horrible conditions at the state mental hospital.

Former political editor Reg Murphy served as editor from 1970 to 1975, before moving to the *San Francisco Examiner* and later becoming publisher of the *Baltimore Sun*. Columnist Lewis Grizzard gained a national following with his folksy humor. Polls in the 1960s and 1970s ranked the *Constitution* as one of the ten best newspapers in the United States. It won another Pulitzer in 1989 for reports about discrimination against blacks applying for home mortgages. Editor Hal Gulliver (1975–1983) was succeeded by Tom Teepen at the *Constitution*. Jack Spalding and Durwood McAllister provided editorial leadership at the *Journal* from the 1970s to 1990s.

Atlantic Monthly

Beginning as an unillustrated literary magazine in 1857, the *Atlantic Monthly* became noted in the twentieth century for its political commentary. Throughout its history, the *Atlantic* has attracted the best-known writers of the day, and its editors have been among the most proficient in periodical history.

When the *Atlantic Monthly* was established, there were more than 150 journals published in Boston alone. Seeking distinction from others, some of New England's literary elite, including Ralph Waldo Emerson and Henry Wadsworth Longfellow, collaborated to launch the *Atlantic*. The first editor was author James Russell Lowell, and the periodical was named by a frequent contributor, Oliver Wendell Holmes. During its early years, essays and poetry by Emerson, Lowell, Holmes, Harriet Beecher Stowe, and John Greenleaf Whittier graced its pages, although the claim that it was a national journal could hardly be justified. Except for Julia Ward Howe's "Battle Hymn of the Republic," the journal scrupulously avoided comment on the Civil War.

In 1861, Lowell was succeeded as editor by James T. Fields, who was also a partner in the new ownership. Fields continued the purely literary slant of the *Atlantic*, but with the editorship of midwestern novelist William Dean Howells (1871–1881), the provincial New England flavor faded. Later, editors such as Thomas Bailey Aldrich (1881–1890) and Horace E. Scudder (1890–1898) included social and political material, but the literary dominance remained.

In 1909, Ellery Sedgwick bought the *Atlantic* for $50,000 when circulation dropped to 15,000 and it began losing money. Also serving as editor, Sedgwick moved the subject matter of the *Atlantic* decidedly toward politics. He invited political leaders such as Woodrow Wilson, Al Smith, and Wendell Willkie to contribute their political philosophy. Although it was not in the vanguard of the muckraking middle-class reform movement, the *Atlantic* included frequent articles on reform issues.

During the editorial tenure of Edward Weeks from 1938 to 1966, the *Atlantic*'s diversity increased. Among the contributors were American novelists James Thurber and Saul Bellow, foreign policy expert George F. Kennan, French existentialist author Albert Camus, Welsh poet Dylan Thomas, American humorist Fred Allen, and scientist Albert Einstein. Weeks advertised the *Atlantic* to youthful potential subscribers by frequently addressing college audiences.

Weeks's successor was former Kennedy administration official Robert Manning, whose years from 1966 to 1977 were marked by a greater focus on political issues. The *Atlantic* featured a regular column by Elizabeth Drew about Washington political affairs. When Michael Janeway became editor in 1977, the *Atlantic*'s circulation was 340,000, greater than that of its longtime rival *Harper's*. When it appeared that the *Atlantic*'s debts would force its dissolution in 1980, real estate entrepreneur Mortimer Zuckerman—who later bought *U.S. News & World Report*—purchased the magazine and revitalized it.

Because of its purely literary beginnings, the original owners refused to include advertising in the *Atlantic*, but the pressures of balance sheets led to the first ads in 1860. By the end of the Civil War, both the inside page and the back cover contained only advertising, in addition to spots on other pages. The advertisers ranged from Steinway pianos to billiard tables to patent medicines. The monotonously similar covers of the nineteenth century were replaced in the mid-twentieth century by pictures of prominent subjects such as T. S. Eliot and Robert Frost.

Reference Howe, M. A. D., *The Atlantic Monthly and Its Makers* (1919).

Baltimore Sun

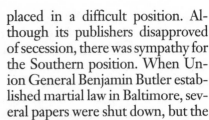

Baltimore's close proximity to the North-South border in the pre–Civil War era and to the nation's capital has often influenced the *Baltimore Sun*. The newspaper began in 1837 as part of the penny press phenomenon and has continued throughout its history to take determined editorial stands and to maintain its integrity by accurately reporting the news.

After James Gordon Bennett's *New York Herald* began the era of penny press journalism in the mid-1830s, it spread beyond the bounds of New York City to places such as Philadelphia and Baltimore. Arunah S. Abell, the founder of the *Baltimore Sun*, first introduced penny papers in Philadelphia as a partner in the *Philadelphia Public Ledger*, established in 1836. The *Baltimore Sun* began publication in May 1837 on the occasion of a bank panic and the start of a depression. The *Sun*'s inaugural issue featured a story about the city council appropriating emergency funds to meet the crisis. Despite the depression, the *Sun*'s circulation rose to 12,000 by the end of its first year of operation.

Abell not only used Samuel Morse's telegraph (introduced in 1844) to gather news but also demanded that Congress subsidize the extension of telegraph lines. Because the *Sun* received news of the 1846 declaration of war against Mexico by telegraph, it scooped rival papers. The *Sun* cooperated with Bennett's *Herald*, especially during the Mexican War (1846–1848), to share news accounts. The publisher also engineered other scoops, such as having President Martin Van Buren's 1837 inaugural address sent to Baltimore by train so that it could be published in the next day's edition. Abell established the first Washington bureau in 1837, a practice that was eventually copied by all the major national dailies. Almost from its inception, the *Sun* gained respect from other media leaders for its accuracy and completeness in news reporting. The *Sun* emulated other penny press papers in its focus on local news, human-interest accounts, and entertainment.

During the Civil War, the *Sun* was placed in a difficult position. Although its publishers disapproved of secession, there was sympathy for the Southern position. When Union General Benjamin Butler established martial law in Baltimore, several papers were shut down, but the *Sun* avoided Butler's interference by wisely adopting a policy of printing no political commentary.

The Abell family continued to publish the *Sun* until it was sold in 1910 to another Baltimore publisher, Charles H. Grasty. During the late nineteenth and early twentieth centuries, the *Sun* had clung to some antiquated financial practices. For example, it was not until 1905 that the *Sun* accepted advertising. Another financial blow was the destruction of the *Sun*'s headquarters by fire in 1904. Grasty also purchased the *Baltimore World* and transformed it into the *Evening Sun*. Grasty's editorial positions supported progressive reformers, especially Woodrow Wilson, and opposed corruption. Yet Grasty could not restore the *Sun*'s ailing financial condition and sold to Van-Lear Black in 1914.

The major revival of the *Baltimore Sun* came during the ownership of Paul C. Patterson from 1918 to 1950. Patterson hired Hamilton Owens as editor, and the *Sun* became lively and popular once again by focusing on national politics, literature, and social issues. Owens recruited sparkling writers such as Henry L. Mencken (a former *Sun* reporter and editor), Virginius Dabney, and Gerald W. Johnson to contribute essays. Mencken accompanied publisher Patterson on a famous tour of the South in 1926 that was recounted in the *Sun*. The pair visited several state capitals and conversed with leading southern journalists and intellects. During the 1940s, four *Sun* reporters received Pulitzer Prizes, and the paper earned a reputation for its foreign news reporting. After World War II, the *Sun* expended considerable effort to improve its local news reporting.

The *Sun* was sold in 1986 to the Times Mirror Company, parent of the *Los Angeles Times*, for $600 million. The editors in 1994 were Edward Hewitt and Tom Linthicum. By the 1990s, the trend showed a decline in the evening circulation and a gain in morning sales. The morning *Sun*'s circulation totaled 250,000 in 1994, a gain of 27,000 from the 1991 figure. The afternoon edition lost 50,000 subscribers between 1991 and 1994, for a total of 127,000. The Sunday edition remained steady at around 490,000 subscribers.

Reference Johnson, Gerald W. et al., *The Sunpapers of Baltimore* (1937).

Bell, Alexander Graham
See Telecommunications.

Bennett, James Gordon (1795–1872)
Beginning his career as a reporter and moving to the positions of editor and publisher, James Gordon Bennett founded the pioneering *New York Herald*. Bennett's *Herald* followed the *New York Sun* as the city's second major penny press daily. Bennett was controversial because he assailed not only politicians but also some fellow journalists. The *Herald* provided extensive accounts of Washington politics and also became the first New York daily to send reporters to cover the Mexican War.

James Gordon Bennett was born in Scotland to Catholic parents. His education included a brief tenure in a Catholic seminary as well as at the Universities of Aberdeen and Glasgow. Immigrating to Halifax, Nova Scotia, in 1819, Bennett found employment as an economics tutor. After a short stint in New York City during 1821, Bennett obtained a newspaper position in Charleston, S.C. Other newspaper reporting jobs followed in New York, Washington, D.C., Philadelphia, and finally back to New York by the mid-1830s. As a reporter and sometime editorial writer, Bennett gave hints of his controversial nature by opposing the recharter of the national bank, which was supported by most big city newspapers. His experiences reporting national and state politics were crucial in helping Bennett formulate in his mind the type of newspaper he wanted to run himself, focusing on subjects such as election campaigns, financial news, and court trials.

When James Gordon Bennett founded the New York Herald *in 1835, he single-handedly wrote every article. His sensational journalistic style contributed to making the* Herald *the highest-circulated daily in the world by the early 1860s.*

Despite Bennett's experience and talent, he failed twice in newspaper ownership. Undaunted, he obtained $500 credit and, with no staff other than himself, founded the politically nonpartisan *New York Herald* in 1835. Inspired by Benjamin Day's successful penny press daily, the *New York Sun*, Bennett added new journalistic techniques to the stock penny press sensationalism. He had reporters write about sensational criminal trials in intricate detail. Bennett sensed the public's voyeurism and appetite for violent stories. The *Herald* also carried full information on financial and business affairs, which appealed to New York businessmen. Bennett's editorials were informed, unequivocal, and persuasive, and he encouraged readers to write letters to the editor. The *Herald* made a practice of gathering news from foreign and national as well as state and local sources. Bennett pioneered the society and sports sections of the modern newspaper.

By the time of the Civil War, the *New York Herald* had the largest circulation of any daily in the world, with 77,000 subscribers. Bennett weathered a well-organized boycott of his paper in 1840 that was started by his oft-criticized rival editors but supported mainly by local clergymen, who disliked the *Herald*'s antireligious tone. Bennett's response was to send reporters to cover religious and church activities, which became a regular part of the *Herald*.

James Gordon Bennett always seized on any innovation that would allow the news to be disseminated more effectively. He quickly began using the telegraph to obtain stories from his reporters in beats such as Washington, D.C., and the *Herald* was the first New York daily to send reporters to cover the Mexican War. His system of couriers between New Orleans and New York City was more efficient than the government's postal service. Continually embroiled in controversy, Bennett suffered numerous libel suits, bomb threats, and even physical beatings from his enemies.

The Mexican War also revealed that Bennett would cooperate to improve the news, even if his competitors also benefited. The *Herald* and Horace Greeley's *New York Tribune* shared telegraphic dispatches from Mexico in their news accounts. After the war ended in 1848, Bennett led five other New York publishers—including Henry J. Raymond, James Watson Webb, and Horace Greeley—to found the Associated Press news service. The group began selling news items gathered by its reporters to other papers outside of New York.

In 1867, Bennett added an afternoon daily, the *New York Evening Telegram*, to complement the morning *Herald*. By the time of his death in 1872, the *Herald* was the leading newspaper in the United States in style, technique, and circulation. Its reporters were placed in numerous news locales at home and abroad. Although he left his son James

Gordon Bennett Jr. a financially secure newspaper, the *Herald*'s position was soon rivaled and undermined by the advent of yellow journalists Joseph Pulitzer and William Randolph Hearst. However, it is fair to state that another reason for the *Herald*'s decline was the authoritarian administration of the younger Bennett, who lacked many of the qualities that made his father successful.

Reference Carson, Oliver, *The Man Who Made News* (1942).

Blair, Francis Preston (1791–1876)

As the editor of the pro-Jacksonian *Washington Globe* in the 1830s, Francis P. Blair helped fashion the journalism of political democracy in the United States. Blair was not merely a spokesman for the president; he helped formulate government policy as a member of the famous "kitchen cabinet."

Francis P. Blair, a native of Virginia, moved to the young state of Kentucky on the American frontier. The Blair family was prominent in Kentucky politics: an uncle was governor, and his father was attorney general. Francis Blair was trained in the law at Transylvania College in Lexington and became a successful farmer and banker as well as editor of the state Democratic Party's *Argus of Western America*. Blair was tutored on the *Argus* by Democratic partisan Amos Kendall, who left the paper to join President Andrew Jackson in the nation's capital.

Jackson depended on Democratic editors to elect him in 1828. One of the most influential, Duff Green of St. Louis, was brought to Washington after the election to launch the *United States Telegraph*, the official organ of the administration. The *Telegraph* depended on government printing contracts to finance itself, since its subscription rates were so high that many of Jackson's constituents could not afford to buy it. By 1830, Green had sided with Vice President John C. Calhoun in a dispute with President Jackson, and he also supported the recharter of the national bank, which Jackson opposed. Thus, Green and the *Telegraph* had to be replaced.

Editor of the government-subsidized Washington Globe, *Francis Preston Blair was heard through both his editorials and his membership in the "kitchen cabinet."*

Kendall, being the president's confidant, persuaded Jackson to bring Francis Blair to Washington from Kentucky to establish a new administration paper, the *Washington Globe*. Like Green's *Telegraph*, Blair's *Globe* depended on government printing contracts voted by Congress, amounting to $50,000 a year. Kendall contributed articles to the *Globe*, and another Kentuckian, John C. Rives, was the paper's astute business manager. Blair not only wrote editorials blistering the national bank and its supporters but also quickly became a leading influence in Democratic Party circles and within the kitchen cabinet.

Although Blair continued at the *Globe* during the succeeding administration of Democrat Martin Van Buren (1837–1841), the *Globe* lost its printing contracts with Congress. The result was a struggle to maintain the paper during the lean years under Van Buren and the succeeding Whig administration. When another Democrat, James K. Polk of Tennessee, was elected in 1844, he quickly dismissed Blair as editor of the *Globe* and named his own choice. Blair and his partner John Rives continued to print the *Globe* until 1849.

Although Blair's journalistic career was over, he remained politically active. He helped found the Republican Party in the 1850s and was a strong backer of Abraham Lincoln. He returned to the Democratic Party after the Civil War because of his opposition to Republican corruption in the Grant era. One of Blair's sons was appointed postmaster general by Lincoln, and another served in both the House of Representatives and the Senate. The house that Blair purchased in Washington in 1836 remained in the family until the federal government bought it in 1942. Thereafter, Blair House became the residence for visiting foreign dignitaries and occasionally for vice presidents.

Reference Smith, William E., "Francis P. Blair, Pen-Executive of Andrew Jackson," *Mississippi Valley Historical Review* (1931).

Bok, Edward W.
See Ladies' Home Journal.

Boston Globe
The *Boston Globe* got a late start in the historically intense Boston newspaper competition, but it emerged in the twentieth century as the most successful and influen-

tial. Charles H. Taylor rescued the *Globe* from financial losses after a rocky beginning in the 1870s. Taylor used sensationalism and extensive New England regional coverage to attract readers. William O. Taylor continued the *Globe* traditions in the twentieth century.

Son of a clergyman, author and magazine editor Maturin Ballou convinced investor Stephen Niles and others of the need for a quality daily in Boston. With $150,000 capitalization, Ballou inaugurated the eight-page, four-cent morning *Boston Globe* in 1872. Ballou promised readers thoughtful editorials and major coverage of arts and literature. Despite very talented assistants, the *Globe* was hardly able to dent the circulation of newspaper rivals. The *Globe* never got above 5,000 readers compared to the *Herald*'s 90,000. Ballou lost two-thirds of the initial investment in six months and resigned in mid-1873.

The *Globe* stockholders, led by Eben Jordan of the Jordan and Marsh department stores, hired Charles H. Taylor as business manager and part-owner in late 1873 at the same time that Edwin Munroe Bacon became the new editor. Taylor proved to be a shrewd business manager; he cut the price of the *Globe* to two cents, started an evening edition and in 1877 a Sunday edition, and hired an advertising manager. Within weeks, the circulation grew to 30,000 and doubled again in three years. Taylor and Jordan led a reorganization of the company in 1877 to clear away remaining debts. A former *New York Times* correspondent, Bacon shifted the *Globe* to support for the Democratic Party which proved attractive to increasing numbers of Irish immigrants. The *Globe* used bold headlines and increased crime coverage as well as extending news accounts to most of New England. Serialized fiction and features articles added variety to the content.

Taylor proved fortunate in recruiting two talented editors to take over from the uninspiring Bacon in 1878. Edward C. Bailey, formerly of the Concord, New Hampshire paper, became editor and former *Post* editor Frederick E. Goodrich took on the assignment of chief editorial writer. Content improved quickly with clear, crisp editorials, new society and arts sections, increased sports coverage, and more and better reporters. When Bailey retired in 1880, Taylor took the title of editor and soon offered support to progressive measures such as direct election of U.S. senators and women's suffrage. Florence Finch added a Sunday column, "The Woman's Hour," in 1881 and soon did reporting and wrote editorials as well. James Morgan became chief editorial writer after serving a term as the *Globe*'s Washington correspondent. Taylor regularly hired graduates of Harvard as staffers and gave them their own bylines. In 1890, the *Globe* pioneered newspaper photo-engraving. By the mid-1880s, the *Globe* circulation of 70,000 topped all its Boston competition; circulation passed 200,000 in 1892 and a record 627,000 copies were sold after election day in 1898.

Charles Taylor's sons began to enter their father's business in the 1890s. Charles Taylor, Jr. and William O. Taylor worked in the business office. After his father purchased the Boston Red Sox baseball team in 1904, John Taylor became president of the ball club. Because it could not support Democratic free-silver candidate William Jennings Bryan in 1896, the *Globe* became more politically independent thereafter. The *Globe* did not clamor for war against Spain in 1898 like the yellow press, but it got considerable circulation boosts from Spanish-American War coverage. Circulation dropped to 180,000 by 1900 and the *Globe* soon lost its leadership to the *Post*'s aggressive editor Edwin Grozier. Moreover, William Randolph Hearst started the *Boston American* in 1904. Yet, the sound business practices, strong advertising income, and talented reporters and writers at the *Globe* kept it at the forefront of Boston newspapers.

The *Globe* had uncharacteristically supported Republican Theodore Roosevelt in 1904, but found itself more comfortable backing Democrat Woodrow Wilson in 1912. Social reformer Lucien Price began a 50-year stint as *Globe* essayist in 1914, M. E.

Hennessy made a national reputation as political reporter, and veteran war correspondent Richard Harding Davis covered World War I. Laurence Winship was named Sunday editor in 1918; he became managing editor in 1937 and editor in 1955. Taylor reduced the price of the evening edition to one cent in 1914 as circulation remained in the doldrums.

Initially after the death of Charles H. Taylor in 1921, brothers Charles, Jr. and William shared management of the *Globe*. Most expected Charles, Jr., already a former president of the American Newspaper Publishers Association, to take charge, yet William was named publisher by his father with Charles, Jr. serving as business manager until 1937. William O. Taylor guided the *Globe* through its most difficult financial times in the Great Depression years. Determined to maintain control of the *Globe*, Taylor rejected many offers to sell the paper. He also brushed aside suggestions that the *Globe* purchase the *Post* and the *Transcript* in the 1950s. William O. Taylor died in 1955, the same year long time staffers James Morgan and M. E. Hennessy passed away.

William Taylor's son Davis became publisher in 1955 and began a remarkable era of expansion for the *Globe*. Davis Taylor remade the *Globe* into a reform and exposé oriented paper which attacked local corruption in particular. The *Globe* won the first Pulitzer among Boston papers in forty-five years in 1966 for "meritorious public service" in blocking the appointment of an unqualified lawyer to the federal bench. A prize for investigative reporting went to four *Globe* reporters in 1972 and Paul Szep won for a cartoon in 1974. The *Globe*'s Washington correspondents, Tom Winship and Robert Healy, helped establish the paper's reputation outside Boston. Davis Taylor risked *Globe* finances in 1970 by refusing cigarette advertising. The *Globe* joined the *New York Times* in 1971 to fight Nixon administration prior restraint efforts over the publication of the "Pentagon Papers."

Davis's son William O. Taylor II became general manager of the *Globe* in 1969 and gradually took over management from his father. Tom Winship moved up to become editor in the 1970s, followed by Michael Janeway and John Driscoll (1986–1993). By 1989, the *Globe* ranked fourteenth nationally in circulation with almost 510,000 daily readers. The Sunday edition held the eighth position with 787,000. Those numbers remained steady through 1994. The *New York Times* acquired ownership of the *Globe* in 1993 but kept William O. Taylor II as publisher.

Reference: Lyons, Louis M., *Newspaper Story: One Hundred Years of the Boston Globe* (1971).

Boston News-Letter

After the removal of Parliament's Licensing Act, the *Boston News-Letter* became the first continuous newspaper in the American colonies. Even though it lacked style and quality writing, the *News-Letter*'s innovations included direct reporting of news, advertising, and illustrations.

American colonial newspapers depended heavily on news from England, which would be stale by the time it was printed. Such was the nature of the first issue of the *Boston News-Letter* on 24 April 1704, printed on both sides of a half sheet of paper measuring about six by ten inches. Other than a few notices about ship traffic in Boston, there was no local news—only reprinted months-old news accounts from London papers. More news appeared in subsequent issues, but the weekly *News-Letter*'s main function was to publicize meetings, government proclamations, legal notices, and commercial shipping lists. The only exciting accounts in its pages concerned piracy on the high seas.

The publisher of the *News-Letter* was a Scotsman, John Campbell. There was not a lot of investment capital at stake for Campbell, who was also a postmaster and a bookseller. Indeed, Campbell was surprised at the demand for his paper. Although he obtained more advertising as time went by, at 2 pence a copy or 12 shillings a year, he constantly faced payment arrears from his 300 subscribers. Publication of the *News-Letter* was briefly suspended twice because of financial troubles. The provincial government extended loans on those occasions to keep the paper solvent, since it was cheaper to have the *News-Letter* publish proclamations than to pay a printer for publication.

Not until 1719, with the appearance of the *Boston Gazette*, did the *News-Letter* have any competition. Campbell was proud of the fact that the *News-Letter* did not print opinion or debate ideas. In order to avoid government scrutiny, Campbell cleared each copy of the *News-Letter* with the governor of Massachusetts. On the masthead below the title were printed the words "Published by Authority." Yet even with competition that was willing to print editorial opinion, the *News-Letter* survived.

In 1722, the paper's new publisher was Bartholomew Green, who had been the printer for the paper as well as for Harvard College. As a deacon at Boston's Old South Church, Green was noted for his religious piety, which kept him from publishing anything controversial. When Green died in 1732, ownership passed to his son-in-law, John Draper, who enlarged the *News-Letter* to four and sometimes six larger pages, featuring increased advertising and more local and colonial news than foreign. By the 1750s, the *News-Letter* had about 600 subscribers and was able to break even financially. At the death of John Draper in 1762, his son Richard became publisher. Always conservative, the *News-Letter* supported the crown's policies against the growing patriot cause that led to the American Revolution. When British troops departed Boston in 1776, the last publisher of the *News-Letter*, Margaret Draper, fled, and the paper died after 72 years of operation.

Reference Kobre, Sidney, "The First American Newspaper: A Product of Environment," *Journalism Quarterly* (1940).

Boston Post

Founded as a Jacksonian Democratic paper in 1831, the *Boston Post* became the most important paper in Boston until the advent of the *Globe* after the Civil War. Charles G.

Greene edited the *Post* for 44 years with humor and skill. Edwin Grozier after 1891 made the *Post* the largest circulation morning daily in the nation by resorting to sensationalism. After the Grozier family sold the *Post* in 1952 to John Fox, it declined rapidly and closed in 1956.

Other than Philadelphia, Boston was the most competitive newspaper city in America in the early nineteenth century; 15 papers were born and died in the 1830s alone. Charles Gordon Greene worked at various times for his brother at the *Boston Statesman* from 1825 to 1829, and briefly published his own paper, the *Spectator*, in 1826. Greene also edited the Democratic Party paper in Washington, D.C., the *United States Telegraph* for a short time in 1828. He finally succeeded in establishing his own paper, the *Boston Post*, as a morning daily in 1831. It joined several other mercantile format papers that sold only through paid subscriptions of four dollars per year. The four-page *Post* had only four columns initially but enlarged to the standard eight columns by 1839.

The penny papers with their human interest and crime stories challenged the *Post* in Boston during the 1830s, but did not last. Greene had become an ardent Democrat in the late 1820s and used the *Post* to champion party principles such as a low tariff. When President Andrew Jackson vetoed the bank bill in 1832, some Democrats bolted from the Democratic Party but Greene remained loyal. He also supported local issues such as ending tolls for bridges and debt imprisonment. Greene wrote a lively column entitled "All Sorts."

The *Boston Post*'s shop was damaged by a major fire in 1872 causing a temporary suspension of operations. The city of Boston paid the *Post* for the property which allowed it to return to printing at a new location. The depression following the Panic of 1873 caused Charles Greene and his son Nathaniel to sell the *Post* in 1875 to a Republican prohibitionist, Reverend E. D. Winslow, publisher of the *Boston Daily Mail*, for $160,000. Winslow engaged in a stock swindling scheme that forced his departure

from Boston to avoid arrest in 1876. The *Post*'s ownership was assumed by Democratic Party leader William Gaston and merchant Leopold Morse. They depended too much on business manager G. F. Emery to straighten the paper's finances. Emery fired the union printers and hired less than competent replacements. Another reorganization followed Gaston and Morse's departure in 1885, and two additional shakeups came later in the 1880s, none of which resolved the *Post*'s crisis. Edward Munroe Bacon, former editor of the *Boston Globe*, provided able if conventional editing from 1886 to 1891. Finally, in 1891 with circulation down to 23,000, Edwin Atkins Grozier took control of the *Post*.

Grozier gained his first newspaper experience as a reporter for the *Boston Globe* (1881–1883). Later, he edited Joseph Pulitzer's evening *New York World* before coming to the *Post*. Grozier lowered the price of the paper to one cent and began introducing sensational stories about crime and personalities. He lobbied for lower streetcar fares and cheaper fuel prices. By the end of the 1890s, the *Post* circulation of 450,000 made it the largest circulation morning paper in the United States. The *Post* held its circulation leadership until after World War I; in 1918, circulation totaled 540,000. Talented writers for the *Post* included Kenneth Roberts and Olin Downes. The *Post* won a Pulitzer Prize in 1921 for meritorious public service in unveiling a financial swindle. Upon the death of Edwin Grozier in 1924, his invalid son Richard took charge of the *Post*.

During the 1920's, the *Post* departed from its Democratic roots and supported Calvin Coolidge. It also opposed Roosevelt's New Deal in the 1930s, so its influence in the national Democratic Party waned. However, managing editor Clifton Carberry issued instructions for local Democrats through his pseudonym "John Bantry." Columnist Bill Cunningham provided lively discussions of subjects from science to sports from the 1920s to the 1940s. Nonetheless, the absence of Edwin Grozier's hand at the helm caused circulation declines to 375,000 by 1930. The price of the *Post* was raised to two cents in the 1920s and five cents in 1948.

The Grozier family wanted to sell the *Post* in 1951 and Grozier trustee Chester Steadman tried to persuade W. O. Taylor of the *Boston Globe* to buy the *Post* for $7.5 million. Taylor declined and Steadman solicited offers from the Knight and Cowles chains without agreement. Joseph P. Kennedy wanted to buy both the *Globe* and the *Post*, but since the *Globe* was not for sale he had no interest in the *Post* alone. The *Post* was finally sold in 1952 to Western Union's John Fox for $3 million. An alcoholic and fierce anti-communist who wanted to use his paper for tirades against communism, Fox promoted editorial writer John Griffin to editor. Griffin's competence could not overcome Fox's extremism. Fox also spent much time and capital unsuccessfully lobbying for a television station for the *Post*. When Fox endorsed Republican Dwight Eisenhower for President in 1952, angry Boston Democrats flailed the *Post*. Fox also demanded and received $500,000 from Joseph Kennedy to support son John Kennedy's senate candidacy. When Fox surrendered control of the *Post* in 1956, creditors tried to revive it but also failed after a few months.

Reference Kenny, Herbert A., *Newspaper Row: Journalism in the Pre-Television Era* (1987).

Bourke-White, Margaret (1904–1971)
Photojournalist Margaret Bourke-White was the first female photographer to be certified by the U.S. armed forces, was the first photographer for *Fortune* (1930), and produced the inaugural cover of *Life* (1936). She covered World War II from Russia, North Africa, Italy, and at sea. Afterward she documented the British denouement in India and photographed the Korean War.

Margaret Bourke-White was born to Irish American Minnie Bourke and Polish Jew Joseph White in New York City. Because her father constantly tinkered with machines and dabbled in amateur photography, Bourke-White developed a keen interest in technology and cameras. During her high school years in Plainfield, New Jersey, she edited the yearbook. An English teacher urged Bourke-White to pursue a writing career. She took photography classes at Columbia University under the noted Clarence H. White and taught photo classes at summer camps. Her first commercial venture was the production of picture postcards. While attending graduate school at the University of Michigan, she was selected as photographer for the student yearbook.

In 1926, after a failed marriage, Bourke-White entered graduate school at Cornell University in New York. She continued her photographic pastime, selling pictures to the alumni magazine. Upon finalizing her divorce in Cleveland in 1928, some Cornell alumni paid Bourke-White to photograph a new school featured in *Architecture* magazine. Her photographic essay of industrial Cleveland, featuring the newly constructed 28-story Terminal Tower, became an entree to five years of photographic work for a local bank magazine, *Trade Winds*.

Before her employment by *Fortune* in 1930, Bourke-White produced photos for the Lincoln Electric Company in Cleveland and the *Cleveland Plain Dealer* newspaper; she took estate shots for *House and Garden* magazine and industrial photos for *Architectural Record*. Her work was included in a New York City museum exhibit in 1930. Her newfound publicity caught the eye of Henry R. Luce, publisher of *Time* and *Fortune*, a new journal chronicling U.S. business. Luce hired Bourke-White to become a full-time photojournalist for his newest venture.

In 1930, Bourke-White traveled with a *Fortune* editor to Europe, where she took photographs of the newly industrialized Soviet Union. Her lectures on photography were so popular there that she was invited back for a second visit in 1931. Bourke-White chronicled her tours of Russia in a photo documentary, *Eyes on Russia*. On a third trip to Russia in 1932, she traveled to Joseph Stalin's native Georgia for additional photo opportunities. By 1931, besides her regular job with *Fortune*, Bourke-White had opened her own studio in the recently constructed Chrysler building in Manhattan. She secured advertising contracts with the Buick automobile company and the Goodyear tire company, as well as doing illustrated ads for the *Saturday Evening Post*. By 1935, she was engaged by Trans World Airlines to do a series of aerial photographs to promote commercial flying.

Before 1935, Bourke-White's professional photography had been almost entirely commercial, but by the mid-1930s, she began to diversify. Her first noncommercial venture in 1934 was photographing the impact of the Dust Bowl drought in the Midwest. In 1935, she launched another facet of her career by doing news photos for the Newspaper Enterprise Association. She did a photographic sequence of President Franklin Roosevelt in 1936 and covered the 1936 presidential campaign for the wire services. A charter member of the American Artists' Congress founded in 1936, Bourke-White was elected vice president by her peers. Bourke-White was invited to exhibit some of her photographs at the New York Museum of Modern Art in 1937.

Although high salaried for the depression era, Bourke-White was sensitive to the economic troubles in her profession. During a photo tour of the South, she began an affair with Erskine Caldwell. Their picture book collaboration, *You Have Seen Their Faces*, published in 1937, featured downtrodden tenant farmers coping with the depression.

In 1936, Bourke-White undertook another assignment with the Luce conglomerate—doing photographs for *Life*, a unique pictorial newsmagazine. The premier cover featured her photo of a Columbia River Public Works Administration dam. Her pictorial essays dominated the early years, including a spectacular series from an Arctic Circle voyage, a selection of Hollywood's motion picture stars, and a peek inside Nazi Germany. Bourke-White's photographs for *Life* contrasted with her earlier work, which focused on U.S. industry and business. In 1939, Bourke-White embarked on her greatest professional adventure, documenting the beginnings of World War II in Europe for *Life*. From London, Bourke-White flew to the Balkans, which were threatened by both the Nazis and the Soviets. She was arrested for taking photographs in Romania. Her travels took her east to Turkey and then to Syria in 1940.

In 1940, publisher Ralph Ingersoll lured Bourke-White and Erskine Caldwell to his new paper in New York, *PM*. Bourke-White's nature photos were a regular feature. But when the experimental paper foundered after four months and was bought by Marshall Field, Bourke-White resigned and reclaimed her position at *Life*. Before returning to the war in Europe, Bourke-White and Caldwell embarked on another national tour that resulted in a second book collaboration, *Say, Is This the USA*, published in 1941. Bourke-White and Caldwell flew to Russia via China in 1941 to cover the German invasion. During the initial German assault, Bourke-White was the only foreign photographer in Russia. She sent photos to *Life* showing the German bombing of Moscow. She also persuaded the Russians to allow the first live U.S. radio broadcast via CBS. Through Presidential Adviser Harry Hopkins's intercession, Bourke-White was allowed to photograph Joseph Stalin, another first for a foreign journalist. She published her account of the Russian experience, *Shooting the Russian War*, in 1942.

While covering the war in North Africa in 1942 and 1943, Margaret Bourke-White became the first woman given permission to accompany a bombing mission. The event resulted in a huge splash in *Life*. She then followed the Allies as they invaded Italy in late 1943 and focused on the artillery. Her exploits in Italy were later published as *They Called It "Purple Heart Valley."* Bourke-White then documented General Patton's troops as they moved into Germany and liberated the concentration camp at Buchenwald. She published the German photos in a book entitled *Dear Fatherland, Rest Quietly*, which reflected her anger at the German people.

In 1946, Margaret Bourke-White traveled to India to photograph Mahatma Gandhi's campaign for independence from Great Britain. Her account of the granting of independence in 1947, the division of India into Hindu and Muslim parts, and the assassination of Gandhi was published in the book *Halfway to Freedom*. Bourke-White continued her relentless search for stories ranging from South Africa's departure from the British Commonwealth in 1949 to the Strategic Air Command's airborne strike force in 1951. In her venture into the Korean War in 1952, Bourke-White's photos concentrated on the gruesome impact of war on native peoples. For the last 20 years of her life, Bourke-White struggled with Parkinson's disease, which finally claimed her life in 1971.

See also Photojournalism.

Reference Goldberg, Vicki, *Margaret Bourke-White: A Biography* (1986).

Bradford, Andrew (1686–1742)

Andrew Bradford founded the first newspaper in Pennsylvania, *The American Weekly Mercury*, in 1719. He also established the first magazine in the British colonies, *The American Magazine*, in 1741. A contemporary of Benjamin Franklin, Bradford was part of a newspaper family that included his father William Bradford, his brother William Bradford Jr., and his nephew William Bradford III, who was trained by Andrew.

Born into a Philadelphia Quaker family in 1686, Andrew Bradford moved to New York City at age seven when his father became editor of the *New York Gazette*. His chief education was working as an apprentice for his father. As early as 1711, Andrew had become a partner with his father, but he moved back to Philadelphia in 1712. His first business in Philadelphia was printing the journals of the colonial assembly, and he soon earned the title of official government printer, which he held exclusively until 1730. By the 1730s, Bradford's printing business had expanded to include a book bindery and sale of writing materials.

The American Weekly Mercury, inaugurated in December 1719, was the first newspaper in Pennsylvania and the first published in the British colonies outside of Boston. The paper was printed by Bradford until his death in 1742. Bradford's main purpose in launching the paper was to encourage business for Philadelphia. As a result, there was scant coverage of local news, literature, or even obituaries normally found in colonial papers. Instead, Bradford's paper concentrated on foreign news and trade reports from ports such as New York City and Boston as well as Philadelphia. Other than his editorial work, Bradford himself contributed little to the paper and clearly lacked writing talent.

After moving to a larger printing shop in 1738, Andrew Bradford launched the first magazine in the British colonies in 1741. *The American Magazine or Monthly Review of the Political State of the British Colonies* was followed in short order by another journal published by Benjamin Franklin. Neither of the magazines was successful, however; these ambitious and diverse publications seemed to be ahead of their time. Bradford found that almanacs were more popular than sophisticated magazines and published many at his press. He also printed various works of the Society of Friends in Philadelphia, even though he was no longer a member of the sect.

Like so many early publishing efforts, Bradford's printing career suffered from the vagaries of government censorship. During a financial crisis in Pennsylvania in 1721, Bradford printed a brief appeal for the assembly to remedy the crisis. The provincial council and governor reprimanded Bradford and told him not to publish any more material concerning the operation of the colonial government. But a few years later, Bradford printed excerpts from a pamphlet that mildly suggested that a change in current officeholders was needed to ensure a selfless civic spirit in government. Bradford was arrested and imprisoned for printing the material, and his property was searched in order to seize the offending publication. After his release from jail, voters elected Bradford to the Philadelphia city council; he continued to serve until his death.

Andrew Bradford was a pioneer in American journalism of the early eighteenth century. Although no radical, he believed that people had a right to know what their government and its officials were doing. He demonstrated a civic spirit by promoting the commercial interests of Philadelphia in his newspaper as well as serving many years as postmaster and city councilman. Bradford used the best technology available in the printing of his publications because he maintained close contacts with printers in England.

Reference DeArmond, Anna J., *Andrew Bradford: Colonial Journalist* (1949).

Brady, Mathew
See Civil War; Photojournalism.

Brisbane, Arthur
See New York World.

Broadsides
During the colonial era, the broadside was a popular method of disseminating information quickly. It involved a single sheet of paper printed on only one side. If it was printed on both sides, it was called a "broadsheet." Usually, the broadside was distributed in conjunction with a particular event or occasion—political campaigns, labor strikes, social or religious events, military preparations—and often the author was not identified.

Printed materials were regulated during most of the colonial period of English rule by the Licensing Act (1662), which did not lapse until 1694. Even after the end of government licensing of printers and publishers, the government used libel prosecutions to intimidate antigovernment writers. Thus, controversial publications had to resort to surreptitious methods to get their ideas into circulation. The authors of such published works normally avoided prosecu-

tion by remaining anonymous. The result was that the printers were often prosecuted, since they were the only ones who could reliably be associated with the publication.

The result of government regulation and censorship and the threat of prosecution was the phenomenon known as the broadside, which began appearing in America during the seventeenth century and continued periodically through the American Revolution. The broadside allowed the author and, to a lesser degree, the printer to remain anonymous and free from the threat of legal action.

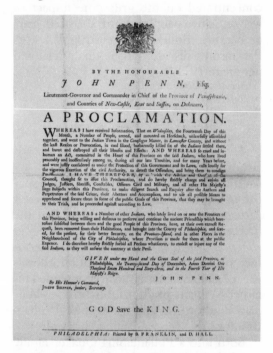

This 1763 broadside, "A Proclamation," argued against the massacring of Indians.

The first broadside known to have been printed in the English colonies was "The Freeman's Oath" (1639) at Stephen Daye's press in Cambridge, Massachusetts. It preceded by a year the publication of the first book in the colonies. The types of broadsides varied considerably, from didactic poetic verse to ballads to political commentary and satire. They were also used by the government itself to distribute official decrees—laws, thanksgiving or holiday proclamations, military recruitment, announcements—to the public. The most popular mid-seventeenth-century category of broadsides was the elegy or funeral broadside attached to the coffin, although almost none of the early examples survive. A variation on the funeral broadside was the "last dying words" of notable persons.

Eventually, many broadsides were illustrated to allow the author to make a point more dramatically and concisely. In the 1830s, the Cold Water Army temperance organization distributed its appeals through a variety of broadsides. Debates ranging from religion to politics were often facilitated by broadsides. Printer's apprentice Benjamin Franklin authored numerous ballads on broadsides printed by his brother James. P. T. Barnum relied on purple prose advertisements to solicit audiences for his "Greatest Show on Earth" circuses.

Because a broadside could be printed and circulated quickly, it could preempt the slower newspapers in getting specific news events into the public realm. The broadsheet was especially popular during the American Revolution, when authors such as Paul Revere were anxious to avoid the authorities but committed to circulating information or instructions to patriots. Isaiah Thomas (1749–1831) was perhaps the best-known colonial printer implicated in printing patriotic broadsides. These included commentary by Samuel Adams's Committee of Correspondence as well as copies of the Declaration of Independence in 1776.

Broadsides continue to be used today, mostly for advertising or political campaign purposes, but their messages are usually transmitted by newspapers, radio, or television. Because of their nature, the collection and preservation of broadsides in archives were slow to develop. After American independence, several organizations such as the Massachusetts Historical Society, the New York Historical Society, and the American Antiquarian Society began to collect and preserve broadsides.

References Bumgardner, Georgia, ed., *American Broadsides, 1680–1800* (1971); Hutchings, Sinclair, "A Broadside View of America," *Lithopinion* (1970).

Broun, Heywood Campbell (1888–1939)

Heywood Broun was the quintessential press reporter, covering events ranging from wars to theater to sports. As a columnist first at the Pulitzer-owned *New York World* and later for the Scripps-Howard *New York Telegram,* Broun was on the cutting edge of a growing trend in twentieth-century print media. He led the fight against publishers in the 1930s to establish a journalists' union—the American Newspaper Guild—to protect professional rights.

Heywood Campbell Broun was born into a middle-class family in New York City, the son of Scottish immigrant Heywood Cox Broun and German American Henrietta Brose. Broun's father owned a prosperous printing business, and Broun attended a first-class private school, where he edited the student paper. His years at Harvard College (1906–1910) included the frustration of being denied employment on the Harvard *Crimson* three successive times as well as failing to graduate. Broun's classmates at Harvard included future Bolshevik chronicler John Reed and future columnist Walter Lippmann.

Heywood Broun's journalistic career began inauspiciously in 1910 as a $20-a-week reporter for the obscure *New York Morning Telegraph.* His first assignments led him to launch a column that dealt mostly with Broadway plays but occasionally included Broun's favorite pastime, baseball. Broun soon took a position with a Broadway theatrical agency and traveled to China to develop background for a play about the Orient. Upon his return from China, Broun became a sports reporter for Whitelaw Reid's *New York Tribune.* In 1915, he became the *Tribune*'s drama critic, where his reviews sometimes alienated stars such as Ethel Barrymore.

Heywood Broun married suffragist Ruth Hale in 1917, the day before both sailed for Europe to cover the war. As a war correspondent, Broun covered all aspects of the U.S. involvement, from the first arrival of the American Expeditionary Force (AEF) to individual battles. Chafing from censorship restraints, Broun sent back numerous stories that were critical of inefficiencies in the U.S. effort and of commanding General John J. Pershing. Despite having his press credentials revoked by the AEF, Broun summarized his war experiences in two books published in 1918, *The AEF: With General Pershing and the American Forces* and *Our Army at the Front.*

Journalist crusader Heywood Campbell Broun spoke out against social injustices, a controversial position that resulted in his dismissal from two U.S. newspapers in the 1920s.

After returning to New York from France, Broun resumed duties as the *Tribune's* chief literary and drama critic. Broun praised emerging postwar talents such as novelist Sinclair Lewis and playwright Eugene O'Neill. In 1921, Broun left the conservative *Tribune* for an editorial position with the more liberal *New York World*, owned by the Pulitzer family. Broun's col-

umn, "It Seems to Me," personalized his byline with a characteristic libertarian debunking of pretensions while championing justice and tolerance. The columns were published collectively in 1935. He also contributed articles on a regular basis to *Collier's*, *Vanity Fair*, and *Atlantic Monthly* and even offered an occasional radio commentary. Broun was an original member of a literary clique known first as the Thanatopsis Club and later as the Algonquin Round Table, which promoted spirited discussions around a poker table. The group eventually included Jazz Age celebrities such as Edna Ferber, Harpo Marx, Noel Coward, and Ring Lardner.

As a journalistic crusader, Broun assailed the violence of the Ku Klux Klan in the mid-1920s, consistently trumpeted equal rights for women, advocated releasing imprisoned Socialist Eugene V. Debs, and condemned the miscarriage of justice in the Sacco-Vanzetti case. Indeed, Broun's outspoken position on the Sacco-Vanzetti affair led to his dismissal from the *New York World* in 1921. Broun quickly took an editorial post with *The Nation*, where subjects were unrestricted. Although Broun was rehired in 1928 by the *World*, he continued writing for *The Nation*. A *Nation* article that criticized New York newspapers for being too tepid led to a second dismissal from the *World*.

Broun was quickly offered a column with a lucrative salary at the *New York Telegram* in 1928. He then shocked his employers by announcing his candidacy for Congress on the Socialist Party ticket in 1930. Despite garnering public backing from celebrities such as George Gershwin, Theodore Dreiser, Walter Winchell, and the Marx brothers and gaining media attention by being arrested in a garment workers' strike, Broun finished a distant third in the election. In 1931, Pulitzer's *New York World* was bought by the owners of the *Telegram*, the Scripps-Howard chain. In the midst of offering his column as a clearinghouse for depression-era jobs and warning of the Nazi threat, Broun coproduced a Broadway play, *Shoot the Works*, which was panned by critics and lasted for only 89 performances.

Heywood Broun's activism in the 1930s led him to found a professional journalists' union, the American Newspaper Guild. His first experience in labor organization came in 1923, when he tried unsuccessfully to organize magazine and newspaper reporters into a professional association. The advent of the depression, combined with publishers' increasing fixation on balance sheets in an era of fierce competition, spurred Broun to use his *Telegram* column as a sounding board for the unionization of press professionals. The American Newspaper Guild was initially a New York entity, but it spread in 1933 to other cities, despite the vocal opposition of publishers. Soon Broun's hope that the guild would spur employment in the industry was eclipsed by concerns over Communist infiltration and unproductive strikes. After the American Newspaper Guild joined the Congress of Industrial Organizations in the late 1930s, it admitted nonprofessional press employees.

Throughout his career, Broun found time to pen a variety of books and magazine articles. Broun coauthored with Margaret Leech Pulitzer a biography of the antipornographer Anthony Comstock in 1927. In 1931, he and George Britt wrote a work excoriating U.S. anti-Semitism entitled *Christians Only*. He also wrote a whimsical tale of baseball, *The Sun Field*, in 1923 and a morose fantasy, *Gandle Follows His Nose*, in 1926. Collections of Broun's columns other than "It Seems to Me" were also published, including *Seeing Things at Night* (1921), *Pieces of Hate and Other Enthusiasms* (1922), and *Sitting on the World* (1924).

Reference O'Connor, Richard, *Heywood Broun: A Biography* (1975).

Bryant, William Cullen (1794–1878)

Although his reputation was made as a poet, William Cullen Bryant's greatest and longest contribution was as editor of the *New York Evening Post*. Bryant changed the old Federalist paper into a Democratic Party organ. Later, as an opponent of slavery, Bryant led the *Post* to support Lincoln during the Civil War.

As the editor of the New York Evening Post, *William Cullen Bryant did not surrender the paper's style to the sensationalism of the penny papers in the mid-1800s.*

William Cullen Bryant was born in Massachusetts to a physician father but showed an early predilection for literary writing. His first published poem was printed in a local newspaper when he was ten years old. He studied the law, was admitted to the bar, and practiced for ten years. In 1825, Bryant left Massachusetts for New York City, where he was employed to edit a literary magazine, the *New York Review*. When the magazine faltered in 1826, Bryant was able to obtain the position of assistant editor of the old Federalist paper, the *New York Evening Post*. During the three years of his tenure as assistant editor, Bryant became involved in supporting the rights of labor, opposing Henry Clay's protective tariff, and backing the new Democratic Party of Andrew Jackson.

After becoming editor of the *Post*, Bryant committed the paper to supporting Democratic policies, especially those that championed the causes of the common man. Bryant's reading of British classical liberals gave him a staunch moral fortitude in his editorials, which analyzed contemporary political, social, and economic issues. He was also an adept mediator, which was required after his return from a two-year trip to Europe in the 1830s. Bryant's associate editor had alienated business advertisers with some caustic antislavery rhetoric. Although Bryant's attitude toward slavery was identical with his associate's, he was able to placate the advertisers and avoid a financial crisis.

The pro-slavery tendencies of the Democratic Party eventually forced Bryant to withdraw his support. He backed the antislavery Free-Soil Party in 1848 and later endorsed the new Republican Party in 1854 and supported the nomination of Abraham Lincoln in 1860. Because of his knowledge of literature, the *Post*'s style remained refined and readable in the era of sensationalism in the penny papers.

During the Civil War, Bryant and the *Post* strongly supported the Radical Republican agenda of emancipation of slaves and severe military measures against the Confederacy. The *Post* had several contacts among Union generals, which allowed the paper to remain well informed about the progress of the war. Although Bryant gave up editorial supervision of the *Post* to his associate editor and son-in-law Parke Godwin in 1870, he remained active in charting the paper's course. The *Post* remained a Republican paper, but it did not always endorse the controversial actions of the administrations in the postwar era. Bryant died in 1878, just short of his fiftieth anniversary as editor of the *Post*. The liberalism of Bryant's editorials was matched by the dignity of his arguments throughout those decades.

Reference Brown, Charles H., *William Cullen Bryant* (1971).

Buckley, William Francis, Jr. (1925–)

The leading spokesman for Cold War conservatives, William F. Buckley, Jr. founded the *National Review* in 1955 to rival the liberal *New Republic* and *The Nation* as a conservative journal of opinion. Though circulation remained modest, the *National Review* became a platform of expression for a new breed of young conservatives. Buckley ventured into television commentary and in 1965 initiated "Firing Line," a distinctive interview show on public television.

William F. Buckley, Jr. was the sixth child born to Will Buckley and staunch Catholic Aloise Steiner in Sharon, Connecticut. Will Buckley had been deeply involved in the Mexican Revolution and much of his father's intrigue rubbed off on the son. The Buckleys were literally world travelers, living in Venezuela in 1926, Europe from 1929 to 1933, and in England during 1938–1939. William F. Buckley thus got some of his schooling at a private academy in England before finishing high school at a similar institution in New York. After graduation in 1943, Buckley went with his family to Mexico City where he learned Spanish.

Buckley was drafted, inducted into the army in 1944, and admitted to officer candidate school but by the time he completed his training the war was over. Upon discharge, Buckley enrolled at Yale University in 1946. He secured positions on the *Yale Daily News* and the debating team, and debated a law professor on a radio show, all as a freshman. Buckley eventually was named editor of the *Yale Daily News* his senior year. Buckley maintained a very strong anti-communist editorial line and irreverently attacked the irreligious views of a Yale anthropology professor. Buckley and his debating partner were the only Ivy League team to defeat a touring debate team from Oxford University in 1949.

Because of the outbreak of the Korean War in 1950 just as Buckley graduated from Yale, he was persuaded by political science professor Willmoore Kendall (himself a former CIA agent) to join the Central Intelligence Agency. Still smarting from some of his confrontations with the Yale administration, Buckley published *God and Man at Yale* in 1951 just prior to being employed by the CIA. He charged that Yale had forsaken

Christianity and the free enterprise system, and had make a mockery of academic freedom. Buckley favored allowing the alumni to set policies for Yale.

Buckley left for his first CIA assignment in Mexico City in 1951 where his main task was to edit an anti-communist tract to be circulated in Latin America. Meanwhile, Buckley's *Man and God at Yale* predictably was condemned in liberal organs such as *Atlantic Monthly* and the *New Republic*. After only nine months with the CIA, Buckley resigned and made his way to New York City to plunge into journalism. Editor William Bradford Huie of the *American Mercury* offered Buckley the position of associate editor which Buckley accepted. Very soon, Buckley quarreled with the other associate editor and quit.

Buckley joined his brother-in-law and Yale debating partner Brent Bozell to write *McCarthy and His Enemies* in 1953 about the infamous Wisconsin senator's fierce anti-communist crusade. Although not uncritical of McCarthy's methods, the work showed clear sympathy with the theme of examining government operations. The book was published in 1954 just prior to McCarthy's climactic nationally televised Army hearings. Having secured his reputation as a pariah among the eastern liberal elites, Buckley longed for a permanent vehicle to express his conservative views. Buckley desired a magazine directed at the political elites rather than the general public and one which could unify the disparate elements of libertarians, classical conservatives, and anti-communists.

Despite difficulties raising capital for the venture, plans moved forward to launch *National Review* in 1955. Buckley was assisted by Austrian expatriate Willi Schlamm, a former editorial assistant at *Time*, to recruit personnel. They got James Burnham to serve as senior editor, but failed to lure Russell Kirk or David Lawrence. Yet, staff unity disappeared in 1956 when Burnham advocated a policy of liberating Eastern Europe from Soviet domination instead of containment. Schlamm vigorously disputed Burnham's position and resigned in 1957 to

be replaced by William Rusher as publisher. From its inaugural issue, *National Review* showed disdain for "moderate" (i.e., Eisenhower) Republicanism, injected humor into its zealous partiality, and helped to create the concept of the "liberal establishment." In short, Buckley and his colleagues sought to reinvent the Right. Circulation grew slowly to 18,000 in 1957 and 25,000 in 1958.

In 1959, Buckley wrote *Up From Liberalism* which summarized his political philosophy from previous editorials and essays. He argued that the liberal obsession with "democracy" was creating a gargantuan government which would impede individual freedoms. Liberals had confused the means for the ends they sought. *National Review* refused to endorse either Republican Richard Nixon or Democrat John Kennedy in the 1960 election, yet its circulation grew from 34,000 in 1960 to 54,000 in 1961. Buckley was instrumental in founding the Young Americans for Freedom in 1961, a sign that the new conservatism was becoming vital. In 1962, Buckley began a syndicated column initially entitled "A Conservative Voice" which gave him a much wider audience than *National Review*. Soon Buckley engaged in public debates with the darlings of the liberal intelligentsia—Norman Mailer, Gore Vidal, and James Baldwin. The culmination of the reinvention of conservatism for Buckley was the Republican nomination of Senator Barry Goldwater for president in 1964. Even Goldwater's crushing defeat at the hands of Lyndon Johnson did not dismay Buckley.

Following defeat in the New York mayoral election in 1965, Buckley launched his television interview-debate show "Firing Line." It aired on a private station, WOR, in 1966. Buckley engaged guests such as columnist Max Lerner and historian Staughton Lynd with caustic challenges, yet the show was a success. Buckley was featured in the *Wall Street Journal, Harper's*, and *Time*. ABC television invited Buckley to analyze the two presidential nominating conventions in 1968 opposite Gore Vidal. The violent demonstrations at the Chicago

Democratic Convention provoked vituperative exchanges on the air between Buckley and Vidal. It was good theater, but not very informative. During the 1970s, Buckley's "Firing Line" exchanges with liberals such as Daniel Ellsberg and Germaine Greer were tame and civil compared to the earlier era.

As Buckley became less controversial and part of the conservative establishment in the late 1970s, both *National Review* and "Firing Line" lost some of their edge. Rather than challenging debates, there were plodding intellectual forays. Buckley spent more of his time writing a series of spy novels which were themselves *passe* by the 1970s. Still, *National Review*'s circulation totaled a respectable 110,000 in the late 1970s and grew to 186,000 by 1994 when John O'Sullivan was editor.

Reference Judis, John B., *William F. Buckley, Jr.: Patron Saint of the Conservatives* (1988).

Cable News Network (CNN)
See Cable Television.

Cable Satellite Public Affairs Network (C-SPAN)
See Cable Television.

Cable Television
The first experiments with cable systems took place in Oregon in 1948, leading to the rapid expansion of the 1970s. Today, cable is available to most urban communities in the United States. Cable allows customers to receive a wide array of stations and services, relying on both broadcast and satellite reception through a community antenna. The improved technology using fiber-optic cable to replace coaxial cable will further increase viewers' options. The Federal Communications Commission (FCC) allowed cable company regulation by local governments in the 1970s, but Congress began passing regulatory legislation in the 1980s.

The development of the community antenna system originally designated CATV used a powerful antenna to receive broadcast signals more clearly than home antennas. Cable companies charged a fee to customers who subscribed to the community antenna offerings. L. E. Parsons launched a CATV system in Astoria, Oregon, in 1948 to pull in signals from a distant Seattle broadcast station to the local community. John Walson established a similar system in Mahoney City, Pennsylvania, later in 1948 to receive signals from Philadelphia stations. Slowly, other primarily rural communities began to create CATV systems to bring in otherwise weak signals from distant broadcast stations.

In 1972, the FCC changed the rules, allowing cable companies to acquire broadcasts from other sources such as satellites. New York City's Manhattan Cable Company inaugurated the Sterling Movie Network, which allowed cable subscribers to receive commercial-free movies for an additional fee. The same year, Home Box Office began selling "premium" movie channels to cable distributors via satellite from its headquarters in Wilkes-Barre, Pennsylvania. The number of cable companies multiplied rapidly, and by the 1990s, 50 million customers subscribed to cable television. Multiple system operators also became more common as local companies were bought by large conglomerates such as Telecommunications, Inc. (TCI), Times Mirror Company, Cox Enterprises, and Time Warner, Inc. TCI cable became the largest national company, with over 6 million subscribers and revenues of $1.7 billion.

Coaxial cable wiring remains the most common means of transmitting cable channels to customers. However, because fiber-optic cable can carry a larger volume of transmissions than coaxial, it will gradually displace the older technology and allow dozens of channel options. Cable companies operate through franchises granted by local government authorities so that they become monopolies. Most franchises extend over a 15-year period to give companies the ability to recoup construction costs.

Cable companies usually offer customers groups of channels. Basic service includes local broadcast television stations, one or more of the "superstations" beamed by satellite—such as WTBS in Atlanta, WGN in Chicago, and WWOR in New Jersey—and some specialized channels such as Cable News Network (CNN) and ESPN, an all-sports channel. The so-called premium movie channels are grouped separately for additional fees. Cable systems also offer "pay-per-view" movies, which customers buy individually per showing for a flat fee and are handled through a computer registering system. Most cable systems include one channel that operates as a viewer guide to programming on all the channels offered. The variety of cable channels is extensive. Many cable channels are highly specialized: the Weather Channel offers continuous local, national, and international reports; the Arts and Entertainment Channel emphasizes fine arts programs; the Nashville Network has country-and-western music; Viacom's MTV features rock music videos; Black Entertainment Television caters to ethnic interests; and Turner Network Television (TNT) offers continuous movies from the film libraries of Metro-Goldwyn-Mayer and United Artists.

In 1979, cable systems financed the launching of the commercial-free Cable Satellite Public Affairs Network (C-SPAN), which began televising live debates in the House of Representatives. Later, C-SPAN broadened its programming to cover press conferences and public affairs seminars as well as interviews, book reviews, and roundtable discussions of political issues. In the 1990s, C-SPAN 2 began televising Senate proceedings. Brian Lamb is the chief executive officer of C-SPAN, which was viewed by 60 million cable customers in 1994.

Also launched in 1979 was Ted Turner's experiment in all-news programming, CNN. It placed immediate pressure on the news divisions of the three broadcast networks. Headquartered in Atlanta, CNN operates bureaus in Washington, New York, Chicago, and Los Angeles. CNN maintains 24-hour coverage of news and provides in-depth treatment of topics as well as weather, financial, and sports reports, reaching 62 million cable subscribers on 14,600 cable systems. CNN also broadcasts "Headline News" on a separate cable channel, which provides 30-minute capsules of news, weather, sports, and business information every half hour. CNN began operating an international service in 1985 with several foreign bureaus in Europe, Latin America, Asia, and Africa, providing service to 58 nations.

Thirteen western broadcasters tried to force the FCC to regulate cable systems in the 1956 case *Frontier Broadcasting v. Collier*, but the FCC refused. In 1962, after congressional criticism, the FCC assumed responsibility for regulating cable development because of its use of interstate microwave transmissions. By 1966, the FCC had issued a series of guidelines to cable companies. In *United States v. Southwestern Cable Co.*, a San Diego cable company unsuccessfully fought FCC regulation. The Supreme Court endorsed the FCC's jurisdiction based on the interstate commerce clause of Article I of the Constitution. Nonetheless, the FCC gradually delegated most regulatory authority to local governments during the 1970s.

Congress's Copyright Act of 1978 required cable systems, as commercial bodies, to acquire compulsory licenses to sell their video services. Local broadcast stations pressured the FCC to require cable systems to carry local television stations (the so-called must-carry rule), but the courts held that such a requirement would abridge First Amendment rights. The Cable Communications Policy Act of 1984 established a national cable policy. Congress wanted to ensure the diversity of cable services and established quality standards that were useful for franchise renewal reviews. In response to complaints about unreasonable rate increases by cable companies, Congress passed the Cable Television Consumer Protection and Competition Act of 1992, which gave the FCC the right to review rate increases and eliminate excessive charges. The act also required cable systems to carry at least one educational, noncommercial station and at least three local commercial stations. The must-carry rule that had been declared unconstitutional in two previous court decisions (*Quincy Cable TV v. FCC* in 1985 and *Century Communications Corporation v. FCC* in 1987) was thus tried again in a different form. Congressional scrutiny of the cable business in the 1990s was a barometer of both the increased availability of cable systems and the concerns of cable customers.

Reference Parsons, Patrick, *Cable Television and the First Amendment* (1987).

Cartoons

One of the most effective types of illustrations in the media is cartoon commentary, which became a regular feature of print media in the twentieth century. Cartoons and comic strips allow humor to be injected into otherwise serious subjects for the purpose of making concise but important points.

Editorial comment, not to mention cartoon commentary, emerged rather slowly in American journalism. Isaiah Thomas's *Massachusetts Spy* revived on its 1774 masthead the 1754 *Pennsylvania Gazette* emblem of a severed snake originally drawn by Benjamin Franklin. The snake symbolized division among the colonies and was intended to provoke unity in the struggle against Great Britain. It may have been the first editorial use of an illustration in American media history. It demonstrated the possibilities of concise, salient comment through illustration. Yet duplication of the *Spy*'s device occurred only sporadically until Andrew Jackson's presidency.

During the 1832 presidential campaign, The *United States Telegraph*, a national Republican paper supporting Henry Clay, printed some woodcut cartoons accompanied by verses satirizing Democratic incumbent Andrew Jackson. Still, it was not until after the Civil War that cartoon illustrations emerged from obscurity. In 1867, James Gordon Bennett's two-cent *New York Evening Telegram* began featuring large front-page cartoons with brief descriptive text on Fridays. Most of the subjects were politicians.

Unquestionably, it was Thomas Nast, cartoonist for *Harper's Weekly* and the *New York Times*, who ushered in the heyday of editorial cartoons with 50 drawings attacking the infamous Tweed Ring in New York City during 1871. Originally hired by George William Curtis of *Harper's* to illustrate Civil War battles, Nast caricatured Boss Tweed and his corrupt Tammany Hall coterie so effectively that the public demanded the prosecution of the gang in the early 1870s. The Nast cartoons also happened to triple the sales of *Harper's Weekly*, which encouraged other publications to follow suit with their own political cartoons. The *New York Daily Graphic* became the first fully illustrated newspaper in 1873. Periodicals such as Joseph Keppler's *Puck* (1877) and Bernard Gillam's *Judge* (1881) used political cartoons almost exclusively for their material.

Joseph Pulitzer's *New York World* began the sensational yellow journalism trend during the 1884 presidential campaign by relying on cartoons drawn by Walt McDougall and Valerian Gribayedoff. Editorial cartoons became a fixture in the Sunday *World*, and when the rival *New York Herald* began using them in daily editions in 1889, the *World* followed suit. The 1896 presidential campaign between Republican William McKinley and Populist-Democrat William Jennings Bryan sparked a wave of cartoons. Artist Homer Davenport lampooned Republicans, especially party boss Mark Hanna, in William Randolph Hearst's *New York Journal*. Veteran artists Charles G. Bush and Charles Lederer became featured cartoonists for Pulitzer's *World*. *Washington Post* cartoonist Clifford K. Berryman made his biggest splash with the "Remember the Maine" slogan in 1898. Pulitzer Prize–winner John T. McCutcheon's pointed drawings appeared regularly in the *Chicago Tribune* after 1903. Of course, politicians were not amused, and the California legislature passed an 1899 law prohibiting cartoon caricatures. The law was never enforced and invited further satires of the legislature.

The popularity of editorial cartoons expanded in the twentieth century. Rollin Kirby of the *New York World* unmercifully parodied prohibitionists in the 1920s. Edmund Duffy of the *Baltimore Sun* was known for his caustic satire and caricatures. Both won Pulitzer Prizes three times. Bill Mauldin won a Pulitzer in 1944 for his memorable portrayal of World War II GIs Willie and Joe in *Stars and Stripes*. He won a second Pulitzer in 1958 while drawing for the *St. Louis Post-Dispatch* and was syndicated by the *Chicago Sun-Times* in 1962. Two-time Pulitzer winner Herbert L. Block, who signed his syndicated drawings "Herblock," became the most influential political cartoonist for the *Washington Post* beginning in 1946. Another popular syndicated cartoonist since the 1960s has been the *Denver Post*'s Patrick Oliphant. Periodicals devoted to current affairs also employ cartoons as a regular feature.

The comic strip, a complement to editorial

cartoons, began in 1896 as a result of the fierce competition in New York City between Pulitzer and Hearst for readers. The use of a series of cartoon panels featuring regular characters such as "Yellow Kid," "Buster Brown," or "Little Nemo" became instantly popular with readers. The longest-running series, the "Katzenjammer Kids," was begun in color by Rudolph Dirks in 1897 for Hearst's King Features syndicate. H. C. Fisher's "Mutt and Jeff," the first regular daily cartoon series, appeared in the *San Francisco Chronicle* in 1907. The most popular comic strip, "Blondie," started by Chic Young for King Features in 1930, has 1,600 newspaper subscribers. Besides the lovable stock "comic" characters in successful strips, there have also been long-running adventure series, such as Chester Gould's detective "Dick Tracy" (1931) and Harold Gray's "Little Orphan Annie" (1924). Children can be popular cartoon subjects, as proved by Hank Ketcham's "Dennis the Menace" in the 1950s and Charles Schulz's "Peanuts" characters since the 1960s.

Comic strips also occasionally offer social and political commentary—sometimes bluntly, through Al Capp's indignant parodies played out by his hillbillies in "Li'l Abner" (1935–1977), or more subtly via Walt Kelly's swamp animals in "Pogo," beginning in 1948. Both Capp (1947) and Kelly (1951) won the National Cartoonists Society's "Reuben" prize. The most recent effective practitioner of comic strip political and social commentary has been Gary Trudeau, inspired by Schulz and Kelly. Trudeau's oddball characters in "Doonesbury" can be so politically slanted that some editors place the strip on the op-ed page instead of with the other comics.

References Becker, Stephen, *Comic Art in America: A Social History of the Funnies, the Political Cartoons, Magazine Humor, Sporting Cartoons, and Animated Cartoons* (1959); Hess, Stephen, and Milton Kaplan, *The Ungentlemanly Art: A History of American Political Cartoons* (1975).

Cash, Wilbur Joseph (1900–1941)

North Carolina journalist and author W. J. Cash wrote perhaps the most original and controversial work ever penned on the modern South, *The Mind of the South*, in 1941. But upon being catapulted into fame, Cash committed suicide.

Wilbur Joseph Cash was born into a plain Scotch-Irish family in Gaffney, South Carolina. Cash's view of the South was shaped by his parents' primitive Baptist views, by Thomas Dixon's racist novels and the movie *The Birth of a Nation* based on Dixon's *Clansman*, and by the frequent racial clashes common to the segregationist era. In 1912, the Cash family moved to Boiling Springs, North Carolina, where Cash received a sound education in the classics at a Baptist secondary school. After briefly attending Wofford College in nearby South Carolina and Valparaiso University in Indiana, Cash settled at Wake Forest, a North Carolina Baptist college. There Cash met moderate southern liberals, including college president William Louis Poteat. Cash's first writings included poetry and short stories published in the student literary magazine, but his real talent was revealed in the student newspaper, where Cash once defended Poteat against racial reactionaries.

Cash taught English at Georgetown College in Kentucky and worked one summer as a reporter for the *Charlotte Observer*. Determined to pursue his love of journalism, Cash struck out for Chicago, where he did a stint on the *Chicago Post*, but a hyperthyroid condition forced him back to North Carolina to concentrate on creative writing. Although Cash's favorite literary work was Joseph Conrad's *Heart of Darkness*, his unquestioned stylistic and intellectual mentor was Henry Louis Mencken. Mencken's attacks on southern fundamentalism and obscurantism coincided with Cash's philosophy. Moreover, Mencken wanted to encourage southern iconoclasts in his own image. After failing to produce a Dostoyevsky-like novel, Cash began writing pieces for journals such as Mencken's *American Mercury*. With Mencken's inspiration, Cash had already developed his concept of the "savage ideal" to explain the South's intolerant cultural provincialism.

That ideal was most evident in fundamentalist preachers such as Billy Sunday, who espoused a "cocksure certainty in a world in which nothing is certain but that nothing is certain."

After a trip to Europe in 1927 for his health, Cash returned to the *Charlotte News* as an editorial writer, columnist, and book reviewer. Cash relished defending "modernism" as reflected in Freud's and Darwin's science and in avant-garde writers such as Theodore Dreiser. Neurasthenia forced him back to Boiling Springs in 1928, but after his condition stabilized, Cash began editing a twice-weekly county newspaper, the *Cleveland Press*, owned by a liberal Democrat. The position allowed Cash great freedom to espouse his liberal views, including defending controversial 1928 Democratic presidential candidate Al Smith and flailing the Ku Klux Klan's anti-Catholic bigotry.

Although his first essay sent to the *American Mercury* was rejected, Cash submitted another in 1929, attacking North Carolina Senator Furnivold M. Simmons for refusing to back Smith's candidacy. Mencken eagerly agreed to publish the essay. Soon Cash sent another piece intriguingly entitled "The Mind of the South," which the *Mercury* also published in 1929. It was, of course, the outline of a larger work that would occupy Cash's attention over the next decade. Mencken's journal also published another Cash essay in 1930 that was sympathetic to a controversial Gastonia, North Carolina, textile strike the previous year. Cash soon negotiated with Alfred A. Knopf a deal to publish a book-length version of his "Mind of the South" treatise.

Cash sought advice from the South's leading sociologist, Howard W. Odum, in developing the themes in *The Mind of the South*. These included the continued hold of Old South culture in the post–Civil War New South, the rigid deference to authority centered in the plantation tradition, undue sentimentality and romanticism mostly revolving around the Confederate "lost cause," and the intractable, all-pervasive issue of race. Moreover, all the themes were linked intricately and indelibly together in a unified southern culture.

During the early 1930s, Cash lived at home with his parents, where he often relapsed into the debilitating neurasthenia. In 1932, Cash wrote an article ridiculing Charlotte as a mecca of Presbyterians, Rotarians, and Babbittry. Another 1933 essay in the *American Mercury* assailed the Methodist college at Durham funded by the Duke family but predicted that it would one day become a haven of liberalism. A 1934 essay by Cash made light of southern clergy predictions that Herbert Hoover was God-ordained. Cash's last essay published in the *Mercury* in 1935 dealt impolitely with the origins of the southern "cracker." Cash also authored two pieces on local North Carolina politics and culture published by the *Baltimore Evening Sun* in 1935.

In 1936, Cash dispatched his first chapters of *The Mind of the South* to Knopf. There followed many months of delay after the publisher asked for revisions that Cash did not initially pursue. Meanwhile, Cash took an editorial position with the *Charlotte News*, where he was limited to writing about European events or literature but not about local or state affairs. Cash spent the next five years writing varied pieces for the editorial page. He was promoted to associate editor after two years.

In 1938, Cash fell in love with divorcée Mary Ross Northrop, and the two were soon married. She inspired him to resume writing *The Mind of the South*. Even then, there were further delays as Cash became sidetracked in his editorials by Nazi and Japanese threats to world peace. Cash also became a heavy drinker during 1939 and 1940, and it began to affect his health and his work. Despite Knopf's frustrations with Cash, the author delivered the complete 160,000-word manuscript in July 1940, and the long-awaited *The Mind of the South* was published in February 1941. Cash was nervous about the critical response to his masterpiece, but reviews across the South were almost entirely laudatory. National reviews in organs such as *Time* magazine, the *New York Times*, and the *New Republic* were even more favorable, much to the surprise of Cash. *The Mind of the South*, a journalistic commentary rather than a history, has never been out of print since its first publication in 1941.

Obviously, the South consumed Cash in more ways than one. He loved the region yet believed that it was imprisoned by its own history and culture. His inability to be detached from his subject hampered his objectivity, yet it also imbued his story with realism. The tragedy of the South on a grand scale was in many ways reflected by the life of Wilbur Joseph Cash, who committed suicide in Mexico City in 1941.

Reference Clayton, Bruce, *W. J. Cash: A Life* (1991).

Cather, Willa (1873–1947)

Although known primarily for her poetry and fiction, Willa Cather regarded herself as a journalist. She had considerable experience writing for the *Pittsburgh Daily Leader* and *McClure's* magazine early in her career.

Willa Cather was born in Virginia in 1873. A decade later, she moved with her family to Nebraska, where her father operated a farm credit agency. Educated at the University of Nebraska at Lincoln (1891–1895), Cather edited the student yearbook, the *Sombrero* (1894), in which she collaborated with future Pulitzer Prize winner Dorothy Canfield (Fisher) on an essay. Cather also wrote a column for the *Daily Nebraskan*, the student newspaper, and she was associate editor of two student literary magazines. During her student days, Cather also served as drama critic and columnist for the *Nebraska State Journal* in Lincoln. Upon graduation in 1895, Cather continued to write for the *Journal* as well as for the weekly *Lincoln Courier*.

In 1896, publisher Charles Axtell of Pittsburgh's *Home Monthly* magazine made Cather assistant editor, a position that allowed her to publish some of her short stories. Because of Cather's reviewing experience in Lincoln, she gained the post of part-time drama critic for the *Pittsburgh Daily Leader*. In 1897, *Home Monthly* was

sold and Cather left to accept the position of telegraph editor with the newspaper. She also began to write more short stories in her spare time, and her contributions were accepted by *Cosmopolitan* and the *Saturday Evening Post* as well as lesser journals. During the years 1901 to 1906, Cather broadened her experience by teaching high school English. A 1902 trip to Europe inspired her first publication of poetry in 1903, *April Twilights*, followed by a collection of short stories, *The Troll Garden* (1905).

Because of her emerging reputation, in 1903, Samuel S. McClure invited Cather to write for *McClure's* magazine. Cather contributed a few articles, but her big break came after the departure of *McClure's* elite reporters—Ida Tarbell, Lincoln Steffens, and Ray Stannard Baker—to form their own magazine. In need of immediate help to run his magazine, McClure offered Cather an editorial position, which she accepted in 1906. In 1908, Cather was given the task of editing the text and checking the facts in a controversial biography of Christian Science founder Mary Baker Eddy that McClure wanted to serialize in his magazine. As a result of her successful reworking of that text, McClure asked Cather to write a serialized biography of him.

Despite the diverse responsibilities and opportunities at *McClure's*, Cather followed the encouragement of her literary friends, including Sarah Orne Jewett, to change her career from editing to writing fiction. Cather left *McClure's* in 1912 and never returned to journalism. She went on to publish several famous works, including *O Pioneers!* (1913), *The Song of the Lark* (1915), *My Antonia* (1918), and *One of Ours* (winner of the 1923 Pulitzer Prize for fiction). Although best known for her fiction, Willa Cather owed a great deal to her years as a journalist, which allowed her to develop her writing talent.

Reference Robinson, Phyllis C., *Willa: The Life of Willa Cather* (1983).

Censorship
See Prior Restraint.

Chain Newspapers

The twentieth century has witnessed major consolidations of daily newspapers, reducing competition in major urban markets through mergers and acquisitions. By the 1990s, more than three-fourths of U.S. dailies operated within chains.

The best known and most successful of the early chain pioneers was William Randolph Hearst. Hearst's father, George, bought the *San Francisco Examiner* in 1880, and William became editor and publisher in 1887. Hearst used profits from his California paper and other family business ventures to purchase a former penny paper, the *New York Journal*, in 1895. The primary competition for Hearst's *Journal* was Joseph Pulitzer's *New York World*. The contest between the two was fierce, especially during the era of yellow journalism climaxed by the Spanish-American War in 1898. After the 1901 assassination of Hearst's political enemy President William McKinley, the *Journal*'s name was changed to the *American*. Hearst also moved into Chicago with the evening *American* in 1900 and the morning *Examiner* in 1902. He launched the *Los Angeles Examiner* in 1903 and the *Boston American* in 1904.

Hearst's chief competitor, Joseph Pulitzer, engaged in a more limited expansion. Pulitzer's career began with part ownership of the *St. Louis Post* in 1872, but his influence dates from the purchase of the *St. Louis Dispatch* in 1878. The two papers were combined, and by 1882, the *Post-Dispatch* was the leading St. Louis daily. Pulitzer began his expansion in 1883 by purchasing from Jay Gould the *New York World*, which immediately became the leading paper in New York City.

The other major player in early chain ownership was Edward Wyllis Scripps, who purchased his first paper, the *Cleveland Press*, in 1878. Profits from the *Press* allowed Scripps to buy the *Cincinnati Post* in 1883. During the 1880s, Scripps also became a partner with his half brother, who had established the *Detroit News* in 1873. Scripps invested in short-lived newspapers in Buffalo, St. Louis, Chicago, and Philadelphia as well. Yet his successes outnumbered his failures. In 1889, Scripps formed the Scripps-McRae League of Newspapers with his business manager. By 1911, the league was composed of 18 dailies in eight states, including the *San Diego Sun*, the *San Francisco News*, and the *Los Angeles Record*. Roy W. Howard left the Scripps-owned United Press Association in 1920 to become a partner with Scripps in the newspaper chain. The Scripps-Howard chain tended to be more successful in medium-sized markets such as Akron, Knoxville, Pittsburgh, and Memphis. By the late 1980s, the Scripps-Howard Company had become a multimedia public corporation, but its 23 daily newspapers remained the core of the business.

By 1900, ten chain ownerships, ranging from two to five dailies each, controlled 32 papers and about 15 percent of total daily circulation. Chain ownership doubled during the 1920s to more than 50 groups and increased their share of circulation to just under 40 percent. A select group, including the original chain papers, contributed to an expanding influence after World War I. The most dominant and financially successful chain launched in the 1920s was the Gannett Company. A leader among the chain groups since the 1930s, Gannett owned 28 small newspapers until it became a public corporation in 1967. Its growth into major markets such as Detroit and Louisville was climaxed by the launching of the innovative *USA Today* in 1982. By the end of the 1980s, Gannett owned 89 daily newspapers in addition to television broadcast stations, and it was the largest newspaper chain in the United States.

Other dominant chain owners dating from the 1920s included Ohioan James M. Cox, whose corporate legacy published 29 newspapers by the end of the 1980s. The Knight-Ridder group, which merged in 1974, owned 30 daily papers by the 1980s. Samuel I. Newhouse's chain began in the 1920s in New York and New Jersey and had expanded to 15 papers by 1955 in cities such as Portland, Cleveland, St. Louis, and Birmingham. By the 1980s, the Newhouse chain included 25 dailies in addition to ownership of numerous periodicals and book publishers. The Tribune Company, with only nine dailies anchored by the *New York Daily News* and the *Chicago Tribune*, still ranked high in national circulation in the 1980s. The Thomson Group, owned by a Canadian family, obtained ownership of more than 100 U.S. dailies by the 1980s, mostly in smaller cities. Dow, Jones and Company's ownership is dominated by its flagship paper the *Wall Street Journal*, the largest circulation newspaper, but it also owns about two dozen other dailies.

The phenomenon of chain ownership has reduced the number of dailies and the amount of competition, and the dominance of the chains is unquestioned. By 1986, 127 chains with 1,158 papers controlled almost 80 percent of the daily paper circulation in the United States and owned 70 percent of all dailies. The number of owners of daily newspapers declined from 1,920 in 1920 to 626 in 1986. Yet another trend has also marked the past several decades—public stock ownership of major chains. The Dow Jones Company was the first to go public in the 1960s and was followed by Knight-Ridder, the Tribune Company, the New York Times Corporation, and the Washington Post Corporation, as well as others. Newspaper chains were also caught up in the construction of multimedia conglomerates featuring periodical, television station, and cable television elements.

See also Cox, James Middleton; Gannett Company; Hearst, William Randolph; Newhouse, Samuel Irving; Pulitzer, Joseph; Scripps-Howard Company.

References Ghiglione, Loren, ed., *The Buying and Selling of America's Newspapers* (1984); Sterling, Christopher H., "Trends in Daily Newspaper and Broadcast Ownership, 1922–70," *Journalism Quarterly* (1975).

Charleston News and Courier

Although not the oldest paper in Charleston, the *Courier*—later the *News and Courier*—is one of the longest–running newspapers in the United States. From its beginnings as a Federalist paper, the *News and Courier* has spared no effort to exhibit first-rate reporting and optimum news-gathering techniques.

Three immigrants founded the *Charleston Courier* in 1803: Loring Andrews, Aaron Smith Willington, and Stephen Cullen Carpenter. The first issue of the paper focused on the threat posed by Napoleon Bonaparte and the issue of the Louisiana Territory. Composed of four 12-by-20-inch pages, the daily *Courier* sold subscriptions for $7 a year. Andrews sold his interest in the paper in 1805, and Carpenter served as editor until his departure from Charleston in 1806. By 1813, Willington was the sole owner. The *Courier* showed Federalist partisanship from its founding until the party faded from existence after the War of 1812. Thereafter, the *Courier* assumed a moderate stance on most political issues. As the first U.S. paper to report the Peace of Ghent in February 1815, the *Courier* gained national recognition. In 1827, the paper became the first in the South to place a correspondent in Washington.

During heated debates over nullification of the protective tariff in the early 1830s, the *Courier*'s editorial writer Richard Yeardon stood against nullification and thus opposed native son John C. Calhoun. Willington made Yeardon and William S. King partners in the paper in 1833. Yeardon retired in 1844, and King died in 1852, but Willington continued to lead the *Courier* until his death in 1862. Although the *Courier* continued to oppose talk of secession during the debates on the Compromise of 1850, editorials actually appeared infrequently. Advertising occupied the greatest volume of space, and most of the news was commercial in nature.

During the Mexican War (1846–1848), the *Courier* cooperated with the *New York Sun* to obtain rapid dispatches from the war zone. The *Courier* installed Charleston's first steam-driven presses in 1859. During the bombardment of Charleston by the Union navy in 1863, the paper suspended publication for nine days. After the surrender to Union forces in 1865, the *Courier* was handed over to George Whittemore, who pledged loyalty to the Union. The Willington family regained control of the *Courier* before the end of 1865 and made Thomas Y. Simons editor.

The *Charleston News* began as a daily in August 1865; it was owned by George R. Cathcart, James W. McMillan, and Mandred Morton. In 1867, the *News* was sold to a firm headed by Virginia native Bartholomew R. Riordan and Englishman Francis W. Dawson, who quickly turned the *News* into a sterling paper. The Riordan-Dawson firm purchased the *Courier* in 1873 at auction and combined the two papers as the *News and Courier*. It began a Sunday edition in 1879, and income tripled between 1868 and 1881. Under Dawson's editorial management, the *News and Courier* ended its traditional moderation with campaigns against violent episodes such as dueling, murders, and lynching. Reporters wrote stories about abuses in the convict leasing system and bootleg liquor manufacture. Dawson paid for the coverage by being shot and killed in the paper's office in 1889.

James Calvin Hemphill, an employee since 1880, became editor of the *News and Courier* in 1889. Hemphill continued Dawson's activist editorial regime, promoting the expansion of textile mills, the revival of tobacco crops, and the establishment of the Charleston Navy Yard. The *News and Courier* also had the temerity to oppose the state's most famous demagogue, "Pitchfork" Ben Tillman. When Hemphill left Charleston in 1910 to become editor of the *Richmond Times-Dispatch*, Robert Lathan was named editor.

Just as Hemphill had battled Tillman, Lathan came up against a new demagogue, Cole Blease, as well as bitter political contests in the city of Charleston. Before Lathan resigned as editor in 1927, he received the Pulitzer Prize for his 1924 editorials opposing boss rule in the city and state. Lathan was succeeded as editor by William Watts Ball, dean of the journalism school at the University of South Carolina. Ball had formerly edited the *Columbia State* and had also been Hemphill's assistant editor at the *News and Courier* from 1904 to 1909. Ball kept the paper in the forefront of controversial issues by opposing the Prohibition amendment and Roosevelt's New Deal. Ball's states' rights stands were reminiscent of John C. Calhoun's fights.

When Ball stepped down as editor on the first day of 1951, Thomas R. Waring took his place. Ball had hired Waring as a reporter for the *News and Courier* in 1927. The paper supported Republican Dwight Eisenhower in the elections of 1952 and 1956. The daily circulation in 1992 was 80,000, and the Sunday circulation totaled 122,000. The editor in 1992 was Larry Tarleton, and the publisher was Ivan V. Anderson Jr.

Reference Sass, Herbert R., *Outspoken: 150 Years of the News and Courier* (1953).

Chicago Daily News and *Record*

Founded by Melville E. Stone in 1876, the *Chicago Daily News* became Chicago's circulation leader and major competitor with the older *Chicago Tribune*. Known as the writer's newspaper, the *Daily News* remained a lively paper which specialized in sensational stories and investigative reporting. Beginning in 1881, the *Daily News* published a morning edition known as the *Record*. Both papers opposed corruption and fought for citizen and consumer rights.

Melville E. Stone began his newspaper career as managing editor of the *Chicago Republican* in 1872 at the very moment the name was changed to the *Inter Ocean*. Stone soon left to join the evening *Chicago Mail* where he served as Washington correspondent. He later returned to Chicago as managing editor of the merged *Mail and Post*. Stone became interested in starting a one cent daily patterned after the highly successful *New York Daily News*. With very little capital, Stone published the first issue of the penny *Chicago Daily News* in January 1876. The paper was printed in a modest four-page, five-column format. Stone envisioned his paper as one which would cover all pertinent news, entertain readers and shape public opinion.

Stone recruited some able assistants to achieve his goals. His financial partners were former reporter William Dougherty and Percy Meggy, but they had trouble meeting payrolls and paying for services such as the telegraph. After Meggy withdrew his assets and the *Daily News* was on the verge of bankruptcy, Stone recruited wealthy Victor F. Lawson to become sole owner and business manager. By 1877, circulation grew to 20,000 and advertising stabilized. Stone eventually secured one-third of the stock and Lawson owned the remaining two-thirds. The *Daily News* bought the competing *Post and Mail* in 1878, thereby obtaining an Associated Press membership. Wisely anticipating the importance of new technology, Stone became a major investor in Ottmar Mergenthaler's linotype manufacturing company in the 1880s.

The success of the evening *Daily News* allowed the ownership to launch a morning edition known as the *Record* in 1881 at two cents per copy. In 1885, the *Daily News* topped the 100,000 circulation mark and doubled that figure over the next three years giving the paper the second largest circulation in the nation after the *New York World*. Eugene Field was recruited to write a popular humor column called "Sharps and Flats," and the *Daily News* became famous for its feature articles. Stone recruited guest contributors from the literary, scientific, and professional ranks. When he decided to retire in 1888, Stone sold his share of the business for $350,000 to Lawson who became sole owner.

The *Daily News* retained its circulation leadership and reputation for readability under Lawson's guidance. It became noted for the use of illustrations and often published six editions daily. Managing editor Henry J. Smith, known for his integrity and crusading reform efforts, recruited and developed numerous talented writers including Carl Sandburg. The morning *Record* employed one of the profession's most talented illustrators, John T. McCutcheon, in the 1890s.

The *Daily News* covered mostly local affairs, but beginning with the Spanish-American War of 1898 moved into the foreign news-gathering realm with zest. Edward P. Bell headed a European bureau from 1900 to 1922 and relied upon excellent reporters to give the *Daily News* a superior reputation for its foreign news. John Gunther and Paul Scott Mowrer provided perhaps the nation's best coverage of World War I and the Paris peace conference. The morning *Record*, an innovator in presidential polling, carried on campaigns for more diversity in banking and publicized abuses of private utility companies in the era before World War I. At the death of owner Lawson in 1925, a group headed by former business manager Walter A. Strong purchased the *Daily News* and *Record* for $13.5 million.

The *Daily News* company acquired another rival, the *Journal*, in 1929 and even started its own radio station. Upon Strong's death in 1931, former Hearst general manager Frank Knox and publisher Theodore Ellis joined the ownership. Politically active, Knox was a Republican vice presidential nominee in 1936 and later served as Franklin Roosevelt's wartime secretary of the navy. The *Daily News* received reports on the clouds of war in Europe during the late 1930s from reporter M. W. Fodor. Also, it was only one of a handful of U.S. dailies which had reporters covering World War II.

Knox died in 1944 and was replaced as majority owner by John S. Knight who had begun to build an impressive chain of dailies. Despite becoming part of a larger group of papers, the *Daily News* retained much of its distinctiveness. Because Knight wanted his papers to inform rather than instruct, the *Daily News* showed editorial independence except for national election endorsements. After Knight made Basil "Stuffy" Walters executive editor of the *Daily News*, the famous foreign bureau reports were compressed for the first time. Nonetheless, Korean War reporters Keyes Beech and Fred Sparks won Pulitzer Prizes for their efforts. The *Daily News* also won Pulitzers for public service in 1950 and 1957. Circulation grew from 427,000 in 1944 to 614,000 in 1957, vaulting the *Daily News* from third to second place behind the *Chicago Tribune*.

In 1959, for a record $24 million Knight sold the *Daily News* to Marshall Field IV, whose father had marketed the tabloid *Chicago Sun-Times* in the 1940s. The *Daily News* continued its operations independent of the *Sun-Times*. Marshall Field IV succeeded Walters as editor in 1961 and Marshall Field V followed in 1969 as the *Daily News* continued garnering professional plaudits. It won another public service Pulitzer in 1963, cartoonist John Fischetti received a prize in 1969, reporter William J. Eaton won in 1970 and columnist Mike Royko in 1972. In the 1970s, polls surveying the best daily newspapers listed the *Chicago Daily News* in the top ten. Yet, the *Daily News* suddenly was forced into oblivion in 1978 after circulation dropped to 315,000, punctuated by severe advertising losses. Some analysts blamed the absence of a lucrative Sunday edition for much of the financial difficulties of the *Daily News*, while others credited ineffectual management and editing.

Reference Stone, Melville E., *Fifty Years as a Journalist* (1921).

Chicago Defender

During World War I, the *Chicago Defender* enunciated a clear policy favoring equal opportunity for America's blacks. Founder and editor Robert Abbott remained an outspoken voice for ending discrimination and segregation in American society. The *Defender* gained a national audience in black communities. Publisher John Sengstacke kept the *Defender* at the forefront of the Civil Rights movement after World War II. He transformed the *Defender* from a weekly to a daily in 1956 and acquired a chain of nine newspapers.

The *Chicago Defender* was founded in 1905 as a weekly black newspaper. The fiery editor and publisher through the first three decades of its existence was Georgia-born Robert S. Abbott, son of slave parents. Abbott had learned his printing skills while attending Hampton Institute and working for his stepfather's newspaper. Except for a few acquaintances volunteering assistance, the *Defender* was essentially a one-man op-

eration. By the time of World War I, the *Defender*'s circulation of 230,000 included many readers outside of Chicago. Abbott designed the *Defender* along the lines of the largest mass circulation dailies with sports and women's departments as well as attention to news and editorial comment.

At a time when division among black leaders existed over segregationist social policies and political disfranchisement, Abbott offered a clear voice advocating equal opportunity for blacks in American society, especially in jobs, education, and politics. He called for overturning the segregated policies on public transportation and in the schools. World War I gave Abbott another policy to attack when blacks were called to serve in segregated military units. It was during World War I that unprecedented numbers of southern blacks migrated into major northern cities like Chicago seeking employment and housing. When race riots broke out in Chicago in 1919 stemming from the migration's impact, the *Defender* resorted to sensational retorts to the exaggerated reporting in mainline newspapers. When the riots subsided, Abbott was chosen by Illinois' governor to serve on a race relations commission along with other black leaders. Abbott continued to feature stories about racial violence of the Ku Klux Klan and other mistreatment of blacks during the 1920s. The *Defender*'s circulation successes brought a measure of financial security to Abbott which was disturbed by the Depression years. By 1935, two-thirds of the paper's circulation disappeared and the *Defender*'s focus, like most media of the era, turned to economic recovery. Upon Robert Abbott's death in 1940, the editing and publishing responsibility fell upon his nephew, John Sengstacke.

World War II helped rather than hindered the *Defender*'s sales. Circulation grew from 82,000 in 1940 to 161,000 in 1947. As many black communities obtained their own local papers, the major national black newspapers witnessed another circulation decline during the 1950s. Sengstacke was elected president of the Negro Newspaper Publishers Association in 1942 and negotiated an agreement with the attorney general that black newspapers would soften their criticisms of the government racial policies in return for full access to war information. The *Defender* joined other members of the black press in advocating the "double v" policy—victory over racism at home and victory over foreign enemies abroad.

Due to increased competition from an enlarged local black press and better coverage from the mainline press, Sengstacke added a daily edition to the weekly *Defender* in 1956 so that it could focus more directly upon Chicago. The *Defender* issued three editions, one for Chicago, another for Gary, Indiana, and a third for the nation. Over the next decade, Sengstacke began buying other black dailies including the well-known *Pittsburgh Courier* to establish the largest black-owned chain network with circulation totaling more than 100,000 by the 1970s. Sengstacke became the first black editor elected to the board of directors of the American Society of Newspaper Editors in 1970. The *Defender*'s daily circulation of 20,000 trailed Sengstacke's *Michigan Chronicle* in Detroit which sold 35,000. *Defender* daily circulation declined to a low of 16,000 in 1983 but rebounded to around 30,000 by the late 1980s.

Reference Wolseley, Roland E., *The Black Press, U.S.A.* (1971).

Chicago Sun-Times
See Field, Marshall III.

Chicago Tribune
Always politically outspoken, the *Chicago Tribune* advocated a staunch abolitionist-Republican position under Joseph Medill in the mid-nineteenth century and adopted an archconservative stance during the tenure of Robert R. McCormick in the twentieth century. The *Tribune* remains the most important daily in Chicago as well as one of the largest and most influential in the entire nation.

The *Chicago Tribune* was founded in 1847 by James Kelly, John Wheeler, and J. K. C.

Forrest. Kelly had previously owned a literary weekly, and Forrest had been a reporter. Four hundred copies were printed for the *Tribune*'s first edition, which joined two other Chicago daily papers. Within a couple of months, both Kelly and Forrest left the paper, and Wheeler served as editor. He brought in reporter John Scripps as a major investor and eventually editor in 1858. The circulation grew steadily from 1,000 in 1849 to 1,800 by 1852. Although the *Tribune* focused on religious and moral issues such as temperance and abolition, it also took unequivocal if controversial stands on politics from the outset. In the election of 1848, the *Tribune* endorsed the abolitionist Free-Soil Party; it backed the Know-Nothing (American) Party, with its anti-immigrant stance, in the election of 1852.

Canadian-born Joseph M. Medill was a key figure in the success of the Tribune *after he and a group of investors bought the paper in 1855.*

By 1855, competition among the seven daily papers in Chicago caused a drop in the *Tribune*'s circulation to 1,200, which led the owners to sell the paper to a group of investors headed by Canadian-born Joseph M. Medill, Charles Ray, and Alfred Cowles.

Medill remained the *Tribune*'s guiding spirit over the next several decades. Having become acquainted with cutting-edge trends while editor of a Cleveland daily, Medill retained the *Tribune*'s abolitionist position and moved it quickly into the new Republican Party camp. While Medill supervised the collection of news, Ray wrote editorials. Circulation recovered smartly to 3,000 in 1856 and reached 24,000 by the outbreak of the Civil War in 1861. One of the reasons for the rapid growth of circulation was the purchase of the rival *Democratic Press* in 1858.

Medill went to Washington, D.C., to establish a bureau before the Civil War and kept the *Tribune* abreast of national political developments. Medill was an early supporter of Abraham Lincoln and became one of the future president's primary consultants. The *Tribune*'s vigorous support of Lincoln was instrumental in his nomination for president by the Republicans in 1860. Numerous reporters followed Union armies during the Civil War, and Medill arranged for soldiers to vote in the 1864 election while at the front.

Differences between Medill and the more liberal Ray resulted in Ray's departure from the paper in 1863. A struggle over editorial control followed between Medill and liberal Horace White, elected editor in 1866 by the majority of owners. While Medill served as mayor of Chicago in the early 1870s, White's editorial control was unchallenged. The *Tribune* attacked political corruption in the Grant administrations and championed free trade. When Medill's term as mayor ended in 1874, he secured a majority ownership in the *Tribune* and assumed editorial control. Robert W. Patterson, Medill's son-in-law, became managing editor. Circulation had dropped since the end of the war from 47,000 to about 35,000.

Medill made the *Tribune* more conservative in politics, opposing progressive Illinois Governor John Altgeld and labor leader Eugene Debs. Still, the *Tribune* continued to assail local Chicago corruption among utilities and railroads. An active band of reporters filled the pages with events, and cartoonist John T. McCutcheon complemented editorial positions. Medill's death in 1899 ended the *Tribune*'s most important era.

Medill's daughters married into the McCormick and Patterson families, the future leaders of the *Tribune*. Robert Patterson took over the paper in 1899, but it was the leadership of his son Joseph Medill Patterson and Joseph's cousin Robert R. McCormick that charted the *Tribune*'s future. By 1910, the *Tribune* had secured first place among Chicago's dailies, with a circulation of 241,000. Both cousins served in the army during World War I, and afterwards, they parted ways. McCormick retained control of the *Tribune*, and Patterson launched an experimental tabloid paper, the *New York Daily News*, in 1919.

Robert McCormick's leadership of the *Tribune* would extend into the mid-1950s. He was more conservative than Joseph Medill but was one of the most talented journalists in the United States at the time. McCormick began sending correspondents overseas in the 1920s, and the *Tribune*'s Berlin reporter, Sigrid Schultz, highlighted the rise of Adolf Hitler in 1930s Germany. McCormick chaired the American Newspaper Publishers Association's committee on freedom of the press after 1928. The *Tribune* joined other major dailies in complaining about regulatory codes of the New Deal's National Recovery Administration. Although opposed to government regulation, McCormick kept salaries high and pension plans solvent for his employees during the depression. Some advertising revenues were lost during the economic hard times, but profits remained high.

McCormick remained consistently hostile to presidential administrations, including those of Truman and Eisenhower. Circulation declined slightly from a high of just over 1 million in 1946 to 900,000 by the mid-1950s. The *Tribune* garnered more advertising revenues than its three Chicago rivals combined. News coverage by its 450 reporters was as complete for foreign news as it was for state and local affairs. McCormick inherited control of the *New York*

Daily News upon the death of his cousin in 1946, but he delegated the New York operations to others, preferring to stick close to the *Tribune*. Many professionals agreed with McCormick when he called the *Tribune* the "World's Greatest Newspaper."

At the death of McCormick in 1955, C. M. Campbell became publisher for the next five years, and W. D. Maxwell became editor. The *Tribune* acquired the competing *Chicago American* from the Hearst chain in 1956 for $11 million. J. Howard Wood succeeded Campbell as publisher in 1960. Because of its continued conservative political stance, the *Tribune* began to lose circulation to the *Chicago Sun-Times* in the 1960s. Beginning with the editorship of Clayton Kirkpatrick in 1969, the *Tribune's* archconservatism waned. During the 1970s, the *Tribune* won three Pulitzer Prizes for excellence in local news reporting and another award for international news coverage. By 1976, the circulation was back to 750,000 from its earlier slump, and the *Tribune* remained ahead of the *Sun-Times* as Chicago's leading paper. Former Washington bureau chief James Squires became editor in the 1980s and continued the steady, sprightly style of Kirkpatrick. In 1989, the *Tribune* ranked seventh among the largest dailies published in the United States, just behind the *Washington Post*. In the 1980s, the Tribune Company became a publicly traded corporation, following the trend of the times. The Tribune Company diversified into other investments, including the Chicago Cubs baseball team and WGN radio and television stations.

Reference Wendt, Lloyd, Chicago Tribune: *The Rise of a Great Newspaper* (1979).

Christian Science Monitor

Strictly speaking, the *Christian Science Monitor* is a religious newspaper owned and operated by the Church of Christ, Scientist, headquartered in Boston. Yet throughout the *Monitor's* history, it has been respected as a truly national newspaper with in-depth analysis of domestic, political, and foreign news, despite its failure to sustain a significant circulation.

The founder of the Christian Science Church, Mary Baker Eddy, became concerned not only about sensational journalism that focused on violence and disasters but also about President Theodore Roosevelt's extension of U.S. government authority into other nations as well as private business. Eddy believed that the true essence of humanity was spiritual and thus morally good. She did not suggest that evil be ignored but wanted to focus on humanity's positive contributions and the need for more personal and business freedom. Eddy's ideals were embodied in the concepts of the *Christian Science Monitor*, which she established in 1908 as a public service to everyone rather than as a members-only journal. The church already published denominational publications, including the *Journal* (1883) and the *Sentinel* (1898). The church's publishing society board managed the business affairs of all the publications, but the five-member board of directors of the church maintained final authority over *Monitor* personnel and policies. That issue was decided by Massachusetts courts in 1922 after a bitter internal struggle for control between the two boards.

The *Christian Science Monitor* began in 1908 as an afternoon daily selling for two cents and containing ten pages. The first editor, Archibald McLellan, simply moved from his editorial desk at the *Journal* and *Sentinel*, which he had occupied since 1902. The *Monitor* subscribed to the recently founded United Press wire service as well as the Associated Press, and it started bureaus in Washington and New York. A London edition featured accounts from England, and the international elements of the *Monitor* were evident from the outset. McLellan's successor in 1914 was Frederick Dixon, who had served as editorial page editor from the launching of the *Monitor*.

Although the early circulation of more than 30,000 was confined largely to Christian Science members and some Boston readers, it grew increasingly diverse and totaled 123,000 by 1919. The major attraction for nonmember readers was the full coverage of foreign news, the fine arts, and literature. Church members read the *Monitor* in part because it was devoid of local criminal reports and news of natural disasters. Yet the *Monitor* contained little if any material that could be considered religious.

Dixon's advocacy of U.S. entry into World War I upset some church members and caused an internal crisis. The publishing society board was dominated by Dixon, who wanted freedom to control the *Monitor*, but the church's board of directors claimed authority over the *Monitor*, based on the church manual drawn up by Eddy. In 1919, the publishing board sued in Massachusetts state court to stop attempted interference by the board of directors. The case was not finally settled until 1922, when the state supreme court ruled that the board of directors controlled the *Monitor*. In the interim, the *Monitor*'s circulation had dropped to about 21,000. A number of advertisers left mainly because many church members who viewed the publishing board as rebellious had stopped subscribing. Circulation moved back above 100,000 by 1924.

The end of the dispute over control of the *Monitor* led to the appointment in 1922 of a new editor, Willis John Abbot, who had been an editor for the Hearst papers. Abbot set out to restore the *Monitor*'s circulation and reputation, which he quickly did. Abbot was elected an officer of the American Society of Newspaper Editors and helped formulate the society's "Canons of Journalism." He also proved to be a first-class interviewer on a late 1920s trip to Europe, where he spoke with Italy's Benito Mussolini, Germany's Gustav Stresemann, and Czechoslovakia's Eduard Benes.

Between 1927 and 1939, the *Monitor*'s management was given over to a four-member editorial board. Abbot remained a member of the board for a time, but Roland R. Harrison became the primary leader of the board as executive editor. Yet the rising star of the *Monitor*'s future was Erwin D. Canham, who served as a foreign correspondent with the paper as early as 1926 and headed the Washington bureau from 1932 to 1939. Canham became managing editor in 1940, when the editorial board supervi-

sion lapsed, and was named editor in chief in 1945, where he remained until 1974. Canham was respected among his peers, who elected him president of the American Society of Newspaper Edtiors in 1948. The staff under Canham won two Pulitzer Prizes and one international award, and the *Monitor* won plaudits for being one of the first media organs to resist Senator Joseph McCarthy's assaults in 1950. Washington bureau chief and columnist James Roscoe Drummond (1940–1954) helped confirm the *Monitor*'s credibility. Three polls on newspaper quality in 1960–1961 listed the *Monitor* as one of the top six daily papers in the United States. In the 1960s, the *Monitor* adopted a five-column, larger-type format, which made the paper more attractive. Yet by the late 1960s, the circulation had slipped to 185,000.

John Hughes, a veteran reporter formerly based in South Africa, succeeded Canham as editor in 1974. Circulation under Hughes ranged between 180,000 and 260,000, and the *Monitor*'s national appeal was challenged by the publication of *USA Today* after 1982. The *Monitor* used state-of-the-art technology such as computers to print weekly international editions in Europe and Australia as well as domestic regional editions in New Jersey, Chicago, and Los Angeles. The Washington bureau headed by Richard L. Strout and Godfrey Sperling remained among the most respected in the nation. The *Monitor*'s editorial positions retained a refreshing independence, and the paper continued to focus national attention on issues such as violence on television. Yet circulation declined to 104,000 in 1991 and fell to 92,000 in 1993. The *Monitor* also initiated its own independent television news for syndication during the 1980s.

Reference Canham, Erwin D., *Commitment to Freedom: The Story of the* Christian Science Monitor (1958).

Civil Rights Movement

The decades of the 1950s and 1960s witnessed extensive focus of the nation and the media upon the cause of minority civil rights. Media coverage served to educate the general public about the problem similar to the nineteenth century abolitionist campaign to abolish slavery. Public opinion thus became a lever for government intervention and legislation.

Although segregation of the races in the South became the primary impetus for civil rights action in the 1950s, racial problems existed across the nation beneath a placid surface. The issue of desegregation and equal treatment of minorities began to accelerate after World War II. President Truman integrated the armed forces in the late 1940s. The Democratic Party platform of 1948 called for broad civil rights measures in housing, jobs and voting. Yet, many regard the Supreme Court decision in *Brown v. Board of Education* in 1954 ending segregated public schools to be the starting point of the civil rights movement. The federal government's dilemma in applying the court's desegregation policy was that individual court rulings were necessary for each situation since southern states resisted application of the general judicial dictum of the Brown case.

The first major issue which attracted media attention was the 1955–1956 Montgomery bus boycott called by black citizens to protest segregated public transportation. A dynamic young black preacher named Martin Luther King spearheaded the boycott. Reporters from large northern dailies descended upon Montgomery to write their stories. Many acknowledged that de-facto segregation and discrimination against blacks also existed in large northern cities. The *Montgomery Advertiser* ran stories of northern racial difficulties from big city dailies. Violence during the Montgomery boycott proved that the civil rights issues would not be settled peacefully or soon.

When a federal court ordered a Little Rock high school integrated in 1957, Governor Orval Faubus called out the National Guard to block the order. President Dwight Eisenhower federalized the Arkansas Guard and supervised the integration order again amidst violence covered extensively by television and the print media including a major

pictorial spread in *Life* magazine. *Life* also covered the violence associated with the integration of the University of Mississippi in 1962. Many news organizations began in-depth features stories on the reasons for segregation and black–white cultural clashes. Yet, for the most part, media tended to concentrate on the events rather than analysis.

In the summer of 1963, television and print media covered the violent confrontations in Birmingham between civil rights demonstrators and police using fire hoses and dogs. The same summer media followed the brutal murder of National Association for the Advancement of Colored People (NAACP) executive Medgar Evers in Mississippi. Governor George Wallace of Alabama staged a faint attempt to block the court-ordered entrance of black students to the University of Alabama in 1963 to the full view of a television audience. National Educational Television produced civil rights documentaries including interviews with black leaders such as King and black nationalist Malcolm X. In August 1963, 200,000 civil rights demonstrators gathered before a national television audience in Washington, D. C. to hear King's famous "I Have A Dream" oration.

The civil rights movement in the South combined with racial riots in Los Angeles (1965) and Detroit (1967) forced media organizations to examine their own hiring policies regarding minorities. Blacks began to appear more frequently on network television shows as well as working for print and broadcast media as reporters and editors. Advertisers remained reluctant to sponsor network programs that dealt with civil rights issues.

Despite the passage of the Civil Rights Act of 1964 requiring equal opportunity in public schools, jobs, transportation, and accommodations, acceptance of change in the south remained grudging. Continued voting rights' violations led to the massive Selma to Montgomery march of 1965 which also turned violent. National media attention, highlighted by the *Washington Star*'s Pulitzer Prize-winning Haynes

Johnson, served to influence Congress to pass the Voting Rights Act of 1965 giving the federal government extensive supervisory authority in southern elections to ensure equal treatment.

Assassinations of civil rights leaders in the 1960s caused additional media attention to be focused upon the issues. The murder of Martin Luther King, Jr. in Memphis in 1968 set off another round of racial unrest and some rioting across the nation. Southern editors such as Ralph McGill and Eugene Patterson of the *Atlanta Constitution* and H. G. Davis of the *Gainesville (Florida) Sun* won Pulitzers for their efforts to instill calm and moderation during the civil rights furor. A similar effort by John Strohmeyer of the *Bethlehem (Pennsylvania) Globe-Times* dealt with racial problems in a northern community.

Reference Lewis, Anthony, *Portrait of a Decade: The Second American Revolution* (1965).

Civil War

Because the conflict occurred in many parts of the nation, the Civil War received the closest press scrutiny of any American war until World War II. Further, the partisan nature of coverage meant that papers in the north and south gave different interpretations to events and relations with government often proved sensitive. Due to the bias problem and heated competition in multi-paper markets, coverage of the Civil War was not always accurate or responsible. Nonetheless, some correspondents made positive professional reputations and war correspondents thereafter were regarded as a special breed of reporter. Increased reliance on the telegraph and widespread use of illustrations and photographs also marked the Civil War years.

The issue of bias in the press developed long before the outbreak of hostilities in 1861. Even in northern states, divisions over abolition of slavery affected papers such as Horace Greeley's *New York Tribune* and Joseph Medill's *Chicago Tribune* (pro) versus James Gordon Bennett's *New York Herald* and Samuel Bowles, III's *Springfield (Massa-*

chusetts) Republican (anti) existed for more than a decade before the war. Yet, when the conflict began, regional support for the respective sides fell into place. Some newspapers such as Henry J. Raymond's *New York Times* established credibility for even-handed reporting. President Abraham Lincoln felt criticism from the anti-war Democratic "Copperhead" press as well as certain Radical Republican editors disappointed with the ineffectual prosecution of the war. Likewise, many Confederate newspapers criticized military strategies and political leadership during the war even while remaining loyal to the cause.

Newspaper coverage of the war was detailed and rather thorough, often accounting for one-third of the space in New York dailies. Military concerns about security led to various trial and error episodes involving censorship. The very fact of the greater prosperity and competition among large dailies by the 1860s made them aggressive in seeking news about the war. Due to the increased extension of telegraphs and railroads (compared to the Mexican War era), especially across the northern states, news traveled faster and easier. Early in the fighting, the Post Office Department and the secretary of war forbid the press from using the mails or telegraphs for dispatching military information.

When General George McClellan got major newspapers to sign an agreement in 1861 not to transmit sensitive military information, he offered reporters access to Union military commanders. Yet the plan fell through because of intense competition between the War Department and the State Department, which employed the Union's military censor. Then, when Secretary of War Edwin Stanton was given the censoring powers in 1862, he decreed that reporters must submit copy to the local provost marshal promising that only operational information would be deleted. The clarification did not please all reporters and editors, but at least it made the press–government relationship clear. Problems thereafter concerned the application of policy by field commanders which was not always uniform.

Despite restrictions on war reporting, the northern press maintained considerable freedom to write about the Civil War. Relations with individual generals posed the major problems. After General William T. Sherman charged a *New York Herald* reporter with a violation of regulations, military commanders were given a veto power over which reporters could cover their operations. General Ambrose Burnside suspended the publication of the "Copperhead" *Chicago Times* for several days in 1863 based on his assertion that information harmful to the military had been published. *Times* editor Wilbur F. Storey instructed his reporters to send rumors as well as facts about the war. In 1864 when Manton Marble's "Copperhead" *New York World* and the *Journal of Commerce* published a forged document about massive new enlistment of Union soldiers, General John Dix briefly suspended the papers and scolded the editors.

Some 500 northern newspaper correspondents nicknamed "specials," led by 40 from the *Herald,* flooded the battlefields with Union armies. *New York Times* editor Henry J. Raymond left his editor's desk to personally cover the first Battle of Bull Run in 1861. The *New York Herald* reporter B. S. Osbon accompanied Union naval commanders on expeditions ranging from the bombardment of Fort Sumter to Admiral Farragut's attack at New Orleans. Albert Richardson reported General U. S. Grant's successful western campaign while George Smalley covered Virginia battlefields for Greeley's *Tribune.* The *Cincinnati Gazette's* Whitelaw Reid, writing under the pseudonym of "Agate," reported the Battle of Gettysburg in memorable detail. The military tried to eliminate pseudonyms to encourage accurate reporting. Illustrations from woodcut engravings were frequently offered by publications such as *Frank Leslie's Illustrated Newspaper* and *Harper's Weekly.* Leslie's paper used eighty artists to draw 3,000 illustrations during the war. Photographer Mathew Brady effectively became the official photographer for the Union side recording 3,500 photos of the Civil War.

Only about 100 reporters covered the war in the South. Confederate newspapers depended upon its Press Association for news accounts much the way the Associated Press informed Union newspapers. Yet, the Confederate Press Association gained a superior reputation over the AP for its objectivity. Following unsatisfactory efforts by newspapers in Augusta and Richmond to provide telegraph reports for other papers, Joseph Clisby of the *Macon Telegraph* led other editors to form the Press Association in 1862 whose membership included all 43 southern dailies. The Association's director, J. S. Thrasher, fought against unnecessary military censorship and though it gained support from generals such as P. G. T. Beauregard, failed to get the Davis administration to issue daily pres releases. The Press Association urged its reporters not to engage in editorial comment about events but to report the facts objectively. Because they were located in the Confederate capital, the Richmond papers dominated the Confederate press. The *Dispatch* had the largest circulation and sometimes criticized President Davis, while the *Enquirer* and the *Sentinel* served as apologists for Davis's administration. Paper and ink shortages were notable obstacles for Confederate papers. Best overall reporting and writing was found in the *Memphis Appeal* which moved its press frequently from place to place in the face of advancing Union armies. The most notable southern reporters were the *Charleston Courier's* Felix de Fontaine, especially his account of the Battle of Antietam, and Peter Alexander who wrote for the *Savannah Republican* and other southern papers, noted for his account of the Battle of Gettysburg.

References Andrews, J. Cutler, *The North Reports the Civil War* (1955); Andrews, J. Cutler, *The South Reports the War* (1970).

Cleveland Plain Dealer

Founded in 1842 as a weekly, the *Cleveland Plain Dealer* struggled for a long time before taking its place as the city's premier newspaper. It withstood competition from the local

Scripps paper and produced some of the top reporters in the Midwest. Finally, the local owners sold the *Plain Dealer* to the Newhouse chain in 1967.

The *Cleveland Advertiser* began in 1831 as a weekly, shifted to a daily in 1836, and went back to a weekly during several changes in ownership. Former schoolteacher and attorney Joseph William Gray and his brother A. N. Gray purchased the *Advertiser* in late 1841 for $1,050. The name was changed to the *Plain Dealer*—a title borrowed from a seventeenth-century English play by William Wycherley—and it appeared as a four-page, six-column weekly at the beginning of 1842. The *Plain Dealer* acquired a modern cylinder steam press in 1852. Editor J. W. Gray and business manager A. N. Gray pledged on the paper's masthead to cover politics, the economy, the arts, and foreign news. As Democrats, the Grays supported local and national party candidates.

The *Plain Dealer*'s early success led to its transformation into Cleveland's third evening daily in 1845, with a circulation of 400. The *Plain Dealer* supported Democrat James K. Polk's decision to wage war with Mexico in 1846. The paper also favored federal subsidies for internal improvements, especially roads. Although it opposed slavery, the *Plain Dealer* backed the controversial but popular sovereignty policy, which allowed territories to decide the fate of slavery. Joseph Gray served as Cleveland's postmaster (1853–1858) and was defeated in a bid for Congress in 1858. Gray carried on a raucous political debate for years with Republican editor Horace Greeley of the *New York Tribune*.

Between 1857 and 1860, the *Plain Dealer* employed Charles Farrar Browne, soon known as Artemus Ward, as a humorist. He enlivened reader interest by lampooning social customs and prominent personalities. After the death of Joseph Gray in 1862, Ward attempted to purchase the *Plain Dealer* but could not consummate the deal. Besides local writers such as Ward, W. E. McLaren, and A. M. Griswold, the *Plain Dealer* was able to place correspondents in New York, New Orleans, St. Louis, and Washington with the arrival of the telegraph in 1847. Its external sources were enhanced by a subscription to the Associated Press in 1854.

After some inept management from 1862 to 1865 under John S. Stephenson, the *Plain Dealer* suspended publication for seven weeks, pending its sale. The paper was bought by experienced journalist William Wirt Armstrong, who resumed publication under the old name in 1865. Armstrong continued the openly partisan nature of the *Plain Dealer* as a Democratic Party voice in an era when partisanship was becoming less appealing to readers. Between 1867 and 1874, due to financial losses, Armstrong recruited new backers in William D. Morgan and Frederick W. Green, but neither interfered with Armstrong's direction of the paper. In 1877, the *Plain Dealer* was incorporated, with six stockholders joining Armstrong. The *Plain Dealer*'s circulation of perhaps 2,400 in 1875 trailed that of the *Cleveland Leader* (founded 1854) by several thousand. During the election campaign of 1880, the evening edition was replaced by a morning edition, but after the election, Armstrong returned to an evening publication schedule.

Liberty Emery Holden purchased Armstrong's majority shares in the *Plain Dealer* in 1885, as the circulation approached 30,000. In the same year, the competing *Herald* (founded 1835) was bought by the *Plain Dealer*, permitting a permanent switch to a morning edition followed by its first Sunday edition. These changes allowed the *Plain Dealer* to challenge its main rival, the *Leader*. In 1878, however, Edward W. Scripps had launched a new competitor, the *Press*, which after some mergers became the *Cleveland News* in 1905. After unsuccessful efforts to make the evening *Plain Dealer* independent, the paper was sold in 1905 to the Meridian Company, which operated the *World* as well as the *Leader*. In the meantime, the *Plain Dealer* installed its first linotype machine in 1891 and added three more presses in 1899. Holden made the *Plain Dealer* a staunch advocate for the improvement of education, recreation, and the arts in Cleveland. The paper also backed the reform efforts of Cleveland's Progressive mayor Tom Johnson between 1901 and 1909 against entrenched bosses such as Mark Hanna. Although the *Plain Dealer* backed Woodrow Wilson, it opposed U.S. entrance into World War I.

Seeking fresh financial backing in 1898, Holden brought in *St. Louis Post-Dispatch* staffers Elbert H. Baker as business manager and Charles E. Kennedy as chief editorial writer. Kennedy's withdrawal from management in 1906 left Baker in a position to become chief stockholder at Holden's death in 1913. When Baker determined that there would be no more fudging on circulation figures, he had some difficulty holding advertisers. But within three years, Baker had turned deficits into profits, which were further enhanced when the *Plain Dealer* purchased the *Leader* from Mark Hanna in 1917. Baker was respected by his peers, who elected him president of the American Newspaper Publishers Association in 1912. He was named a director of the Associated Press in 1916.

Benjamin P. Bole became president of the *Plain Dealer* in 1929 and gradually took over the chief executive duties from Baker, who died in 1933. E. C. Hopwood served as editor from 1920 to 1928 and was succeeded by Paul Bellamy. From the beginning of the Progressive era in the 1890s, the *Plain Dealer* gradually loosened its Democratic Party ties and became politically independent. The cycle was complete in 1940 when the paper endorsed Republican Wendell Willkie for president. During World War II, *Plain Dealer* correspondent Peggy Hull joined a growing number of women reporters covering the war. Edward Kuekes won a Pulitzer Prize in 1953 for his cartoons about the Korean War.

Although the *Plain Dealer* acquired the *Cleveland News* after World War II, the afternoon paper was sold again to the Scripps-Howard *Cleveland Press* in 1960. Samuel I. Newhouse added the *Plain Dealer* to his chain of newspapers by paying $50 million—at the time the highest price ever paid for a daily—to the paper's corporation in 1967. The *Plain Dealer* remains a successful part of Newhouse's multimedia conglomerate Advance Publications, with David Hall as editor in 1994. Daily circulation in 1994 totaled 396,000, and Sunday circulation was 543,000.

Reference Shaw, Archer H., *The Plain Dealer* (1942).

Collier's

Although originally founded to promote subscription book sales, *Collier's* became a leading muckraking journal after the turn of the century, promoting a variety of reforms. After World War I, *Collier's* continued its political vein by attacking extremists such as the Ku Klux Klan and Huey Long, as well as opposing Prohibition. It remained committed to sensational subject matter until its demise in 1957.

Peter Fenelon Collier founded *Once in a Week* in 1888 for the sole purpose of publicizing the subscription book trade. When Robert Collier took over the five-cent magazine in 1896, he changed the name to *Collier's Weekly* and recruited well-known writers such as Henry James and artists such as Frederic Remington to be contributors. Collier paid Spanish-American War correspondent Richard Harding Davis to cover the Russo-Japanese War (1904–1905) for *Collier's*. The journal entered the muckraking era in 1906 by printing Samuel Hopkins Adams's series on fraud in the patent medicine industry. *Collier's* led political campaigns for a progressive income tax, direct election of U.S. senators, and women's suffrage. It continued its social activism by calling for standards in the manufacture of food and drugs, removal of slum housing, and workers' compensation for on-the-job injuries. President Theodore Roosevelt cited *Collier's* for siding with the public rather than self-interest in its refusal to accept fraudulent advertising.

In 1919, *Collier's* was sold to the Crowell Publishing Company for $1.75 million. Under the editorship of William L. Chenery, *Collier's* was among the first national

THE GREAT AMERICAN FRAUD

By SAMUEL HOPKINS ADAMS

II—PERUNA AND THE "BRACERS"

This is the second article of this series, which is to contain a full explanation and exposure of patent medicine methods and of the harm done to the public by this industry, founded mainly on fraud and poison. The object of the series is to make the situation so familiar and thoroughly understood by the public that there will be a speedy end to the worst aspects of the evil. The third article of the series will be published in COLLIER'S for November 18. The first article appeared in COLLIER'S for October 7

A DISTINGUISHED public health official and medical writer once made this jocular suggestion to me:

"Let us buy in large quantities the cheapest Italian vermouth, poor gin, and bitters. We will mix them in the proportion of three of vermouth to two of gin with a dash of bitters, dilute and bottle them by the short quart, label them '*Smith's Revivifier and Blood-Purifier; dose, one wineglassful before each meal*'; advertise them to cure erysipelas, bunions, dyspepsia, heat rash, fever and ague, and consumption; and to prevent loss of hair, small-pox, old age, sunstroke, and near-sightedness, and make our everlasting fortunes selling them to the temperance trade."

"That sounds to me very much like a cocktail," said I.

"So it is," he replied. "But it's just as much a medicine as Peruna and not as bad a drink."

Peruna, or, as its owner, Dr. S. B. Hartman of Columbus, O. (once a physician in good standing), prefers to write it, Pe-ru-na, is at present the most prominent proprietary nostrum in the country. It has taken the place once held by Greene's Nervura and by Paine's Celery Compound, and for the same reason which made them popular. The name of that reason is alcohol. Peruna is a stimulant pure and simple, and it is the more dangerous in that it sails under the false colors of a benign purpose.

According to an authoritative statement given out in private circulation a few years ago by its proprietors, Peruna is a compound of seven drugs with cologne spirits. This formula, they assure me, has not been materially changed. None of the seven drugs is of any great potency. Their total is less than one-half of one per cent. of the product. Medicinally this is too inconsiderable, in this proportion, to produce any effect. There remains to Peruna only water and cologne spirits, roughly in the proportion of three to one. Cologne spirits is the commercial term for alcohol.

What Peruna is Made of

Any one wishing to make Peruna for home consumption may do so by mixing half a pint of cologne spirits, 90 proof, with a pint and a half of water, adding thereto a little cubebs for flavor and a little burned sugar for color. It will cost, in small quantities, perhaps seven or eight cents per quart. Manufactured in bulk, so a former Peruna agent estimates, its cost, including bottle and wrapper, is about eight and one-half cents. Its price is $1.00. Because of this handsome margin of profit, and by way of making hay in the stolen sunshine of Peruna advertising, many imitations have sprung up to harass the proprietors of the alcohol-and-water product. Pe-ru-vi-na, P-ru-na, Purina, Anurep (an obvious inversion); these, bottled and labeled to resemble Peruna, are self-confessed imitations. From what the Peruna people tell me, I gather that they are dangerous and damnable frauds, and that they cure nothing.

What does Peruna cure? Catarrh. That is the modest claim for it; nothing but catarrh. To be sure, a careful study of its literature will suggest its value as a tonic, and a preventive of lassitude. But its reputation rests upon catarrh. What is catarrh? Whatever ails you. No matter what you've got, you will be not only enabled, but compelled, after reading Dr. Hartman's Peruna book, "The Ills of Life," to diagnose your illness as catarrh, and to realize that Peruna alone will save you. Pneumonia is catarrh of the lungs; so is consumption. Dyspepsia is catarrh of the stomach. Enteritis is catarrh of the intestines. Appendicitis—surgeons, please note before operating—is catarrh of the appendix. Bright's disease is catarrh of the kidneys.

Heart disease is catarrh of the heart. Canker sores are catarrh of the mouth. Measles is, perhaps, catarrh of the skin, since "a teaspoonful of Peruna thrice daily or oftener is an effectual cure" ("The Ills of Life"). Similarly, malaria, one may guess, is catarrh of the mosquito that bit you. Other diseases not specifically placed in the catarrhal class, but yielding to Peruna (in the book), are colic, mumps, convulsions, neuralgia, women's complaints, and rheumatism. Yet, "Peruna is not a cure-all," virtuously disclaims Dr. Hartman, and grasps at a golden opportunity by advertising his nostrum as a preventive against yellow fever! That almost any length of time without acquiring a drug habit water, with a little coloring matter and one-half of one per cent. of mild drugs, will cure all or any of the ills listed above is too ridiculous to need refutation. Nor does Dr. Hartman himself personally make that claim for his product. He stated to me specifically and repeatedly that no drug or combination of drugs, with the possible exception of quinine for malaria, will cure disease. His claim is that the belief of the patient in Peruna, fostered as it is by the printed testimony, and aided by the "gentle stimulation," produces good results. It is well established that in certain classes of disease the opposite is true. A considerable proportion of tuberculosis cases show a history of the Peruna type of medicines taken in the early stages, with the result of diminishing the patient's resistant power, and much of the typhoid in the Middle West is complicated by the victim's "keeping up" on this stimulus long after he should have been under a doctor's care. But it is not as a fraud upon the sick alone that Peruna is baneful; but as the maker of drunkards, also.

"It can be used any length of time without acquiring a drug habit," declares the Peruna book, and therein, I regret to say, lies specifically and directly. The lie is ingeniously backed up by Dr. Hartman's argument that "nobody could get drunk on the prescribed doses of Peruna."

Perhaps this is true, though I note three wineglassfuls in forty-five minutes as a prescription which might temporarily alter a prohibitionist's outlook on life. But what makes Peruna profitable to the maker, and a curse to the community at large, is the fact that the minimum dose first ceases to satisfy, then the moderate dose, and finally the maximum dose; and the unsuspecting patron, who began with it as a medicine, goes on to use it as a beverage, and finally to be enslaved by it as a habit. A well-known authority on drug-addictions writes me:

"A number of physicians have called my attention to the use of Peruna, both preceding and following alcohol and drug addictions. Lydia Pinkham's Compound is another dangerous drug used largely by drinkers; Paine's Celery Compound also. I have, in the last two years, met four cases of persons who drank Peruna in large quantities to intoxication. They were given to them originally as a tonic. They were treated under my care as simple alcoholics."

The Government Forbids the Sale of Peruna to Indians

Expert opinion on the non-medical side is represented in the Government order to the Indian Department, reproduced on the following page, the kernel of which is this:

"In connection with this investigation, please give particular attention to the proprietary medicines and other compounds which the traders keep in stock, with special reference to the liability of their misuse by Indians on account of the alcohol which they contain. The sale of Peruna, which is on the lists of several traders, is hereby absolutely prohibited. As a medicine, something else can be substituted; as an intoxicant, it has been found too tempting and effective. Anything of the sort under another name which is found to lead to intoxication you will please report to this office." [Signed]
C. F. LARRABEE, Acting Commissioner.

Specific evidence of what Peruna can do will be found in the following report, verified by special investigation:

PINEDALE, Wyoming, Oct. 4.—(Special.)—Two men suffering from delirium tremens and one dead is the result of a Peruna intoxication which took place here a few days ago. C. E. Armstrong of this place and a party of three others started out on a camping trip to the Yellowstone country, taking with them several bottles of whiskey, and ten bottles of Peruna, which one of the members of the party was taking as a tonic. The trip lasted over a week, the whiskey was exhausted, and for two days the party was without liquor. At last some one suggested that they use Peruna, of which nine bottles remained. Before they stopped the whole

ALCOHOL IN "MEDICINES" AND IN LIQUORS

These diagrams show what would be left in a bottle of patent medicine if everything was poured out except the alcohol; they also show the quantity of alcohol that would be present if the same bottle had contained whiskey, champagne, claret, or beer. It is apparent that a bottle of Peruna contains as much alcohol as five bottles of beer, or three bottles of claret or champagne—that is, bottles of the same size. It would take nearly nine bottles of beer to put as much alcohol into a thirsty man's system as a temperance advocate can get by drinking one bottle of Hostetter's Stomach Bitters. While the "doses" prescribed by the patent medicine manufacturers are only one to two teaspoonfuls several times a day, the opportunity to take more exists, and even small doses of alcohol, taken regularly, cause that craving which is the first step in the making of a drunkard or drug fiend.

[The bottle diagrams are labeled, row by row:]

PERUNA 28% | WHISKY BOTTLED IN BOND 50% | CHAMPAGNE 9% | CLARET 8% | BEER 5%

PAINE'S CELERY COMPOUND 21% | WHISKY BOTTLED IN BOND 50% | CHAMPAGNE 9% | CLARET 8% | BEER 5%

HOSTETTER'S STOMACH BITTERS 44.3% | WHISKY BOTTLED IN BOND 50% | CHAMPAGNE 9% | CLARET 8% | BEER 5%

Collier's *featured muckraking articles such as Samuel Hopkins Adams's, which reported on the fraudulent claims of the medicine industry.*

publications to focus on the rise to political power of the second Ku Klux Klan. The journal exposed the demagoguery of ambitious Louisiana Governor Huey Long and led the fight to repeal the Eighteenth Amendment on Prohibition. Circulation increased by 400,000 during the Chenery era, which ended in 1949.

Collier's seemed unsure of its direction after World War II, and circulation began slipping. The editors argued that its raison d'etre was to entertain readers through its sensational stories. An attempt to include at least one exposé each week strained the credibility of some stories. One of the most controversial, albeit popular, issues in 1951 featured an imaginary account of a third world war involving atomic exchanges between the United States and the Soviet Union. That particular issue sold almost 4 million copies, but critics wondered in print about *Collier's* motives. The magazine subsequently devoted more space to nonfiction and shortened its essays.

Concern about losing subscribers to television prompted a reader survey in 1952, which claimed that *Collier's* was less affected by television than other journals such as its principal competition, the *Saturday Evening Post*. Yet in 1953, with circulation at an all-time high of 3.8 million, *Collier's* ended its tradition as a weekly and began publishing only biweekly and oriented its subject matter more toward mystery and western fiction, color photographs, and cartoons. Among its contributors were Pearl Buck and John Steinbeck. The publishers argued that the change would keep circulation above 3.5 million. Even though circulation targets were achieved, advertising revenues continued losing ground to television, and the final issue of *Collier's* appeared in the first week of 1957. Crowell-Collier publishers also closed down its other major magazine, *Woman's Home Companion*, at the same time. Perhaps the fate of *Collier's* was tied as much to the absence of editorial focus and to concerns about the balance sheet as it was to the competition of television.

Reference Powell, Hickman, "*Collier's*," *Scribner's Magazine* (1939).

Columbia Broadcasting System (CBS)

The second of the three major broadcasting networks was born in 1927. The Columbia Broadcasting System (CBS) quickly succeeded under the leadership of William Paley and recruited some of the most famous correspondents in radio and television, including Edward R. Murrow and Walter Cronkite. The network's entertainment and news programs kept it consistently near the top of the ratings. After Larry Tisch of Loews Corporation bought CBS in 1986, major holdings such as Columbia Records and Harcourt Brace publishing house were dispatched.

In early 1927, Arthur Judson created the United Independent Broadcasters to sell ads and programs to radio stations. Columbia Phonograph Broadcasting System was established by the Columbia Phonograph Record Company specifically to infuse funds into United, which made Columbia a major stockholder. Sixteen radio stations made up the original United network, but most of the prospective sponsors opted to deal with NBC. Columbia wanted out and sold its stock to United. New investors from the Philadelphia affiliate were recruited, and United's name was changed to the Columbia Broadcasting System in late 1927. Still, the network remained on shaky financial ground until William S. Paley, son of the Congress Cigar Company owner, bought a majority share of Columbia in 1928. Paley persuaded Paramount to buy 49 percent of CBS's stock to give it a strong credit rating. Paley led the network and increased the number of stations from 16 to 79 by 1931. He also arranged to provide free programs to affiliates as long as the network could select the broadcast time for the programs. The plan allowed CBS to acquire several important NBC affiliate stations.

Musical programs predominated on the CBS network at first, but experiments with dramas began immediately. In 1930, CBS hired former newspaper reporter Hans Van Kaltenborn to do features about the depression and cover the Spanish civil war in 1936. CBS also sent a reporter to cover the 1930 disarmament conference in London. The

England trip produced an agreement for CBS to use the facilities of the British Broadcasting Company to broadcast interviews with celebrities, including George Bernard Shaw, back to the United States. In 1932, CBS tried to launch a full-time news operation but disbanded it after newspaper boycotts. Instead, the network set up a Press-Radio Bureau in 1933 to receive reports from the wire services. The early days were not without their problems. In 1935, when Alexander Woollcott commented on European tensions during his weekly CBS series, the sponsor canceled the show. And when Father Charles Coughlin's strident radio show became an embarrassment to CBS in 1931, he was removed from the airwaves.

CBS blended drama and news in its most popular show, "March of Time," sponsored by *Time* magazine and premiering in 1931. The program featured actors and actresses portraying contemporary historical figures. After CBS hired William B. Lewis as program chief in 1936, several other successful programs aired, including the "Columbia Workshop" series, featuring plays such as Archibald MacLeish's *The Fall of the City*. The biggest single splash caused by radio was Orson Welles's broadcast of H. G. Wells's *War of the Worlds* in 1938 on CBS's "Mercury Theater on the Air." The program caused a wave of momentary excitement about a Martian invasion, which demonstrated the power of radio's influence.

Economic hard times were felt to a lesser degree by the radio networks than by other businesses. CBS sold only 22 percent of its airtime in 1931 and saw its net profits drop from $2.3 million in 1931 to $1.6 million in 1932. Yet the network recovered nicely, and net profits were back up to $2.2 million in 1935. In 1932, Paley shrewdly bought back the huge share of stock held by Paramount since 1928.

The approaching war in Europe was a boon of sorts to the previously suppressed efforts to expand news programming at CBS. Following Kaltenborn's reports on the civil war in Spain, CBS correspondents Edward R. Murrow and William L. Shirer dispatched reports from Europe about the rise of Nazism in 1938. CBS radio followed the Munich crisis blow by blow, and reports by European correspondents were synthesized by Kaltenborn in the United States. CBS became uneasy with Kaltenborn's natural tendency to comment on the news, however, and when he left CBS for NBC in 1940, there was a sense of relief.

When World War II began in 1939, CBS news chief Paul White's correspondents, including Howard K. Smith, Eric Sevareid, and Charles Collingwood, joined Murrow and Shirer in various theaters in Europe and Asia. Murrow's reports on the German blitz on London in 1940 and the liberation of German concentration camps in 1945 mesmerized U.S. listeners.

In 1946, former sociology professor Frank Stanton became president of CBS. Murrow, back from Europe, took charge of the news division and produced a hit documentary called "Hear It Now." A similar television show, "See It Now," followed in 1951. CBS's desire to pursue FM radio broadcasting in the postwar era delayed its entry into television. CBS developed a method of color television broadcasting that could not be received on black and white sets, but it was rejected by the Federal Communications Commission in favor of an RCA system that was compatible with black and white. CBS quickly recovered in 1948 by recruiting star comedians Jack Benny, Edgar Bergen, Red Skelton, and George Burns from NBC. The veteran radio personalities made an easy transition to television. The biggest television bonanza for CBS's future was a 1948 variety show, "Toast of the Town," hosted by Ed Sullivan.

CBS endured the infamous "Red scare" years of the late 1940s and early 1950s along with the rest of the broadcasting and entertainment industry. Many individual performers and professionals were blacklisted because of supposed Communist affiliations uncovered by the House of Representatives Un-American Activities Committee and Senator Joseph McCarthy of Wisconsin. At first, the press tried to ignore the threat, other than reporting events. Gradually, however, more and more journalists challenged the false basis of the anti-Communist hunt. Murrow climaxed the era in 1954 with a televised interview with Senator McCarthy in which the senator was cleverly revealed as a fanatic.

CBS news outstripped its television network competition after World War II with broadcasters such as Murrow and Walter Cronkite. The 15-minute evening news program was anchored by Douglas Edwards beginning in 1948. Walter Cronkite replaced Edwards in 1962 and became one of the most trusted newsmen in history. CBS's "Face the Nation" program successfully imitated NBC's established "Meet the Press." Entertainment shows also topped the most-viewed list, led by Lucille Ball's "I Love Lucy," the popular children's program "Captain Kangaroo," the critically acclaimed drama series "Playhouse 90," and "The Ed Sullivan Show." CBS did have setbacks, such as the scandal involving its pioneering quiz show "The $64,000 Question."

From the 1950s through the 1980s, CBS and other networks spent huge sums to cover the presidential nominating conventions. The lengthy coverage gave more airtime to the news anchors and reporters, who became more familiar to viewers. CBS followed the other networks in covering the Vietnam War, the first U.S. conflict detailed so closely by television. Fred Friendly had succeeded Murrow as head of the news division, and his reporters, including John Laurence and Morley Safer, sent back shocking accounts of reprisals against native civilians, raising questions about U.S. involvement. CBS executives were sympathetic to the Johnson administration and questioned some of Friendly's news reports. The clashes eventually led to Friendly's resignation in 1966. By 1968, the critical media focus on Vietnam had undermined the national consensus about the war.

After a consulting firm recommended in 1961 that CBS use a cash surplus to diversify its holdings, Paley surprised CBS president Stanton by opting to buy the New York Yankees baseball team instead of acquiring either *Newsweek* or the *Washington Post*, as Stanton had recommended. The Yankees proved to be unprofitable and were sold to George Steinbrenner in 1973 at a loss of $3 million. Paley paid $280 million in 1967 to buy publisher Holt, Rinehart & Winston, the largest purchase ever of a public corporation. The publishing house proved much less profitable than expected. CBS also lost $30 million on a film production studio from 1967 to 1972. Paley demonstrated his philanthropy in 1975 when he underwrote the founding of the Museum of Television and Radio in New York City. By 1994, the museum contained more than 60,000 broadcast programs in its archives. It also sponsors various educational programs about broadcasting.

CBS entertainment programming remained competitive during the 1970s with several top-rated shows, led by the news program "60 Minutes" and the prime-time soap opera "Dallas." In 1974, CBS owned nine of the top ten prime-time shows. After the retirement of Walter Cronkite as news anchor in 1981, CBS ratings on the evening news began to slide. Thanks in part to the growth of cable television, the network's ratings dropped to last place among the big three in 1988. Huge salaries and rising production costs reduced profits dramatically in the 1980s. Debts had reached $1 billion by the mid-1980s.

In need of revival, CBS was taken over by Laurence A. Tisch, head of Loews entertainment conglomerate, in 1986. Tisch reduced the employees at CBS by almost 50 percent in two years. He sold some valuable nonbroadcasting interests such as Columbia Records and the Harcourt, Brace, Jovan-ovich publishing house. Grant Tinker, program chief at NBC, was hired in 1986 to shore up CBS's prime-time programming. With the death of Paley in 1990, Tisch assumed even greater control at CBS. Tisch's controversial moves unloaded some financial burdens, but CBS still faces a competitive array of broadcast entertainment and news options.

Reference Smith, Sally Bedell, *In All His Glory: The Life of William S. Paley* (1990).

Comic Strips
See Cartoons.

Computers

Computers have become relevant to all information systems in the 1990s. They directly influence the quantity and quality of information received and disseminated by the media, and multimedia companies have come to view computers as an integral aspect of their operations. Computers are used to prepare copy for print media publications as well as for radio and television. The ability to transmit information from one computer to another has created a new system of communication.

The development of the computer from the transistor of the 1940s to the integrated circuitry of the 1990s has moved so rapidly that technological advances now occur within months rather than years or decades. The electronic computer was invented by John Mauchly and John Eckert at the University of Pennsylvania in 1945 while working under a government contract. The transition in computer technology from vacuum tube to transistor and analog (approximate number) to digital (exact number) hardware occurred during the late 1940s and 1950s. In 1960, there were still only about 6,000 computers operating; they were not cost-effective and had limited business and scientific applications.

Personal computers made their appearance in the 1970s, facilitated by advanced semiconductor integrated circuits or silicon chips, which stored enormous amounts of memory and improved microprocessors, enhancing the speed of computing. Intel, a leading manufacturer of chips and microprocessors, produced the first microprocessor chip in 1971 and introduced the 486 microprocessor in 1989 with over 1 million transistors. Apple Computer's Stephen Jobs created a whole industry based on marketing personal computers to average consumers. Apple's sales rose from $165 million in 1980 to $5.75 billion in 1990. William Hewlett and David Packard formed their electronics company in 1939; by 1990, Hewlett-Packard sales of computer hardware totaled over $13 billion. An early mainframe manufacturer, International Business Machines (IBM), also entered the personal computer market. William Gates built Microsoft into the leading software producer in the same era. By the 1990s, four U.S. computer companies were among the world's top ten: IBM, Digital Equipment Company, UNISYS, and Hewlett-Packard.

Media companies, which were already using "cold type" offset printing in the 1960s, quickly converted from typewriters to computerized writing and editing on video display terminals integrated with a central processing unit—that is, typesetting machinery. The Associated Press became the first major media company to use computerized typesetting in 1970. Subscriptions, bookkeeping, the mailroom, and other newspaper functions were soon computerized. Newspapers were storehouses of personal information such as obituaries and photographs, and computers began to replace microfilm as a more efficient system of storing and retrieving such information. Computers could also be used to organize the layout of the publication through a process called "pagination" that effectively eliminated the composing room functions. Further, computer graphics allowed faster and more sophisticated methods of illustration and design. Computerized desktop publishing could be used for small offices as well as major multimedia publications.

The capacity of computers to interface with other technologies made them even more useful. Personal computers could be linked with other computers, including mainframe systems, via a modem, a device that transmits computer messages through telephone wires. Computer users soon found a method of bypassing traditional communication-information formats by conversing through computer bulletin boards or electronic mail. Computer communications may involve simply dispatching messages, but they have also been used as a means of advertising and to research technical questions. The computer networks include a variety of on-line services that allow personal computers access to information for a fee. Even financial transactions such as buying and selling stocks can be done through on-line connections. The Internet system, originally designed for use by defense contract researchers, connects personal computer users with a variety of mainframe computer databases.

Computers have also been adapted to utilize optical (i.e., laser) information technologies in three formats: read-only memory (CD-ROM), write once read many (WORM), and erasable (Multiple Write). Laser technology uses a light beam to imprint a disc surface in either continuous spirals (CLV for constant linear velocity) or concentric circles (CAV for constant angular velocity). The digital videodisc or laser disc can be used to record and play mixed media, such as movies, with sound, color, and motion intact. Computer discs used for audio only provide a technologically advanced—superior to magnetic tape cassettes—sound that is ideal for musical recordings.

CD-ROM discs can be used directly in personal computers or in disc players to communicate text, audio, graphics, and software, but not motion. CD-ROM formats are ideal for storing a variety of databases. The Philips and Sony companies have developed interactive compact disc systems that allow users to become creative. WORM technology allows the computer itself to write onto a disc, which makes it useful for desktop publishing. The erasable technology creates not only added optical storage capacity but also the option of erasing part or all of the disc, similar to a computer floppy disc.

Computers can also interface with satellite technology in cable television systems. The technology is now available through teletext to read newspapers electronically or reference airline and theater schedules. Textual frames are saved on the television screen by means of an electronic converter. Videotex is an interactive two-way communication system relayed through cable or telephone wires. Videotex technology al-

lows the user to access a particular frame immediately instead of waiting for its sequence in teletext. Computer software programs offer an endless variety of options to computer users, ranging from computer games to word processing. The relationship of artificial intelligence and computers produced a vast array of computer games played on computers or simulated hardware through television sets. The two computer systems designed by IBM and Apple originally required separate formats, but recent hardware makes even those systems compatible.

Even Hollywood became fascinated by computers and publicized their capabilities through science-fiction scenarios in films such as Arthur Clarke's *2001: A Space Odyssey* and Thomas Allen's *War Games*, wherein the computers seize control from their human operators. George Lucas's *Star Wars* trilogy and the *Star Trek* television and movie series relied heavily on computer technology for their story lines and high-tech gimmicks.

References Singleton, L. A., *Telecommunications in the Information Age* (1986); Smith, Anthony, *Goodbye Gutenberg: The Newspaper Revolution of the 1980s* (1980).

Connecticut (Hartford) Courant

The longest-running newspaper in U.S. history is the *Connecticut Courant*, which began publishing in 1764 and continues to publish today. Founded by Thomas Green as a patriot organ in the era of the American Revolution, the *Courant* expressed partisan views for Federalists and later antislavery Republicans. In 1979, the *Courant* became part of the Los Angeles Times Mirror Corporation's multimedia conglomerate.

Thomas Green came from a family of printers and had edited a weekly paper in New Haven before arriving in Hartford and founding the *Courant*. Its early editions lacked uniformity in size (ranging from 6 by 9 inches to 11 by 14 inches), typeface, and number of columns. Nonlocal news accounts dominated, and Green wrote no editorials initially. Within days of the first issue of the *Courant*, however, Green set a pattern of patriotic positions by criticizing Parliament's Revenue Act and later the Stamp Act of 1765. In 1768, Green entered a partnership with Ebenezer Watson and began to withdraw from active participation in the *Courant*.

Watson made several important changes: adding a regular poetry section, local death notices, and marriage announcements and adopting a uniform size of 10 by 16 inches. By the mid-1770s, the *Courant* had 300 subscribers paying seven shillings a year and another 400 who bought the paper on a less regular basis. Because of the paper's hostility to the British, it was forced to start its own paper mill. After the British occupation of New York in 1777, the *Courant* rapidly became the most widely read paper in the states, printing 8,000 copies. The bias of the *Courant*'s war reporting became obvious when it virtually ignored or even denied military setbacks.

After Watson's death in 1777, his widow made George Goodwin a partner. Goodwin referred to himself as editor and continued to guide the *Courant* until 1836. After the Revolution, the *Courant* supported a stronger central government under the Articles of Confederation and approved of the new constitutional government. Goodwin was a staunch Federalist, supporting the policies of President George Washington and Treasury Secretary Alexander Hamilton. When party politics emerged in the mid-1790s, the Federalists had no better friend than the *Courant*. When a string of Democratic-Republican administrations began with Thomas Jefferson's election in 1800, the *Courant* remained loyal to the Federalist cause. Indeed, during Thomas Jefferson's administration, Goodwin landed in jail for criticizing the Democratic-Republicans, but the Supreme Court overturned the case as a violation of freedom of the press. After the Federalist Party disintegrated following the War of 1812, the *Courant* seemed almost uninterested in politics until the Whig Party emerged in the 1830s.

Goodwin was forced by old age and ill health to sell the *Courant* in 1836 to John L. Boswell, a former employee with editorial experience on two Pennsylvania papers as well. As a close friend of Whig leader Henry Clay, Boswell showed a partisan political bias that had not been seen in the *Courant* for many years. Boswell launched a daily edition in 1837 and soon had advertising covering three of the paper's four pages. Boswell was fond of printing illustrations, including maps, to enhance the attractiveness of the paper.

With the death of Boswell in 1854, the *Courant*'s ownership passed to Thomas M. Day, a Yale-educated lawyer and merchant who immediately ended the paper's Whig preference. Day initially backed the American or Know-Nothing Party during 1855 and 1856, with its anti-immigration platform. Soon, however, Day moved into the new Republican Party camp and became a strong backer of Abraham Lincoln's administration. Day managed the *Courant* adeptly, relying on a network of reporters, telegraph information, and material from the new Associated Press in New York. He invited readers to write letters to the editor and express opinions that would be printed in the paper.

Day took in a partner, Abel N. Clark, in 1857 and eventually sold out to Clark in 1864. Clark continued to support Lincoln in the 1864 election and advocated a vigorous military campaign to end the war. Joseph R. Hawley, a Union army general, took over the *Courant* in 1867 after serving a term as governor of Connecticut. The paper remained conservative and Republican in the postwar era. When Hawley was elected to the U.S. Senate in 1880, associate editor Charles Dudley Warner took over active direction of the paper. It was Warner who coined the phrase "politics makes strange bedfellows."

During the twentieth century, the title of the paper changed to the *Hartford Courant*, but it remained a conservative Republican paper that vigorously defended free speech. Former city editor John Reitemeyer served as publisher in the 1950s and 1960s, followed by Edmund Downes in the 1970s.

Richard Mooney left the *New York Times* to become editor in 1976. In 1979, when circulation totaled 215,000, the *Courant* was purchased for $105.6 million by the Los Angeles Times Mirror Corporation, owner of the *Los Angeles Times, New York Newsday*, and *Baltimore Sun*. Local patrons were dismayed by the imported Times Mirror management, which showed callous disregard for the concerns of the community and state. Over 100 reporters and several officers resigned in the 1980s. Editor and publisher Michael Davies, who was elected president of the Association of Managing Editors in 1985, reduced local coverage and increased investigative reporting. The daily circulation in 1993 was 229,000, and the Sunday edition had 320,000 readers.

References Kreig, Andrew, *Spiked: How Chain Management Corrupted America's Oldest Newspaper* (1987); Smith, James Eugene, *One Hundred Years of Hartford's* Courant (1949).

Constitutional Convention

The American press was still young and immature in certain respects in the 1780s when doubts developed about the national government under the Articles of Confederation. The press's role in the calling of the Philadelphia convention that drafted the Constitution in 1787, reporting the delegates actions, and then in taking editorial positions upon the new Constitution, proved to be of great consequence for the nation's future. A concerted press bias in favor of the Constitution and against those who opposed it helped win ratification.

Newspapers had become more numerous and more influential in the United States since the Revolutionary War (1775–1783). A characteristic of this young national press was that it was demonstrably free from external coercion or influence by political parties, governments, or commercial interests. Such an era of freedom cannot be said to have existed at any other time in American history. Yet, the newspapers during the period of the Articles of Confederation (1781–1787) national government re-

flected the fears and frustrations of a nation grappling with economic depression and the conflicts of state sovereignty.

When the Philadelphia convention was called in 1787, 12 of the 13 states sent delegates for what all assumed would be an attempt to strengthen the powers of the Confederation government. The delegates agreed to keep their proceedings secret from the press and public. Thus, for several months working behind closed doors fashioning what became a new constitutional system of government, the American people and the press could not know what the result would be. Despite the pride newspapers exhibited in their fairness on major issues, the press overwhelmingly concluded that the Constitution would be good for America before they had even seen the document. Prior to the announcement of the Constitution in the fall of 1787 in Philadelphia, the vast majority of newspapers prepared their readers to embrace the new government. Moreover, those same papers that had promised impartial accounts of the proceedings browbeat fellow journalists who dissented from their position by branding them disloyal. The conduct of most newspapers reporting the Constitutional Convention demonstrated the worst and most dangerous aspects of American journalism.

The average circulation of America's 76 newspapers in 1787 was 700, although news in the papers invariably found a wider audience through coffee houses, inns, and taverns. Pro-convention newspapers dwelt upon economic and social upheavals in the 1780s such as Shays Rebellion in Massachusetts (1786) over tax policies and tariff wars between states. They also recounted the absence of adequate governing powers for the Congress under the Articles of Confederation in areas such as regulation of commerce and currency. The virtual impracticability of amending the Articles (requiring unanimous approval of all states) was another feature of newspaper coverage favoring the Philadelphia meeting. Pro-convention newspapers touted the prominence and integrity of the delegates to the Philadelphia meeting, including George Washington, Benjamin Franklin, and James Madison. Surely the papers reasoned, those leaders had only the best interests of the nation in mind as they designed a new government.

Letters of commentary in newspapers were frequently reprinted in other papers as a means of distributing opinion more widely. Yet, many pro-convention papers either would not print letters questioning the convention or they would not be widely reprinted in other papers. Those comments which were favorable, on the other hand, got a wide audience through reprints. Pro-convention papers tended to question the patriotism of anyone who doubted either the convention delegates' motives or the type of government they were creating.

The 76 American newspaper accounts about the Philadelphia proceedings became a prelude to debate on ratification of the Constitution. The *Federalist Papers*, printed anonymously in New York newspapers but authored by James Madison, Alexander Hamilton, and John Jay, claimed that the Constitution would create a strong central government necessary to resolve state disputes and economic problems facing the nation. The newspapers which had championed the Philadelphia convention naturally took up the cause of promoting the ratification of the Constitution, usually by reprinting the *Federalist Papers*. Antifederalist arguments, repressed or infrequent during the Convention meetings, expressed similar reservations about the Constitution after it was offered for ratification. Creating a strong central government might endanger both states' rights and individual freedoms. The antifederalists also argued that the nation's troubles were not as serious as the federalists suggested. Just as the pro-convention dominance of the press helped to garner favorable approval of the Constitutional Convention, the federalist press influenced the approval of the Constitution in 12 state ratifying conventions during 1787–1788.

Reference Alexander, John K., *The Selling of the Constitutional Convention: A History of News Coverage* (1990).

Cosmopolitan

Originally a magazine aimed at a family audience in 1886, *Cosmopolitan* went through more than one transformation in order to remain competitive. During the early years of the twentieth century, *Cosmopolitan* participated in the muckraking journalism that used sensational exposés to spur reforms. As part of the Hearst network of profitable magazines since the 1960s, it became a popular women's magazine.

Joseph N. Hallock launched *Cosmopolitan* in 1886 as a family magazine, but because circulation remained mired in the 16,000 range, it was sold to newspaperman John Brisben Walker in 1889. Walker moved the operation from Rochester to New York City and began to imitate the successful genre of illustrated monthlies with a literary bent, led by *McClure's*. Walker recruited contributors such as Mark Twain, Arthur Conan Doyle, and Henry James. He persuaded the former editor of the *Atlantic Monthly*, William Dean Howells, to edit *Cosmopolitan* during 1891 and 1892. The result of these changes and a price reduction to ten cents was a boost in circulation to 400,000 by the mid-1890s.

By the turn of the century, *Cosmopolitan*'s pages were filled with stories by H. G. Wells, verse by Rudyard Kipling, investigative reports on foreign subjects and domestic institutions, and features on the physical beauty of women. The magazine had more advertising than it needed and used illustrations on a vast scale to make it physically attractive.

William Randolph Hearst purchased *Cosmopolitan* in 1905 from Walker. The magazine immediately joined the popular and prosperous muckraking trend with a series by David Graham Phillips, a former editorial writer for Joseph Pulitzer's *New York World*, on the influences of special interests on certain U.S. senators entitled "The Treason of the Senate." Phillips later expanded his investigations to Wall Street financial shenanigans and insurance fraud. Other investigative accounts published in *Cosmopolitan* included an exposé of the International Harvester Company by Alfred Henry Lewis and a dissection of corrupt state governments by Charles Edward Russell.

The muckraking bonanza played out before World War I, and *Cosmopolitan* returned to its previous focus on literature, especially fiction. Illustrations by Charles Dana Gibson became a common feature. In 1914, circulation totaled 1 million. Ray Long served as editor from 1918 to 1931 and recruited contributions from Ring Lardner, Fannie Hurst, and P. G. Wodehouse. In 1925, *Hearst's Magazine*, founded in 1901, was merged with *Cosmopolitan* to become *International Cosmopolitan*. In the post–World War II era, *Cosmopolitan* faced the same intense competition from television that other traditional popular magazines encountered. Yet *Cosmopolitan* was able to shift its focus to special topics in each issue that involved detailed investigative reporting and celebrities from the entertainment industry. More contributions came from female authors such as Edna Ferber and Agatha Christie. Sales were oriented more to the newsstands than subscriptions, and circulation increased to about 500,000 by 1960. Other competing journals were not so successful, and many folded in the 1950s.

The last transformation in the mid-1960s was to deal with rising costs, increased competition, and the division of readers into specialized markets. The result was *Cosmopolitan* being made over into a women's magazine focusing on female sexuality and beauty. Editor Helen Gurley Brown supervised the transition, and the new *Cosmopolitan* was an immediate hit with female readers. By the 1980s, with advertising revenues up 50 percent, it was in the thick of competition with comparable magazines such as *Mademoiselle*, *Glamour*, and *Vogue*, although most sales were through single-copy purchases rather than subscriptions. By 1987, *Cosmopolitan*'s advertising revenue was just under $112 million; in 1991, circulation reached 2.8 million.

Reference Reisig, Robin, "The Feminine Plastique," *Ramparts* (1973).

Cox, James Middleton (1870–1957)

Known for his unsuccessful run as the Democratic presidential candidate in 1920,

James M. Cox started out as a journalist in Ohio. He purchased the *Dayton News* in 1898 and the *Springfield News* in 1903. After a political career that included three terms as governor of Ohio as well as the lost presidential election, Cox returned to newspapers in the 1920s. He bought two more papers in Ohio and added the *Miami News*, *Atlanta Journal*, and *Atlanta Constitution* to his holdings. The Cox Broadcasting Company consisted of several radio and television stations.

James Middleton Cox grew up in rural Ohio, where he did an apprenticeship in the printing business. He became a reporter for his brother-in-law John Q. Baker on the *Middletown Signal* in 1891. Cox then moved to Cincinnati, where he worked as a reporter for the *Cincinnati Enquirer* for a couple of years. Baker arranged for Cox to become a secretary to Congressman Paul J. Sorg in 1896. His patron obtained $26,000 in 1898 for Cox to purchase the *Dayton News*, which had been founded in 1826 as a Democratic Party organ. Cox discontinued the morning edition and added a wire service, a women's section, and photographs. Cox used the *News* to expose a reform platform for the Democratic Party, although it took an anti-immigrant, pro-segregation stance. During the first ten years of Cox's ownership, the *News* circulation grew from 2,600 to 30,000. After five successful years in Dayton, Cox bought the *Springfield (Ohio) Press-Republic* and changed its name to the *Springfield News* and its politics from Republican to Democratic. At the same time, Cox formed the Ohio News League as a holding company for his newspapers.

Cox's experience with newspapers stimulated an interest in politics and more active support for the Democratic Party. He was elected to Congress in 1908 and served two terms. In 1912, he ran as a Progressive for governor of Ohio and was elected. He lost a bid for reelection in 1914 but won second and third terms in 1916 and 1918. During his gubernatorial administration, Cox enacted education reforms, workers' compensation, a direct primary law, the initiative, and the referendum. The 1920 Democratic convention nominated Cox to run for president against Republican Warren G. Harding, a fellow Ohioan. Cox found himself in a no-win situation caused by Woodrow Wilson's obsession with the League of Nations and the resulting disintegration of his presidency. Cox promised to make whatever concessions necessary in the Senate to get the league approved if he was elected, but he lost in a landslide. The Republican theme of "Return to Normalcy" suited national sentiment best.

After the defeat in 1920, Cox returned to active management of his newspapers and expanded his holdings. A winter vacation in Miami in 1923 led to Cox's purchase of the *Miami Metropolis*, which was renamed the *Daily News*. As Miami grew, so did the circulation of the paper. At about the same time, Cox bought the *Canton (Ohio) News*, with Don Mellett as editor. Mellett was killed in 1926 by gangsters who were threatened by the *News*'s campaign against bootlegging, vice, and gambling. An officer in the police department was implicated in the murder. The *Canton News* won the 1927 Pulitzer Prize for meritorious public service in its efforts to thwart organized crime. Cox sold the Canton paper in 1930.

The Knight chain's Springfield, Ohio, morning *Sun* went up for sale in 1928, and Cox acted to secure a monopoly with his existing evening *News*. The depression slowed newspaper expansion in the 1930s, but Cox bought the *Atlanta Journal* in 1939. He also secured and discontinued Hearst's afternoon *Atlanta Georgian* to create a monopoly on evening sales. Cox's *Journal* backed successful reform candidate Ellis Arnall against the Eugene Talmadge machine in the gubernatorial election of 1942. When Cox added the *Atlanta Constitution* to his holdings in 1950, he completed the monopoly in the burgeoning southern metropolis.

Ralph McGill was hired as publisher of the *Constitution* and made it a prize-winning paper. All the Cox papers were noted for their thorough coverage of local news and as guardians of the public trust against corrupt or inefficient state and local governments. The newspapers were also profitable and allowed Cox to venture into radio and television ownership through publicly owned Cox Communications, Inc. The stations extended from Ohio to California to Georgia.

By the time of James M. Cox's death in 1957, his newspaper chain was the eighth largest in the nation in circulation, with 18 dailies. The family kept control of the newspaper and broadcasting operations and combined them in 1985 into the Cox Enterprises conglomerate by buying out the publicly operated Cox Communications, which had branched into the cable industry. Cox Enterprises newspaper holdings included 29 dailies in 1988 and ranked eleventh nationally, with a circulation of 1.3 million. Its broadcasting holdings ranked ninth nationally.

Reference Cebula, James E., *James M. Cox: Journalist and Politician* (1985).

Croly, Herbert D.
See New Republic.

Cronkite, Walter
See Columbia Broadcasting System.

Curtis, Cyrus H. K.
See Ladies' Home Journal; Saturday Evening Post.

Curtis, George William
See Harper's Weekly.

Dallas Morning News

In 1875, Alfred H. Belo acquired the *Galveston News*, founded by Samuel Bangs in 1842. His decision to launch a second paper in Dallas in 1885 proved to be an auspicious one for the new paper as well as for Dallas. Quickly, Galveston's twin paper in Dallas eclipsed the original in importance. The *Dallas Morning News* became the most influential paper in Texas during the twentieth century.

Alfred H. Belo, an ex-Confederate colonel, migrated in 1865 from North Carolina to Galveston—the largest city in Texas—to become a bookkeeper for the *News* there. By 1875, he owned the paper. A decade later, he launched another *News* in Dallas to extend coverage over growing north Texas, thereby engaging in the phenomenon of chain ownership. Belo himself moved to Dallas to oversee the expansion. He named Donaldson C. Jenkins editor and, in 1885, hired George B. Dealey as business manager. The *Dallas Morning News* pledged to remain conservative and honest and to promote civic progress.

Eight weeks after beginning publication, the *News* bought its morning competition, the *Dallas Herald* (founded in 1849), which included the local Associated Press franchise. The acquisition also brought Frank Doremus from the *Herald* as managing editor. At the end of its first year, the *News*'s circulation was three times as great as the old *Herald*'s. The *News* quickly extended its sales into Fort Worth and Houston and routed the St. Louis papers that had become entrenched in north Texas communities. By 1895, the daily circulation totaled 15,000, and growth in advertising and revenues followed growth in circulation. Although unafraid to comment on state or national political issues, the *News*'s clear priority was the promotion of the city of Dallas.

Because of the often violent nature of the frontier around Dallas and the *News*'s commitment to support law and order, the paper may have seemed to give undue attention to crime and violence as well as to the opposition to Prohibition. Yet the *News* was also known for sports coverage and promotion of the local opera house, opportunities for women, and the opening of public lands in west Texas to small farmers. The *News* tended to be sympathetic toward big business because it believed that economic expansion was crucial to Texas's future. Thus, it opposed Governor James Hogg's regulatory measures in the 1890s and the Democratic Party's free silver campaign.

The *Dallas Morning News* tardily supported Republican imperialism, which led to the Spanish-American War of 1898. Postwar circulation increased by more than a third, to 26,000. The *News* sponsored an urban renewal program called the Cleaner Dallas League to promote beautification and cleanup, including storm sewers and garbage collection. Founding publisher Belo died in 1901 and was succeeded by his son, Alfred H. Belo Jr., who had been carefully tutored in the business. Editor Jenkins had resigned in 1900 and was replaced by Luther Clark.

Circulation had increased to 38,000 in 1906 when Alfred Belo Jr. died. George Dealey, business manager since 1885, became publisher of the *News*. Dealey was even more vigorous than the Belos in promoting civic progress. He was succeeded by his son Ted Dealey in 1946. The *News* created an evening counterpart, the *Dallas Journal*, in 1914, edited by Lynn Landrum; it was sold in 1938. At the death of editor Clark in 1920, former Washington correspondent Alonzo Wasson was promoted to editor. Upon Wasson's return to reporting in 1929, the publisher's brother, James Q. Dealey, a political science professor at Brown University, became editor and remained until his death in 1937. The *Dallas Morning News* followed the lead of other newspapers by starting its own radio broadcasting station, WFAA, in 1922, which in turn began a television station in the late 1940s.

Despite competition from major conglomerates, the *Dallas Morning News* has remained in local hands, with Ralph Langer as editor and Burl Osborne as publisher in the 1990s. The Times Mirror Company of Los Angeles gave up ownership of the *News*'s rival, the *Dallas Times Herald*, in the 1980s because the *News* could not be beaten. Its daily circulation of 514,000 in 1994 showed a significant increase of 132,000 over the 1991 figure. Likewise, the Sunday edition increased by 257,000 from 1991, to a total of 809,000 in 1994. The great success story of the city of Dallas was matched at every step by the competence and popularity of the *News*.

Reference Sharpe, Ernest, *G. B. Dealey of the Dallas News* (1955).

Dana, Charles Anderson (1819–1897)

Charles Dana, dominant New York journalist of the post–Civil War era as editor of the *Sun*, demonstrated both the rewards and the dangers of remaining independent. Dana demanded skillful reporting of the news and was not afraid to use sensational stories to increase circulation. The *Sun* was the first successful Democratic daily in New York City, and it became a strong advocate for the working classes in the industrial expansion of the postwar era.

A native of New Hampshire, Charles Anderson Dana was educated at Harvard and participated with leading transcendentalists Nathaniel Hawthorne and Henry David Thoreau in the utopian Brook Farm, Massachusetts, experiment in the 1840s. After a brief tenure as a typesetter for a Boston newspaper, Dana moved to Horace Greeley's *New York Tribune* as city editor and later became the first managing editor of a U.S. paper. As a member of the *Tribune* staff, Dana proved to be a dedicated Free-Soil abolitionist on the slavery question. Because of Dana's advocacy of the use of massive military force against the Confederacy, he was named assistant secretary of war by President Abraham Lincoln during the Civil War. After the war, Dana edited a short-lived Chicago newspaper. Dana's opportunity to establish his own paper came in 1868, when he persuaded some New York financiers to back his purchase of the *New York Sun* from Moses Beach for $175,000.

A lonely Democratic paper in a city dominated by the Republican press, the *Sun* had a circulation of only 43,000 in 1868. Dana was committed to obtaining the most complete news possible and getting it into print quickly. As a two-cent, four-page daily, the *Sun* followed the example of James Gordon Bennett's *Herald* by including human-interest stories about ordinary people, covering crime and scandals, and providing stimulating interviews. Editor Dana recruited reporters who could not only dig up the facts for a story but also write with zest and vigor. The *Sun*'s editorial page was as lively and entertaining as its news accounts, even though it usually resisted taking serious positions on key issues. Dana delighted in expressing an independent and cynical view of politics in an era of greed and graft, especially regarding the Republican Grant administration nationally and Tammany Hall politics locally. One of the *Sun*'s most popular phrases ridiculing the Grant administration was "Turn the rascals out." Yet because of his affection for the working classes, Dana opposed the patrician-led Liberal Republican movement, even though he agreed with its condemnation of corruption. Dana's focus on the interests of common working people created more readers for the *Sun*, and by 1876, the circulation had grown to 131,000—the largest readership in New York City.

The *New York Sun* gave sympathetic coverage to labor issues, such as the brutal suppression of New York's Tompkins Square riot in 1874. Editor Dana consistently supported labor rights and social justice for the working classes. He opposed the nativism movement against foreigners and advocated tolerance toward all. Dana's Brook Farm–inspired philosophy favored a harmonious relationship between management and labor, even though such a view seemed naive in the robber-baron era. Identification with the urban workingman and disaffection from Democrat Grover Cleveland caused Dana to endorse the third-party Greenback Labor ticket in 1884. Dana seemed surprised that the decision cost the *Sun* many readers. By 1886, circulation had fallen to 82,000 from 145,000 in 1884, probably in large part because of the popularity of Pulitzer's *World,* which appealed to the city's working classes in a different way. Dana still relied on the 1840s romantic socialist view of workers as producers trying to divert capitalism from competition to cooperation. Pulitzer understood and appealed to workers as consumers seeking inexpensive leisure activities.

Charles Dana's colleagues included transcendentalists Nathaniel Hawthorne and Henry David Thoreau before he became the New York Sun's *editor in 1868.*

Charles Dana believed that he remained true to his ideals and methods even after the new corporate competition emerged. When other papers lowered their prices in 1884 to one cent to compete with Pulitzer's *World,* Dana kept the *Sun*'s price at two cents and continued to lose money. The *Sun* fell from first place in circulation in 1883 to third place in 1885. As the *Sun* lost

many working-class readers, it tried to attract businessmen by adopting a more conservative stance. The *Sun* opposed the 1886 strikes sponsored by the Knights of Labor favoring an eight-hour day because Dana believed that they promoted anarchism.

Charles Dana feared that the agrarian Populist movement, with its unrealistic reform proposals, would promote class conflict and backed the Republicans against Populist Democratic candidate William Jennings Bryan in 1896. Dana would not resort to yellow journalism's thumping for war in 1898 against Spain, even though he was an imperialist. Hearst's *New York Journal* circulation of 568,000 in 1897 pushed the *Sun* to a distant second, with 150,000 readers, at the time of Dana's death. Yet not even the *Sun*'s apparent proclivity for changes in philosophy could detract from Dana's respect and influence among journalists of the era. Although the old-fashioned belief in personal journalism did not survive his death, Charles Dana's determined editorial independence from advertising influence is nostalgically revered by many modern editors constrained by the pursuit of profits.

Reference Steele, Janet E., *The Sun Shines for All: Journalism and Ideology in the Life of Charles A. Dana* (1993).

Daniels, Josephus
See Raleigh News and Observer.

Day, Dorothy (1897–1980)
Beginning her career as a Socialist, Dorothy Day became the editorial voice of the *Catholic Worker,* which she cofounded in 1933. She showed empathy for the working classes, the poor, and minorities as well as disdain for the political establishment. Her religious convictions stood out in her writings on all subjects.

Dorothy Day was born in New York City to middle-class parents, John and Grace Day. Her father's ancestors from Tennessee had fought for the Confederacy in the Civil War. John Day was a journalist and a horse-racing enthusiast. He helped establish the

Hialeah racetrack in Miami and wrote a racing column for the *New York Telegraph*. The Day family moved to San Francisco in 1904 and experienced the great earthquake of 1906. Shortly thereafter, they moved to Chicago, where John Day became sports editor for the *Chicago Inter Ocean* in 1907. Dorothy matriculated at the University of Illinois at age 16 on a partial scholarship from the Hearst Foundation. She fancied herself a populist-socialist and was determined to pursue a journalism career, emulating her father and two older brothers.

Day left the University of Illinois after two years and traveled to New York in 1915 to work as a reporter for the socialist paper *The Call*. Her writing displayed her passionate commitment to justice for the poverty-stricken lower classes. Day served a jail sentence for participating in a 1917 suffragist march in Washington. At the end of World War I, Day accepted a position with *The Masses*, another socialist periodical that featured writers such as John Dos Passos and Malcolm Cowley. When *The Masses* collapsed, Day moved to a radical magazine, the *Liberator*. She became acquainted with playwright Eugene O'Neill, who proved to be a good friend and strong influence on Day. She continued her radical involvement, once being arrested in Chicago for supporting the International Workers of the World. A trip to Europe after her marriage allowed Day to immerse herself in the European socialist milieu.

Day penned an autobiographical novel, *The Eleventh Virgin*, in 1924 and obtained modest royalties by selling the rights to a movie producer. She was able to purchase a home on Staten Island and soon gave birth to a daughter. In 1927, Day underwent a conversion experience that led her into the Catholic Church. She continued to write for the *New Masses* and *Commonweal* (a Catholic journal), but her religious conversion added a new element to her journalistic pursuits. In 1932, Day observed the "hunger march" on Washington and was moved to establish a journal to feature concerns of the underprivileged classes.

Day joined a fellow advocate for the poor, Peter Maurin, to found the monthly *Catholic Worker* in May 1933, selling for a penny a copy. They printed 2,500 copies of the first issue with virtually no financial resources. Day's regular column was entitled "On Pilgrimage." The *Worker* called on individuals to offer assistance to the poor and underprivileged, a sort of old-fashioned Christian charity. Day and Maurin did not believe that government assistance was the only or the best way to aid the poor or bring about social change. Circulation rose to 190,000 by 1938, in the era of the massive New Deal government welfare schemes. Day wrote about her experiences in two books: *From Union Square to Rome* (1938) and *House of Hospitality* (1939).

The *Catholic Worker* also fought against the anti-Semitism of radio celebrity Father Coughlin as well as that of the German Nazis. During the Spanish civil war (1936–1939), without showing partiality toward the socialist-communist Republicans, Day condemned the fascist dictator Franco and alienated some Catholics, who supported him as an anticommunist. During World War II, the *Catholic Worker*'s unpopular pacifism and criticism of U.S. internment of Japanese Americans caused a major circulation decline of 50,000. The Federal Bureau of Investigation (FBI) began a surveillance of Day and the *Worker* in the early 1940s but determined that she was loyal by 1944. Yet because of what many regarded as an unpatriotic wartime stance, Day was suspected of being a communist sympathizer during the Cold War years after 1945. The FBI reopened Day's file in the 1950s, and she was arrested several times for obstructing air-raid drills. One jailing in 1957 caused major media outlets such as the *New York Times* and *Post* as well as the *Catholic Worker* to protest Day's treatment. Day revealed the difficulties of her isolation in the book *The Long Loneliness* (1952).

Dorothy Day led the *Catholic Worker* to the forefront of the civil rights campaigns of the 1950s. She rode desegregated buses in the South and marched with migrant worker leader Cesar Chavez in California. Day demonstrated her pacifism once more by opposing the Vietnam War in the 1960s. Throughout her participation in demonstrations for peace or civil rights causes, Day manifested a passive religious attitude rather than a confrontational stance. Her unique approach was summarized in her last two books: *Loaves and Fishes* (1963) and *On Pilgrimage: The Sixties* (1973). Day continued to write for the *Catholic Worker* until her death in 1980.

Reference Miller, William D., *A Harsh and Dreadful Love: Dorothy Day and the Catholic Worker Movement* (1973).

Des Moines Register

Emerging slowly from its nineteenth century lethargy, the *Des Moines Register*, under Cowles family ownership after 1903, became one of America's great dailies. The *Register* was noted for its excellence in reporting the news and an ability to give midwesterners a world perspective. Its staff has been the recipient of more Pulitzer Prizes than any other paper its size. The Gannett Company bought the *Register* in 1986.

Barlow Granger founded the *Iowa Star* at Des Moines in 1849, but the paper lacked dynamic qualities and changed its name to the *Iowa State Leader* in 1870. The *Iowa State Register* joined four other Des Moines papers in 1857 as a Free Soil advocate published by James Clarkson, who wanted cheap land for small farmers. Clarkson made the *Register* into a staunch Republican paper by the time of the Civil War. The personal and political nature of journalism in the Clarkson era was the rule rather than the exception. James Clarkson's brother Richard managed the paper after James went to Washington as assistant postmaster general.

Richard Clarkson sold his interests in the *Register* in 1902 to George Roberts, publisher of the *Leader*, resulting in the combined morning *Des Moines Register and Leader*. The move set the stage for the beginning of the Gardner Cowles era. Gardner Cowles and his future editor Harvey Ingham grew up in Algona, Iowa where Cowles got into Republican politics in the legislature and Ingham became editor of a local weekly

paper. When the competition in small Algona became too stiff, Ingham accepted the editorship of the newly combined *Des Moines Register and Leader* in 1902. At Ingham's suggestion, Cowles came from Algona in 1903 to buy the majority shares in the *Register and Leader* from Roberts.

Cowles had assumed control of a troubled paper with serious financial problems and competition from three afternoon papers. Roberts claimed the circulation of the *Register and Leader* was 32,000, but Cowles soon learned that it was only 14,000. Many of the actual subscribers were in arrears. Seeking advertising was made more complicated by the opposition of Cowles to both patent medicines and liquor. Before the end of one-year's ownership, Cowles had resolved debts and was making profits. Circulation passed the 25,000 mark in 1906. Cowles gave the editors and staff great freedom of expression; he only asked that editorial opinion be kept out of news coverage. Editor Ingham was passionate in his abhorrence of war and empathy with the underprivileged. Cowles and Ingham's biggest initial hurdle was fighting corruption in city hall. Ingham's editorials backed Progressive efforts at trust-busting and urged fair treatment of America's black population.

Competition with other papers fortunately resolved itself since the three afternoon dailies—the *News, Capital,* and *Tribune*—had to fight each other for business. The *Tribune* was founded in 1906 by Charles Hellen and its circulation never rose above 10,000 against entrenched competition. Cowles was able to buy the *Tribune* in late 1908 for less than $30,000 at a time when the *Register and Leader* circulation hit 31,000. The *Tribune* continued to be operated as an afternoon daily by Cowles, albeit with much greater zest than before. *Tribune* circulation surpassed its previous best within a year. In 1916, the morning edition's name was changed to simply the *Register*.

The Cowles papers continued to editorially back almost every Progressive measure including the new federal income tax in 1913. The most important Progressive reform in Iowa was railroad regulation. The big railroad companies had dominated all aspects of Iowa politics and economy for decades. Ingham opposed the United States entrance into World War I, but after the declaration of war in 1917 he urged a goal of victory. The *Register* favored approval of the League of Nations in 1919 against the majority sentiment of the isolationist midwest. After the war, the *Register* was among the first papers in the nation to condemn violence by the Ku Klux Klan, which was as powerful in the midwest as in the South. The *Register* also clamored for funds to provide paved highways in the burgeoning era of the automobile.

Circulation for the *Register* and *Tribune* hit a high of 116,000 in 1918, but declined somewhat after the war. The Sunday edition recovered better than the dailies. Subscription prices were raised to compensate for inflation. Because of declining circulation, the Scripps-Howard Company agreed to sell its afternoon *News* to Cowles in 1924. The *News* was merged into the *Tribune*, causing circulation of the combined morning and afternoon edition to rise from 147,000 to 165,000 by 1925. In 1927, Publisher Lafayette Young of the afternoon *Capital* agreed to sell to Cowles for $750,000. The termination of the remaining competition left the morning *Register* and afternoon *Tribune* a newspaper monopoly in Des Moines. By 1930, the combined daily circulation rose to 243,000 and the Sunday edition sold 206,000.

The Cowles papers could not help but feel disappointment toward the disastrous end of native son Herbert Hoover's administration. Franklin Roosevelt was given a reluctant endorsement. Farmers and banks were hit especially hard during the Great Depression in Iowa. Meanwhile, the Cowles sons, John and Gardner, Jr., had obtained control of the *Minneapolis Star* in 1935. When Gardner, Jr. launched *Look* magazine in 1937 and eventually took control of the Des Moines papers, John was left in charge in Minneapolis. Ingham retired as editor of the *Register* in 1943. During the Ingham era, cartoonist Jay Darling won two Pulitzer Prizes while W. W. Waymack and

Forrest Seymour won editorial Pulitzers in 1938 and 1943 respectively.

The post–World War II era at the *Register* saw a continuation of an active Cowles role. Gardner Cowles, Jr.'s nephew David Kruidenier succeeded his uncle as publisher in 1970. The *Register* completed a conversion to offset and computerized printing by 1976. Longtime staffer Kenneth McDonald served as editor after Ingham until 1976. During McDonald's era, more Pulitzer Prizes were won by *Register* writers: Nat Finney (1948), Richard Wilson (1954), Clark Mollenhoff (1958), Nick Kotz (1968), and James Risser (1976) for reporting; John Robinson and Don Ultang (1952) for photography; Lauren Soth (1956) for editorial writing; and Frank Miller (1963) for cartoons. After Mcdonald's retirement in 1976, another *Register* staffer, Michael Gartner, became editor. The Cowles family sold the *Register* to the Gannett Company in 1986 for $200 million.

Reference Mills, George, *Harvey Ingham and Gardner Cowles, Sr.: Things Don't Just Happen* (1977).

Detroit News

James E. Scripps helped formulate a proud newspaper tradition when he founded the *Detroit News* in 1873. Like most Scripps newspapers, the *News* was an inexpensive evening daily noted for its comprehensive news coverage and aggressive editorial page. The *News* distinguished itself by being the first newspaper to start its own radio station in 1920. In the 1980s, the *News* was sold to the Gannett Company.

At the time of its founding, the *Detroit News* faced a successful morning daily, the *Free Press*, founded in 1831. James Scripps had gained experience on papers in Chicago and Detroit but had very little capital to invest. The *News* was tabloid size and sold for two cents, whereas the competing papers all sold for five cents. It was an inauspicious time to launch a newspaper, because in 1873, the nation entered a severe depression that lasted about four years. Following early monetary losses, Scripps engaged a number of relatives, including his half brother Edward W. Scripps, to help keep the paper going. At the end of the second year, the *News* had turned losses into profits. After five years, circulation rose to more than 36,000, making it the eleventh largest evening daily in the nation.

The *Detroit News* maintained a political independence, which was unusual for the times. The *News*'s campaign for open meetings of the aldermanic board proved to be popular with voters. Reflecting a keen civic pride, the *News* promoted city improvements such as parks and recreational facilities. Soon the profits from the *News* paved the way for the Scripps family to launch other papers in Cleveland, Buffalo, St. Louis, and Cincinnati based on the *News* format. The tradition of family newspaper enterprises began with the Scripps family and the *Detroit News*.

The circulation and financial success of the *News* allowed it to buy out much of its competition. As early as 1874, Scripps purchased the *Daily Union*, from which Scripps had recruited some of his staff. With the acquisition of the morning *Tribune* in 1891, the *News* gained the Associated Press franchise for Detroit. Scripps continued to publish the *Tribune* until 1915. In 1921, the *News* bought the morning *Detroit Journal* and terminated its publication.

During the Progressive reform era, the *Detroit News* became a leader. As early as 1890, the paper backed the eight-hour workday championed by organized labor. It favored a public transportation system that would create efficient and economical service. *News* editorials supported Progressive Mayor H. S. Pingree and city government threats to regulate the utilities, which produced lower rates. The *News* carried a feature story on the development of the automobile by Henry Ford in 1899, anticipating the significance of the invention. Circulation grew steadily; it reached 50,000 in 1890, 233,000 in 1920, and 323,000 in 1930.

After James Scripps's death in 1906, publisher George Booth maintained the *News*'s traditions of political independence, civic promotion, and vigorous opposition to corruption and crime. George E. Miller, for-

mer Washington bureau chief who became editor during the 1920s, typified the involved *News* staffer. Miller suggested a project to develop the St. Lawrence waterway to a Michigan senator. He also saw to it that the *Detroit News* had the distinction of being the first newspaper to own and operate a radio broadcasting station. Like most early radio, WWJ began as an experiment, broadcasting the presidential election returns of 1920. Publishers at the *News* believed that radio should be viewed as a complement to newspapers rather than as competition. Such a view would prove profitable for many other newspapers that followed the lead of the *News* in entering broadcasting. WWJ established Michigan's first FM broadcast station in 1941, and television broadcasting began in 1946.

The traditions of pursuing crime and political graft remained intact under recent *News* editors such as Harry V. Wade and Martin Hayden. Despite efforts to champion the cause of labor, the *News* itself was shut down for 267 days by a strike in 1967 and 1968. The competing Hearst afternoon daily, the *Detroit Times*, was bought by the *News* in 1960. In the early 1980s, the *News* was sold to the Gannett Company for $717 million. In 1989, the *Detroit News*'s 676,000 subscribers put it ninth in circulation among the nation's daily newspapers, just ahead of Knight-Ridder's *Detroit Free Press*.

Reference Lutz, William W., *The* News *of Detroit* (1973).

Disney, Walt
See Animation.

Douglass, Frederick (1817–1895)

As a leading abolitionist, former slave Frederick Douglass contributed to antislavery writings and even launched a newspaper of his own, the *North Star*. Douglass's printing business was the first ever established by an African American in the United States. Before the Civil War, Douglass published his autobiography and spoke publicly against slavery in England as well as across the northern states.

Frederick Douglass's mother was a Negro

slave and his father was a white man. One of Douglass's owners taught him to read, and when he escaped from a Maryland plantation, he made his way to New York City. He worked as a carpenter, but his fame emerged when he began speaking to the Massachusetts Anti-Slavery Society. Douglass became acquainted with New England's leading antislavery advocate, William Lloyd Garrison, who often accompanied Douglass on the lecture circuit. Douglass also began writing articles for Garrison's newspaper, *The Liberator*. However, the two did not agree on all aspects of the antislavery campaign. Garrison's view that the Constitution was a document endorsing slavery was rejected by Douglass, who was thereby charged with treachery by Garrison.

After a visit to England in 1845 to continue lecturing on the issue of slavery, Douglass returned to the United States and became associate editor of an abolitionist newspaper, *The Ram's Horn*. The paper failed within a year. In late 1847, Douglass launched his own newspaper in Rochester, New York, the *North Star*. It was the first printing establishment owned and operated by an African American. The circulation, which soon surpassed 3,000, included subscribers in the West Indies and England. Douglass's paper was not popular with all the residents of Rochester, and his house containing most of his personal papers was burned. Douglass renamed his newspaper *Frederick Douglass' Paper* in 1851 during a financial reorganization; the paper was suspended just before the Civil War in 1860. Douglass toured Canada and England during 1859, lecturing again on the evils of slavery.

During the Civil War, Douglass published a monthly magazine that sought English benefactors for the Union war effort. He also helped recruit blacks for a Massachusetts regiment in the Union army. After the war, in 1869, Douglass began to edit a weekly newspaper in Washington, D.C., the *New Era*, which sought assistance for southern freedmen. The paper lasted until 1875, when Douglass's debts became too great. Frederick Douglass participated

fully in government activities, serving as a U.S. marshall and as ambassador to Haiti.

Frederick Douglass founded the North Star *in 1847; it was the first newspaper to be owned by an African American.*

In addition to his varied efforts in the newspaper field, Douglass published several autobiographical accounts. The first installment was entitled *Narrative of the Life of Frederick Douglass*, published in 1845. A second account, *My Bondage and My Freedom*, was issued in 1855, and the final volume, *Life and Times of Frederick Douglass*, was printed in 1878. All three treatises were instrumental in detailing the crisis of slavery and the problems of free blacks in the United States. During the 1880s, Douglass made one final lecture tour that took him to Greece and Egypt. Douglass often spoke in favor of women's suffrage and died in 1895 after attending a suffragist convention.

See also Abolitionist Movement.

Reference Foner, Philip S., *Frederick Douglass: A Biography* (1963).

Dow, Jones and Company
See Wall Street Journal.

Edison, Thomas Alva
See Motion Pictures; Phonograph.

Editor and Publisher

The New York City weekly journal *Editor and Publisher: A Journal for Newspaper Makers* was founded by James Shale in 1901 to cover the technical aspects of newspaper publishing. *Editor and Publisher* outlasted its rivals to become the industry's principal source of specialized information.

At the height of newspaper influence in the 1890s, publisher James Shale of the *McKeesport (Pennsylvania) News* became concerned about providing useful publishing information to newspapers. When United Press collapsed in 1897, Shale helped found the Publishers' Press Association as an alternative to Associated Press's dominance on the East Coast. The time was also ripe for the launching of *Editor and Publisher* in 1901. Shale wanted the manufacturers of newspaper materials such as ink, paper, and presses to use his journal as a prime source of advertising to newspaper executives. Despite his title of editor, Shale was interested mainly in the business side of the journal, leaving the publishing management to Frank L. Blanchard. The earliest issues of *Editor and Publisher* were eight pages with features on publishing giants of the day. For example, the first issue in 1901 featured a story on William Randolph Hearst, complete with a photo.

Although the publication included some hard news, the primary thrust from the journal's beginning to the present was providing practical business information to the industry. *Editor and Publisher* acquired one of its rivals, the *Journalist*, in 1907 and dropped its subtitle in 1915. Partly because circulation never rose above 1,000 and partly because Shale became distracted by business prospects elsewhere, he sold the journal in 1912 to James Wright Brown, a former managing editor with a Louisville paper, and seven silent partners. Brown committed the journal to a high ethical code, opposing fraud in advertising and news reporting and vigorously defending freedom of the press. The Brown family still owns *Editor and Publisher* today.

Editor and Publisher produced special issues on the occasions of large professional conclaves such as the American Newspaper Publishers Association and Associated Press. The journal continued its earlier practice of focusing on the heritage and personalities of the profession in feature articles. Almost immediately after Brown's takeover, the journal was put on a sounder financial footing with increased advertising and circulation. By 1927, when circulation had reached 9,000, *Editor and Publisher* took over its remaining competitor, the *Fourth Estate*.

New departments emerged in the 1920s, including editorial commentary and book reviews. *Editor and Publisher*'s independence allowed it to comment on serious developments, such as tension between editorial and business departments of major newspapers. The journal also began a regular practice of printing statistical facts about publishing. In 1922, the journal published a complementary "yearbook" that listed information about foreign advertisers, professional organizations, and faculties of schools of journalism. Beginning in 1959, the *International Year Book* was published separately and included ownership, staff, and circulation listings for all daily and weekly newspapers. It compiled similar information for Canadian and foreign newspapers. The *Year Book* also provided addresses for news services and equipment suppliers.

Another innovative feature in 1924 was the publication of market guides, with tables on the sizes of all U.S. newspapers. In 1940, *Editor and Publisher* began a preelection poll of dailies indicating their editorial support for presidential candidates.

James Wright Brown died in 1959 and was succeeded by his son, Robert Utting Brown, as president and editor. Robert Brown was a Dartmouth graduate and began his journalism career as a reporter for United Press. He started working at *Editor and Publisher* in 1936 and was made editor in

1944. The company operated bureaus in Washington and Chicago as well as its headquarters in New York City. By the mid-1960s, *Editor and Publisher* had a circulation of 20,000 and gross revenues of over $1 million. In 1994, paid circulation was over 25,000. The *Year Book* became available on CD-ROM in 1994.

Editorials

In addition to their primary functions of presenting the news to readers, listeners, and viewers, the media traditionally have allowed themselves the option of expressing their own or others' opinions about current events or people. When Joseph Pulitzer first conceived the series of journalism awards, one of the first categories included was editorial comment. Historically, the evolution of the editorial has undergone many and varied treatments from integrating opinion with news accounts to separating material on an opinion-editorial page. Editorial commentators even established their own National Conference of Editorial Writers in 1947. There have been distinct differences between editorial formats for print and broadcast media, mostly because of the regulatory aspect for radio and television.

When James Franklin took a stand against smallpox inoculation in the 1721 *New England Courant*, editorial comment began a long and important history in America. Franklin's brother Benjamin later included brief editorial comments in his *Pennsylvania Gazette* despite a belief that newspapers should remain objective. The main difficulty in the colonial period was that no journalist had conceived of a separate editorial page. Thus, most editorializing occurred in essays on public policy issues or letters sent to the paper. Indeed, sometimes editors wrote letters themselves in order to inject opinions. Although pamphlets rather than newspapers were the normal means of expressing opinion, during and after the American Revolution newspapers became openly partisan so that reporting the news itself was an exercise in editorializing.

During the Revolution, the *New York Journal* began isolating its commentary in a section called the "Journal of Occurrences," which used italicized type to set it apart from news accounts. Many papers began to use the column headed local news as the place for editorial comment. English newspapers had begun to use editorial essays called "leaders" before the end of the eighteenth century. The technique attracted Noah Webster who had been using the local New York column for comment in the *American Minerva* before 1796. In that year he started writing editorials under the heading "The Minerva," legitimately the first editorial column. Boston's *Columbian Centinel* copied Webster's technique and in 1800 the *Philadelphia Aurora* set aside its second page for comment utilizing the editorial first person. Most editorials before the 1830s were succinct single paragraphs, however, and did not cover nearly an entire page. The art of writing editorials had not yet been developed to its potential.

In the 1840s, Horace Greeley's *New York Tribune* led the way to establishing a full page of editorial comment. The process was completed in the 1850s when the *Tribune* expanded to eight pages. Greeley's editorial page utilized several writers on topics including politics, society, the economy, and even literature. James Gordon Bennett's *New York Herald* featured short editorial paragraphs noted for their harsh tone. The *New York Times* in the 1850s sought to provide balance and instruction through its editorials with editor Henry Raymond often elucidating both sides of issues. William Cullen Bryant at the *New York Post* used the editorial page to crusade for an end to slavery and speculation in public lands. Smaller weeklies began to emulate the dailies, although their editorials rarely entertained subjects other than politics.

After the Civil War, editors and publishers quickly moved to focus upon accurate and thorough news gathering by talented reporters rather than simply using their papers to espouse opinions. Although some predicted the end of the editorial, many editors such as Henry Watterson at the *Louisville Courier-Journal*, E. L. Godkin at the

New York Post, and Harvey Scott of the *Portland Oregonian* showed that commentary remained important when it was forceful and informed. When Joseph Pulitzer designed the *New York World* as the prototype of the modern newspaper in the 1880s, the editorial page became a lively feature to attract readers. Arthur Brisbane introduced a new format—large type face and wide columns—and style to the editorial pages of the Hearst papers in the early 1900s. Brevity and a clear style were important Brisbane rules, but many topics could be covered in both prose and cartoon form.

News magazines led by *Time* in the 1920s introduced the integrated news and interpretation scheme on a sophisticated level. The idea that events and facts had become too complex to cover in great detail allowed Henry Luce's staff to shape the articles on news topics so that readers could obtain a point of view about events. The *Time* method led to a proliferation of signed newspaper columns which provided interpretation as well as opinion. In due course, there were specialized columns on politics, foreign affairs, economics, culture, etc. The syndication of columns allowed the writers to establish national audiences for their comments. In the era since World War II, large and even medium-sized dailies have an editorial page editor to coordinate the opinion and comment section. Indeed, the larger dailies utilize an editorial conference of writers and editors to determine the paper's position on issues.

Concern that editorial pages had become stale and uninviting led to a conference in 1947 sponsored by the American Society of Newspaper Editors and the American Newspaper Institute which created the National Conference of Editorial Writers. The Conference sought to develop methods to improve editorial writing. The Conference's 1975 statement of principles advocated that editorialists present facts honestly, draw fair conclusions from the facts, avoid seeking personal favor, and encourage a serious approach to public policy issues.

Unlike the print media, broadcasters have labored under the scrutiny of regulatory licensing agencies, chiefly the Federal Communications Commission (FCC). Because news accounts on radio broadcasts emerged only gradually, it was not until World War II that the FCC made a condition of licensing that stations would not comment on news events. The ban was altered in 1949 with the so-called Fairness Doctrine, which allowed comment by the stations but required them to allow rebuttals by listeners. Although a majority of radio and television stations thereafter presented occasional editorials, there was no regularity. In 1977, only 22 percent of television and 16 percent of radio stations offered daily editorials. In short, editorials were not a regular feature of broadcast media as they were in the print media. Network television news shows occasionally featured commentary with the appropriate disclaimers, but networks too have shown reluctance to engage in the practice regularly. Talk media shows have become popular over the past two decades, in part because they often mingle views of the host with viewer-listener phone calls expressing personal opinions.

Reference Stonecipher, Harry W., *Editorial and Persuasive Writing: Opinion Functions of the News Media* (1979).

Engravings

Although illustrations emerged slowly as a media technique, since the nineteenth century they have complemented textual content as well as being independent expressions. The technology of engravings moved from the early woodcuts to halftone photoengraving to offset printing, which reproduced the most realistic images.

The first illustrations were colophons on newspapers or magazines, which were used as printers' trademarks. The first decorative title design was created in 1707 for the *Boston News-Letter*. Early illustrations were made from woodcut engravings upon which ink and paper were applied. Since these required artistic skill and considerable production time, they were rarely used in newspapers except for mastheads, which could be used over and over. The "Join or Die" snake symbol on the patriotic *Massachusetts Spy* masthead in the 1770s demonstrated the impact of illustrations. The *Connecticut Courant* used a woodcut diagram to show the path of Lexell's comet in 1770. The *Albany Evening Journal* featured a spread-winged eagle woodcut to represent Whig electoral victories in 1838. The *New York Herald* created a full page of engravings depicting Andrew Jackson's funeral in 1845 and other engravings showing battle scenes from the Mexican War. Woodcuts depicting battles were also used frequently during the Civil War.

The *Pictorial Drawing-Room Companion*, published weekly in Boston during the 1850s, sought to emulate the popular *Illustrated London News* by including numerous woodcuts. *Frank Leslie's Illustrated Newspaper* (begun in 1855) and *Harper's Weekly* (started in 1857) included numerous woodcut illustrations in their pages. But it was *Graham's Magazine*, published in Philadelphia during the 1840s, that demonstrated the potential of technologically sophisticated illustrations. Engravings on copper and steel, although expensive, were a regular feature of *Graham's*, which undoubtedly enhanced its popularity. *Godey's Lady's Book* used hand-colored engravings of women's fashions from the 1830s to the 1870s.

Another technological advance in engraving was zincographs, which were first used in Europe during the 1860s and became popular with U.S. printers in the 1870s. This expensive technique used acid to etch lines on zinc plates. It was a short jump from zincographs to photoengraving, since photos could be printed directly on zinc plates. Frederic Ives followed early research into photoengraving in England to

Godey's Lady's Book *featured engravings such as this one on women's fashions in 1875.*

develop the product known as halftones at Cornell University between 1878 and 1886. Stephen H. Horgan demonstrated the application of halftones to the new stereotyped printing presses for the *New York Herald.* Other papers such as the *New York Daily Graphic* and Joseph Pulitzer's *New York World* used the new halftones as a central element. With the emergence of photoengraving, photographers displaced most artists on major publications.

When yellow journalism brought the use of halftones to a peak in newspapers, it was only a matter of time until photography itself became an art form for the news media as well as for advertising. Joseph Medill Patterson's *New York Daily News*, pioneer tabloid of the 1920s, featured a photograph on the front of each issue. Indeed, the success of the tabloids led Henry R. Luce to launch his pictorial magazine *Life* in 1936. Gardner Cowles's *Look* appeared in 1937, imitating *Life*'s pictorial journalism. The addition of color photos enhanced the attractiveness of magazines even more. The emergence of facsimile transmissions via telephone lines in the 1970s allowed photographs to be sent in minutes from the source of origin to the publisher. Only television's great expansion in the 1950s would blunt the popularity of photojournalism.

See also Graphic Design; Photojournalism.

Reference Schuneman, R. Smith, "Art or Photography: A Question for Newspaper Editors in the 1890s," *Journalism Quarterly* (1965).

Fairness Doctrine
See Prior Restraint.

Federal Communications Commission (FCC)

Created by the Federal Communications Act of 1934, the Federal Communications Commission (FCC) replaced the Radio Commission as the chief regulator of the commercial broadcast industry. Within a few years, the FCC also took on the responsibility of regulating the new television industry. The primary method of regulation has been the issuance of licenses to stations, which allows control over operations and programming.

Government supervision over broadcasting began in the 1920s after radio stations mushroomed and engaged in various conflicts. The industry itself requested federal government intervention because states could not effectively regulate a technology involved in interstate commerce. The Radio Act of 1927 allowed a seven-member Radio Commission to license broadcasting stations, but it shared regulatory authority with the Commerce Department. The Federal Communications Act of 1934 created an independent regulatory agency whose jurisdiction was expanded to include the telegraph and telephone industries; television would be added later.

The FCC issued licenses to broadcast stations as long as they operated "in the public interest." Thus, although the FCC could not censor program content, any programs that were viewed unfavorably by the commission could become a factor in license renewal or even revocation. Section 315 of the act provided "equal time" to political candidates using the broadcast airwaves. So stations selling airtime to one candidate for campaign advertising would have to grant equal time to all other candidates. The FCC, like the Radio Commission before it, prohibited "obscene" and "indecent" program content. In addition to potential loss of license, violation of this provision (added to the license code by Congress in 1948) could result in fines, imprisonment, or both upon conviction.

The Federal Communications Act allowed the president to assume control of broadcasting during a national emergency. This provision allowed the federal government free use of the airwaves to make important announcements in time of war or natural disaster (later through the Emergency Broadcast System). In 1941, after some criticism of the government by the Mayflower Broadcast Corporation, the FCC ruled that broadcast stations could not editorialize on the air. After many complaints about this ruling, the "Fairness Doctrine" was adopted in 1949, allowing stations to air their views only if contrary views were also given free expression. Obviously, the broadcast industry found itself with much greater interference in its freedom of operation than the print media. Certainly, the First Amendment did not apply equally to broadcasting. Yet it was the broadcasting companies that first called on the government to intervene in the 1920s.

FCC policies could affect commercial operations in many ways. For example, in 1940, the FCC finally gave approval for frequency modulation (FM) radio broadcast stations to operate on channel one of the television band. After World War II, the FCC reversed its position by assigning FM stations the upper rather than the lower end of the frequency band, making earlier receiving sets obsolete. The FCC also approved duplicate programming on AM and FM stations, which retarded the growth of FM broadcasting. Another example was the FCC's sanctioning of a color broadcast method for television. Columbia Broadcasting System (CBS) had developed a clear color system in 1946 that would not be compatible with older black and white sets. Radio Corporation of America (RCA), which owned the National Broadcasting Company (NBC), argued for its black-and-white-compatible system. The FCC gave approval in 1947 to RCA's technology, thus eliminating any CBS competition. During the 1970s, when numerous mergers of newspapers eliminated local competition, the FCC ruled that a company could not monopolize both newspaper and broadcast outlets in local communities. The ruling forced media giants such as Rupert Murdoch to divest his newspaper holdings in New York City and Chicago in order to retain ownership of television stations in the same cities.

The FCC "Report on Chain Broadcasting" in 1941 brought regulation to the networks. It led to a policy that restricted network control over affiliate stations. The policy also forced NBC to divest one of its two networks (the "red" and the "blue") because the FCC would not allow more than one affiliation in a town. In *National Broadcasting Company v. United States*, the Supreme Court upheld the FCC's authority to issue such a ruling. Thus, in 1943, NBC sold its blue network to the American Broadcasting Company (ABC).

In 1946, the FCC's "Blue Book of Broadcasting" established program standards for the first time. During the 1950s, FCC commissioner Frieda Hennock lobbied for more educational stations. After 1961, FCC chairman Newton Minnow made the commission more active in program regulation. Minnow charged that television programming was a "vast wasteland" in a speech before the National Association of Broadcasters. Favoring more time for newscasts, public affairs, and children's programming, Minnow met resistance from the television industry, other commissioners, and Congress. Broadcasting companies—always mindful of their profits—were tied inexorably to the ratings system to determine their programming. Minnow was instrumental in getting Congress to pass a bill in 1962 requiring television sets to receive both the older VHF stations and the newer UHF broadcasts. The FCC revoked the licenses of 14 stations during Minnow's tenure on the FCC, but there was less disturbance of network power than Minnow desired.

Bowing to the fears of broadcasters, the FCC initially restrained the growth of community-access television (CATV) via cable

in the 1960s. The FCC also played a role in the development of satellite technology. It approved the creation of the commercial Communications Satellite Corporation (COMSAT) in 1963 but limited broadcast company control to 50 percent of shares. After 1981, FCC chairman Mark Fowler favored deregulation of the broadcast companies. This began in 1985, accompanied by the ending of its enforcement of the Fairness Doctrine. The new policy changed the number of stations (AM, FM, and television) that one company could operate from 7 to 12. The change spurred a number of broadcast and multimedia company mergers.

Reference Ray, W. B., *FCC: The Ups and Downs of Radio-TV Regulation* (1990).

Field, Marshall III (1893–1956)

Grandson of the Chicago department store magnate, Marshall Field III expressed his liberal philosophy through some innovative newspapers. Field became owner of the experimental *PM* started in New York in 1940 by Ralph Ingersoll, but he sold it in 1948. Field launched his own paper, the *Sun*, in 1941 and added the *Times* in 1947 to produce the tabloid *Sun-Times*. Field's son later acquired the *Chicago Daily News* in 1959.

Marshall Field III inherited a huge fortune from his grandfather's mercantile operations in Chicago. He was educated at Eton and Cambridge University in England and served as both an enlisted soldier and an officer in World War I. When former *Fortune* magazine editor Ralph M. Ingersoll sought financial backers for an innovative newspaper called *PM* in 1940, Field underwrote 13 percent of the investment. Within a few months, Field became the majority stockholder in *PM*. Field was attracted to Ingersoll's publication not only because it expressed a liberal point of view but also because it featured skilled writing and numerous pictures. Veteran journalist Max Lerner became the chief editorial writer. Regular features covered New York, labor, business, theater and movies, food, and sports. Reporters wrote stories about social issues and monopolistic business practices

Marshall Field III's Chicago Sun *sold almost 900,000 copies on the first day of its release in 1941.*

as well as uncovering tax evasion and insurance scandals.

Ingersoll financed the *PM* experiment through sales; no advertising was accepted. Scoffers seemed correct when *PM* showed a circulation drop from 60,000 charter subscribers to 31,000 after only eight weeks of publication. Of course, the fact that the *New York Daily News* organized a boycott of distributors that handled *PM* did not help either. Within a year, *PM*'s cash reserves were depleted. Field gained control over the reorganized company in 1941 and gradually got the circulation back up to 100,000, but *PM* needed more than twice those numbers to break even. Internally, staffers engaged in debilitating arguments over the merits of capitalism and communism. When Field decided that he had to accept advertising in 1946 to help defray rising costs, Ingersoll resigned in protest. Field was forced to sell *PM* in 1948 to Bartley C. Crum, and its name and format were changed.

Meanwhile, Marshall Field III had developed his own liberal Chicago newspaper in 1941 to contest Robert McCormick's conservative *Chicago Tribune*. Careful preparation in collecting charter subscriptions and involving the public in a contest to name the new paper helped get the *Chicago Sun* off to a rousing beginning. The first daily issue sold almost 900,000 copies at two cents apiece, and the initial Sunday edition sold 1 million copies. The *Sun*'s first extra featured the Japanese attack on Pearl Harbor. Field persuaded Silliman Evans of the *Nashville Tennessean* to become publisher. Evans named Rex Smith of *Newsweek* the first editor of the *Sun*, but he was called to military service in 1942. Next, Evans recruited Turner Catledge from the Washington bureau of the *New York Times* as editor. Catledge, in turn, hired Robert Lasch from the *Omaha World-Herald* to be his chief editorial writer. Under Catledge and Lasch, the editorial page reflected Field's philosophy perfectly.

Meanwhile, the war dampened the initial enthusiasm for and sales of the *Sun*. Circulation, which had fallen dramatically, finally stabilized at around 260,000 during the war.

Even though Field was pleased with Catledge, Evans—who managed the paper—and Catledge quarreled often. Catledge resigned in 1943 and returned to the *Times*. Evans brought in E. Z. Dimitman from the *Philadelphia Inquirer* as editor. The *Sun*'s editorial policy was liberal Democratic, but not as radical as *PM*'s. The *Sun* was forced to bring legal action against the *Chicago Tribune* and Associated Press for denying it access to the wire service. The 1942 court ruling that Associated Press was a monopoly and in violation of antitrust laws opened the way to easier access to Associated Press for other newspapers as well as the *Sun*. The *Sun*'s daily circulation grew to 363,000 by 1947, and the Sunday edition sold 422,000 copies.

In 1947, Field purchased from Samuel E. Thomason the liberal tabloid the *Chicago Times*, founded in 1929 as an evening daily. Field retained talented Richard Finnegan as editor of the *Times*. In less than a year, the morning *Sun* (now also a tabloid) and the evening *Times* were combined as the *Sun-Times* and published continually throughout the day. Before the merger, Field had suffered staggering losses: $5 million on *PM* and $25 million on the *Sun*. The *Sun-Times* established a reputation for accurate and thorough reporting, and its circulation grew during the 1950s but never seriously challenged the supremacy of the *Tribune*. Field detailed his liberal philosophy in *Freedom Is More Than a Word* (1945).

Marshall Field III formed a multimedia corporation called Field Enterprises in 1944 to coordinate a variety of media ventures. The corporation took over the Sunday newspaper supplement magazine *Parade*, an idea originally developed by Henry Luce and taken up by Ingersoll's *PM* in 1941. Within six months, *Parade* had 12 major Sunday subscribers, but its real growth occurred after World War II. Ken Purdy edited *Parade* after the war, and it became the leading Sunday supplement in newspapers across the nation. By 1958, *Parade* circulation totaled 8.6 million in 62 papers, with $24 million advertising revenue. Field also owned the World Book Encyclopedia and

Simon and Schuster book publishers. Field Enterprises branched into broadcasting in the 1940s when Field purchased Chicago radio station WJJD to compete with the *Tribune*-owned WGN. Field Enterprises added radio stations in Cincinnati, Seattle, and Portland, Oregon.

Marshall Field IV had been trained on the job to succeed his father and took control of the *Sun-Times* in 1950. Just three years after Marshall Field III's death, his son sold *Parade* magazine in 1959 to raise cash to purchase the *Chicago Daily News* from the Knight chain for $24 million. The *Daily News* continued to operate separately from the *Sun-Times*. Marshall Field V sold the *Sun-Times* in 1984 to Australian media mogul Rupert Murdoch for $63 million. The *Daily News* was terminated in 1978 after massive circulation and advertising losses.

Reference Becker, Stephen, *Marshall Field III: A Biography* (1964).

First Amendment
See Freedom of the Press.

Fleeson, Doris (1901–1970)
A noted reporter, syndicated columnist, and war correspondent, Doris Fleeson became one of the first female crusading, independent journalists. Fleeson championed labor rights, including the minimum wage, and she participated in the founding of the American Newspaper Guild. She wrote a widely read column for the *New York Daily News* about Washington politics in the 1930s.

Doris Fleeson was born in Kansas and educated at the University of Kansas. She was inspired to become a journalist by reading native Kansans William Allen White and Edgar Watson Howe. Her early newspaper experience included service as a reporter for the *Pittsburg (Kansas) Sun*. She became society editor for the *Evanston (Illinois) News-Index* in the hope of coming to the attention of a major Chicago daily. Failing to secure an offer in Chicago, she fixed her sights on New York City and served as city editor for the *Great Neck News* on Long Island, New York. She finally got her big break when the *New York Daily News* offered her a job as a general assignments reporter in 1927. Fleeson quickly gained a reputation as a crusader with her articles on state government corruption and mayoral scandals in New York City. Moved to the Washington bureau in 1933, Fleeson wrote a column with her husband, John O'Donnell, entitled "Capitol Stuff."

Fleeson actively supported a minimum wage for reporters during the depression, and she helped found the reporters' union, the American Newspaper Guild, in 1933. She was elected president of the Women's National Press Club in 1937. Fleeson became the first woman reporter to cover the White House during Franklin D. Roosevelt's administration. After her divorce and a brief trip to Europe, Fleeson resigned from the *Daily News* in 1943 and agreed to become a war correspondent for *Woman's Home Companion* magazine in Europe. She published ten articles for the magazine about varying aspects of the war.

After the war, Fleeson worked briefly for the *Washington Star* and the *Boston Globe*. Based in Washington again, Fleeson wrote a column for the Bell Syndicate beginning in 1945; after 1954, her column was syndicated through the United Features Syndicate. The distribution of her column grew to include about 100 newspapers by the late 1950s. Fleeson had several reporting coups, including the revelation of a dispute between Supreme Court Justices Robert Jackson and Hugo Black. She carefully cultivated her sources and rarely used the canned briefings offered by bureaucrats or congressmen.

Doris Fleeson received several awards during her career. The women's journalism society Theta Sigma Phi recognized Fleeson with its Headliner Award in 1950. Fleeson was the first woman to win the American Society of Newspaper Editors' Raymond Clapper award for meritorious reporting in 1954. Fleeson retired from her column in 1969 and died the next year.

Reference Hynes, Terry, "Doris Fleeson," in *Dictionary of Literary Biography: American Newspaper Journalists, 1926–1950*, ed. Perry T. Ashley (1984).

Foreign Language Media

It was only natural that immigrants from non-English-speaking nations would establish their own means of communication upon arriving in the United States. The German press was the first foreign language press in the colonial era and remained dominant during the next great influx of the 1830s through 1850s as well. Only in the late nineteenth century did Polish and Italian immigrants begin to introduce their newspapers. In the twentieth century, Asians and Hispanics have become the largest groups of immigrants to establish their native language presses and radio stations. Mainline English-language media have become more conscious of ethnic populations in recent decades. Many Hispanic broadcast companies are owned by English-language companies.

Benjamin Franklin founded the first foreign language newspaper in the colonies in 1732—the *Philadelphische Zeitung*, written in German. The editor was Louis Timothy, a French Protestant who had married a Dutch woman. The *Zeitung* was four pages and included mostly obscure European news. Subscribers were few so that when Timothy left Philadelphia in 1733 to edit a Charleston paper, the *Zeitung* died. The second German paper, the *Germantown Zeitung*, was started in 1739 and published by Christopher Saur. It lasted for 40 years, first as a monthly and later as a weekly. Heinrich Miller, a Franklin protégé, printed the *Wochenliche Philadelphische Staatsbote*, a successful weekly. Several other German-language papers were established in Pennsylvania during the late eighteenth century.

Because of upheavals caused by the French Revolution, a number of French refugees arrived in America, seeking asylum. French immigrants started America's first foreign language daily, the *Courrier Francais*, in Philadelphia between 1794 and 1798. In the nineteenth century, New York rather than Philadelphia became the center of the foreign language press, since it was the port through which most immigrants entered the United States. San Francisco followed New York in foreign language papers, with dailies in German, French, Spanish, and Italian by 1860. The premier French paper became New York City's *Courrier des Etats-Unis*, started in 1828 and published for 110 years.

The next great period of European immigration to the United States began in the 1830s and included mostly Irish and Germans. The German immigrants increasingly moved to midwestern cities such as Cincinnati, St. Louis, and Chicago. Reading newspapers was a tradition among Germans that they carried over into their new residence. Founded in 1834 by Jacob Uhl, the *New Yorker Staats-Zeitung* became the most successful German-language paper of the nineteenth century, especially during the editorships of Oswald Ottendorfer from the 1850s to 1890 and Herman Ridder after 1890. By 1880, the *Staats-Zeitung* circulation was 50,000, making it the most widely read German newspaper in the world. German papers remained dominant throughout the remainder of the nineteenth century. There were several German-language papers in New York, Philadelphia, Chicago, Cincinnati, St. Louis, and Milwaukee by the 1890s. The second largest number of foreign language papers were Scandinavian, with about 100 by the end of the century, concentrated in the Midwest. The *San Francisco Wah-Kee*, edited by Yee Jenn, became the first Chinese newspaper in the United States and was published during the 1870s.

In the three decades before World War I, the number of foreign language newspapers reached 1,300, written in 18 languages. Only about 160 were dailies, reaching 2.6 million readers; New York City had 32 dailies. The German press—with 97 dailies in 1892—lost its dominance and fell from 80 to 30 percent of the foreign language papers by 1914. Yet Ridder's *Staats-Zeitung* in New York City and Paul Mueller's *Abendpost* (founded in 1889) in Chicago retained the largest circulations. The Scandinavian weeklies in mostly small towns in the Midwest continued to thrive. Italian, Polish, and Yiddish papers appeared in many eastern cities, and Japanese papers outdistanced the

Chinese press on the West Coast. New York's Yiddish *Vorwarts*, edited by socialist Abraham Cahan, had the largest foreign language circulation—175,000 in 1914. During World War I, Congress's Trading with the Enemy Act (1917) allowed the confiscation of German-owned papers. Half of the prewar German papers disappeared by 1919, and in 1940, only 13 German dailies survived out of the 45 in 1914.

The first Spanish-language newspaper began in Taos, New Mexico, in 1835, although the bilingual *El Misisipi* had begun publication in New Orleans in 1808. Border states such as Florida, Texas, and California attracted most of the Hispanic settlers, although major urban centers such as New York and Chicago also gained a measurable share. New York City's *El Diario* had 68,000 readers in the 1970s, and Miami's *Diario de las Americas* had a circulation of 55,000. Cesar Chavez's fight for migrant workers in California led to the founding of *El Malcriado* by the United Farm Workers in 1964. In Los Angeles, *La Raza* became the dominant Spanish-language paper after 1967. Hispanic radio stations numbered 400 by the 1970s, along with 60 television stations. About 100 Spanish-language magazines were published in the 1970s, and 50 newspapers were started by the Chicano Press Association. Intense competition has led the Hispanic media to become more market-driven than political.

Mainline media have become more interested in the Hispanic market in the last two decades. Cable News Network and MTV produce Spanish programs for the Telemundo Group of five Spanish-language television stations. The top two dozen television advertisers buy commercial time on the largest Hispanic television system, Univision. The *Miami Herald* publishes a Spanish-language edition, *El Nuevo Herald*, with a circulation of 95,000. The *Los Angeles Times* began publishing *Nuestro Tiempo*, a bilingual monthly journal, in 1989.

Asian language media shifted from the previously dominant Japanese and Chinese to Korean, Vietnamese, and Filipino after World War II. Some publications, such as the magazine *AsiAm*, were aimed at all Asian groups, but most publications reflected national origins. New York City had 11 Chinese dailies in the 1980s with a circulation of 250,000. Vietnamese publications have become numerous in California since the exodus caused by the Vietnam War in the 1960s and 1970s. Japanese and Koreans publish their own papers as well as import native products from their homelands.

Native American publications were not numerous in the nineteenth century. In the twentieth century, about 350 publications exist, most of which are owned by the tribes. The *Cherokee Phoenix*, published from 1828 to 1832 in Georgia, was the first Native American newspaper. Others in the nineteenth century included the *Cherokee Advocate*, published in Oklahoma, and the Sioux-language *Shawnee Sun*. In 1994, the American Indian Press Association cited 325 newspapers in 34 states. The Mohawks published a national semimonthly journal in the 1970s with 80,000 subscribers. The American Indian Historical Society sponsored publication of *Wassaja*, a national bimonthly paper dedicated to educational improvements.

References Gutierrez, Felix, "Spanish-Language Media," *Journalism History* (1977); Wittke, Carl, *The German Language Press in America* (1957).

Fort Worth Star-Telegram

Inaugurated by local entrepreneur Amon G. Carter in 1906, the *Fort Worth Star*—soon called the *Star-Telegram*—became the journalistic voice not only for Fort Worth but also for much of west Texas. The *Star-Telegram* never lost sight of its obligation to the local community, even after its purchase by the powerful conglomerate Capital Cities Communications in 1974.

Fort Worth was a vital part of the expanding Texas frontier after the Civil War and became a center for the cattle industry. As early as 1905, businessman Amon G. Carter and some local reporters discussed establishing an afternoon newspaper to challenge the *Fort Worth Telegram*. Having honed his sales skills, Carter believed that he could sell enough advertising to make a newspaper profitable. Carter and his journalist friends A. G. Dawson and D. C. McCaleb convinced grocer Paul Waples to become the principal financial backer.

The *Fort Worth Star*, a 16-page, two-cent afternoon daily, hit the streets on 1 February 1906. Carter served as advertising manager, Dawson as business manager, and McCaleb as managing editor; Waples named Louis J. Wortham as editor. Carter sold more advertising than space allowed in the first editions. The *Star* promoted itself as conservative and independent and promised more local news than competing papers. The early circulation was less than 5,000, but colorful news stories included accounts of the activities of cereal magnate C. W. Post and controversial presidential daughter Alice Roosevelt Longworth.

Although the *Star* began auspiciously, it soon encountered trouble with the defection of Dawson and McCaleb and losses of $27,000 by 1908. The *Fort Worth Telegram* tried to hire Carter away from the *Star*, but Carter convinced Wortham and Waples to buy the *Telegram* for $100,000. The newly merged paper became the *Fort Worth Star-Telegram* on 1 January 1909. Carter was determined to make the newspaper widely read across west Texas, and he had 13 editions composed by 600 correspondents. The papers were sent by stagecoach, train, or bus to 1,100 towns covering 375,000 square miles west of Fort Worth. By 1913, the *Star-Telegram* was the fourth largest daily in Texas; three years later, it was the largest newspaper in the state, with 66,000 circulation. In 1920, the paper moved into a state-of-the-art printing plant, hailed as the finest in the Southwest.

The success of the *Star-Telegram* coincided with the decline of its morning competitor, the *Record*. In 1918, William Randolph Hearst offered to buy the *Star-Telegram*, and when Carter refused to sell, Hearst bought the *Record*. Although the *Record* published considerable national and international news, it could not compete with the *Star-Telegram* in local news. After losses

mounted in 1924, Hearst sold the *Record* to the *Star-Telegram*. The Scripps-Howard chain also entertained ideas of purchasing the *Star-Telegram*, but after being turned down by Carter, it started its own paper, the *Fort Worth Press*.

Like many newspapers, the *Star-Telegram* decided to enter the radio broadcasting industry in the early 1920s with station WBAP. In 1928, the station affiliated with the National Broadcasting Company, and in 1938, it was permitted to raise its power to 50,000 watts. WBAP launched a television station in 1948, the first station between St. Louis and Los Angeles. WBAP-TV also pioneered the first local news program in 1948. In the 1950s, WBAP-TV became the first all-color station west of the Mississippi River.

Publisher Carter continued to recruit the best talent to run the *Star-Telegram*, including editors such as James M. North and circulation genius Harold Hough. The paper survived the Great Depression without laying off a single employee. Carter struck oil in 1937 and sold his interest to Shell for $16.5 million, thereby permanently relieving the *Star-Telegram* of financial trouble. An early promoter of airplane technology, Carter persuaded the federal government to make Fort Worth a center of military aircraft development at the outset of World War II. General Dynamics soon built a huge facility, and the Air Force established a major air base at Fort Worth. The *Star-Telegram* championed the expansion of city parks, including a zoo, and the establishment of Big Bend National Park along the Rio Grande. The paper almost single-handedly convinced the legislature to establish the Texas Technological College at Lubbock. The *Star-Telegram* always led charitable efforts in the Fort Worth area, whether it was for handicapped children or the humane society.

Amon Carter died in 1955 and was succeeded by his son, Amon G. Carter Jr., as publisher. Capital Cities Communications purchased the *Star-Telegram* in 1974 as part of a growing multimedia conglomerate. Mike Blackmon served as editor during the

1990s. The trend has been gains for the morning edition and losses for the evening paper. The 1994 morning circulation of 180,000 was 30,000 more than the 1991 figures. The afternoon edition slipped 26,000—to 77,000—over the same period. The Sunday edition continued to grow slowly to 337,000 in 1994.

Reference Meek, Phillip J., *Fort Worth Star-Telegram* (1981).

Fortune

Part of the Henry R. Luce media empire, *Fortune* was founded in 1930 specifically to report on and publicize U.S. business. It has remained true to its original purpose, and although it has many competitors, none quite fits the *Fortune* mold for sophistication and professional production.

Henry Luce established *Time* in 1923 as a weekly newsmagazine. Its success was one reason for the consideration of a specialized journal covering U.S. business. Even though *Fortune* was launched at a most inopportune time—just after the Great Depression began—Luce correctly intuited that because business was such an integral aspect of the American character the magazine would succeed despite the depression. Luce wanted his magazine to flesh out for readers the vitality and even the beauty of business—from balance sheets to shiny office towers.

By relying on artistic photography and quality paper and production techniques, *Fortune* started out as an aesthetically attractive journal that garnered the attention Luce desired. Luce was quite specific about *Fortune* not attempting to provide advice or simply engaging in name-dropping of business elites. The literary standards would remain high, along with the goal of keeping *Fortune* stunning in appearance. Through advertising and promotion in *Time*, 30,000 subscribers awaited the first issue of *Fortune* in January 1930. It took only three years for the magazine to begin making a profit.

Initially, articles concentrated entirely on business, but by the end of the 1930s, subjects such as government regulation and so-cial aspects of business were added. The research and writing of *Fortune* articles were done largely through a cooperative staff approach, similar to the method used at *Time*. Thus, a research staff compiled the raw material, another group collected interviews, and a writing staff put the pieces together, often with accompanying photographs. *Fortune* articles aimed for completeness as well as accuracy, but the purpose was always to foster understanding of the subject rather than controversy. Avoiding both propaganda and cynicism about business, the magazine featured various regular sections dealing with investing trends, cutting-edge technology, entrepreneurial personalities, and even reviews of publications about business. There were also occasional pieces on specialized topics such as minorities and education. William H. Whyte's best-selling 1950s novel, *The Organization Man*, began as an assignment for *Fortune*.

By the end of World War II, the circulation of *Fortune* was only 170,000, but it rose to just under 500,000 by the 1960s. Because the vast majority of its readers were business executives, *Fortune* never expected to compete with magazines that appeal to a popular audience. Its expensive production costs required the price to start at $1 an issue in 1930, beyond the reach of most working-class consumers during the depression. Most of the advertising came from U.S. corporations, but *Fortune* has never had a problem filling its advertising quotas, which provide the profit margin. In 1987, *Fortune*'s income from advertising was more than $122 million. In addition to publishing the monthly magazine, *Fortune* publishes a special midyear issue, listing the 500 largest U.S. corporations (the Fortune 500). The categories include financial institutions, life insurance companies, manufacturing industries, transportation corporations, and utility companies. The corporate assets, earnings, number of employees, and other statistics are included. *Fortune* also publishes an annual directory of the 200 largest international industrial corporations outside the United States.

See also Luce, Henry Robinson.

Fox Broadcasting Company
See Murdoch, Keith Rupert.

Franklin, Benjamin (1706–1790)

One of America's most talented colonial leaders, Benjamin Franklin established his reputation as a journalist. In 1729, he acquired control of the *Pennsylvania Gazette* and made it the most successful colonial newspaper. He made considerable profits selling his *Poor Richard's Almanack* from 1732 to 1757. Franklin also played a significant role in launching a number of other colonial papers and training future journalists.

Benjamin Franklin was apprenticed to his older brother James, who was a printer in Boston. James Franklin printed the *Boston Gazette* before starting his own paper, the *New England Courant*, in 1721. At age 17, Benjamin became interim editor of the *Courant* while James served a jail term. Earlier, Benjamin had written some ballads as well as several satirical essays under the pseudonym "Silence Dogood" about topics such as matrimony and college professors. Benjamin eventually left his brother's employ and traveled to New York City, where printer William Bradford sent him to Philadelphia to seek work from Bradford's son Andrew, who published the *American Weekly Mercury*.

Franklin was determined to start a newspaper of his own to compete with Bradford's, but printer Samuel Keimer got the jump on him. Keimer employed Franklin in the new printing establishment in 1724. Franklin traveled to England to secure the required printing presses and even worked for a London printer for a brief period before returning to Philadelphia. Longing for his own paper, Franklin withdrew from Keimer's business. Meanwhile, Franklin organized a debating society called the Junto in 1727, which was later renamed the American Philosophical Society.

Keimer started publication of the *Pennsylvania Gazette* in 1728, in part to prevent Franklin from launching a paper. Franklin wrote a series of satires called the "Busy-Body Papers" for Bradford's *American*

Weekly Mercury, many of which ridiculed Keimer. After only nine months of publication, Keimer agreed to sell the *Gazette* to Franklin. The new editor-publisher promised to obtain the freshest news from the colonies and England. The *Gazette* also included weather reports and perhaps the first cartoon. Franklin's establishment sold a variety of writing materials as well as advertising for the *Gazette*. Editorially, the *Gazette* maintained a neutral position on controversies and gave accounts of both sides of issues. In Franklin's "Apology to Printers" (1731), he reprised John Milton's argument about printing all shades of opinion.

In 1732, with his printing business prosperous, Franklin began issuing the annual

Poor Richard, 1733.

A N

Almanack

For the Year of Chrift

1733,

Being the Firft after LEAP YEAR:

And makes fince the Creation	Years
By the Account of the Eastern *Greeks*	7241
By the Latin Church, when ☉ ent. ♈	6932
By the Computation of *W. W.*	5742
By the *Roman* Chronology	5682
By the *Jewish* Rabbies	5494

Wherein is contained

The Lunations, Eclipfes, Judgment of the Weather, Spring Tides, Planets Motions & mutual Afpects, Sun and Moon's Rifing and Setting, Length of Days, Time of High Water, Fairs, Courts, and obfervable Days.

Fitted to the Latitude of Forty Degrees, and a Meridian of Five Hours Weft from *London*, but may without fenfible Error, ferve all the adjacent Places, even from *Newfoundland* to *South-Carolina*.

By *RICHARD SAUNDERS*, Philom.

PHILADELPHIA:
Printed and fold by *B. FRANKLIN*, at the New Printing-Office near the Market.

Benjamin Franklin's print shop began publishing Poor Richard's Almanack *in 1732. The profitable* Almanack *ran for 25 years.*

Poor Richard's Almanack, which served to advertise the *Gazette*. The *Almanack* included not only prognostications for the year but also humorous quips and self-help advice that touted diligence, hard work, common sense, and frugality. Franklin's famous adages included "Some are weather-wise, some are otherwise," "Three may keep a secret if two of them are dead," and "He that lives upon hope will die fasting." Other items of interest to readers were recipes, tide schedules, and even jokes. The *Almanack* became a best-seller, with 10,000 copies sold across the colonies. Not all of Franklin's publishing efforts were successful, however. In 1741, in competition with Andrew Bradford, Franklin launched a periodical called *General Magazine and Historical Chronicle for all the British Plantations in North America*. The monthly journal contained informative essays on money and books, literary material, and political documents in its 75 pages, which sold for sixpence. Although Franklin's magazine was published longer than Bradford's *American Magazine*, it lasted only six months.

Franklin had friends in England and arranged for book exchanges across the Atlantic between colonial and London booksellers. Perhaps more than any other individual, Franklin helped secure the English heritage among colonials before the American Revolution. Franklin also aided the establishment of other publications in the colonies. In 1732, he financed the first foreign language paper in America, the *Philadelphia Zeitung* in German. Other papers were either funded in part or staffed by Franklin, including the *South-Carolina Gazette* in Charleston. Franklin began work on his autobiography in 1771 and continued writing until his death. He also wrote some bagatelles (short stories) while serving as ambassador in France during the 1780s.

Franklin demonstrated to future American journalists that newspapers and magazines could be entertaining as well as informative. He showed that good business practices would turn a nice profit in the publishing business. Franklin's efforts also went a long way toward making U.S. newspapers respectable and influential with the public.

Reference Clark, Ronald W., *Benjamin Franklin: A Biography* (1983).

Freedom of the Press

The First Amendment to the Constitution guarantees freedom of the press, among other protected personal freedoms. The historical definition of limits on that freedom has been crucial to the survival of the republic. A free press naturally tends to be critical of government due to close scrutiny of its operations and personnel. On frequent occasions in U.S. history, the press's freedom to inquire or investigate has saved the nation from egregious danger.

During most of the seventeenth century, colonial printers and publishers were licensed by the royal government, which would not allow critical publications to exist. Thus, America's first newspaper, *Publick Occurrences*, could print only one issue in 1690 before it was shut down because it lacked a government license. The Licensing Act of 1662 was suspended by Parliament in 1694 so that government regulation over the press was limited thereafter to the libel laws. Censor-free newspapers such as the *Boston News-Letter*, started in 1704, could publish without government permission. Yet both Parliament and colonial governments successfully intimidated editors and publishers from printing critical accounts in the early decades after the suspension of the Licensing Act. Most publishers sought government sanction for their publications.

The accord between government and the press ended when John Peter Zenger was prosecuted in 1734–1735 for publishing negative stories about New York's government in the *New York Weekly Journal*. Zenger was charged with "seditious libel" in 1734, suggesting that he had maliciously defamed New York's government and its officials. Zenger's lawyer, Andrew Hamilton, argued that as long as published material was truthful, there could be no libel—no matter how damaging the truth might be. The jury acquitted Zenger, and the case became a landmark in the history of freedom of the press, even though publishers still remained hesitant to vigorously criticize governments.

The next challenge to the government came during the crisis leading to the American Revolution. After some initial conflicts with the crown following the French and Indian War (1754–1763), colonists were alarmed by the tax implications of the Stamp Act (1765). The act placed a duty on paper used for printing and made publication more expensive for publishers. Even though the Stamp Act was eventually repealed, the law actuated a patriotic opposition that grew in strength. Isaiah Thomas began his *Massachusetts Spy* in 1770 to lead the patriot papers as revolution came closer. Thomas Paine's 1776 pamphlet "Common Sense" suggested that the colonies should fight for political independence from Britain. It was overwhelmingly popular and had a direct influence on the Continental Congress's issuing of the Declaration of Independence.

After independence in 1783, the press was unregulated until the ratification of the Constitution in 1787. Anti-Federalists feared that a strong central government might trample individual liberties, including press freedom. States such as Virginia incorporated "Bills of Rights" into their constitutions to protect individual freedoms. The first Congress under the Constitution passed a similar Bill of Rights, the First Amendment of which included a clause guaranteeing freedom of the press. After the First Amendment was ratified in 1791, the government—Congress and the president—was required to respect the right of free expression.

The first test of freedom of the press was the Sedition Act of 1798, passed by a Federalist-dominated Congress in an attempt to muzzle Democratic-Republican criticism. Although unconstitutional on its face, eight editors were convicted under the Sedition Act before it lapsed in 1801 without a constitutional test. It was a dangerous moment in U.S. history; the Constitution had effectively failed. Soon the shoe was on the other

political foot when Harry Croswell, pro-Federalist editor of the weekly paper *The Wasp*, was indicted in 1804 by New York State for seditious libel. Croswell had copied another paper's charge that President Thomas Jefferson had bribed an editor to slander ex-President George Washington. Federalist Party chief Alexander Hamilton defended Croswell with the same argument used by Andrew Hamilton to defend Zenger—that the truth can be published with impunity. Hamilton lost the case, but New York's legislature passed a law in 1805 providing that truth was a defense in a libel case. The U.S. Supreme Court ruled in 1812 that the English common law of seditious libel was not applicable in the United States.

The press had extensive freedom to cover wars in the nineteenth century, including the War of 1812, Mexican War (1846–1848), Civil War (1861–1865), and Spanish-American War (1898). Except for some New England press criticism of the War of 1812 and partisan divisions during the Civil War, most of the press coverage was favorable to the military and the government. The government's attitudes about freedom of the press changed during World War I (1917–1918). Because of concerns about sabotage by pro-German elements, Congress passed the Espionage Act (1917), which allowed the suppression of German and socialist newspapers on the grounds that they were disloyal. About 75 papers were denied First Amendment protection under the guise of protecting national security. The Wilson administration also took the extraordinary measure of establishing the Committee on Public Information, headed by journalist George Creel, to control the flow of war news to the press. Such drastic action seemed unnecessary, because the nation generally supported the war effort, and it was of short duration.

Even more dangerous to the press's constitutional protection was the Sedition Act (1918), which prohibited publication of disloyal language about the federal government, the Constitution, the military, or the flag. The Post Office and a Censorship

Board were given broad powers of search and seizure of the mails to enforce the act. Socialist leader Eugene V. Debs was convicted under the Sedition Act and imprisoned. He challenged the constitutionality of the Espionage and Sedition Acts, both of which were upheld by the Supreme Court.

The pattern of government control over the press was repeated during World War II (1941–1945). An Office of Censorship was established in 1941, with Associated Press's Byron Price as director. The office sought voluntary censorship by publishing a code (1942) that set guidelines for the press. The counterpart to World War I's Committee on Public Information was the Office of War Information, created in 1942, that provided the news media with releases about the war. Again, there were few complaints about press restrictions during the war because patriotic attitudes were widespread.

The federal courts have been called upon to interpret the First Amendment more in the twentieth century than previously. The Supreme Court extended First Amendment protection for the press by overturning a state law in *Near v. Minnesota* (1931). The American Newspaper Publishers Association challenged the constitutionality of a Minnesota law prohibiting scandalous or malicious publications. The Supreme Court threw out the Minnesota law by applying the First Amendment through the Fourteenth Amendment's due process clause. The Court did not, however, rule out all cases of prior restraint. At the behest of Governor Huey Long, the Louisiana legislature passed a 1934 law to tax the advertising revenue of larger newspapers that opposed the governor. In 1936, the Supreme Court found the tax to be punitive in nature and thus unconstitutional *(Grosjean v. American Press Company)*. In *Bridges v. California* (1941), the Supreme Court used the First Amendment to strike down contempt charges against the *Los Angeles Times* for printing a labor leader's threatening telegram and editorials that were critical of a judge.

The classic case of prior restraint was *New York Times v. United States* (1971), involving the publication of the so-called Pentagon Papers. After the *Times* published the first of a series of summaries detailing the origins of the Vietnam War, the Justice Department under President Richard Nixon asked for a restraining order to stop further publication. The government's case was based on the argument that because the papers were top secret, their publication endangered national security. The Supreme Court ruled that the papers were historical, did not threaten national security, and could be published. The Court warned the government not to apply prior restraint unless there was an overwhelming basis to support it.

The Supreme Court has also been engaged in the debate about obscenity laws. In 1943, *Esquire* was denied its second-class postage rate because it did not contribute to the public welfare. The Supreme Court found that mere opinion of Post Office officials was an insufficient basis for punitive treatment and ruled in favor of *Esquire*. In *Roth v. United States* (1957), the Supreme Court established the obscenity standard, ruling that publications could be censored if they appealed solely to "prurient interests." The Court refined its position in *Miller v. California* (1973) by suggesting that local community standards could be the basis for defining obscenity. The decision meant that different standards might apply in different communities.

The concern about government secrets and the collection of information about individuals in government files led to the passage of the Freedom of Information Act (1966). It allowed individual citizens to have access to government files containing information about them, but matters of national security would still be protected by the law. The act also allowed media access to government documents, which could be copied or cited in news stories.

See also Prior Restraint.

References Chafee, Zechariah Jr., *Government and Mass Communications* (1947); Hatchen, William A., ed., *The Supreme Court on Freedom of the Press: Decisions and Dissents* (1968).

Freedom's Journal

The first black-owned and -edited newspaper in the United States, *Freedom's Journal*, was begun in 1827 by Samuel Cornish and John Russwurm in New York City. The weekly publication was oriented primarily toward the abolition of slavery, but it carried literary items and proved the potential of Negro publications during its brief history.

The abolitionist movement began to generate activity during the 1820s, although it was not until the 1830s that white-owned abolitionist newspapers appeared. The debate over slavery advanced in northern states, where it had been outlawed since the turn of the century. Born in Jamaica to a white father and a slave mother, John Brown Russwurm (1799–1851) was one of the earliest Negro graduates of a U.S. college in 1826, when he received a degree from Bowdoin College in Maine. Russwurm recruited an experienced editor of weekly papers, Presbyterian minister Samuel Eli Cornish (1795–1858), to become a partner in Freedom's Journal. The two stated their conviction that Negroes should be allowed to speak for themselves about abolition or other issues.

Russwurm and Cornish decided to establish their paper in 1827 following a vicious attack on the abolitionist movement by editor Mordecai Noah in the *New York Enquirer*. In particular, Noah blasted the emergence of various black antislavery societies in major northern cities. Russwurm and Cornish printed the *Journal* on four pages measuring 10 by 15 inches. Although the principal focus was the abolition of slavery, the *Journal* also carried news items about the black community, sermons, poetry, literary essays, and reprints from other papers. The paper's motto was the biblical phrase "righteousness exalteth a nation," and it advocated education for blacks and a self-help philosophy. David Walker penned a famous "appeal" in the *Journal* for a slave uprising to overthrow the system. *Freedom's Journal* circulated fairly widely in several southern states as well as major northern cities.

Soon, Russwurm and Cornish clashed over the issue of whether American blacks should return to Africa and establish colonies. Most abolitionists opposed the colonization movement, since they believed that it would leave slavery entrenched in the United States. Cornish was against colonization, but Russwurm had been converted to the idea of African colonization promoted by the American Colonization Society (founded in 1816). Russwurm was able to editorialize favorably on the issue when Cornish returned to the ministry after the first 27 issues. Then, when Russwurm left the United States to edit a paper in Liberia in 1829, Cornish resumed control of the *Journal* and editorially opposed colonization once more. Cornish changed the name of the *Journal* to *Rights of All* and pledged to lobby for citizenship for Negroes, but financial troubles forced the paper to end publication in 1830. Cornish continued to support the abolitionist cause as a member of the American Antislavery Society.

It was not until six years after the death of *Freedom's Journal* that another black-owned paper began publication. Yet the precedent had been set by the *Journal*, and newspapers published and edited by blacks became a regular occurrence thereafter. The most successful of those papers was Frederick Douglass's *North Star* in the 1840s.

References Barrow, Lionel C., "'Our Own Cause': *Freedom's Journal* and the Beginnings of the Black Press," *Journalism History* (1977); Bryan, Carter R., "Negro Journalism in America before Emancipation," *Journalism Monographs* (1969).

Gannett Company

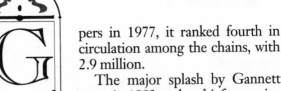

Founder of a modest newspaper chain made up of medium-sized dailies in New York and New Jersey, Frank Gannett paved the way for the establishment of a $3 billion multimedia conglomerate. By the 1930s, the Gannett chain was already among the six largest in the nation. After Gannett's death, his corporation converted to public ownership and became the largest newspaper company in the nation. It also pioneered the successful national publication *USA Today* in the 1980s.

A native of New York, Frank E. Gannett (1876–1957) worked his way through college at Cornell and purchased the *Elmira Star-Gazette* in 1906 after a brief newspaper stint in Ithaca and Pittsburgh. By the end of the 1920s, Gannett owned 15 dailies in medium-sized markets in New York as well as a few papers in New Jersey, Connecticut, and Illinois. Determined that his papers would reflect editorial independence, Gannett allowed local editors to set editorial policy. Gannett showed a keen business sense as well as a regard for the nurturing of public goodwill. The principal supplier of newsprint, International Paper Company, owned stock in four Gannett papers in the 1920s and sought to influence their policies. After the Federal Trade Commission publicized the extent of International's newspaper influence in 1928, Gannett quickly paid off his debts to International and ended dealings with the company.

The major expansion of the Gannett chain, directed by chief executive Paul Miller, came after its founder's death in 1957. Miller anticipated an important trend in media industries in 1967 when he made Gannett a publicly owned company. The company possessed only about 16 dailies in 1957, but 20 years later, its 73 dailies made Gannett the largest newspaper chain in the United States. Much of the expansion came by purchasing smaller chains rather than individual properties: Westchester Rockland (1964), Federated and the *Honolulu Star-Bulletin* group (1971), and Speidel (1976). Although Gannett had the most papers in 1977, it ranked fourth in circulation among the chains, with 2.9 million.

The major splash by Gannett came in 1982 under chief executive Allen Neuharth with the launching of the national-circulation, computer copy-set *USA Today*. It was a serious gamble that has made Gannett even more influential and wealthy. *USA Today* was published five days a week and featured concise news stories interspersed with charts, graphs, pictures, and lots of color. It targeted a vast general-interest audience, with a focus on national and international news events, entertainment, financial news, and sports. Gannett spent a lot of money to research its future product before beginning publication. After one year, the circulation surpassed the 500,000 figure; by 1989, its circulation of 1.3 million was second only to the *Wall Street Journal*. However, advertising did not keep pace with sales, and *USA Today* lost money from the outset. *USA Today* was also published in Singapore, Hong Kong, and Switzerland.

The *USA Today* experiment did not divert Gannett from its previous newspaper acquisition program. In fact, Gannett began to purchase some major dailies under Neuharth's successor John Curley. The company paid $315 million for the *Louisville Courier-Journal* and obtained the *Des Moines Register* from the Cowles family for $200 million, both in 1986. It also added the *Detroit News* to its holdings for $717 million. By 1987, Gannett revenues passed the $2.7 billion mark, compared with 1967 revenues of $186 million. In 1988, Gannett newspapers numbered 89 dailies with a circulation of over 6 million—no longer first in the number of papers, but number one in circulation. Gannett had also diversified into broadcast ownership (12 percent of revenues) and advertising (7 percent of revenues), but newspapers continued to dominate company holdings. Gannett established its own news service—open only to company newspapers and broadcast stations. The company also founded a Center for Media Studies in New York City, headed by Everette Dennis, to examine various elements in media such as technology and ethics.

Reference Williamson, Samuel T., *Imprint of a Publisher: The Story of Frank Gannett and His Newspapers* (1948).

Garrison, William Lloyd (1805–1879)

As the leading abolitionist publicist, William Lloyd Garrison demonstrated the power of the press in rallying support behind a social policy. Garrison's single-minded newspaper, *The Liberator* (1831–1865), educated northerners about the repressive institution of slavery for the purpose of legislating it out of existence. The end of slavery in 1865 also meant the end of Garrison's newspaper, which achieved its only aim.

William Lloyd Garrison was born in coastal Massachusetts to a hard-drinking seaman father and a devoutly evangelical mother. Most of Garrison's education came from practical work experience. He eventually settled on printing, working at the pro-Federalist *Newburyport Herald* from 1818 to 1825. Seeking a paper of his own, Garrison borrowed money to launch the *Newburyport Free Press* in 1826. Other than reflecting staunch, if outdated, Federalist views, the *Free Press* became increasingly puritanical as Garrison fell under the influence of transcendentalist poet John Greenleaf Whittier. The paper was a financial failure, and Garrison sold it in late 1826 and left Newburyport to seek employment in Boston.

Garrison was introduced to antislavery sentiments by merchant Caleb Cushing in 1821 and to the abolitionist cause by Quaker journalist Benjamin Lundy in 1828. After serving briefly as editor of a temperance paper, the *National Philanthropist*, Garrison accepted the invitation of the Bennington, Vermont, owners of the *Journal of the Times* to edit the anti-Jacksonian paper. Garrison's independence and increasing infatuation with abolition led him away from Vermont in early 1829 and back to Boston. He agreed to spell Lundy as editor of *The Genius of Universal Emancipation* in 1829,

but his radical stance on emancipation led to a libel suit and a jail sentence.

Subsidized by Arthur Tappan, publisher of New York's *Journal of Commerce*, Garrison printed 400 copies of his abolitionist newspaper *The Liberator* on 1 January 1831, promising readers to be "as harsh as truth." Even in Massachusetts, such a venture was tenuous. White subscribers in 1834 numbered only about 600; another 1,700 copies were distributed without charge to philanthropic societies and to free blacks. Despite contributions mainly from black communities in northern cities, Garrison was losing $1,700 annually.

Meanwhile, backed by friends such as Samuel Sewall, Garrison founded the New England Antislavery Society in 1832, the first organization of its kind. The following year, the American Antislavery Society was established by merging Garrison's society with a New York group led by Arthur and Lewis Tappan. Some of the same abolitionists who failed to support Garrison's newspaper also hesitated to participate in his antislavery society. Garrison's support of immediate emancipation, albeit nonviolently, ran against the vanguard of more moderate abolitionists, who favored gradual emancipation. Garrison received some blame for Virginia's bloody Nat Turner slave revolt in 1831, mainly because many southern newspapers freely quoted from *The Liberator*. Soon it became a crime in many southern communities to possess a copy of *The Liberator*.

Garrison used *The Liberator* as a vehicle of education. His column "Refuge of Oppression" listed factual examples of the cruelties of slavery, especially physical violence. Garrison faced mobs on many occasions, including one that ransacked his Boston offices in 1835. Actually, the 1835 attack was aimed at a visiting English abolitionist, George Thompson, who was supposed to have been at *The Liberator* offices. The event seemed to galvanize the abolitionist elements to recognize that not only slavery but also freedom was at stake.

Garrison slowly continued toward his goal of convincing northern public opinion to oppose slavery into the 1850s. Garrison opposed the Compromise of 1850 and favored allowing the Confederate states to leave the Union in 1861. Soon after the Civil War began, he realized that defeat of the Confederacy and preservation of the Union were the only viable means of ending slavery. As Garrison lost some of his youthful zeal, *The Liberator* sometimes reflected a lack of direction in its goals. Yet in the crucial election of 1864—the eve of the end of slavery—when Radical Republicans offered lukewarm support for President Abraham Lincoln's reelection, *The Liberator* and Garrison rallied behind the president without equivocation.

Reference Thomas, John L., *The Liberator: William Lloyd Garrison* (1963).

Gazette of the United States

The most important Federalist Party newspaper was the *Gazette of the United States*, established and directed by party leader Alexander Hamilton at the outset of George Washington's administration. The editor of the *Gazette* was John Fenno, a former schoolteacher who had developed some journalistic talents in Boston. The *Gazette*'s fade from prominence paralleled the Federalist Party's decline during the Virginia dynasty of Democratic-Republican presidents after 1801.

Following the election of George Washington in 1789, future Federalist Party organizer and Secretary of the Treasury Alexander Hamilton decided to establish a newspaper to act as the voice of the administration. The new government under the Constitution of 1787 was facing many serious national crises that had developed under the Articles of Confederation. Hamilton knew that public support for the administration was crucial to the success of the Constitution itself. The *Gazette of the United States* was thus launched in 1789 just prior to Washington's inauguration.

Hamilton and his fellow Federalists recruited John Fenno of Boston as their editor, despite his lack of any apprenticeship in newspaper management. A schoolteacher by profession, Fenno had demonstrated loyalty to the Federalist cause as a contributor to newspapers in Massachusetts. The Gazette was first issued on a semiweekly basis with no advertising. Although Fenno believed that the paper could establish a national circulation, such ambitions were never realized, largely because the subscription cost of $3 a year was beyond most commoners' means. Yet the paper served its purpose of backing administration policies and attacking those who opposed the administration, such as Thomas Jefferson. Even though Fenno's proclivity toward royalism was occasionally embarrassing, party leaders and contributors Hamilton and Vice President John Adams maintained the appropriate tone for the Gazette. The paper included reports on debates in Congress and foreign news as well as timely political treatises. The Gazette engaged in regular partisan exchanges with the principal Democratic-Republican newspaper, the National Gazette, edited by Philip Freneau.

The *Gazette* was printed in New York City—the first temporary national capital—until 1790, when the paper moved with the capital to Philadelphia. The official circulation did not move much above 1,000, and there were numerous delinquent subscribers. The *Gazette* obtained some government printing contracts, but they were not enough to forestall the necessity of selling advertising, which was placed on the front page. At one point, Fenno had to appeal for a loan from Hamilton to keep the paper going. The *Gazette* became a daily in 1793, but it never obtained a solid financial footing, even when the subscription price rose to $8 a year in 1797. After Fenno's death in 1798, the editorship was given to his son, who saw the decline of the Federalist Party coincide with the paper's slow demise. The *Gazette* was sold in 1818, ending its brief but significant history.

Godkin, E. L.
See New York Post.

Good Housekeeping

Founded in 1885 by Clark W. Bryan to provide a service to women, *Good Housekeeping* kept track of trends in fashion, beauty, child care, and homemaking. Although retaining a strong literary bent at first, *Good Housekeeping* solicited opinions and ideas from its readers throughout its history. Gradually, the addition of more illustrations and the founding of the Good Housekeeping Bureau in 1912 brought circulation to 3.5 million in the 1950s.

Clark W. Bryan became a newspaper editor in rural Massachusetts in the 1850s. In the 1870s, Bryan left the *Springfield Republican* to manage a publishing house in Holyoke. It was there in 1885 that Bryan launched the fortnightly magazine *Good Housekeeping: A Family Journal Conducted in the Interests of the Higher Life of the Household;* a subscription cost $2.50 a year. During its first ten years, *Good Housekeeping* carried mostly poetry, fiction, and short stories. There were also articles that gave advice about the management of the household, including cooking, sewing, house design, and furnishing. Bryan invited readers to submit literary pieces, recipes, and household hints and to offer advice. Prizes were offered for the best submissions in various categories. Thus, *Good Housekeeping* kept in close touch with its readers and household trends. Unlike *Ladies' Home Journal, Good Housekeeping* had few regular or noted outside contributors. Bryan himself was a frequent contributor, mostly of poems.

Bryan changed the publication to a monthly in 1891, with about 50 pages per issue. Circulation had risen to about 25,000. Illustrations became more frequent, and regular departments were featured each month. When Bryan committed suicide in 1898 after an illness, John Pettigrew purchased *Good Housekeeping* and continued to publish it. More ownership changes occurred over the next two years before the magazine settled in the hands of publisher E. H. Phelps, who had worked with Bryan in Springfield. Phelps hired James E. Tower to edit the magazine and made some technical improvements in its appearance, but the content remained familiar. In 1901, Phelps inaugurated the Good Housekeeping Institute, which provided laboratories to test appliances, clothes, and cleaning products to determine whether they should receive the Good Housekeeping Seal of Approval. The seal was quickly sought by manufacturers of consumer products.

By 1908, *Good Housekeeping's* circulation passed the 200,000 mark, and there were up to 30 pages of advertising per issue. The magazine now featured more fiction—usually serialized novels about domestic life—as well as humor. Tower paid greater attention to household affairs, particularly home economics. Estimates of the nutritional value of food began to appear after 1905. The Good Housekeeping Institute was complemented in 1912 by the creation of the Good Housekeeping Bureau of Food, Sanitation, and Health, headed by former Department of Agriculture chemist Dr. H. W. Wiley. The bureau tested the quality of food products in the same manner that the institute tested manufactured items.

Phelps sold the magazine to the Hearst company in 1912, and the production offices were moved to New York City. Tower was succeeded as editor in 1913 by William Frederick Bigelow, who had worked at Hearst's *Cosmopolitan.* Serialized fiction by famous authors such as Somerset Maugham, John Galsworthy, and Kathleen Norris became more prominent, along with short stories by Ellen Glasgow, Booth Tarkington, and Ring Lardner. Francis Parkinson Keyes wrote a column of public affairs from Washington that followed the suffragist movement, among others. *Good Housekeeping's* length often reached 250 pages and produced the largest profits of any national monthly by the time Bigelow's editorship ended. The Federal Trade Commission filed a legal complaint against the Seal of Approval in 1938, claiming that it was misleading and often exaggerated. After lengthy hearings, the commission ordered *Good Housekeeping* to modify its Seal of Approval claims in 1941.

Herbert Raymond Mayes followed Bigelow as editor in 1942 and began reducing the amount of fiction. Extended works were condensed, although recognized authors such as Daphne du Maurier and Sinclair Lewis continued to appear. More variety was offered to readers, including reviews of motion pictures and articles on baby care and hairstyles. *Good Housekeeping* remained aloof from news subjects as well as from topics such as gardening. Circulation grew from 2.5 million in 1943 to 3.5 million a decade later. The former editor of *Redbook*, Wade Nichols, became editor of *Good Housekeeping* in 1959 when Mayes was hired by *McCall's*. Circulation moved past 5 million in 1962. New departments entering the magazine's pages in the 1960s included medical updates and diets.

Grady, Henry
See Atlanta Constitution.

Graham's Magazine
Begun by staffers at the *Saturday Evening Post*, *Graham's Magazine* became the prototype for the modern popular magazine that appeals to a literate middle-class audience. The journal attracted both male and female readers and set the standard for quality illustrations.

As early as 1826, two Saturday Evening Post staffers, Samuel C. Atkinson and Charles Alexander, began publishing a monthly magazine known as the *Casket*. It tended to be a virtual replica of the *Post* until George R. Graham, also affiliated with the *Post*, purchased the *Casket* in 1839, along with another journal called *Gentleman's Magazine*. Graham combined elements of both in his new publication launched in Philadelphia in 1840—*Graham's Lady's and Gentleman's Magazine*—which featured essays, short stories, and poetry.

Graham sought quality editors such as Edgar Allan Poe in the early 1840s and successfully solicited manuscripts from Henry Wadsworth Longfellow, William Cullen Bryant, and James Fenimore Cooper. Graham departed from tradition by not

only printing the authors' names with the articles but also advertising their participation. Another Graham innovation was the use of original engraved illustrations. He hired English artist-engraver John Sartain to work for *Graham's*, and a sample of his work appeared in each issue. These illustrations were certainly one of the primary reasons for the magazine's popularity.

Graham also mimicked a popular women's magazine, *Godey's Lady's Book*, by printing illustrations featuring fashions or domestic scenes and romantic stories to attract women readers. But unlike *Godey's*, *Graham's* promoted an intellectual image of women by publishing the writings of women such as Ann Stephens and Lydia Sigourney. By 1842, the circulation of *Graham's* was an impressive 40,000. Graham used the profits from his magazine to promote his Whig political sentiments through newspaper publishing in Philadelphia. He bought into not one but three newspapers and began losing money. The newspaper failures directly affected the publisher's ownership of *Graham's Magazine*, which he surrendered in 1848. The journal continued to publish until its final demise in 1852.

Reference Smyth, Albert H., *Philadelphia Magazines and Their Contributors, 1741–1850* (1892).

Graphic Design
Technology changed the art of graphic design during the nineteenth and twentieth centuries as much as any other aspect of media production. Graphic design engaged the talents of not one but several contributors. In the nineteenth century, the illustrator or artist was assisted by the engraver and the printer. In the twentieth century, photography and computers became part of the design mix. Graphic design, which enhances or explains text, has been important in virtually all media products beginning with newspapers and later extending to magazines, broadcasting, advertising, and motion pictures.

In the early days of newspaper layout, there was no specialization—certainly no profession of graphic designer. Writing the copy, designing and producing typeface, setting type, and printing were all done by one or a few people in newspaper offices. By the early nineteenth century, some degree of specialization had been established for these tasks, although someone still had to visualize—hence design—the final product and oversee its production. When the first illustrations appeared regularly in early-nineteenth-century newspapers and magazines, the artist or illustrator would pass along the drawing to an engraver, who would etch the illustration onto a wooden block, metal plate, or lithographic stone, which would be given to the printer for production. Throughout these stages, the product would be altered in varying degrees by each creative participant. The production materials themselves, including paper and ink, determined the quality of the final product. Further, the early presses had both qualitative and quantitative limitations.

Fortunately, printers had access to several published manuals dating from the seventeenth century to consult about the design and production processes. Of all the limitations facing graphic design in the early nineteenth century, the quality of ink may have been the most difficult, since most inks faded or stained easily. By the time the new cylinder presses appeared in the 1820s, the quality of inks had improved dramatically. Coincidentally, typography technology improved to allow greater variety in the production of typefaces. But it was illustration technology that provided the greatest opportunity for design diversification in newspapers and magazines.

The intaglio process of printing illustrations from a metal plate had existed since the seventeenth century. The process involved using a tool to engrave lines onto a metal plate; it was used mostly to reproduce artworks. Intaglio engravers were highly skilled and thus were paid handsomely to engrave plates. But the cost of intaglio was so great that it could not be used by most printers on a regular basis. *Graham's Magazine*, published in Philadelphia in the 1840s, made extensive use of intaglio line engravings.

The invention of lithography in the 1790s by German artist Aloysius Senefelder provided an inexpensive method of illustration that was ideal for newspapers and magazines. Lithography involved drawing images with a crayon on fine-grained limestone. The water-dampened rock surface was rolled with an ink-charged roller. The paper picked up the ink-stained engraved portions, leaving the undrawn portions of the stone blank. Lithography required much less skill than intaglio, since drawing on the stone face was identical to drawing on paper. However, lithography had to be printed on special presses, because it was not suited to the printer's letterpress. Nonetheless, lithography became popular in commercial printing and advertising.

Publishing still lacked a practical method of using illustrations with the typefaced presses. Wood engraving became the most popular and practical solution to the dilemma. Wood engraving had been used in the eighteenth century for decorative borders on newspapers or illustrations on broadsheets, but it did not compete effectively at first with line engraving. Engravers in the early nineteenth century switched from soft to hard wood blocks, which made greater detail possible. Publications such as *Frank Leslie's Illustrated Newspaper* and *Harper's Weekly* in the 1850s made considerable use of woodcut engravings.

The advent of photography in the 1830s spelled important changes in graphics, but before the development of the photomechanical process of halftones in the 1870s, illustrators were still required to transpose photographs into engravings. One of the first newspapers to make regular use of halftones was the *New York Daily Graphic*, begun in 1873. Of course, photography meant that older engraved or painted products could be reproduced in halftones as well. By the time the yellow press emerged in the 1890s, front-page photographs had become standard fare for newspapers. Gradually, some magazines also resorted to the regular use of halftones in their design. The chief advocate of the photomechanical process was artist Joseph Pennell, whose manual *Modern Illus-*

tration (1895) influenced European as well as U.S. publishing. Photomechanical processes also facilitated the use of color in printing, as colored inks and color-separation technology improved. Graphic design also benefited from the superior typesetting system of the linotype in the 1880s. The advertising industry benefited from each of these technical advances as well.

After World War I, graphic design became a recognized specialty for publishing. New art forms such as cubism and surrealism were represented by graphic designers using collages or photomontages. The Bauhaus architectural school in the 1920s influenced the design principle that "form follows function," meaning that art and technology should have practical applications. The principle was applied in fashion magazines such as *Harper's Bazaar* and *Vogue.* Tabloid newspapers such as the *New York Daily News,* begun in 1919, featured sophisticated layouts that included headlines and halftones to attract readers. Daniel Updike's classic *Printing Types,* published in 1922, outlined the variety of typography available for printing. Henry Luce em-

ployed T. M. Cleland to give an aesthetic design to his slick business magazine *Fortune,* begun in 1930. The ultimate publishing application of halftones was Luce's pictorial magazine *Life,* launched in 1936. Even before 1936, many popular magazines featured photographic covers, and since the 1930s, all magazines as well as many newspapers, such as *USA Today,* use professional graphic designers.

Advertisers of motion pictures also used designers for their posters and signs. Television provided new opportunities for graphic designers beginning in the 1940s. By the end of the twentieth century, most media products, including newspapers, magazines, motion pictures, advertising, and television, employed art directors or graphic designers to assist editors in conceptualizing and producing the end product.

See also Engravings; Photojournalism.

Reference Meggs, Philip, *A History of Graphic Design* (1983).

Greeley, Horace
See New York Tribune and *Herald Tribune.*

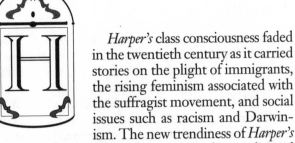

Harper's Monthly

Much to the dismay of American writers, *Harper's Monthly Magazine* began in 1850 with almost entirely English contributors. The magazine has endured in large part because of the diversity of its content and the quality of its style. It began as a literary magazine, but its orientation changed toward public affairs with a liberal bent beginning in the 1920s.

Fletcher Harper of the Harper Brothers book publishing firm started *Harper's New Monthly Magazine* in 1850 mainly to advertise the company's books. Indeed, for a long time, the journal would not accept any other advertising, and most of its articles were serialized versions of books by English authors such as Thomas Hardy, Charles Dickens, and William Thackeray. Other features included essays on travel, leisure, science, and art. *Harper's* also followed the trend of earlier illustrated monthlies by featuring pen-and-ink fashion plates. Editor Henry J. Raymond included an account of current events in each issue. Circulation reached 50,000 by the end of the first year and 200,000 by the outbreak of the Civil War. From the outset, most *Harper's* readers came from the educated upper class.

Gradually, *Harper's* began to include more American authors such as Mark Twain, Helen Hunt Jackson, and Thomas Nelson Page, but English writers continued to dominate. American artists also found opportunities to contribute to *Harper's*. After the Civil War, longtime editor Henry Mills Alden kept the literary and artistic quality of *Harper's* ahead of its competition. Circulation held steady at 200,000 by 1890, with the magazine still managing to avoid political and social commentary. The muckraking era of journalism, however, required *Harper's* to consider current issues such as imperialism, reform, and socially avant-garde trends. Thus, Henry Cabot Lodge's coverage of the Spanish-American War in Cuba tended to romanticize the affair. A certain snobbishness that was evident in the tone of the writing kept readers limited to the upper class before the turn of the century.

Harper's class consciousness faded in the twentieth century as it carried stories on the plight of immigrants, the rising feminism associated with the suffragist movement, and social issues such as racism and Darwinism. The new trendiness of *Harper's* did not retain the interest of its traditional readers; circulation dropped to 150,000, and revenues followed. The losses required the book publishing component of the company to subsidize the magazine. Other early characteristics of *Harper's* also changed by the twentieth century. Outside advertising equaled that in its trade rivals, and the monochrome illustrations were replaced by colorful, artsy covers.

THE JANUARY NUMBER CONTAINS

White Man's Africa, by POULTNEY BIGELOW.—The Martian, by DU MAURIER.—Farce, by W.D.HOWELLS.—Short Stories,by Miss WILKINS, BRANDER MATTHEWS, and E. A. ALEXANDER.—Science at the Beginning of the Century, Illustrated.—Literary Landmarks of Rome, by LAURENCE HUTTON, etc., etc.

Founded in 1850, Harper's Monthly *appealed largely to the educated upper class throughout the nineteenth century.*

When John Fischer took over as editor from Frederick Lewis Allen in 1953, he tried to blend the original literary elements of *Harper's,* including regular columns on the fine arts, with public affairs and current events. A more drastic turn toward public affairs occurred under the editorship of Willie Morris (1967–1971). Lengthy articles dealing with contemporary politics or cultural developments became the norm. Morris fostered a personal brand of journalism without editorial direction for contributors. David Halberstam contributed articles on the Vietnam War, and Joseph Kraft wrote a regular column of political commentary. However, even though circulation expanded in 1968 from 295,000 to 411,000, it slid back to 360,000 by 1971. At that time, the magazine was sold to a Minneapolis newspaper conglomerate headed by John Cowles. When Cowles released Morris, six staff and contributing editors resigned in protest.

New editor Lewis Lapham picked up the pieces in 1971 and steered the content of *Harper's* toward an analysis of the malaise affecting U.S. institutions and society. The balance sheets continued to bleed red until 1980, when the owners—facing $4 million in debt—announced that they would be shutting *Harper's* down. Its demise was prevented by its purchase for $250,000 by the MacArthur Foundation and Atlantic Richfield Corporation. The new owners installed Michael Kinsley, former *New Republic* editor, at the editorial helm.

Reference Allen, Frederick L., *Harper's Magazine, 1850–1950* (1950).

Harper's Weekly

In sharp contrast to *Harper's Monthly*, which disdained political and social commentary in the 1850s, *Harper's Weekly* used political reporting and editorial illustrations to become a major social force in the United States. Its strong editorial commentary and sensational reporting, combined with quality short stories, serialized books, and poetry, gave the weekly journal a distinctive flavor until its demise in 1916. *Harper's* employed the most talented artists of the era, including Thomas Nast, Frederic Remington, and Charles Dana Gibson.

Fletcher Harper, the youngest of the Harper brothers, was trained as a printer and proved to be a skilled businessman. From its birth in 1857, *Harper's Weekly: A Journal of Civilization* set the tone for a new breed of periodical that relied on stinging investigative articles and realistic political cartoons to educate the public about corruption and mismanagement in government. Harper named lawyer Theodore Sedgwick editor but retained major decision-making authority himself as publisher. Both publisher and editor were Democrats until they switched their support to Abraham Lincoln during the Civil War. The 16-page weekly featured unsigned editorials—initially placed on the front page but later removed to the second—and three pages of advertising. In its first year, *Harper's* used full-page illustrations almost as a substitute for prose descriptions in order to make a point with its readers. The number of illustrations increased, and although they were not intentionally sensational, they sometimes had that effect. *Harper's* also contained serialized fiction, mostly by English authors such as Charles Dickens, and a few short stories. Circulation grew from 60,000 the first year to 120,000 by 1861.

The magazine's greatest impact occurred during the Civil War, when artists such as Thomas Nast provided pen-and-ink illustrations of the horrors of the battlefield. *Harper's* also utilized the photographs of Mathew Brady, although most were portraits of Union army commanders and lacked the realism of illustrations. Publisher Harper and managing editor John Bonner had to defend the magazine's existence against Secretary of War Edwin Stanton's attempt to stifle it for supposed revelations about Union fortifications. President Abraham Lincoln revoked Stanton's order and thanked Harper for helping recruitment efforts.

In the post–Civil War years, New York City came under the grip of the infamous William Marcy Tweed. Boss Tweed and his cronies obtained protective laws from the state legislature that made prosecution difficult. *Harper's Weekly* was edited from 1863 to 1892 by reformer George William Curtis, an early contributor to the journal. Curtis wrote editorials and Nast drew cartoons exposing Tweed's graft in 1870. Although *Harper's* had no legal method of proceeding against the Tweed ring, Curtis's editorials and Nast's cartoons held the Tammany crowd up to ridicule. Although most of the New York media carefully avoided offending Tweed, the courage displayed by *Harper's* inspired the *New York Times* to join in the fray. Eventually, New York Attorney General Samuel J. Tilden was able to obtain incriminating evidence and prosecute the Tweed ring, but not before Tammany thugs attacked the offices of *Harper's* and offered bribes to Nast. The campaign against the Tweed ring was profitable for *Harper's*, and circulation grew to 160,000 by 1872.

Despite its penchant for reform, *Harper's* ridiculed the presidential candidacy of Liberal Republican Horace Greeley in the 1872 election. Curtis and Nast did not always agree on tactics, although their combined impact was unquestioned. Fletcher Harper retired from active control of the weekly in 1875. *Harper's* produced a huge pictorial spread of the 1876 Philadelphia Centennial Exposition. Although *Harper's Weekly* never again gained the prominence or circulation that it had in the 1870s, its reputation for independence and integrity was permanently emblazoned in the public's mind. Nast retired in 1887, and editor Curtis died in 1892.

Harper's Weekly stayed with its format of current news and editorial and cartoon commentary. Longtime reform advocate Carl Schurz succeeded Curtis as editor in 1892. Frederic Remington became the principal illustrator in the 1890s, and halftone photographs appeared regularly. Rudyard Kipling and Arthur Conan Doyle contributed short stories, and William Dean Howells added serialized novels. *Harper's* broke with the Republicans in 1884 when it backed Democrat Grover Cleveland for president over James G. Blaine. The magazine opposed the free silver movement of the 1890s and thus did not back Democrat William Jennings Bryan in the 1896 and 1900 elections. War correspondent Richard Harding Davis sent reports from Cuba during the Spanish-American War (1898). George Harvey became president of the company in 1900 and editor in 1901. Charles Dana Gibson rendered many

of his famous illustrations in *Harper's* after 1900. Harvey favored Progressive reforms and became a strong advocate of Democrat Woodrow Wilson. *Harper's* was sold in 1913 to muckraking publisher Samuel S. McClure, who named Norman Hapgood editor, but the magazine continued to lose money. It was sold again in 1916 and merged into the *Independent*.

Reference Keller, Morton, *The Art and Politics of Thomas Nast* (1968).

Hearst, William Randolph (1863–1951)

The name most often associated with the era of yellow journalism is that of William Randolph Hearst. He began his newspaper career with his father's *San Francisco Examiner* but became best known nationally as publisher of the *New York Journal* after 1895. It was the *Journal* that plunged the New York press into the era of sensational yellow journalism, climaxed by the agitation for war against Spain in 1898 over Cuba. Hearst built one of the great chains of dailies across the United States and became a true captain of the newspaper industry. Hearst papers were always noted for their aggressive marketing methods but were not always rated highly for other journalistic qualities.

William Randolph Hearst's father, George Hearst, struck it rich in the California gold rush before the Civil War and became a U.S. senator. In 1880, George Hearst bought the failing morning daily the *San Francisco Examiner* and made it the voice of the Democratic Party. William was sent to Harvard in 1882, where he showed skill in editing the student humor magazine *Lampoon*. He also spent considerable time at the offices of the *Boston Globe*. Hearst was dismissed from Harvard for misconduct and served as a cub reporter for his boyhood idol Joseph Pulitzer at the *New York World*.

Upon returning to San Francisco, Hearst overcame his father's misgivings about letting him run the *Examiner*. He hired some talented reporters and began a newspaper campaign to regulate the railroads, especially the powerful Southern Pacific.

Although Hearst's methods initially proved costly, the *Examiner*'s circulation rose quickly and soon passed that of Michel De Young's *Chronicle*. When the *Examiner* showed a profit by 1895, Hearst began looking for a new challenge. Joseph Pulitzer's brother Albert had founded the *New York Journal* in 1882, but it never rose above its reputation as a scandal sheet. John R. McLean, owner of the *Cincinnati Enquirer*, bought Albert Pulitzer's *Journal* in 1894 for $1 million but was unable to make it competitive in New York City. Thus, suffering losses daily, McLean agreed to sell the paper to Hearst in 1895 for $180,000.

Although Hearst quickly increased the *Journal*'s circulation to second place behind Pulitzer's *World* by reducing the price from two cents to one cent, he suffered considerable financial losses in the process. Hearst's mother agreed to sell the family's Anaconda copper business to provide more capital for the *Journal*. Hearst had always paid his staff well, and better pay lured many of the *World*'s best executives and reporters to the *Journal*, including Morrill Goddard, S. S. Carvalho, and Arthur Brisbane. Color printing and comic strips were added to make the *Journal* more attractive and distinct from the *World*. An original comic strip transferred from the *World* to the *Journal*, the "Yellow Kid," supplied the label for the new type of journalism Hearst developed.

In addition to using sensational headlines and stories about crime and violence, the *Journal* crusaded for reforms in municipal government. By 1896, the daily circulation reached 437,000; in 1897, the Sunday edition, with its innovative magazine supplement, equaled the *World*'s 600,000. Because the *Journal*, like the *World*, depended more on street sales than subscriptions, its circulation numbers fluctuated with the type of stories making news. The issue reporting the 1896 election results sold 1.5 million copies. Yellow journalism reached its peak of influence during the events leading to war with Spain over Cuba in 1898. The *Journal*'s reporters in Cuba sent back daily reports of events that were exhibited with lurid headlines and half-truths. Hearst sim-

ply exploited a tradition of U.S. imperialism and territorial expansion that manifested itself often in the nineteenth century. Richard Harding Davis became one of many star reporters in Cuba, along with artist Frederic Remington. Hearst spent $500,000 to cover the conflict with Spain.

Little did William Randolph Hearst know that when he printed the comic strip "Yellow Kid" in the New York Journal, *the term* yellow journalism *would be coined and used to describe his own paper's style.*

After the successful Spanish war, Hearst turned his *Journal* toward domestic issues, advocating a variety of Progressive reforms such as direct elections and a graduated income tax. The *Journal* ridiculed President William McKinley in the election of 1900 and received some blame when it was discovered that McKinley's assassin possessed a copy of the *Journal*. Hearst soon changed the name of the morning paper to the *American*. He also decided that he wanted to be president of the United States himself and entered politics. Hearst was elected to two terms in the House of Representatives in 1902 and 1904. He received a respectable vote at the 1904 Democratic convention as a presidential candidate but shifted his interest to the New York mayoral race in 1905 and the governor's race in 1906, both of which he lost. Hearst ditched his political ambitions to pursue a newspaper empire.

Originally, the idea of expanding newspaper ownership to other cities was to promote his presidential ambitions. He campaigned against boss rule and corporate trusts to attract middle- and working-class voters. Critics grew suspicious of his journalistic motives and noted the absence of in-depth reporting and any sincere concern for social reform. Hearst started the Chicago evening *American* in 1900 and the morning *Examiner* in 1902, the Los Angeles morning *Examiner* in 1903, and the Boston evening *American* in 1904. The familiar quality reporting and writing as well as sensational content, headlines, and comic strips appeared in each of his new acquisitions. Labor unions received their strongest support from Hearst papers. Hearst later acquired the King Features Syndicate, International News and Photo Services, 13 magazines, and eight radio stations.

The Great Depression in the 1930s proved especially harmful to the Hearst newspaper chain, which was always subsidized by the family's corporate interests. In 1935, the Hearst chain reached a peak of 26 dailies in 19 cities, with almost 14 percent of national daily circulation. Yet financial hardship caused Hearst to consider declaring bankruptcy at one point during the depression, when he lost nine daily papers, magazines, and radio stations. Large portions of Hearst real estate were auctioned. Perhaps age and hard economic times caused Hearst to exhibit uncharacteristic conservatism in the 1930s. He fought against the emerging writers' union, the American Newspaper Guild; he backed Republican Alfred Landon against Roosevelt in the 1936 election and opposed U.S. intervention in World War II until after the bombing of Pearl Harbor. Anticommunist campaigns were backed strongly by Hearst

papers in the early days of the Cold War. Hearst's health began to fail, and he died in 1951, leaving an indelible if controversial mark on U.S. newspapers. Hearst's five sons continued the Hearst tradition and gave the remaining eight papers greater credibility with solid reporting, balanced news accounts, and independent editorial control. The Hearst Foundation provided scholarships to journalism students.

See also San Francisco Examiner; Yellow Journalism.
Reference Swanberg, W. A., *Citizen Hearst* (1961).

Higgins, Marguerite
See Korean War; World War II.

Howe, Edgar Watson (1853–1937)
The iconoclastic Kansan E. W. Howe established a national reputation as editor of the *Atchison Globe* in the 1870s. Along with fellow Kansan William Allen White, Howe became the symbol of the small-town country editor and earned the sobriquet "The Sage of Potato Hill." After retiring from his newspaper, Howe edited *E. W. Howe's Monthly*, featuring more of his homespun truisms. Touting capitalism and translating it into small-town terms became a hallmark of Howe's writing in early-twentieth-century media outlets.

Edgar Watson Howe was born in Bethany in northern Missouri during the turbulent era of the struggle over slavery. His father, Henry Howe, was a hellfire-and-damnation preacher and newspaper publisher. Howe became seriously troubled when his father demonstrated the height of hypocrisy by leaving his family and moving to Iowa with a female church member. Twelve-year-old Ed assisted his brother James for two years running the *Bethany Weekly Union of States*, which his father had bought in 1863. Howe left home in 1865 and wandered about for the next dozen years.

Howe purchased his first newspaper in Golden, Colorado, in 1873. When the paper failed in 1875, Howe moved to Falls

City, Kansas, to start another newspaper. Finally, Howe founded his third newspaper, the *Atchison Globe*, in 1877 with about $200 capital. Serving as reporter, typesetter, and editor, Howe approached his task diligently. He was especially skilled at gaining the confidence of people who could supply him with news items. It was Howe's considered opinion that the primary function of a newspaper was to entertain rather than inform. He also desperately wanted to establish a reputation beyond the bounds of Atchison and even Kansas. Howe was able to make profits from the *Globe* immediately, averaging about $25,000 a year.

By the time he retired in 1911 to launch his magazine, Howe was making $40,000 a year on the *Globe*, and the paper's circulation was just under 7,000 for the daily edition and 8,000 for the weekly edition. In 1891, Howe had started to publish a quarterly journal but issued only two installments before giving it up. *E. W. Howe's Monthly*, launched in 1911, had a longer run. Many of the essays that first appeared in the *Monthly* were included in two books: *Success Easier Than Failure* (1917) and *The Blessing of Business* (1918). Howe's pen pal H. L. Mencken also reprinted selected Howe essays under the title *Ventures in Common Sense* (1919), which even merited a printing in England. The *Monthly* was discontinued in 1933.

Because he had such curiosity about people, Howe gleaned a host of human-interest stories. He also formulated a lengthy list of adages about people that were quoted in major papers across the nation. Howe could stir feelings with his adamant stands on controversial subjects. For example, he often ridiculed religion in a region that took the subject seriously. Another common theme was that women should accept their role as mothers and homemakers rather than seek political or other rights. Howe once wrote that small-town residents' sins became the stock of gossip almost simultaneously with their commission. Despite his many followers in the South, Howe offered harsh criticism of the region, which he believed was blighted by its historical past and current affliction of one-party rule.

Howe took time between his editorial duties to write about 25 books. His best-known novel was *The Story of a Country Town* (1883), which was based on Howe's youthful experiences in Bethany, Missouri. He also wrote a memoir entitled *Plain People* (1929) that further reflected his insight into small-town traditions. Edward Bok's *Ladies' Home Journal* contracted in 1911 to serialize another Howe book, *Ante-Mortem Statement*. Howe believed fervently in the idea of progress, especially scientific and technological advances, because he felt that all humankind must become self-made and self-sufficient. These sentiments, combined with his championing of free enterprise, made him popular with eastern financial leaders. John D. Rockefeller purchased 200 copies of one issue of *Howe's Monthly* because it featured such maxims. Howe authored similar pro-business items for the *Saturday Evening Post* and *Collier's*.

Reference Pickett, Calder M., *Ed Howe: Country Town Philosopher* (1968).

International News Service
See United Press.

Iran-Contra Hearings
During the administration of
Ronald Reagan, Congress prohib-
ited military aid to the Nicaraguan anticom-
munists. An aide on the National Security
Council, Colonel Oliver North, spearheaded a covert operation to continue military shipments to Nicaragua. Monies to
fund the operation were diverted from the
sale of weapons to Iran; the weapons sale
was part of a scheme to obtain the release of
American hostages held in Lebanon. A joint
House-Senate select committee held televised hearings in the summer of 1987 to
uncover the covert operations and determine responsibility for violations of congressional directives. The nation followed the
proceedings with considerable interest.

Because of the complexity and secrecy of
the Iran-Contra scheme, the public had little knowledge of it through news outlets
until the congressional hearings.
Since television naturally gravitates
toward strong or controversial personalities, it was not surprising that
North became the focal point of
media coverage. The Iran-Contra
Congressional Committee heard
24 witnesses prior to North's six-day testimony, yet his presence dominated the hearings. Prior to the hearings, print media outlets such as *Newsweek* had carried stories
considering North as both hero and villain.
The *New York Times* argued in its reports
that Reagan administration officials had attempted to make North a scapegoat for
their own failings. Thus, the buildup to
North's testimony was not artificial.

The television networks did in-depth biographical analyses of North from his child-
hood through his Vietnam service to the
assignment at the National Security Council. The reports, especially those on ABC
and CBS, provided largely favorable views
of North. When North's testimony began,
television cameras followed the drama live.

*Fired National Security Council aide Lieutenant Colonel Oliver North is surrounded by photographers and
reporters as he leaves his home on 18 December 1986.*

Critics of the administration and North were appalled at the attempts to subvert congressional directives and at North's lying before previous committees about the Nicaraguan activity. Apologists reveled in North as the antihero, antigovernment patriot willing to do whatever was needed to assist the cause of freedom. Congressional comments decried the ends-justifying-the-means approach of North and his compatriots.

North's ability to sway public opinion through media coverage became obvious in polls about providing aid to the anticommunist Nicaraguan Contras. Prior to the Iran-Contra episode, the public opposed the aid by 70 percent, but after the televised hearings featuring North's defense of the cause, almost half of the public polled favored the Contra effort. Thus, even as the Reagan administration set North up as the scapegoat, its Central American policy benefited from North's testimony. The power of personality in conjunction with the media was clearly demonstrated. Caught up in the climate of opinion in which they were the reflectors rather than the molders of thought, the media were being manipulated by their own innate influence.

Network ratings during the six days of North's testimony showed that more people watched the hearings than normally tuned in to the regularly scheduled soap operas. Indeed, five times as many viewers watched North as watched the top-rated daytime show, ABC's "General Hospital." The avant-garde *Village Voice* lamented that such ratings proved that television audiences preferred mediocrity. Amazingly, the television publicity propelled North into becoming a successful lecture circuit attraction and best-selling book author as well as a political candidate in the 1994 Virginia senatorial election, which he lost.

Reference Anderson, Robin, "Oliver North and the News," in *Journalism and Popular Culture*, ed. Peter Dalhgren and Colin Sparks (1992).

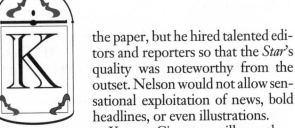

Kansas City Star

During its early history, the *Kansas City Star* (Missouri) was synonymous with its founder, William Rockhill Nelson. The *Star* favored reforms and attacked corruption in the Progressive era. Nelson nurtured civic pride and promoted improvements for Kansas City as a political independent, and that tradition was continued by Roy Roberts in the twentieth century. The *Star* was one of the most respected and financially prosperous newspapers in the nation. In 1977, the evening *Star* and its morning counterpart the *Times* became part of Capital Cities Communications conglomerate.

William Rockhill Nelson grew up in Indiana, where he was dismissed from Notre Dame in his second year for misbehavior. He made a small fortune in the contracting business in Indiana but lost most of his money in a disastrous Georgia cotton land deal. He joined with partner Samuel Morss in 1879 to take control of the *Fort Wayne (Indiana) Sentinel*, which Nelson's father had owned at one time. The *Sentinel* began a campaign for municipal reforms, and Nelson developed feature writing at the paper.

Soon the *Sentinel* owners decided that they needed a larger publishing outlet and determined that Kansas City would be an appropriate location. Nelson and Morss launched the *Kansas City Star* in September 1880 as a four-page evening daily facing two poorly run competitors. The *Star*'s price of two cents beat the nickel price of its competition but required sizable advertising revenue, which came slowly at first. Rival editor Eugene Field referred to the *Star* as Kansas City's "twilight twinkler." Morss retired after one year and sold his interest to Nelson, who had to borrow money to keep the paper solvent. In 1882, Nelson bought one of his evening competitors with an Associated Press franchise. Circulation reached 10,000 by 1883. Nelson did very little writing for the paper, but he hired talented editors and reporters so that the *Star*'s quality was noteworthy from the outset. Nelson would not allow sensational exploitation of news, bold headlines, or even illustrations.

Kansas City was still mostly a frontier town in the 1880s, with a parasitic government and inadequate utility services. The *Star*'s principal campaign over a 15-year period called for improved and inexpensive transportation, including paved streets and a streetcar system. Nelson fought boss rule in Kansas City and inspired the creation of a commission form of municipal government. The *Star* promoted urban beautification projects such as parks and tree-lined boulevards, advocated affordable housing for the working classes, and opposed the liquor interests. Nelson believed that the primary purpose of a newspaper was to be an advocate for civic improvements in partnership with citizens. He had been a Democrat before coming to Kansas City, but the *Star* tended to be politically independent, although it strongly endorsed Progressive candidates such as Theodore Roosevelt.

Despite the *Star*'s staid appearance in comparison with yellow press journals, circulation continued to grow, hitting 50,000 in 1893 and holding first place in Kansas City. Nelson began a weekly edition of the *Star* in 1890 that had 250,000 subscribers by 1914. A Sunday edition was inaugurated in 1894. In 1901, Nelson purchased the morning *Times* (founded in 1868) and kept it as a complement to the afternoon *Star*. During the Progressive era, the *Star*'s chief editorial writer Alexander Butts led the paper's reform impetus. At the time of Nelson's death in 1915, the daily *Star*'s circulation was 170,000. Nelson left much of his fortune to endow an art gallery in his name. Nelson's widow and daughter operated the *Star* through a trust, and Nelson's son-in-law Irwin Kirkwood served as editor until his death in 1928. In 1917, former President Theodore Roosevelt became a contributing editor, using the *Star* as a platform to urge more rapid military preparations for World

War I. The trust offered the *Star* for sale in 1926, and a stock company made up of 90 *Star* employees offered the high bid of $11 million to acquire title to the paper. The *Star* became one of many newspapers to move into radio broadcasting in 1922 with station WDAF. The radio and later television station were divested in 1957 because of a Justice Department prosecution based on news monopoly.

Nelson had put Oberlin College graduate Henry Haskell in charge of the editorial page in 1910 after the death of Butts. Haskell had started with the *Star* in 1898 as assistant telegraph editor and served two years as Washington correspondent. During Haskell's tenure as editor from 1928 until 1952, he wrote a Sunday column entitled "Random Thoughts." The *Star* received two editorial Pulitzer Prizes during Haskell's era—in 1931 and 1944. Editorial campaigns for lower gasoline prices led to a $54 million libel suit by Teapot Dome principal Harry Doherty against the *Star*, but the paper stood firm, and the suit was eventually dropped. The *Star* altered some of Nelson's practices by increasing its coverage of foreign news and adding illustrations and comic strips. The *Star* and *Times* were left as Kansas City's only newspapers in 1942 when the rival *Journal-Post* folded.

Roy Roberts became the *Star*'s Washington correspondent in 1915 and returned to Kansas City in 1928 to become managing editor under Haskell. Roberts was elected president of the American Society of Newspaper Editors and an Associated Press director; he helped found the Associated Press Managing Editors Association in 1931. He won election as president of the *Star-Times* company in 1947, where he remained until 1965. During his tenure at the *Star*, Roberts often counseled leaders in the Republican Party and made the *Star* a dependable backer of the party in elections.

When University of Michigan graduate William W. Baker took over the editorship in 1967, the morning *Times'* circulation of 345,000 led the evening *Star*'s by 7,000. Baker had begun his career at the *Star* as a reporter in 1947 and had served as editorial

writer and associate editor before being named to the top spot. An opinion poll in the early 1960s ranked the *Star* among the top 15 dailies in the nation.

Circulation fell off during the 1970s, prompting the employee stockholders to sell the company to Capital Cities Communications in 1977 for $125 million. Sales continued to decline during the 1980s amidst frequent staff turnover; the combined circulation of the *Star* and *Times* in 1989 was just under 500,000, compared with almost 650,000 in 1973. By 1994, however, the improvement was notable; the *Star*'s circulation was moving back close to 300,000 under editor Arthur S. Brisbane, grandson of a famous Pulitzer editor.

Reference Johnson, Icie F., *William Rockhill Nelson and the* Kansas City Star (1935).

Kefauver Hearings

The first major public exposure of government operations by television came in 1951 when the hearings of the Senate Subcommittee on Interstate Crime were televised in several major cities. Committee chairman Estes Kefauver may have seen television as a tool for his presidential aspirations, which became evident in the 1952 election, but even he could not have foreseen the actual results. An estimated 20 to 30 million Americans followed the televised hearings with great interest, which proved the capacity of the medium to both inform and entertain.

Senator Estes Kefauver—a Democrat from Tennessee—believed that even though the federal government could not take over state and local governments' responsibility for prosecuting criminals, it could set an important example of leadership, particularly when it came to organized crime. New Orleans Mayor DeLesseps Morrison had urged Kefauver to create an interstate crime committee and offered New Orleans as a site for one of the hearings. The Senate approved the creation of the Subcommittee on Interstate Crime in early 1950. Senator Kefauver assumed that the committee's work would concentrate on gambling. Following the repeal of Prohibition in 1933, organized crime had moved mostly into gambling, perhaps a $25 billion industry by the 1950s. Other cities on the committee circuit included Miami, Tampa, St. Louis, Kansas City, Chicago, Las Vegas, Los Angeles, San Francisco, Detroit, Cleveland, Philadelphia, and New York. The committee's chief investigator, Rudolph Halley, planned the hearings in great detail. During the questioning, Senator Kefauver remained emotionless and proper.

Early television accounts of the committee hearings did not include live coverage but only short summaries on news programs. The live coverage began with the visit to New Orleans in January 1951, when Mayor Morrison claimed that New York mob boss Frank Costello had gotten his start in New Orleans. A local New Orleans television station, WNOE, telecast the entire proceedings, and other stations outside of New Orleans decided to tune in as well. Kefauver made no effort to invite the television coverage. Live coverage continued when the committee visited St. Louis and Los Angeles; San Francisco television stations followed suit with similar coverage, setting the stage for the finale in New York City. Kefauver soon realized that the television cameras forced the senators to alter their questioning to suit the pace and content that viewers demanded.

When the committee arrived in New York City in March 1951, *Time* magazine offered to sponsor the television coverage. The hearings increased morning television viewing time from an average of 2 percent to 25 percent, and afternoon viewing time from 12 percent to 30 percent. National networks began to buy time for the coverage when reputed crime boss Frank Costello appeared to testify over a seven-day period. At one point, Costello asked the television cameras not to show his face; they focused instead on his hands. Costello's testimony revealed links between organized crime and former New York City Mayor William O'Dwyer, who was also called to testify. There were some angry exchanges between O'Dwyer and the senators, which made great theater for the cameras.

Undoubtedly, the media climax of the committee tour was in New York City. Television viewers were so enthralled at the proceedings that local newspapers featured stories about housework being neglected, movie and theater attendance down, and sluggish department store sales. The *New York Times* suggested that the hearings brought television to the forefront of U.S. society. The Kefauver hearings capsuled television's future political era, with politicians posturing over concerns about the crime problem and the media exploiting a serious issue for ratings points and profits.

Some of the committee's colleagues in the Senate thought that the televised proceedings set a bad precedent, since they unfairly held witnesses up to public ridicule. One witness who would not allow his face to be shown claimed that television invoked the "fright factor" for those called to testify. The committee cited two witnesses who refused to appear on television at all for contempt of Congress. A federal judge later dismissed the contempt charge based on the improper use of the congressional hearing mandate. Kefauver wanted the public to pressure Congress to pass new laws regarding organized crime and understood that publicity through television would help achieve that objective. The Kefauver committee spent $315,000 to interview 800 witnesses and produced four reports that concluded that organized crime syndicates succeeded in part because of inaction or collusion with public officials. The committee also concluded that Chicago was the headquarters of an organized crime network that extended into other large cities. Kefauver authorized a ghost-written, best-selling book entitled *Crime in America*, summarizing the findings of the committee.

Although Kefauver did not invite television coverage of his Subcommittee on Interstate Crime hearings, his decision in 1952 to seek the Democratic presidential nomination fueled speculation that he had been motivated by a desire for media attention. If that was the case, he achieved his objective in some respects by defeating incumbent President Harry Truman in an early primary and forcing the president's withdrawal from the contest. Kefauver led the first two ballots at the Democratic convention in 1952 before losing to Illinois's Adlai Stevenson.

The nature of the Kefauver hearings was itself sensational, since it dealt with the extent of organized crime's influence on government at all levels. The high ratings for stations and networks no doubt surprised broadcast executives as well as the print media. The major revelations concerned graft in the Internal Revenue Service (IRS), which led the secretary of the treasury to demand resignations from several employees, including the commissioner of the IRS. More than two dozen IRS officials were implicated, along with an assistant attorney general. In 1952, the publicity stemming from the hearings forced President Truman to appoint a special prosecutor to pursue the links between crime bosses and federal employees.

Reference Moore, William Howard, *The Kefauver Committee and the Politics of Crime* (1974).

Kendall, Amos (1789–1869)

Perhaps the most important journalist in President Andrew Jackson's "kitchen cabinet," Amos Kendall edited a Kentucky newspaper as well as the Democratic Party organ in Washington. Kendall authored the famous "Kendall Report" authorizing the removal of federal funds from the national bank in 1833 and was named postmaster general by Jackson in 1835.

Born into a New England farming family, Amos Kendall had a slight physique that made him favor learning over manual labor. He graduated from Dartmouth College in New Hampshire in 1811 with a law degree and moved in 1814 to Kentucky, where he tutored the Henry Clay family. In 1816, Kentucky's Democratic-Republican Party leader Richard M. Johnson (vice president, 1837–1841) recruited Kendall to become editor of the party's weekly newspaper, the *Argus of Western America* (founded in 1808). Kendall editorialized against tax policies that burdened small farmer-debtors and in favor of public funding of schools. When

the legislature enacted debtor relief, Kendall railed against judicial efforts to overturn the law during the so-called relief war of 1823 to 1826.

Kendall was attracted to the leadership qualities of General Andrew Jackson during the War of 1812 and followed Jackson into politics. Jackson depended on Kendall to take his ideas and write them into articulate speeches. Angered by the failure of debtor relief in Kentucky, Kendall joined other journalists as leaders of the new Jacksonian Democratic Party after Jackson's bitter loss in the 1824 presidential election. The *Argus* lampooned Jackson's enemies President John Quincy Adams and Secretary of State Henry Clay, preparing for the 1828 election. After Jackson's election, Kendall was invited to Washington in 1829 to become an auditor in the Treasury Department.

Amos Kendall

An innovator throughout his career, Andrew Jackson rarely sought advice from his nominal cabinet officers. Instead, he created an unofficial body of advisers nicknamed the "kitchen cabinet" because of their deliberations in the kitchen of the White House. Most of the members of this group were journalists, including Kendall. Whenever

Jackson developed a policy position, he called on the kitchen cabinet for direction and for the proper wording of his ideas.

Until 1830, the editorial voice of the Jackson administration was the *United States Telegraph*, edited by Duff Green. When Green sided with John C. Calhoun in a dispute with the president, Jackson's backers launched the *Washington Globe* as the new conduit for the administration. Francis P. Blair, the editor who had succeeded Kendall at the *Argus*, was named editor of the *Globe*, and Kendall became a regular contributor.

In 1832, in order to embarrass Jackson, the new Whig Party forced a bill before Congress that would have rechartered the national bank. After his reelection, Jackson sought to effectively eliminate the bank by removing the federal funds, but the secretary of the treasury insisted that some provision be made to secure the funds when they were withdrawn. Jackson gave the task to Kendall, who issued the so-called Kendall Report in 1833, which directed the funds to selected state banks in cities where branches of the national bank were located. Jackson was criticized by the Whigs in the Senate for his actions, but the policy remained intact. Kendall served from 1835 to 1839 as postmaster general, directing the office with considerable efficiency. In addition to establishing a pony express service between New York City and Philadelphia (and eventually New Orleans), Kendall cooperated with slave interests trying to prevent dispersion of abolitionist literature through the mails.

After leaving his political appointment, Kendall continued to dabble in journalism. He served briefly as editor of the biweekly *Kendall's Expositor* in 1841 and edited the *Union Democrat* in 1842. Because of his interest in the news, Kendall became deeply involved in promoting the extension of the telegraph system across the nation during the 1840s. He was an investor and chief publicist for the Magnetic Telegraph Company, which utilized the talents of telegraph inventor Samuel F. B. Morse. The telegraph became an essential tool for disseminating news during the Mexican War

(1846–1848). Kendall was also engaged in various philanthropic causes; he founded the Columbia Institute for the Deaf and Dumb (later Gallaudet College) in Washington, D.C. He was awarded an honorary doctor of laws degree from his alma mater, Dartmouth, in 1849.

Reference Stickney, William, ed., *Autobiography of Amos Kendall* (1872).

Kennedy Assassination

The 1960s proved to be a violent decade in U.S. history, and nothing was more shocking than the assassination of President John F. Kennedy in 1963. The news media followed the aftermath of the assassination with considerable tenacity and curiosity, even after the government's Warren Commission provided authoritative answers. More than 30 years after the event, occasional media attention to unresolved questions about the assassination still engenders considerable public fascination.

President John F. Kennedy was personally popular and appealing because of his youth and vigor. Thus, it was especially shocking for Americans to learn of his assassination while riding in a Dallas motorcade on 22 November 1963. United Press International's Merriman Smith was in the presidential motorcade and radio-telephoned the report to the Dallas bureau four minutes after the shooting. ABC radio broke the story in New York six minutes after the first shots had been fired. Ten minutes after the shooting, Walter Cronkite interrupted a CBS television soap opera to announce the event. For the next four days, network television coverage continued almost without interruption, covering the president's funeral, the succession of Vice President Lyndon Johnson, and the investigation of the assassination. A national audience soon became international thanks to satellite relays.

Dallas police—anxious to abate an image of hostility toward the president and the press—offered free access to accused assassin Lee Harvey Oswald, who had been arrested the same day of the shooting. That situation made it easy for nightclub owner Jack Ruby to fatally shoot Oswald a few days later while Oswald was in police custody, as a live NBC television audience watched. The networks agreed to use pool coverage of the president's funeral the following Monday. Meanwhile, extensive investigations into Oswald's background were undertaken by the broadcast and print media. The networks carried no commercials from Friday through Monday to ensure continuous coverage, although some local stations did air commercials. Ratings showed that television viewer attention in New York City rose from 25 to 70 percent during the first hours after the assassination. An estimated 80 percent of potential viewers tuned in to watch the aftermath of the Oswald murder on Sunday. The president's funeral on Monday was watched by 93 percent of viewers, the highest level in the history of television. Certainly, television facilitated the national sense of mourning for the fallen president. It also helped create a legend surrounding a president whose record had been unimpressive before his assassination. The Kennedy presidency seemed all the more attractive in hindsight because it was followed by controversial and eventually unpopular presidents, Lyndon Johnson and Richard Nixon.

Months and years after the event, both broadcast and print media featured detailed studies of the assassination scenario. The Zapruder home movie film of the assassination scene was made available to television networks and was replayed hundreds of times. When the Warren Commission's official findings were announced, the media remained skeptical and continued investigating the assassination ad nauseam. In the 1970s, a special House of Representatives investigating committee held hearings about the Warren Commission Report. The House committee, covered extensively by the media, concluded that a conspiracy probably existed, but it could not determine the responsible parties.

Encircled by reporters, U.S. Attorney General Robert Kennedy looks at the rocking chair used by his brother, the late President John F. Kennedy.

Kennedy-Nixon Debates
See Presidential Debates.

Knight-Ridder, Incorporated
The international communications conglomerate Knight-Ridder, Inc., began in 1974 with the merger of two successful family-owned newspaper chains. By the 1990s, the company owned 30 daily newspapers and the *Journal of Commerce* and had also ventured into cable television, business information, and financial and news services. The publicly owned company was worth more than $2 billion in the early 1990s. It employed almost 25,000 people and had received 53 Pulitzer Prizes.

Herman Ridder (1851–1915) established a family-owned newspaper business in 1890, beginning with the daily German-language paper *New Yorker Staats.* The *Staats* was later merged with a competitor purchased by Ridder to become the *Staats-Zeitung.* Before World War I, it had the largest circulation among foreign language papers at 120,000, but it was sold at the beginning of World War II. Ridder also established Intertype, the first production company manufacturing linotypes in the United States prior to 1914.

Ridder's three sons—Bernard, Victor, and Joseph—gained ownership of several English-language publications after World War I, including the *New York Journal of Commerce* purchased in 1926, the *St. Paul Dispatch* and *Daily News*, the *Seattle Times*, and midsized papers in South Dakota, Minnesota, California, Indiana, Kansas, and Michigan. By the mid-1950s, the Ridder family owned 14 dailies in whole or in part. Brothers Herman H. Ridder and Bernard H. Ridder Jr. headed the company in the 1960s and 1970s. Educated at Princeton, Bernard Ridder Jr. served as an officer in the Inland Daily Press Association and Associated Press.

John S. Knight (1894–1981) began his newspaper career at the *Akron Beacon Journal*, which his father edited. Knight became editor and publisher of the paper after his father's death in 1933. In 1937, Knight purchased the *Miami Herald* and the *Miami Tribune* and merged the two. He added ownership of the *Detroit Free Press* in 1940. Knight was elected president of the American Society of Newspaper Editors in 1944, the same year he bought majority ownership in the *Chicago Daily News.* The *Daily News* was sold to Marshall Field IV in 1959 for $24 million, a record price at the time. In the 1970s, Knight chairman Lee Hills felt that the company needed a broader base than its Detroit-Miami-Philadelphia operations. The stage was set for a merger of the Ridder and Knight family newspapers.

By the time of the merger of the Ridder and Knight newspapers in 1974, both companies had been publicly owned since 1969. The newspaper division—with 35 dailies, 23 Sunday editions, about 4 million subscribers, and 18,000 employees—remained the primary revenue producer and included noteworthy papers such as the *Philadelphia Inquirer, Miami Herald, Charlotte Observer,* and *Detroit Free Press.* The company also owned several television broadcasting stations in New York and New Jersey until 1988, when they were sold. Knight-Ridder also operated a national news service, a commodity news service, and a business information service provided through its financial paper, the *Journal of Commerce.* The computerized Dialog database system purchased in 1988 and the company's Vu/Text computer retrieval service provided the largest news databank in the world to commercial subscribers. Knight-Ridder's annual revenues consistently hovered above the $1 billion mark.

Lee Hills of the Knight firm became the first chairman of Knight-Ridder, with Bernard Ridder Jr. serving as vice chairman. Another former Knight executive, Alvah Chapman, succeeded Hills as chairman in 1976. The company directors are elected by over 11,000 shareholders and operate from corporate headquarters in Miami. Currently, the chairman is James L. Knight, a son of John S. Knight. The president of the newspaper division, P. Anthony Ridder, is a grandson of Herman Ridder. The Knight-Ridder firm sells photographs and illustrations, in addition to news stories, to other media. Its foreign and financial bureaus operate in 23 nations and Hong Kong.

Reference Whited, Charles, *Knight: A Publisher in the Tumultuous Century* (1988).

Korean War

Because of the close proximity of the end of World War II and the outbreak of the Korean War, the media had considerable experience to draw on in covering the Asian conflict. Despite broadcast media inroads, the print media continued to lead war coverage; television was not a factor in this war. The Korean War produced special notice for correspondents Marguerite Higgins and Keyes Beech, as well as radio veteran Edward R. Murrow and photographer David Douglas Duncan. Government censorship was handled by the military commanders in the field rather than a government agency, but many conflicts resulted. American reporters often challenged the accuracy of United Nations press releases and showed alarm at Korean brutalities.

U.S. involvement in Korea began in 1945 with the joint occupation of the peninsula by the Soviet Union in the north and the United States in the south. The failure to unify resulted in two separate nations being created in 1948. Yet the onset of war in 1950 caught many by surprise, and the media had few personnel covering Korea. Walter Simmons of the *Chicago Tribune* accompanied Secretary of State John Foster Dulles on a trip to Seoul just before the North Korean invasion and remained to begin coverage. United Press correspondent Jack James had the privilege of alerting the nation's press to the North Korean invasion by wireless communication.

Media organizations responded promptly by dispatching sizable contingents to report the conflict. Eventually, over 200 journalists, representing several allied nations, arrived in Korea: about 100 daily newspaper reporters, 50 from magazines, 17 broadcasters, and 50 photographers. World War II veteran reporter Marguerite Higgins of the *New York Herald Tribune* arrived two days after the invasion. Joining

her was Keyes Beech of the *Chicago Daily News*, Burton Crane of the *New York Times*, and *Time* magazine's Frank Gibney. *Life*'s David Douglas Duncan had photographs of the early retreat in the first edition after the invasion began. In 1951, the Pulitzer Prize committee divided its reporting prize among several journalists: Higgins and Homer Bigart of the *Herald Tribune*, Beech and Fred Sparks of the *Daily News*, and Associated Press's Relman Morin and Don Whitehead. Broadcast coverage was still limited to radio and newsreels, with CBS veteran Edward R. Murrow again leading the coverage, as he had during World War II.

As the allied counteroffensive led by General Douglas MacArthur got under way, reporters joined the Inchon landings. Scripps-Howard reporter Jim Lucas, who covered the bloody battle for "Porkchop Hill" and the recapture of Seoul, won a 1954 Pulitzer for a story about the GIs' everyday lives. Associated Press photographer Max Desfor also received a Pulitzer for a photo of war refugees crossing a partially destroyed bridge. General MacArthur did not formally censor press coverage at first. After Associated Press reporter Tom Lambert and United Press correspondent Peter Kalischer filed stories without military review, MacArthur had their credentials revoked, beginning a period of strain between the military and reporters. The tensions were especially noteworthy after the Chinese intervention in late 1950. Photos by Duncan and stories by Beech enraged MacArthur, who instituted formal censorship. Reporters were not allowed to use terms such as "retreat" to describe allied movements. When President Harry Truman relieved MacArthur as commander, censorship regulations were relaxed, although some military officers refused to cooperate with the media and criticized their reports. The Defense Department eventually issued uniform censorship rules that were more reasonable.

The military paper *Stars and Stripes* began early publication from Tokyo but soon operated near the front lines. A *Stars and Stripes* reporter was killed during the second week of fighting. Eleven American correspondents died covering the Korean War, and several other non-U.S. journalists were killed as well. The communists refused to allow reporters to cover the peace negotiations at Panmunjom at first, but the United Nations diplomats insisted, and 20 correspondents were allowed to view the first of many peace discussions in 1951.

Labor Unions

The organization of workers in media businesses was a gradual process that did not emerge in the form of labor unions until the middle of the nineteenth century. From the first printers' strike in Philadelphia in 1786 to the founding of the first successful union—the National Typographical Union—in 1850, labor organizations experienced numerous vagaries. Labor's fortunes improved after the Civil War, and unions dominated the media workplace during the twentieth century.

The training of printer's devils (i.e., apprentices) under an apprenticeship system continued from colonial times into the early nineteenth century. A journeyman printer earned about $6 a week in the late eighteenth century, but the hours were long and the work difficult. Wages were the main cause of labor disputes in the eighteenth century. When employers attempted to reduce wages in Philadelphia in 1786, the printers organized and went on strike. They were able to restore their wage rate, but afterwards the organization dissolved. Some labor groups in New York City were able to negotiate a wage of $8 a week by the turn of the century.

During the early nineteenth century, several labor organizations existed, although they were mainly self-help groups and rarely entertained the idea of unionization. Because jobs for printers were numerous and the wages were adequate, there were few reasons for unionization. Furthermore, in addition to being publishers and editors, the proprietors of most small papers were essentially printers who labored alongside the apprentices and journeymen to get the paper into print. The first agitation for labor rights came with the publication of several labor newspapers in the late 1820s. The most important, the *Working Man's Advocate*, was printed in New York from 1829 to 1847 and attempted to raise workers' consciousness about their working conditions. The result of such agitation was the revival of labor unions. The Typographical Association in New York City was founded in 1831 and started to raise the issues of technology eliminating workers' jobs and child labor practices.

The first national printers' union was established in 1836 but foundered almost immediately in the Panic of 1837. Top wages were paid by New York City papers—$12 a week in the 1830s. Workers in other cities soon clamored for comparable wages, and printers' strikes became more numerous in the 1840s. The New York Printers' Union, founded in 1850, was the forerunner of the National (later International) Typographical Union launched in 1852; it enrolled 34 locals by 1860 and had 3,500 members. Prominent editors such as Horace Greeley and James Gordon Bennett applauded and supported the efforts of labor unions. After the Civil War, the Typographical Union obtained pledges from employers to train workers whenever new equipment was introduced. The International Typographical Union followed the lead of other unions in advocating an eight-hour workday, but that goal was not achieved until 1908, after a major strike in 1906 and in the face of opposition from the American Newspaper Publishers Association. During the 1890s, the International Typographical Union began to admit underpaid reporters into its organization.

During the New Deal era of the 1930s, labor rights were expanded. The Wagner Labor Relations Act of 1935 recognized the right of collective bargaining and stopped management from interfering with union activities. The Fair Labor Standards Act of 1938 established a minimum wage and maximum hours for workers. In 1933, several local guilds of reporters and copyreaders met in Washington, D.C., to organize the American Newspaper Guild, which proposed to protect the interests of professional writers in journalism. Nationally known columnist Heywood Broun was elected the first president of the guild. Gradually, the guild became involved in an increasing number of strikes due to failed contract negotiations. In 1936, the American Newspaper Guild joined the American

Federation of Labor (AFL), and its success helped the existing typographical unions improve their members' working conditions during the depression years. Another media guild, the National Federation of Telephone Workers, was established in 1939. Its name was changed in 1947 to the Communications Workers of America; that union also joined the AFL.

Although the main problem for media publications during World War II was a shortage of labor, immediately following the war, rising inflation caused unions to press for higher wages. In 1945 alone, the International Typographical Union supervised strikes at 30 daily newspapers. Strikes crippled newspaper publication for weeks to months at a time. In addition to wage demands, unions were concerned about the new offset technology employing "cold type," which required retraining of linotype operators. Despite the restrictions imposed on labor unions under the Taft-Hartley Act (1947), both the International Typographical Union and the American Newspaper Guild attracted record membership in the late 1940s and 1950s. The union had 782 locals with 100,000 members by 1960, and the guild's membership grew to 30,000 by 1958, partly because it allowed clerical workers to join after 1946. Although the unions' influence increased, so did the number of strikes idling newspapers, especially in the early 1960s. Telecommunications and broadcasting technologies produced additional labor organizations, including the International Brotherhood of Electrical Workers and the Communications Workers of America.

References Douglas, Sara, *Labor's New Voice: Unions and Mass Media* (1986); Leab, Daniel J., *A Union of Individuals: The Formation of the American Newspaper Guild, 1933–1936* (1970).

Ladies' Home Journal

Setting the standard for women's magazines in the late nineteenth century was Cyrus H. K. Curtis's *Ladies' Home Journal*. The *Journal* promoted the expansion of women's knowledge on subjects from pat-

ent medicines to venereal disease. It provided educational opportunities for women and promoted recognition of their contributions as wives and mothers.

Cyrus H. K. Curtis got an early start by publishing a newspaper in Boston at age 13. He had learned all aspects of the publishing business by the time he founded *The Tribune and Farmer*—a four-page weekly aimed at farmers—in Philadelphia in 1879. Curtis persuaded his wife, Louisa May Knapp, to edit a women's section for the *Tribune*. That women's section led to Curtis's launching of the *Ladies' Journal and Practical Housekeeper*, an eight-page weekly featuring articles on domestic matters, in 1883. Mrs. Curtis became the editor of the *Journal*. By the end of the first year, the *Ladies' Home Journal*, as it was soon called, had a circulation of 25,000, and Curtis sold his interest in *The Tribune and Farmer* in order to concentrate on the *Journal*.

Curtis was able to obtain considerable advertising, and he provided group subscriptions for women's clubs to attract readers. He sought talented contributors; among the earliest was Louisa May Alcott. Circulation grew to 100,000 by the end of the second year of publication and to 700,000 by 1889. Increased readership allowed Curtis to raise the subscription price, eventually to a dollar a year or ten cents per monthly issue. The *Journal* quickly eclipsed its main competition, *Godey's Lady's Book*, which ended publication in 1892.

When Mrs. Curtis asked to be relieved from editorial duties in 1889, Curtis hired Edward Bok, an employee of Charles Scribner's Sons, to be the *Journal*'s editor. Bok began a tradition of reader surveys to find out what they wanted to see in the *Journal*. One of the innovations that resulted from the surveys was Bok assuming the pseudonym "Ruth Ashmore" in a regular column of advice to young women who wrote inquiries to the magazine. Under Bok, *Ladies' Home Journal* became the first magazine to feature a different cover illustration for each issue as well as other illustrations inside. It was the first magazine to use four-color printing and expanded its length to 48 pages in its fifteenth year. Serials, essays, and verse by authors such as William Dean Howells, Mark Twain, Eugene Field, Sarah Orne Jewett, Kate Douglas Wiggin, and James Whitcomb Riley were published in the *Journal*. It attracted equally well-known illustrators, including Charles Dana Gibson. The *Journal* also prided itself on its true-life stories, such as a series of reflections by the daughters of Charles Dickens, Nathaniel Hawthorne, Horace Greeley, and William Dean Howells.

The *Ladies' Home Journal* helped reshape the image of women around the domestic framework of the home. Women were the moral inspirations for their families as wives, mothers, and daughters. The *Journal* helped promote women's interest in beauty and fashion, home decoration, sewing, and cooking. It maintained a working kitchen to test each recipe before it was printed. In 1895, the *Journal* began to publish house plans with simple and practical designs, which speeded the demise of the Victorian house. The *Journal*'s house made extensive changes, including built-in cabinets in the kitchen, practical furniture, and even wall pictures. Bok also launched a campaign to spruce up neighborhoods through the planting of flowers and shrubs and the removal of billboards in residential areas.

Ladies' Home Journal actually began the muckraking reform era in journalism in 1892 by banning patent medicine advertising. Other publications quickly followed its lead. Bok used the *Journal* after 1904 to assail the patent medicine industry by listing the ingredients of 22 potions. The magazine hired Mark Sullivan to expand the exposé into adulterated foods. President Theodore Roosevelt was so inspired by the *Journal*'s investigations that he recommended the Pure Food and Drug Act of 1906, which allowed the government to set standards for production and established regular inspections of manufacturing facilities.

Beginning in 1909, editor Bok took on the Paris fashion designers by launching a series of women's clothing designs in the *Journal*. Generally, Bok favored an attractive but restrained look for women's clothes.

He invited readers to submit suggestions and created a committee of designers to develop a new fashion line. The campaign to undercut Paris fashions failed, however, as did another cause to stop women from wearing the feathers of the egret bird.

Cyrus H. K. Curtis first published the Ladies' Journal and Practical Housekeeper *in 1883. By seeking talented contributors, Curtis boosted its circulation to 700,000 within six years.*

Bok's most controversial effort was to eliminate venereal disease. He was influenced by an editor of a Christian journal, Lyman Abbott, to begin the publicity. Curtis left the decision to Bok, and after his first editorial on the subject in 1906, readers began to cancel subscriptions. Despite losing 75,000 regular readers, the *Journal* continued with the topic, including articles by personalities such as Jane Addams, the president of Harvard, and the bishop of London. Among other information revealed in the articles was that 70 percent of surgery on women concerned venereal diseases.

After Edward Bok's resignation as editor in 1919, the *Journal*'s circulation grew more slowly to 3 million by 1928. It languished in the early 1930s until Bruce and Beatrice Gould became coeditors in 1935. In addition to traditional subjects of interest to women, the new editors broadened the magazine's coverage to include articles on foreign affairs, science, education, and politics. The *Journal* also featured serialized fiction and biographies of prominent women. Whenever something new emerged, such as diets, the *Journal* was always on the cutting edge of its publicity.

By the time the Goulds resigned as editors in 1962, *Ladies' Home Journal* was losing ground to other women's magazines such as *McCall's*. Advertising also slipped in the face of competition from television as well as other magazines. The Curtis Publishing Company tried to cut costs by reducing the size of the *Journal* but finally sold it to Downe Communications, Inc., in 1968 for more than $5 million. Even with its slippage since the early 1960s, the *Journal*'s circulation in 1991 was more than 5 million—80 percent from subscriptions—which ranked it eleventh among periodical publications. It was only nineteenth in the ranking of advertising revenues, however, with just under $77 million. Donna Galotti became editor in 1991.

Reference Bok, Edward W., *The Americanization of Edward Bok* (1920).

Lawrence, David
See U.S. News & World Report.

Life
Following the success of illustrated magazines in the nineteenth century, Henry R. Luce made *Life* the premier pictorial newsmagazine of the twentieth century. It combined information with entertainment to reach one-fourth of the adult population before meeting its match in television.

Henry R. Luce began his periodical ventures with *Time* in 1923 and soon recognized the potential of a new type of illustrated magazine using photographs instead

of engravings. The new technology relied on the rotogravure printing press and Leica portable camera, both of which had been invented in Germany and imported into the United States before World War I. The preparation for the first issue of *Life* was deliberate and followed the methods used by the German photomagazine *BIZ*. The first printing of *Life* in November 1936 produced 466,000 copies, about twice the number of subscriptions. Within four months, *Life*'s printing run numbered over a million. Luce underestimated the costs of the new magazine, and it lost about $3 million a year until 1939, when it began making a profit.

Luce intended *Life* to provide information in a picture-dominated format for both news and entertainment. The reading audience sought by Luce included the younger generation, educated Americans, and those engaged in participatory sports and recreation. *Life* sought attention through sensational, albeit realistic, photography of glamorous people, acts of violence, natural disasters, and even a daring 1938 photoessay on childbirth.

Life's editors sought to keep readers abreast of new scientific technology and medical information as well as business and industry. It did not ignore art and employed almost as many artists as photographers. Occasionally, the editors concentrated on the past as well as the present in articles dealing with the Renaissance or the Middle Ages. Over its history, *Life* gradually reduced the number of photos and increased the amount of text. More book abstracts and serials as well as literary essays began to appear. Special issues such as the half-century retrospective in 1950 were also part of *Life*'s stock.

Life's photographers were more famous than its editors. Initially, Luce contracted with the Black Star Picture Agency, headed by Ernest Mayer, to supply most of the photos for *Life*. Eventually, many agency photographers became staff photographers. Among the original staff photographers were Margaret Bourke-White and Robert Capa. During World War II, *Life* photos allowed the public to follow events. The war helped raise circulation to 4 million in the

United States and more than 300,000 overseas. Natural photography, including outer space in the 1960s, was another important attraction for *Life*'s readers. The increased emphasis on text allowed more in-depth reporting on subjects such as organized crime and the decline of the railroads.

In 1950, *Life* was reaching 20 percent of American readers; by 1961, the number had risen to 25 percent of households, with a 7 million circulation. Rising circulation numbers in the 1950s and 1960s were often misleading about the financial health of magazines, however. *Life* was not exempt from rising production costs and lower advertising income as a result of competition from television. In fact, it was especially vulnerable to television, since both relied on visual images for their impact. Clearly, television had advantages over still photography, especially in the realm of entertainment. Luce retired as editor of *Life* in 1964 and was replaced by Hedley Donovan. Circulation declined from 8.5 million in 1970 to 5.5 million in 1972, and the corporation decided to drop *Life*. It was revived again as a monthly in 1978, but it never achieved the stature or profitability of the original. Circulation in 1992 was only 1.5 million.

Reference Wainwright, Loudon, *The Great American Magazine: An Inside History of* Life (1986).

Linotype
See Printing Press.

Lippmann, Walter (1889–1974)

Epitomizing the thoughtful commentator, Walter Lippmann became the conscience of American journalism through his syndicated columns and his monograph called *Public Opinion*. Lippmann's early training came at the liberal journal the *New Republic* during World War I. He wrote for and edited Pulitzer's *New York World* beginning in 1922. Lippmann's political column "Today and Tomorrow," concentrating on international matters, appeared in the *New York Herald Tribune* in 1931 and became

syndicated in 165 papers by the outbreak of World War II. Lippmann won a Pulitzer Prize at the *Herald Tribune* in 1962.

Born into a well-to-do New York City family of German Jewish extraction, Walter Lippmann was not close to his parents and sought heroes among the rich and famous in an age of unbridled capitalism and yellow journalism. He had the advantage of private schooling and tours through Europe, and when Lippmann entered Harvard College in 1906, he was already determined to become an art historian. Stimulated by the exciting atmosphere at Harvard, Lippmann soon fancied himself a Fabian socialist, sensitive to society's inequities. Lippmann's class included future radical socialist journalist John Reed, future radio commentator Hans Van Kaltenborn, poet T. S. Eliot, and future colleague Heywood Broun. Lippmann wrote boldly for student publications such as the *Harvard Monthly* and gained the congratulations of psychology professor William James. Much of Lippmann's freethinking philosophical bent he derived from philosophy professor George Santayana.

During a lecture, visiting Fabian socialist Graham Wallas questioned human motivations and whether citizens could make rational political judgments, causing Lippmann to become skeptical of his own idealism. Upon leaving Harvard in 1910, Lippmann signed on with Ralph Albertson's *Boston Common*, a Progressive paper that promoted government ownership of utilities and railroads. After only a few months, Lippmann persuaded the famous muckraker Lincoln Steffens to hire him to write for *Everybody's* magazine. He also contributed occasional pieces to the socialist-anarchist journal *The Masses*, edited by Harvard classmate John Reed. Lippmann left *Everybody's* in 1911 to become a speechwriter for the socialist mayor of Schenectady, New York, George Lunn. Impatient with Lunn's reform schedule, Lippmann criticized him in the socialist weekly *Call*. His departure from Lunn's staff was followed by the writing of a short treatise, *A Preface to Politics*, which applied Freud's personality theories to politics.

Herbert Croly invited Lippmann to join

the inaugural publication of the liberal weekly the *New Republic* in 1914. Soon Lippmann was in England debating socialist philosophy with Beatrice and Sidney Webb, George Bernard Shaw, and other Fabian socialist founders. When World War I broke out, Lippmann, in characteristic Fabian language, opposed U.S. participation in an imperialist venture. Nonetheless, by the time the United States entered the war in 1917, Lippmann had changed his position and favored the U.S. commitment to promote Woodrow Wilson's ideals. Lippmann took a leave of absence from the *New Republic* to assist Secretary of War Newton Baker, but he criticized George Creel's suppression of free expression through the Committee on Public Information. Lippmann helped Wilson draft the Fourteen Points peace plan that was later debated at the Paris peace conference in 1919. Suspicious of the League of Nations proposal, Lippmann fought against it and President Wilson's sponsorship.

In 1919, Lippmann returned to the *New Republic*, but disagreements with the magazine's Anglophobic Francis Hackett caused him to leave in 1922. *New York World* editor Herbert Bayard Swope hired Lippmann to take charge of the editorial page; he became executive editor in 1929. On three separate occasions in the 1920s, Lippmann refused to allow himself to be nominated for a Pulitzer Prize. Lippmann also wrote three books in the 1920s: *Public Opinion* (1922), *The Phantom Public* (1925), and *A Preface to Morals* (1929). In his most important work, *Public Opinion*, Lippmann abandoned the notion that an informed electorate could make rational political decisions because government and the media distort the facts. Upon the sale of the *World* in 1931 and its merger into the Scripps-Howard *Telegram*, Lippmann got an offer from the *Herald Tribune* to be a columnist.

Lippmann's column "Today and Tomorrow" was launched at the *Herald Tribune* in 1931, and he gained a national audience through syndication in over a hundred papers after one year. By 1937, Lippmann was read in 155 dailies. He published the column four times a week initially, then cut back to three times in 1934 and twice a week in 1955. Lippmann's newly won fame coincided with a softening of his radical views. His writing exuded a stronger conservative tone beginning in the 1930s. Lippmann's *The Good Society*, published in 1937, assailed the economic planning of collectivism, which was central to New Deal programs. Yet Lippmann still argued the merits of genuine liberal social reform. He criticized the U.S. tactics of using the United Nations as a tool in the Cold War strategy. The Pulitzer Prize committee awarded Lippmann a special citation in 1958 for his service to journalism. Lippmann became the confidant of many politicians—from senators to secretaries of state and presidents. In 1961, he warned President John Kennedy about the dangers of tinkering in Indochina.

The last part of Lippmann's career was spent writing for Philip Graham's *Washington Post* and *Newsweek*. Under a 1962 deal, he was obligated to write two columns a week for the *Post* and 16 articles a year for *Newsweek*, for which he would be paid $1 million over ten years. Lippmann persuaded Graham's widow Katherine to change the *Post*'s editorial position to oppose Lyndon Johnson's Vietnam policy. An interview with the Soviet Union's Nikita Khrushchev in 1962 brought Lippmann a Pulitzer Prize for international reporting. In a 1965 speech to the International Press Institute in London, Lippmann both praised the media's intellectual maturity and warned of the temptation to abuse their power.

Reference Steel, Ronald, *Walter Lippmann and the American Century* (1980).

Literary Digest

Founded by the publishing firm of Funk and Wagnalls in 1890, the *Literary Digest* was intended to provide information to educators. Gradually, it became more involved in reporting and commenting on the news. Under publisher Robert Cuddihy, the *Digest* gained a wide circulation, advertising volume second only to that of the *Saturday Evening Post*, and a national reputation. The magazine's straw polls proved influential until the disastrous prediction of the 1936 election.

Isaac K. Funk and Adam W. Wagnalls, both former Lutheran pastors, became partners in 1878 in a book publishing company in New York City. They conceived of and launched the *Literary Digest* in 1890 as a reference source summarizing periodical literature. The editors reprinted excerpts from the nation's newspapers and magazines on current issues. Funk and Wagnalls were especially determined to present both sides of issues. The categories in the *Digest* included current events, foreign news, science and technology, literature and the arts, religion, and finance. Initially, the *Digest* did not take an editorial position on the issues. Due to its nonpartisan approach, the *Digest* became a popular resource in school courses in literature, civics, debate, and history.

Beginning in 1905, the *Literary Digest* included general news coverage and editorial comment. The change occurred when Robert J. Cuddihy became the majority stockholder and named William Seaver Woods as editor, a post he held until 1933. Publisher Cuddihy and editor Woods solicited subscriptions from names in telephone books and boosted both circulation and profits. Just before the United States' entry into World War I in 1917, circulation neared the 700,000 mark. The greatest innovation under the new ownership was presidential straw polls beginning in the 1920 election between Democrat James M. Cox and Republican Warren G. Harding. When the poll accurately predicted Harding's sweeping victory, the *Digest*'s reputation and circulation benefited.

By 1920, the *Literary Digest* had the second highest gross revenues among U.S. magazines, trailing only the *Saturday Evening Post*. Circulation hit the 2 million mark in 1920. That year was the magazine's highwater mark, for despite its accurate poll in the 1924 presidential election, revenues fell by 40 percent in 1925. *Literary Digest* purchased ownership of *Current Opinion* magazine in 1925, but circulation continued its decline to less than a million in 1933. Arthur Draper succeeded Woods as editor in 1933 and made some changes in the magazine's format, including new typeface, and implemented some subscription gimmicks. Still, the circulation declined to 686,000 in 1936. Draper resigned in 1935 and was succeeded by Morton Savell and then Wilfred Funk, son of one founder.

The magazine's poor financial health was already taking its toll when the 1936 poll incorrectly predicted a close victory for Republican Alfred Landon over incumbent Democrat Franklin D. Roosevelt. The 1936 poll had relied on the magazine's 1932 mailing list to cut costs. The publishers let the industry know that the magazine was for sale, and rumors flew about potential purchasers, including William Randolph Hearst. Albert Shaw, publisher of *Review of Reviews*, bought the *Literary Digest* in July 1936 for $200,000. The two journals were merged into a single publication known as *The Digest*, whose format included a summary of the week's news, a photographic portfolio, a review of new books, and excerpts from important magazines. The initial printing of 600,000 copies was not sustained by its reception. *The Digest* was sold in November 1937 to George Havell for the same price Shaw had paid the previous year. Havell reissued the magazine as the *Literary Digest*, but it lasted only six months. It was bought by Henry Luce's magazine empire and terminated.

Look

Soon after the publication of Henry Luce's *Life*, the Cowles family produced the second major magazine of picture journalism in 1937. The purpose of *Look* was clearly to entertain more than to inform, and the market responded positively. Only with wider availability of television in the 1960s did *Look* and *Life* lose their niche.

Gardner and John Cowles, publishers of the *Des Moines Register* and the *Minneapolis Star*, set out to emulate Henry Luce's new pictorial magazine *Life*. The first issue of

Look was published in January 1937, just two months after *Life*'s inaugural issue. *Look*'s first editor, Daniel D. Mich, and his successor, William B. Arthur, were able to overcome *Life*'s head start and production quality. *Look* used the rotogravure photographic reproduction method; it had been introduced in the United States in 1914 and was widely used by U.S. newspapers by the 1930s. The editors pledged to cater to readers' broad interests, including world affairs, sports and recreation, beauty, science, and education. But from the beginning, *Look*'s emphasis was on celebrities. Published monthly at first, *Look* went to a fortnightly schedule after the first four issues. The Cowles family moved the operations of *Look* from Des Moines to New York City in 1940.

The editors of *Look* sought sensational rather than merely informative topics. Indeed, an early editor admitted that *Look* sought the subjective, whereas *Life* strove for an objective approach to its subject matter. Still, *Look* was able to recruit well-known figures to contribute articles, including political leaders such as Adlai Stevenson and Thomas Dewey, journalists John Gunther and Walter Lippmann, and writers Robert Sherwood and Ernest Hemingway. By the 1960s, *Look* was on a par with *Life* in virtually every area—from circulation to quality of pictures and writing. Gradually, *Look* gave more space to print and less to photographs, although its basic nature changed very little over the years.

Look ran detailed features in the 1960s on the assassination of Senator Robert Kennedy, the Central Intelligence Agency, Castro's Cuba, the Catholic Church, and rural poverty in the South. It retained the best writers—from political investigative reporter Theodore H. White to sociologist Julian Huxley to Reverend Norman Vincent Peale, who responded to readers' questions in a regular column. *Look* began a trend of catering to the younger generation in the 1960s, in its advertising as well as its content.

Look's circulation numbers were always impressive. By the end of World War II,

circulation reached 2 million; ten years later, it doubled. By the end of the 1960s, circulation doubled again to about 8 million—fourth among U.S. magazines. But sales alone could not keep the magazine afloat. *Look*'s advertising revenue dropped 5 percent in 1967 and another 2 percent in 1969. Rising production costs combined with television's appeal to advertisers were the main factors leading to the termination of *Look* in 1971 and *Life* in 1972.

Los Angeles Times
Although it did not reach prominence until many decades after its founding in 1881, the *Los Angeles Times* eventually achieved its place as the third best newspaper in the United States. Its history before World War I was dominated by Harrison Gray Otis and afterwards by the Chandler family. Otis chartered the Times Mirror Company in 1884; a century later, it was the sixth largest multimedia conglomerate in the United States, with $3 billion in revenues. Among national dailies in 1989, the *Times* ranked fourth in circulation, with 1.1 million readers.

Thomas Gardiner and Nathan Cole launched the *Los Angeles Times* in 1881 as a four-page penny daily, but they lost their investment in the first month. Their creditors assumed control and recruited Harrison Gray Otis as editor and one-fourth owner in 1882. An Ohio native, Otis had learned the newspaper craft in Louisville before moving to Santa Barbara to found the *Daily Press* in 1876. Upon assuming command at the *Times*, Otis increased the space for telegraph news and letters to the editor. He also convinced his partners to incorporate the Times Mirror Company in 1884. Harry Chandler was employed as circulation manager, rose to become business manager, and married Otis's daughter. The *Times* assumed a partisan Republican editorial position and was anti-union and pro-business, although it fought the railroad monopolies. The *Times* vigorously opposed Hiram Johnson, California's Progressive governor.

When Otis died in 1917, his son-in-law

Chandler took over as publisher. The *Times* began to thrive after World War I because the real estate boom brought enormous advertising revenues to the paper. Chandler became Los Angeles's chief promoter, encouraging growth of the movie industry and the construction of a massive 240-mile water aqueduct. He helped found the California Institute of Technology in 1920. Chandler also proved instrumental in obtaining New Deal monies to build the Hollywood Bowl and convinced the railroads to build a centralized Union Station in 1939. As the population of Los Angeles grew through World War II, the *Times* was one of many beneficiaries.

Harry Chandler's son Norman became publisher in 1944. Norman Chandler launched the experimental *Mirror* in 1948, an evening tabloid with a growing circulation until it was suspended in 1962 due to rising costs. Chandler employed several talented managing editors during his tenure: J. Edward Murray, Loyal Hotchkiss, and Nick Williams (1958–1971). Otis Chandler succeeded his father as publisher in 1960 and became the most aggressive of the *Times*'s leaders. Otis Chandler sought to hire the most talented reporters and writers. Because of skepticism about Republican Party nominees Richard Nixon and Barry Goldwater, Chandler announced in 1973 that the *Times* would no longer make presidential endorsements. When Hearst's *Examiner* closed in 1962, it left the *Times* as the only morning Los Angeles daily.

After Chandler failed to persuade talented Washington bureau chief Robert Donovan to become managing editor in 1971, he named city editor William Thomas to the position. Thomas had led the *Times*'s reporting of the Watts riots in 1965, which earned the paper a Pulitzer Prize in 1966. In 1988, the *Times* maintained 25 correspondents overseas, second only to the *New York Times*. By the 1980s, the *Los Angeles Times* was rated the third best daily in the nation behind the *New York Times* and *Washington Post*. In 1989, the *Times* had the fourth largest daily circulation in the United States at more than 1.1 million, with $1 billion in advertising and $3 billion in revenues. The *Times* operated 36 news bureaus—22 overseas—and it launched the bilingual *Nuestro Tiempo* in 1989, serving 420,000 Spanish-speaking residents in the Los Angeles area.

Meanwhile, the Times Mirror Company became a multimedia conglomerate; it concentrated on newspapers but also included magazines and broadcast properties. The *Times* began its first broadcasting operations under Harry Chandler in 1922 with radio station KHJ. In the mid-1980s, the company sold some of its less competitive newspaper properties such as the *Dallas Times Herald* and the *Denver Post*; it also acquired new papers such as the *Baltimore Sun*. William Thomas served as editor in the late 1980s, and Shelby Coffey III since 1990; Richard Schlosberg became chief executive officer of Times Mirror in the 1990s. By 1994, circulation had eroded slightly from the highs of the late 1980s.

Reference Berges, Marshall, *The Life and Times of Los Angeles: A Newspaper, a Family and a City* (1984).

Louisville Courier-Journal

Founded in 1831 by George Prentice, the *Louisville Journal* merged in 1868 with Walter Haldeman's *Courier*. The *Courier-Journal* came to national attention between 1868 and 1919 under the editorship of Henry Watterson. Aristocratic by nature, Watterson led the *Courier-Journal* to prominence for its authoritative reporting and respected editorials. The Bingham family bought the *Courier-Journal* and the afternoon *Times* in 1917 and operated the papers successfully until their sale to the Gannett Company in 1986.

George Prentice, the *Louisville Journal*'s founder, was a former Connecticut journalist. The paper quickly embraced the new Whig Party, which had a large western following. Because of Prentice's spry aphorisms and political commentary, the *Journal*'s editorial page was widely quoted and reprinted by other Whig papers. As the clouds of sectional conflict darkened in the 1850s, Prentice turned to the Democratic

Party upon the failure of the Whigs. He criticized the Republicans and their 1860 presidential candidate Abraham Lincoln. Yet Prentice was opposed to secession as a remedy to the southern plight. He led the successful fight in the *Journal* to keep Kentucky part of the Union. Still, Prentice's two sons served in the Confederate army during the Civil War.

The *Louisville Courier*, edited by Walter Haldeman at the outbreak of the Civil War, had been a strong advocate of secession. Haldeman joined the Confederate army when the federal government ordered his paper closed in late 1861. He returned after the war to reopen the *Courier* and also purchased the *Louisville Democrat* in 1868. That same year, Haldeman bought the *Journal* from Prentice and formed the morning daily *Courier-Journal*. Haldeman obtained the services of *Journal* editor Henry Watterson, an experienced journalist who had worked for Charles Dana and Horace Greeley in New York City before the Civil War. Watterson had also worked with several pro-Confederate papers in Chattanooga and Atlanta as well as serving as editor of *The Rebel*, a Confederate army journal. After the war, Watterson accepted the editorship of the *Cincinnati Times* but missed his southern roots and worked briefly at the *Nashville Banner* before becoming editor of the *Louisville Journal* in 1867.

Watterson actually brought Haldeman and Prentice together in 1868 for the merger of the *Courier-Journal*. He became its editor at age 28 and also bought one-third ownership. Despite his Confederate sympathies, Watterson admired Lincoln and supported the president's plan for Reconstruction of the South. When the Radical Republicans seized the initiative in Reconstruction, Watterson became a critic of their punitive measures. At the same time, Watterson did not hesitate to favor suffrage rights for the freedmen and condemn Ku Klux Klan violence.

In the 1872 presidential election, Watterson's *Courier-Journal* followed other Democratic papers in endorsing Horace Greeley's Liberal Republican candidacy. The *Courier-Journal* held presidents, including Democrats like Grover Cleveland, to a high standard of accountability. Watterson's most consistent political principle was free trade. The paper bolted from the Democrats in 1896 when they nominated William Jennings Bryan. Watterson was a sound money man and feared the consequences of the free silver movement. The decision to oppose Bryan proved costly to the *Courier-Journal*'s circulation, but it recovered most of the losses by 1900, when the paper endorsed Bryan's second nomination. Watterson showed little enthusiasm for the Progressive movement, opposing Theodore Roosevelt and William Howard Taft and offering only lukewarm support for Democrat Woodrow Wilson. Although Watterson had grave doubts about German intentions, he counseled U.S. restraint toward involvement in World War I. Once the United States entered the war, however, Watterson unleashed patriotic rhetoric urging the defeat of Germany. Two of those editorials were the basis of Watterson's winning the Pulitzer Prize for editorials in 1918.

Watterson's national fame resulted from his stimulating editorials, which were widely reprinted, but the *Courier-Journal* paid most attention to state and local matters. The weekly edition had more readers than any other southern newspaper until the *Atlanta Constitution* surpassed it in 1887. The daily edition ran a close second in southern daily circulation to the *New Orleans Picayune* through the 1880s. Watterson was no friend of the yellow press and avoided sensational headlines or news stories in the 1890s.

Watterson's decision to retire was affected by the *Courier-Journal*'s sale in 1917 to Judge Robert W. Bingham. The new owner also bought the afternoon *Louisville Times* and maintained publication as a complement to the morning *Courier-Journal*. The fact that Bingham approved of U.S. membership in the League of Nations, whereas Watterson opposed such action, led to the editor's decision to retire in 1919 and sell his shares to

Bingham. Bingham provided sound management to both papers until his death in 1937. He also started radio station WHAS in the 1920s. *Courier-Journal* reporter William B. Miller won a 1926 Pulitzer Prize for reporting on his own efforts to save the life of a cave explorer. Barry Bingham succeeded his father but made Mark Ethridge publisher and gave over the editorial duties to Herbert Agar in 1939.

By the 1950s, Russell Briney and George Burt handled the editorial pages at the *Courier-Journal* and the *Times*, respectively. The papers continued to be Democratic partisans but expanded their coverage of national and international affairs. Support of civic improvements in the fine arts and education as well as sympathy for labor rights and civil rights also found expression in the two papers. Barry Bingham Jr. succeeded his father as editor and publisher of both papers in 1971. Circulation continued to increase at the *Courier-Journal*, from 220,000 in 1963 to 325,000 in 1983, but it gradually declined at the *Times*.

In 1974, Carol Reeves became the *Courier-Journal*'s managing editor—the first woman in the nation to hold that position. The *Courier-Journal* received a public service Pulitzer Prize in 1967 for a campaign to regulate strip mining. Reporter John Fetterman won a Pulitzer in 1969 for coverage of a local Vietnam War hero's death and burial. Polls in the early 1960s rated the *Courier-Journal* in the top eight among national daily newspapers, and another in 1970 ranked it in the top five. Internal disagreements in the Bingham family resulted in the sale of the *Courier-Journal* and *Times* to the Gannett Company in 1986 for $315 million. In 1989, editor Michael Gartner was succeeded by David Hawpe.

Reference Wall, Joseph F., *Henry Watterson: Reconstructed Rebel* (1956).

Luce, Henry Robinson (1898–1967)

Likened to a press lord by some, Henry R. Luce became the most successful magazine publisher in the twentieth century. His magazines—*Time, Life, Fortune,* and *Sports Illustrated*—used cutting-edge innovations and reporting to dramatize the development of U.S. government, society, personality cults, and big business. Luce also influenced U.S. media through his radio and newsreel productions of the "March of Time."

Native Pennsylvanian Henry Winters Luce became a Presbyterian minister after attending Union Theological Seminary and Princeton. He married a New York native, Elizabeth Root, just prior to traveling to China as a teaching missionary in 1898. The couple's first child, Henry Robinson Luce, was born in China during their first year of residence. Growing up in China, the young Luce showed a keen interest in education and patriotism. He also evidenced an early fascination with journalism and eventually decided to pursue it as a vocation. At age 15, Luce was sent to the Hotchkiss School in Connecticut, where he edited a literary monthly. He also worked for a Springfield, Massachusetts, newspaper the summer before entering Yale, where he wrote for the student newspaper.

Influenced by Theodore Roosevelt's staunch patriotism, Luce joined the army in 1918 after the United States entered World War I. Luce never saw action in Europe and returned to Yale at the end of 1918. Upon graduation from Yale, in a 1920 class that included Thornton Wilder and Stephen Vincent Benét, Luce traveled to England to study history at Oxford for one year. In 1921, Luce's benefactor, the McCormick family, obtained a reporter's post for him at the *Chicago Daily News*. Unhappy with the overly serious, structured system at the paper, Luce retreated to Baltimore to join his longtime friend Briton Hadden on the *Baltimore News*. The two planned a weekly news journal for a national audience that would treat news as stories, in the tradition of the nineteenth-century *Niles' Weekly Register*.

Luce and Hadden launched *Time* magazine as a weekly summary of news in 1923, seeking to restore the "idea of progress" shattered by World War I. Politically, Luce and Hadden reflected the progressive, entrepreneurial, Republican views of Herbert Hoover. Journalistically, the editors of

Time mimicked the philosophy of Walter Lippmann. They aimed for an audience of young, college-educated males who would be typical readers of the *New York Times*, distinguished from subscribers to the *Literary Digest*. The first issue of *Time* in February 1923 was composed of 30 pages featuring categories such as national affairs, education, and religion. First-year subscriptions totaled 20,000, and the magazine suffered modest financial losses before posting a profit in its second year.

By 1925, *Time*'s circulation surpassed that of H. L. Mencken's popular *American Mercury*. Strangely, Luce decided to move the magazine's operations from New York City to Cleveland in 1925, only to discover the inadequacies there; he returned to New York in 1927. After Hadden's death in 1929, Luce bought his partner's stock and began to move *Time* into the business of reporting the news as well as summarizing it. Luce required strict coordination among the reporting staff so that the writing appeared to be by one person. In addition to treating news as stories, *Time* always focused on the role of individuals, which proved attractive to its readers. Circulation increased from 100,000 in 1925 to 300,000 by 1930, with growth mainly among the middle class. By the 1930s, *Time* was being imitated as well as quoted in all the major media outlets.

Profits from *Time* allowed Luce to pursue his true passion in publishing, *Fortune*, which was launched in February 1930 as a stylish magazine of U.S. business. Rather than dissuading him, the depression made Luce even more determined to trumpet the virtues of U.S. capitalism and new management techniques in his publication. Unlike *Time*, *Fortune*'s articles were fewer and consisted of more detailed explorations. Luce utilized expensive production processes, including lavish illustrations. Despite the price of $1 a copy, circulation increased from 34,000 in 1930 to 96,000 in 1934. Luce recruited high-quality staffers, including photographer Margaret Bourke-White, essayist Archibald MacLeish, and editor Ralph Ingersoll.

Although Luce did not conceive of the "March of Time" radio and newsreel series, he supported its production, since it was originally designed to promote his newsmagazine. The radio program was launched in 1931 on the Columbia Broadcasting System network, and the newsreel feature followed in 1935. The "March of Time" focus was on personalities; actors portrayed contemporary newsmakers such as Roosevelt, Hitler, and Mussolini. Despite Luce's reservations, the radio program continued until 1945. The newsreel version was awarded an Oscar by the Academy of Motion Picture Arts and Sciences in 1937.

Life magazine was another Luce venture that exploited new technologies, especially a new portable German camera called the Leica. In 1934, Luce found himself persuaded by Daniel Longwell to consider a photographic newsmagazine that would feature a higher grade of paper than that used by newspapers or other magazines. His second wife, Clare Boothe Brokaw, convinced Luce to pursue the new venture in 1935. The initial issue of *Life* in November 1936 sold 435,000 copies. Within four months, the circulation rose to over 1 million, so fast that production was unable to keep copies on the newsstands. But the depression's impact on advertising revenue led to financial losses in the late 1930s. The subjects of *Life*'s famous photo-essays were determined by the photographers as much as by the editors.

The Luces became more political in the 1940s. Henry Luce favored U.S. support of Britain against Germany in 1940 and worked hard for Republican Wendell Willkie's presidential campaign. His wife Clare was elected to Congress from Connecticut in 1942 and reelected in 1944. Both Luces worked on behalf of Dwight Eisenhower's presidential campaign in 1952, and afterwards, Clare was appointed U.S. ambassador to Italy. Luce publications predictably indulged in partisan lapses during the 1940s and 1950s. Nonetheless, circulation continued to rise—*Life* sold over 5 million copies a week in 1953.

Despite a lack of interest in spectator sports, yet consumed by a desire to produce another magazine, Luce decided to publish a weekly sports journal in mid-1954 entitled *Sports Illustrated.* Luce realized that his middle-class audience had moved to the suburbs and increasingly pursued leisure activities. *Sports Illustrated* possessed elements of Luce's other entities—current news of various sports and fewer and longer articles, replete with photographs of athletes. Patient as always, Luce stuck with *Sports Illustrated* for ten years before it showed a profit.

By the time of Luce's death in 1967, his magazines had numerous imitators and rivals. The publishing empire was forced to adjust to television as well as other publications. Still, Henry Luce had established a standard for quality periodicals that raised the entire industry to new heights of respect and influence.

See also Fortune; Time.

Reference Baughman, James L., *Henry R. Luce and the Rise of the American News Media* (1987).

McCarthy Hearings

Undoubtedly, television's first major sensation involving government operations was the climactic Senate subcommittee hearings chaired by communist-hunter Joseph McCarthy. The coverage on national television brought the anticommunist political struggle into the homes of millions of Americans. Edward R. Murrow's confrontation with Senator McCarthy in 1954 on CBS's "See It Now" became a television interview classic.

The advent of the Cold War in the late 1940s resulted in a new "Red scare," reminiscent of the post–World War I era. As the Iron Curtain descended across Eastern Europe, Western ignorance about the aims of Soviet dictator Joseph Stalin and fears about the communist threat of international subversion created an exploitative climate for some politicians. The House of Representatives' Committee on Un-American Activities became the first institutional venue for "Red-baiting" in the late 1940s. President Harry Truman contributed to the hysteria by requiring a loyalty oath from defense industry and government employees.

Republican Senator Joseph R. McCarthy from Wisconsin sensed the fear that a strong anticommunist politician could exploit and conducted himself accordingly. During a 1950 speech in West Virginia, McCarthy held forth a piece of paper that allegedly contained the names of 205 communists holding positions in the U.S. government. The evidence to support McCarthy's charges never materialized, but because of his position, the charges were taken seriously by the press and public—at least until they could be closely examined. After McCarthy's speech in 1950, several print media outlets, including the *Christian Science Monitor*, *Time*, the *Washington Post*, and the *Milwaukee Journal*, questioned and criticized the accusations but found it difficult to prove that they were untrue. The *Journal* in McCarthy's home state printed over 200 critical editorials. McCarthy bullied the opposition press, which he labeled as "bleeding-heart, left-wing." Of course,

initially, he received a fair share of editorial support from newspapers such as the *Cleveland Plain Dealer*, *Houston Post*, and *Los Angeles Times*.

The highlight of the McCarthy era was a 1954 series of televised hearings about the supposed communist infiltration in the U.S. Army. Viewers were treated not only to the familiar McCarthy methods of slur and innuendo but also to army counsel Joseph Welch's passionate defense of individuals implicated by Senator McCarthy. Just prior to the hearings, CBS's premier reporter/interviewer Edward R. Murrow had persuaded McCarthy to appear on the program "See It Now." After the interview, Murrow presented his own opinion of McCarthy and "McCarthyism." Anticipating McCarthy's methods on the upcoming subcommittee hearings, Murrow was especially concerned that the government's investigative authority might lead to persecution. CBS announced that it received 12,000 telephone calls following the broadcast and that callers endorsed Murrow's analysis by a ratio of 15 to one. McCarthy responded to Murrow on a network radio show a few days later and suggested that Murrow himself was sympathetic to communism.

Television viewers were able to watch the first day's army hearings before McCarthy's subcommittee live on the NBC, ABC, and Du Mont networks, with CBS providing a filmed summary at night. ABC and Du Mont continued live coverage, but NBC ended its after two days because of fear of losing daytime viewers to CBS. The ratings showed audiences equal to those of some popular network prime-time variety shows. The McCarthy hearings attracted more newspaper and magazine reporters than any previous congressional committee hearings. Although some media were intimidated by the McCarthy tactics and the "Red scare" environment, others ably confronted McCarthy and his methods to demonstrate the important role of a free press. The episode would be cited in classrooms and textbooks as an illustration of the do's and don'ts of handling news coverage.

See also Murrow, Edward Roscoe.
Reference Bayley, Edwin R., *Joe McCarthy and the Press* (1981).

McClure, Samuel Sidney (1857–1949)

The leading spirit behind the muckraking era in the early twentieth century, Samuel S. McClure gave his magazine *McClure's* a reputation for accurate reporting and quality writing. Although McClure came to his reform platform rather slowly, he entered the fray against corrupt government and business with zest beginning in 1902. The muckraking influence produced the greatest era of reform in the history of the United States.

Samuel Sidney McClure was one of four sons born into a Scotch-Irish Protestant family in Northern Ireland. They immigrated to rural Indiana in 1866 after his father's death. McClure's first experience with newspapers was working as a printer's devil (i.e., apprentice) for the Valparaiso paper before attending Knox College in Illinois. He edited the student newspaper at Knox and helped found the Western College Associated Press, which elected him president. McClure published a *History of Western College Journalism*, which yielded modest profits from advertising. After graduation in 1882, McClure edited *The Wheelman*, a bicycling magazine published by a manufacturer in Boston. McClure did some freelance writing that was published in *Harper's Weekly* and *The Modern Age* while editing his journal. In 1884, McClure also created a service in New York City that syndicated features, mostly fiction, to newspapers. By 1887, McClure's syndicate had over 100 clients.

McClure's years of operating the syndicate brought him into contact with both authors and publishers on a wide scale, despite yielding only modest profits. As early as 1890, McClure conceived of a literary magazine that was eventually inaugurated in 1893 as *McClure's Magazine*. The publisher of *The Wheelman*, along with others, contributed capital to help launch *McClure's*, which sold for a dime. McClure sold only 8,000 of an original printing of 20,000, but after a year, *McClure's* had 60,000 subscribers and ample advertising. By 1900, circulation had grown to 370,000, second nationally behind *Munsey's*. In the early years, the theme of *McClure's* was American ingenuity and the work ethic; it featured articles on successful leaders in government and business. Ironically, some of these same figures, including Philip Armour and Andrew Carnegie, later became targets of *McClure's* muckraking.

By 1897, McClure began to question his own assessment of U.S. success by dealing with the realities of how robber-baron fortunes had been acquired. Writers such as Ida Tarbell were instructed to explore the underlying dilemma of working-class America in the age of big business. When the Spanish-American War diverted attention from the emerging domestic agenda, McClure sent several reporters and photographers to cover the imperial campaign. By 1901, *McClure's* began taking stock of the United States' urbanization and development in the West and South as well as the problems of labor and poverty. McClure hired *Chicago Record* reporter Ray Stannard Baker in 1899 and the *New York Commercial Advertiser*'s Lincoln Steffens in 1902 to join Tarbell as *McClure's* lead reporters. Other writers employed by *McClure's* included Kansas journalist William Allen White, author Willa Cather, and Finley Peter Dunne, who wrote a humorous column of commentary entitled "Mr. Dooley."

After a serial on the life of Abraham Lincoln, Tarbell began the muckraking technique in 1902 by researching the life and career of John D. Rockefeller and his Standard Oil monopoly. One result of Tarbell's revelations was the eventual breakup of the Standard Oil trust. Steffens's first contribution focused on corrupt boss rule in St. Louis, and he penned a similar exposé about Minneapolis. Steffins's collected essays were later published as *The Shame of the Cities* and directly influenced municipal reform in the Progressive era. Baker researched the history of labor unions and their relations with antilabor big business and later focused on railroad monopolies. Burton Hendrick wrote a series on fraud in the life insurance industry, which led to reforms.

In each case, the articles in *McClure's* were less like typical reporting and more like carefully documented histories. *McClure's* not only set the tone for the muckraking era but was also imitated by many other journals that joined the campaign. The upshot of the muckraking theme was to focus middle-class readers' attention on a pervasive social, economic, and political phenomenon that had been neither understood nor questioned previously.

Samuel McClure became almost delirious by the success of *McClure's* muckraking articles, which raised circulation to 500,000 by 1906. He planned to build an expensive state-of-the-art production facility, but managing editor John Phillips, Tarbell, Steffens, and Baker thought that the idea was half-baked, and they all resigned. Although McClure still had capable reporters such as George Kibbe Turner, who continued Steffins's investigation of municipal reform, circulation and advertising declined sharply in 1907, forcing McClure to jettison his construction scheme. McClure's poor health caused him to reduce his participation in the management of *McClure's* after 1911, and he eventually sold the magazine. *McClure's* survived the transition and recovered to a circulation of over 500,000 by 1918. Although bankruptcy loomed after World War I, McClure came back as editor. But even with an infusion of capital from the Hearst group in 1926, *McClure's* declined until its demise in 1931.

See also Muckrakers.

Reference Lyon, Peter, *Success Story: The Life and Times of S. S. McClure* (1963).

McGill, Ralph
See Atlanta Constitution.

McLuhan, Marshall
See Telecommunications; Television.

Media Education

Before the twentieth century, training for media professionals was essentially on-the-job rather than academic. After the turn of the century, beginning with the University of Missouri in 1908, several colleges began to establish schools of journalism. At the end of the twentieth century, a degree in journalism or media studies was virtually a prerequisite to entering the profession.

The concern for professional training in media businesses was evident by the 1870s, when several colleges launched courses in printing and journalism. The University of Pennsylvania offered the first degree in journalism after 1893, but it lapsed in 1901. The University of Illinois offered the first four-year program in journalism beginning in 1904. Departments of journalism soon became regular features at several colleges and universities, but the greatest boost came with the establishment of the first school of journalism at the University of Missouri in 1908. Joseph Pulitzer endowed the Columbia University School of Journalism with $2 million in 1912; endowment gifts from the publisher of the *Minneapolis Tribune* to the University of Minnesota (1918) and from the publisher of the *Chicago Tribune* to Northwestern University (1921) followed the Pulitzer example. As schools of journalism were established, they immediately became sensitive to the need for credibility within the academy.

Early journalism courses in colleges and universities focused on technical rather than stylistic aspects of media professions. In 1904, professor Willard G. Bleyer at the University of Wisconsin recognized the need to make media studies an integral part of emerging social science programs. The result was a rapid movement to complement technical knowledge with proficiency in English, history, and the social sciences—political science, psychology, and sociology. As more schools of journalism opened their doors, the curriculum became more diverse and the degree attained legitimacy in academic circles. Students began to study media other than daily newspapers, and instructors wrote textbooks that included a historical and social perspective. By the 1920s, media schools had introduced ethics courses into their curricula.

Professional organizations appeared concurrently with the advent of organized schools. Founded at DePauw University in 1909, Sigma Delta Chi has remained the most prestigious journalism society, and its annual awards for quality are highly prized. Kappa Tau Alpha, founded at the University of Missouri in 1910, promoted the development of professional skills. Theta Sigma Phi became the primary women's journalism society after its founding in 1909 at the University of Washington. Two organizations for journalism teachers were founded early in the century. The American Association of Teachers of Journalism was formed in 1912 and sponsored the publication of the *Journalism Quarterly* (before 1930, the *Journalism Bulletin*), edited by Frank Luther Mott, and the *Journalism Educator*. The American Association of Schools and Departments of Journalism was founded in 1917. More recent ventures include the International Communication Association (1953), which publishes the *Journal of Communication*, and the Broadcast Education Association, sponsor of the *Journal of Broadcasting*. By the 1930s, schools of journalism such as Northwestern and Columbia offered graduate degrees. Selected institutions in the 1940s founded mass communications research agencies to produce statistical and behavioral studies.

In 1939, an effort to link media education with its practitioners bore fruit with the creation of the American Council on Education for Journalism. Professional schools of journalism cosponsored the council with the American Society of Newspaper Editors, the American Newspaper Publishers Association, the National Newspaper Association, the Inland Daily Press Association, and the Southern Newspaper Publishers Association. Other professional groups representing broadcasting, magazines, advertising, and public relations later affiliated with the council. The primary contribution of the council was to inaugurate an accreditation program to approve media curricula.

By the end of the 1940s, there were 40 schools accredited by the council.

Further consolidations of professional groups occurred in the 1940s. The American Association of Teachers of Journalism, reconstituted as the Association for Education in Journalism, merged in 1949 with the American Association of Schools and Departments of Journalism and the recently established American Society of Journalism School Administrators. Cooperation among the centers of education, research, and business fostered the preparation of future media professionals. Another type of cooperation was the Nieman Foundation Fellowships at Harvard, established by a grant from the estate of Lucius W. Nieman of the *Milwaukee Journal* in 1937. Each year the foundation selected 12 working journalists to attend Harvard for intensive study of their profession. The American Press Institute, founded at Columbia University in 1946, sponsored frequent conferences for media professionals.

Reference Lindley, William R., *Journalism and Higher Education* (1976).

Media Humorists

An important trait throughout U.S. history has been a delight in humor, especially the ability to laugh at ourselves, as an outlet for all classes and types of people. The use of the media, both print and broadcast, as a means of expressing humor also has a long tradition, beginning in the nineteenth century. Some of the United States' best-loved personalities have been humorists—from Mark Twain to Will Rogers to Garrison Keillor—and certain publications such as the *New Yorker* have featured subtle humor as a trademark.

By the early nineteenth century, newspaper editors often injected humor or satire into their editorials, but the function of humor as an art form developed more gradually. One of the earliest examples before the Civil War was Charles F. Browne, whose fictional character "Artemus Ward" began writing humorous letters in colloquial jargon to the *Cleveland Plain Dealer*. Imitating

Artemus Ward was Charles Henry Smith (1826–1903), who published a series of humorous letters beginning in 1861 in the *Atlanta Constitution* under the pseudonym "Bill Arp." Arp enjoyed painting caricatures of southerners, highlighting local customs.

Certainly Mark Twain (Samuel Langhorne Clemens) became one of America's best-loved humorists after the Civil War. Born along the Mississippi River, which was the source of many of his stories and characters, Twain apprenticed at the *Hannibal (Missouri) Gazette* in 1847 and later wrote for the *Hannibal Journal* from 1850 to 1853. Traveling widely for additional newspaper experience—from St. Louis to Virginia City, Nevada to San Francisco—Twain began to perfect his technique. While writing for the *Alta California* in San Francisco (1866–1867), Twain produced a series of letters recounting a journey through Central America to Palestine, which became the basis for his first book, *The Innocents Abroad*, a satire on Old World social conventions. In 1874 and 1875, he wrote a series of stories for the *Atlantic Monthly* that became *Life on the Mississippi*, featuring the familiar characters of Tom Sawyer and Huckleberry Finn in adventures peppered with humor.

Mark Twain's contemporaries Bret Harte and Eugene Field added new elements to journalistic humor. Harte, like Twain, traveled to California in the 1850s to write articles in the *San Francisco Golden Era*. After the Civil War, Harte became editor of the *Overland Monthly* (1867–1871), which printed many of his humorous short stories imitating the style of Washington Irving and Charles Dickens, with heavy doses of sentimentality and realism. Harte then spent several years (1871–1876) writing short stories for the *Atlantic Monthly*. The subjects of Harte's sardonic humor included fashion fads, cultural values, and the eccentricities of vernacular language. Eugene Field's popular column "Sharps and Flats" began appearing in the *Chicago Daily News* in 1883. His satirical quips covered numerous subjects, including baseball, Christmas, delinquent children, politicians, and stereotypical husbands and wives. He also enjoyed lampooning classical authors such as Dante and Petrarch.

Another writer for the *Chicago Daily News* and the afternoon *Record* was cynic George Ade, whose essays of ridicule appeared from 1887 to 1900. Ade began his column entitled "Stories of the Streets and of the Town" in 1893 in the *Record*. Ade enjoyed portraying the culture shock of rural Americans as they experienced urban life for the first time. His syndicated "Fables in Slang," begun in 1897, gave Ade his greatest fame; 500 fables were written over the next several decades featuring naive and foolish characters such as "Artie" and "Pink Marsh." Ring Lardner used Americans' favorite pastime—baseball—as the backdrop for his humorous essays. A sports writer and editor at the *Chicago Examiner* and *Tribune* as well as the *Boston American*, Lardner's syndicated column at the *Tribune* (1913–1919) and through the Bell Syndicate (1931–1933) gave him a national following. Lardner also created fictional characters such as the vain, semiliterate baseball player "Jack Keefe" as vehicles for his sports humor.

After World War I, "cowboy philosopher" Will Rogers became perhaps the best-loved American humorist ever. Rogers's column "Weekly Sayings" appeared first in the *New York Times* in 1922 and later spread to the *World*, the *Boston Globe*, the *Chicago Daily News*, and many other papers through the McNaught Syndicate. During the same period, Rogers contracted to write a series of essays for George Lorimer's *Saturday Evening Post* on subjects as diverse as the Democratic Party political misfortunes, Mussolini's Italian Fascists, the backwardness of the Soviet Union, and the competition between Florida and California for migrating populations. Rogers traveled widely across the nation, making appearances and commenting on contemporary events. His death in an airplane crash in 1935 produced a national mourning of unprecedented magnitude.

Also following World War I, the premier magazine of sophisticated humor, the *New Yorker*, produced some of the best examples of the genre. Robert C. Benchley, a former essayist for *Vanity Fair*, wrote a column called "The Wayward Press" beginning in 1927 that parodied or mocked conventional logic. A. J. Liebling took over Benchley's column in 1945 and became noted for puncturing the affectations of editors and publishers. Though known more for his children's stories, E. B. White contributed witty paragraphs and humorous editorials for the *New Yorker* from 1925 until 1982. Harold Ross named James Thurber editor of the *New Yorker* in 1927, with no trial employment. Thurber produced essays and short stories filled with irony, drew his trademark cartoons, and contributed to the popular "Talk of the Town" section. Thurber enjoyed satirizing social fads such as self-help manuals and creating impractical characters who dealt comically with ordinary life circumstances.

Will Rogers

Another contributor of humorous essays to the *New Yorker* beginning in 1931 was better known as a screenwriter for movie comedies. S. J. Perelman wrote the classic screenplays for the Marx brothers' films *Monkey Business* and *Horse Feathers* in the 1930s. Perelman won an Oscar for his screenplay of *Around the World in Eighty Days* in 1955. He also penned screenplays for television programs in the 1950s. Perelman's 278 essays in the *New Yorker* usually concerned problems of home ownership such as plumbing, pets, visiting relatives, and the quest for fun and pleasure through travel.

Art Buchwald and Russell Baker have been among the most popular humor columnists since World War II. As a GI in Europe, Buchwald did some work for *Variety* and the international *Herald Tribune* in Paris following the peace. After returning from his stint with the *Tribune* in 1962, Buchwald began a syndicated column based in Washington and eventually carried by 550 newspapers—the most of any humorist. Buchwald's writing featured incongruous parodies of personalities and politics; for example, he used football metaphors to describe labor boss Jimmy Hoffa. Since 1972, Russell Baker's informal essays in his syndicated *New York Times* "Observer" column have included satire and wry humor. Baker followed the Will Rogers style of casual philosophy about the human condition, including notes about relatives, politicians, taxes, and daily routines.

Publisher Bennett Cerf's columns, "Trade Winds" in the *Saturday Review* (1942–1957) and "Cerfbound" in *This Week* during the 1950s, made him noteworthy for humorous puns and anecdotes. He also wrote a syndicated column of humor, "Try and Stop Me," for King Features. Cerf's celebrity gained even wider credence when he appeared as a regular panelist on television's "What's My Line" show (1952–1966). Erma Bombeck began writing in the 1950s about humorous episodes in the life of a housewife for the *Dayton Herald*. *Newsday* syndicated her column in 1965, and it appeared in 900 newspapers by 1984. Bombeck's humor stemmed from her skill in getting people to laugh at their own foibles. She also wrote essays for *Good Housekeeping* and made regular appearances in the 1980s on ABC television's "Good Morning America." Garrison

Keillor's Saturday evening public radio program, "Prairie Home Companion," aired in 1974, mixing music with Keillor's monologue about the fictional Lake Wobegon. Keillor satirized popular cultural fads such as pop psychology, polls on everything from food to politics, country-and-western music, new food labeling, and minority rights in essays published in the *New Yorker* beginning in 1970.

Early television stand-up comics such as George Burns, Bob Hope, and Jack Benny had learned their craft in vaudeville or radio. They used commentary on current events and personalities as a regular vehicle for their humor. Late-night television also became a popular medium for extemporaneous humor by talk-show hosts and guests. NBC's "Tonight Show," begun in the 1950s, led the way with the dry wit of host Jack Paar, followed in the 1960s through 1980s by the physical humor of Johnny Carson. Political satire and jokes about prominent cultural icons enlivened studio and broadcast audiences. A different approach came in the late 1970s, with "Saturday Night Live" skits lampooning politicians and cultural fads.

Reference Gale, Stephen H., ed., *Encyclopedia of American Humorists* (1988).

Medill, Joseph
See Chicago Tribune.

Memphis Commercial Appeal

From its beginning as a weekly organ of Jacksonian democracy in 1841 to its management by the Scripps-Howard Company after 1936, the *Memphis Commercial Appeal* has been a major journalistic voice for Tennessee and the South. The paper promoted the growth of and pride in Memphis through difficult periods such as the Civil War and the twentieth-century civil rights era.

When Henry Van Pelt founded the *Memphis Appeal* in 1841 as a weekly four-page Democratic paper to rival the Whig *Enquirer*, the town of Memphis had just over 1,800 residents. A native of Kentucky, Van Pelt had 20 years of newspaper experience in Nashville and Franklin. The *Appeal*'s philosophy sanctioned the tenets of states' rights and strict construction of the Constitution. On economic matters, the *Appeal* promoted banking and mercantile interests, despite its agrarian orientation. It consistently fought for better schools and covered social issues, including crime, with a class-conscious perspective.

During the 1840s, most of the *Appeal*'s attention was focused on western expansion, which included matters such as railroads and the annexation of Texas. Thus, the *Appeal* defended President Polk's entry into and prosecution of the Mexican War. Anxious to start another paper, Van Pelt sold the *Appeal* in 1847 to the paper's assistant editor, S. T. Sewall, and a local attorney, W. N. Stanton. Within a few months, the new owners made the *Appeal* a daily, but their split over the slavery issue soon resulted in Sewall's departure. Several short-term changes occurred before Van Pelt resumed ownership of the *Appeal* in 1848.

Although moderate by the standards of most southern newspapers, editor John R. McClanahan led the *Appeal*'s defense of the southern way of life during the abolitionist campaigns leading up to the Civil War. For two years following the election of 1848, the *Appeal* stopped its daily editions. After Van Pelt's death in 1851, McClanahan joined the business manager and a third investor as co-owners of the *Appeal*. The paper strove for southern unity in the face of Whigs, Know-Nothings, and Republicans in the 1850s. Benjamin F. Dill of Georgia became a fourth partner and associate editor in 1855. By 1857, daily circulation reached 1,000, making it the largest Memphis paper.

The *Appeal*'s moderation became glaringly evident in 1860 when it backed Stephen Douglas of Illinois for the Democratic presidential nomination against southerner John Breckinridge. After the election, however, the *Appeal*'s attitudes toward secession and war changed to support because of the desire for southern unity. Having already been jolted by two fires in the 1850s, the

Appeal faced its most serious predicament in 1862 when a Union army occupation of Memphis forced it to move operations to northern Mississippi. Retreating before further Union advances, the paper moved to Jackson, Atlanta, Montgomery, and Columbus from 1862 to 1865, with numerous interruptions in printing. Relying on correspondents and the telegraph, the *Appeal* was able to maintain broad coverage of news during its exile from Memphis.

Before publication could be resumed in Memphis after the war, editor-partner McClanahan died, leaving Dill to get the paper back into publication in November 1865. Dill died the following January. The new editor, J. H. McMahon, carried on the editorial tradition of moderation and got circulation back to 4,000 in 1866, despite competition from seven other Memphis dailies. Recovery was followed by collapse when Dill's widow fired McMahon and lost half the *Appeal*'s circulation. The paper went bankrupt in early 1867 and was acquired by John Ainslie, J. S. C. Hogan, and Albert Pike, with Pike assuming the editorial duties.

Pike sold his share of the *Appeal* to John M. Keating, who became editor in 1868 after his own paper failed. By 1879, Keating and M. C. Gallaway were the sole owners of the *Appeal*. They shifted away from a narrow editorial focus on Democratic politics toward the "New South" theme of economic growth, especially manufacturing and railroads. Circulation was back up to the 1866 level of 4,000 by 1870, but the *Appeal* was no longer the most widely read paper in Memphis. Because of disastrous yellow fever epidemics in 1873 and 1878, the *Appeal* urged water and sewage construction and health measures to stymie the disease. A sports page was added to the paper's format in the mid-1870s.

During the 1880s, the *Appeal* joined the chorus of Progressive sentiment calling for regulation of big business, especially railroad monopolies. It took a moderate stance on the Negro question—preferring education rather than suffrage—and on the labor issue—supporting peaceful strikes. Although favoring temperance, the *Appeal* opposed total prohibition of alcohol. Led by W. H. Collier, a group of investors bought Gallaway's half interest in 1887 and Keating's half in 1889 to take control. Collier bought new linotype machines and a stereotyping press to modernize the *Appeal*'s format and increase printing speed. He also obtained the Associated Press monopoly in Memphis. The *Appeal*'s circulation of 18,000 in 1890 made it the largest paper in Memphis. After a heated senatorial race pitted the Memphis papers against candidate D. P. Hadden, he formed his own newspaper, the *Commercial*, with John Keating as editor. In the aftermath of the Panic of 1893, the *Appeal* went bankrupt in 1894 and was purchased by the *Commercial* to form the *Commercial Appeal*.

The businessmen owners of the *Commercial Appeal* hired Edward W. Carmack, a former editorial writer in Nashville, as editor. A free silver advocate who feared Populist competition with Democrats, Carmack resigned in 1896 when a majority of the owners opposed his strident pro-silver position. The growth in circulation to 25,000 at the turn of the century was aided by sensational coverage of crime and violence as well as the Spanish-American War.

When former managing editor C. P. J. Mooney became editor of the *Commercial Appeal* in 1908, daily circulation had almost doubled since 1900. Trained on Hearst papers in New York and Chicago, Mooney promoted straightforward editorials, thorough reporting, and lucid writing until his death in 1926. The *Commercial Appeal* opposed longtime Memphis Mayor E. H. Crump, supported Prohibition—even though the issue divided the state Democratic Party—and urged cotton farmers to diversify crops. The *Commercial Appeal* backed Woodrow Wilson's goal of membership in the League of Nations and opposed the neo-isolationism of the 1920s. Mooney's campaign against the violence of the Ku Klux Klan in the early 1920s won the paper a Pulitzer Prize. Daily circulation grew from 81,000 in 1918 to 100,000 by 1925. The *Commercial Appeal* launched its own radio station, WMC, in 1923 and added a television station in 1948.

Soon after launching an afternoon edition in 1926, the *Commercial Appeal* was sold to Luke Lea, publisher of the *Nashville Tennessean*. Editor George Morris offered bland editorial backing of flood control and suppression of crime and corruption. The *Commercial Appeal* also shifted from opponent to supporter of "Boss" Crump. The depression sent the paper into receivership in 1930, and it was sold three times over the next six years. Finally, the Scripps-Howard Company, owner of the afternoon daily *Press-Scimitar*, acquired the *Commercial Appeal* in 1936. The two papers were run separately, accented by their frequently opposing editorial positions. Frank Ahlgren became editor of the *Commercial Appeal* and restored some of its traditions during his tenure, which ended in 1968.

As the city of Memphis grew after World War II, so did the *Commercial Appeal*'s circulation—from 120,000 in 1940 to 216,000 by 1970. Scripps-Howard did not interfere with editorial policy in local and state elections, although it did insist on uniformity for national elections. Thus, the traditionally Democratic *Commercial Appeal* backed Republican presidential candidates from 1940 to 1972, except in 1964, when it supported Democrat Lyndon Johnson. By 1994, the *Commercial Appeal*'s daily circulation had only grown to 226,000.

Reference Baker, Thomas Harrison, *The Memphis Commercial Appeal* (1971).

Mencken, Henry Louis (1880–1956)

A noted iconoclast and critic of U.S. institutions, Henry Louis Mencken was the *enfant terrible* of the U.S. journalistic community for years after World War I. Mencken was affiliated with journals such as *The Smart Set* and *American Mercury* as well as the *Baltimore Sun* newspaper. He positively influenced the development of creative geniuses in both literature and journalism more than any other intellectual.

From the time Henry Louis Mencken received a toy printing press at seven years of age, he knew that he would be a writer.

Mencken was valedictorian of his class at Polytechnic High School in Baltimore. His first published work was poetry, and he produced a prose account of George Bernard Shaw's plays and a study of Friedrich Nietzsche's philosophy before his thirtieth birthday. Proud of his German heritage, Mencken suffered through the anti-German prejudice accompanying World War I. Mencken was tied directly or indirectly to Baltimore newspapers throughout most of his career. His early experiences were recounted in *Newspaper Days, 1899–1906* (1941). He began as a police reporter with the *Baltimore Herald*, a penny morning daily. Mencken rose rapidly to become a feature writer, drama critic, city editor, and editor in chief. When the *Herald* went bankrupt in 1906, Mencken joined the staff of the *Evening Sun*, where he maintained a working relationship until 1948. One of his closest confidants in this era was *Sun* editor

H. L. Mencken challenged traditional religious and social mores from rural America to Woodrow Wilson's White House by embracing almost every avant-garde view of his time.

Hamilton Owens, who joined Mencken on various crusades.

Mencken also contributed to a prominent magazine, *The Smart Set*, as early as 1908. From 1914 to 1923, he was coeditor with the journal's founder, drama critic George Jean Nathan. Mencken wrote monthly essays on a variety of subjects, but his favorite topic was literary criticism. He was determined to shake the foundations of the U.S. literary community by assailing their status quo neo-Puritanism. Thus, he challenged traditional religious and social mores from rural America to Woodrow Wilson's White House.

Mencken's philosophy of modernism embraced almost every avant-garde view, including Darwin's biology and arguments that the Founding Fathers were atheists. His positive views on capitalism were shaped by reading William Graham Sumner. Mencken's favorite authors included Jane Austen and Joseph Conrad. Among contemporary writers, he approved of Sherwood Anderson, Willa Cather, Theodore Dreiser, and Sinclair Lewis, in large part because they too engaged in debunking U.S. traditions. Mencken expounded on literary criticism and waxed philosophically in six series of essays entitled *Prejudices*. From 1904 to the 1940s, he regularly visited Baltimore's Saturday Night Club to talk, drink, and listen to classical music with compatriots.

Mencken's most vicious blows were directed against the South in the essay "The Sahara of the Bozart," published in a 1920 installment of *Prejudices*. Yet in the midst of his ridicule about the cultural barrenness of the South, Mencken provoked progressive southern writers into a southern Renaissance. He even went so far as to marry a Montgomery writer, Sara Haardt. Mencken took considerable pride in the southern network that emerged in the 1920s. He lent encouragement to Julian Harris of the *Columbus (Georgia) Enquirer* and Grover C. Hall of the *Montgomery Advertiser*, both of whom won Pulitzer Prizes in the decade for attacking Ku Klux Klan violence. Mencken commiserated with other southern journalists, including Nell Battle Lewis, Gerald W. Johnson, Virginius Dabney, and Wilbur J. Cash. He admired the work of novelist James Cabell Branch and North Carolina sociologist Howard W. Odum.

One of the primary vehicles used to promote southern writers was the *American Mercury*, which Mencken founded with Nathan in 1924, thanks to financial backing from Alfred A. Knopf. Mencken was the sole editor of the journal between 1925 and 1933, when articles by his southern friends appeared regularly. Paid circulation reached 75,000 by the second year of publication. Mencken and his colleagues attacked symbols of the Old South such as intellectual obscurantism and Ku Kluxism.

As an outgrowth of his freethinking skepticism, Mencken never embraced politicians of any philosophical stripe, in part because he was unconvinced of the merits of democracy. Basically, Mencken surmised that politicians were opportunists who played on the fears and ignorance of the voters, who were lampooned as "Boobus Americanus." Mencken was openly skeptical of and hostile to Franklin Roosevelt's New Deal programs designed to remedy the Great Depression of the 1930s. Some of his earlier followers grew somewhat tired of Mencken's constant criticism of the New Deal. By the time of World War II, Mencken's style had been eclipsed, even though his contribution could not be ignored.

Mencken's most lasting contribution may have been the publication of *The American Language*, which first appeared in 1919 and went through four editions and two supplements by the late 1940s. The work was a comprehensive study and commentary on the history and traditions of the English tongue.

Reference Bode, Carl, *Mencken* (1969).

Mexican War

The Mexican War (1846–1848) was the first foreign war that received significant coverage in the U.S. press. New York newspapers organized a cooperative system to obtain rapid reports from the front lines. The *New Orleans Picayune* provided the best coverage of any newspaper. Americans also started bilingual newspapers in Mexico during the war that were regulated by military commanders.

Territorial expansion became a major issue among westerners in the 1840s. It was instrumental in helping to elect Democrat James K. Polk president in the 1844 election. Many politicians and speculators promoted the notion that the United States should expand from the Atlantic coast to the Pacific. The quest caused tensions in three places: in Oregon, where a dispute with Great Britain was resolved peacefully by treaty, and in California and Texas, which led to the war with Mexico. In 1845, *United States Magazine and Democratic Review* editor John L. O'Sullivan said that Texas's annexation by the United States was part of the "fulfillment of our manifest destiny to overspread the continent allotted by Providence for the free development of our yearly multiplying millions." Other pro-expansionist editors began to repeat the phrase "manifest destiny," and in January 1846, congressmen echoed the term in speeches advocating territorial acquisition.

Once the fighting began along the Rio Grande, newspapers showed a thirst for news about the conflict. *New Orleans Picayune* editor George Kendall traveled to the front to report the war for his paper. Kendall covered all the major battles from Monterey to Mexico City, and the *Picayune* also had five other reporters following the war. The *New Orleans Delta* sent two correspondents to Mexico, and the *Bee* and *Crescent* shared reports from one reporter. The *Philadelphia North American* and *Boston Atlas* each had one reporter in Mexico. James Gordon Bennett's *Herald* also sent a correspondent to Mexico; it had operated a horse courier service before the war but had been forced by the postmaster general to stop competing with the U.S. mails. Because the closest telegraph to the East Coast was at Richmond, it took over two weeks to receive reports from the front lines. *New York Sun*

publisher Moses Beach and an editorial writer went to Mexico City on a peace mission for President Polk in 1847. The trip allowed firsthand reports about the war to be published in the *Sun*. The *Sun, Herald, Tribune, Courier and Enquirer*, and others formed the Harbour News Association to coordinate the acquisition and reduce the cost of war news.

Printing presses began to appear at many places inside Mexico once the U.S. armies captured territory—a phenomenon known as "war newspapers." Two dozen of the bilingual papers were sold to both American soldiers and local Mexicans. At Matamoros on the Rio Grande, Isaac Fleeson and William Dryden set up the *Republic of the Rio Grande* in 1846; it urged states in northern Mexico to revolt and form their own nation. General Zachary Taylor was ordered to close the *Republic*. Shortly thereafter, Fleeson started the *American Flag*, which continued to publish until after the war. Some hostile Mexican papers were also suppressed by the military. As U.S. forces captured California, two newspapers emerged. Reverend Walter Colton and Dr. Robert Semple started the *Californian* at Monterey and later moved to San Francisco. Mormon settler Sam Brannan opened the *California Star* in San Francisco in 1846. In the United States, the Polk administration's suppression of newspapers in Mexico was approved by the *Baltimore Sun* and the *Washington Union*.

The East Coast penny press tended to view the Mexican War not only in nationalistic terms but also in economic ones. The war helped sell newspapers, but it also allowed publishers to develop more efficient news-gathering techniques. Although there was some interference with reporters and papers in Mexico by the military, the incidents were minor. President Polk became alarmed in a few instances by what he regarded as leaks about his strategy and diplomacy, but he did not take any repressive actions. Generally, the press was permitted considerable free access to information during the Mexican War.

Reference Bauer, Jack K., *The Mexican War, 1846–48* (1974).

Miami Herald

Consistently ranked in the top ten among U.S. dailies, the *Miami Herald* has mirrored the growth of Miami throughout the twentieth century. The *Herald* became the most valuable property of the Knight newspaper chain after its purchase in 1937. Its reporters have won numerous Pulitzer Prizes, and the paper maintains the most important Latin American coverage of any U.S. daily.

The city of Miami was only 14 years old when Frank B. Shutts launched the *Herald* in 1910 with the financial backing of railroad tycoon Henry M. Flagler. Frank B. Stoneman served as editor from 1910 to 1941. Shutts obtained the first Associated Press contract in Miami in 1911. Circulation grew slowly at first, from 2,000 in 1912 to 4,000 in 1917, but the *Herald* positioned itself to capitalize on Miami's growth after World War I. Although there was some experimentation with sensational headlines, such as the sinking of the *Titanic* in 1912 and coverage of the Mexican revolution (1913–1916), Shutts maintained a conservative approach in format, imitating the *New York Times*.

The postwar real estate boom in Miami brought profits to the *Herald* because of voluminous advertising and changed the focus of news from the foreign to the local scene. The *Herald* faced serious competition when James M. Cox of Ohio bought the *Miami Metropolis* and changed it to the *Daily News* in 1924. Shutts was active in supporting the establishment of the Hialeah Park horse-racing track in 1925. The 1926 hurricane devastated the burgeoning city—causing $100 million worth of damage—and caused a rapid slowdown in growth, including the *Herald*'s advertising sales. Circulation of the *Herald* also declined from 47,000 in 1927 to 38,000 in 1934.

Although the depression of the 1930s caused further delays in Miami's recovery, Miami Beach was developed, and Pan American offered international flights from Miami to Latin America and the Far East. Eastern Airlines made Miami its headquarters in 1931. Circulation of the *Herald* recovered to 55,000 by 1937. Soon after Moses Annenberg launched the tabloid *Miami Tribune* in 1934, John S. Knight of Ohio became interested in Miami newspapers. He bought both the *Tribune*, which had ceased publication, and the *Herald* in 1937; Knight paid $2.25 million for the *Herald*. Although some new staffers appeared in Miami, Stoneman remained as editor in chief. New columnists were added, including Walter Winchell, Westbrook Pegler, and Heywood Broun.

After an outbreak of undulant fever in 1939, the *Herald* pressed for an ordinance requiring pasteurization of milk, which was opposed by the mayor. Although the Knight papers opposed U.S. entry into World War II, they supported the war effort after 1941. Following the death of editor Stoneman in 1941, Knight promoted former city editor Lee Hills to managing editor. Hills immediately enlarged the paper's Latin American coverage and soon departed to cover the war in Europe. Although Hills was given the additional task of editing the *Detroit Free Press* in 1951, he continued as executive editor at the *Herald*. Another former city editor, John Pennekamp, served as editorial page editor from 1941 to 1956. Pennekamp took a jaundiced view of politicians and business tycoons. He was held in contempt of court for editorials criticizing a Florida judge, but the decision was overturned by the U.S. Supreme Court. Pennekamp's influential column, "Behind the Front Page," remained the talk of Miami in the 1940s and 1950s.

The *Herald* successfully endured a strike by the International Typographical Union local that lasted from 1948 to 1950. The *Herald* uncovered corruption in the sheriff's department and a bookmaking syndicate in the postwar era, the basis for a Pulitzer Prize in 1951. Circulation rose to 200,000 by 1952. Throughout the Knight era, the *Herald* employed some top-notch reporters, including Pulitzer Prize winners Edna Buchanan and Gene Miller, as well as state reporter Steve Trumbull, Jeanne Bellamy, and future Gannett chief Al Neuharth. The $30 million *Herald* plant that opened in 1963 was the largest building in the state of

Florida. In 1966, the *Herald* took over the production, advertising, and circulation tasks of the *Daily News*.

The paper began printing its Spanish-language section, *El Miami Herald*, in 1976, followed by a full Spanish edition, *El Nuevo Herald*, in the 1980s. The primary audience for these publications was the growing Cuban population in Miami. Spanish editions of the *Herald* were also published in several Latin American countries.

In 1974, the Supreme Court ruled in *Miami Herald v. Tornillo* that, contrary to a Florida law, politicians did not have a guaranteed right to reply to newspaper criticism. Tornillo, a candidate for the state legislature, had been criticized in *Herald* editorials for breaking the law and had asked for space to reply, based on a state statute. The *Herald* was criticized by some and praised by others for its coverage of Democratic presidential candidate Gary Hart's romantic adventures in 1987, which effectively torpedoed his campaign.

The *Herald* remained the flagship of the Knight-Ridder chain throughout the 1970s and 1980s. *Time* magazine placed the *Herald* on its "ten best newspapers" list in 1974. Professional polls in 1960 and 1970 ranked the *Herald* among the top 15 newspapers. In 1977, the *Herald* ranked seventeenth among U.S. dailies in circulation and third in advertising volume. Writers Madelaine Blais and Shirley Christian won Pulitzer Prizes in 1980 and 1981, respectively. The *Herald* received a 1983 Pulitzer for its reporting on the poor treatment of Haitian refugees and two more Pulitzers in 1988. Daily circulation in 1994 totaled 404,000; circulation for the Sunday edition was 528,000. David Lawrence Jr. was publisher and chairman in 1994.

Reference Smiley, Nixon, *Knights of the Fourth Estate: The Story of the* Miami Herald (1974).

Milwaukee Journal

Like many great papers, the *Milwaukee Journal* has fought against crime and corruption as well as for civic progress and tolerance. The *Journal* broke out of the pro-vincial mold of many papers its size and maintained a national perspective. It has examined its own colorful home-state politicians from Robert LaFollette to Joseph McCarthy. The *Journal* personnel has included notables such as editor Lucius W. Nieman and publisher Harry J. Grant.

Democratic Congressman Peter V. Deuster founded the four-page daily *Milwaukee Journal* in 1882, joining six other dailies. At the time, Deuster edited one of three German-language newspapers in Milwaukee. In less than a month, with circulation unable to rise above 1,000, Deuster sold out to partner Michael Kraus, who called on Lucius William Nieman to take over the editor's chair at the *Journal*. Nieman had begun his newspaper career in the composing room of the *Milwaukee Sentinel* and later served as a reporter and managing editor. Promising that the *Journal* would be "independent and aggressive," Nieman targeted political bosses as objects of scrutiny. In its third month of publication, the *Journal* became the only Milwaukee paper to call for an investigation into a hotel fire that had killed dozens of people. It succeeded in getting the city council to adopt a new building and fire code. By 1884, Nieman acquired a United Press franchise for the *Journal*, and circulation grew to about 5,000.

The *Journal* campaigned for improvements at the state mental hospital and for an end to speculators' control of public lands. It showed sympathy for the labor union movement. Nieman promised readers that congressmen and senators from Wisconsin would be closely scrutinized. In 1884, the *Journal* endorsed Democrat Grover Cleveland in its first presidential coverage. Nieman announced in 1889 that the *Journal* would become the mouthpiece for the Democratic Party thereafter. The reason for the partisan turn was Nieman's belief that ousting the Republicans entrenched in the statehouse was the only way that reforms could be enacted. State treasurers had been pocketing the interest on state funds for years. The *Journal* helped the Democrats achieve victory in the election of 1890. The reform era in Wisconsin had begun.

Because Nieman was a sound money advocate, he opposed the free silver movement that was so popular in the West. The *Journal* endorsed the Democrats' gold splinter party in 1896 because it could not back the free silver ticket headed by William Jennings Bryan. Nieman vowed not to commit the *Journal* to a political party again. On the state level, the *Journal* was attracted to Progressive Republican Robert M. LaFollette, who won the governorship in 1898 and was reelected in 1902 with *Journal* support. LaFollette led the enactment of the so-called Wisconsin Idea, a package of Progressive measures that included elimination of the free pass given by railroads to political supporters, creation of a railroad regulatory commission, direct primary votes to replace conventions, a graduated income tax, and civil service reform. LaFollette was elected U.S. senator in 1906.

The *Journal* was not as successful in bringing reform to the city of Milwaukee, which elected a Socialist Party government in 1910. The *Journal* organized a nonpartisan party for the elections of 1912 and unseated the Socialists. Meanwhile, the *Journal* continued to prosper. The price of the paper was reduced from two cents to one cent in 1899, almost doubling circulation to 22,000 and making it the circulation leader against its three rivals. The paper acquired a new press in 1902 and a new printing facility in 1906. The *Journal* published its first Sunday edition in 1911. Talented reporters working at the paper included Zona Gale, Edna Ferber, and Carl Sandburg.

On national issues, the *Journal* remained independent: it supported Republican Theodore Roosevelt in 1904, endorsed neither major candidate in 1908, and favored Democrat Woodrow Wilson in 1912. The *Journal* favored neutrality when World War I began in 1914 and criticized the German-language papers backing Germany. After the United States entered into the war in 1917, the *Journal* called for vigorous prosecution and received criticism from many German-speaking Milwaukeeans. The *Journal* won a Pulitzer Prize for meritorious public service in 1919 for its critique of German propaganda. Support for the League of Nations after the war also proved an unpopular stand for the paper.

Circulation at the *Journal* passed the 100,000 mark in 1915, and Harry J. Grant was hired in 1916 as advertising manager. Grant quickly rose up the hierarchy to become publisher in 1919. He hired Marvin H. Creager from the *Kansas City Star* as managing editor in 1920, and Donald Ferguson as chief editorial writer in 1923. Led by Grant's vision of radio complementing the newspaper, the *Journal* cooperated with Marquette University to operate a noncommercial radio station in 1925 and started its own commercial station, WTMJ, in 1927. Lucius W. Nieman died in 1935. After his widow's death in 1936, the bulk of the Nieman estate was used to create an endowment at Harvard to promote journalism standards. The Nieman Foundation (established in 1938) awards about a dozen short-term fellowships each year to working journalists.

Nieman was replaced as editor by Grant. Within two years, Grant had reorganized the *Journal* company to distribute stock to the employees. The *Journal* began carrying the Sunday supplement *This Week* in 1935. Grant stepped down as editor in 1938 to become chairman of the board. Creager served as editor from 1938 to 1943, when ill health forced his retirement. Ferguson followed Creager as editor and served until 1961. Nieman's successors continued the *Journal*'s tradition of thorough coverage of local, state, national, and international issues. The *Journal* endorsed Democratic presidential candidates with regularity in the 1920s and 1930s but broke with Roosevelt in 1940 to support Republican Wendell Willkie. Following its pattern in World War I, the *Journal* favored neutrality before the bombing of Pearl Harbor, then backed the war effort and sent Robert Doyle to cover the war in the Pacific. No candidate was endorsed in the presidential election of 1944. In the postwar era, thanks to the efforts of new publisher Irwin Maier, the *Journal* led the nation in volume of advertising.

The *Journal* fought long and hard against

the anticommunist crusade of Wisconsin Senator Joseph McCarthy, which climaxed in 1954 with televised Senate hearings. McCarthy's unfounded and injurious insinuations were rejected from the outset in dozens of *Journal* editorials. In presidential elections, the *Journal* continued to prove its independence, endorsing Republican Thomas Dewey in 1948 and Democrat Adlai Stevenson in 1952 and 1956. When Donald Ferguson stepped down as editor in 1961, Lindsay Hoben became editor after 35 years of service at the paper. Following a crippling strike at the morning *Milwaukee Sentinel* in 1962, its Hearst owners agreed to sell the paper to the *Journal* for $3 million. The *Sentinel* continued to be published by the new owners; in 1994, circulation totaled 175,000 with Keith Spore as editor. After Hoben's death in 1967, managing editor Richard Leonard became editor and solicited reader comments to identify ways to improve the paper. The *Journal* won a second Pulitzer in 1967 for an investigation of water pollution. The paper oppposed U.S. involvement in Vietnam as early as 1963. In the 1970s, the *Journal* company acquired television and printing businesses to become more diversified. The *Journal*'s circulation in 1994 was 232,000 for the daily and 496,000 for the Sunday edition. Mary Jo Meisner served as editor in the 1990s, and Robert Kahler as chairman.

Reference Wells, Robert W., The Milwaukee Journal: *An Informal Chronicle of Its First 100 Years* (1981).

Motion Pictures

After the first daguerreotype in 1839, the technology of motion pictures was only a matter of time. Thomas A. Edison's Kinetoscope (1888) began the era, and it blossomed into a major industry after the turn of the century. The impact of motion pictures on popular culture has been enormous in the twentieth century.

Edison's Kinetoscope, perfected by assistant William Dickson, utilized the new Kodak camera of George Eastman to produce a series of still photographs in rapid succession. In 1896, Edison premiered the first public U.S. motion picture with an improved projector known as the Vitascope, and newsreel footage appeared on a regular basis in 1897. In 1903, *The Great Train Robbery* became the first motion picture— only 12 minutes long—produced from a story line by Edwin S. Porter. Motion pictures, which began as a novelty, became a major media industry by World War I.

Edison convinced his major competitors to organize the Motion Picture Patents Company in 1908 to regulate the new technology as a monopoly. The attempt failed partly because the government sued the Patents Company under the Sherman Antitrust Act and also because independent producers moved ahead on their own. The first ambitious undertaking by a filmmaker was David W. Griffith's three-hour production of *The Birth of a Nation* in 1915. The project cost just under $100,000 but yielded profits of $5 million. Despite the controversy created by the racist subject matter, Griffith's use of a detailed story and his techniques of editing and directing set the standard for future motion pictures.

Most of the early producers were immigrants—Adolph Zukor, Marcus Loew, Samuel Goldwyn, William Fox—and most of the capital investment came from banks, insurance companies, and other businesses. The Paramount Group, founded in 1912 and headed by Zukor, was the first major production company that controlled the distribution of films. During the 1920s, the motion picture industry was centered in Hollywood, California, where 20 production companies operated. Ultimately the large studios became dominant, including Metro-Goldwyn-Mayer, founded in 1924, and Warner Brothers, established in 1923. The U.S. industry produced four-fifths of the movies made throughout the world and owned about 20,000 theaters during the 1920s. Motion picture "stars" were rapidly becoming household names across the country. In 1921, motion picture producers made 700 films that played in 14,000 theaters, with box-office sales of $300 million. In 1922, after investigations of the industry by the Federal Trade Commission, the Motion Picture Producers and Distributors of America (MPPDA) was founded. Headed by politically connected Republican Postmaster General Will H. Hays, the MPPDA established industry guidelines about the content of films to avoid government scrutiny. The MPPDA code forbade sex, excessive violence, and untoward language.

Technology continued to challenge the motion picture industry and offer new opportunities. The first color films were produced in England as early as 1906, but it was not until the advent of Technicolor in 1922 that cost-effective production of color films was feasible. Sound introduced the era of "talkies"; the first was 1927's *The Jazz Singer*, starring Al Jolson. The age of "silent" films was immediately eclipsed. Some early productions have become classics, including *Gone with the Wind* in 1939, based on Margaret Mitchell's best-seller, and Orson Welles's *Citizen Kane* in 1941, still regarded by many critics as the best motion picture of all time. Labor disputes in the 1930s led to the creation of the Screen Actors' Guild and the Screen Writers' Guild.

Motion pictures remained popular in the late 1940s, but income began to slip in the face of competition from television. Movies would never again sell 4 billion tickets as happened in 1946; ticket sales in 1987 were just over 1 billion. New technology such as wide-screen Cinemascope, first used in the 1953 movie *The Robe*, based on the Lloyd C. Douglas best-seller, revitalized the appeal of motion pictures. Special-effects photography became increasingly sophisticated by the 1970s in films such as Steven Spielberg's *Jaws* and George Lucas's *Star Wars* trilogy. By 1980, the average cost of making a film was about $16 million, and some elaborate productions such as *Superman* surpassed the $50 million mark. The most financially suc-

Thomas Alva Edison's Vitascope premiered the first public U.S. motion picture in 1896, and newsreel footage began appearing on a regular basis in 1897.

cessful film, Spielberg's *E.T.: The Extra-Terrestrial*, grossed $228 million in 1982.

Merger and consolidation in the face of other broadcast media competition were the rule for motion picture companies beginning in the 1970s. Paramount continued to claim about 20 percent of the share of motion picture revenues through the 1980s, but it was purchased by the Gulf and Western telecommunications conglomerate, whose properties included the cable television network USA. Warner Brothers held about a 12 percent share of profits in the 1980s, but it merged with Time, Inc., in 1989. Walt Disney productions, which began in 1923 and controlled about 18 percent of the industry, was best known for its massive theme parks. Twentieth Century Fox, started as Fox Films before World War I, controlled only about 9 percent of the industry when it was purchased by Australian Rupert Murdoch and became part of his huge multimedia communications conglomerate. Founded in 1912, Universal Pictures became part of the entertainment conglomerate MCA, Inc. The Japanese Sony Corporation bought Columbia Pictures in 1989. The trend of consolidation and ultimate reduction of the number of motion picture companies seemed inevitable.

Reference Harpole, Charles, ed., *History of the American Cinema* (1990).

Muckrakers

The muckraking phenomenon in the early years of the twentieth century was unique in media annals. It involved the use of sensational journalistic exposés to promote the Progressive era, encompassing the most sweeping reforms of business and government in U.S. history.

Muckraking journalists were given their moniker by President Theodore Roosevelt, who likened their investigative efforts to John Bunyan's character in *Pilgrim's Progress* who cleaned out the gutters with a rake. The nature of muckraking journalism involved in-depth research and factually documented accounts rather than mere opinion. The muckrakers focused on two related areas of concern: the abusive methods of building private business fortunes through monopolistic practices, and corruption in government from city councils to Congress. The primary audience targeted by the muckrakers was the middle class, which had the ability to bring about reforms through the ballot box.

Although newspapers were not neglected as a tool of the muckraking campaign, the primary vehicles for muckrakers were mass-circulation magazines, which allowed lengthy, detailed analysis of a subject. Participants in the reform movement spawned by the muckrakers were quite varied, from Prohibitionists to municipal reformers. Above all, the muckrakers did not seek to destroy the U.S. capitalist-representative system but to improve it. Whatever their limitations or inadequacies, the muckrakers' record for influencing substantive reforms remains unparalleled in U.S. history.

The magazine credited with inaugurating the muckraking era in 1902 was *McClure's*, published since 1893 by Samuel Sidney McClure as a stylish general-interest magazine. By 1900, *McClure's* had a respectable circulation of 370,000, but its articles on U.S. business and entrepreneurs were laudatory until 1902. Samuel McClure's conversion from adulation to critical analysis of U.S. business occurred gradually. During coverage of the Spanish-American War of 1898, McClure speculated about national as well as business motives for acquiring parts of the dilapidated Spanish empire.

The groundwork for investigative writing was laid when McClure hired Ida Tarbell and Ray Stannard Baker in 1899, followed by Lincoln Steffens in 1902. Tarbell's father had been put out of the oil business by John D. Rockefeller, so her motives for investigating the Standard Oil Company were partly personal. Baker had traveled to Cuba to cover mismanagement in military supply during the 1898 war. Steffens's journalistic career was generally a failure before he was employed by McClure. In the fall of 1902, Steffens began a series on boss rule in St. Louis, Tarbell began her account of the Standard Oil Company, and Baker studied the problems of labor. Steffens eventually revealed details of boss rule in Minneapolis, Pittsburgh, Philadelphia, Chicago, and New York in his essays. Tarbell's series on Standard Oil and Rockefeller continued for two years. Baker wrote articles on child labor and problems of working black Americans. Each entry was carefully documented with names, dates, and places, shocking readers with revelations of public and private elites flaunting laws and trammeling the public interest for the sake of private gain.

Ida Tarbell was a pioneer of the investigative writing that became known as muckraking.

By 1907, circulation of *McClure's* rose to 500,000, demonstrating that literate middle-class readers supported the muckraking exposés. Congress was pressured to strengthen antitrust laws against big business, and voters elected reformers to clean up the graft in government at all levels. Although publisher McClure's primary

motivation in pursuing the investigations was not to increase the magazine's profit potential, success led to unrealistic expansion plans followed by the departure of his top reporters in 1906. By 1911, when McClure left the magazine, its heyday had passed. Even so, *McClure's* was the pioneer in the muckraking era and spurred other magazines to imitate the exposé technique.

After Steffens, Baker, and Tarbell left *McClure's* in 1906, they formed their own journal, *American Magazine,* by purchasing *Frank Leslie's Illustrated Monthly* for $360,000. Yet the reporter-owners departed from the hard-hitting articles that had brought them fame at *McClure's* and relied on an optimistic analysis of the United States' future. The effort was financially unsound, and the company was sold in 1911.

Cosmopolitan, owned by William Randolph Hearst, began a muckraking series in 1906 on special-interest influence in the U.S. Senate, written by David Graham Phillips. Thomas W. Lawson published in *Everybody's* magazine a 1904 series about the emotional influences on Wall Street investment firms. *Collier's* featured a series by Samuel Hopkins Adams on fraud in the patent medicine business during 1905 and 1906. Edward Bok's *Ladies' Home Journal* reinforced the attack on patent medicines and added questions about adulterated processed foods through articles written by Mark Sullivan. After Upton Sinclair's 1906 fact-based study *The Jungle* horrified the public by exposing the lack of safety and sanitation in meat-packing plants, Congress passed the Pure Food and Drug Act to establish production standards and government inspections of manufacturing plants.

See also McClure, Samuel Sidney.

References Chalmers, David M., *The Social and Political Ideas of the Muckrakers* (1964); Wilson, Harold S., *McClure's Magazine and the Muckrakers* (1970).

Munsey, Frank Andrew (1854–1925)

Although not as well known in the newspaper field as contemporaries Scripps, Pulitzer, and Hearst, Frank Munsey created controversy by viewing papers as commodities rather than institutions. Munsey began by building a newspaper chain in the late nineteenth century and later consolidating those papers. His *Munsey's Magazine* was a leader in the muckraking era around the turn of the century.

Afforded little schooling during his youth in Maine, Frank Munsey worked at several jobs, including postmaster, general store clerk, and telegraph operator for Western Union. Upon moving to New York City in 1882, Munsey began publication of *Golden Argosy*, a children's weekly that was later changed to an adult fiction format as *Argosy*. Two other magazine ventures, *Puritan* (1897) and *Junior Munsey* (1900), were merged into *Argosy*. None of these unremarkable efforts hinted at his later success.

The 36-page *Munsey's Weekly*, founded in 1889, was changed to the 96-page monthly *Munsey's Magazine* in 1891. It was a concoction of several elements: satire, fiction, commentary on public affairs, and flamboyant illustrations. The weekly's circulation never rose past 40,000 and lost money. Only after cutting the price from 25 to 10 cents in 1893 did the magazine show any potential. Managing editor Richard Titherington recruited interesting contributors such as Theodore Dreiser, Conan Doyle, Bret Harte, and William Dean Howells. After *Munsey's* took up the muckraking theme in the 1890s, circulation boomed; it became the largest magazine in the United States by 1898, with a circulation over 700,000. *Munsey's* joined other muckraking journals to advocate reforms in government and business that would end corruption and monopolies. During World War I, *Munsey's* reverberated a staunch patriotism and featured articles by government officials. Serialization of novels by P. G. Wodehouse, Joseph Conrad, and others became a regular feature after 1913. *Munsey's Magazine* ended publication in 1929, four years after its founder's death.

Although Munsey's contributions to the magazine industry may have been more notable, he is best remembered for his influ-

ence on the emergence of chain newspapers and the subsequent consolidation in the newspaper industry. Munsey used his large profits from the magazine to buy newspapers. In 1891, Munsey spent $40,000 to rehabilitate the *New York Star* as the tabloid *Continent*, featuring human-interest stories, but it lasted only four months. Then, in 1901, Munsey bought the *Washington Times* and the *New York Daily News*, followed by purchase of the *Boston Journal* in 1902 and the *Baltimore News* and *Philadelphia Times* in 1908. All of Munsey's newspapers backed Republican Party candidates.

Frank Andrew Munsey is best remembered for his influence on the newspaper industry and the emergence of chain newspapers.

Although Munsey made the appearance of the *New York Daily News* more attractive, he lost many of the paper's working-class patrons and some advertising. By 1906, he had lost $750,000 and sold the *Daily News*. After paying $600,000 for the *Boston Journal*, Munsey reduced the price to a penny, removed front-page advertising, and used banner headlines. The *Journal* lost circulation, and Munsey sold it at a loss in 1913.

Munsey made the *Washington Times* the major newspaper force behind the political ambitions of Theodore Roosevelt. Despite having more success with the *Times* than with other dailies, Munsey sold it in 1917 to Arthur Brisbane. Munsey paid $1.5 million for the *Baltimore News* and made few changes; it succeeded financially before being sold in 1915 to Stuart Olivier. The *Philadelphia Times* initially backed labor groups in a local strike, but after Munsey switched editorial positions, the paper's circulation declined until Munsey terminated it in 1914.

About the time of World War I, Munsey shifted his emphasis from building a chain ownership to consolidating the *New York Press* and *Sun* in 1916. The *Press* had been founded in 1887 and proved successful even after Munsey acquired it in 1912 for $1 million. Circulation stayed steady at about 100,000. The *Sun*, once famous under the guidance of Charles Dana, saw its circulation decline to 65,000 by the time Munsey bought it in 1916 for almost $2.5 million. The *Press* was merged into the morning *Sun*, whose editor, Edward Mitchell, remained, and the price was reduced to a penny. In 1920, after failing to move the morning *Sun*'s circulation significantly, Munsey paid $4 million for the *New York Herald* along with the afternoon *Telegram* and merged the morning *Sun* into the *Herald*. After the merger, the evening *Sun* was simply known as the *Sun*.

Munsey tried to purchase the *New York Tribune*, once edited by Horace Greeley and Whitelaw Reid, and merge it with the *Herald*. When the Reid family refused to sell, Munsey sold his *Herald* to the *Tribune* for $5 million in 1924. The new daily became the *Herald Tribune*. Meanwhile, seeking an Associated Press franchise for the evening *Sun*, Munsey bought the *New York Globe* (founded in 1904) for $2 million in 1923 and merged it into the *Sun*. The move doubled the circulation of the *Sun*. Next, in 1924, Munsey purchased the *New York Mail* (founded in 1867) for $2.2 million and merged it with the *Telegram*.

Soon after regaining control of the debt-ridden *Baltimore News* in 1918, Munsey sought to inject new life into the paper by acquiring the *Baltimore American* and the *Star* in 1921. The *Star* was merged into the *News*, but Munsey could not make a profit. He sold the *News* in 1922 and the *American* in 1923 to the Hearst chain. Munsey was negotiating to buy the *Chicago Daily News* in 1925 when he died. Ridiculed by professional contemporaries for his cutthroat tactics, Munsey left a fortune of over $20 million and endowed the Metropolitan Museum of Art in New York City with about half his assets.

Reference Britt, George, *Forty Years—Forty Millions, the Career of Frank A. Munsey* (1935).

Murdoch, Keith Rupert (1931–)

Beginning with a small newspaper foothold in Australia, Rupert Murdoch became one of the world's great multimedia barons by the 1970s. He acquired reputable and large-circulation newspapers in England as well as expanding his holdings in Australia. Murdoch began building a similar empire in the United States. He eventually owned the *New York Post* and *Chicago Sun-Times* as well as television's Fox Broadcasting Company.

Rupert Murdoch was born in Adelaide, Australia, where his father, Sir Keith Murdoch, published the *Adelaide News* and *Sunday Mail* and edited the *Melbourne Herald*. Rupert was just finishing school at Oxford University in England when his father died in 1952. Before he left England, Murdoch's friendship with legendary newspaperman Lord Beaverbrook led to a junior editor's post with London's *Daily Express*. After returning to Australia in 1953, Murdoch spent the remainder of the decade parlaying his two newspaper properties in Adelaide into a major chain. He ultimately bought control of Brisbane's *Sun*, Perth's *Times*, and, most importantly, *The Australian*, *Daily Mirror*, and *Daily Telegraph* in Sydney. He also acquired numerous smaller papers in several other Australian cities as well as venturing into television and a women's magazine.

In 1960, Murdoch moved to London, where he began investing in major London dailies. Murdoch acquired the tabloid *Sun* and England's largest circulation daily, *News of the World;* he even bought the ancient symbol of newspaper respectability, the *Times*, and the much larger circulation *Sunday Times*. In England, Murdoch began his first takeover battles with another international media mogul, Robert Maxwell.

Tiring of the media and union wars in England, Murdoch came to the United States in 1973 to begin building another portion of his empire. Murdoch's first media purchase was in San Antonio: the morning *Express*, the evening *News*, and the combined Sunday edition—all for $19.7 million. The San Antonio papers were redesigned along familiar Murdoch lines: banner headlines and concentration on sensational accounts of crime, sex, and celebrities to the detriment of hard news. Circulation of the *News* increased from 61,000 in 1973 to 75,000 in 1975, but it remained flat for the other editions.

Murdoch wanted a tabloid-type newspaper with a national circulation, but no such property was for sale. Thus, he established the *National Star* (later, simply the *Star)* in 1976 as a nationally distributed weekly. It proved to be serious competition for the well-established and high-circulation *National Enquirer*, passing the 3 million mark in readership within a few years. Following the *Star*'s success, Murdoch paid Dorothy Schiff $30 million for the shaky but venerable *New York Post*, which was the city's only evening daily by the mid-1970s. As was typical after a Murdoch takeover, *Post* editor Paul Sann and other staffers resigned, giving way to former *Time* senior editor Edwin Bolwell at the editorial helm. Through Murdoch's promotion efforts, the *Post* became a major player again in the New York circulation wars. Although employees dreaded the thought of Murdoch as their boss, the slick *New York* magazine and avant-garde *Village Voice*—two rather different weeklies—also became Murdoch properties in the 1970s after he successfully outmaneuvered Clay Felker. Murdoch made James Brady editor of *New York* and David Schneiderman editor of the *Village*

Voice. Circulation for *New York* stabilized at 325,000 and about 150,000 for the *Village Voice*.

Rupert Murdoch built a world multimedia empire consisting of newspapers, magazines, and television interests.

For a brief time after the flurry of U.S. activity, Murdoch became reengaged in both Australia, buying television stations, and Britain, acquiring the *Times*. But he was not finished by any means with his U.S. plans. Murdoch was attracted to Hearst's *Boston Herald American*, which had become a tabloid in 1981 to regain some of its readers lost to the rival *Globe*. The change did not help circulation, and Murdoch offered $1 million down and $7 million in payments for the *Herald American* in 1984. The offer was accepted, and Murdoch changed the name to the *Herald* and brought staffers from the *Post* and the *Star* to enliven the new acquisition. Sports coverage was expanded, and more crime stories and personalities were featured. Although circulation increased by 100,000 the first year, advertising rose only 1 percent.

Murdoch quickly moved from Boston to Chicago in 1983. The Marshall Field–owned liberal *Sun-Times* trailed the conservative *Tribune* narrowly in daily circulation but by a two-to-one margin for the Sunday edition. When Marshall Field V put the Sun-Times up for sale in 1983, publisher James Hoge tried to convince Field not to sell to Murdoch. But Murdoch's bid of $90 million topped a Hoge group offer of $63 million and the *Washington Post* bid of $50 million, and Field agreed to sell to Murdoch in 1984. Publisher Hoge, editor Ralph Otwell, and nationally syndicated columnist Mike Royko all resigned in protest. Murdoch's subscription gimmicks increased circulation by 80,000, and the *Sun-Times* proved to be a profit maker.

The next venture for Rupert Murdoch involved television. To prepare the way for television ventures, Murdoch became a naturalized U.S. citizen to avoid legal penalties against foreign ownership. He was forced by the Federal Communications Commission to divest ownership in the *New York Post* and *Chicago Sun-Times* in 1988 in order to retain control of television stations in those cities. In 1985, Murdoch's company News Corporation paid $575 million for a one-half interest in Twentieth Century Fox, with the idea of transforming it into a new television network. Thanks especially to the cable phenomenon, Fox Broadcasting Company programs reached 80 percent of American homes within two years. The television network was initially built around Murdoch's $1.5 billion purchase of six Metromedia television stations in major markets such as New York, Los Angeles, and Chicago. By 1987, Fox was producing its own television shows and filled most of the prime-time slots. Several of its shows ranked high in the Nielsen ratings. In 1994, Fox outbid CBS to acquire the rights to televise National Football League games.

Forced out of the newspaper markets in New York and Chicago because of his television pursuits, Murdoch bought the publishing house of Harper and Row in 1987. Murdoch's last blockbuster deal came in 1988, when he paid a record $3 billion for Annenberg's Triangle Publications, publisher of *TV Guide* and *Seventeen* magazine. By the 1990s, the Murdoch media holdings in the United States tilted strongest toward broadcasting, followed by magazines and then newspapers. Murdoch had accumulated a debt of almost $3 billion to acquire his U.S. media empire. That empire was acquired without any master plan simply by making moves when opportunities presented themselves.

Reference Leapman, Michael, *Arrogant Aussie: The Rupert Murdoch Story* (1984).

Murrow, Edward Roscoe (1908–1965)

A pioneer broadcaster, Edward R. Murrow guided CBS radio and later television news from the 1930s to the 1960s. Noted for his serious approach and dedication to the truth, Murrow's commentary became familiar to Americans during World War II. He created the television news interview show with his "See It Now" program in the early 1950s. Murrow gained recognition for hard-hitting interviews with controversial figures such as Senator Joseph McCarthy. The end of his career was spent as director of the U.S. Information Agency.

Egbert (later changed to Edward) Roscoe Murrow was born into a North Carolina Quaker family who moved shortly thereafter to Washington. Murrow entered Washington State College in 1926, where he became involved in student affairs, serving on the debate team and as class president and student government president. Murrow's speech instructor at Washington State persuaded him to change his major from business administration to speech. After graduation, Murrow served a year's term as president of the National Student Federation of America in New York City, where he gained his first radio broadcasting experience.

In 1931, Murrow became assistant director of the Institute of International Education, a cultural exchange agency founded by the Carnegie Endowment for International Peace in 1919. The position allowed Murrow to travel in Europe, where he established important contacts and got an early view of the Nazis. The Nazi takeover in Germany in 1933 led to Murrow's editorial service on behalf of a committee to defend academic freedom and free expression. The committee acted as a liaison between exiled German professors seeking employment and U.S. universities. After several years with the institute, Murrow was offered the post of director of talks and events at the Columbia Broadcasting System in 1935.

Edward R. Murrow, a pioneer of broadcast media, invented the television interview show in 1951.

Murrow immediately began to utilize his European contacts and knowledge to obtain news and interviews for CBS about rapidly unfolding international events. The news operation was extremely austere, even for the depression years; CBS's only on-air news reporter was Robert Trout. Murrow coordinated the network's coverage of the 1936 presidential nominating conventions. He also oversaw the weekly overseas commentaries from London and Paris by editorial writers. Murrow convinced CBS to cover the 1936 constitutional crisis created in England by King Edward VIII's decision to marry an American divorcée.

CBS made Murrow its correspondent and director of European news in 1937, with a mandate to break the monopoly held by NBC in Central Europe. Murrow arrived in London, where he remained until the end of World War II. He recruited William L. Shirer to take a post in Berlin and follow Hitler's moves. Murrow went with Shirer to Berlin to demand that the Nazis give CBS the same access to news that NBC enjoyed. There were similar problems with NBC privileges in other nations, including Austria. Yet Murrow was able to broadcast Austria's collapse at the hands of the Nazis in the spring of 1938. When he returned to London, Murrow began broadcasting regular reports about prewar activities to the United States using facilities of the British Broadcasting Corporation. Later in 1938, Murrow in London and Shirer in Prague broadcast reports of the Sudeten crisis in Czechoslovakia.

After World War II began in September 1939, CBS authorized Murrow to hire additional correspondents to cover the conflict. CBS's 14 broadcast reporters contributed to the 30-minute program "European News Roundup" anchored by Hans Van Kaltenborn, giving CBS and NBC an equal footing in Europe for the first time. Murrow continued to engage in reporting himself, covering the Nazi bombing of London during the Battle of Britain in 1940. In 1943, Murrow accompanied Allied bombers on a raid on Berlin and reported the events in a subsequent broadcast. Many of Murrow's broadcasts were part of a bestselling recording of CBS news from 1933 to 1945 sold as "I Can Hear It Now" in 1948.

Murrow was elevated to a vice presidency at CBS following the war. He also handled public affairs for the network, but the administrative duties took him away from broadcasting. A postwar "Hear It Now" radio series occasionally featured Murrow's commentary and interviews. Murrow launched his television series "See It Now" in 1951, modeled after the "Hear It Now" radio show. "See It Now" combined Murrow's interviewing talent and skill at description with the new video medium. Early shows focused on the Korean War and gave viewers a visual representation of modern warfare.

Meanwhile, Senator Joseph McCarthy became a leader in the anticommunist Cold War furor. Some media cooperated with McCarthy's tactics, and others were intimidated by his approach. Murrow consistently questioned McCarthy's methods and brought the issue to the American people on his television program in 1954. The televised interview occurred just prior to network coverage of the McCarthy subcommittee hearings on supposed communist infiltration into the U.S. Army. Following the interview, Murrow gave his own analysis of McCarthyism and the danger of government persecution of individuals. CBS received overwhelming endorsement of Murrow's views from postshow telephone calls.

In 1954, Murrow developed another television interview show for CBS called "Person to Person," which featured celebrities rather than news personalities and paid Murrow almost $100,000. "Person to Person" allowed viewers to see a less serious side of Murrow. The "Person to Person" show was sold to CBS by Murrow's own production company, called Jefferson Productions. Murrow tried to launch spin-offs of "See It Now" with an international setting, and "Small World" was broadcast in 1957, focusing on international events and personalities. Murrow traveled widely for "Small World," but the program was canceled in 1960.

When President Kennedy offered Murrow the post of director of the U.S. Information Agency in 1961, he accepted. Recommended for the job by CBS president Frank Stanton, Murrow was ideally suited to run the agency, which provided foreign news to media outlets and operated the Voice of America radio network. Murrow was frequently interviewed on network television shows by old colleagues such as Howard K. Smith and Harry Reasoner. After conflicts with Vice President Lyndon Johnson and health problems, Murrow resigned in 1963.

See also McCarthy Hearings.

Reference Sperber, Ann M., *Murrow: His Life and Times* (1986).

Mutual Broadcasting System
See Radio.

Nast, Thomas
See Cartoons; *Harper's Weekly.*

Nation, The
Founded by Edwin L. Godkin in 1865 as a liberal journal of news and opinion, *The Nation* had a long and distinguished career as a trendsetter. Godkin's magazine exhibited empathy with what he regarded as the exploited classes, including labor and blacks. Godkin attracted many reputable scholars to write for *The Nation.* Oswald Garrison Villard, Freda Kirchwey, and Carey McWilliams continued to champion civil liberties as editors in the twentieth century.

Edwin Lawrence Godkin was born in England and began his journalism career there before immigrating to the United States in 1856. He wrote some editorials for the *New York Times* but soon evidenced a desire to publish his own weekly journal. Godkin obtained some investors and started *The Nation* in 1865 as a liberal weekly that commented on current affairs. The money ran out quickly, however, and Godkin had to form his own company in 1866 to publish the magazine. Because *The Nation* was intellectually oriented, its circulation rarely rose above 10,000, and the magazine remained on shaky financial ground. Godkin committed *The Nation* to improving conditions for groups such as blacks and labor that could not protect themselves from exploitation.

The early contributors to *The Nation* read like a who's who of the intellectual leadership in the United States. They included Henry and Charles Francis Adams, Henry and William James, and Francis Parkman. Godkin became a leading spokesman for the Liberal Republican movement in the 1870s, which condemned political corruption and called for reconciliation with the former Confederacy. *The Nation* also included literary and art criticism, but its focus remained on the political, social, and economic developments in the nation.

In 1881, Godkin was offered an editorship at the *New York Post* by publisher Henry Villard, who also agreed to purchase *The Nation.* Godkin remained editor of the magazine, which was published under the auspices of the *Post.* During the 1884 presidential campaign, the *Post* and *The Nation* refused to back the Republican candidate James G. Blaine. The election of Democrat Grover Cleveland proved to Godkin that there was a new block of independent voters, which the *Post* and *The Nation* nurtured thereafter. Despite his sympathy with the rights of labor, Godkin vigorously opposed the labor union movement, which he believed was the wrong solution to labor-management problems. Godkin retired as editor of the *Post* and *The Nation* in 1899 and died in 1902.

At the death of publisher Henry Villard in 1900, his son Oswald Garrison Villard became the driving spirit behind the *Post* and *The Nation.* Villard sold the *Post* in 1918 but remained at the editorial helm of *The Nation* until 1933. During this era, the editorial board featured some talented journalists such as Heywood Broun, H. L. Mencken, Max Lerner, Carl Van Doren, and George Seldes. *The Nation* continued to attract literary writers as contributors, including Allen Tate, Dorothy Thompson, Raymond Clapper, and Reinhold Niebuhr. *The Nation* ran afoul of the U.S. Postal Service in 1918 for what the government regarded as unpatriotic writing. It opposed ratification of the Treaty of Versailles in 1919, identified the dangers of totalitarian dictators such as Mussolini and Hitler before other news media, publicized corruption such as the Teapot Dome scandal, and lamented nativist antiforeign sentiments in the Sacco-Vanzetti case. Reporter Louis Fischer dispatched numerous articles about the Soviet Union from Moscow during the late 1920s.

Oswald Villard retired as editor and publisher of *The Nation* in 1933, although he continued to write for the journal. Freda Kirchwey succeeded Villard as editor and publisher. She continued the liberal foreign and domestic commentary of the past and added some feminist touches, such as promotion of birth control. She advocated a collective response against the European dictators to prevent a worldwide catastrophe. During World War II, *The Nation* ridiculed the United States' friendly relations with Vichy France and Franco's Spain. In 1951, after editor Kirchwey refused to allow certain targets of editorials the space to respond, several staffers resigned. Kirchwey stepped down as editor and publisher in 1955 in favor of Carey McWilliams as editor and George Kirstein as publisher, both of whom sought to restore *The Nation*'s traditions. McWilliams had been with *The Nation* since 1926.

Editor McWilliams committed *The Nation* to racial equality in the late 1950s during the advent of the civil rights movement. Exposés of corruption focused on the city of New York in 1959 and on the Central Intelligence Agency in 1961. Ralph Nader wrote his first major piece advocating greater attention to safety by automobile manufac-

E. L. Godkin founded The Nation *in 1865 as a liberal weekly committed to improving conditions for minorities and exploited workers.*

turers in 1959. Circulation remained modest but respectable, totaling just under 120,000 in 1968. Most influential American writers read *The Nation* regularly. By 1994, when Neil Black served as president and Richard Lingeman as executive editor, *The Nation*'s circulation had fallen to 95,000.

Reference Ogden, Rollo, *Life and Letters of Edwin Lawrence Godkin* (1907).

National Association of Broadcasters (NAB)

In 1923, soon after radio broadcasting began to spread across the United States, broadcasters organized a professional association. The National Association of Broadcasters (NAB) represents virtually all the television stations and more than half the radio stations broadcasting today. The association promotes the business interests of the industry but has also adopted a code of ethical conduct.

Although radio broadcasting stations invited government regulation of the airwaves long before the Radio Act of 1927 created the Federal Radio Commission, they did not have to wait to organize their own professional association. Broadcasters began convening national conferences in Washington, D.C., in 1922, and the idea emerged for a national professional association. The issue that precipitated the founding of the NAB in 1923 was the demand by the American Society of Composers, Authors, and Publishers (ASCAP) for more lucrative fees for the right to broadcast ASCAP's music. Paul Klugh was the NAB's first managing director.

The NAB has focused much of its attention on the issue of advertising, as indicated in its 1929 code of conduct. It formed the Broadcast Ratings Council in 1963, with the approval of the three major networks; it offered verification to advertisers that their messages are reaching the intended audiences. Many of the NAB's historic concerns have revolved around the tendency of the federal government to regulate the industry. The association favored the enactment of the Radio Act of 1927, which established a system of licensing broadcast stations through the Federal Radio Commission. The NAB sought resolution of conflicts over stations' interference with one another's signal power and broadcast band frequency. The NAB urged the commission to avoid the temptation of censorship. The association's *Broadcasting in the United States*, published in 1933, defended the industry as a promoter of diverse educational and cultural programs.

When the Federal Communications Commission (FCC) was created in 1934, it assumed the functions of the Radio Commission. Although the NAB's revised 1939 code opposed editorials on the air, it could not enforce the policy, in large part because most stations were not members. In 1941, during a license renewal application, the FCC raised objections to editorials being broadcast by the Mayflower Broadcasting Company's WAAB in Boston. Thereafter, broadcast stations were prohibited by the FCC from expressing an editorial point of view. Although this was comparable to its own policy, the NAB opposed the 1941 FCC decision as a violation of the First Amendment. The NAB preferred a voluntary adherence to a noneditorial policy. During World War II, the NAB urged broadcasters to cooperate with the government regarding war news but continued to oppose government censorship. A 1949 compromise, the FCC's so-called Fairness Doctrine, allowed stations to state their editorial views but guaranteed others holding different views equal response time on the station.

Eventually, separate radio and television codes were developed in 1952. The codes vaguely sought integrity and restraint from broadcasters and the avoidance of "horror, suspense and undue excitement." Whenever questions arose concerning the code, they were submitted to an NAB committee in Washington. At first, only about half the broadcasting stations—mainly larger ones—subscribed to the NAB code, even though all the national networks were members. By 1974, only 57 percent of broadcasting stations were members of the

NAB—although about 90 percent of television stations were members—and not all its members subscribed to the codes of ethics. In 1992, 940 television stations and 4,900 radio stations were members of the NAB. Those that did not follow the NAB codes argued that federal regulation made the codes superfluous. Then, in 1982, a federal court ruled that portions of the code restricting the number and length of commercials violated the Sherman Antitrust Act. The NAB promptly suspended the codes, and nothing has been produced to take their place.

The NAB also published books on careers in broadcasting, legal questions, and how to start a broadcasting station. The principal public notice of the NAB derived from its annual conventions in Washington, which usually concentrated on mundane matters such as technology and management. Only occasionally did the convention create excitement, such as the 1961 meeting. NAB president Leroy Collins chided the membership for their obsession with balance sheets while ignoring the public interest. Collins's surprising remarks were followed by another stunner from recently appointed FCC chairman Newton Minnow. He cited television's trends toward violence, contrived formula comedies and dramas, and an absence of realism in human relations. Minnow concluded: "when television is bad, nothing is worse. I invite you to sit down in front of your television set . . . you will observe a vast wasteland."

National Broadcasting Company (NBC)

Created as the broadcasting arm of the Radio Corporation of America (RCA) in 1926, the National Broadcasting Company (NBC) dominated the early years of network radio with two networks. A ruling by the Federal Communications Commission (FCC) in 1943 forced NBC to divest itself of its less profitable "blue" network to the American Broadcasting Company (ABC). NBC also led the development of television broadcasting in the 1940s. NBC programming attracted the biggest stars in the entertainment business, and its programs remained on top in ratings. General Electric purchased RCA—and with it NBC—in 1986 for $6.3 billion. The NBC radio network was sold to Westwood One in 1987 for $50 million.

Electronics industry leader RCA engineered the formation of NBC in 1926, with RCA holding 50 percent ownership, General Electric 30 percent, and Westinghouse 20 percent. WEAF in New York City, previously owned by American Telephone and Telegraph (AT&T), became NBC's anchor station. Owen D. Young became chairman and James G. Harbord president of NBC. Within a few months, NBC had established two networks. Originally, WEAF headed the "red" network, which transmitted via telephone lines owned by AT&T; a former Westinghouse station, WJZ, anchored the "blue" network, which transmitted via radio waves. Because advertisers favored the red network, it quickly established its supremacy over the blue network, despite NBC's efforts to offer evenhanded support. By 1931, both NBC-red and NBC-blue had 61 radio stations coast to coast.

Because the Justice Department objected to the monopolistic tendencies of the cooperative venture involving RCA, General Electric, and Westinghouse, RCA president David Sarnoff worked out a dissolution of the partnership in 1932. Agreeing to accept other assets as compensation, General Electric and Westinghouse withdrew from NBC, leaving RCA the sole owner.

NBC radio programs included ratings winners such as "Amos and Andy," "Edgar Bergen–Charlie McCarthy," and "Jack Benny." The "March of Time," a quasi-documentary program originally sponsored by *Time* magazine, ran from 1931 to 1945 on NBC's blue network, with 18 million listeners. Following a dispute with newspapers and wire services about news access, A. A. Schechter established NBC's news-gathering agency in 1933, relying on affiliate stations to contribute news stories. Lowell Thomas became NBC-blue's first newscaster with a regular program. NBC lured news broadcasting pioneer Hans Van Kaltenborn from CBS in 1940 and spent large sums to obtain regular reports from battlefields in Europe during World War II.

The FCC's 1941 "Report on Chain Broadcasting" spelled trouble for NBC's two radio networks. The FCC argued that NBC used one network to shield the other from competition. The end result of FCC pressure and an unsuccessful lawsuit was RCA's sale of its NBC-blue radio network of 168 stations to ABC in 1943 for $8 million. Meanwhile, NBC's television broadcasts emerged gradually after Sarnoff announced the company's first television development project in 1935. Television programming advanced steadily after World War II, with sporting events and dramatic presentations highlighting early programming. NBC won an important victory over CBS in 1947 when the FCC approved its color television system, which was compatible with older black-and-white sets. CBS's incompatible technology would have required scrapping older sets. NBC's first network telecast in color was the 1 January 1954 Tournament of Roses parade preceding the Rose Bowl. Yet even with NBC's early advantage in color television programming, the competition among the three television networks was a fairly even match.

NBC television news programs were headed by the "Camel News Caravan" hosted by John Cameron Swayze, a 15-minute early evening broadcast started in 1949. "Meet the Press" originated in an interview format on radio in 1945 and moved to television in 1947. Network coverage of presidential nominating conventions began in earnest in 1952 and 1956. The successful pairing of Chet Huntley and David Brinkley at the 1956 conventions led to their installation as coanchors of the nightly newscast, replacing Swayze. Following Huntley's retirement in 1970, NBC "Nightly News" was anchored by various newsmen, including John Chancellor and Tom Brokaw. In 1948, NBC's Pauline Frederick was the first woman reporter to cover a political convention. When executives at NBC decided to cover the coronation of Queen Elizabeth II from England in 1953, they produced a rapid film-development technique that allowed the network to scoop its U.S. competition. NBC news began a series of programs known as "White Papers" beginning in 1960, offering in-depth examination of important public policy issues such as civil rights, the U-2 affair with the Soviet Union, and the Vietnam War.

Sylvester L. Weaver moved from vice president in charge of television to president of NBC between 1949 and 1953. He proved to be a successful innovator of the popular TV magazine format and specials or spectaculars. Weaver began NBC's early morning "Today" show in 1952 with host Dave Garroway; the format involved repeating news briefs every half hour, interspersed with "magazine" variety-interview segments. NBC also pioneered late-night television programming with its 1954 "Tonight" show hosted by Jack Paar. The other networks borrowed NBC's ideas and often competed effectively, but NBC also copied its competitors and presented its own daytime soap operas. Some NBC innovations proved embarrassing, such as its quiz show, "Twenty-One." In 1959, when one of the winning contestants, Charles Van Doren, admitted to receiving answers to the questions in advance, NBC found its integrity damaged.

Robert Sarnoff succeeded his father as chairman of RCA in the 1950s and remained until the late 1970s. As part of the media merger fever of the 1980s, former partner General Electric paid $6.3 billion in 1986 to acquire RCA and NBC. Prior to its purchase of NBC, General Electric owned only a single television station in Denver. In 1987, General Electric agreed to sell the NBC radio network to Westwood One, headed by Norm Pattiz, which already owned Mutual Broadcasting Company.

With NBC's prime-time programming and news shows suffering losses in the ratings, there were various executive shuffles. When NBC reduced the news division staff by 400 in 1987, NBC News president Larry Grossman resigned. Michael Gartner, a

Gannett print media news executive, became president of NBC News in 1988 to enliven formats on the evening news and on programs such as "Meet the Press." By 1987, for the first time in history, the three networks held less than a 50 percent share of the television audience—a sign of cable television's impact on viewers.

See also Radio Corporation of America.

Reference "NBC: 50th Anniversary; Spearhead of Broadcast Industry Marks Beginning," *Television/Radio Age* (1976).

National Gazette

Democratic-Republican leaders Thomas Jefferson and James Madison created the *National Gazette* as a rival to the Federalist newspaper, the *Gazette of the United States*. The *National Gazette* served as the principal mouthpiece of Jefferson and Madison in their battles with Alexander Hamilton and the Federalist majority in Congress during the 1790s.

As political parties emerged in the 1790s, newspapers became the primary vehicle of communicating partisan ideas. Because the Federalists had already established their own newspaper—the *Gazette of the United States*—to promote the Washington administration policies in 1789, the political opposition led by Thomas Jefferson and James Madison saw the need for their own newspaper as a counterweight. It was Madison who suggested Philip Freneau as the editor of the semiweekly paper, to be called the *National Gazette*. Descended from a French Huguenot family, Freneau had been a classmate of Madison's at Princeton, was a Revolutionary War veteran and former prisoner of war, and was an experienced journalist. He agreed to edit the *National Gazette* for $250 a year and a part-time position as translator in Jefferson's State Department. The paper began publication in the temporary capital of Philadelphia in 1791.

Freneau immediately launched into attacks on the Hamilton fiscal program, especially the proposal for a national bank. The editor used satire to lampoon the Federalist

foes, including Hamilton, Vice President John Adams, and, to a lesser degree, President Washington. The most controversial issue raised by the *National Gazette* was the administration's anti-French foreign policy in the Anglo-French conflict in Europe. It was easy for the staunchly anti-British Freneau to make the Jefferson-Madison sympathy toward France crystal clear, even to the point of collecting money for France.

This 16 April 1792 edition of the National Gazette *contains an anti-Federalist letter on the front page. The* Gazette *was founded by Democratic-Republican leaders Thomas Jefferson and James Madison to combat Alexander Hamilton and the Federalist majority Congress.*

Hamilton and the Federalists smarted from the Freneau attacks but responded in kind through the *Gazette of the United States*. Hamilton questioned the patriotism of the *National Gazette* and charged that it was simply the personal vehicle for Jefferson's partisan attacks. President Washington himself was enraged at some of the more caustic Freneau statements about the administration. Washington demanded that Jefferson fire Freneau from his post in the State Department. For his part, Jefferson rejected Federalist charges that the *National Gazette* was a personal mouthpiece and argued that the rivalry between editors Freneau and Fenno of the *Gazette of the United States* was based on ideological grounds. Jefferson believed that the *National Gazette* served a high purpose in protecting the Constitution from being undermined by a tendency toward monarchy.

The end of the *National Gazette* came suddenly and was precipitated by Jefferson's decision to resign as secretary of state at the beginning of Washington's second term in 1793. Both advertisers and subscribers showed reluctance to continue support for the *National Gazette* with Jefferson out of office. Moreover, a yellow fever epidemic in Philadelphia in the fall of 1793 forced all newspapers to suspend publication. Unlike the *Gazette of the United States*, which was bailed out by Hamilton's subsidies, Freneau found no patron to save the *National Gazette*.

Because they served political parties, the *National Gazette* and its Federalist counterpart were not typical newspapers. Yet the times demanded vehicles to disseminate political ideas. Partisan newspapers were practical and relatively inexpensive methods of airing the debates over issues and personalities, with the ultimate benefit of informing the public. The continued existence of a free press, especially one that allowed open partisanship, was ensured by a constitutional government able to accommodate criticism and political debate in print.

Reference Axelrad, Jacob, *Philip Freneau: Champion of Democracy* (1967).

National Intelligencer

In the age of intense partisan journalism around 1800, the *National Intelligencer* set the standard for media coverage of Congress. Editor-publisher Samuel Harrison Smith began reporting congressional debates just after the capital was moved to its permanent site in the District of Columbia in 1800. Smith was hampered by Congress itself and by federal judges before gaining full access to both the House and Senate chambers. The *National Intelligencer* became the chief source of congressional action for newspapers across the young nation. Smith sold the *Intelligencer* to Joseph Gales Jr. in 1810; he and William Seaton continued to publish the paper into the 1860s.

Samuel Harrison Smith was born in Philadelphia. His father had been an ardent patriot during the Revolution. Smith graduated from the University of Pennsylvania in 1787 and added a master's degree three years later. He began a printing establishment in 1791 but had only modest success in the highly competitive Philadelphia market. Smith was acquainted with pro-Jefferson journalists Philip Freneau and Benjamin Franklin Bache. During 1796 and 1797, Smith published his own newspaper called the *New World*, which supported Jefferson's Democratic-Republican Party. In 1797, Smith bought Joseph Gales's weekly *Independent Gazetteer* (founded in 1782) and changed its name to the *Universal Gazette*. Most news in the *Gazette* concerned government activities in the temporary capital of Philadelphia, but Smith pledged editorial neutrality toward political issues and personalities.

Smith was already considering leaving Philadelphia for New York City in 1800 when Democratic-Republican presidential candidate Thomas Jefferson and his future Secretary of the Treasury Albert Gallatin persuaded Smith to start a Democratic-Republican paper in the District of Columbia. Smith maintained ownership of the *Universal Gazette* until 1810 but began the *National Intelligencer and Washington Advertiser* at the end of October 1800. The *Intelligencer* was published three times a week at a subscription price of $5 a year. Smith promised to pursue the truth but also intended to include opinion. The Speaker of the House of Representatives refused to allow Smith a place on the House floor to report debates, so he obtained information from the clerk. By 1802, however, he was allowed to record the debates in shorthand for both the House and the Senate. Verbatim excerpts of congressional debates were printed in the *National Intelligencer*. The paper also published government proclamations and advertisements.

Smith's reports did not always please congressmen, who tried to exclude him when accounts reflected poorly on them or the institution. The Federalists tried to obtain an indictment for libel against Smith on one occasion, but a grand jury refused to vote the bill. Editors of other national newspapers recognized and applauded the service rendered by Smith's congressional reporting. Smith insisted that despite his sympathies for Jefferson, the *National Intelligencer*'s reports were objective. Still, Federalist editors charged that the *Intelligencer* was simply the mouthpiece of President Jefferson, as evidenced by the frequent meetings between Smith and Jefferson.

In 1808, Joseph Gales Jr. joined Smith's paper as a reporter. Gales's father had sold Smith the *Philadelphia Gazette* back in 1797, and young Gales had worked for his father in Raleigh after attending the University of North Carolina. In 1809, Smith made the younger Gales a partner in the *Intelligencer*, planning to retire when possible. A year and a half later, in 1810, Smith sold both the *National Intelligencer* and his *Philadelphia Universal Gazette* to Joseph Gales Jr. A business partner, William Winston Seaton, was recruited in 1812 to assist Gales in managing the *Intelligencer*. Gales and Seaton published the *National Intelligencer* until the eve of the Civil War.

The *National Intelligencer* continued to act effectively as the official organ of the James Madison administration (1809–1817). Editorially, the paper supported the movement toward war with Great Britain, and Gales often discussed policy with the so-called War Hawks. British troops destroyed the *Intelligencer*'s offices during their assault on the capital in 1814. After the war, under the administration of James Monroe (1817–1825), the *Intelligencer* recouped

some of its financial losses from the war by obtaining the government printing contract. Congressional reports continued to dominate the pages of the *Intelligencer* during these years. Perhaps 600 papers copied congressional reports from the *Intelligencer*.

The *Intelligencer* lost its printing contract when Andrew Jackson became president in 1829. The Democratic Party had its own collection of editors and newspapers for support and patronage. Despite Democratic opposition, Gales and Seaton obtained a government contract to publish the *American State Papers* in 1831, a project that continued until 1861. The *National Intelligencer* strongly backed Henry Clay and the new Whig Party in the presidential election of 1832. The paper remained critical of Democrats such as Martin Van Buren and opposed the Mexican War (1846–1848) during Democrat James K. Polk's term.

Gales and Seaton underestimated the furor over slavery and backed the Compromise of 1850 as a permanent settlement of the issue. They did not give credence to radical southern notions about secession because they were devoted to the union of states. Although they admired Abraham Lincoln personally, the *Intelligencer* supported the Democrats in the elections of 1860 and 1864. The *Intelligencer*'s circulation rarely rose above 2,000, and by the 1850s, the *Washington Star* had more than twice as many subscribers and led the eight capital dailies. After Gales's death in 1860, Seaton continued to edit and write for the *Intelligencer* until he sold the paper at the end of 1864 to Snow, Coyle and Co. The new owners tried to enliven the format and content of the *Intelligencer* but failed to find a following. The paper ended publication in 1869.

Reference Ames, William E., *A History of the National Intelligencer* (1972).

National News Council
Amidst the growing public criticism of the integrity of the news media, the National News Council was established in 1973 to serve as a clearinghouse for ethical prob-

lems. Although the council was backed by many major media, it was also opposed as unnecessary by others, including the *New York Times*. Thus, the controversy about how to deal with public criticism was not resolved by the council's creation. Not surprisingly, with an absence of consensus, the council lost its funding in 1984.

Because of the press's visibility in reporting the Vietnam War, the violent Democratic Party convention in 1968, and the Watergate affair during 1973 and 1974, public confidence in the accuracy and impartiality of the news media concerned many of its owners and ethicists. Another factor was the celebrity status of many newspeople as television became a widespread source of the public's news. An article in the respected *Columbia Journalism Review* characterized professional journalists of the early 1970s as a "separate and subversive class." Many organizations set about to create internal codes of conduct or appoint ombudsmen to investigate complaints. By 1985, about 35 ombudsmen operated in different parts of the nation, trying to rectify public concerns and set internal standards. Organizational codes of ethics concentrated on limiting activities of employees that might compromise the integrity of the media employer.

Other professionals advocated an external, independent agency to oversee media ethics. The Newspaper Guild funded a number of local news councils in states such as California, Illinois, and Colorado, which featured members of the media and the public addressing ethical questions. Modeled after the British Press Council (created in 1953 and revamped in 1964 to receive public complaints about press coverage in order to reduce libel suits), the National News Council was inaugurated in the United States in 1973 and headquartered in New York City. The council was recommended and funded by the Twentieth Century Fund and several other foundations to "make press freedom more secure" while retaining independence from any media corporate influence. The council's objectives were to hear complaints about the media, champion press freedom, and analyze ethical issues. Its membership included 18 public and media officials; the executive director was William B. Arthur, former editor of *Look* magazine. Major media organizations such as the *Washington Post, Wall Street Journal, Christian Science Monitor*, Columbia Broadcasting System, and Associated Press supported the creation of the council. Arthur O. Sulzberger of the *New York Times* led opposition to the council, which was regarded as an unneeded intrusion into an area that was already adequately self-policed.

The News Council proved reluctant to intervene in "local" matters and arbitrarily focused only on questions of national import. It did not deal with "editorial" matters, except for factual questions. Moreover, the council did not investigate any question that was not brought to it by an outside principal. It made no attempt to scrutinize ethical practices on its own investigatory authority. Further, there were no penalties provided for actions that the council might condemn.

Except for the period from 1976 to 1982, when former *Louisville Courier-Journal* editor Norman Isaacs chaired the council, it lacked aggressive leadership. Thus, because many media companies had opposed the council when it was founded and initial supporters showed unhappiness with its performance, the funding was dropped in 1984, and the council dissolved. Of the 249 complaints heard by the council, 35 percent were judged to be warranted. Two-thirds of the complaints concerned television networks, and the remaining third dealt with newspapers. The complaints or decisions were not widely publicized, since only journals such as the *Columbia Journalism Review* regularly reported council activities.

Reference Brogan, Patrick, *Spiked: The Short Life and Death of the National News Council* (1985).

Natural Disasters

Media have always been drawn to report natural disasters, because humans are awed by such events. They are usually unpredictable and unavoidable, and the public is fascinated by the ferocity of nature. As the era of electronic media dawned in the twentieth century, television offered more dramatic coverage of such disasters—from small-scale fires to major hurricanes and earthquakes. This media attention creates a heightened public awareness of such dangers.

Major urban fire disasters often got only local news coverage. An 1835 fire in New York City destroyed over 500 structures. The great Chicago fire of 1871, following 14 weeks of drought, destroyed about $2 million worth of property and killed 250 people. A fire in Boston destroyed over 800 buildings in 1872. Fires in theaters, clubs, and hotels accounted for the greatest loss of life. The Chicago Iroquois Theater fire in 1903 killed over 600. The 1942 Cocoanut Grove nightclub fire in Boston killed 491. There were 146 fatalities in Atlanta's Winecoff Hotel fire in 1946. Improved fire-prevention techniques reduced the deaths from fires in the second half of the twentieth century. For example, only eight died in the Las Vegas Hilton hotel fire in 1981. Forest fires periodically ravage the woodlands and sometimes threaten residential areas, especially on the West Coast, where fires ravaged 6 million acres in 1988.

Earthquakes are often associated with specific areas of the nation, such as California, but they have occurred in a wide variety of locations. Many reporters, including Henry Grady of the *Atlanta Constitution*, covered the Charleston, South Carolina, earthquake of 1886. Probably the most memorable earthquake was the 1906 San Francisco quake, which destroyed most of the city because it was accompanied by numerous fires. The city's major newspaper buildings were among the losses, and over 500 people died. Although sophisticated earthquake monitoring technology has become available, it cannot predict or prepare communities for the actual quakes.

Floods have occurred on small and large scales throughout the history of the nation. They are usually associated with heavy rains, storms, and hurricanes. The Johnstown, Pennsylvania, flood of 1889, caused by a dam break, led to the deaths of 2,200

people and was covered extensively by New York, Philadelphia, and Pittsburgh newspapers. Over 700 deaths were attributed to flooding in Ohio and Indiana in 1913. Destructive floods along the Mississippi River have been numerous; 250 people were killed in 1937, and in 1993, there was $12 billion worth of damage but only 24 deaths. Flooding tends to do more physical than human damage, especially as more people move into floodplains. Television shots from helicopters provide especially dramatic visual representation of flood damage.

Hurricanes strike only coastal areas, but their power can devastate the topography. The Galveston hurricane of 1900 caused 6,000 deaths because the city is located on a coastal island that was flooded. A 1938 hurricane that struck New England left 600 dead, partly due to associated flooding. Even after the National Weather Service developed the technology to predict the course of hurricanes, they still destroyed at will. Camille in 1969 struck the Mississippi Gulf coast with 200-mile-an-hour winds and a storm surge of 24 feet, killing 140. Hurricane Agnes in 1972 caused flooding and 118 deaths along the Atlantic coast. Hurricane Andrew, which struck south Florida below Miami in 1992, produced the greatest amount of property damage in the history of hurricanes. Television coverage of hurricanes provides viewers with firsthand evidence of the power of such storms.

Tornadoes are sometimes by-products of hurricanes, but more often they occur in the plains areas of the Midwest, especially Texas, Oklahoma, and Kansas. Modern technology can warn of tornadoes, as it does with hurricanes, but tornado paths are more unpredictable. The single greatest tornado disaster occurred in 1925 when a storm in the Midwest killed 689 people. A series of tornadoes struck Illinois, Kentucky, and Ohio in 1974, the deadliest blow coming at Xenia, Ohio. Altogether, 310 people in 12 states died as a result of the storms. The event caused NBC television to produce a special program on tornadoes.

Other types of natural disasters also occur periodically in particular parts of the nation. Blizzards have hit the northeastern states especially hard over the years. The famous 1888 blizzard in New York and New England left 400 dead. The *New York Times* and other papers provided considerable coverage. The blizzard of 1958 caused the death of 345, and a similar one in 1960 left 354 dead. Droughts have affected agricultural areas where the land has been ploughed extensively, making the loosened soil susceptible to strong winds. The worst drought occurred in the so-called Dust Bowl during the 1930s in Oklahoma, Texas, Kansas, and New Mexico. The social and economic impact was chronicled by John Steinbeck's *The Grapes of Wrath* as well as by local newspapers. The publicity caused the Department of Agriculture to create the Soil Conservation Service. Volcanic eruptions are among the rarest form of disaster in the United States, but the Mount St. Helens eruption in 1980 killed 60 people and caused ecological damage to a wide area of the Northwest.

In recent decades, environmental concerns have been heightened by ecological disasters, some of which were caused by human fault. The near-catastrophic Three Mile Island, Pennsylvania, nuclear reactor accident in 1979 received so much adverse media attention that it virtually halted the nuclear power industry's development. Likewise, the 240,000-barrel oil spill by the *Exxon-Valdez* off the coast of Alaska in 1989 created a public backlash against oil exploration and transportation efforts as well as the Exxon corporation itself.

New England Courant

James Franklin, brother of Benjamin Franklin, boldly published the first antigovernment newspaper in the American colonies from Boston. Although the *Courant* lasted only a few years, it established an important American newspaper tradition of remaining independent of government and proved that the style and quality of newspaper writing could be improved.

Between 1719 and 1721, James Franklin

gained experience as the printer of the *Boston Gazette* and of inflammatory pamphlets. Backed by several dissidents from the local Boston government, Franklin published the first issue of the two-page weekly *New England Courant* in August 1721. The paper attacked the clergy's influence on government and opposed Dr. Zabdiel Boylston's use of experimental inoculations designed to slow the spread of a smallpox epidemic. The *Courant* reprinted biting essays by Whig writers in England such as Richard Steele and Joseph Addison. The satirical format of an English journal, the *Spectator*, was unashamedly copied. The *Courant* also included humorous items to enliven and distinguish the paper from its five Boston rivals.

Franklin employed controversial Anglican minister John Checkley as editor. Checkley immediately attacked the Calvinist clergy led by Cotton Mather for their backing of the untested smallpox inoculations. Although Franklin soon removed Checkley as editor, the *Courant* continued its anti-inoculation campaign. Franklin's opponents referred to his group as the "Hell-Fire Club" after a similar antiestablishment political coterie in England. Unquestionably, James Franklin pioneered the type of crusading editorship that would become popular throughout U.S. journalism.

Franklin's ability to criticize the government and its backers so freely was due in part to a diversionary struggle between the governor and the legislature over executive licensing powers. In 1722, however, Franklin's criticism of the government's failure to protect shipping from pirates landed him in jail, charged with seditious libel. During his jail term, Franklin's 17-year-old brother Benjamin kept the *Courant* going. After his release from jail, James Franklin was forbidden by the Massachusetts government from printing without its approval. Franklin refused to submit to prior restraint and was arrested again. However, a grand jury refused to indict him, and Franklin allowed his brother to remain as nominal editor so as to avoid government control over publication of the *Courant*. Benjamin wrote a series of satirical essays for the *Courant* under the pseudonym "Silence Dogood."

After a quarrel with his brother about apprenticeship in late 1723, Benjamin Franklin left Boston for Pennsylvania. James Franklin was soon overwhelmed by debt and forced to give up the *Courant* in 1726. He continued in the newspaper business in Rhode Island until his death in 1735. Although its defiance of the government did not sustain the *New England Courant*, James Franklin's determined independence established an important precedent for future American journalists.

See also Franklin, Benjamin.

Reference Smith, Jeffrey A., "James Franklin," in *Dictionary of Literary Biography: American Newspaper Journalists, 1690–1872*, ed. Perry J. Ashley (1985).

New Journalism

The term "new journalism" has been used to describe two periods of media history. The first era at the close of the nineteenth century ushered in true mass communication through new types of news gathering, newspaper formats, advertising, and photojournalism. It is associated most often with pioneers such as Joseph Pulitzer and William Randolph Hearst. The second era in the 1960s produced nonfiction reportage as well as advocacy, alternative, underground, and precision journalism—all published outside of the traditional media outlets.

Joseph Pulitzer got his start as a publisher with the *St. Louis Post-Dispatch*, but his major splash on the newspaper scene came after 1883 through his direction of the *New York World*, which became the largest-circulation daily in the United States. Pulitzer instructed his reporters not to be satisfied with a superficial approach to news gathering but to dig beneath the surface to discover the complete and unvarnished story. The news stories in Pulitzer's papers were accompanied by bold headlines that invited curious readers to purchase the paper to read the full account. Thus, Pulitzer relied more on newsstand sales than subscriptions to extend circulation.

William Randolph Hearst's origins were with the *San Francisco Examiner* (1887), but he followed Pulitzer into the New York competition by purchasing the *Journal* in 1895. Hearst outdid even Pulitzer in resorting to sensational stories and features to attract readers. Hearst's influence in moving the nation to war with Spain in 1898 over Cuba demonstrated the capacity of the "new journalism" to influence a nation's destiny.

Both Pulitzer and Hearst relied on the latest technology, such as the linotype, to print a greater quantity of papers more efficiently; the telephone to speed news gathering; and photographs to portray life more realistically. The format of the modern paper was also constructed by this "new journalism" of the 1880s and 1890s. New departments covered sports and recreation and women's and society news, and entertaining comic strips were added. More women became involved in the reporting and editing of newspapers in the era, especially during the muckraking period. The "new journalism" featured lively editorials that buttressed a paper's crusades or point of view. The other major change in the "new journalism" era was the expanded role of the business manager. Newspapers and other media increasingly relied on financial expertise to guide their policies. Tremendous competition for circulation and its related element of advertising required careful attention as never before. A number of general-interest magazines such as *McClure's, Cosmopolitan, Ladies' Home Journal*, and the *Saturday Evening Post* followed the lead of newspaper innovators in making their product more attractive to readers.

The second era of "new journalism" emerged in the 1960s when several enterprising young reporters departed from the traditional method of news gathering through questions and began to pursue interpretive reporting with new language and style. There were several types of "new journalism" in this era: nonfiction reportage, alternative journalism akin to muckraking, advocacy journalism, underground journalism, and precision journalism.

The new nonfiction reporting focused on social trends, celebrities, and public affairs. The stories used a fictional veneer, but careful research ensured that they were factually based. Tom Wolfe wrote magazine articles that featured descriptive prose designed to shock and enlighten. Truman Capote's novel *In Cold Blood* told the story of a grizzly murder from the point of view of the murderers. Gay Talese wrote numerous articles for *Esquire* featuring biographical treatments of celebrities. He also examined the inner workings—especially the personalities—of the *New York Times* in a work entitled *The Kingdom and the Power.* Columnist Jimmy Breslin used the new style to examine sports organizations from within. Syndicated tabloid television newsmagazines relied on sensational insider stories about celebrities to attract audiences in the 1990s.

Advocacy journalism simply endorsed a particular point of view with regard to issues or causes. The most colorful example was Hunter S. Thompson, who criticized mainstream journalists for their overly friendly approach to covering presidential candidates in 1972. Alternative journalism pursued accurate detail in investigations to portray the essence of people or issues that were dealt with only superficially by the mainstream press. Most of the alternative newspapers, such as the *San Francisco Bay Guardian* or New York's *Village Voice*, had modest and usually local circulations. Alternative journalism also fostered the birth of several analytical media reviews, including the *Columbia Journalism Review* (1961) and the *Washington Journalism Review* (1977). Such journals gave professionals the opportunity to critique and improve the profession.

Underground journalism referred to a series of unauthorized publications that challenged or offered a contrary perspective to the existing official publications in schools, universities, and military bases. The underground papers invariably criticized aspects of the establishment and offered their pages as forums for discussion of taboo subjects, such as the drug culture.

Precision journalism also criticized the typical methods of the mainstream reporters. This field relied heavily on social science methods such as surveys and random sampling. The primary leader in defining the precision methodology was professor Philip Meyer at the University of North Carolina journalism school. Statistical analysis has not found its place in traditional media circles because private firms can be hired to do surveying or sampling.

References Dennis, Everette E., and William L. Rivers, *Other Voices: The New Journalism in America* (1974); Johnson, Michael L., *The New Journalism* (1971).

New Orleans Times-Picayune

Begun as the *New Orleans Picayune* by George W. Kendall and Francis A. Lumsden in 1837, the morning daily won plaudits for its aggressive and accurate coverage of the Mexican War. A merger with the *Times-Democrat* in 1914 created the *Times-Picayune*, owned by L. K. Nicholson. Purchase of the *States* in 1933 gave the paper an evening edition, which expanded with the acquisition of the *Item* in 1958 to produce the *States-Item*. Samuel Newhouse bought the *Times-Picayune* in 1962.

Francis Asbury Lumsden, a native of North Carolina, and George Wilkins Kendall of New Hampshire came to New Orleans in 1835. Both had newspaper experience, Lumsden with the *Raleigh Observer* and Kendall at the *Mobile Register.* They met while they were both working at the *National Intelligencer* in Washington, D.C. When they arrived in New Orleans, Kendall and Lumsden found employment at different newspapers. After one year, they pooled their savings to launch the morning *Picayune* in 1837 without a printing press; a hand press was purchased in a few months. Despite the Panic of 1837 and the depression that followed, the *Picayune* rose in circulation and advertising. In fact, the paper had to stop accepting subscriptions after 2,500 because its antiquated presses could not keep pace. Editor Kendall sought to provide more thorough local news, keep news accounts brief, and avoid political entanglements. Kendall used humor to expose pretense and promote fair play.

The *Picayune* was noted for promoting literary products—from its backing of a new library to its reviews of plays. It also promoted the growth of public education, which was entirely absent when the paper began publishing. By 1839, the *Picayune* began establishing correspondents in major cities, beginning with New York. Circulation remained at about 2,500 for the daily edition, but the weekly edition sold 10,000 copies and spread the paper's influence to many parts of Louisiana and Texas. A new infusion of capital occurred in 1839 when businessman Alva Morris Holbrook became a partner with Kendall and Lumsden.

Because of an interest in the Texas revolution against Mexico in 1837, the *Picayune*'s Kendall joined a Texas expedition to Santa Fe in 1841, which led to his capture by the Mexicans. The U.S. government intervened and secured Kendall's release in 1842. These events were detailed in the pages of the *Picayune*. When the Mexican War began in 1846, New Orleans readers were kept abreast of events when Kendall once again ventured to Texas to cover the war. Even Lumsden spent a few months at the war front. The *Picayune* had the earliest and best news about the Mexican War among newspapers in the United States. It cooperated with eastern papers by organizing a pony express system.

In 1848, Kendall traveled to Paris to report on the revolution in France for the *Picayune*. His tour took him to other European capitals as well, from which he sent detailed letters for publication in the paper. The *Picayune* began an afternoon edition in late 1848 at the same time that telegraph service was introduced in New Orleans. The destruction of the paper's plant and equipment in 1850 required the purchase of more modern presses. The *Picayune* did not neglect the promotion of civic progress in New Orleans, especially transportation improvements such as railroads and steamboats.

At the outset of the secessionist movement in 1860, the *Picayune* favored reconciliation with the North in part because the odds against the South were tremendous. Once war began, the *Picayune* showed loyalty to the Confederate cause. The war caused the paper to be reduced from eight pages to six, but news coverage did not suffer. After New Orleans was captured in 1862 by Union forces, the *Picayune* remained restrained in its opinions in order to keep publishing, but the loss of reports by telegraph and mail made it difficult to obtain accurate news. The postwar era brought changes to the *Picayune*, beginning with Kendall's death in 1867 and Holbrook's addition of additional business investors in 1872. The new management, conscious of growing competition from other papers, cut the price of the *Picayune* from ten to five cents.

The *Picayune*'s chief competitors in the 1870s were the *Times* (founded in 1863 by carpetbaggers), the *Democrat* (founded in 1875), the *Item* (founded in 1877), and the *States* (founded in 1880). Editor Holbrook died in 1876, leaving his widow Eliza Jane a significant debt. Mrs. Holbrook decided to continue operating the *Picayune* with George Lloyd as managing editor. A yellow fever epidemic in 1878 killed almost 4,000 residents, followed by a major flood in 1882. When the *Times-Democrat* merger occurred in 1881, it became the second major daily after the *Picayune*. The *Picayune*'s circulation grew from 6,000 in 1878 to 19,000 by 1891. Fifteen Mergenthaler linotypes were installed in 1892, complementing two new stereotype presses.

After the death of publisher Eliza Jane Nicholson (after her remarriage) in 1896, new management led by T. G. Rapier and Harry McEnery allowed the *Picayune* to drift for several years. The *Times-Democrat* had passed the *Picayune* in circulation and advertising by 1914. A merger in that year created the new *Times-Picayune*, which dedicated itself to being not just a New Orleans paper but one that served the South. A Washington bureau was established in 1914, and the paper sent reporters to cover World War I in Europe, one of whom died there in 1918. During the rise of

Ku Klux Klan influence in the 1920s, the *Times-Picayune* became one of the first southern newspapers to condemn Klan tactics and philosophy. Circulation during the 1920s grew at the fastest pace in the paper's history, from 74,000 in 1920 to 100,000 by 1930.

The depression in the 1930s allowed president Leonard K. Nicholson to buy the afternoon *States*, with a circulation of about 40,000, from James L. Ewing for $525,000. The *States* continued to be published as the afternoon edition of the *Times-Picayune*. The New Orleans papers battled powerful Governor and then Senator Huey Long in the 1920s and 1930s. Long tried to retaliate by getting the legislature to pass a tax on advertising in 1934, but the U.S. Supreme Court declared the tax invalid as a violation of freedom of the press. The *States* spearheaded an investigation of Long's cronies that resulted in prison terms for several.

Former managing editor George W. Healy served in the Office of War Information (1942–1945) with two other editors to coordinate war news to the U.S. media. Newsprint shortages during World War II drove production costs much higher for newspapers, especially those in competitive markets. Costs proved to be one important factor in the purchase of the *New Orleans Item* by the *States* and their subsequent merger into a new afternoon daily, the *States-Item*. The historic tradition of great newspaper competition in New Orleans ended in 1958 with one company operating the only two dailies left.

Just four years later, the Samuel I. Newhouse Company bought both New Orleans papers for $40 million, adding to Newhouse properties in the South. Circulation was at a peak when Newhouse acquired the New Orleans papers: the morning *Times-Picayune* with 194,000 and the afternoon *States-Item* with 157,000. George Healy Jr. continued to edit the *Times-Picayune* until 1974, when he was succeeded by Edward Tunstall. Walter Cowan edited the *States-Item* through much of the 1970s. In 1981, the papers ended their separate publications and began printing all day. Charles Fer-

guson edited the combined paper, which soon dropped the *States-Item* label, in the 1980s. Jim Amoss has been editor since 1990.

Reference Dabney, Thomas Ewing, *One Hundred Great Years: The Story of the* Times-Picayune *from Its Founding to 1940* (1944).

New Republic

Founded by Willard Straight and Herbert Croly in 1914 in the tradition of the older *Nation* magazine, the *New Republic* has remained at the top of the opinion journal category in quality and substance. The *New Republic* was inspired by the Progressive reform movement and national leaders such as Theodore Roosevelt and Woodrow Wilson. Because of subsidies that do not depend on healthy circulation and advertising revenues, *New Republic* editors have been free to maintain their own philosophical purposes, which have lurched from the far left to the moderate center.

Willard Straight, trained as an architect, immigrated to China as a young man, where he met and married Dorothy Whitney, daughter of rich and politically connected Americans. Willard and Dorothy read Herbert Croly's liberal manifesto, *The Promise of American Life*, while in China and, upon their return to the States in 1912, offered Croly financial backing to publish a liberal journal. The Straights and Croly idealized democratic social reform, the superiority of capitalism, and the positive role that the United States should play in world affairs. Croly's historical inspiration was Alexander Hamilton, although his system sought balance between the power of the federal government and the individualism embodied in democratic ideals.

The idea for the *New Republic* emerged in discussions between the Straights and Croly in 1913. Talk led to the formation of an editorial board, which would include economist and author Walter Weyl, critic Francis Hackett, and Harvard-trained journalist Walter Lippmann. The first unillustrated issue of the 32-page weekly *New Republic: A Journal of Opinion* appeared in

November 1914 and sold for ten cents a copy or $4 a year. The format included an introductory editorial comment, four or five editorial articles, signed articles by contributors, book reviews, and advertising. By the end of the first year of publication, circulation reached 15,000.

Among the early contributors to *New Republic* were cutting-edge pioneers such as legal scribe Felix Frankfurter, sociologist John Dewey, and historian Charles Beard. Some young poets whose writing later became internationally known found space in the *New Republic:* Robert Frost and William Faulkner. There were few contributors outside of East Coast elites, however. By 1920, circulation had grown to 43,000—still modest in view of *New Republic*'s claim to be a national journal. Many general readers were repelled by its superiority complex and elitist style. Editor Croly remained less concerned about the magazine's ability to inform or entertain than its ability to cause readers to examine their traditional beliefs.

Although the *New Republic* was often criticized for its vague philosophy, it espoused specific progressive ideals, including labor rights, railroad regulation, women's suffrage, legal and prison reform, and academic freedom for educational institutions. The journal felt free to disagree on occasion, but it generally endorsed Wilson's domestic and foreign policies, including the decision to enter World War I. The magazine expressed alarm at the intolerant peace at the end of the war and could not take comfort in the ideals of the League of Nations. Meanwhile, the *New Republic* lost some of its most important founding spirits with the death of Willard Straight in 1918 and the resignations of associate editors Weyl, Hackett, and Lippmann by 1921.

The *New Republic* raised its price to 15 cents in 1919, and its circulation eroded in the 1920s. Croly's philosophy reflected a less political and more spiritual slant in the 1920s. The magazine also featured greater emphasis on cultural areas such as music, books, and the theater by authors such as Lewis Mumford, Edmund Wilson, and Van Wyck Brooks. More articles appeared by English writers, including H. G. Wells, Harold Laski, Lytton Strachey, Virginia Woolf, Bertrand Russell, and John Maynard Keynes. Croly's distaste for national parties led him to endorse third-party candidates such as Robert LaFollette during 1920s presidential campaigns. The *New Republic* continued to take liberal stands against Prohibition, the government's "Red scare" repression, the prejudices elicited by the Ku Klux Klan and the Sacco-Vanzetti case, and scandals such as the Teapot Dome episode.

Upon the death of Herbert Croly in 1930, experienced staffer Bruce Bliven became editor. Bliven and associate editor George Soule reverted to practical as opposed to philosophical liberalism. Associate editor Edmund Wilson even questioned the future of capitalism during the depression and resigned over conflicts with Bliven. Many among Franklin Roosevelt's brain trust that outlined the New Deal policies had written for the *New Republic,* which endorsed most of the planned-economy tenets of the Democrats. Circulation had dropped to 10,000 by the time of Croly's death, but it climbed back to 25,000 in the 1930s. The *New Republic*'s finances were aided by a bequest from the Straight estate and sales of its brief paperbound books on social and economic issues.

Although initially isolationist in the face of the totalitarian threat to peace in the 1930s, the *New Republic* backed U.S. intervention in World War II even before the bombing of Pearl Harbor in December 1941. Concerned about losing the peace, as had occurred after World War I, the *New Republic* resisted praise for the creation of the United Nations. The *New Republic* solidified its reputation as a left-leaning journal with its sympathetic view of the Soviet Union, especially during the editorship of controversial former Vice President Henry A. Wallace during 1946 and 1947. Wallace's term brought significant increases in circulation—from 41,000 to 96,000—but they fell away after he left the *New Republic* to run for president. Willard Straight's son Michael became publisher in 1946 and added a few innovations: color covers, cartoons, and new departments, including one on the United Nations and another on farm-labor issues.

After the 1948 election, the *New Republic* lapsed into a tame liberalism that sympathized with Harry Truman's "Fair Deal" and backed Democrat Adlai Stevenson's 1952 presidential candidacy. The editorial offices of the *New Republic* moved from New York City to Washington, D.C., in 1952. Political coverage continued to be balanced by considerable cultural content, which was reflected in contributors such as W. H. Auden, Gerald Johnson, and John Crowe Ransom. When the Straight estate withdrew its subsidy in 1953, editor Michael Straight recruited new publisher Gilbert Harrison, who advanced monies from the International Harvester fortune. Michael Straight resigned as editor in 1956, and editorial supervision fell solely to Harrison.

During the mid-1950s, the *New Republic* retreated from its pro-Soviet stance without yielding its liberal views on foreign policy. Most of the space in the 24 pages was devoted to domestic politics, international affairs, and book reviews. The shift from political philosophy to political journalism did not stimulate circulation, which rarely rose above 30,000. Garth Hite became publisher in 1966, succeeding Harrison, who remained as editor in chief. Circulation recovered to about 80,000 by the late 1970s.

In the mid-1980s, publisher Jeff Dearth broadened the *New Republic*'s narrow approach to examine conflicting issues within U.S. liberalism and also sought new advertisers to boost revenues. After 1985, editor Michael Kinsley orchestrated a much more balanced view of political opinion by recruiting conservative writers such as Fred Barnes as senior editors. As a result of these changes, circulation moved past the 100,000 mark in the late 1980s. Martin Peretz was chairman in 1992, and Andrew Sullivan was editor. Circulation was holding stable, just below the 100,000 mark.

Reference Levy, David W., *Herbert Croly of the New Republic* (1985).

New York Herald

See Bennett, James Gordon; *New York Tribune* and *Herald Tribune*.

New York Post

The venerable *New York Post* has experienced a wide variety of changes since its founding in 1801. Created as a Federalist Party vehicle, the *Post* was edited by poet William Cullen Bryant from the mid-1820s until the late 1870s, backing first the Democratic and later the new Republican Party. Under publishers Henry and Oswald Villard after 1881, *Post* editors E. L. Godkin and Horace White attacked New York's Tammany Hall power block and bolted from the Republican Party to back Democrat Grover Cleveland. Briefly owned by Cyrus Curtis in the 1920s and 1930s, the *Post* declined in both circulation and influence. After 1939, owner Dorothy Schiff retained Democratic Party endorsements and modernized the *Post* in a tabloid format. Schiff sold the *Post* in 1977 to Australian media magnate Rupert Murdoch.

After the Democratic-Republican rout of the Federalists in the election of 1800, Federalist Party leader Alexander Hamilton raised money to establish a Federalist paper in New York City. The *Evening Post* began publication in November 1801 with lawyer William Coleman as editor, although Hamilton retained control of editorial policy until his death in 1804. The *Post* dutifully assailed President Thomas Jefferson's policies, including the trade embargo, and opposed the War of 1812 against Great Britain. In addition to political coverage, the *Post* had especially thorough news about commerce through the port of New York and first-rate reviews of books and the theater. By the 1820s, circulation had grown to 2,000.

Poet William Cullen Bryant arrived in New York to edit a literary journal, and he was hired by Coleman in 1826 as assistant editor of the *Post*, although he was effectively in control because of Coleman's ill health. Bryant became editor in 1829 and quickly moved the traditionally Federalist paper to endorse the Democratic Party, supporting Andrew Jackson and opposing the protective tariff. Inspired by English liberal authors, Bryant's *Post* exuded moral fortitude to champion causes of the common man. Bryant also gained assistance from talented writers such as Parke Godwin and business manager and part owner John Bigelow, who made the *Post* quite profitable. Thanks to Bryant's writing talents, the *Post* retained a dignified style and refined taste in the era of penny press sensationalism.

During the 1840s, Bryant became discouraged by the Democratic Party's refusal to condemn slavery. The *Post* backed the antislavery Free-Soil Party in the 1848 election and endorsed the newly established Republican Party in 1854. Bryant became a staunch backer of Abraham Lincoln in 1860 and condemned secession by southern states as an act of rebellion. During the Civil War, Bryant favored immediate emancipation of the slaves and vigorous prosecution of the war against the Confederacy. Coverage of battles by *Post* reporters, assisted by several Union army generals, was among the best of northern papers.

The *Post* continued to support the Radical Republicans during Reconstruction after the Civil War, although it did not condone the various scandals associated with the administration of Ulysses Grant. Bryant gave up editorial supervision of the *Post* to his associate editor (and son-in-law) Parke Godwin in 1870 but remained active in guiding the paper's course until his death in 1878. The talented but somewhat naive Godwin became editor in 1878 only to be undercut by business manager and half owner Isaac Henderson when the *Post* was sold to Henry Villard in 1881.

Villard also bought *The Nation* magazine along with the *Post*, which resulted in E. L. Godkin becoming an editor with both publications. Former senator and Liberal Republican Carl Schurz was named the *Post*'s editor in chief, but Godkin and Horace White, former editor of the *Chicago Tribune*, handled the day-to-day editorial duties. Villard put the *Post*'s finances into a trust so that monetary matters would not influence

editorial policy. After quarreling with Godkin about a labor strike in 1883, Schurz resigned, allowing Godkin to become editor and White associate editor. Godkin evoked a strong free trade economic policy and attacked the corrupt spoils system.

Under Godkin's editorship, the *Post* switched its political loyalties from the Republican to the Democratic Party, beginning with the 1884 endorsement of Grover Cleveland for president. The *Post* also began a belated campaign against the powerful Tammany Hall organization in New York City. Its exposure of Tammany leaders led to libel suits, harassment, and the arrest of Godkin. Finally, after a legislative investigation into Tammany, the organization was overthrown with the election of a reform mayor in 1894. Although refusing to engage in the sensationalism used by the new yellow journal sheets, the *Post* did expand its size from four to eight pages and reduced its price to three cents. Circulation never got much above 20,000, but the paper continued to make modest profits.

Upon the death of Henry Villard in 1900, his son Oswald Garrison Villard became publisher of the *Post*. Godkin had retired as editor the previous year and was succeeded by Horace White. When White died in 1903, the editorship was given to Rollo Ogden, an editorial writer since 1891. The *Post* under Oswald Villard and Ogden remained Democratic, except that it did not support the candidacy of William Jennings Bryan in 1908. Publisher Villard's pacifism during World War I led to criticism of the Wilson administration. Villard sold the *Post* in 1918 to banker Thomas W. Lamont for $1 million.

Lamont made few changes in the *Post*'s traditions during his brief ownership. Ogden stepped down as editor in 1920 to be replaced by Harvard economics professor Edwin F. Gay. Lamont sold the *Post* in 1923 to Cyrus H. K. Curtis for $1.6 million. Curtis operated the successful *Saturday Evening Post* and *Ladies' Home Journal* and also owned a newspaper in Philadelphia. *Post* editor Julius Mason backed the Republican Party and big business. After Curtis's death in 1933, the *Post* was purchased by J. David Stern, owner of newspapers in Philadelphia and New Jersey, for much less than $1 million. Although circulation recovered to 250,000, the *Post* continued losing money. Thus, Stern sold the *Post* in 1939 to liberal millionaire George Backer, who instituted some format changes, increased advertising, and gave more prominence to columnists such as Max Lerner. The *Post* had developed a strong foreign news service with reporters such as Dorothy Thompson and even published a Paris edition during 1945 and 1946.

After Backer's retirement from management of the *Post* in 1942, his wife Dorothy Schiff Backer took over. When the two were divorced in 1943, Dorothy Schiff married the *Post*'s managing editor Ted Thackery. The *Post* acquired the *Bronx Home News* in 1948 and changed the paper's name temporarily to the *Post Home News*. James Wechsler became editor of the *Post* in 1949. The paper was the only New York City daily to back Democratic presidential candidate Adlai Stevenson in 1952 and 1956. By the 1960s, the *Post* was the only afternoon daily left after several newspaper collapses. Even with less competition, the *Post* seemed mired in a rut.

Australian entrepreneur Rupert Murdoch offered Dorothy Schiff $30 million in late 1976 for the *Post*. She accepted, and the innovative Murdoch revitalized the paper's appearance and circulation, partly by issuing a morning as well as an evening edition. Murdoch brought in his own editor, Edwin Bolwell, to take over from Paul Sann. A decade after Murdoch's purchase of the *Post*, its circulation of 740,000 ranked eighth nationally among daily papers, although it remained third in New York City behind the morning *Daily News* and the *Times*. Subscription gimmicks and sensational news coverage broke the long traditions of the pre-Murdoch *Post*. Because of his interest in television ownership, the Federal Communications Commission forced Murdoch to sell the *Post* in 1988 in order to retain a New York television station. By 1989, the *Post*'s circulation had fallen to 535,000 and its national ranking to thirteenth.

References Brown, Charles H., *William Cullen Bryant* (1971); Nevins, Allen, *The* Evening Post: *A Century of Journalism* (1922).

New York Sun
See Dana, Charles Anderson.

New York Times
Regarded by most as the best newspaper in the United States, the *New York Times* was founded by Henry J. Raymond in 1851 to cover the news without attendant opinion. It quickly earned respect for its accuracy and thoroughness. The *Times* held true to its founding ideals during difficult competition with the sensational yellow press. Under Adolph Ochs and Arthur Sulzberger, the *Times* set the standard of quality for other U.S. dailies. The *Times* has won more Pulitzer Prizes than any other U.S. newspaper.

Henry Jarvis Raymond began his newspaper career as a reporter for Horace Greeley's *New Yorker* while a student at the University of Vermont. Raymond became Greeley's right-hand man upon the launching of the *New York Tribune* in 1841, but the two men quarreled over Raymond's pay. After leaving the *Tribune*, Raymond entered politics and served as a state senator. The dream of running his own newspaper did not fade, however, and Raymond persuaded his friend George Jones to join him in founding the daily *New York Times* in 1851. Raymond wanted the paper to concentrate on reporting news rather than injecting personal opinion, in contrast to most dailies. The *Times* started as a four-page sheet that sold for a penny. After the first year's profits totaled $100,000, the paper was enlarged to eight pages and the price was raised to two cents. Fifteen dailies in New York City guaranteed plenty of competition.

The *Times* became respected immediately for its sober, tasteful, and objective reporting of news and its extensive coverage of European news. Raymond moved more directly into politics as lieutenant governor in 1854 and as an early spokesman for the new Republican Party. That left Jones to take greater editorial command of the *Times* until the Civil War. The *Times* provided extensive coverage of the Civil War; Raymond himself reported the first Battle of Bull Run, and 15 correspondents continued to follow the progress of the war. Raymond returned to politics, serving one term in Congress after the Civil War, and he died in 1869.

Henry J. Raymond founded the New York Times *in 1851 to cover news without the editorial opinion and commentary so prevalent in other newspapers of the day.*

George Jones succeeded Raymond as chief manager of the paper and hired Louis Jennings as editor. The *Times* uncharacteristically became deeply embroiled in the scandals of New York City's Boss Tweed. During 1870, *Times* reporters and editorials assailed the Tweed ring's corruption to the point that Tweed tried unsuccessfully to buy the paper for $5 million. The *Times*'s prestige helped keep circulation above 30,000 during the 1870s, and its reporting remained stellar. But during the 1880s, when a new era of sensationalism emerged, the conservative *Times* seemed out of step

with its lack of illustrations and demure headlines. After Jones's death in 1891, editor Charles Miller and some partners engineered the purchase of the paper for just under $1 million. The Panic of 1893 hit the new owners especially hard with losses in advertising and circulation. The circulation in 1896 was only 9,000, compared with the *World*'s 200,000.

Tennessee newspaper owner Adolph Ochs offered to bail out the *Times* in 1896 by selling bonds, on the condition that Ochs would take control of the company, although Miller remained as editor. Ochs's plan did not involve pursuing the popular sensationalism of the day but rather restoring the original goal of thorough reporting of the news. Ochs adopted a new slogan for the *Times*, "All the news that's fit to print." He increased coverage of business and financial news, including a weekly financial review. A book review section was added in the Saturday edition, along with a Sunday magazine supplement and space for letters to the editor. In 1898, Ochs reduced the price from three cents to one cent—the same price of the sensational dailies—and circulation grew from 25,000 to 75,000 in one year. By 1901, circulation surpassed 100,000, and the *Times* was profitable again.

In 1904, Ochs hired Carr Van Anda from the *New York Sun* as the *Times*'s managing editor. Van Anda brought dynamic, competent control to the staff. He gave detailed coverage to international events such as the Russo-Japanese War, polar expeditions, and the sinking of the *Titanic*. He also introduced extensive science stories. During World War I, Van Anda spent huge sums to ensure thorough coverage of events in Europe. In 1917, the *Times* founded a news service, which was sold to subscribers through a leased wire. By the 1970s, the service was used by over 400 subscribers in 54 countries. The *Times* won the 1918 Pulitzer Prize for meritorious public service for its war coverage. By 1921, circulation topped 330,000 for the daily edition and 500,000 for the Sunday paper. Ochs switched the *Times*'s political allegiance to the Democratic Party, except during the campaigns of William Jennings Bryan. Although he curtailed his management after 1925, Van Anda remained in his post until 1932. Publisher Ochs died in 1935 and was succeeded by his son-in-law, Arthur Sulzberger.

Sulzberger made a few changes at the *Times;* he directed reporters to sign their articles and added an interpretation of the week's news in the Sunday edition. Sulzberger relied on experienced professionals such as managing editor Edwin James and city editor David Joseph to uphold the tradition of thorough and accurate reporting. *Times* reporters—including Walter Duranty on Stalin's regime, European correspondent Anne O'Hare McCormick, Berlin correspondent Otto Tolischus, and World War II reporter Hanson Baldwin—garnered Pulitzer Prizes in the 1930s and 1940s. The paper's star interviewer, Arthur Krock, won the Pulitzer Prize for correspondence in 1935 and 1938. Another veteran editor, Charles Merz, maintained the forcefulness of the paper's editorials from 1938 to 1961. Former Washington correspondent Turner Catledge succeeded James as managing editor in 1951. Sulzberger retired in 1961 in favor of his son-in-law Orvil Dryfoos.

Beginning in 1962, the *Times* experimented with a West Coast edition in Los Angeles, but the resulting losses led to its termination in 1964. After the death of Dryfoos in 1963, there were major shake-ups in management. An inexperienced Arthur Ochs Sulzberger (son of Arthur Sulzberger) became publisher, causing the business manager to resign. Catledge was named executive editor, and Tom Wicker replaced James Reston as head of the Washington bureau. Other changes at the Washington bureau—from James Greenfield to Max Frankel, to Hedrick Smith—highlighted internal struggles through the late 1960s and 1970s. Eventually, Sulzberger stabilized the management and expanded the company into ownership of medium-sized dailies and television stations. Pulitzer Prize–winning reporter Abe Rosenthal moved from managing editor to executive editor of the *Times* in 1977. Meanwhile, the *Times*

continued its tradition of extensive international reporting with Pulitzer Prize winners Harrison Salisbury (1955), David Halberstam covering the Vietnam War (1964), and Hedrick Smith on the Soviet Union (1974). National reporting Pulitzers were won by James Reston and Anthony Lewis, along with urban environment writer Ada Louise Huxtable. The *Times* consistently ranked number one among various surveys of the best U.S. newspapers in the 1970s. It ranked fifth nationally in daily circulation with 1.1 million in 1989 but first in Sunday circulation at 1.6 million.

The *New York Times* has been instrumental in defending press rights in the courts. Although the paper excused the repressive Espionage Act during World War I as a necessary patriotic precaution, the *Times*—led by former Vietnam reporter Neil Sheehan—published the so-called Pentagon Papers in 1971 against the wishes of the Nixon administration. The Supreme Court upheld the right of the press to publish the sensitive documents, finding that doing so did not violate national security, as the Justice Department had claimed. In New York Times *v. Sullivan* (1964), the Supreme Court held the press to a lower standard of accuracy in the material it printed about public officials in order to avoid libel suits.

References Berger, Meyer, *The Story of the* New York Times, *1851–1951* (1951); Talese, Gay, *The Kingdom and the Power* (1969).

New York Times *v. Sullivan* (1964)

News media concerns about being sued for libel were at the heart of this important Supreme Court case. The court held that news accounts that contained errors of fact involving public officials could not be the basis for libel suits unless it could be proved that the errors were intentional. Thus, publicly elected officials would not necessarily obtain the same stringent protection as private individuals in the case of inaccurate printed statements.

A number of students at a predominantly black college in Montgomery, Alabama, who had been demonstrating against the segregation of public facilities were the object of violence by whites. The students bought an ad in the *New York Times* that contained the signatures of 64 students asking for financial support for their demonstrations. The ad referred in part to the presence of "truckloads of police armed with shotguns and tear gas" used to break up the demonstration with force. Montgomery Police Commissioner L. B. Sullivan sued the *New York Times*, claiming that the ad libeled him by its references to police actions.

The local court found the *Times* guilty and awarded Sullivan $500,000 in damages. That same year, the *Times*'s reporting of civil rights violence resulted in 11 other libel suits in Alabama involving $5 million in potential damages. CBS News was also the object of five libel suits. The Sullivan case was appealed by the *Times*, and the Supreme Court overturned the lower court's decision.

Justice William Brennan wrote the majority opinion in which he suggested that the case involved more than just the reputation of a public official; it involved the very right of the press to investigate and report critically on actions of the government and its agents. Brennan suggested that the plaintiff was attempting to resurrect the eighteenth-century technique of "seditious libel" in order to muzzle the press. The plaintiff's attorneys argued that the Sullivan case was different because the printed matter was in an advertisement, which had not previously been protected by the First Amendment. The Supreme Court distinguished the ad in question as one expressing social or political views and found that it was covered by the First Amendment protection. In order for the ad to be libelous, the plaintiff would have to prove that the defendant was guilty of "actual malice" toward the plaintiff.

The Sullivan case was important not only in enabling the news media to report controversial civil rights incidents without danger of being sued but also in allowing the press to investigate government agencies and public officials without fear of retali-ation in libel suits. No longer would inadvertent errors in print become the basis for trivial lawsuits designed to obstruct reporting or investigations by the media. The new judicial position on libel involving public officials became known as the "public law of libel." The decision in the Sullivan case was extended in 1967 to include "public figures" as well as "public officials." Courts have not, however, excused media organs from using proper care and concern for reputations in printing controversial material.

Reference Pfaff, Daniel W., "Race, Libel and the Supreme Court," *Columbia Journalism Review* (1969).

New York Tribune and *Herald Tribune*

Founded by Horace Greeley in 1841, the *New York Tribune* became both an outspoken newspaper on the issues and a profitable financial venture throughout most of its history. Greeley and his more conservative successor Whitelaw Reid established and maintained the quality of the *Tribune*. When Frank Munsey sold the *New York Herald* to the Reids in 1924, the resulting *Herald Tribune* continued the great traditions of strong Washington and foreign bureaus and indomitable columnists. In 1966, the *Herald Tribune* followed other New York papers into oblivion.

Horace Greeley began his career as a printer, worked at the *New York Evening Post*, edited a literary journal called *New Yorker*, and wrote political treatises for the Whigs before launching the *New York Tribune* in 1841. Greeley used $1,000 of his own money and borrowed another $2,000 to start his paper. His partner and business manager Thomas McElrath kept the financial operations efficient. The *Tribune* consisted of four pages with five columns per page in what would later be called a tabloid sheet. The *Tribune* joined some illustrious New York company, including Benjamin Day's *Sun*, James Gordon Bennett's *Herald*, and James Watson Webb's *Courier and Enquirer*. Greeley secured a circulation of 11,000 within a few months and launched a weekly edition that grew to 200,000 readers, including a truly national audience.

Horace Greeley was no intellectual, but the *Tribune*'s forceful writing and serious content offered the masses something other than the vulgar sensationalism of its competitors. Since Greeley's partisan politics was the main reason for starting the paper, the *Tribune* always took unequivocal stands on issues dear to Greeley. Those issues included support for Whig Party nationalism and public education and opposition to slavery and alcohol. Greeley's irascible nature made many employees uncomfortable, but opportunities for aspiring journalists to hone their craft were readily available. Henry J. Raymond, founder of the *New York Times*; transcendentalist Margaret Fuller; future editor of the *Sun*, Charles Dana; and Whitelaw Reid, later editor of the *Tribune*, all trained under Greeley. Yale- and Harvard-educated George Smalley gave the *Tribune* some of the best coverage of Civil War campaigns, and he later became the paper's European correspondent.

Horace Greeley is remembered for his 1862 call to easterners, "Go west young man, go west."

Because of Greeley's fervent interest in politics, he ran for a number of posts, including the House of Representatives, U.S. Senate, New York comptroller, and president of the United States in 1872. Greeley lost all his political contests in part because of his outspoken, immoderate positions on issues. Nonetheless, despite his defeats, Greeley figured prominently in national politics. The *Tribune* was an early and avid backer of Abraham Lincoln in 1860. Greeley and Lincoln conferred on many occasions about political policy. At the end of the Civil War, Greeley endorsed Lincoln's conciliatory stand toward the ex-Confederacy and even campaigned to release Confederate President Jefferson Davis from prison. Greeley's *Tribune* railed against the political corruption of the Reconstruction era and called for civil service reform to end the spoils system.

Greeley's national reputation for radical positions came more from the weekly edition of the *Tribune*, which sold in virtually all parts of the nation. Many Americans remembered him for the clarion call to easterners, "Go west young man, go west," uttered in support of the 1862 Homestead Act. The Liberal Republican movement for reforms to end corruption and reconciliation with the South was led mainly by journalists, including George William Curtis and E. L. Godkin. Greeley was among the group and obtained the party's nomination for president in 1872, running against incumbent Radical Republican Ulysses S. Grant. Most of the journalists had various bones to pick with Greeley, and many were no doubt jealous of the honor bestowed on him. Thus, some Liberal Republican papers did not back Greeley with enthusiasm. Greeley campaigned hard, traveling across much of the nation. The grind took its toll, and one month after his devastating 1872 defeat, Greeley died.

By the time of Greeley's death, he actually owned very little of the *Tribune*, which had been divided into numerous shares. The associate editor, Whitelaw Reid, emerged as the new editor when he borrowed money from controversial financier Jay Gould to buy a majority of shares. Reid had come to the *Tribune* in 1868 as chief editorial writer from the editor's chair at the *Cincinnati Gazette*. He immediately changed the political tone of the *Tribune* to conform with conservative Republicans rather than Greeley's Liberal Republicans; Reid favored the protective tariff and the gold standard and opposed labor unions. The *Tribune*'s news coverage and writing, however, remained superb. Still, Greeley's absence was reflected in significant declines in circulation for both the daily and the weekly editions.

The *Tribune* became the most dependable Republican daily in New York, backing even controversial candidates such as James G. Blaine. Reid became a serious confidant of Republican bosses. President Benjamin Harrison named Reid ambassador to France in 1889, and Reid ran unsuccessfully with Harrison as the Republican vice presidential candidate in 1892. Reid tended to recruit colleges graduates as staffers at the *Tribune*. They included future Secretary of State John Hay as an editorial writer and literary writers John Hassard and William Winter. Ellen "Nelly" Hutchinson made a reputation in feature writing and replaced George Ripley in 1882 as literary editor. Smalley continued as the European correspondent. Reid brought out the first Sunday edition of the *Tribune* in 1879, concentrating on features and literary material. The first Mergenthaler linotype machines in the United States were installed at the *Tribune* in 1886.

By the 1880s, the *Tribune*'s circulation had recovered to 50,000 for the daily, 100,000 for the weekly, and more than 50,000 for the Sunday edition. Reid often appealed to the educated youth as the core of the *Tribune*'s readership. He challenged them to use high-minded knowledge rather than resorting to the emotional ploys of some competing newspapers. *Tribune* "extras" on science subjects and prominent lectures exemplified the approach. Although the *Tribune* did not ignore sensational subjects such as crime, natural disasters, or political corruption, those matters were dealt with forthrightly as news rather than as gimmicks to increase sales.

By the time of Whitelaw Reid's death in 1912, the *Tribune*'s circulation had dropped to 25,000, suffering from competition from yellow press papers such as the *World* and the *Journal*. Reid's son Ogden took the editorial reins, and World War I helped circulation recover somewhat. Ogden Reid's wife, Helen Rogers Reid, served capably as advertising director. When Frank Munsey of the *New York Herald* (circulation 175,000) sought to buy the *Tribune* (circulation 140,000) after the war, the Reids would not sell. Indeed, it was the Reids who bought Munsey's *Herald* in 1924 for $5 million and created the *Herald Tribune*, which further stimulated circulation.

Despite its sound financial condition with a 275,000 circulation, the *Herald Tribune* became a leader in innovations such as the three-line banner headline in 1931 and the radiotelephone for overseas communications. The *Herald Tribune* was one of a handful of U.S. papers that sent its own correspondents to cover World War II. The international edition of the *Herald Tribune*, based in Paris, was suspended for four years during the Nazi occupation but resumed in 1944. Talented personnel also kept the *Herald Tribune* a leader in competition. Assistant editor Arthur Draper, editorial writer and Pulitzer winner Geoffrey Parsons, and managing editor Grafton Wilcox were complemented by columnists such as Walter Lippmann, Dorothy Thompson, Mark Sullivan, and Joseph Alsop.

Upon Ogden Reid's death in 1947, Helen Rogers Reid was ably assisted by her sons Whitelaw and Ogden Jr. in keeping the *Herald Tribune* afloat. Nonetheless, management and financial difficulties caused the family to sell the paper to Ambassador to England John Hay Whitney in 1958. Whitney bought the Sunday supplement magazine *Parade* from Marshall Field IV in 1959 and added radio and television stations to Whitney Communications Corporation. Whitney put Walter Thayer in charge of management and personnel at the *Herald Tribune*. Thayer named Robert M. White

editor in 1959. Although White was unable to restore the paper to its earlier heights, he was rewarded by a poll in 1960 that listed the *Herald Tribune* as the sixth best paper in the nation.

Thayer agreed that the paper needed more dynamic leadership and replaced White with John Denson of *Newsweek* in 1961. Denson possessed many of the qualities of Horace Greeley and brought more life to the *Herald Tribune*, but he also failed to fit the paper's needs and was replaced in 1962 by James Bellows. The *Herald Tribune* converted to a tabloid format. A four-month strike in 1963 was a crippling blow to the *Herald Tribune*, on top of increased production costs. The *Herald Tribune* ended its long string of Republican endorsements when its refused to back Senator Barry Goldwater in the 1964 election. Whitney was forced to sell the *Herald Tribune* to a conglomerate in 1966, which ended publication. However, Whitney obtained new partners, including the *New York Times*, to continue the international edition and added Asian and Latin American editions.

Reference Kluger, Richard, *The Paper: The Life and Death of the* New York Herald Tribune (1986).

New York World

Founded in 1860 as a religious paper, the *New York World* became a staunch Democratic organ during the Civil War under editor Manton Marble. Under publisher Joseph Pulitzer after 1883, the *New York World* became noted for sensationalizing the news as part of the era of yellow journalism in the 1890s. The *World* became a leader in news-gathering techniques, especially while covering the Spanish-American War, and had the largest circulation of any U.S. daily. Some of the most famous reporters in newspaper history worked for the *World*.

The *New York World* was founded in 1860 by Alexander Cummings, the successful publisher of the *Philadelphia Evening Bulletin*. It promoted religious and moral issues and refused to accept advertising from liquor or entertainment businesses. Many religious businessmen invested in the *World*, which was forced to raise its price from one cent to two cents a copy because of slow sales. By 1861, the *World*'s original investors had sold out to financiers including August Belmont, who hired Manton Marble as editor and made the *World* a general morning daily. Marble brought competent and literate editing to the paper and bought the majority ownership in 1869.

As a Democrat, Manton Marble and his *World* ran against the majority Republican press during and after the Civil War. The failure of the Democratic Party to prevail in the disputed presidential election of 1876 and stiff competition from Charles Dana's *Sun* led Marble to retire from journalism. He sold the *World* to a group of investors headed by railroad owner Thomas Scott, who in turn sold to another railroad owner, Jay Gould, in 1879. The new editor was William Henry Hurlbert, who provided able direction. Still unable to compete effectively with Charles Dana's thriving *New York Sun*, Gould's paper was losing $40,000 a year. He agreed to sell to Joseph Pulitzer in 1883 for $346,000.

At the time Pulitzer bought the *World* in 1883, its circulation was only 11,000, but it rose to 60,000 by the end of the first year and reached a national record for dailies of 200,000 by 1887. Pulitzer brought John A. Cockerill from his St. Louis paper to be managing editor and began to recruit reporters to add flavor and depth to news writing. Elizabeth Cochrane, known by the pen name Nellie Bly, came from the *Pittsburgh Dispatch*, where she had written a detailed exposé of the Mexican government. She relied on undercover methods to discover facts about New York's hospitals for the insane and women's prisons. Frank I. Cobb, formerly of the *Detroit Free Press*, graduated from reporter to editor at the *World*. War correspondents who made reputations during the Spanish-American War and World War I included Edward Harden and Heywood Broun. Other notable reporters who later gained fame in their own right included Walter Lippmann, Maxwell Anderson, and Allan Nevins.

The *World* started an evening edition in 1887, developed a worldwide news service,

utilized numerous photographs and illustrations, and added cartoons, sports, and women's coverage. Its advertising revenues passed those of the rival *Herald* in 1884. Pulitzer's most successful innovation was the Sunday edition. Although some papers, such as the *Herald*, published Sunday editions, they were rare among U.S. dailies. The Sunday *World* included considerable entertainment features aimed at women, sports followers, and younger readers. Profuse illustrations, literary installments, and five-color cartoon supplements also appeared on a regular basis in the 48-page edition. Sunday circulation passed the 250,000 mark in 1887. The Sunday *World* stimulated other dailies to launch their own Sunday editions, imitating the *World*'s content.

The Spanish-American War was the height of yellow journalism in the United States. The banner of this 17 February 1898 edition of the New York World *reads "Maine Explosion Caused by Bomb or Torpedo?" The* World *went so far as to hire divers to search for the cause of the explosion.*

Pulitzer's crusading spirit was revealed often as the *World* championed reforms to aid immigrants and the poor by attacking shoddy tenement construction, white slave traffic, and police brutality. The *World* sponsored giveaways of ice, fuel, medical care, holiday trips, and Christmas dinners for the poor. Monopolistic practices of the New York Central Railroad, Standard Oil, and Bell Telephone were criticized by the *World*. Pulitzer also frequently assailed political corruption.

Despite Pulitzer's antiwar stance in the 1895 Venezuelan boundary dispute involving Great Britain, the *World* participated in the anti-Spanish jingoism and promoted war over the Cuban situation in the 1890s. However, William Randolph Hearst's New York Journal demonstrated even more egregious behavior in its promotion of war. The Pulitzer-Hearst rivalry was intense and was best illustrated by Hearst hiring away many *World* staffers, such as editor Arthur Brisbane, for higher salaries. The World hired divers to check the sunken USS Maine in Havana harbor and blamed Spain for the sinking. Novelist Stephen Crane was hired to write stories for the World, and reporter Edward Harden sent back the first report of the naval engagement at Manila in the Philippines. The Spanish-American War represented the height of yellow journalism, but profits were considerable, as the *World*'s circulation rose to over 1 million during the war.

Although Joseph Pulitzer wanted to keep the *World* in the family at his death in 1911, none of his three sons had the ability or the training to succeed. Still, the *World* continued to hold its own with talents such as editorial page editor Frank Cobb, who kept the editorials pungent and authoritative until his death in 1923. Management decided to raise the price of the paper to three cents in 1925, just as the new tabloids were making inroads into the major dailies. The *World* began to show losses after 1926, eventually reaching just under $2 million. In 1931, the Scripps-Howard chain offered to buy the *World* for $5 million. The sale by the Pulitzer family led to the merger that created the *World-Telegram*, which dispensed with the morning and Sunday editions.

See also Pulitzer, Joseph.

Reference Juergens, George, *Joseph Pulitzer and the* New York World (1966).

New Yorker

Although the first *New Yorker* was a literary magazine edited by Horace Greeley in the 1830s, its modern issuance was started in 1925 by Harold Ross. Designed as a magazine of humor and comment on urban lifestyles, the weekly *New Yorker* also offered incisive essays and candid reporting on public affairs. Intended to attract well-educated readers mostly from the East Coast, the *New Yorker* was also appreciated by many non-New Yorkers.

A native of Colorado and a high school dropout, Harold Ross's early career as a reporter took him from San Francisco to New Orleans to Atlanta. As a soldier in World War I, he became editor of the military newspaper *Stars and Stripes*. After the war, Ross briefly edited a veterans' magazine called *Home Sector* while contemplating a weekly magazine of his own. Some *Stars and Stripes* staffers, including Franklin Adams and Alexander Woollcott, helped Ross launch the *New Yorker* in 1925, with the financial backing of bakery magnate Raoul Fleischmann.

The first issue in February sold 15,000 copies, but Ross hoped to obtain a readership of 50,000 or more. Succeeding issues lost circulation, however, as Ross struggled to locate the type of staff he desired. Ralph Ingersoll served as managing editor before leaving for *Fortune* magazine in the 1930s. Ross used talented artists such as Peter Arno, Helen Hokinson, and Charles Addams to draw the famous *New Yorker* cartoons. Helen Mackay wrote a popular series about young women frequenting cabarets. Other writers recruited to contribute to the magazine included James Thurber, Ogden Nash, and S. J. Perelman. There were also regular columns such as E. B. White's gossipy "Talk of the Town" and the biographical "Profiles" series, which focused on various personalities rather than worldly achievers.

Ross tended to focus on what was happening in New York City, Europe, and Hollywood, but not much else. The sophisticated *New Yorker* intentionally did not appeal to the masses, although it avoided the label highbrow. Irascible and tactless, Ross's pursuit of perfection proved difficult for most staffers. Outside observers could not understand the prosperity of the *New Yorker*. Advertising demand was so great that not all applicants could be included. The *New Yorker* consistently led U.S. periodicals in the ratio of net income to gross revenues.

After Harold Ross's death in 1951, William Shawn became editor. New bylines appeared as the older contributions faded away, and some readers complained that the *New Yorker* had become fat and sassy in its prosperous old age. Articles about far-flung locales and peoples displaced the traditional New York fare. Still, the *New Yorker* attracted excellent writers such as James Baldwin and Hannah Arendt and focused reader attention on subjects such as pesticide contamination of the food chain. Circulation in 1963 held steady at 468,000. Quite a few *New Yorker* articles by authors such as Thurber and John Updike resulted in book-length publications. Understanding *New Yorker* humor required insight, and its cartoons proved more important than the brief captions.

Although the *New Yorker* had weathered the transition from the Ross era by the 1970s, it faced shrinking advertising revenue. Controversial reporting by Jonathan Schell on the Vietnam War may have caused some advertisers to shy away from the *New Yorker*. Nevertheless, circulation grew slowly to 490,000 by 1977. The Newhouse media conglomerate bought the *New Yorker* in 1985, and editor Shawn resigned in January 1987. Former Knopf editor Robert Gottlieb became only the third editor at the *New Yorker*. New advertising policies admitted sexier formats that had previously been banned. Newhouse advertised the magazine widely on television to boost circulation on a national scale. Still, the *New Yorker* did not lose all its original charm and literary bent. Attempts to mimic the *New Yorker*'s style in other metropolitan markets have not been nearly so successful.

Reference Kramer, Dale, *Ross and the* New Yorker (1951).

Newhouse, Samuel Irving (1895–1979)

Beginning with small dailies in New York and New Jersey, Samuel I. Newhouse established a competitive chain of newspapers in the 1950s and 1960s. Newhouse papers in cities such as St. Louis, Birmingham, New Orleans, and Portland, Oregon, created extensive national influence. By 1977, the chain owned 30 dailies with a combined circulation of 3.5 million. In 1988, the Newhouse chain was the third largest in the United States. In 1990, Advance Publications conglomerate, run by Newhouse's sons, was a $2.2 billion operation that included magazine ownership, book publishing, and broadcast media.

Samuel Irving Newhouse was born in New York City to immigrant Russian Jewish parents. He took control of the circulation department of the *Bayonne (New Jersey) Times* while still in high school. Newhouse attended law school at night and was admitted to the bar at age 21. By 1922, he had saved enough to purchase 51 percent of the weekly *Staten Island Advance*; in less than a year, with the circulation over 10,000, the paper showed a profit. By 1931, circulation approached 25,000, allowing the *Advance* to weather the depression years. Over the next ten years, Newhouse bought five newspapers on Long Island, including the *Long Island Daily Press*, which became the object of a strike by the American Newspaper Guild in 1934. Newhouse purchased 51 percent of the financially troubled *Newark Ledger* in 1934 from L. T. Russell for $110,000. Within four years, the circulation of the *Ledger* had doubled to 60,000.

In 1938, after several years of legal and labor problems, Newhouse began adding to his newspaper collection. He bought part ownership in the *Long Island Star*, closed it temporarily, and reopened it after obtaining a favorable labor arrangement. When the *Long Island Journal* went bankrupt because of a labor strike in 1938, Newhouse moved into the subscriber area with the *Star*, renamed the *Star-Journal*. With considerable experience and some profits behind him, Newhouse moved out of the metropolitan

New York City area in 1939 to buy two evening papers in Syracuse, the *Herald* and the *Journal*, for $1.9 million and merged them as the *Herald-Journal*. Three years later, Newhouse obtained the morning *Syracuse Post-Standard* to become the only daily newspaper publisher in the city. Also in 1939, Newhouse bought the assets of the failed *Newark Star-Eagle* and blended it with the *Ledger*, creating the *Star-Ledger*. At the end of World War II, Newhouse obtained half-interest in the *Journal* in Jersey City.

After the war, Newhouse had to fend off several libel suits before continuing his expansion in newspaper properties. He bought the *Harrisburg (Pennsylvania) Telegraph* in 1947 for $1 million. Three months later, Newhouse announced that he was suspending publication and selling the *Telegraph* to the rival *Patriot-News*. In fact, Newhouse had obtained a large share in the *Patriot-News*, which increased to majority control by 1950. The pace of acquisitions picked up and began to focus on larger properties. The 100-year-old morning *Portland Oregonian* was bought in 1950 for $5.25 million; the evening *Oregon Journal* was added in 1961 for $6 million. In 1955, Newhouse claimed the morning *St. Louis Globe-Democrat* for $6 million and the evening *Birmingham* News for $18 million. Newhouse bought a minority interest in the *Denver Post* in 1960 for $3.6 million. The combined *New Orleans Times-Picayune* and *States-Item* were acquired in 1962 for $40 million. The *Mobile Press-Register* became a Newhouse property in 1966 for $15 million. Finally, the *Cleveland Plain Dealer* was obtained in 1967 for $50 million.

In part because of Newhouse's libertarian philosophy, he did not give strong editorial direction to his newspapers. This allowed local editors more leeway in determining the best stance for the papers in the communities. From the beginning, Newhouse viewed newspapers as a business rather than a service, but he argued that only a soundly run business could maintain its integrity against those who would control or manipulate it. He believed that a paper's key staff members were its reporter-

writers and circulation-advertising managers. Shortly before his death in 1977, Newhouse newspapers ranked second nationally behind the Knight-Ridder chain, with 30 dailies and 3.5 million circulation.

During the 1950s, Newhouse started diversifying his media holdings through the formation of a holding company, Advance Publications. Magazines acquired by Advance included *Vogue, Mademoiselle, Vanity Fair, House and Garden, Bride's,* and the *New Yorker*. Also in the 1950s, Newhouse shrewdly began to purchase television stations in the major markets where his newspapers were located—Portland, Syracuse, Birmingham, and St. Louis. When Newhouse's sons, Donald and Samuel Jr., realized in 1980 that the networks' influence was waning because of cable, they sold the television stations and reinvested in cable companies. The Newhouse companies also include major publishing houses such as Alfred A. Knopf, Random House, and Vintage. In 1990, Advance Publications produced $2.2 billion in revenue, making it the seventh largest media conglomerate; nearly two-thirds of the revenues still derived from newspaper holdings.

Reference Lent, John A., *Newhouse, Newspapers, Nuisances: Highlights in the Growth of a Communication Empire* (1966).

News Gathering

Methods of acquiring news have undergone innovative changes, including the application of new technologies, since the eighteenth century. The idea of a reporter gathering news was foreign to early papers and was not developed until well into the nineteenth century. The advent of the telegraph provided the first technological boost to news gathering. In the twentieth century, electronic news gathering using satellite and computer technology has made the craft extremely sophisticated and rapid.

In the eighteenth century, editors relied on others to gather the news that they printed in their newspapers. The *Boston News-Letter* was typical of such early papers. Mercantile papers like the *News-Letter* used printed reports of commercial shipping interests as a large part of their published material. Letters from individuals who were not associated with the paper became a major source of news both domestically and abroad. American readers thirsted for news from England, and no paper could be successful without reprinting items from English newspapers. Domestic news, usually referred to as "intelligence," relied on some form of correspondent, usually postmasters. The *News-Letter*, for example, used correspondents in New York City and Newport, Rhode Island, even though their accounts were sporadic and concentrated on maritime matters.

As more colonial papers appeared in the eighteenth century, editors sent their papers to one another and freely copied pertinent news in their publications. Invariably, news reports were outdated by days or weeks because of weekly publication schedules and communication delays. Sometimes, weeklies would print an edition early if significant news occurred before the regular publication date. This practice became known as the "extra," which was well established in the eighteenth century. Because most urban centers were still quite small, newspapers did not feel any urgency to report local news, which was already widely known. Papers regarded their function as one of recording historical events rather than keeping readers abreast of breaking news. Such a view meant that most news that was printed concerned political and military events rather than social, economic, or cultural affairs. Still, crime and natural disasters such as fires and storms always received proper attention. Also, papers regularly published obituaries and marriage notices.

During the Revolutionary War, American newspapers were ill equipped to provide accounts of the conflict to readers, since they still relied on personal letters or government announcements. Yet some precedents for news gathering had developed before the fighting. Patriots in Boston issued a newsletter called "Journal of Occurrences" in 1768 and 1769; it featured daily accounts of events in Boston that were reprinted in regular newspapers. The *Boston Gazette* printed a detailed account of the Boston Massacre a week after the event in 1770. During the conflict, many newspapers issued "extras" to describe the results of particular battles. The accounts came mostly from letters written by observers or by word of mouth to the editor. During the war, papers continued to print news of remarkable events such as crop yields, crimes, and epidemics.

By the end of the eighteenth century, some editors began to edit news accounts gathered from other papers or letters so that they could provide summaries. New England papers that pioneered edited news included the *Columbian Centinel*, the *Farmer's Weekly Museum*, and the *Salem Gazette* and *Register*. News accounts continued to be outdated; it took two months for European news to reach the East Coast, and one month or more for papers in the interior to obtain East Coast news. It took almost a month for the news of George Washington's death in 1799 to reach Cincinnati and Lexington. The first "reporters," including Joseph Gales, James Callender, and William Duane, gathered information about federal government activities for Philadelphia papers in the 1790s.

In 1811, Samuel Topliff of Boston developed a news-gathering technique that became widely used. He rowed out to meet incoming foreign ships to obtain their packages of newspapers before the ships docked. Topliff then distributed the papers in the reading room of the Exchange Coffee House in Boston. Editor A. S. Willington of the *Charleston Courier* applied the news-boat technique to acquire the earliest possible foreign news accounts for his paper. Willington employed James Gordon Bennett, who soon took the concept to New York, where he launched the *Herald* in the 1830s. James M. Bradford became perhaps the first war correspondent during the War of 1812, covering the Battle of New Orleans for the *Orleans Gazette*.

Except for mercantile news, obituaries, marriage notices, and occasionally items from the nation's capital, local news continued to be neglected by small and large papers well into the nineteenth century. Elias Kingman established a Washington news bureau in 1822 that supplied items to several major dailies. Before he launched the *New York Herald,* reporter James Gordon Bennett sent some juicy items from the capital to the *New York Enquirer* in the 1820s. When the penny press emerged in the 1830s, the speed of news transmission became more important. Horse expresses were used to transmit items from neighboring cities to urban centers such as Philadelphia and New York. Many of these services, such as that run by New York's *Journal of Commerce* to Washington, were faster than the postal service but expensive. The penny press papers made a habit of gathering election returns for early printing and also regularly featured presidential messages. Charles Dana's *New York Sun* began using carrier pigeons as a method of acquiring distant news quickly. Daniel Craig established a news agency in New York that relied exclusively on the pigeon method and sold items to subscribing papers. The *Baltimore Sun* was well positioned to become the first to use both railroads and the telegraph to obtain news from nearby Washington in the mid-1840s. Samuel F. B. Morse's invention of the telegraph led to the promotion of its use by newspapermen such as William Swain of Philadelphia and Amos Kendall of Washington. By 1846, all New York dailies featured a column of "telegraph news."

The Mexican War (1846–1848) led to the first serious use of war correspondents by several papers in New Orleans and New York. The war also produced a permanent news-gathering agency in New York, the forerunner of the Associated Press, in 1848. The Associated Press relied principally on the telegraph to dispatch news to its subscribers. By the 1850s, major dailies employed reporters full-time to collect news either locally or in places such as Washington. The Civil War stimulated a proliferation of reporters who followed the battles. By the time of the era of yellow journalism at the end of the century, reporting had become a generic feature of all daily and most weekly newspapers. As the public demanded and responded to more and better news, the quest for greater sales drove editors to place a premium on news gathering.

The advent of broadcasting in the 1920s slowly led to a new feature of news gathering. News reporting on the radio developed rather slowly and was not a serious network venture until the early 1930s. Live broadcasts of events such as presidential nominating conventions and sports competitions created considerable listener interest. The application of news gathering to television also lagged the early history of the medium. So-called electronic news gathering developed with technological improvements in portable cameras and the invention of magnetic videotaping in the 1950s and the emergence of satellite transmission in the 1960s. By the 1970s, television news gathering moved into a new realm of instant news—broadcasting live from the news scene. Live broadcasts placed more responsibility on reporters, whose accounts would not be screened by editors. In the 1980s, local television stations in major cities joined the networks in relying on satellite feeds by establishing bureaus in major news centers such as Washington. Satellite news coverage helped obliterate the traditional local-national news dichotomy more than any other factor.

References Stephens, Mitchell, *A History of News: From the Drum to Satellite* (1988); Yoakum, Richard D., and Charles F. Cremer, *ENG: Television News and the New Technology* (1989).

Newsday

Begun as a Long Island daily in 1940, *Newsday* expanded into New York City and became a major force among metropolitan newspapers. Founded by Alicia Patterson, daughter of the publisher of the *New York Daily News, Newsday* expanded its circulation rapidly after World War II. It gained a reputation for crisp, accurate reporting embodied in an attractive tabloid format. The Times Mirror Company purchased *Newsday* in 1970 after a successful stint by Bill Moyers as publisher. A New York City edition begun in 1983 became an instant success. *Newsday* won Pulitzer Prizes in 1954, 1970, 1974, 1984, and 1985.

Joseph Medill Patterson had launched the circulation blockbuster the *New York Daily News* as a sensational tabloid in 1919. His daughter Alicia had a similar dream for her own paper and, with her father's advice and support, got the opportunity to make it a reality. Alicia Patterson married Harry Guggenheim, who became an integral part of the newspaper project in both financing and planning. After considerable calculations and several dry runs, *Newsday* was launched on Long Island in 1940 as a two-cent five-day-a-week paper in a tabloid format. The 32-page first edition went to 11,000 prepaid subscribers, and another 6,000 were sold at newsstands. Alicia Patterson raided her father's *Daily News* for *Newsday*'s first two managing editors—Harold Davis (1940–1944) and Alan Hathaway (1944–1967), both reporters at heart. In 1942, *Newsday* began publishing a Saturday edition.

After World War II, *Newsday* began to find its niche among the competition on Long Island. Circulation grew from 38,000 in 1944 to 64,000 in 1946. Its direct competitor in Nassau County, the *Review-Star*, founded in 1926, was purchased by Samuel Newhouse in 1949, the same year that *Newsday* passed the 100,000 mark in circulation. Even Newhouse could not sustain the *Review-Star*, and it closed in 1953. Meanwhile, *Newsday* had started a Suffolk County edition in 1944, which further expanded its readership on Long Island. *Newsday*'s success also took a toll on another Newhouse paper, the Queens-based *Long Island Press*, founded in 1820. The *Press* refused to challenge *Newsday* in Nassau and Suffolk Counties, so when *Newsday* moved into Queens in the 1970s, it resulted in the *Press*'s collapse in 1977.

Publisher Patterson insisted on articulate, well-researched reporting for *Newsday*, and the policy paid dividends in recognition from the profession. Reports about graft in a Long Island labor union run by the De-Konig family became the basis for its first

Pulitzer Prize for meritorious public service in 1954. *Time* magazine not only gave top billing to the award but also placed Patterson on the cover. Patterson was constantly at the forefront of decision making at *Newsday* until her untimely death from stomach ulcers in 1963. Her husband Harry Guggenheim had no experience or interest in managing the paper, so he hired veteran Mark Ethridge, formerly of the *Louisville Courier-Journal*, to become interim editor. Ethridge made some changes, such as starting a Saturday magazine edited by Joseph Albright. At Ethridge's suggestion, Guggenheim persuaded John Steinbeck to write a column for *Newsday* in 1965.

At the end of 1966, Guggenheim found the management leader he sought in Bill Moyers, former press secretary to President Lyndon Johnson. Moyers agreed to become publisher just before Alan Hathaway's retirement in 1967 as managing editor. Al Marlens was named as Hathaway's replacement, and Bill McIlwain became editorial page editor. Moyers recruited David Laventhol from the *Washington Post* to assist him in developing a stronger news orientation. Marlens clashed with both Guggenheim and Laventhol, and he left *Newsday* in 1970, just before Moyers quit as publisher under the new ownership. *Newsday* reporters led by Bob Greene uncovered political corruption in Suffolk County, which brought the paper another Pulitzer in 1970. The same year, editorial cartoonist Tom Darcy won a Pulitzer for his drawings about the Vietnam War.

The *Newsday* Pulitzers of 1970 were overshadowed somewhat by Guggenheim's decision to sell the paper to Otis Chandler's Times Mirror Company. The sale resulted in major shake-ups, beginning with Moyers's resignation and replacement by William Attwood. Laventhol had just been named executive editor and remained in place. The new owners immediately doubled the price of *Newsday* from a nickel to a dime. Circulation fell from 450,000 to just above 400,000 and did not recover until 1976. A Sunday edition was launched in 1971 and soon stabilized as a profitable venture, which spread *Newsday*'s influence around the metropolitan New York area. The new Times Mirror team began emphasizing national and international news, which led to a 1974 Pulitzer for Bob Greene's investigative stories of heroin trafficking traced from Turkey to the United States. The same year, art commentator Emily Genauer also won a Pulitzer.

Attwood stepped down as publisher in 1978 to be replaced by Laventhol; Anthony Insolia took Laventhol's spot as executive editor. Profits were increasing dramatically for *Newsday* in the 1970s, partly because of the price increase. By 1976, the Sunday edition passed the 500,000 circulation mark. *Newsday* benefited from a 1978 New York City newspaper strike, which left the Long Island paper as the only advertising outlet for a time. Initially, plans to start a New York City edition were based on the impending collapse of the *Daily News*. When the *News* weathered its difficulties and survived, *New York Newsday* was begun anyway in 1983. By 1985, the edition sold 60,000 copies and reached 100,000 circulation in 1986. Donald Forst became editor of the New York edition in 1986, the same year that Robert Johnson became publisher of *Newsday*.

Newsday entered the cable television field briefly in 1983 and 1984 when Bob Greene anchored a local news show as a complement to a videotex of the paper, but the show was canceled when executives refused to invest more money. Meanwhile, quality writing won *Newsday* yet another Pulitzer Prize in 1984 for its 1983 "Baby Jane Doe" series, involving legal issues surrounding medical care for a baby born with spina bifida. The next year, *Newsday* reporters covering famine in Africa won a Pulitzer Prize for reporting, and columnist Murray Kempton won the commentary award. Anthony Marro became executive editor of the Long Island edition of *Newsday* in 1986. In 1987, several changes occurred when David Laventhol was elected president of Times Mirror. Former staffer Steven Isenberg was recruited as deputy publisher. The New York edition passed the 200,000 circulation

mark in 1988 and became distinguished from its Long Island parent with its sportier, crisper look. The Long Island edition, with 700,000 circulation in 1990 (the eighth largest daily in the United States), switched to morning publication and created several regional editions for metropolitan boroughs to stave off competition from revitalized weeklies.

Reference Keeler, Robert F., Newsday: *A Candid History of the Respectable Tabloid* (1990).

Newspaper Preservation Act (1970)

Increased consolidation and merger of newspapers in major cities led the federal government to try to prevent monopolies from developing. Major publishing companies opposed government regulation and lobbied successfully to have Congress pass the Newspaper Preservation Act in 1970. The act effectively exempted major publishers from antitrust laws and allowed competing papers to combine functions in the face of financial difficulties.

During the Great Depression of the 1930s, when newspaper costs were rising and technological improvements expensive, some newspapers competing in the same markets wanted to share production facilities to stave off bankruptcy. Congress approved joint operating agreements when it could be demonstrated that without such sharing a newspaper would fail. Although joint operating agreements did not end the process of consolidation and merger among daily newspapers, they became standard in most major urban markets by the 1960s, when less than three dozen cities had competing daily newspapers. Generally, it was the small daily and weekly newspapers rather than the big-city dailies that provided the greatest employment for newspaper workers. Therefore, the public was not alarmed at the elimination of competition as long as the process itself seemed fair. In addition, the expansion of broadcast media after World War II, especially television, had created a new form of competition for print media.

Major publishing companies were disturbed by a 1969 Supreme Court decision that a joint operating agreement between two supposedly competing daily papers was a violation of the antitrust laws. The Court's reasoning was that joint operating agreements required "proof" that failure to engage in the cooperation would cause one of the competitors to go bankrupt. The Court's concern was that joint operating agreements had been abused because of the print media's focus on competition with broadcast media rather than with their own print rivals. Many key publishers were alarmed that their system could be unraveled by Court actions and sought relief in Congress.

The original legislation drafted at the urging of print publishers and the American Newspaper Publishers Association was called the Failing Newspaper Act, but it was soon renamed the Newspaper Preservation Act—a more palatable designation. The act would exempt newspapers with joint operating agreements from regulation under the antitrust laws. The rationale behind the law was that since joint operating agreements preserve different points of view in major markets, they function "in the public interest." Allowing competing newspapers to use common facilities for production did not taint the free expression of ideas. The act passed easily in 1970 and was signed into law by President Richard Nixon.

Not all publishing interests approved of the Newspaper Preservation Act. Some believed that it indeed promoted monopolies. The publisher of the *San Francisco Bay Guardian* challenged the constitutionality of the act because it allowed preexisting joint operating agreements in 11 cities to continue in effect. The *Bay Guardian* argued that a 1965 agreement had caused the San Francisco market's three competing dailies to be reduced to two papers, the *Chronicle* and the *Examiner*, which shared not only production facilities but also profits. The case was settled out of court, with the *Bay Guardian* being compensated more than $1 million, thus protecting the Newspaper Preservation Act from potential adverse court action.

A 1987 investigative study by Stephen Lacy showed that newspapers operating under joint operating agreements were more similar to openly competing newspapers than to monopolies in their content, especially their editorial positions. By 1990, the number of joint operating agreements declined to 19. Although monopolistic tendencies continued after the Newspaper Preservation Act, its passage demonstrated the influence of powerful print media concerns and ended attempts by the federal government to intervene in the decline of daily newspaper competition.

References Ghiglione, Loren, ed., *The Buying and Selling of America's Newspapers* (1984); Lacey, Stephen, and Todd F. Simon, *The Economics and Regulation of United States Newspapers* (1993).

Newsprint

Other than the printing press, the most fundamental ingredient in publishing is paper. The quality of the paper used by newspapers and magazines improved over time, but it also became more expensive. Newsprint is the one aspect of publishing for which there is no substitute.

In the colonial period, most paper for printing was imported from England. By the time of the American Revolution, however, there were about 70 paper mills operating in the colonies. The first such mill was established in 1690 near Philadelphia by William Rittenhouse, a Mennonite preacher, who had learned how to make paper in his native Netherlands. The paper produced in America was at first crude and remained insufficient to satisfy all the demands for colonial printing. Paper in the eighteenth century was made from cloth rags, which, although rough in texture, lasted longer than modern paper made from wood. The value and scarcity of paper were demonstrated when it was included among the six imported items to be taxed in Parliament's Townshend duties in 1767.

During the American Revolution, the importation of paper from England was cut off entirely, and the scarcity caused the price of paper to increase. One patriot paper, the *Connecticut Courant*, built its own paper mill during the Revolution. Other publishers soon followed the example of the Hartford publisher. Because Americans produced paper with insufficient bleaching, a blue dye was often used, giving paper a blue tint. The demand for cloth rags led to appeals that equated saving rags with doing one's patriotic duty. There were even contests with prizes for those who could collect the most rags. The price of rags rose to ten shillings per pound by the end of the war. Despite paper-mill expansions that continued after the war, newspapers often had to reduce their size because of paper shortages.

In the early nineteenth century, U.S. paper manufacturers Thomas Gilpin and John Ames developed a paper-making machine that produced paper on a continuous roll, similar to a model invented by Englishmen Sealy and Henry Fourdrinier. Gradual improvement in paper production drove the price of paper down from 13 to 8 cents a pound. The price reduction came just in time to accommodate the new penny papers of the 1830s. Shortages caused by the Civil War drove paper prices up again to between 22 and 28 cents a pound by 1863. By 1874, the price was back down to just slightly above prewar levels.

The most important factor affecting the cost of newsprint after the Civil War was the technology to produce paper from wood pulp. The manufacturing process had been developed by a German, Friedrich Keller, and his machines were imported into Massachusetts in 1867. Rag paper did not entirely disappear, however. Initially, the paper manufacturers used a composite of about 40 percent wood pulp and 60 percent rag for their paper. It was not until the 1880s that paper made entirely of wood pulp, mainly spruce, was used on a regular basis. The conversion to wood pulp paper significantly reduced the cost of paper for printing—down to less than two cents a pound by the turn of the century. The cost would never again be so low.

World War I, like all wars, led to the inflation of prices, and paper was not exempt from increases. Although the Federal Trade Commission placed price controls on newsprint during the war, once controls were removed, the cost rose from about two cents a pound in 1914 to six cents by 1920. Increased demand—1.5 million tons in 1914—also affected prices. Manufacturers were unable to keep pace even when, at the urging of the American Newspaper Publishers Association, the tariff on imported paper from Canada was lowered and finally eliminated between 1909 and 1913. Most newsprint manufacturing soon migrated to Canada, which provided 79 percent of newsprint used in the United States by 1948.

In the 1920s, an overproduction of newsprint led to a gradual decline in price, to about three cents a pound by 1929. During the Great Depression, newspaper publishing was less affected by economic upheaval than other industries, because newsprint remained cheap. In 1940, a group of southern publishers and chemists produced a quality grade of newsprint from young pine trees cut before the resin content became too high. The first mill built to utilize the new pine pulp production process in Texas had a capacity of 50,000 tons per year. The discovery allowed the plentiful southern pine forests, where the growth rate was much faster than in Canada, to temporarily resolve shortages of newsprint and competition from Canada.

World War II caused even greater scarcity of imports that were traditionally obtained from nations such as Norway. Prices were again frozen by the federal government, but shortages caused rationing of newsprint by 1943. Once the price controls were ended at the beginning of 1946, the price of newsprint rose by $35 a ton over the prewar price. It continued to rise to $100 a ton in 1948, double the prewar price. Although manufacturers were getting more for their paper, the production rate of 2,000 feet per minute was still inadequate to meet demand. Newspapers experimented with methods of reducing paper consumption, ranging from cutting classified advertising to eliminating special editions. More paper mills were built in the South during the postwar era to use the pine pulp raw material.

The Korean War caused another 25 percent spike in newsprint prices, and consumption increased to 6.5 million tons by the mid-1950s. The next major price jolt for newsprint came during the inflationary era of the late 1960s, with paper prices more than doubling by the early 1970s. By the 1980s, newsprint was the second highest cost for newspaper publishing—after staff salaries—requiring about 20 percent of revenues. The cost had again more than doubled to about $650 a ton. Major dailies such as the *Los Angeles Times* used almost half a million tons of newsprint annually.

Reference Ellis, L. Ethan, *Newsprint: Producers, Publishers, Political Pressures* (1960).

Newsweek

Established as an obvious imitator of *Time* in 1933, *Newsweek* has found it difficult to establish its distinctiveness ever since. Started by Thomas Martyn as a news digest, *Newsweek* has been more careful than *Time* about separating news reports from editorials. As part of the *Washington Post* conglomerate, *Newsweek* continues to show profits and maintain a large circulation.

Thomas J. C. Martyn was born in England and obtained his first major journalism assignment as editor of foreign news for *Time* in the 1920s. He left to join the *New York Times*, where he conceived the idea of starting his own newsmagazine. *News-Week* was launched in 1933, with publisher Martyn promising advertisers that he could sell 50,000 copies. Martyn used much the same format as *Time*, but he instructed his writers to approach their subjects objectively and avoid the editorializing for which Henry Luce's *Time* had become noteworthy. Whenever opinion columns appeared, they were always signed, in contrast with *Time*'s anonymity of authorship. Martyn's scheme of placing seven photo blocks on the cover—depicting one event for each day of the week—was soon discarded because it confused prospective purchasers.

By 1937, despite an impressive circulation of 250,000, *News-Week* faced serious financial problems. The company agreed to merge with another well-financed journal, *Today*, owned by the Astor and Harriman families of New York. *Today*'s editor, Raymond Moley, had been a member of Franklin Roosevelt's brain trust, and he was made editor at *News-Week*. Later in 1937, Malcolm Muir, former president of McGraw-Hill publishing company, became publisher and president of the magazine, which dropped its hyphen to become *Newsweek*. Muir announced that the magazine would concentrate on reporting the news, providing detailed background to stories, and interpreting events—all of which *Time* had been doing, albeit through a different scheme. *Newsweek* pioneered the "Periscope" entry, which encapsulated major news events of the week. It also established a foreign bureau in Europe during World War II to coordinate reports from its many war correspondents. Muir was succeeded as publisher by Theodore Mueller in 1949, and when Mueller died in 1958, Gibson McCabe took the reins.

Newsweek established its own bureaus and employed more researchers than reporters to help prepare its articles. In 1950, *Newsweek* started a ten-cent magazine called *People Today*, a precursor of today's successful *People* magazine; it was sold after only eight months, despite acquiring a circulation of 500,000. Meanwhile, *Newsweek*'s circulation continued to grow steadily through the 1940s and 1950s, reaching 1.5 million in 1961 when the Astor, Harriman, and Muir families sold the magazine to Philip Graham of the *Washington Post* for almost $9 million. Under editors Osborn Elliot and Edward Kosner, the magazine became more vigorous in its editorial policy and was compartmentalized into categories such as national news, foreign news, science and technology, religion, sports and leisure, and the press. It also carried book, movie, and theater reviews and was embellished throughout with bright photographs. *Newsweek* columnists have always been taken from the cream of writers, including Walter Lippmann, Stewart Alsop, and economist Milton Friedman. Circulation continued increasing to 2.3 million in 1969 and 3 million in 1977, but *Newsweek* still trailed its principal rival *Time*.

Since the 1960s, each issue of *Newsweek* featured a lead story with an accompanying cover photograph. Wars, peace, racial issues, education crises, medical or technological breakthroughs, and social trends have been among the topics included as lead stories. *Newsweek* followed the lead of other U.S. journals by marketing its product overseas, and the foreign circulation soon passed the 2 million mark. By 1987, *Newsweek* ranked fifth in magazine revenues at $239 million. Philip Graham's widow, Katherine, has headed the *Washington Post* conglomerate since 1963.

Nielsen, A. C.

Broadcast ratings determine not only the advertising rates but also the popularity of radio and television programs. The A. C. Nielsen Company pioneered the technique in the 1930s and continues to be the bellwether of the ratings system.

Arthur C. Nielsen was able to utilize technology developed at the Massachusetts Institute of Technology in 1936 to begin measuring radio audiences. He soon founded a company based on audience research, and the controversies surrounding the ratings game have continued ever since. The critics claim that the ratings are inaccurate because, like political polls, they take only a sample from the total audience to establish their scale. Even though the Nielsen ratings are independent of the radio and television networks, the future of programs revolves more around their ratings than any other factor. People who follow a particular program that is canceled because of bad ratings tend to blame the ratings service rather than the network.

The sampling procedure begins with a decision about the size of the sample—500 or 1,000, for example. Then a random selection process is followed to choose the individuals to be surveyed. Usually, for broadcast samples, the survey does not include more than one member of a family. The samples are taken from a demographic cross section of the geographic area surveyed. Data are collected through personal or telephone interviews, weekly diaries, or electrical meters attached to the broadcast receiving sets.

The Nielsen Company pioneered the use of meters for radio in 1942 and later the television Audimeters in the 1950s. Typically, Nielsen distributes 1,700 Audimeters to sample households. From the Nielsen center in Florida, telephone calls can collect the audience data instantaneously. In 1986, Nielsen experimented with the "people meter" developed by AGB Research Co., which can track the programming preferences of each member of a sample household. Gradually, the number of meters distributed in the sample has risen to 4,000.

The Nielsen statistics are useful for understanding general audience behavior patterns as well as providing information for advertisers and networks. For example, Nielsen estimated that in 1986 there were about 86 million households with television. Nielsen surveys can determine the average length of television viewing per day for different household members.

References Belville, H. M., *Audience Ratings: Radio, Television, Cable* (1988); Field, Harry, and Paul F. Lazarsfeld, *The People Look at Radio* (1946).

Nieman, Lucius W.
See Milwaukee Journal.

Niles' Weekly Register

Niles' Weekly Register combined the elements of a newspaper and a magazine. It was committed to covering national news and reproducing government documents and major speeches of political leaders. Published first in Baltimore and later in Washington, D.C., the *Register* garnered wide respect for its accuracy and effort to print both sides of political issues.

Hezekiah Niles gained his first publishing experience with a Wilmington, Delaware, magazine in 1805. He was then copublisher of the *New York Evening Post* for over five years following the magazine's collapse.

Two weeks after the sale of the *Post* in 1811, Niles launched the *Weekly Register* from Baltimore. The six-by-nine-inch, 16-page paper featured no advertising and scant illustrations. It sold for $5 a year, and the circulation grew from 1,500 to 3,300 by the end of the first year.

Niles aimed for a national audience from the outset, and subscribers were distributed across all the states and some foreign nations. Major political leaders, including John Adams, Thomas Jefferson, James Madison, and Andrew Jackson, praised the *Register* and helped enhance its reputation for accurate and complete political news. As a Quaker, Niles promoted religious tolerance through his editorials, but he was best known for a strong nationalism; he abhorred sectional issues that tended to divide the nation. During the War of 1812, the *Register* opposed the antiwar sentiments coming from New England, and when the slavery issue emerged during the Missouri Compromise debate in 1819 and 1820, Niles urged reconciliation and cooperation. The *Register* encouraged American authors and fought against the literary dominance of English writers.

Niles' Weekly Register became known for its verbatim printing of government documents, important speeches, and excerpts from the personal papers of principal political leaders. The *Register* thus became the closest thing to an official agency for government news, and it was the most quoted media source in the first half of the nineteenth century. Niles ensured that quotations were full and complete rather than edited so as to guarantee fairness.

When a partisan press revived during the Jacksonian era, Niles was critical of the undue influence of newspapers affiliated with political parties. Niles believed strongly that the press could not remain free and independent if it was subsidized by partisan organizations. Economic issues also attracted Niles's attention; he championed the growth of agriculture, trade, and industry and opposed what he considered limitations on their expansion. Niles's economic ideas most closely resembled the nationalistic American System of Kentucky's Henry Clay.

By the time Hezekiah Niles retired in 1836 and was succeeded by his oldest son, William Ogden Niles, as editor and publisher, the *Register*'s circulation surpassed 4,000. Although the son pledged to follow his father's lead, William failed to achieve Hezekiah's success. The younger Niles made two important changes in the paper: he moved the printing operations from Baltimore to Washington, D.C., in 1837, and he changed the name of the paper to *Niles' National Register*. The new editor devoted more space to coverage of congressional debates, which squeezed out other significant news. When failing finances forced the suspension of publication for two months in 1839, Niles reluctantly announced that the paper was for sale.

William Ogden Niles sold the *Register* in 1839 to his father's friend Jeremiah Hughes. Experienced in Maryland publishing circles, Hughes promised a return to the broad type of coverage *Register* readers had come to expect from Hezekiah Niles. Difficulty in collecting subscriber arrears further complicated the precarious finances of the paper. By 1848, Hughes's old age and a lack of enthusiasm for publishing caused a four-month suspension of publication just prior to his death. George Beatty purchased the *Register* and moved the paper to Philadelphia. Beatty attempted to resolve the financial dilemma by selling advertising, but past problems were compounded by Beatty's untalented editorship. The *Register* terminated publication in 1849, ending an auspicious history.

Reference Luxon, Norval Neil, Niles' Weekly Register (1947).

North American Review

The first magazine to last more than five years, the *North American Review* became the United States' premier journal of literature, history, and criticism from 1815 to 1940. It retained a Boston-Harvard flavor until its move to New York City in 1878. The *Review* was noted for allowing both sides of an issue to use its pages as a forum for debate. The list of the *Review*'s editors read like a who's who, including Jared Sparks, Edward Everett, James Russell Lowell, Henry Adams, and Henry Cabot Lodge.

The *North American Review* was founded in 1815 as a bimonthly journal by the Anthology Club of Boston to publish literary and historical items. The first editor, William Tudor, had talented assistants in Edward Tyrell Channing and Richard Henry Dana. Anxious to end the English literary dominance in the United States, Tudor deliberately recruited an entirely American participation in the *Review*. Although its circulation never got much above 3,000 in the early years, the *Review*'s mark on U.S. literature was permanent.

The literary bent of early editors such as Edward Everett and Jared Sparks shaped the type of contributors. One of the nation's most famous orators, Everett served as the *Review*'s editor from 1820 to 1824, following a stint as professor of Greek at Harvard; he later served as congressman and governor in Massachusetts. The editor of the writings of George Washington and Benjamin Franklin, Sparks edited the *Review* from 1824 to 1831; he later served as president of Harvard College.

The work of New England poets such as Ralph Waldo Emerson, Henry Wadsworth Longfellow, and William Cullen Bryant appeared regularly in the *Review*. Bryant's well-known "Thanatopsis" appeared first in the *Review*. Historians such as Francis Parkman, John L. Motley, and W. H. Prescott contributed essays. Writings of short-story connoisseur Washington Irving and even former President John Adams graced the pages of the *Review*. During the pre–Civil War era, when social issues such as slavery were prominent, editors James Russell Lowell and Charles Eliot Norton made readers fully aware of the journal's editorial position.

After the Civil War, editor Henry Adams recruited novelists Henry James, Mark Twain, and William Dean Howells to write for the *Review*. James serialized his novel *The Ambassadors* in the *Review;* Twain published chapters of his autobiography. After Adams stepped down from the editor's chair, Allen Thorndike Rice moved the journal to New York City and made it a monthly in 1878. Rice treated readers to varying symposia on current issues such as public education and morals on the stage. During 1879 and 1880, Rice invited five suffragist leaders, including Elizabeth Cady Stanton, to use the *Review* to express their views. Francis Parkman and others responded, opposing women's suffrage. Editors such as Henry Cabot Lodge brought a greater political consciousness to the *Review* with critics such as H. G. Wells and E. P. Whipple and political figures such as Theodore Roosevelt. Circulation reached a peak of 76,000 in 1891.

As owner and editor from 1899 to 1926, George Harvey maintained the *Review*'s quality and readers' interest in its offerings. Harvey began his journalism career as a reporter for the *Chicago Daily News* and later served as managing editor for Joseph Pulitzer's *New York World*. In 1924, after a hiatus as ambassador to Great Britain, Harvey changed the publication to a quarterly; circulation had declined to 13,000. When lawyer Walter Butler Mahony purchased the *Review* in 1926, he restored it to a monthly publication schedule. Although not at its peak of the late nineteenth century, the *North American Review* retained its reputation for distinctive writing into the 1930s.

In 1938, the *Review* was sold to Joseph Hilton Smyth, who turned out to be an agent of the Japanese government, which was seeking U.S. publications as propaganda outlets. When the link between Smyth and the Japanese was revealed, it led to the termination of the *Review* in 1940.

Noyes, Frank B.
See Washington Star.

On-Line Services

The spread of personal computer ownership led to the establishment in 1979 of the first on-line computer network. For a modest monthly fee, the on-line system connects personal computers via a modem—telephone line linkage—to a mainframe system with various databases. The networks provide a variety of useful services ranging from computer games to educational reference materials to information bulletin boards.

The range of services offered by the on-line systems began with text-only material and extended to graphics. The systems operate on IBM-compatible or Apple Macintosh personal computers, the two most popular personal computer formats. The "bulletin board" system allows computer owners to communicate with one another by leaving messages, and some on-line services provide "live" discussions with instant exchanges. Computer games may be played with the mainframe computer or with other subscribers. Informational resources on the on-line systems include news, sports, entertainment schedules, movie and television reviews, and soap opera recaps. There is also access to some encyclopedias. Graphics capabilities include weather maps as well as those used in games.

CompuServe was the first on-line system offered publicly to subscribers in 1979. It began in 1969 on a limited time-sharing basis; by the 1990s, it had over 1.5 million subscribers. CompuServe charges a basic monthly fee and adds fees for extended services not included in the basic package. There are about 2,000 different databases in the CompuServe system.

The Delphi on-line service began in 1981 and remains a text-only service with no graphics capabilities. Its options include financial news, home shopping services, and news wire reports. GEnie on-line service was established in 1985 by General Electric. The system offers computer games as well as the text-only options similar to most on-line systems. Its main attraction is the conversation group format, which touches on a variety of topics. The America Online service claims to provide greater graphics offerings than any other network. Its reference sources include the National Geographic Society, Library of Congress, and Smithsonian Institution. The latest on-line service is Prodigy, founded in 1990 as a cooperative venture between IBM and Sears. It was the first service to offer on-screen graphics continuously, and it boasts over 700 types of information databases, but Prodigy does not provide live discussion formats. Prodigy's chief information source is Grolier's Encyclopedia.

All the commercial on-line services cooperate with one another through the Internet system, which allows access to thousands of computer networks worldwide. Internet began in 1969 as a cooperative venture by the Defense Department to connect several research universities with defense contractors. It soon expanded with connections to other on-line services; it included 100 networks in 1985 and grew to about 4,000 by 1991. In 1993, the number of Internet subscribers was growing 15 percent a month and was projected to reach 100 million by 1998. The chief use of the Internet system is multiuser dimension, or MUD, by which groups of users are connected together to a particular computer system for joint access. Commercial on-line services have begun to offer connection to Internet as part of their packages. Internet and all the commercial on-line services provide electronic mail capabilities. There are many published manuals with instructions about joining and using Internet. Gradually, broadcast media are connecting their systems with on-line services to allow more viewers or listeners easier access. Libraries can subscribe to on-line reference services, which speed their ordering and interlibrary loan capabilities.

See also Computers.

Paine, Thomas (1737–1809)

An English firebrand who arrived in America on the eve of the Revolution, Thomas Paine wrote the pamphlet *Common Sense* in 1776, which inspired the Continental Congress to draft the Declaration of Independence. He also penned the widely read "Crisis" essays in the revolutionary press. Later, he traveled to France to promote individual rights in another revolution.

After quarreling with his Anglican mother, Thomas Paine was attracted to his father's Quaker faith, with its stress on individualism and opposition to institutions such as slavery. He worked at various occupations, including corset maker and exciseman, but remained restless and in poverty. Paine met Benjamin Franklin in England, and Franklin advised him to travel to America to make a fresh start. Paine arrived in Philadelphia in 1774 and began contributing to Robert Aitken's *Pennsylvania Magazine*. Writing on a variety of subjects from politics to matrimony in both prose and verse, Paine developed his skills quickly. He also wrote an entry in the *Pennsylvania Journal* advocating an end to slavery; in other papers, he proposed manhood suffrage and public funding for education.

Aitken apparently thought that Paine's writing was too incendiary and released him in December 1775. By then, the Revolutionary War had been under way for several months. In early January 1776, Paine anonymously published a pamphlet entitled *Common Sense* that assailed the person of King George III as well as the institution of monarchy. Paine argued that England's past constitution had no relevance to present circumstances and thus deserved no reverence. *Common Sense* further suggested that the colonials should not be fighting merely for a restitution of Britain's laissez-faire colonial policy but for political independence from Britain. The pamphlet was soon quoted in many newspapers and sold 120,000 copies in 25 editions within three months. Certainly, Common Sense caused representatives in Congress to consider its proposals seriously.

Yet not all patriots supported independence. William Smith, head of the future University of Pennsylvania in Philadelphia, writing under the pseudonym "Cato" in the *Pennsylvania Gazette*, rejected the necessity of independence and said that Paine was promoting "common nonsense." Using the pseudonym "Forester," Paine countered Smith's arguments in the *Pennsylvania Packet*. The more that was said about *Common Sense*—whether pro or con—the more currency it received across the colonies.

Thomas Paine is best known for writing the historic pamphlet Common Sense *in 1776, inspiring Thomas Jefferson to write the* Declaration of Independence.

Meanwhile, Paine joined George Washington's Continental Army during its retreat from New York City toward Pennsylvania. Paine wrote a series of rhetorical blasts called the "The American Crisis" (1776–1783) that first appeared in the *Pennsylvania Packet* and was reprinted in many other publications. Washington had Paine's essay read to his dejected troops to instill esprit de corps on the eve of the American attack at Trenton. The first "Crisis" entry began with the famous phrase "These are the times that try men's souls" and sold even more copies than *Common Sense*. While Washington's army endured hardships and setbacks, Congress adopted Paine's concept of independence in a document largely written by Thomas Jefferson. This document, which we know as the Declaration of Independence, was approved by Congress on 4 July 1776. The course of the American Revolution and the history of the United States was fundamentally altered thereafter.

Satisfied with the achievement of American independence and the rejection of monarchy and aristocracy, Paine continued the radical cause by publishing another popular pamphlet, *The Rights of Man*, in 1791 and 1792. Paine responded to Edmund Burke's questioning of the philosophical grounds for the French Revolution and his predictions of chaos. At the invitation of President Thomas Jefferson in 1802, Paine returned to the United States from England. He was greeted by a hostile Federalist Party press that was still incensed by Paine's 1796 criticisms of Federalist leaders George Washington and John Adams. Paine settled on some New York property he had been granted for his Revolutionary War service, died in New York City, and was buried on his estate. Paine consistently defended the rights of the individual against monarchy and favored various schemes of social and political reform in England and France as well as in America. He also believed that the press had a duty to present controversial ideas that the public could then judge.

References Aldridge, Alfred O., *Man of Reason: The Life of Thomas Paine* (1959); Foner, Eric, *Tom Paine and Revolutionary America* (1976).

Paley, William S.

See Columbia Broadcasting System.

Pearson, Drew (1893–1969)

Among the most potent and controversial political columns was Drew Pearson's syndicated "Washington Merry-Go-Round," which appeared daily in 600 papers across the United States and had 40 million readers. Noted for his exposés and fearless attacks on political power brokers, Pearson was an expert at using investigative techniques and confidential sources to get his story. Pearson made his philosophy clear and unequivocal, and presidents feared running afoul of the columnist.

Drew Pearson was born in Kansas, but his parents left the farmlands for university life. The family's Quaker pacifism was an enduring influence on Pearson. His father, Paul, attended Northwestern University in Illinois and Harvard while young Pearson grew to school age. Paul Pearson obtained a position teaching English at Swarthmore in Pennsylvania, where Drew attended a prep school and then the Quaker college where his father taught. Drew Pearson followed his father's involvement in the Chautauqua movement, which broadened his perspective. Pearson avoided service in World War I and traveled with Chautauqua tours after the war. He also began some freelance writing in the early 1920s. Pearson married the daughter of newspaper publisher Eleanor Medill Patterson, granddaughter of the founder of the *Chicago Tribune*.

Drew Pearson obtained the position of foreign editor at David Lawrence's *United States Daily*, the forerunner of *U.S. News & World Report*. The primary task of the *Daily* was reprinting important government documents, so Pearson had little opportunity to develop his writing skills. He was able to cover some important European diplomatic conferences during the late 1920s, however. The experience at *United States Daily*, combined with Pearson's friendship with the son of the *Baltimore Sun*'s publisher, got him a post as diplomatic correspondent on the *Sun* in 1929. Pearson angered the State Department by criticizing the British ambassador to the United States and shocked many by suggesting that President Hoover tried to censor the press. It was the first of many episodes wherein Pearson clashed with the rich and powerful in Washington.

Encouraged by Henry L. Mencken to write a gossipy insider's view of Washington society, Robert S. Allen of the *Christian Science Monitor* sought a collaborator in 1929. Allen engaged Pearson as coauthor of the book entitled *Washington Merry-Go-Round*, issued in 1931 without the authors' identities. The book was hard on the politicians but even more critical of weak-kneed journalists. President Hoover used the Federal Bureau of Investigation (FBI) to identify the authors and vowed never to speak to Pearson again. A sequel, *More Merry-Go-Round*, appeared in 1932 but lacked the clout and energy of the first book. More importantly, United Features Syndicate offered Pearson and Allen their own political column under the byline "Washington Merry-Go-Round" in 1932.

Although the column tended to criticize almost all politicians, Franklin D. Roosevelt fared better than most because his political philosophy of the welfare state paralleled Pearson's. Other New Deal brain trusters were not as fortunate as the president in avoiding the Pearson barbs. The first of many libel suits against Pearson was filed quickly by General Douglas MacArthur but later dropped. Altogether, Pearson was sued for libel 275 times during his career, but only once did he have to pay damages. Pearson had remained a pacifist until the Spanish civil war (1936–1939) caused him to accept the notion of stopping aggression by dictators. On the domestic front, Pearson attacked Louisiana's Huey Long and anti–New Deal radio host Father Charles Coughlin. Pearson's acquaintances with congressmen allowed him to introduce pet legislation indirectly over the years.

During World War II, Pearson moved his Washington column from his mother-in-law's *Times-Herald* to the *Post*, in part because of Mrs. Patterson's isolationism. He also began broadcasting commentary about the war via radio. Pearson's partner Allen left to serve in the military and was seriously wounded, thus ending his tenure with "Washington Merry-Go-Round" in 1942. After trying several replacements, Pearson settled on Jack Anderson as a junior partner in the column. Pearson broke the story about General George Patton striking an enlisted man in Italy, as well as Roosevelt's decision to make Senator Harry Truman his 1944 running mate.

Washington, D.C., columnist Drew Pearson used investigative techniques and confidential sources to wage war against political impropriety and corruption.

Pearson's fame spread to other parts of the globe after World War II. His column was printed in European, Asian, and Latin American papers. President Truman was angered by a Pearson column that charged Truman with anti-Semitic statements. The Ku Klux Klan threatened Pearson when he exposed its violent revival in the South. The "Merry-Go-Round" regularly featured assaults on the House Committee on Un-American Activities because of its witch-hunt tactics against communists. Pearson was an early and loud critic of Senator Joseph McCarthy's method of using his Senate position to hurl unsubstantiated charges about disloyalty. Pearson cooperated with the FBI in uncovering activities of organized crime and encouraged Senator Kefauver's senatorial investigation of crime links with government figures in 1950 and 1951.

During the administration of Dwight Eisenhower—a hero of Pearson's during World War II—the president got the "Merry-Go-Round" treatment for allowing lobbyist Bernard Golfine too much influence, which led to Chief of Staff Sherman Adams's resignation. Pearson also revealed an emerging military-industrial complex through big-business manipulation of executive departments. The "Merry-Go-Round" also supported the civil rights movement and attacked the ultra-right-wing John Birch Society in the 1950s. Democratic Senate majority leader Lyndon Johnson was befriended by Pearson during Johnson's political journey to the presidency. In 1958, Pearson mistakenly charged that John Kennedy was not the author of *Profiles in Courage*, for which he had won a Pulitzer Prize. Although Pearson wielded considerable influence with both Johnson and Hubert Humphrey, it tended to compromise his journalistic independence.

During 1965, Pearson trained his sights on congressional misuse of power and privilege by Congressman Adam Clayton Powell of New York and Senator Thomas Dodd of Connecticut. Powell was soon defeated in a reelection bid, and Dodd was censured by the Senate. The Dodd revelations were the basis of a Pulitzer jury nomination for Pearson and Anderson, which was rejected by the advisory board in 1967. Pearson's reputation for loosely applying facts to facilitate exposés allowed his conservative enemies to attack him ceaselessly toward the end of his career.

Reference Pilat, Oliver, *Drew Pearson: An Unauthorized Biography* (1973).

Pennsylvania Gazette

Founded by Samuel Keimer in 1728, the weekly *Pennsylvania Gazette* gained its greatest fame after Benjamin Franklin became the owner-editor in 1729. Franklin made the Gazette outspoken for the times and very lively. He also trained many other printers who served the colonies. After retiring in 1766, Franklin sold the *Gazette* to David Hall, whose family operated the paper until its demise in 1815. Under Hall, the *Gazette* became the largest-circulation English-language newspaper in the Americas.

After being released from his apprenticeship to his brother, Benjamin Franklin came to Philadelphia from Boston in 1728. Franklin opened a printing shop with Hugh Meredith and planned a paper to compete with Andrew Bradford's *American Mercury* (1719). Before Franklin could act, however, a printer named Samuel Keimer issued a weekly entitled the *Pennsylvania Gazette* in December 1728. Keimer conceived of the idea to reprint Chamber's encyclopedia in the *Gazette*. He also proposed to print some local news as well as accounts from English papers, and he began serializing a novel by Daniel Defoe. Franklin was not amused that Keimer had beaten him to the punch, so he composed a series of essays called the "Busy-Body Papers" that were printed in Bradford's *Mercury*, satirizing Keimer's journalistic effort. When the *Gazette*'s circulation fell below 100, Keimer agreed to sell the paper to Franklin and Meredith, less than ten months after beginning publication.

Franklin immediately discontinued the encyclopedia reprints and the Defoe serial. He devoted the *Gazette* to effective news gathering, attractive advertisements, and an appealing format. Franklin sometimes had to print eight pages—twice the normal length—in order to accommodate all the advertising. Editor Franklin believed that literate readers should be given all the facts available so that they could make intelligent decisions. Franklin trained a number of printers at the *Gazette* who later established half a dozen newspapers in other colonies.

The *Gazette*'s main rival continued to be Bradford's *Mercury*, which received a lucrative government subsidy as the official printer for the colony. Franklin succeeded in attracting the attention of the colonial legislature by sending printed copies of documents to demonstrate the quality of his work. Within a year, the *Gazette* received the contract for government printing previously held by the *Mercury*. In 1732, Franklin bought out his partner Meredith to become the sole owner of the *Gazette*. In addition to publishing the *Gazette*, Franklin's print shop published other profitable items, including *Poor Richard's Almanack* (1732–1757). Franklin also helped start the first foreign language newspaper, the *Zei-*

tung, in Philadelphia in 1732 and briefly published a magazine in 1741.

When Franklin decided to retire as publisher of the *Gazette* in 1747, he brought in a partner from London, David Hall, who had been trained by William Strahan. By the 1760s, the circulation of the *Pennsylvania Gazette* increased to 3,000, giving it the largest circulation in the colonies. Because of Hall's connections with Strahan, the *Gazette* carried the freshest news from England among all the colonial papers. The sometimes rash Hall wanted to attack the Stamp Act of 1765 more vigorously than Franklin, because Hall feared that it would end colonial newspapers. The Hall family became the sole owners of the *Gazette* in 1766 and continued to operate it until 1815. The *Gazette* published John Dickinson's famous "Letters from a Farmer in Pennsylvania," questioning British policy toward the colonies, in 1768. The paper backed the patriot cause in the American Revolution and briefly moved from Philadelphia during the British occupation. David Hall's son and coeditor William Sellers so staunchly backed the strong new central government being fashioned in secret at the Philadelphia convention of 1787 that they branded any opponents as traitors. The *Pennsylvania Gazette* printed not only the first copy of the newly drafted Constitution in 1787 but also the first commentary advocating its ratification.

See also Franklin, Benjamin.

References Harlan, Robert D., "David Hall and the Stamp Act," *Papers of the Bibliographical Society of America* (1967); Simpson, Lewis T., "The Printer as a Man of Letters: Franklin and the Symbolism of the Third Realm," in *The Oldest Revolutionary: Essays on Benjamin Franklin*, ed. J. A. Leo Lemay (1976).

Penny Press

The journalistic corollary to political democracy in the Jacksonian era was the advent of the penny press, a newspaper oriented to the common man. The penny press revolutionized journalism in the 1830s and 1840s not only because it engaged the common man in U.S. society but also because of its novel methods of selling through vendors and financing through advertising rather than subscriptions.

When Benjamin Day launched the first penny newspaper, the *New York Sun*, in 1833, big-city dailies cost six cents a copy and were financed almost exclusively on a subscription basis. The front page of the *Sun* consisted of three columns containing stories on local events, especially those with a violent angle. The news in the *Sun* did not resemble items in the traditional dailies, which aimed at middle- and upper-class interests such as politics. The circulation of the *Sun* outstripped that of its rivals within six months after the inaugural issue. Day hired veteran English reporter George Wisner to locate crime stories that would appeal to the *Sun*'s audience. The result was a focus on the frailties and problems of common people. Page four of the *Sun* was devoted to advertising and classified ads, the key to financing the paper.

The ability to mass produce was due to Day's purchase of the new Napier cylinder presses manufactured by the Hoe Company; it was capable of printing 1,500 papers an hour. Day sold the *Sun* in 1837 to his brother-in-law, Moses Beach, for $40,000, although profits had risen as high as $120,000. Beach and his successor, Charles A. Dana (1868), continued to focus on the ingredients that had made the *Sun* a success: modern technology, reporters, and advertising.

Reputable journalists were horrified at the sensational nature of the penny papers, especially at the tendency to manufacture spurious stories such as a description of life on the moon in 1835, which tripled sales of the *Sun*. The mass circulation phenomenon allowed penny publishers to focus on the relationship between advertising and news gathering. The public's appetite for news spurred innovations, such as gathering the news through reporters, which directly affected an advertiser's interest in a publication. At first, the penny papers were sold primarily at newsstands on the streets of the big cities rather than through subscriptions. Street vendors bought a volume of papers from the publisher at a discount and sold them to their customers for profit. The penny press placed a premium on reporting

THE BOOM IN JOURNALISM.

Unlike the traditional dailies, which were aimed at middle- and upper-class readers and derived their income from subscriptions, the new penny newspapers appealed to the industrial working class and were largely financed by advertising. The sensationalism of these popular dailies was deplored by traditional publishers, but it was the innovative practices of the penny press that came to influence modern newspaper journalism.

the news rather than trying to mold opinions on political issues or reprinting news stories from other papers. Hiring reporters was regarded as scandalous by traditional publishers.

After Day's *New York Sun* established the pattern, other publishers tried to imitate the *Sun* and its success. James Gordon Bennett launched his *New York Herald* in 1835, and although its orientation toward sensationalism was not as pronounced as the *Sun*'s, the *Herald* was definitely a by-product of the first penny paper. William M. Swain and Arunah S. Abell, friends of Benjamin Day, joined publisher Azariah H. Simmons to launch their version of the penny paper in 1836, the *Philadelphia Public Ledger*. It catered to the sensational but was in better taste than the *Sun* or the *Herald*. By 1838, the *Public Ledger* was selling more than 20,000 copies a day. Abell then persuaded his partners to back another venture, the *Baltimore Sun*, founded in 1837. Despite the national depression that greeted the *Sun*, it prospered and had a circulation of 12,000 by the end of its first year. The *Baltimore Sun* exchanged news with the *New York Herald* via the new telegraphic service (1846) and also shared reports from the Mexican War in the 1840s. Even Horace Greeley's *New York Tribune* began as a penny paper in 1841. All the penny press publishers were businessmen first and foremost, a new breed of journalist.

Clearly, the penny press phenomenon was a reflection of changes occurring in the United States in addition to those occurring within journalism itself. The advent of industrial expansion in northeastern cities had a social and economic impact on the working classes. They had a desire to know what was happening to their livelihoods and why. Industrialization was accompanied by dramatic technological advances in machinery, some of which involved the production of printed materials. The expansion of adult male suffrage led to a new interest in politics and government. Commoners were concerned about the criminal justice system, which often touched their lives. They were curious about the unknown and the mysterious. Yet with all the innovations pioneered by the penny press, its publishers wanted respectability rather than to lead revolutions. Although they were on the cutting edge of technology, advertising techniques, and appeal to the masses, the penny press hesitated at assuming the role of social arbiter of issues such as labor rights or slavery.

See also News Gathering.

References Nerone, John C., "The Mythology of the Penny Press," *Critical Studies in Mass Communications* (1987); O'Brien, Frank M., *The Story of the Sun* (1928).

Persian Gulf War

Instant television coverage loomed larger than ever in the 1991 war known as "Desert Storm." President George Bush was more careful than Vietnam-era administrations in controlling media coverage, however. The result was that although American civilians saw more of this war than any other in U.S. history, what they viewed on their television sets was carefully constrained by military and government controls. During Desert Storm, Cable News Network (CNN) rivaled the three major networks in reporting, elevating the cable giant into international prominence. Satellite feeds back to the United States allowed simultaneous "real-time" television coverage.

When Iraqi dictator Saddam Hussein invaded the Persian Gulf state of Kuwait in August 1990, the U.S. media, like the U.S. government, had virtually no warning and thus lacked advance preparations. Over the next several months, however, as U.S. and allied forces converged along the Kuwait–Saudi Arabia border, journalists swarmed into the previous void. The youthful CNN sent reporters not only to Saudi Arabia but also to Iraq. When U.S. bombing of the Iraqi capital, Baghdad, began the Desert Storm offensive in January 1991, CNN correspondents Bernard Shaw and Peter Arnett reported live by satellite to the United States. Some reporters disliked the military's requirement that all reporters in the Gulf have medical exams before receiving their credentials.

Shortly after an air attack on Baghdad by allied aircraft, TV reporters use a satellite phone to communicate with the outside world.

The military provided ample official briefings in the Persian Gulf theater as well as at the Pentagon. They allowed television cameras to film military preparations and even provided videotape of high-tech weapons hitting their targets. Because the enemy had been successfully portrayed as lacking scruples or principles, the press tended to mimic World War II reporters by engaging in patriotic asides. Although the print media were able to provide detailed maps showing troop and weapon positions, television clearly dominated coverage thanks to live satellite transmissions. Technology gave the media a new means of gathering news, but it also caused disruptions in the normal patterns of reporting.

The United States was better able to identify military heroes, something that was difficult in the Vietnam era. Chairman of the Joint Chiefs of Staff General Colin Powell and field commander General Norman Schwarzkopf became excellent focal points for patriotic fervor. Since the war was extremely short and resulted in the smallest loss of life in any major war, the American public showed overwhelming support. With few exceptions, the public perception of the media was much more positive than during the Vietnam War. From the government's point of view, such circumstances proved invaluable, since television's omnipresence on the foreign scene magnifies, distorts, and sometimes modifies government policy. For example, when television showed a rout and massacre of Iraqis after the allied invasion of Kuwait, the Bush administration stopped the offensive to avoid alienating its Arab allies by an appearance of bloodthirstiness. Certainly, political leaders in the television era realize that they must use the media to build a consensus and support the use of force. Such a perspective was unnecessary during conflicts such as World War II and had yet to be discovered in the Vietnam era.

The typical news reports during the Persian Gulf War followed the preparations and departure of local military units in the United States. Even local newspapers, radio, and television played an important part in that coverage. During congressional debates over the authorization of military force, reporters interviewed legislative leaders. Because of the United Nations involvement, reporters followed activities at UN headquarters in New York City. Correspondents at military sites in the Persian Gulf theaters provided further coverage of unit preparations. The U.S. government took great care to protect local Arab culture from undue scrutiny by the media. Press briefings—in Saudi Arabia and at the Pentagon—by the military became an important if limited source of information as well, especially when the fighting began. Coverage extended into Israel after Iraq began firing missiles at sites there. Some reporters ventured toward enemy lines without approval, and a few were captured by the Iraqis. Once the allied attack began, the reporters in Baghdad were gradually removed, although they occasionally got invitations to return to view bomb damage. The television networks employed military experts to explain the various scenarios and options in the conflict.

There was no shortage of official sources for reporters to consult during the Gulf War. Besides U.S. agencies, representatives of the Saudi, Kuwaiti, British, and French governments and military were interviewed by reporters. Participating in the coverage with U.S. television networks—NBC, CBS, ABC, and CNN—were Israeli, British, and French broadcasters. The print media were represented by the major dailies and newsmagazines, along with wire service correspondents. The visual images provided by television and photographers lacked the sordid, bloody elements evoked in Vietnam. The Gulf War images were mostly of eager warriors and sophisticated weapons wreaking destruction, not of dead soldiers or civilians. A poll at the outset of the war in January 1991 revealed that 70 percent of the public followed Desert Storm events very closely.

Reference Bennett, W. Lance, and David L. Paletz, eds., *Taken by Storm: The Media, Public Opinion and U.S. Foreign Policy in the Gulf War* (1994).

Philadelphia Inquirer

The longest running daily in newspaper-rich Philadelphia was the *Inquirer*, founded in 1829. Jesper and William Harding made the *Inquirer* first a Whig and later a Republican organ through the Civil War. Rarely a leader in newspaper trends or even circulation in Philadelphia, the *Inquirer* nonetheless proved to be a survivor. Moses Annenberg bought the *Inquirer* in 1936, and his family ran the paper until it was sold to the Knight chain in 1969, after which it won numerous Pulitzer Prizes.

From its birth in 1829, the *Philadelphia Inquirer* exhibited a partisan bent. Initially, editor Jesper Harding backed Andrew Jackson's new Democratic Party but broke with the president over the extension of the Bank of the United States, headquartered in Philadelphia. Harding soon became an ardent backer of the emerging Whig Party led by bank proponents Henry Clay and Daniel Webster. The *Inquirer* found it difficult to make the transition when the Whig Party died in the 1850s. It reluctantly supported Republican Abraham Lincoln in the 1860 election, when William Harding was editor, but it remained strongly Republican long afterwards.

William Harding reduced the *Inquirer*'s price to two cents in 1860. The paper offered perhaps the most thorough coverage of the Civil War among Union papers. Its circulation rose to 60,000 in 1862, and it became the most respectable paper in Philadelphia. At the end of the century, the paper was bought by James Elverson, who had begun his career as a telegraph messenger. The *Inquirer* continued to prosper in the highly competitive Philadelphia market. James Elverson Jr. succeeded his father as publisher in 1911 and constructed a massive building in 1925 with state-of-the-art equipment for the paper.

After Elverson's death in 1929, his widow sold the *Inquirer* to Cyrus H. K. Curtis, publisher of the *Saturday Evening Post* and *Ladies' Home Journal*, who had obtained the *Philadelphia Public Ledger* in 1913 and the *Press* in 1920. Curtis merged the *Press* and the *Public Ledger* into the *Inquirer*, and Mrs.

Elverson repurchased the paper in 1934. Then in 1936, she sold the *Inquirer* to Moses Annenberg for $13 million. Annenberg had worked in circulation departments at Hearst newspapers in Chicago, New York, and Wisconsin. He had made a success of the *Daily Racing Form* after 1922 and started the *Miami Tribune* in 1934, among several other publishing ventures.

Annenberg pushed hard to increase circulation, which rose from 288,000 in 1936 to 390,000 by 1940 and passed the million mark for the Sunday edition. The *Inquirer* increased the space devoted to news and added columnists and cartoon strips. Annenberg launched various promotions to attract subscribers and lowered the price from two cents to one. The publisher installed city editor Eli Zachary Dimitman as editor, where he remained until the paper was sold to John Knight in 1969. Moses Annenberg became embroiled in Pennsylvania politics trying to influence legislation. He was indicted and convicted of income tax fraud and served a brief prison sentence before his death in 1942.

Walter Annenberg had been groomed to take his father's place at the head of Triangle Publications, the publishing company created shortly before Moses Annenberg's death. The *Inquirer* witnessed the failure of one of its rivals, the *Record*, in 1947. Walter Annenberg tried in 1951 to purchase another, Robert McLean's *Bulletin*, but failed. In 1951, the *Inquirer*'s daily circulation was 644,000, and the Sunday edition's totaled 1.125 million. In 1957, Annenberg bought the 32-year-old evening *Daily News*, eliminating yet another competitor. The Annenbergs broke the long-standing tradition of the *Inquirer* backing Republican Party candidates. The paper backed some local Democratic candidates in the 1950s but did not endorse a Democratic presidential candidate until Lyndon Johnson in 1964.

Samuel Newhouse offered to buy the *Inquirer* in 1969, but John Knight intervened with an offer of $55 million, which Annenberg accepted. As part of the Knight-Ridder group, the *Inquirer* reached new heights of journalistic competence. Under editor

Gene Roberts, the paper won numerous awards, including Pulitzers. The paper was rated in the top five among national dailies. In 1994, under editor Max King, daily circulation totals were more than 500,000, and Sunday's was just under 1 million.

Reference Cooney, John, *The Annenbergs* (1982).

Phonograph

Recorded music has been at the center of the entertainment industry since Thomas Edison's invention of the phonograph. Technological improvements in the original machine, such as stereophonic sound, digital recording, and laser disc players, have enhanced the phonograph's significance in media such as popular music, motion pictures, radio, and television.

Thomas Alva Edison began tinkering with inventions as a young man in Ohio. He produced a mechanical voting machine and an electric stock ticker. Edison also invented the first working phonograph in 1877 while experimenting with a means of recording telegraphic messages. The machine consisted of a cylinder covered with tin foil, which vibrated from the sound waves. Edison's first recording was the verse "Mary had a little lamb." The decade between the initial invention and the manufacture of phonographs required cooperation from Edison's team of chemists, physicists, and electrical and acoustical engineers. The phonograph was not only Edison's favorite invention but also the first to be mass produced—200 sets a day—at the Edison Phonograph Works, which opened in 1887 in West Orange, New Jersey. The factory was part of a massive production facility that grew into the giant General Electric Company.

In 1885, Chichester Bell and Charles Tainter took a different approach. In their Graphaphone, the recording cylinder was coated with wax instead of tin foil. Tainter incorporated the Volta (later American) Graphaphone Company in 1886 after Edison's original patents lapsed. Emile Berliner's Gramophone, invented in 1887, used a disc instead of cylinder; the recording needle moved in a lateral direction on the wax disc.

The production of recordings for the talking machines began with a master disc imprinted on a metal form. This allowed the mass production of duplicate records, which used a shellacked surface. The sound waves, transcribed directly on the grooves in the record, were limited to three and one-half octaves at first. Although Edison visualized the phonograph's primary use as a dictating machine, music reproduction quickly became the ideal function for the device. Musicians played into a large megaphone to produce the recording. Musical sounds reproduced more poorly than singing voices on the early phonographs. In 1924, Western Electric scientists demonstrated the Orthophonic electrical method of recording, which allowed clearer reproductions for musical instruments.

Because of the fragility of the talking machines and their poor-quality sound reproduction, there was no guarantee that they could be sold in large numbers. In 1888, Edison leased his phonograph's marketing rights to Jesse Lippincott, who had also obtained a similar grant from Tainter's American Graphaphone Company. Lippincott founded the North American Phonograph Company but touted the machine mainly for office dictating. The first major sales of the phonograph, however, were to penny arcades, where they were used as coin-operated music boxes. The National Phonograph Company took over marketing for the defunct North American Phonograph Company in 1891. Edison began improving his version, but competition soon expanded.

The Columbia Phonograph Company began manufacturing amusement machines in 1891 based on Edison's cylinder design. The Victor Talking Machine Company, founded in 1901 by Eldridge R. Johnson, used the Berliner disc machines. The company's new model, the Victrola, debuted in 1906. The works were totally enclosed in a piece of furniture—a design that would attract American households. Edison imitated the Victor design with the Amberola enclosed set. By 1912, Victor had sold 186,000 machines, compared with Edison's 61,000. There were only three phonograph manufacturing companies in 1912, but by 1916 there were 46. The new company that provided the most competition to the established firms was the Brunswick-Balke-Collender Company of Iowa, founded in 1916. Phonograph sales in 1914 totaled 27 million and rose to 159 million by 1919.

During the 1920s, competition was fierce. Victor bought Western Electric's electrical recording rights, and General Electric and Westinghouse developed similar technology for Brunswick. The major surge in record sales, and thus phonographs, was due to the emergence of jazz, played mostly by black musicians. Record and phonograph sales began to decline by the mid-1920s due to the popularity of another technological breakthrough—radio broadcasting. There was some recoupment in the 1930s, but the combination of declining revenues and the onset of the depression led to takeovers of phonograph companies by broadcasting-entertainment interests. The Columbia Phonograph Company was subsumed by the new radio network, Columbia Broadcasting System (CBS), in 1928. Broadcasting giant Radio Corporation of America (RCA) bought Victor in 1929 for $32 million. Edison's company had been slow to adopt the electrical recording system and collapsed in 1929. Brunswick was bought by Warner Brothers in 1930.

Although radio hurt phonograph sales initially, broadcast stations relied on phonographs to play their music. Edison's idea of using the phonograph to record talk never materialized. The National Broadcasting Company (NBC) and CBS radio networks prohibited their stations from using recorded speeches except for special occasions, such as year-end reviews. RCA-Victor and Decca Records dominated the sale of records, with Columbia a distant third during the 1930s and 1940s. World War II caused a shortage of raw materials for the shellac to manufacture records, which limited sales. But in 1947, 400 million records, with revenues of $204 million, and 3.5 million phonographs were sold.

The postwar 1940s witnessed several technological flurries affecting the industry. In 1945, record manufacturers touted their "full frequency range reproduction" techniques to improve sound quality. The most significant advance, however, was Columbia Records' successful 1948 production of a long-playing (LP) record. Experimentation with the technique dated from the 1920s, but previous efforts had proved infeasible. To enhance volume capacity, Columbia produced a vinylite plastic record with 300 microgrooves to the inch, compared with the normal 85 grooves. The length of playing time, 23 minutes on each side, was due to the new speed of 33-1/3 revolutions per minute (rpm) instead of the old 78. RCA refused to follow Columbia's lead and developed a 45-rpm record in 1949. After other companies followed the LP trend, RCA also began producing the records in 1950. Still, the 45-rpm records gained a 50 percent share of sales in the mid-1950s because of the popularity of rock-and-roll singles. Record sales skyrocketed from $213 million in revenues in 1954 to $603 million in 1959.

Sound technology also experienced innovations in the 1940s. Greater amplification of sound, known as "high fidelity," became popular during 1947 and 1948. Other than using two speakers and amplifying the treble and bass sounds, there was nothing revolutionary about the system, but the timing was right for the marketing of phonographs. Magnetic tape recording began to be used in 1949 to enhance the sounds transmitted over radio. It encouraged further experimentation, which produced "stereophonic" sound in 1957. The ability to combine sounds on tape meant that two microphones could simultaneously feed two channels to create a "two-eared listening" phenomenon played through two separate amplifiers and speakers. Eventually, stereophonic sound would be followed by quadraphonic sound (four channels, amplifiers, and so on). These technological advances helped spur sales of records, which broke the $1 billion mark in 1967. By 1975, 73 million Americans had phonographic sound systems.

The most recent technological advance in the 1980s was digital recording, which relied on binary codes to store every detail of the recorded sound and remove distortions. A laser beam reads and translates the binary digits onto a compact disc for crystal-clear reproduction. Playing the discs requires a disc player, the ultimate successor to Edison's tin-foil cylinder. Compact disc sales tripled between 1984 and 1985.

Reference Gelatt, Roland, *The Fabulous Phonograph, 1877–1977* (1977).

Photojournalism

The photograph as an element of media history predates the halftone processes as well as the publication of pictorial magazines such as *Life* and *Look*. Initially, photographs were unaccompanied by written explanations or comment, fully adhering to the adage that a picture is worth a thousand words. Photos became stock features of news stories, accounts of famous personalities, historic events, and entertainment in all forms of print media, thereby creating a new aspect of media history known as photojournalism.

Louis Daguerre revealed his method of making positive photographic plates with copper and silver to the French Academy of Sciences in 1839. For a long period thereafter, photographs were called daguerreotypes, despite a rival English system developed contemporaneously by William H. F. Talbot. Photographs appeared in U.S. publications as early as 1840 using an improved camera lens combined with different chemicals to soften tones. Two British inventors produced a positive-negative process that allowed the production of multiple copies of daguerreotypes. The collodion process developed in 1851, using a glass negative and a much shorter exposure time, allowed the portrait photography business to emerge. By 1871, the use of dry plates with the collodion process cut the exposure time to seconds.

Photographic journals, such as Henry Snelling's *Photographic Art-Journal* begun in 1851, featured portraits of public figures accompanied by biographical essays. Widely circulated photographs enhanced the renown of national celebrities such as political leaders. Using technology advanced by John Plumbe, political magazines

Mathew Brady traveled with the Union army and safely transported glass plates in his buggy and wagon, pictured here. The Civil War helped popularize photographs in newspapers and magazines.

such as the *United States Magazine and Democratic Review* and the *American Whig Review* reprinted photographs of their respective political leaders in the 1840s. Both Plumbe and Mathew Brady launched unsuccessful picture magazines in the 1840s. By the early 1850s, engravings from daguerreotypes were appearing in newspapers depicting train wrecks, fires, and civil unrest as well as occasional portraits of newsworthy personalities. The introduction of "stereographic" photography provided a three-dimensional image that gradually became very popular.

With the development of John A. Whipple's process (patented in 1850) to produce inexpensive negatives, newspapers such as *Frank Leslie's Illustrated Newspaper* (1855) and magazines such as *Harper's Weekly* (1857) found it easier to use photographs. Leslie used photographs as a method of following news events. Mathew Brady, who had started a portrait photo business in New York City in 1844, provided many of the photographs from which the engravings were made for the *Illustrated Newspaper*. Fletcher Harper's magazine offered competition to Leslie by introducing photographs in its eighteenth issue. Photographers such as Brady established a brisk business supplying the print media with their products. Actually, established newspapers and magazines were reluctant to introduce photographs because of the expense and the view that they wasted precious space.

Photojournalistic coverage of the Civil War helped elevate the popularity of pictures associated with news events. Brady was allowed to travel with units of the Union army during the war and photographed scenes of the first major battle at Bull Run in 1861. Twenty photographers worked for Brady to document the war on the Union side. In Richmond, the *Southern Illustrated News* (1862–1864) borrowed the techniques of photographic reproduction from the Union press. Leslie's photos of survivors at the Confederate prison camp at Andersonville demonstrated war's reality.

After the Civil War had made photojournalism an integral part of the U.S. media scene, the opening of the western frontier became the next great attraction for illustration. Cowboys, Indians, railroad construction, and the awesome natural beauty of the West were portrayed in photographs published in new journals such as *Scribner's* and *Lippincott's* as well as in veterans such as *Harper's* and *Leslie's*. When Frederick Ives and Stephen Horgan developed the halftone process in the 1870s, it was possible to transfer photographs directly to the printed page. Halftones made reproducing photographs easier and less expensive so that no publication needed to avoid their use. Soon newspapers such as Horgan's *New York Daily Graphic* (1873) made halftones the centerpiece of their publication. Publishers such as Joseph Pulitzer and William Randolph Hearst realized that photographs could enhance their newspaper sales. The advent of news photographers gradually removed artists from their prominent role in journalism. News syndicates such as Associated Press maintained photographers as well as reporters on their staffs.

The next phase in the history of photojournalism was the emergence of the tabloids in the 1920s. Although the tabloid size had been used before, the format was borrowed from English newspapers in the late nineteenth century. Beginning with the *New York Daily News* (1919), tabloid journalism depended on the ample use of photographs, especially large front-page features, to make the publications appealing to the masses. Soon after the decline of the tabloids, publisher Henry Luce devised a pictorial magazine that would raise the level of taste for its readers. *Life* magazine was begun in 1936, using photographs from the new 35-mm camera. The entire front page was a photograph, and photographs made up a substantial portion of the interior pages of *Life*. John Cowles produced an imitator called *Look* in 1937. Photojournalists such as Margaret Bourke-White, Robert Capa, David Douglas Duncan, Dorothea Lange, and Ansel Adams made careers of media photography. The Pulitzer advisory board at Columbia University inaugurated a photography award in 1942. Once again, war proved a boon to the new product, as *Life* reporter-photographers brought the war graphically to civilians at home.

The success of *Life* and *Look* made photojournalism even more attractive and acceptable for traditional print media. Certainly, all mass audience magazines, including *Sports Illustrated, Better Homes and Gardens,* and *National Geographic,* relied heavily on photographs to sell their products. The nationally marketed *USA Today* employed hundreds of news photographers to collect pictures for publication. It was not until the 1970s that photopicture agencies were established to provide magazines such as *Time* and *Newsweek* with photographs from around the globe. The Associated Press developed filmless cameras, portable photo transmitters, and electronic darkrooms. Motion pictures introduced newsreels in its earliest era before World War I, and some producers made documentaries on film in the 1920s. The ultimate technological advance for photojournalism was television, which did not supplant still photography but added a unique dimension to news coverage.

See also Graphic Design.

References Carlebach, Michael L., *The Origins of Photojournalism in America* (1992); Kerns, Robert L., *Photojournalism: Photography with a Purpose* (1980).

Portland Oregonian

Founded in 1850 as a weekly by Thomas Jefferson Dryer, the *Portland Oregonian* became a daily in 1861 and began a Sunday edition in 1880. Publisher Henry Pittock led the *Oregonian* from the post–Civil War era to the early twentieth century. The *Oregonian* was edited during that time by Harvey W. Scott, who established a national reputation for himself and the paper. In 1950, the *Oregonian* was bought by Samuel I. Newhouse, who also acquired the evening *Oregon Journal* in 1961.

Self-taught Thomas Jefferson Dryer came west from New York and gained some newspaper experience in San Francisco. He founded his own paper in 1850 at the junction of the Willamette and Columbia Rivers on the site soon called Portland. The *Oregonian* began as a weekly printed on Dryer's Ramage hand press. Dryer urged area gold prospectors to seek more stable employment and endorsed the Republican Party in what was strongly Democratic country. After accepting many subscribers' word that they had paid their subscriptions when they had not, Dryer hired 18-year-old Henry Pittock as business manager in 1853. Dryer later established another paper at Olympia, Washington, known as the *Columbian.* Upon being named diplomatic envoy to the Hawaiian Islands in 1861 by Secretary of State William Seward, Dryer gave the *Oregonian* to Pittock as payment for past services. Pittock's major task as publisher would be to find a suitable editor, especially since he had decided to transform the *Oregonian* into a daily by purchasing a Hoe cylinder press.

Harvey W. Scott worked his way through college and practiced law before starting part-time at the *Oregonian* as an editorial writer in 1865. At Pittock's request, Scott agreed to become editor of the paper later that year. Scott had a knack of unraveling difficult issues for his readers and presented forceful, logical editorial opinions. Scott always considered the public's interest ahead of personal whims. Although the *Oregonian* remained a supporter of the Republican Party after the Civil War, Scott was not hidebound by Republican positions. Scott favored a low tariff and territorial expansion but opposed the free silver and Asian immigrant exclusion movements, which were especially popular in the West. The *Oregonian* became the largest-circulation paper in the state of Oregon, rising from 10,000 to 15,000 during the 1870s and 1880s. Scott's editorial reputation, which reached across the nation, was interrupted between 1872 and 1876 while he served as a federal customs collector in Portland. In 1877, Scott became a partner with Henry Pittock in the ownership of the *Oregonian,* the same year that Pittock purchased the evening *Portland Telegram,* which continued publication until it was sold in 1914. From 1900 to 1910, Scott served a term as director at the Associated Press. After Scott died in 1910 and Pittock in 1919, their heirs continued to operate the *Oregonian*.

Edgar B. Piper followed Scott as editor of the *Oregonian*. He had been the state capital correspondent for the paper and moved up to city editor in 1894. Piper was more interested in local news stories than Scott had been, and he persuaded management to start radio station KGW in 1922. Ronald G. Callvert served as acting editor after Piper's death in 1928, until Paul Kelty got the permanent post. During the Great Depression, the *Oregonian* felt the impact endured by most papers—declines in circulation and advertising. A financial restructuring was handled by Guy T. Viskniskki working with the Pittock trustees. Editorial management was entrusted to Edwin Palmer Hoyt from 1933 until 1946, when he resigned to become publisher of the *Denver Post*. Hoyt renewed the *Oregonian*'s editorial reputation during those years. The son of a preacher and a graduate of the University of Oregon, Hoyt had risen through the ranks at the *Oregonian* beginning in 1926—from copy editor, reporter, and news editor to the top spot. The board also elected him publisher in 1938. During 1943, Hoyt spent six months as a member of the Office of War Information in the Roosevelt administration. Hoyt also helped found Radio Free Europe after World War II. Chief editorial writer Ronald Callvert won a Pulitzer Prize in 1939 for a patriotic theme.

Arden Pangborn took over the editorial duties after Hoyt became publisher in 1938. When Pangborn assumed control over the radio station, city editor Robert C. Notson was named managing editor, and Michael J. Frey became business manager. The *Oregonian* celebrated its 1950 centennial in a curious fashion; the Scott and Pittock heirs sold the paper to chain newspaper owner Samuel Irving Newhouse for $5 million. Newhouse kept the management executives such as Frey and Notson in place. In a separate agreement, Newhouse purchased radio station KGW for $600,000. Newhouse bought the Oregonian's competitor, the evening *Oregon Journal*, in 1961 and

made Pangborn editor. *Oregonian* reporters Wallace Turner and William Lambert won a Pulitzer Prize in 1957 for revealing corruption in the Teamsters union. Editor Robert C. Notson, who was serving as president of the American Society of Newspaper Editors, became publisher in 1967. *Oregonian* assistant managing editor Edward M. Miller became managing editor until 1970, when former city editor J. Richard Nokes succeeded him. Fred A. Stickel followed Nokes as publisher in 1975. Circulation grew during the 1960s to 250,000 before declining in the late 1970s. Former city editor and assistant managing editor William Hilliard became editor in 1983, when circulation had risen above the 335,000 mark.

Reference Notson, Robert C., *Making the Day Begin: A Story of the* Oregonian (1976).

Presidential Debates

The U.S. political tradition of debates advanced into the electronic age in the late twentieth century, giving voters a chance to see and hear presidential candidates firsthand. The movement toward formal debates, however, was a difficult and slow change from presidential candidates remaining above the fray and letting their spokesmen hold forth on their behalf. Television has been at the forefront of the dramatic changes in presidential elections, and increasingly traditional debates since 1960 represent that adjustment better than anything else.

After the emergence of political parties in the 1790s, political leaders most often expressed their positions through partisan newspapers. Party leaders Thomas Jefferson and Alexander Hamilton used the press as practically the only vehicle for expressing viewpoints or vilifying political enemies. Long before American independence from Great Britain, however, the debating tradition had been used as a means of educating citizens and developing their civic awareness. Traditionally, Americans respected debate as a way of promoting independent

The televised Nixon-Kennedy debates set the precedent for presidential debates in the late twentieth century.

thought. Presidential candidates themselves did not engage in any debate—direct or indirect—until the election of 1896, because it was deemed unseemly for the candidates to lower themselves to that level. Instead, surrogates spoke for the candidates, as Abraham Lincoln did on behalf of Republican nominee John C. Frémont in 1856. Even under the nineteenth-century system, politicians and the press resorted to military and sports metaphors, which remain commonplace on the campaign trail today—broadsides, battles, heavy artillery, struggle, winning, teamwork, and rally are among many overused terms.

The debating format gradually emerged under the old system before the end of the nineteenth century. The debates of the twentieth century have involved face-to-face confrontations under a format that provides equal treatment and time for the candidates to respond to formal questions. Congressional debates, such as the Webster-Hayne debate in 1830 over the constitutionality of state nullification of federal laws, helped prepare the way for presidential contests. So too did formal campaign debates such as those between Abraham Lincoln and Stephen Douglas for a U.S. Senate seat in 1858. The first significant change at the presidential level came in the election of 1896, however. Democratic Populist candidate William Jennings Bryan took his campaign directly to the people by making over 600 speeches in 27 states, stressing his single-issue free silver theme. In the 1872 campaign, Horace Greeley had made a direct appeal to the voters, but almost never in person as Bryan did in 1896. The Bryan model became the new campaign method for the twentieth century.

Secretary of Commerce Herbert Hoover worked with Congress to enact the Federal Radio Act of 1927 and suggested that broadcasting would revolutionize political debate in the nation. For the presidential election of 1928, the League of Women Voters organized weekly radio debates on specific issues that featured spokesmen for the two major parties but not for the presidential candidates. Another radio program called "American Forum of the Air" on the Mutual Broadcasting System offered contrasting speakers' views on a set topic. Invariably, some observers charged that the broadcasts were flawed, and politicians since the 1920s have often claimed distortions in broadcast coverage. Radio networks, anxious to demonstrate evenhandedness, created programs such as NBC's "America's Town Meeting of the Air" in 1935 as a public service to educate citizens about issues. Candidates were using radio broadcasts as part of their campaign appeal, and presidents began using radio to broadcast their news conferences. Republican presidential candidate Wendell Willkie appeared on "America's Town Meeting of the Air" to make points in his 1940 contest with Franklin Roosevelt.

Gradually, the debate format began moving toward the presidential process. During the 1948 Republican primary in Oregon, Thomas Dewey agreed to a radio debate with Harold Stassen on the issue of whether to outlaw the Communist Party. Although Dewey took the less popular position of opposing abolition of the party, he articulated his views better and won the primary and the nomination. In 1956, an ABC-televised discussion of a variety of issues between Democratic candidates Adlai Stevenson and Estes Kefauver proved less rewarding, as did a similar debate between Democratic candidates John Kennedy and Hubert Humphrey in 1960. The candidates took almost identical positions on foreign and domestic issues, so viewers had no real basis for making distinctions. Television offered a potentially troubling aspect in that candidates might "look good" even if they did not provide substantive answers to issues. Hence, the political rule in television campaigns became that appearance was more important than content. Dwight Eisenhower's 1952 television campaign speeches were formulated by a Madison Avenue advertising firm to ensure the proper look. Television advertising also

places a premium on succinctness, since airtime is so costly.

The idea of having presidential candidates face each other over the issues developed gradually. In 1952, the League of Women Voters and *Life* magazine cosponsored a presidential debate moderated by John Daly in which surrogates represented candidates Eisenhower and Stevenson. It was the televised, face-to-face Kennedy-Nixon debates in the 1960 campaign that changed forever the approach to electioneering. The four debate sessions in an otherwise close contest gave Kennedy the edge over Nixon because of his appearance and demeanor rather than anything of substance that separated the two men. About 80 million viewers watched the first Kennedy-Nixon debate, about 60 percent of the voting population.

After the precedent had been set in 1960, it was not until 1976 that the tradition resumed. If either candidate refused to participate, there could be no debates; that was the case in 1964, 1968, and 1972. The League of Women Voters continued to sponsor presidential debates featuring a moderator and a panel of journalists to ask questions. The Gerald Ford–Jimmy Carter debates in 1976 used a three-session format—one on domestic policy, one on foreign policy, and one general—but attracted only about one-third of the voting population as viewers. The 1976 debates also featured one debate between the parties' vice presidential candidates, which became part of the format for the future.

The 1980 debate between Jimmy Carter and Ronald Reagan gained the highest ratings of any broadcast debate, with 120 million viewers. The numbers dropped to 85 million for the 1984 debate between Reagan and Walter Mondale. A debate among Republican candidates preceding the 1988 primaries gained only about 10 million viewers, indicating that voter interest tends to peak just a few weeks before the general election. Debates were held in 1988 between George Bush and Michael Dukakis using the 1976 format. In the 1992 debates, three candidates were included for the first time: Bush, Bill Clinton, and third-party candidate Ross Perot. The debates since 1960 have become somewhat less oriented toward appearance and based more on substance. Certainly, presidential debates have been an important, if not the most important, element in the campaigns since 1976. Yet the debates have not improved the overall voter turnout in presidential elections.

Reference Jamieson, Kathleen Hall, and David S. Birdsell, *Presidential Debates: The Challenge of Creating an Informed Electorate* (1988).

Presidential Election Campaigns

One event that Americans have followed with great interest since the founding of the republic has been the presidential election. Although the media have had little if any influence over elections until very recent decades, elections were regarded as important news even before reporters began covering the campaigns. Beginning with the presidential nominating conventions of 1832, there was greater scrutiny of campaigns as reporters followed the candidates. The broadcast era in the twentieth century brought even closer attention to the campaigns—first with radio and then with television.

Since President George Washington had no formal opposition in his elections of 1789 and 1792, there was little coverage of the event. Beginning with the contested election of 1796, newspapers focused on presidential campaigns. Early newspapers such as the *National Gazette* (Democratic-Republican) and *Gazette of the United States* (Federalist) were partisan sheets that assumed a one-sided stance in their reports. When the Federalist Party collapsed after the War of 1812, Boston's *Columbian Centinel* described James Monroe's presidency (1817–1825) as "an era of good feelings," in part because of the absence of party hostility. The election of 1824 resulted in a bitter division within Jefferson's old party between Democrats led by Andrew Jackson and National Republicans led by John Quincy Adams and Henry Clay. The Democrats recruited partisan editors such as Duff Green, Amos Kendall, and Isaac

Hill to assail the Adams administration (1825–1829) in preparation for Jackson's successful challenge in the 1828 election.

When the parties began selecting their presidential candidates at nominating conventions in 1832, the penny press thirst for news allowed much greater coverage of the unique events. By the election of 1840, the Whigs had as many partisan papers as the Democrats and waged a modern campaign, replete with campaign songs, floats, banners, and parades. Horace Greeley published the *Log Cabin*, a Whig campaign paper that sold as many as 85,000 copies in one issue. Abraham Lincoln won the election of 1860 with only 40 percent of the popular vote and only one-third of the newspapers backing him. By 1864, Lincoln gathered support from the great majority of northern newspapers for his reelection. Republican Ulysses S. Grant, who won easily in 1868 and 1872, got fewer newspapers to back him in 1872 because of the issue of corruption, which was played up by the Liberal Republican press. The New York Times outlined a new position for dailies by attempting to be impartial in the reporting of political news but still editorially "endorsing" a particular candidate or party. In the post–Civil War era, most newspapers attempted to follow the Times's lead by recognizing that the public wanted accurate facts more than mere opinion. The history of press endorsements has shown that rarely does such approval affect the outcome of elections.

In the disputed election of 1876 between Democrat Samuel Tilden and Republican Rutherford B. Hayes, the *New York Times* urged the creation of an electoral commission to resolve the dispute. When the Republicans nominated controversial James G. Blaine for president in 1884, a large number of traditionally Republican papers, including the *New York Times, New York Post, Harper's Weekly,* and *The Nation*, refused to endorse Blaine. Democrats had the same problem in 1896 when Populist presidential nominee William Jennings Bryan got very few endorsements from traditionally Democratic papers. Progressive Republican

Theodore Roosevelt was opposed by much of the eastern Republican press and the Hearst papers in the election of 1904, but he had considerable support in the rest of the nation. In the three-way race of 1912, eventual winner Democrat Woodrow Wilson gained more newspaper endorsements than either Roosevelt or William Howard Taft.

In the 1920s, press approval for Republicans returned, with an average of about 60 percent of newspaper endorsements for Harding, Coolidge, and Hoover. Even in 1932, Hoover received the same majority support in the press against landslide winner Democrat Franklin Roosevelt. Republican Wendell Willkie got 63 percent of newspaper endorsements in the 1940 election against Roosevelt. Radio coverage of elections began in earnest in 1936 after initial broadcasts at the 1920 conventions. NBC radio coverage was moderated by Lowell Thomas; guest commentators included Walter Lippmann and Dorothy Thompson. Mutual radio broadcasts were handled by the popular Gabriel Heatter, and CBS's coverage was led by Robert Trout and commentator Hans Van Kaltenborn. When Roosevelt won an unprecedented fourth term in 1944, he had only one-fourth of the newspaper support.

The advent of television in the 1940s led to new elements in presidential campaign coverage. Television cameras were present for the first time at both parties' 1948 conventions held in Philadelphia. Douglas Edwards moderated the CBS television and radio coverage, assisted by ten reporters; John Cameron Swayze represented NBC's broadcasts, heading a dozen correspondents. ABC utilized 50 personnel to produce its broadcasts in 1948. DuMont television network also covered the 1948 events. The radio audiences of 60 million in 1948 outnumbered the 10 million television viewers, but the roles would be reversed beginning in 1952. Presidential candidates Dwight Eisenhower and Adlai Stevenson were forced to depend on television coverage to get their messages to voters. Eisenhower's campaign was managed by a New York public-relations firm, which planned half-hour campaign programs that were carefully orchestrated to create the appropriate visual image of Eisenhower. The Republicans also used 30-second "spot" announcements effectively. Stevenson decided not to follow the Republican strategy and lost the election in a landslide. Permanent lessons were learned from the 1952 campaign about the use of television in the future.

The 1960 election featured the first televised debates between candidates Richard Nixon and John Kennedy. Again, images proved crucial in the close election. Kennedy appeared more comfortable and spoke extemporaneously, but Nixon seemed nervous and read from a prepared text. During the 1960s, the television networks spent huge sums to cover the party nominating conventions from gavel to gavel. The 1968 coverage of the Democratic convention also showed the violent antiwar demonstrations and negatively impacted the party's electoral chances. Broadcast debates reappeared in the 1976 campaign and have continued since. However, televised coverage of the party conventions lessened beginning in the 1980s, and greater attention has been focused on the party primaries.

See also Presidential Debates.

Press Clubs

As competition among newspapers in the late nineteenth century transformed the institutions into commercial operations, low-paid reporters became anxious not only about job security but also about their public and self-image as professionals. Press clubs were formed to provide a sense of professionalism and camaraderie for reporters and media executives. The earliest organization was the Press Club of Chicago founded in 1880, but the best known today is the National Press Club founded in 1908 in Washington, D.C.

The ability to report the news objectively almost necessitated reporters' isolation from the social circles of the community. The stereotype of the hard-drinking reporter who commiserated with all classes of people to dig up their stories made it difficult for reporters to find a niche in local society. Moreover, as the journalistic profession expanded after the Civil War, reporters faced meager wages offered by executives who were more interested in financial statements than in the quality of the news. The idea of an organization that would allow reporters to seize a measure of social respectability as professionals became attractive. The Press Club of Chicago was founded in 1880 to bestow respectability on the profession and allow journalists a chance to socialize together. The club included Chicago's media elite such as Melville Stone, Victor Lawson, and Joseph Medill as well as ordinary reporters. The Press Club was rather formal, but it helped mold a more positive image of the profession.

A more casual organization founded in 1889 was Chicago's Whitechapel Club. It attracted mostly reporters, who could unwind and engage in radical political debates in the bohemian atmosphere. The Whitechapel Club made a point of not admitting media executives, since the club disdained pretense and sham. Reporters collectively internalized their role as social critics through the Whitechapel Club, whereas the Press Club enhanced their external public image as respectable members of society.

Although Chicago showed leadership in developing the press club concept, Washington, D.C., became the center of activity of national organization. Major dailies found it necessary to maintain at least one correspondent in the nation's capital—by 1870, there were 130 Washington correspondents. Soon whole bureaus of reporters would be created by the largest papers. The Washington correspondents felt even more detached from their communities, since they were almost always absent from the cities they represented. Washington became more of a home to them, but it was not a typical existence. The Washington corps of correspondents founded the Gridiron Club in 1885—an exclusive club that elects only 50 members from the Washington press corps. The club's first president,

Ben:Perley Poore, had been a capital correspondent for the *Boston Journal* since the 1850s. The Gridiron Club provided a social release from the isolation and tedium of covering government far from home. Scheduled meetings featured guest speakers, and humor was the most frequent ingredient of deliberations. The major event of the Gridiron Club was its annual banquet, when members and political figures were roasted with tongue-in-cheek barbs. Presidents are frequent speakers at the Gridiron Club, where their remarks are strictly off the record.

By the 1890s, most states had organizations of editorial writers that met periodically. The New York club maintained swank quarters in New York City for its periodic meetings. What became the most famous of the press clubs, the National Press Club, was founded in Washington in 1908. Its luncheons and banquets continue to feature regular guests from the political or professional elite. Recordings of addresses to the club since 1952 are housed at the Library of Congress. Also, the club sponsors workshops and seminars on reporting. The club's National Press Foundation funds a library and journalism awards. The principal awards are the Sol Taishoff Award for excellence in broadcasting and the Editor of the Year Award for print media. In 1990, the National Press Club had 4,600 members from both print and broadcast media.

World War II was the occasion for the founding of the Overseas Press Club of America in 1939. It focused initially on correspondents covering the war but afterwards specialized in international reporting. The Overseas Press Club eventually found a permanent home in New York City, where it sponsored important surveys and studies of foreign press reporting as well as social events. In 1892, the International League of Press Clubs held its inaugural convocation in San Francisco.

The status of press clubs has been affected by internal political divisions among members and by the admission of members who were not part of the profession. Press clubs have a tendency to curry favor with political figures in order to gain easier access to news events or information. Hence, their original purpose of social and professional advancement has been undermined somewhat in the twentieth century.

Press Conferences

Beginning with Theodore Roosevelt, presidents have relied on the press conference to both inform the public and promote good relations with the media. Roosevelt's informal meetings with reporters featured the president doing most of the talking. Presidents Wilson and Harding regularized the process, and Franklin Roosevelt set the record for the most press conferences of any president. The advent of broadcasting added an important wrinkle to the press conference, especially when television demonstrated the importance of projecting images. Presidential access to the media is usually gauged by the frequency of press conferences.

Major daily newspapers dispatched correspondents to cover Washington, D.C., events by the 1890s. William McKinley's private secretary was a former editor, and two cabinet members had journalism experience. Although McKinley (1897–1901) did not hold regular press conferences, he occasionally spoke to reporters collectively and provided them with official statements. A White House clerk named George Cortelyou prepared daily press reports for McKinley and was soon assigned to draft and distribute official executive statements. Theodore Roosevelt (1901–1909) retained Cortelyou as press secretary and provided a small room in the White House for reporters to use; when the executive office building was constructed, a press room equipped with telephones was included. Roosevelt gave interviews to selected reporters whom he liked but made important announcements to all White House reporters. Verbal retaliation against critical reporters was also a Roosevelt characteristic.

When former reporter William Howard Taft became president (1909–1913), he outlined a plan for regular press conferences but did not adhere to it. In his infrequent meetings with reporters, he prohibited any quotes from being used. Woodrow Wilson (1913–1921) held regular press conferences with reporters for the first two and one-half years of his administration. Because of Wilson's reticence, he allowed reporters to ask questions rather than simply speaking to them, as Roosevelt had done. Also unlike Roosevelt, Wilson allowed all correspondents equal access to the conferences. In the later years of his administration, Wilson sought other means of communicating with the public and neglected press conferences.

Warren G. Harding (1921–1923), a former newspaper editor in Ohio, made the press conference part of the routine business of the White House. The conferences were held twice weekly, alternating at different times so as not to discriminate against morning or evening newspaper editions. Reporters submitted their questions ahead of time and Harding selected certain ones to respond to. It was during Harding's administration that quotations appeared in print under the rubric of "White House spokesman." During Calvin Coolidge's term (1923–1929), 520 press conferences were held following the Harding format. Coolidge often allowed follow-up questions for written questions he had addressed. Before the stock market crash of 1929, Herbert Hoover (1929–1933) held more regular news conferences than any president before or after. However, the situation changed after the onset of the depression. After 1929, Hoover usually selected a few reporters to converse with, and even those meetings decreased as the economy faltered.

Franklin Delano Roosevelt (1933–1945) obviously had the best press relations and used the press conference more frequently than any U.S. president. Roosevelt did not require preconference written questions, but he often spoke "off the record" to reporters. If the president wanted to be quoted, he gave reporters a written statement. The twice-a-week routine for conferences was followed without pause during the Roosevelt years. Roosevelt's confident, easy nature made him ideally suited to the format of press contact. Because of the massive legislative agenda of the New Deal, the press conferences often functioned like a classroom to explain the details of laws and agencies. About half of Roosevelt's press conferences were introduced with a presidential statement on topics he wanted to air. Roosevelt began to assign Stephen Early the task of preparing for the press conferences.

Harry Truman (1945–1953) reduced his press conferences to one a week. Since 150 reporters now covered the White House, Truman's press secretary Charles Ross moved the proceedings to larger facilities at the executive office building. The president also insisted that reporters identify themselves and their employers when rising to ask questions, but he allowed more direct quotes than his predecessors. Crisis situations led to curtailments in the regular press conference schedule. Staff preparations for anticipated questions at the conferences occupied more time and effort. Newsreel films and radio became regular aspects of news conferences during the Truman era.

Under Dwight Eisenhower (1953–1961), the frequency of scheduled press conferences fell back to every other week, but Eisenhower allowed complete tapes of the conferences to be used by broadcast media. Most importantly, television cameras were allowed to record press conferences for the first time. Press secretary James Hagerty considered but did not inaugurate live television coverage of the president's conferences. Secretary of State John Foster Dulles showed skill in using the press conference to promote the administration's foreign policy agenda. Beginning with Eisenhower, presidential staffs were forced to focus on the significant image problems created by television coverage.

John F. Kennedy (1961–1963) began live radio and television broadcasts of press conferences but scheduled fewer of them than Eisenhower. The president and his press secretary Pierre Salinger thought that the dangers of live coverage were outweighed by the advantage of allowing the president to speak directly to the public without possible distortion by reporters. Critics of the new format charged that it allowed reporters and the president to posture for public-relations benefit. Certainly, a great deal of the president's time was spent rehearsing for press conferences to ensure a successful performance. During the 1960s, other executive departments often held press conferences and employed press officers.

Lyndon B. Johnson (1963–1969) felt compelled to follow Kennedy's precedent of broadcasting press conferences live, even though he was not as comfortable in front of the cameras. Johnson sat behind a desk rather than standing as his predecessors had done. Johnson altered the times and places for his news conferences to the distraction of the press. As the Vietnam War widened and criticism of Johnson's policy increased, the president's relations with the press were strained and his credibility questioned. Johnson did not hesitate to telephone the media's chief executive officers to complain about coverage.

A similar situation developed under Richard Nixon (1969–1974), who was never at ease or on good terms with the press. The 39 press conferences held by Nixon—the fewest since Hoover—were almost never longer than 30 minutes and were tightly controlled by press secretary Ron Ziegler. The unfolding celebrity status of many reporters in the television era often led to clashes with President Nixon and an adversarial atmosphere. During Gerald Ford's term (1974–1977), virtually all press conference questions were related to Nixon and Ford's pardon of him following the Watergate fiasco. Ford held 41 press conferences in two and one-half years at various sites.

Jimmy Carter's press conferences (1977–1981) were both more frequent—twice a month—and more formal, with reporters being assigned seats according to their seniority and media status. Responding to recommendations of a study by the University of Virginia, Ronald Reagan (1981–1989) pledged to meet monthly with the press and have questioners chosen by lot. Reagan also agreed to meet informally with reporters on occasion and not use live broadcasts.

Reference French, Blaire Atherton, *The Presidential Press Conference: Its History and Role in the American Political System* (1982).

Printing Press

The technology of printing changed very little between the advent of the earliest movable type in the fifteenth century and the nineteenth century. The application of steam and later electric power changed the speed and quantity of printing. The invention of the linotype in the 1880s further increased the efficiency of printing. The latest technology of photo-offsetting has brought printing into the age of computers in the late twentieth century.

Johannes Gutenberg's first printing press using movable type was launched in Germany in about 1450. When the first printing press was set up in British North America at Cambridge, Massachusetts, in 1638, the technology had changed very little. Printers had to set the type by hand and used a press imported from England. The typical machine was seven feet high, weighed about 1,500 pounds, and was bolted to the floor and ceiling. Making an impression, or "token," of the type required considerable skill, so much early printing was of inferior quality. A wheel and pulley rolled the bed of the press over the type, which had been set into a form and inked by an apprentice called a "printer's devil." The paper was placed in a tray of water so that the impression would be clear. Once the press was rolled over the paper and type, a pressure plate was pushed down by a screw or lever. The pressure plate was then released, the press rolled back, and the 10-by-15-inch paper was removed. The process had to be repeated for another copy. The printer and his devil could produce about 200 impressions an hour. Illustrations were made from a woodcut that was inked and pressed in the same manner.

Printing presses continued to be imported from England until Isaac Doolittle of Connecticut began manufacturing the presses in 1769. The next major technical innovation was the invention of the "Columbian press" by George Clymer of Philadelphia in 1813. It used levers instead of screws to push the pressure plate. Peter Smith made a further improvement in 1822 by increasing the lever speed. In 1827, Samuel Rust of New York added some automatic features to the hand press, including the press bed and paper rollers.

The most dramatic advance was the steam-powered cylinder printing press, first invented in 1811 by German Frederick Koenig, working in England. He soon added a second cylinder that allowed paper to be printed on both sides at once and was known as the "perfecting press." The Koenig press was improved by Englishman David Napier, who tripled its speed. The first Napier press was purchased by the *New York Daily Advertiser* in 1825, and it was capable of producing 2,000 papers an hour. Although it cost ten times more than a hand press, its efficiency more than made up for the cost.

In 1832, Richard Hoe of New York invented a double-cylinder press with a capacity twice that of the Napier press. Hoe's company had already become the principal manufacturer of printing presses in the United States. The increased productivity of printing presses had a direct effect on all printed materials—from newspapers to books. Mass production allowed costs for items such as newspapers and periodicals to remain modest.

After the Civil War, the next technological development was stereotyping, which had actually originated as early as the 1720s. Instead of putting type into the press, a papier-mâché mat with type formations was used to reduce the wear on the type. Previously, type for daily newspapers lasted only about three months before it was worn down. Although the technology existed, no press had been invented before the Civil War that used stereotyping. The Hoe Company built the web-perfecting stereotype press with a curved plate in 1870. It allowed printing on both sides of a continuous roll of newsprint and could produce

The linotype enabled keyboarders to set type mechanically, ending the time-consuming burden of setting type by hand. This innovation, when combined with the stereotype, revolutionized the speed of production and the physical appearance of newspapers.

48,000 twelve-page papers an hour. Of course, it required new equipment to cut and fold the rolls, but that was quickly added. A German inventor, Ottmar Mergenthaler, perfected the linotype machine in 1886. From a keyboard similar to that of a typewriter, an operator could assemble a line of type in a lead slug. The linotype ended the chore of setting type by hand. The stereotype press and the linotype combined in the 1880s to provide attractive new possibilities for printing, including bold headlines and advertising.

The use of color printing in the 1890s allowed comic strips to become a regular feature of the newspaper format. Halftone photoengraving also added a new dimension to the printing of illustrations by the 1880s. This technology was only a prelude to another revolutionary process known as offset printing. As early as the 1950s, photographic productions were being transferred to printing plates without the use of metal type. Web-fed offset printing essentially revived the ancient art of lithography by photographing the pasteups and producing a "cold-type" flat printing plate without either typesetting or photoengraving. A daily newspaper in Louisiana inaugurated offset printing, but it did not become popular until the 1960s. By the mid-1970s, more than half the daily newspapers were using offset. In 1980, almost three-fourths of newspapers used the offset system. Another system called "di-litho," developed in the 1970s, used an offset plate attached to an older letterpress machine. The di-litho had obvious monetary advantages, since it allowed printers to use their old presses. About 20 percent of newspapers were using the di-litho system in 1980.

The computer age closely followed offset technology. By the 1970s, most large printing establishments were using computers to set type as well as store information from reporters. Composing rooms featured a process of tapping the computer's memory for the stories to be produced in print. Computerized typesetting eliminated the old linotypes, and it combined with telecommunication satellites to allow print to be distributed anywhere in the world from a single computer station. A 1990s system called pagination allowed computers to do page layouts, thereby eliminating the composing room.

Reference Moran, James, *Printing Presses* (1973).

Prior Restraint

An ancient and frequently used form of censorship by governments is prior restraint—the prevention of publication or production. It was part of the early colonial-era controls embodied in the Licensing Act, which required government permission to publish. Prior restraint was revived during the twentieth century through the licensing powers of the Federal Communications Commission (FCC) and the Pentagon Papers case in the Nixon administration.

The English Licensing Act was passed by Parliament in 1662 and continued to be applied until its lapse in 1694. During the seventeenth century, the law covered the English colonies in America as well as England proper. The effect of the Licensing Act was to make printing without government permission a crime. Obviously, there were always some illicit publications printed underground or smuggled into the English territories from abroad. Essentially, however, the Licensing Act allowed the government to outlaw undesired publications.

Once the First Amendment to the Constitution was approved in 1791, government control of printed materials was reduced to issues of national security and Post Office regulations. Effectively, freedom of the press meant that only during wartime could the government deny access to the news media by claiming that information made public might endanger national security. During the Civil War (1861–1865), the War Department warned but did not prosecute violators of a prohibition against providing military information to the enemy. The first major war in which coordinated control of news access occurred was World War I (1917–1919). The Creel Committee was given the authority to filter news presented to the American public, but there were few questions raised because of strong patriotic feeling during the short war.

The U.S. Post Office has sometimes assumed carte blanche control over printed items sent through the mails. In 1914, the post office stopped the distribution of birth-control advocate Margaret Sanger's newspaper *The Woman Rebel*. In 1959, the New York City postmaster banned the mailing of D. H. Lawrence's novel *Lady Chatterley's Lover* on the grounds that it was obscene, but the courts overturned the post office's actions. The Supreme Court in *Near v. Minnesota* (1931) overturned a state's prior restraint law, but its obiter dictum suggested that there might be legitimate occasions when prior restraint could be used by governments.

The advent of radio broadcasting in the 1920s eventually forced Congress to establish first the Radio Commission in 1927 and then the FCC in 1934 to formulate and enforce broadcast regulations. The principal means of regulation was the granting of licenses to broadcasting companies by the commissions. The threat of license revocation allowed the government to control broadcast content in a manner that had never applied to the print media. Prior restraint had been reborn because of a new method of communication.

In 1949, after numerous complaints of interference by the FCC, Congress passed revised codes for the FCC that established the "Fairness Doctrine." The doctrine required broadcast stations—radio and television—to allow equal access to all points of view on public issues; newscasts were exempt. When FCC chairman Newton Minnow openly encouraged better programming for television in the early 1960s, many in Congress and the broadcasting industry claimed that what Minnow advocated was a form of censorship. Fourteen radio and television stations lost their licenses during Minnow's tenure, most on the basis of unsatisfactory programming. Broadcasters challenged the constitutionality of the Fairness Doctrine in the courts, but the Supreme Court upheld it in 1969. Finally, in 1987, the FCC succumbed to pressure from

broadcasters to give them the same First Amendment rights as the print media and repealed the Fairness Doctrine.

The 1971 Supreme Court case New York Times *v. United States* involved the printing of portions of top-secret documents analyzing the origins of the Vietnam War—known as the Pentagon Papers—by the *Times, Washington Post,* and *St. Louis Post-Dispatch*. The Justice Department began prosecuting two former Rand Corporation employees, Daniel Ellsberg and J. Anthony Russo, who had worked on the project and allegedly leaked the papers to the press. It took three months for *Times* reporters led by Neil Sheehan to condense the 47 volumes of the Pentagon Papers. When the first intallment was printed, the Justice Department went to court to stop further publication, based on a national security justification. A temporary restraining order was issued, sending alarms throughout the media. The Supreme Court ruled in a six-to-three decision that the papers revealed no secrets that would endanger national security and allowed the *Times* and other papers to print any parts of the Pentagon Papers they desired. The Court warned the government against invoking prior restraint without considerable justification.

In a more recent Supreme Court decision, the Hazlewood case of 1987, the Court gave high school officials the power of prior restraint over student publications. The decision interpreted the regulatory authority of the school system broadly. At the college and university level, however, judicial opinions have backed the right of student publications to force administrations to reveal information about on-campus crime statistics and arrest records.

See also Freedom of the Press.

Reference Simmons, Steven J., *The Fairness Doctrine and the Media* (1978).

Public Broadcasting Service (PBS)
See Radio; Television.

Public Relations
Although the practice of using press agents to promote something or someone goes

back at least to the nineteenth century, the birth of the public-relations industry occurred in the early 1900s. Public relations can be distinguished from advertising because publicity tries to educate the public about a product, service, or cause that has sufficient newsworthiness to be disseminated by the media without charge. Edward Bernays pioneered the psychology of public relations in his writings after World War I. Eventually, every major industry employed a public-relations department to help maintain a positive image with consumers and to market new products. Politicians and celebrities also hired press agents to protect a favorable public image.

In 1850, the Illinois Central Railroad envisioned a north-south railroad line connecting Chicago with southern cities. The company organized a public-relations campaign that sought to stress the importance of economic unity between North and South and thereby head off talk of secession and civil war. Railroads continued to be an industry leader in altering the public's perception of railroads as greedy and anxious to avoid government regulation. Even when the Interstate Commerce Act was passed in 1886, railroads played a major role in controlling the method of regulation by placing their own executives on the regulating commission. It was the Association of American Railroads that first used the phrase "public relations" in a business context in 1897.

Before his days as a circus entrepreneur in the 1870s, Phineas T. Barnum used press agent Richard Hamilton to promote his scams. By the end of the nineteenth century, most industries that operated as monopolies, such as utility companies, hired public-relations agents to help mollify their customers about rates and service. The Mutual Life Insurance company hired Charles J. Smith in 1888 to promote a better image of the company and the life insurance industry. Westinghouse Electric Company established the first corporate publicity department in 1889. Gradually, the profession of public relations gained credence as independent agencies appeared, including the Publicity Bureau in Boston (1900) and William Wolff

Smith's agency in Washington (1902).

Former newspaperman Ivy Lee and George Parker formed the New York City public-relations agency Parker and Lee in 1904. Lee was hired by several major companies, including the Pennsylvania Railroad and coal mining companies, as well as by millionaire John D. Rockefeller, who wanted his negative image refurbished. Lee's philosophy was that companies and their executives are held in higher regard by the public when their dealings are open—even to the point of grappling with negative issues. Lee made himself available to the media, promising to provide them with any facts they needed to inform the public. Nonetheless, reform journalists such as Upton Sinclair mistrusted Lee's methods and referred to him as "Poison Ivy."

George Creel's Committee on Public Information during World War I became a model of how effective public relations can be managed. Private charitable and philanthropic institutions such as the Red Cross and the Salvation Army learned that public relations had a direct bearing on their fundraising schemes. State and regional utility corporations followed the lead of Illinois' Samuel Insull in focusing on favorable publicity. Edward Bernays, a member of the Creel Committee, began his own agency in 1919; in 1923, he published *Crystallizing Public Opinion*, the first of three books on methods of cultivating public opinion that became textbooks for future practitioners. Bernays argued that good public relations required a careful understanding of the public's desires and fears. He advocated business methods that were orderly and oriented toward the public interest as the surest means to good public relations. Gaining and holding the public trust meant much more than spending lavishly on advertising alone.

Other industries soon found that public-relations experts were a necessary adjunct of their business functions. General Motors Corporation hired Paul Garrett in 1931 to research consumer preferences about automobiles and to publicize its products as responsive to those desires. Consumer products were touted by public-relations agents for their dependability and quality. The Public Relations Society of America was established in 1948 from a merger of smaller associations. The society adopted its "Code of Professional Standards for the Practice of Public Relations" in 1954.

Certainly, Creel's committee also taught many lessons to political leaders about the importance of a good public image. By the 1920s, presidents regularly employed press secretaries to help shape the chief executive's public image in relations with the media. During World War II, another government agency headed by Elmer Davies, the Office of War Information, operated in the fashion of the Creel Committee. The Voice of America was created in 1942 to publicize U.S. democratic principles but continued to be used after the war in the publicity battles of the Cold War. The U.S. Information Agency was established in 1953 to use a variety of propaganda methods to facilitate a positive image for the United States in all parts of the globe.

As with most areas of public information, television made public relations both more important and more complex. A report—either positive or negative—carried on television news can have dramatic repercussions on how the public views political leaders, celebrities, products, and companies. Those who are part of the power elite in either the private or the public sector understand that a positive public image requires constant nurturing and that negative publicity is difficult to overcome. The Public Relations Society of America, which labors constantly for professional standards, offers accreditation to public-relations practitioners after five years of successful work. Accreditation requires two independent endorsements of the subject's integrity. Only about half of the organization's members are accredited, however.

Reference Grunig, James E., and Todd Hunt, *Managing Public Relations* (1984).

Publick Occurrences

In 1690, *Publick Occurrences* became the first newspaper published in America—before the removal of government licensing. But precisely because the paper lacked authority to publish, it was immediately suspended after its first and only issue.

The origin of U.S. newspapers was inextricably and appropriately linked with a time-honored American tenet—freedom of the press. A London bookseller and publisher with Whig sympathies, Benjamin Harris was arrested and imprisoned in 1679 by royal authority for printing a supposedly seditious pamphlet. Again in 1686, under James II, a warrant was issued for Harris's arrest for publishing seditious material. Fearing another prison sentence, Harris and his family immigrated to Boston. Harris's Boston bookshop prospered, especially after he wrote and published a popular spelling book known as the *New England Primer*.

Harris arrived in New England during the infamous rule of Governor Edmund Andros, who, with the backing of King James II's government, began to undermine colonial autonomy and religious freedom. Spurred by the removal of King James in the so-called Glorious Revolution in 1689, Bostonians removed the unpopular Governor Andros as well. In the interim, with new governments taking over in both England and Massachusetts, Harris decided to issue his own newspaper. Unfortunately, he made no effort to obtain the requisite license from the government before publishing. According to the 1662 Parliamentary Licensing Act, all printers had to obtain permission from the government before publication.

Harris published *Publick Occurrences Both Forreign and Domestick* on 25 September 1690, promising monthly issues. The four-page, six-by-nine-inch paper known as a half-sheet was printed on only three pages and included local and foreign news. In addition to failing to obtain a license from the Massachusetts government, *Publick Occurrences* contained some pointed descriptions of sexual indiscretions by France's Louis XIV; more importantly, by describing Indian barbarities in the colonial war between France and England, it seemed to be critical of colonial policy regarding Indian allies. The governor of Massachusetts and the executive council immediately objected to both the content of *Publick Occurrences* and the fact that it lacked authority to publish. They decreed that Harris had to stop publication after only one issue.

Harris returned to England four years after the suspension of *Publick Occurrences*, where he started another newspaper. The example of Harris's experience made it clear that no press freedom meant no real newspapers in the colonies until the Licensing Act was removed. Indeed, soon after Parliament allowed the act to lapse in 1694, the first American newspapers were able to publish without government authority. Harris had proved by his defiance what all potential publishers knew—that no real newspapers could exist as long as any form of censorship remained.

Reference Paltsits, Victor H., "New Light on 'Publick Occurrences,'" *American Antiquarian Society Proceedings* (1949).

Publishers' Weekly

From its beginning in 1872, *Publishers' Weekly* became the Bible of the book publishing industry by publicizing new book issues. Frederick Leypoldt created the *Weekly* in Philadelphia. In addition to book announcements from publishers, the *Weekly* featured news about libraries and antiquarian and historical societies. The *Weekly* assisted libraries as well as individuals in deciding which books to acquire.

In 1851, Charles Norton founded *Norton's Literary Advertiser*, also in Philadelphia; it provided a monthly account of books published in the United States and much of Europe. It also reviewed the literature in print, including major English and American magazines, and included advertising. Correspondents sent library and historical association news to Norton from Boston, New York, New Haven, and Cincinnati. Initially, the *Advertiser* was free, but it began charging a subscription fee after it acquired *Wiley's Literary Telegraph* in 1854. Book publisher George Childs bought the *Advertiser* in 1855 and changed the name to *American Publishers' Circular and Literary Gazette*. When the *Gazette* bought the *Criterion* in 1856, the latter's editor, Charles Rode, became editor of the *Gazette*.

Another book publisher, Frederick Leypoldt, began issuing the *Literary Bulletin* in 1868. Modeled after a German circular, the *Bulletin* was designed to list new foreign publications sold through the firm of Leypoldt and Holt. Leypoldt expanded the publication in 1869 and changed its name to *Monthly Book Trade Circular*. By 1871, Leypoldt left the book publishing firm to pursue his bibliographical interests. The *Publishers' and Stationers' Weekly Trade Circular* superseded the monthly publication in January 1872. A month later, Leypoldt purchased the *American Publishers' Circular and Literary Gazette* begun by Childs. Finally, in 1873, Leypoldt changed the name of his publication to *Publishers' Weekly*, which focused entirely on the book trade.

Soon the *Weekly* sought to publish announcements of all new books published in the United States. Publishers also bought advertising in the *Weekly* to tout their new issues. The *Weekly* normally carried eight to ten pages of advertising, but its largest ad issue was at Christmas, which was the major sales season for publishers. In addition to book announcements and advertising, *Publishers' Weekly* included publishing news, reading trends, biographical information about publishers, occasional bits about authors, and any trade issues of importance. The first January issue featured an annual review of the book publishing industry.

Leypoldt entered into partnership with R. R. Bowker in 1879, mainly because Leypoldt needed a fresh infusion of capital into the publication. Bowker had been editing the *Library Journal*, and he assumed control of *Publishers' Weekly* upon the death of Leypoldt in 1884. Bowker continued to control the direction of the magazine until his death in 1933. More attention to English publishing characterized Bowker's editing of the *Weekly*. Bowker wrote essays about copyright law and eventually published a treatise on the subject. Circulation of *Publishers' Weekly* remained around 2,000 from the 1880s until World War I. Circulation then rose to 7,000 by the time of the Great Depression. By the 1890s, the length of the *Weekly* had increased, in large part due to more advertising. Advertisers used considerable ingenuity to make their ads appealing and informative. Frederick Melcher became coeditor and vice president of the *Weekly* in 1918 and succeeded Bowker as editor and president in 1933. As the era of multimedia conglomerates emerged in the 1960s, book publishing became more intertwined with broadcast and print media. *Publishers' Weekly* thus follows the ancillary developments of media companies very closely.

Pulitzer, Joseph (1847–1911)

Perhaps the greatest immigrant success story in U.S. media history is that of Joseph Pulitzer, who gave the modern newspaper its basic format. The *St. Louis Post-Dispatch*, purchased in 1878, became the training ground for Pulitzer and his staff, and his *New York World* led the nation's dailies in circulation. Pulitzer showed considerable sympathy with reform movements, but he also used sensational methods and joined the yellow journalism phenomenon in the 1890s. An endowment left to Columbia University was the basis for the establishment of the Pulitzer Prizes, the most prestigious awards in U.S. journalism.

Joseph Pulitzer was born in Hungary to Jewish parents; his father was a successful merchant. Pulitzer remained self-conscious about his Jewish heritage, especially after he left for the United States in 1864, following unsuccessful efforts to enlist in the army. He joined the Union army during the last months of the Civil War and then moved to St. Louis. After having several odd jobs, Pulitzer was hired in 1868 by Carl Schurz to work on a German-language newspaper, the *Westliche Post*. He became a U.S. citizen following language and law studies and won election to the Missouri legislature in 1870. His political career ended after he wounded a lobbyist who opposed legislation that Pulitzer had introduced.

Pulitzer bought majority ownership in the *Westliche Post* in 1872 and used it to campaign for Horace Greeley and the Liberal Republican Party. He then sold the *Post* for $30,000 to purchase another German-language paper, the *Staats-Zeitung*, which had an Associated Press franchise. Chicago newspaperman Joseph McCullagh bought the *Staats-Zeitung* from Pulitzer in 1874 because he needed the Associated Press franchise to further his plans to merge the *Globe* and *Democrat*. Pulitzer left journalism for a time and traveled to Europe and the East Coast. He agreed to do some reporting for Charles Dana's *New York Sun* and covered the 1876 electoral commission created to resolve the disputed presidential election. Pulitzer finally returned to St. Louis in 1878, prepared to reenter the newspaper profession.

When the *St. Louis Dispatch* (founded in 1864) went bankrupt in 1878, Pulitzer bought the paper and its Associated Press franchise at auction for $2,500. Within days, Pulitzer joined John Dillon's *Post* (founded in 1875) as a partner and merged the two papers, creating the *St. Louis Post-Dispatch*, an evening daily. Dillon retired within the year, leaving Pulitzer in command. Because the Liberal Republican Party had gone bust, Pulitzer gave editorial support to the Democratic Party, which he hoped would become the champion of reform. Pulitzer's crusading spirit and energy demanded excellence among his staff. The most important staff member was John A. Cockerill, formerly of the *Cincinnati Enquirer*, who became managing editor in 1880. When Pulitzer left St. Louis a few years later for New York, Cockerill kept the *Post-Dispatch* moving in the direction Pulitzer wanted. Pulitzer insisted that reporters dig until they knew their stories inside and out. The *Post-Dispatch* scrutinized venal politicians, the rich, police graft, and inefficient private utilities. Cockerill also used sensational stories about crime and violence as well as humorous gossip to attract readers. Unlike the *World* in New York City, the *Post-Dispatch* sought readers from the middle classes rather than the working classes.

Joseph Pulitzer seized an important opportunity in 1883 to purchase the moribund

New York World from financier Jay Gould for $346,000. Pulitzer's concept of using the *World* to reach a national audience proved to be innovative. The *World* announced a plan to tax wealthy individuals and monopolistic big business, lower the tariff, end corrupt elections, and inaugurate civil service reform. Pulitzer soon brought Cockerill from St. Louis to be managing editor of the *World*. Just as he had done in St. Louis, Pulitzer hired capable staffers such as "Nellie Bly" (Elizabeth Cochrane) to do investi-

Joseph Pulitzer gave the newspaper its modern format. Realizing that newspapers needed to be profitable, Pulitzer experimented with sensational stories and yellow journalism in order to boost circulation.

gative reporting on mental hospitals, prisons, and patent medicines. Other famous reporters working for the *World* included Arthur Brisbane, Frank I. Cobb (later editor), Herbert Bayard Swope, Walter Lippmann, and Heywood Broun. Because Pulitzer did not pay his reporters well, many were hired away by William Randolph Hearst when he bought the *New York Journal* in 1895. Pulitzer's *World* used banner headlines and halftone photographs for the first time. The *World* targeted every known audience with extensive sections on sports and women. Many of the *World*'s editorial crusades promoted greater educational opportunities, labor rights, tax equity, and religious toleration for the poor and immigrant populations. Pulitzer believed that the pursuit of wealth in the United States aimed to create a European-style aristocracy.

When Pulitzer acquired the *World* in 1883, its circulation was a meager 15,000. Before the end of his first year, sales rose to 60,000. They hit 200,000 in 1887, making the *World* the largest-circulation paper in the United States. An evening edition was added in 1887. The Sunday edition reflected many of Pulitzer's experimental ideas. Sensational techniques had already been introduced in the *Post-Dispatch*, but they expanded in the *World*. Pulitzer never apologized for methods that were designed to sell more papers; he accepted the fact that profits were an integral fact of life for publishers. More than any other journalist before him, Pulitzer gave the counting room at least an equal standing with the newsroom.

Pulitzer withdrew from active management of the *World* in 1890, somewhat disappointed that his reform campaign had languished. The arrival of Hearst at the *Journal* in 1895 introduced full-blown yellow journalism. Though not an imperialist at heart, Pulitzer's competitive spirit caused the *World* to follow Hearst's lead in agitating the Cuban situation, which resulted in the Spanish-American War of 1898. *World* reporters rivaled those from the *Journal* in getting scoops from Cuba and the Pacific theaters. Pulitzer eventually ordered his reporters to stop bending the truth in accounts of the war.

Toward the end of his life, Pulitzer decided to leave a positive heritage by endowing a journalism school at Columbia. His bequest of $2 million would become the basis for the Pulitzer Prizes, which were outlined in his will. The prizes were granted beginning in 1917 and immediately became the most prestigious journalism awards in the United States. Although the Pulitzer family sold the *New York World* to the Scripps-Howard chain in 1931, it continued to operate the *St. Louis Post-Dispatch*.

See also New York World; Pulitzer Prizes; *St. Louis Post-Dispatch*; Yellow Journalism.

Reference Swanberg, W. A., *Pulitzer* (1967).

Pulitzer Prizes

Famed yellow journalist Joseph Pulitzer endowed the Graduate School of Journalism at Columbia University in 1912. The school inaugurated the Pulitzer Prizes in journalism in 1917, honoring its benefactor. The number and categories of awards have changed over the years, but the prize remains the most prestigious in the profession.

In 1902, Joseph Pulitzer, publisher of the *St. Louis Post-Dispatch* and *New York World*, learned that fellow publisher James Gordon Bennett Jr. planned to endow a school of journalism. Although Bennett's idea never came to fruition, Pulitzer seized the moment and began negotiating with Columbia University in New York City to found a journalism school there. Pulitzer had donated scholarship money to Columbia in the past. The agreement with the trustees of Columbia University in 1903 provided for a donation of $2 million to establish a graduate school of journalism. The crucial element in the agreement was the role of the advisory board—including who would appoint the members and what would be the extent of their authority. Actually, Pulitzer's main concern related to the board's control over the awarding of the prospective writing prizes. Because of Pulitzer's delay in paying the full $2 million and appointing the advisory board, the journalism school did not open until 1912, just after Pulitzer's death in 1911.

Pulitzer himself outlined the types of prizes and the amounts of the awards in each category. The journalism prize categories were meritorious public service, best editorial, and best reporting; the arts awards were for the best American novel, play, history of the United States, and biography. Because Pulitzer's will specified that the prizes could not be awarded until the school of journalism had operated successfully for three years, the first awards were not made until 1917.

The journalism prizes required nomination by a jury of Columbia's journalism faculty or a member of the advisory board and were limited to journalists on U.S. daily or weekly newspapers. The advisory board then voted for a winner from the nominees in the different categories. The advisory board typically included some members of the Columbia faculty or administration as well as representative journalists from around the nation. In 1950, the advisory board severed its ties with the Graduate School of Journalism and became simply the agency to award the Pulitzer Prizes. In 1954, at the recommendation of Arthur Krock of the *New York Times*, the board voted to limit members' terms to no more than three four-year terms and required the sitting board to resign and make way for new appointments.

Because there was little room for questions about the integrity of the selection process, the Pulitzer Prizes were immediately both coveted and respected by American journalists as the ultimate recognition for contributions to the profession. It was sometimes difficult to obtain acceptable nominees in each category, so in some years, no prizes were awarded in certain categories. In the first three years of awards, 12 of 27 prizes were not granted because of a lack of qualified nominees. It was not until the early 1920s that recipients came from outside the eastern establishment newspapers.

Gradually, the advisory board added new categories for the prizes. In 1953, the reporting award was divided into categories of local reporting and specialized or investigative reporting. In 1942, both international and national reporting prize categories were created. A correspondence award for national or international service was begun in 1929 but ended after 1947. An editorial cartoon award was initiated in 1922, in addition to the original editorial writing award. The photography prize instituted in 1942 was divided in 1968 into spot news and features photography. A prize for commentary and another for criticism began in 1970, and special citations have been awarded whenever the occasion merited since 1938.

The Pulitzer Prizes have been awarded to journalistic veterans as well as enterprising novices. The advisory board takes into account not only demonstrated talent but also commitment to public service. The *New York Times* received the first meritorious public service award; Henry Watterson garnered the second editorial prize, and Herbert Bayard Swope won the initial reporting prize. Often, winning the prize launched or secured a successful career for the recipient. Individual winners brought encomiums for their employers, and vice versa. Major newspaper giants accumulated many prizes over the years, but a number of small papers received prizes as well.

The history of the Pulitzer Prizes closely follows the social and political history of the nation in the twentieth century. Winning subjects have included social issues such as Ku Klux Klan violence; sensational murder trials such as the Sacco-Vanzetti, Leopold-Loeb, and Lindbergh baby cases; and the impact of the depression, the 1930s Dust Bowl, and major disasters and accidents. Prizes have been awarded for reporting overseas events such as World War II, the Korean War, and the Vietnam War. Other topics associated with Pulitzer winners include the civil rights campaigns of the 1950s and 1960s, activities of organized crime or labor racketeering, the urban riots of the 1960s, and the Watergate fiasco of the 1970s.

Reference Hohenberg, John, *The Pulitzer Prizes* (1974).

Radio

Throughout its history, radio's variety of offerings, including entertainment, music, news, and talk, has made the medium remarkably resilient. The technology of radio has changed little from its beginnings, but the number of people who rely on radio has grown to include almost the entire population in the United States.

As early as the 1870s, British scientist James Maxwell discovered the possibility of radio wave transmissions. Through the coincidental 1906 inventions of the audion tube by Lee DeForest, which allowed the transmission of radio waves, and the crystal receiving set by Henry C. Dunwoody, radio broadcast and reception became a reality. The first experimental radio station, started by Professor Charles D. Herrold as part of his radio school in San Jose, California, broadcast news and music one night a week in 1909. The station was later moved to San Francisco as KCBS. In 1917, another professor at the University of Wisconsin, Earle M. Terry, began broadcasting as station 9XM. In 1922, the station became a commercial operation as WHA in Madison.

One of the most important trends in early radio was newspaper ownership of broadcast stations. The trend began with publisher William E. Scripps of the *Detroit News*, who visualized radio as a potential ally to news gathering. Following an experimental broadcast in 1920 that reported Michigan election returns, the *News* quickly established its own broadcasting station, WWJ. Programming by WWJ, including news, sports, and music, set the pattern for future radio stations. Another important radio development, regular programming, was begun by Westinghouse's station KDKA in Pittsburgh in 1920. The brainchild of Westinghouse engineer Frank Conrad, the station had begun transmissions in 1916 on an experimental basis.

From individual stations, the next step in radio was the creation of networks. The Radio Corporation of America (RCA) was founded in 1919 as a consortium, initially by two major manufacturing giants that had cooperated with the government during World War I: American Telephone and Telegraph (AT&T) and General Electric joined as a partner in 1920. The consortium bought out the patent rights for radio from the American Marconi Company. General Electric's Owen D. Young became the first chairman of the board at RCA. RCA's initial business involved selling radio receiving sets as the number of radio broadcasting stations rose from five in 1921 to 700 by 1927. Almost half of U.S. households owned radios by 1930, when David Sarnoff became president of RCA.

Meanwhile, AT&T had launched radio station WEAF in New York City using its telephone lines rather than a wireless broadcast; it was financed with "tolls" paid by advertisers. This experiment ultimately led AT&T to withdraw from RCA in 1926 to pursue its telephone interests. RCA purchased WEAF for $1 million and inaugurated its National Broadcasting Company (NBC) network. NBC was financed by selling advertising—the principal financial basis for all broadcasting systems thereafter. Because of an agreement with AT&T, NBC continued to use telephone lines to broadcast on its "red" network anchored by WEAF; it also developed a wireless "blue" network around WJZ, purchased by RCA from Westinghouse. The two networks offered different programming so that, in a sense, they were rivals, even though both were owned and operated by NBC. Another rival, the Columbia Broadcasting System (CBS) headed by William S. Paley, launched its radio network in 1928 by purchasing 16 stations from United Independent Broadcasters.

Although several newspapers were involved in launching radio stations, a conflict about news gathering invariably occurred. Newspapers jealously guarded their control of wire service news because they did not want competition from radio. Eventually, by the 1930s, radio networks began their own news-gathering organizations through their affiliate stations. However, a truce

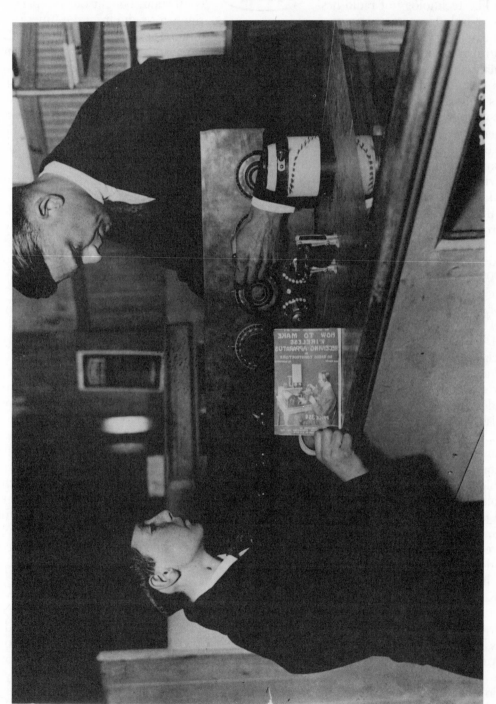

Radio building was a popular trend of the 1920s. In this photo, a Brooklyn radio store owner instructs a young teen in the art of making his own wireless set.

with newspapers in 1933 allowed radio stations to have access to wire service reports—on the condition that they not start news programs. A Press-Radio Bureau was set up in 1934 to distribute news reports from the wire services to stations. Over time, radio networks and stations increased their news coverage despite newspaper efforts to restrain the process.

During the 1930s, new developments in radio broadcasting expanded its horizons. Edwin Armstrong at Columbia University developed FM broadcasting technology in 1933 from the superheterodyne circuit produced during World War I. The circuit changed the frequency of radio waves—hence the name frequency modulation, or FM—to produce a static-free signal. Although Armstrong worked for RCA, it seemed uninterested in his inventions, which were purchased by Westinghouse. Indeed, RCA opposed Armstrong, who struggled to get Federal Communications Commission (FCC) approval to begin an FM station in New Jersey in 1936. It was not until after World War II, however, that FM broadcasting emerged from its infancy to rival and eventually surpass AM (amplitude modulation) stations. By 1993, there were 4,963 AM stations compared with 6,312 FM stations.

Another important development in the 1930s was President Roosevelt's use of radio to communicate his New Deal plans to the nation in a series of "Fireside Chats." Roosevelt demonstrated that radio was a more effective vehicle than the print media for communicating with citizens; the voice of the speaker could offer a tone of assurance that print could not provide. Thereafter, political leaders and candidates resorted to radio as their principal means of communicating with the voters.

By the 1930s, radio programming—with its considerable variety of comedies, westerns, and melodramas—was producing its own "stars" to rival Hollywood and vaudeville celebrities. Indeed, movie stars were featured in some radio programs such as "Lux Radio Theater." Actor-director-producer Orson Welles relied on stage,

movies, and radio to showcase his talents. He and coproducer John Houseman planned the 1938 broadcast of H. G. Wells's *War of the Worlds* on Halloween eve for the CBS network's "Mercury Theater on the Air." Welles's recounting of Martians landing in the United States stirred many listeners—unaware of the fictional source—to genuine panic. The Associated Press issued a warning about the fictional broadcast to all its subscribers.

Government scrutiny of radio and later television broadcasting was evident from the earliest era. The relationship between the public and private sectors of broadcasting has not always been amicable, but the early history of cooperation was noteworthy. At an international conference in London in 1912, participants agreed to allow each nation to regulate radio individually. Congress passed the Radio Act, establishing a licensing system for radio operators, but the legislation did not limit broadcast signal power or address wave-frequency conflicts. Secretary of Commerce Herbert Hoover organized a series of national radio conferences for broadcasters from 1922 to 1925 to help write new regulatory legislation. Congress finally passed the Federal Radio Act of 1927, which created a five-member commission to issue licenses and establish station power and wave frequency. The legislation viewed the broadcast airwaves as "public," so that protecting the public's interest must be the basis for licensing provisions.

The Federal Radio Commission was replaced in 1934 by the FCC, which broadened its regulatory authority to cover all telecommunications. The FCC's rules for licensing were similar to the Radio Commission's, but the FCC began to interfere with private companies because of its concern about monopolistic tendencies. For example, a 1941 FCC report viewed NBC's two networks not as rivals but as part of a larger monopoly. FCC pressures on NBC led to the 1943 sale of NBC's 168-station blue network to Edward J. Noble, who formed the American Broadcasting Company (ABC). Meanwhile, another radio network, the Mutual Broadcasting System, had been created; it started with four stations in 1934 and expanded to 160 stations by 1940. CBS enlarged its network to 113 stations by 1938.

Other than the postwar growth of FM broadcasting, boosted by the medium of stereophonic sound, the next technological breakthrough affecting radio was the invention of the transistor to replace vacuum tubes in receiving sets. William Shockley, working at the Bell Laboratories in 1947, developed the silicon crystal transistor. The small size of the transistor changed the physical characteristics of radio sets, which could also be powered by batteries.

Radio's darkest moments came when station disc jockeys, in collusion with recording companies, agreed to accept cash gratuities to play the companies' records. One disc jockey in 1959 received over $36,000 from eight record companies. The scheme, known as "payola," ran afoul of FCC regulations, and several disc jockeys were prosecuted. Despite its embarrassing moments, radio has been profitable because of steadily rising advertising revenues. In 1988, one New York station sold for $79 million, and total radio station sales topped $1.8 billion—more than television station sales.

FCC chairman Newton Minnow often complained in the 1960s about the absence of noncommercial broadcasting. Members of Congress responded with passage of the Public Broadcasting Act of 1967, which established the Corporation for Public Broadcasting, a quasi-public agency designed to improve noncommercial radio and television programs. The Public Broadcasting Service (PBS), funded by the Corporation for Public Broadcasting, was founded in 1970 to organize noncommercial stations and distribute programs. Launched in 1971, National Public Radio offered in-depth reporting of major news and public affairs issues that commercial networks avoided. PBS's signal was distributed by a satellite to individual stations, which selected the programs they wanted to air. A rival to National Public Radio, American Public Radio, began broadcasting in 1982 with its own programming and news

accessed from the *Christian Science Monitor* and the British Broadcasting Corporation World News Service.

References Barnouw, Erik, *A History of Broadcasting in the United States* (1966–1970); Lichty, Lawrence W., and Malachi C. Topping, eds., *American Broadcasting: A Sourcebook on the History of Radio and Television* (1975).

Radio Corporation of America (RCA)

The pioneer in the development of radio technology after World War I was Radio Corporation of America (RCA). The company began as a consortium and at first concentrated on wireless technology. RCA began producing radio receiving sets as well as broadcasting technology. The National Broadcasting Company (NBC) became a subsidiary of RCA. The company was also at the forefront of television technology, and its system of broadcasting color images was adopted by the Federal Communications Commission (FCC).

Because of the obvious military uses of wireless and radio communications, the federal government spurred three companies to pool their resources to develop the technology during World War I. Two of the three giants—American Telephone and Telegraph (AT&T) and General Electric—jointly formed RCA in 1919 and obtained all key patents for the new technology. General Electric's Owen D. Young, RCA's first chairman, ensured that RCA would remain a strictly U.S. corporation by limiting the role of foreigners. Edward J. Nally, formerly of American Marconi, became president of RCA; another Marconi employee, David Sarnoff, was named business manager and began to push Young toward broadcasting. Westinghouse launched the first commercial radio broadcast station with regular programming in 1920—KDKA in Pittsburgh—and was soon invited to join the RCA conglomerate. AT&T inaugurated broadcasting with an advertising-supported New York City station, WEAF, in 1922; it used telephone lines to broadcast, which led to the establishment of a network of more than a dozen stations. Even with its initial dominance, AT&T decided to withdraw from the RCA consortium in 1926. WEAF was sold to RCA, and NBC was created as a subsidiary to oversee the acquisition and management of broadcast stations nationwide.

By 1923, there were over 500 radio broadcasting stations in the United States and more than 600,000 radio receiving sets. General Electric and Westinghouse manufactured radio sets for RCA, and sales netted $11 million in 1922. Radio sales grew to $50 million by 1925 and to $135 million by 1929. About half of U.S. households owned radio sets by 1930. Because of antitrust questions, General Electric and Westinghouse were forced to sell their shares of RCA in 1932. RCA moved to new offices at Radio City in New York in 1933. David Sarnoff, promoted to president of RCA in 1930, had acquired the Victor phonograph rights and founded the RCA-Victor subsidiary to manufacture phonographs, radio sets, and electronic parts such as tubes. RCA also operated a worldwide radio and telegraph service, and in 1928, it formed Radio-Keith-Orpheum (RKO) as a motion picture subsidiary. By 1934, NBC owned 127 broadcast stations but faced competition from the Columbia Broadcasting System (CBS) and Mutual Broadcasting Company.

As experiments with television broadcasting began in the 1920s, RCA was at the forefront of manufacturing the receiving sets. RCA displayed its television technology publicly at the 1939 New York World's Fair. The post–World War II competition to make color and black-and-white broadcasts compatible began when CBS failed to convince the FCC to approve its color system, which would have made existing black-and-white receiving sets obsolete. RCA gained FCC approval in 1947 to manufacture its system, which allowed television sets to receive broadcasts in either color or black and white.

By the 1950s, three-fourths of RCA's income came from areas outside of broadcasting. It created a defense electronics division in 1956 to manage its increasing government military contracts. Sarnoff was a principal adviser for the government's Radio Free Europe and Radio Liberation. In the 1960s, RCA's broadcast satellite, *Relay*, sent television pictures to 23 countries. The television cameras set up by astronauts during their moon walk in 1969 were manufactured by RCA. By the 1970s, RCA followed the trend of multimedia conglomerates by obtaining several publishing houses, including Random House and Alfred A. Knopf. One of the largest business mergers in history occurred in 1986 when RCA—including its subsidiaries such as NBC—was bought by General Electric for more than $6 billion.

References Lyons, Eugene, *David Sarnoff: A Biography* (1966); Sobel, Robert, *RCA* (1986).

Raleigh News and Observer

Founded at the end of the Civil War, the *Raleigh News and Observer* became the voice of North Carolina well into the twentieth century before other dailies challenged its dominance. The guiding spirit throughout much of the formative era was Josephus Daniels, whose editorials espoused a progressive, Jeffersonian Democratic philosophy.

For most of the period before Josephus Daniels acquired control of the *Raleigh News and Observer*, the paper was run by archconservative publisher Samuel A. Ashe, an ex-Confederate officer. After two years as editor of the *Raleigh State Chronicle*, Daniels proposed a merger in 1887 with Ashe's *News and Observer*, which included Daniels becoming editor of the combined paper. The merger did not occur until 1894, when North Carolina Democratic fortunes seemed doomed by the advent of Populism. The new owner of the faltering *State Chronicle*, banker and tobacco magnate Julian S. Carr, purchased the *News and Observer* and made Daniels editor.

At both the *State Chronicle* (1885–1893) and the *News and Observer*, editor Daniels challenged power blocs from the Southern Railway to the Duke tobacco fortune. He supported expansion of public education, including compulsory schooling, and lobbied for North Carolina's public universities, which were overshadowed by private institutions. On national issues, Daniels mostly wrote in favor of civil service reform to end political corruption.

A fervent supporter of William Jennings Bryan in 1896, Daniels campaigned with the Democratic presidential candidate throughout the East. Daniels's accounts of the campaign in the *News and Observer* were overly optimistic, as Bryan lost badly. Anxious to silence Daniels's campaign for rate regulation in the *News and Observer*, Southern Railway interests financed two rival papers in Raleigh during 1897, but neither dented the popularity of Daniels's paper. Because Democrats feared Republican and Populist attempts to manipulate the black vote, Daniels somewhat reluctantly supported disfranchisement legislation in North Carolina, which reduced black voters to a slim few.

During the Progressive era after 1901, Daniels and the *News and Observer* pressured governors and the legislature to enact reform measures, including antitrust and child-labor laws, railroad regulation, Prohibition, and the breakup of monopolies such as the American Tobacco Company. The *News and Observer* lobbied relentlessly for more school funding, which quadrupled between 1900 and 1913. Daniels's attention turned to Democratic Progressive candidate Woodrow Wilson during the 1912 presidential campaign. After Wilson's election, the new president named Daniels secretary of the navy, and the editor took a leave of absence from the *News and Observer*. While he was away, the paper's building burned to the ground not once but twice—in 1913 and again in 1915. Yet the *News and Observer* never missed publishing an issue, thanks to the use of the *Raleigh Times*'s presses. Daniels made many new friends during his eight-year tenure in Washington, including Franklin Delano Roosevelt, who served as Daniels's assistant secretary.

Forced to return to Raleigh in the face of a Republican landslide in 1920, Josephus Daniels resumed direct control of the *News and Observer*. He rejected a $1 million offer from William Randolph Hearst to buy the paper. The *News and Observer* renewed its battles to regulate monopolies such as the utilities, which were now run by the powerful Duke family. Daniels also pushed hard in 1927 for legislation to suppress Ku Klux Klan violence. Josephus and his son Jonathan disagreed about the continuation of Prohibition—father for and son against. Josephus Daniels and the *News and Observer* strongly backed controversial Democratic presidential candidate Al Smith in 1928, despite Smith's opposition to Prohibition. The *News and Observer* had other notables writing for it in the 1920s and 1930s, including columnist and book reviewer Nell Battle Lewis, who consistently piqued the southern conscience.

Josephus Daniels seriously considered running for governor of North Carolina in 1932, but an automobile accident caused him to drop the notion. After Jonathan Daniels left *Fortune* magazine in 1932 to assume an editorial position with the *News and Observer*, it seemed clear who Josephus's successor would be. When Josephus left Raleigh to become the U.S. ambassador to Mexico under the Roosevelt administration in 1933, Jonathan began to provide more personal direction for the *News and Observer*. After the repeal of national Prohibition, North Carolina held a wet-dry referendum. Because Jonathan and his father differed on the Prohibition issue, Jonathan assigned a colleague to write editorials on the subject for the *News and Observer*.

Josephus Daniels returned to Raleigh in 1941 after his two-term ambassadorial stint to resume control of the *News and Observer*. In 1943, Jonathan Daniels served as a special assistant to President Roosevelt on racial issues and urged the recruitment of more black military officers. Meanwhile, in its continuing commitment to funding for public education, the *News and Observer* led the fight to expand the medical school at Chapel Hill to a four-year program in 1947. The paper remained a staunch voice for labor rights despite the antilabor surge that culminated in the Taft-Hartley Act of 1947. When North Carolina's own Senator Josiah Bailey opposed Jonathan Daniels's appointment as ambassador to New Zealand under

President Truman, Jonathan agreed to accept a presidential assistant's post during 1946 and 1947. The *News and Observer* quickly opposed the Dixiecrat bolt from the Democratic Party in 1948. Josephus Daniels died at the end of 1948, ending a long career directing the *News and Observer*. Jonathan succeeded his father as editor, and the family has continued its ownership and management of the paper into the 1990s. Jonathan's son Frank Daniels Jr. became president of the company; his grandson, Frank Daniels III, was editor in the 1990s. Daily circulation in 1994 was 144,000, and Sunday sales totaled 183,000.

Reference Morrison, Joseph L., *Josephus Daniels: The Small-d Democrat* (1966).

Raymond, Henry J.

See New York Times.

Reader's Digest

Although not a new idea, DeWitt Wallace's *Reader's Digest*, begun in 1922, became the most successful magazine that reprinted and condensed articles. *Reader's Digest* became the largest-circulation magazine in the United States and worldwide by the 1950s. It demonstrated Americans' desire for concise and selective reading choices.

A native of Minnesota and son of a Presbyterian minister and college president, DeWitt Wallace resonated optimism regarding progress for the United States. He conceived of the idea of a compact literary digest while working for a magazine and book publisher in St. Paul before World War I. In 1920, after serving in the army during the war, Wallace collected a variety of articles and sent a prospectus to a dozen New York publishers, all of which rejected his idea. Wallace and his wife Lila Acheson formed the Reader's Digest Association in New York City in 1921 and began clipping articles and advertising for subscribers. When they had secured 1,500 subscriptions, the first issue of *Reader's Digest* was readied for sale at 25 cents a copy in February 1922.

The monthly *Digest* originally targeted women as the primary audience but quickly included men as well. The Wallaces' criteria for articles to be selected included their relevance to readers; they had to retain more than a passing interest to readers and reflect a positive outlook. In short, they were looking for interesting, informative, and inspirational subjects. The nonfiction selections were taken from journals such as *Harper's, Atlantic, Forum*, and *North American Review*. After one year of publication in Greenwich Village, New York, the Wallaces moved their operations to Pleasant-ville, New York, and eventually built a large production facility in the town. The early staff of the *Digest* was inexperienced in magazine production. The first professional editor, Kenneth Payne, had edited the *North American Review* before coming to the *Reader's Digest* in 1930. Other professionals soon joined the staff from *Scribner's, Review of Reviews*, and *Literary Digest*.

At first, Wallace did not allow newsstand sales because he thought that the *Digest* would not appeal to such consumers. Although the publishers kept the circulation figures secret in the early years, the best estimate for the first year is 7,000. By 1929, when newsstand sales began, the number had risen to 109,000; *Reader's Digest* passed the million mark in 1935. Many publishers were anxious for their material to be reprinted in the *Digest* at first, but by the late 1930s, several decided not to extend their reprint agreements. Because of a potential paucity of sources, DeWitt Wallace began to print original material in 1933. Some of the pieces were so popular that they were reprinted in newspapers and other magazines. By 1940, more than half the articles in the *Digest* were original compositions. Wallace even commissioned articles for publication in other magazines, which he then reprinted or excerpted in the *Digest*.

The potential for overseas sales of the *Digest* became apparent when Wallace issued a British edition in 1938. By the 1960s, the *Digest* had 29 international editions in 13 languages. Wallace even lowered the foreign price to ensure sales. Subscription and newsstand sales were the only source of revenue for 33 years of the *Digest*'s history because it did not accept advertising. Advertising initially appeared in April 1955 after rising production costs created the first deficits. Ad revenues totaled $60 million by the early 1960s and $107 million by the late 1980s. The *Digest* produced a number of consumer-interest articles beginning in the 1930s that tested manufacturers' claims about their products. Competitors often quoted the *Digest* without permission to exploit the consumer exposés for their own benefit.

Reader's Digest began selling condensed books through a club in 1950, further enhancing the company's profit margins. Circulation climbed from over 9 million in 1950 to 17 million in 1970, far outstripping its second-place competition *TV Guide* as the largest-circulation magazine in the United States. Worldwide circulation to 39 countries reached 29 million by 1970. The Wallaces gradually removed themselves from the day-to-day management of the *Digest* in the early 1960s. Paul W. Thompson assumed the new position of editor in chief in 1969. By 1974, *TV Guide* surpassed *Reader's Digest* for the leadership in domestic circulation. Publisher Richard L. McLoughlin attributed the decline to a reduction in newsstand sales.

Reference Bainbridge, John, *Little Wonder, or Reader's Digest and How It Grew* (1946).

Reid, Whitelaw
See New York Tribune and Herald Tribune.

Religious Broadcasting
From the earliest radio era to the advent of television and its cable derivative, religious broadcasting has been a prominent adjunct to traditional religious practices in the United States. By the 1970s, more Americans were reached by religious broadcasts than attended religious services in person. Over 1,400 religious radio stations and 30 television stations operated in the 1980s, not to mention religious programs purchased by nonowned stations. Surveys have shown that Protestants listen to religious broadcasts most, followed by Catholics and Jews. An association called the National Religious Broadcasters was created, which established a code of ethics and awarded prizes. Religious broadcasting has also had its share of scandal, which undermined its popularity and made skeptics and the mainline media even more jaded toward religion.

The first religious broadcast over Westinghouse's radio station KDKA in Pittsburgh occurred in 1921 during Sunday evening services at the Calvary Episcopal Church. The response was so positive that it became a regularly scheduled program. After a 1922 broadcast by Reverend Paul Rader at the Chicago Gospel Tabernacle, a regular Sunday evening broadcast became part of the programming at station WBBM. The listening audience was much greater than those attending the services in person. Rader also pioneered the "Breakfast Brigade" over the Columbia Broadcasting System (CBS) network in the 1930s, reaching a national audience.

Reverend Robert R. Brown broadcast the first nondenominational service over station WOW in Omaha in 1923. The initial broadcast led to a regular program called "Radio Chapel Service" carried by dozens of stations to an audience of 500,000 a week. Brown soon became known by the nickname "Billy Sunday of the air." "Radio Chapel Service" remained on the air until 1977. By 1923, ten churches were using radio broadcasts as part of their ministry; in 1927, 50 stations operated by religious organizations held broadcasting licenses. Independent evangelists such as Aimee Semple McPherson in California also relied on radio broadcasting to attract a large following. After the creation of "public-interest" licensing standards by the Federal Radio Commission in 1927, many religious stations found it impossible to meet the prohibitive costs required for licensing. The number of religious stations declined from a peak of 60 in 1928 to 30 in 1933.

Some religious broadcasting stations began providing programs that could be used by religious organizations around the nation. WMBI was founded in 1925 by the Moody Bible Institute in Chicago and broadcast music and lectures six days a week. A Bible class was soon made available to subscribing stations to allow audio students to obtain credit at the institute. Ultimately, 30 different programs were produced at WMBI for various religious constituencies. Nationally syndicated programs became a regular part of religious broadcasting in the 1930s. Starting in 1930, Reverend Walter Maier hosted "The Lutheran Hour" from WHK in Cleveland and was eventually heard by 5 million listeners over the Mutual Broadcasting System network. After using radio in his own church for several years, Reverend Charles Fuller began the "Old Fashioned Revival Hour" in 1933, eventually broadcast on 152 Mutual stations across the nation and heard by 10 million listeners. The Mutual network soon garnered one-fourth of its income from religious broadcasts. M. R. De Haan's "Radio Bible Class" proved its popularity and endurance and made the transition to television under his son Richard. Paul Myers began his "Haven of Rest" program in 1934 from Los Angeles and continued it until his death in 1973.

Invariably, some religious broadcasters stepped over the line into political and social commentary. Roman Catholic priest Father Charles Coughlin gained a national radio audience from Detroit in the early 1930s by criticizing President Roosevelt's New Deal. Reverend Robert Schuler used his Los Angeles radio program to attack local political corruption. In the post–World War II era, broadcasting featured both commercial and noncommercial, nonprofit stations. Well-known black evangelist Frederick Eiderenkoetter, or "Reverend Ike," began preaching his blended message of capitalism and Christianity on an 85-station network in the 1960s. Other popular black evangelists who used radio and television included Cleophus Robinson of St. Louis, Clay Evans of Chicago, and Fred Price of Los Angeles. Also after World War II, the use of radio for evangelical missionary outreach

expanded. Led by experimental station HCJB in Ecuador, started in 1931, the network expanded across Latin America and into Europe. The Far East Broadcasting Company began operations in Asia after 1945.

The National Religious Broadcasters (NRB), founded in 1944, grew out of the National Association of Evangelicals. The NRB adopted a constitution and code of ethics for its 50 charter members. By 1979, the NRB had over 800 members, including the broadcasting departments of several denominations. The NRB began granting awards in 1959; Billy Graham's "Hour of Decision" program won the first merit prize, and Fuller's "Old Fashioned Revival Hour" received recognition in 1960.

The advent of television opened up new avenues for religious broadcasting, and enterprising ministers recognized the opportunity. Following Marshall McLuhan's dictum about the medium being the message, televised religion has grown to look more like show business. Roman Catholic Bishop Fulton J. Sheen began the first regular televised program in 1950 on the National Broadcasting Company (NBC) network. He continued the program for 16 years and had a wide following in various denominations. Rex Humbard started a weekly televised service from his church in Akron in 1952; it was eventually broadcast to dozens of stations across the nation. Oral Roberts was refused the use of network airwaves after he launched his television program in 1954 because of his belief in divine healing. In 1969, under a more sophisticated format oriented toward entertainment at his university in Tulsa, Roberts began broadcasting to 50 million viewers. Billy Graham also used television to cover his revival crusades so that he could reach much larger audiences. The Religion in Media Association, a nonprofit California organization started in the 1970s, operates as an intermediary between religious organizations and the media to improve religious broadcasting.

In the same way that Father Coughlin used radio as an essentially political platform in the 1930s, Jerry Falwell and Pat

Robertson relied on television to offer a mixture of gospel religion and social-political commentary. Falwell's "Old Time Gospel Hour" originating from his church in Lynchburg, Virginia, became the launching pad for the "Moral Majority" political movement in the 1980s, which sought to influence social issues such as school prayer and abortion. Pat Robertson relied on satellite technology at his Christian Broadcasting Network in Virginia Beach, Virginia, to reach a national audience. Robertson's "700 Club" mixes religious topics with advice on finance, political commentary, and newscasts. Robertson offered himself as a presidential candidate for the Republican Party in 1988, buoyed by a nationwide following from his television program.

Television creates the images of popular religious broadcasters, who occasionally give the medium a bad name. Televangelists Jim Baker of the Praise the Lord network and the Church of God's Jimmy Swaggart became the objects of scandal in 1986 and 1987. Oral Roberts was criticized for putting pressure on listeners to send donations for his university in Tulsa. Even though many other television ministries survived, almost all felt some financial impact from these embarrassments. Television ministries supported by listeners tend to thrive most when the programs have dominant personalities using entertainment techniques. Thus, if questions arise about the personality, the whole ministry is threatened.

References Hill, George H., *Airwaves to the Soul: The Influence and Growth of Religious Broadcasting in America* (1983); Schultze, Quentin J., *Televangelism and American Culture: The Business of Popular Religion* (1991).

Revolutionary War

It was during the American colonial revolt against Great Britain that the press fully realized its potential to influence public opinion. From the revolutionary preliminaries in the 1760s to the adoption of the Constitution in 1787, the press played an enormous part in nation building. Propaganda has been a vital part of all major political revolutions, and the American revolt was a classic example. Reporting military campaigns and diplomacy was largely a new experience for American journalists. Editors staked out a vital claim for freedom of the press as a result of their experience in the revolutionary era.

By the end of the French and Indian War in 1763, American journalism had matured in several important ways. Newspapers had made important strides to end prior restraint censorship, and continuous daily publications existed in all the major colonial cities. Printers who had endured skirmishes with government officials recognized and championed free expression as part of English liberties. There were a large number of printing presses in the colonies and considerable importation of printed materials from England. In short, literate Americans were accustomed to getting much of their knowledge from newspapers or news sheets.

The first event that caused concern among colonial printers about British policy was the Stamp Act of 1765. The precedent-setting act by Parliament became the first direct, internal tax upon the colonies. Previous Parliamentary taxes had applied only to trade. Although the tax itself was not onerous, colonial printers were most affected because the act required taxes on all printed materials—from newspapers to playing cards. Therefore, first and foremost, the Stamp Act threatened the printers' economic survival. But because of their natural inclination not to criticize government—especially Parliament—and because many of them held printing contracts with colonial governments, the printers largely kept their feelings private. The dean of colonial printers, Benjamin Franklin, urged a cautious approach. Franklin argued in person before Parliament that the Stamp Act should be repealed because of the economic hardship it caused rather than for any constitutional reasons. Fortunately, from both an economic and a political perspective, the colonial printers were relieved of the stamp tax burden when Parliament agreed to repeal the measure in 1766.

As the tensions between England and the colonies continued to mount after 1766, colonial printers were forced to opt out of their neutrality. Eventually the patriot printers outnumbered the Tories by a two-to-one margin, but the choices were almost always difficult before the fighting began in 1775. Making a constitutional argument against the Townshend Duties in 1767, John Dickinson published 14 essays entitled "Letters from a Farmer in Pennsylvania" in the *Pennsylvania Chronicle*. Several other colonial papers such as the *Boston Chronicle* printed the "Letters" without comment because editors believed that they were newsworthy. In 1768, Samuel Adams persuaded the Massachusetts assembly to pass a condemnation of the Townshend Duties as taxation without representation. Adams then printed the legislative resolution in the "Massachusetts Circular Letter" and forwarded it to the other 12 colonial legislatures.

The greatest patriot agitation before the Revolution was carried out by the Sons of Liberty, first organized by Boston's Samuel Adams in 1765. Local associations gradually spread to other port cities, and coordination developed through correspondence. The Sons of Liberty valued the role of propaganda to motivate the majority of colonials, who were neutral at first. Adams formalized a Committee of Correspondence for Boston in 1772; other committees were established in the colonies to carry out the propaganda plans by issuing broadsides or news sheets condemning various aspects of British policy. Before 1775, the Committees of Correspondence were much more effective than the patriot press in spreading the growing hostility toward Parliament and crown governance.

After the Revolutionary War began in 1775, the number of newspapers expanded, especially in the interior and in smaller communities. At the time of the Stamp Act in 1765, 16 communities supported 27 papers. By the outbreak of the Revolution in 1775, 24 cities published 44 newspapers; about one-fourth remained Tory. At the end of the war in 1783, 26 cities had 58 newspapers; others begun during the war did not survive. More than ever, people depended on the press for information about and interpretation of events, and editors who did not reflect majority opinion risked their businesses. Tory printer James Rivington's *New York Gazetteer* office was ransacked by a patriot mob in 1775. Margaret Draper, another Tory editor, was forced to shut down the colonies' oldest continuous paper, the *Boston News-Letter*, in 1776 when the British withdrew. Although pamphlets such as Thomas Paine's 1776 *Common Sense*, advocating independence, had a life of their own, newspaper printers almost always printed such pamphlets and reprinted them in their papers. Newspapers included accounts of battles and campaigns as well as urged support for the revolutionary cause.

As decisions about support for or opposition to the war were replaced by economic and political options for the peace, citizens looked to the press for a thorough airing of the pros and cons of various policy positions. American newspapers accepted their newfound responsibility of protecting a free press in order to ensure the vitality of a republican form of government. They also recognized the need to nurture their local economies and promote civic responsibility.

Several new names became familiar to Americans because of their Revolutionary War editing. Isaiah Thomas had become well known in New England through his pro-patriot *Massachusetts Spy* and later founded the American Antiquarian Society. Daniel Fowle, publisher of the *New Hampshire Gazette*, trained a number of printers who established newspapers after the Revolution. Benjamin Edes of the *Boston Gazette* gained the confidence of the public through his support of the patriot cause. William Goddard, editor of the *Maryland Journal* and *Pennsylvania Chronicle*, began a colonial postal system in 1774 that was continued by the Continental Congress. Editors in the revolutionary era were obligated only to themselves and their constituents. Newspapers were not yet controlled by political parties or by governments, local or national, as many would be later. In many respects, the press during the Revolution was freer than at any other time in American history. Certainly the movement to include freedom of the press in the First Amendment to the Constitution grew directly from the revolutionary era.

See also Franklin, Benjamin; Paine, Thomas; Thomas, Isaiah.

Reference Bailyn, Bernard, and John B. Hench, eds., *The Press and the American Revolution* (1980).

Richmond Times-Dispatch and *News Leader*

The principal Richmond newspapers trace their origins to before the Civil War, but in the twentieth century, the Bryan family ownership has dominated both papers. The *Times-Dispatch* and the *News Leader* have been noteworthy for their literate, urbane editors and nationally known columnists.

The *Richmond Dispatch* was founded in 1850 by James A. Cowardin as a nonpartisan daily paper in a very partisan era. By 1860, the *Dispatch*'s circulation of 18,000 made it larger than all other Richmond papers combined. During the Civil War, the *Dispatch* assumed a staunch pro-Confederate stance in the capital of the Confederacy. Possibly the best Civil War reporting by a southern newspaper was done by the *Dispatch*. Its war correspondents included Peter W. Alexander, perhaps the most respected of all wartime reporters, as well as James B. Sener and John H. Linebaugh.

Richmond businessman and Confederate veteran Lewis Ginter started the *Richmond Times* in 1886 but knew nothing about the management of a newspaper. In 1887, he gave the paper to fellow Richmond businessman Joseph Bryan, who also took over the editorial duties. Both the *Dispatch* and the *Times* showed discretion during the Republican carpetbag governments of Reconstruction. Charles Cowardin, the publisher's son, took on the editorial duties at the *Dispatch* from Henry K. Ellyson in 1870 and exhibited a reactionary editorial policy toward racial issues, whereas the *Times* was more restrained. Still, both papers eventually supported the institution of the Jim Crow segregation system.

After the death of Charles Cowardin in 1900, the *Dispatch* was purchased by John L. Williams, who had just started the evening

Richmond News in 1899. In 1903, Williams exchanged the *Dispatch* for Joseph Bryan's afternoon *Richmond Leader*, founded in 1888. John Stewart Bryan assumed control of the 1903-merged *Times-Dispatch* upon his father's death in 1908 and bought the *News Leader* in 1909 from Williams, who had merged the two papers in 1903. Bryan then sold the *Times-Dispatch* in 1914 to concentrate on the *News Leader*. Charles Hasbrook and Mark Ethridge both served as publishers of the *Times-Dispatch* during the 1920s and 1930s. John Stewart Bryan was recognized by his peers when they elected him president of the American Newspaper Publishers Association in 1926. Bryan repurchased the *Times-Dispatch* in 1940 and directed both papers until his death in 1944.

John Stewart Bryan made Douglas Southall Freeman, the future Pulitzer Prize–winning biographer of Robert E. Lee and George Washington, editor of the *News Leader* in 1915. Freeman remained editor until 1949 and brought a high degree of literate, albeit conservative, gentility to the paper. Freeman was succeeded by the equally conservative James J. Kilpatrick, who had joined the *News Leader* in 1941 as a reporter; he became chief editorial writer in 1949 and served as editor from 1951 until 1967. Kilpatrick launched a successful syndicated column in 1964, which he continued after his retirement from the editor's desk. He also served as a contributing editor to William Buckley's *National Review*.

One of Freeman's trainees was reporter Virginius Dabney, son of University of Virginia history professor and dean Richard Dabney and Lily Davis Dabney, who traced her Virginia lineage back to Thomas Jefferson. Dabney worked at the *News Leader* from 1922 to 1928 and then took an editorial post with the *Times-Dispatch*. Dabney served as editor from 1934 to 1969 and won a Pulitzer Prize for editorial writing in 1948. He also wrote *Liberalism in the South* (1932); *Below the Potomac* (1942), a study of southern journalism; *Dry Messiah* (1949), a biography of Prohibitionist Bishop Cannon; and a history of the city entitled *Richmond* (1990). Dabney's moderate liberalism opposed intolerance and political demagoguery while maintaining pride in Virginia and the South. In the 1940s, he urged repeal of the poll tax and an end to segregated public transportation.

The Richmond papers have also produced prize-winning cartoonists. Jeffrey MacNelly, a syndicated cartoonist, won Pulitzers for *News Leader* cartoons in 1972 and 1978. Fred O. Seibel, a transplanted New Yorker, used subtle humor in his cartoons for the *Times-Dispatch* from 1926 to 1968. He refused to submit his widely reprinted cartoons for Pulitzer consideration; otherwise, he too would probably have won a prize. Charles McDowell of the *Times-Dispatch* established a solid reputation for his columns as the paper's Washington correspondent since 1965. McDowell joined the *Times-Dispatch* in 1949 as a reporter and began a column of political commentary in 1957. In 1967, the Richmond papers' holding company, Media General (which also owned the *Tampa Tribune* and *Winston-Salem Journal-Sentinel*), became a publicly held corporation. During the merger mania of the 1980s, Media General fought off some unwanted conglomerate suitors. In 1994, the daily circulation of the morning *Times-Dispatch* was 143,000, and the evening *News Leader*'s circulation totaled 104,000. John Stewart Bryan III currently serves as publisher of the *Times-Dispatch* and chairman of the board of Richmond Newspapers; his son John Stewart Bryan IV is publisher of the *News Leader*.

The two Richmond papers were involved in a major First Amendment case in 1980 when the Supreme Court reversed both a state court ruling and a prior Supreme Court decision by allowing reporters to cover trials even when the defendant opposes such coverage. The seven-to-one decision involved a 1978 murder trial, but it did not clarify whether the decision included pretrial hearings. Nonetheless, the *Richmond Newspapers v. Commonwealth of Virginia* case suggested that the right to report trials was protected by the Constitution.

Reference Dabney, Virginius, *Richmond: The Story of a City* (1990).

Rocky Mountain News

Founded in 1859 during the gold rush in Colorado, the *Rocky Mountain News* became the most important daily in Denver. Owner-editor William N. Byers focused on accurate coverage of local news. The *News* bought out several competitors but had its fiercest rivalry with F. G. Bonfils's *Post*. John Shaffer owned the *News* in the early twentieth century until it was bought by the Scripps-Howard chain in 1926.

William Newton Byers brought a printing press with him when he came to Denver from Omaha in 1859. He founded the *Rocky Mountain News* in the midst of unregulated growth caused by the mining boom along Cherry Creek. At first, Byers's primary concern was to accurately report the lawless activities in the mines. Careful attention to facts earned the paper the nickname of "Old Reliable." The *News* began as a weekly but added a daily morning edition in 1860 after acquiring a new press. The rival *Commonwealth* was bought by Byers in 1864 for $4,000. Because of Denver's isolation, gathering news was expensive, so Byers had to charge 25 cents for the *News*. Using the pony express to obtain the text, Byers reported a summary of Abraham Lincoln's inaugural address in 1861.

Byers showed a keen interest in politics and founded the Republican Party in Colorado at a time when statehood was a prime concern. Territorial status was granted by Congress in 1861, and statehood efforts failed in 1864, 1865, and 1867. The discovery of silver in the 1870s brought a new flood of settlers to the area. A state constitution was submitted to Congress in 1875, and Colorado was finally admitted as a state in 1876. Byers reorganized the *News* in 1876 to allow outside investors for the first time. He decided to retire in 1878 when circulation reached 2,000 and sold the *News* to Democratic Party supporter William A. H. Loveland for $30,000. Loveland made James T. Smith vice president and editor.

Little changed at the *News* until John Arkins became editor in 1880. Perceptive and witty, Arkins became very aggressive toward the *News*'s competition and wanted to give the paper a more modern format. Arkins acquired a Hoe double-cylinder press, took ads off the front page, and began using bold headlines. He increased the size of the *News* to ten pages and added sports coverage, illustrations, and cartoons. Arkins secured the *News*'s first wire service in 1890; this was crucial for western papers, which were so distant from population centers in the East. Gradually, Arkins and his family became principal owners of the *News*.

In 1890, political leader Thomas M. Patterson purchased a one-third interest in the *News* and eventually obtained majority ownership. As a Democrat, Patterson had led the fight for statehood in the 1870s and later served as U.S. senator (1901–1907). Daily circulation of the *News* reached 16,000 by 1891, and the Sunday edition had 25,000 readers. Its most serious and combative competition began in 1892 with the founding of the *Denver Post* by Frederick Gilmer Bonfils, who resorted to sensational yellow journalism. Patterson and the *News* strongly backed the presidential campaign of Democrat William Jennings Bryan in 1896. Bryan's free silver platform appealed directly to the powerful silver mining interests in Colorado. Patterson continued the changes begun by Arkins, and the *News* prospered. It bought the evening *Denver Times* to compete with the *Post*. Liberal reporter George Creel, who had worked at Bonfils's *Post*, came to the *News* in 1911; he promoted civic reform and ridiculed the obstructionism of the *Post*. Creel later served as head of the Committee on Public Information during World War I.

Patterson sold the *News* and the *Times* in 1913 to financier-philanthropist John C. Shaffer of Chicago. Immediately thereafter, Shaffer also purchased the *Denver Republican* from Crawford Hill and merged it with the *Times*. That left only four dailies in Denver, two of which were owned by Shaffer. Publisher Shaffer stated that the *News* and *Times* would promote citizenship rather than partisanship but ended the *News*'s support for the Democratic Party and backed Republicans. When editor Henry Carbery resigned, Shaffer made himself editor but

hired William Forman as managing editor and William Chenery as chief editorial writer.

During World War I, the *Rocky Mountain News* demonstrated greater focus on international affairs than ever before. A number of military camps were established in the Denver area. Circulation grew during the war years and was soon pushing the 100,000 threshold. The Ku Klux Klan moved into Denver in 1920 and the *News* proved soft in dealing with the Klan, partly because managing editor Forman was a member. Shaffer gave less attention to the management of the paper in the early 1920s; staff turnover increased, and circulation began a steady decline.

Not surprisingly, Shaffer agreed to sell the *News* and *Times* to the Scripps-Howard Company in 1926 for $1 million. Scripps-Howard already operated the evening *Denver Express*. The new owners combined the *Express* and *Times* into an evening *News* edition. Recognizing the vulnerability of the outside ownership, Bonfils at the *Post* began a morning edition in 1927 designed to knock out the *News*. Bonfils had recently been forced to resign from the American Society of Newspaper Editors for fraudulent handling of the Teapot Dome oil scandal. A fierce and ugly battle ensued, illustrated by a *News* editorial calling the *Post* a "blackmailing, blackguarding, nauseous sheet which stinks to the high heaven." The morning *Post* experiment proved very expensive for Bonfils as well as for Scripps-Howard; both operations lost over $2 million during the year-long battle. The truce in 1928 involved the *News* buying the morning *Post* and Bonfils purchasing the evening *News*, thereby ending the head-to-head competition.

The circulation of the *News* eroded steadily from the time of the Scripps-Howard purchase until the mid-1930s. The low point in 1934 was 33,000. In addition to the depression factor, the *News* went through seven editors in 11 years through 1940. The situation stabilized in 1941 when Jack C. Foster became editor. A writing editor formerly with the *New York World-*

Telegram, Foster was popular with employees because he was a good listener. When Foster took over, circulation had recovered slightly to 42,000 for the daily edition and 45,000 for the Sunday paper. Howard William Hailey joined the *News* as business manager shortly after Foster arrived and put the paper's finances on a sound footing for the first time in two decades. Circulation rose to 48,000 for the daily edition by 1942, when the *News* adopted the tabloid format. By 1948, circulation was 100,000 and hit 160,000 in 1958. The recovery of the *Rocky Mountain News* was complete.

During Foster's later years as editor in the 1960s, the *News* began to close the circulation gap between it and the *Post*. By the end of the 1970s, the *News* had passed the *Post* with just under 300,000 circulation; the margin grew in the 1980s during the editorship of Ralph E. Looney, formerly editor of the *Albuquerque Tribune*. The Times Mirror Company of Los Angeles bought the rival *Post* in the mid-1980s but resold it to Media-News Group in 1988 after failing to dent the *News*'s circulation lead. By the 1990s, the *News* held steady at almost 350,000 daily circulation. Larry Stratton was publisher and chairman in 1994.

Reference Perkin, Robert L., *The First Hundred Years: An Informal History of Denver and the* Rocky Mountain News (1959).

Rogers, Will
See Media Humorists.

St. Louis Globe-Democrat

Founded by Free-Soil Democrats in 1852, the *Missouri Democrat* secured a position among stiff competition before the Civil War. When Joseph B. McCullagh came from Chicago to edit the *Globe* in 1878, it merged with the rival *Democrat.* Lansing Ray owned the *Globe-Democrat* from World War I to 1955 and continued its focus on civic affairs and conservative politics. Samuel Newhouse added the *Globe-Democrat* to his chain in 1955. The paper ended publication in 1988 because of mounting costs.

St. Louis had six newspapers in 1850, so there seemed to be no need for another. The *Missouri Democrat* was founded in 1852 for the express purpose of supporting the senatorial candidacy of Free-Soiler Thomas Hart Benton. The editor was Francis P. Blair Jr., son of Andrew Jackson's staunch editor-ally, but Blair's cousin B. Gratz Brown also helped write editorials. Because the paper had no printing facilities, Blair and Brown were forced to sell it to printers William McKee and William Hill. The next year, the *Democrat* bought one of its rivals, the *Union*, for $16,000 and used the old *Union* offices for printing.

Editorially, the *Democrat* supported all of Benton's positions, especially federal funding of internal improvements such as a transcontinental railroad. It also printed many of Benton's speeches. In 1854, Hill sold his half interest to the previous editors, Blair and Brown, and McKee made lawyer-politician Brown editor. Gradually, the *Democrat* edged closer to an antislavery position during the 1850s. Typical of most papers of the era, the *Democrat* mixed news facts with opinion in its columns. By 1859, when Brown resigned as editor, the daily *Democrat* had over 2,000 readers, and the weekly edition had 14,000 subscribers.

Blair and McKee hired a 17-year-old reporter named Joseph B. McCullagh in 1859. He and others working on the paper wrote articles about transportation improvements, business activity, and treatment of cholera and tuberculosis, which were common in St. Louis. McKee also insisted that the paper feature some literary items such as poetry, fiction, and biographies. Other information typically found in the *Democrat* included court cases and steamboat schedules. Advertising filled more than half of the four-page, ten-column paper, allowing its owners to retire debts and begin reaping profits in 1859.

New editor Peter Foy led the *Democrat* to openly endorse the Republican Party and favor emancipation of the slaves. The *Democrat* campaigned hard for Abraham Lincoln's election in 1860. When Lincoln appointed Foy postmaster for St. Louis in 1861, McKee persuaded antislavery advocate John Hume to become editor. Francis Blair sold his one-sixth interest in the *Democrat* in 1862 to Daniel Houser. The *Democrat*'s former owner-editor Gratz Brown became a Missouri senator in 1863.

Despite the *Democrat*'s strong support for Radical Republican Charles Drake during the Civil War, the paper's new editor, Yale-educated New Englander William Grosvenor, began a gradual movement toward Liberal Republicanism in 1866. Grosvenor became the campaign manager for fellow editor Carl Schurz, who ran successfully for senator in 1868 as a Liberal Republican against the Radical Drake. The *Democrat* backed former Senator Gratz Brown as the Liberal candidate for governor in 1870. Grosvenor left the paper as editor in 1871 and was replaced by former *Democrat* reporter Joseph McCullagh.

By the time the McCullagh era began, the *Democrat* had been able to invest in a new plant and equipment to collect and print the news more efficiently. The paper employed Henry Morton Stanley to cover western railroad expansion and Indian wars. *Democrat* reporters uncovered the local beginnings of what became a national scandal known as the Whiskey Ring. It involved whiskey manufacturers bribing internal revenue collectors not to report their full income. The *Democrat* was also one of the first dailies to give regular space to sports activities, especially baseball after 1870.

After a quarrel among the principal owners in 1872, George W. Fishback outbid McKee and others to purchase the paper for $456,000. McKee used the profits from the sale of the *Democrat* to launch a new paper called the *Globe*. The *Democrat* and the *Globe* had some bitter exchanges for a few years. When McCullagh had a falling-out with publisher Fishback in 1873, he resigned and was hired by McKee to edit the *Globe*. Fishback also blocked the *Globe*'s attempt to subscribe to a wire service. In 1874, McKee made a deal with Joseph Pulitzer, who agreed to buy a small paper with a wire service and sell it to the *Globe*. Pulitzer used the profits from the sale to obtain the *Post-Dispatch*. When the circulation of the *Globe* surpassed that of the *Democrat*, McKee was able to buy the *Democrat* from Fishback in 1875 for $325,000, producing the *Globe-Democrat*, with a circulation of 25,000.

The Whiskey Ring scandal, which existed on a small scale in 1870 when the *Democrat* first uncovered the scheme in St. Louis, expanded to a national scale by the mid-1870s. After several arrests, one of those charged implicated *Globe-Democrat* publisher William McKee. McKee was tried, convicted, and sentenced to two years in prison for accepting kickbacks. Despite the embarrassment, McCullagh was able to maintain circulation and respectability for the paper. McKee died in 1879 after serving only six months in prison and receiving a presidential pardon.

After McKee's departure, the *Globe-Democrat* reflected more than ever the journalistic philosophy of editor McCullagh. While co-owner Daniel Houser nurtured advertising revenues, McCullagh recruited reporters such as Theodore Dreiser and Walter B. Stevens, sending them from the inner city of St. Louis to Mexico to gather news. Gambling and mob violence were criticized, and sympathy for labor unions was expressed. The more sensational the story, the better it was for circulation. The *Globe-Democrat* never missed an opportunity for an interview with a famous personage. The sports and women's departments were expanded. Nor did McCullagh neglect editorials, which usually promoted civic pride or Republican candidates. After a long illness, McCullagh committed suicide in 1896. He was succeeded as editor by Henry King.

The *Globe-Democrat* began to feel competition from Pulitzer's *Post-Dispatch* in the 1890s. In 1892, the circulation of the *Globe-Democrat* was more than 53,000, and that of the *Post-Dispatch* totaled almost 34,000. By 1914, however, the *Post-Dispatch*'s circulation was 177,000, compared with the *Globe-Democrat*'s 135,000. The *Globe-Democrat*'s longtime rival, the *Republic* (founded in 1808 as the *Missouri Republican*), was no longer a serious competitor, having lost half its subscribers by the end of World War I. In 1919, with only 30,000 circulation, the *Republic* was sold to the *Globe-Democrat* for $734,000. The *Globe-Democrat* was then the only morning daily in St. Louis.

Upon the resignation of editor King in 1915, city editor Joseph McAuliffe was named editor. At the same time, Casper Yost, a *Globe-Democrat* staffer since the early 1890s, became editorial page editor. Yost was a principal founder of the American Society of Newspaper Editors in 1922. At war's end, Vice President E. Lansing Ray became publisher. Ray eliminated the weekly edition of the paper and raised the price of the daily to three cents. The *Globe-Democrat* prospered, as did much of the United States, in the 1920s. By 1929, circulation passed 500,000, and subscription revenues alone totaled almost $1.5 million. The printing operations were moved into a new, modern facility in 1931.

During the depression, circulation fell to 212,000 and did not recover quickly. Nonetheless, *Globe-Democrat* readership was comparable to that of the *Post-Dispatch*. In 1941, Lon Burrowes replaced McAuliffe as editor, and Louis LaCoss took over the editorial page position. The paper's price was raised in 1946 and again in 1952 due to rising production costs and lower profits. The financial difficulties led publisher Ray to sell the *Globe-Democrat* to Samuel Newhouse in 1955 for $6.25 million. The new owner promised St. Louis that the *Globe-*

Democrat would fight for the right side on issues and provide constructive news and analysis. Newhouse brought Charles Pierson from the *Pittsburgh Press* to be editor in 1956. The *Globe-Democrat* became a crusader for honest, efficient city and state government. The paper faced a major strike by the American Newspaper Guild in 1959, which weakened its finances. Although the *Globe-Democrat*'s circulation remained even with that of the *Post-Dispatch* as late as 1984, declines to 141,000 under publisher John Prentis combined with rising costs to force the closing of the *Globe-Democrat* in 1988.

Reference Hart, Jim Alle, *A History of the* St. Louis Globe-Democrat (1961).

St. Louis Post-Dispatch

Created through a merger engineered by Joseph Pulitzer in 1878, the *St. Louis Post-Dispatch* became a reform-oriented Democratic daily. Its early success under editor John Cockerill was followed by some neglect when both publisher and editor moved to the *New York World* in 1883. The *Post-Dispatch* continued to be operated by the Pulitzer family even after the *World* was sold in 1941. The paper has won 16 Pulitzer Prizes for editorial and reporting efforts as well as numerous other awards. Recent polls surveying leading U.S. newspapers consistently ranked the *Post-Dispatch* in the top ten.

Joseph Pulitzer's first newspaper enterprise, the German-language *Westliche Post*, was used to foster the Liberal Republican campaign of 1872. Disappointed by the breakup of the party and its failure to assure reform, Pulitzer sold the paper and left St. Louis for a few years. Upon his return, Pulitzer bought the bankrupt *St. Louis Dispatch* (founded in 1864) at an auction in 1878 and joined it with his partner John Dillon's *Post* (founded in 1875). Within a year, Pulitzer bought Dillon's share of the business and brought John A. Cockerill from the *Cincinnati Enquirer* to be editor. Because of Pulitzer's interest in reform, the *Post-Dispatch* pursued sometimes sensational stories about crime and corruption.

Moreover, Cockerill tended to emphasize graphically violent murders, lynchings, and similar episodes. Cockerill's penchant for violence became personal in 1882 when he shot and killed an angry political opponent in self-defense in the *Post-Dispatch* offices. Pulitzer aimed his paper primarily at a middle-class audience, and it quickly became a profitable enterprise.

The *Post-Dispatch* retained its original traditions even after Pulitzer left for New York in 1883 and Cockerill followed soon thereafter to take control of the *World*. However, a brief episode in 1895 and 1896 disturbed those traditions. Charles H. Jones was a maverick editorial writer at the *New York World* whom Pulitzer wanted to remove. Jones negotiated the purchase of a one-sixth share of the *Post-Dispatch* from Pulitzer in 1895, along with carte blanche editorial control. Jones fired several loyal staffers, and Pulitzer sued to regain control but failed. After Jones's presidential candidate William Jennings Bryan was defeated in 1896, he agreed to resell the shares to Pulitzer and retire. Meanwhile, the *Post-Dispatch* continued to introduce modern innovations, including color comics in 1894 and photographs in 1898.

Joseph Pulitzer retained control of policy after 1896 until his death in 1911. His son Joseph Pulitzer II received his training at the *Post-Dispatch* and took control from 1911 to 1955. Young Pulitzer showed both talent and daring over his several decades of management. He led the company's entrance into broadcasting in 1922 when radio station KSD began; a television station was added in 1947. Certainly, the most controversial action took place in 1929, involving the establishment of an advertising censorship board to review ads for false or misleading statements. The *Post-Dispatch* turned away $200,000 in advertising over the first decade of censorship. Still, the paper remained profitable during Pulitzer's tenure, despite the depression in the 1930s. Joseph Pulitzer II purchased the rival *Star-Times* from Elzey Roberts in 1951 for $5 million. The *Star-Times* had a circulation of 180,000 compared with the *Post-Dispatch*'s 282,000.

The merger allowed the *Post-Dispatch* to move ahead of its remaining rival, the *Globe-Democrat*. Pulitzer became interested in purchasing the *Globe-Democrat* in 1955, but Samuel I. Newhouse got there first.

Joseph Pulitzer II's staff consistently demonstrated impeccable talent. Skilled editorial writing was provided by George S. Johns, Charles G. Ross, and Robert Lasch, among others. Cartoonist Daniel R. Fitzpatrick won Pulitzer Prizes in 1926 and 1955. Bill Mauldin, well known for his World War II cartoons, was hired to replace Fitzpatrick in 1958 and promptly won another Pulitzer. Longtime managing editor Oliver K. Bovard guided the many excellent reporters from 1908 to 1938. Paul Anderson urged Bovard to give the *Post-Dispatch* a national perspective after World War I. It was Anderson who broke the story of the Teapot Dome oil-leasing scandal during the Harding administration. John Rogers won a 1927 Pulitzer Prize for revealing misconduct by a federal judge in Illinois. Washington correspondent Edward Harris won a Pulitzer in 1947. The *Post-Dispatch* successfully fought a state judge in 1940 for the privilege of criticizing judicial conduct and assailed a two-term governor in 1948 for graft, despite having its reporter, Theodore Link, indicted. The governor was defeated in a reelection bid, and the indictment was dropped. Since Joseph Pulitzer first switched to the Democratic Party in 1880, the *Post-Dispatch* has tended to back Democratic presidential candidates. Exceptions included the endorsement of Republicans Alfred Landon in 1936 and Thomas Dewey in 1948.

Joseph Pulitzer III also trained at the *Post-Dispatch*'s Washington bureau in the late 1930s after graduating from Harvard. After three years' service in the navy, Pulitzer moved up to associate editor in 1948; he gradually assumed more responsibility and became publisher in 1955, whereupon he continued the sterling record and reputation of the *Post-Dispatch*. Washington bureau chief Marquis Childs won the 1970 Pulitzer for commentary. The *Post-Dispatch* followed other media companies in 1986 by becoming a publicly owned corporation; at the same time, Joseph Pulitzer III retired as editor and publisher. William F. Woo became editor of the *Post-Dispatch*, and Joseph Pulitzer IV became a vice president. The Pulitzer Publishing Company owns two daily papers besides the *Post-Dispatch* and two radio and five television stations. Broadcasting accounts for almost two-thirds of the revenues of the company.

See also Pulitzer, Joseph.

Reference Wilensky, Harry, *The Story of the* St. Louis Post-Dispatch (1981).

San Francisco Chronicle

Started in January 1865 as a theater newsletter by teenagers Charles and Michel De Young, the *San Francisco Chronicle* became a general-circulation daily in 1868, and its circulation doubled the first year. Attacks on local graft cost Charles De Young his life in 1880 when a disgruntled political rival shot him. Battling corruption became a trademark of the *Chronicle* far into the twentieth century. It also remained locally owned in an age of multimedia conglomerates.

Because San Francisco had a number of theaters in the 1860s, two young brothers, Charles and Michel Henry De Young, decided to start a playbill in January 1865. The De Young boys had been born in St. Louis and moved with their parents to San Francisco in the early 1850s. Almost from the outset, the *Dramatic Chronicle* was more than just a specialized theater news sheet. The De Youngs included news items, both original and telegraphic, in the early issues of the *Chronicle*. One of the original contributors was Mark Twain, who spent several years on the West Coast and worked as a correspondent for San Francisco's first daily, the *Alta California*. Bret Harte also wrote some satirical pieces for the *Chronicle*, including poetry. Expenses for editing and printing the paper were paid for by advertising, since the *Chronicle* was distributed gratis. The De Youngs were able to scoop the regular press with an extra about the assassination of President Abraham Lincoln. Other extras about the assassination investigation followed, complete with illustrations. The future course of the *Chronicle* seemed to be set by those rapid events in 1865.

The steady movement away from theater billings toward becoming a newspaper was complete in September 1868 when the paper's title was changed to the *Daily Morning Chronicle* and readers were charged two cents a copy. Charles De Young assumed the editorial duties and Michel Henry handled business affairs. It was now a four-page paper and larger than its original size, with seven columns per page. The month after the transition, the *Chronicle* issued an extra with illustrations to report an earthquake and the resulting damage. The *Chronicle* became San Francisco's first eight-page paper in 1869 when it published a Sunday edition. Henry George, the single-tax advocate of later years, wrote editorials for the *Chronicle* between 1870 and 1873 about ending the land monopoly. George later became editor of the *Post*, where he continued his crusade. Also during the 1870s, the *Chronicle* added a sports editor.

During the drafting of a new state constitution in 1878, the *Chronicle* distinguished itself as the only newspaper to campaign for the reform-oriented constitution that championed labor rights and established a railroad regulating commission. Railroad interests had pushed a press muzzling law in the 1878 legislature, but the *Chronicle* vigorously defended freedom of the press, and the bill was rejected. The De Youngs spent much of their money promoting the approval of the constitution, which was ratified by the voters. The railroad barons pressured *Chronicle* advertisers to stop doing business with the paper, but they failed. The new constitution was approved in 1879— the same year the *Chronicle* moved into a new four-story building complete with advanced web-perfecting presses.

Editor Charles De Young was shot and killed in 1880 after leading opposition to the Workingman's Party. De Young had wounded the party's leader, and the man's son sought vengeance by murdering De Young. Michel Henry De Young did not change the principles of the *Chronicle* after his brother's death. Its news reporting continued to be the most thorough on the West Coast, and editorial independence was maintained despite the publisher's support for the national Republican Party. The *Chronicle* distributed weather bulletin boards beginning in 1885 to warn farmers of approaching inclement weather. The paper established its own Pacific wire service, which became an extension of the New York Associated Press in 1875. De Young became a founding director of the Western Press Association in 1881. By the 1880s, the *Chronicle* had a correspondent covering the Pacific and Far East. De Young was rewarded for his civic promotions by being named chief executive of the 1894 San Francisco Exposition. The *Chronicle*'s circulation leadership was eclipsed in 1893 by William Randolph Hearst's *Examiner*.

Although the *Chronicle* gave extensive coverage to U.S. interests in Hawaii and Cuba in the 1890s, it opposed intervention in Cuba before war was declared in 1898. The *Chronicle*'s traditional but solitary stand against local corruption was joined in 1895 by Freemont Older of the *San Francisco Bulletin*. The San Francisco earthquake of 1906 provided a major setback to the city's progress and destroyed the *Chronicle* building. The paper cheered the reconstruction of the city by building a skyscraper for its own headquarters. It pioneered the daily comic strip in 1907 with Bud Fisher's "Mutt and Jeff." De Young bought one of his two morning competitors, the conservative *Call* (founded in 1856), in 1913 from John Spreckels. The *Chronicle* opposed U.S. intervention in World War I before the declaration of war in 1917.

After the death of Michel Henry De Young in 1925, the family retained control of the *Chronicle*. George Cameron held the title of publisher in the 1930s and 1940s, and Chester Rowell served as editor. After World War I, the *Chronicle* became noted for its extensive news coverage of national and international events. Reporter Royce Brier won a 1934 Pulitzer for a story about lynchings. George De Carvalho received a

1952 Pulitzer for reports about an Asian racket in San Francisco. By the 1950s, under editor Scott Newhall, the *Chronicle*'s format shifted to more emphasis on features and columns, with news items becoming briefer. By the 1960s, only two dailies remained in San Francisco, the morning *Chronicle* and the evening *Examiner*. The two agreed to publish their Sunday editions jointly beginning in 1965. Since 1985, Richard Thierot has served as editor and publisher of the company, which owns cable television operations as well as three television broadcast stations. *Chronicle* circulation in 1994 was 544,000.

San Francisco Examiner

Although founded in 1865, the *San Francisco Examiner* lacked distinction until George Hearst bought the paper in 1880. Upon its transfer to his son William Randolph Hearst, the *Examiner* became the linchpin in an eventual chain of modern newspapers that altered journalism forever. The *Examiner* was Democratic throughout its history and, in addition to sensational treatment of the news under the Hearsts, was known for its quality writing and reporting. The *Examiner* engaged in crusades and championed civic improvements.

William Moss operated the *Democratic Press* in San Francisco at the end of the Civil War. Because of its "copperhead" antiwar stance, the *Press* became the target of an angry mob when the news broke of President Abraham Lincoln's assassination in 1865. Moss then found four financial backers to start a new evening Democratic paper, the *San Francisco Examiner*, in 1865. Democracy remained unpopular, however, and even Democratic legislator and *Examiner* columnist James Coffey could not create a large following for the paper, which went through several owners over the next 15 years. In 1880, with circulation struggling to reach 4,000, George Hearst purchased the *Examiner* from W. T. Baggett to foster Hearst's campaign for the U.S. Senate and changed the paper to a morning edition.

Despite the personal motive for acquiring the *Examiner*, Hearst treated the project with great seriousness. In order to stimulate circulation, Hearst used a variety of devices, including games and puzzles. His personal attorney Clarence Greathouse became editor and built the circulation to 20,000 by 1887, when Hearst left San Francisco to serve in the Senate. Hearst's son, William Randolph, was given charge of the *Examiner*. Immediately, William Randolph Hearst started making changes in format and personnel. He hired managing editor Samuel Chamberlain, former employee of James Gordon Bennett Jr. and Joseph Pulitzer. Ambrose Bierce assumed the task of writing essays and commentary as well as a satirical column called "Prattle," and Homer Davenport became the *Examiner*'s political cartoonist. Winifred Black, writing under the pseudonym "Annie Laurie," contributed stories about women as well as some sterling reporting.

The *Examiner* became involved in crusades to a lesser degree than its morning rival the *Chronicle*, but it assailed the Southern Pacific Railroad monopoly in California and championed free trade. The *Examiner*'s technical expert, George Pancoast, hired in 1888, gave the paper an attractive look with bold typeface and symmetrical headlines. He soon convinced Hearst to buy improved printing presses using the new linotype typesetting machines. Circulation grew rapidly under William Randolph Hearst—to 30,000 in the first year and to 60,000 by 1893, when it passed the *Chronicle* in readership. Yet the paper continued to lose money until about 1895 because of Hearst's lavish spending habits. Thereafter, the *Examiner* became a model for West Coast newspaper success, even after Hearst left to take charge of the *New York Journal*.

In 1908, the *Examiner*'s circulation passed the 100,000 mark. In 1913 Hearst bought both the evening *Call* (founded in 1855) and the evening *Post* (founded in 1871), which had an Associated Press franchise. Subsequently, the *Post* was merged into the *Call*. Another evening rival, the *Bulletin* (founded in 1856), was purchased in

1929, creating the *Call-Bulletin*. Hearst also started the *American Weekly* Sunday magazine supplement, featuring colored comic strips, in the 1890s. William Randolph Hearst Jr. assumed control of the *Examiner* at the death of his father in 1951. His paper won a Pulitzer Prize for reporting in the Soviet Union during 1956. In 1959, the *Examiner* acquired the Scripps-Howard *News* to form the *News-Call-Bulletin* afternoon paper. Production and labor costs rose dramatically in the 1960s in the face of stiff competition from television. In a joint agreement in 1965, the *Examiner* agreed to terminate its afternoon *News-Call-Bulletin* and switched the *Examiner* to an evening rather than a morning daily. That left the morning *Chronicle* and the evening *Examiner* as San Francisco's only dailies. The two papers agreed to publish their Sunday editions jointly in 1965.

Although William Randolph Hearst Jr. remained chief executive officer, his son W. R. Hearst III became editor and publisher in the 1980s. Circulation continued to erode gradually, down from 150,000 in 1984 to 125,000 in 1994. Of course, the *Examiner* benefited from the joint Sunday edition with the *Chronicle*, which retained profitability and a tenth-place national circulation ranking.

See also Hearst, William Randolph.

Sarnoff, David
See Radio Corporation of America.

Satellites
The communications industries were revolutionized by the advent of satellite technology beginning in the 1960s. An orbiting satellite receives signals from an earth transmitter known as an "uplink"; after the signal bounces off the satellite, it returns to an earth receiving station known as a "downlink," which is often merely a satellite dish. Both print and broadcast news media depend heavily on satellite technology to report global news events as they occur. The cable television industry also benefits directly from the new technology in marketing its product. Consumers are faced with a seemingly limitless number of choices and variety in both news and entertainment because of satellite technology.

When the "space race" between the Soviet Union and the United States began with the launching of the Russian *Sputnik* satellite in October 1957, the impact on mass media was just as great as the impact on scientific and military technology. Congress passed the Communications Satellite Act in 1962 to encourage private commercial development or "common carriers" of satellite technology, although at first only the National Aeronautics and Space Administration (NASA) was authorized to orbit satellites in agreements with American Telephone and Telegraph (AT&T) for *Telstar I* in 1962, Radio Corporation of America (RCA) for *Relay* in 1963, and International Telecommunications Satellite Organization (INTELSAT) for *Early Bird* in 1965. AT&T's *Telstar I* sent the first live televised pictures from Europe to the United States in 1962. The first synchronous-orbit satellite, *Syncrom II*, was launched in 1963. It could remain stationary over the earth at any designated position to send continuous signals. In 1972, the Federal Communications Commission (FCC) allowed private companies to launch their own satellites. Western Union delivered its first *Westar* satellite into orbit in 1974; RCA immediately followed with its *Satcom* satellite, and General Telephone and Electronics' (GTE's) *Spacenet* was launched in 1981.

The first public investment venture in satellite technology was the Communications Satellite Corporation (COMSAT), which sold stock in 1963. Commercial media companies were allowed to purchase stock in the corporation, and AT&T, GTE, and RCA quickly bought almost all the corporate shares. In 1977, COMSAT launched a satellite that allowed 6,000 voice circuits and two television channels to broadcast to 80 nations.

The international implications and uses of the satellites were obvious from the beginning. In 1964, the consortium called

INTELSAT enrolled 19 nations as participants in a global system of satellite access; by 1983, 109 countries had joined INTELSAT, and nonmembers were allowed to purchase time on the network. INTELSAT sold 1,000 hours of television in 1970 and almost 10,000 in 1980. After 1982, television users could contract for daily access from INTELSAT's operational satellites, which numbered seven in 1993. INTELSAT's monopoly on international relays ended in 1977 when a European consortium established a rival system. The United States' COMSAT owned the majority shares in INTELSAT until the early 1970s, when its share dropped to 40 percent, an indication that although the United States dominated the satellite industry, it would not obstruct expansion or participation. Media gurus such as Marshall McLuhan argued that the new technology would blur the cultural distinctions among nations. Satellite technology combined with computers to enhance the speed, capacity, public accessibility, mobility, and cost-effectiveness of mass media—from the traditional realms of print to the newer broadcast media.

Gannett's *USA Today*, begun in 1982, utilized satellite transmissions to distribute each day's paper to 33 printing sites around the nation as well as to three overseas locations. The *Wall Street Journal* used a similar system for its U.S. and foreign outlets. In the television entertainment field, there is a new system known as direct broadcast satellite (DBS). A signal is sent from an earth station to the satellite and then directly into homes through individual antennas. More than 2 million homes received DBS by 1990. A consortium including Hughes Communications, General Electric, Cablevision, and Rupert Murdoch will launch a 100-plus-station DBS system by the mid-1990s. If DBS becomes cost-effective, it could be a threat to local cable systems.

References Marks, Leonard H., "Communication Satellites: New Horizons for Broadcasters," *Journal of Broadcasting* (1965); Rees, David W. E., *Satellite Communications: The First Quarter Century of Service* (1990).

Saturday Evening Post

The *Saturday Evening Post* was founded in Philadelphia as a weekly literary magazine in 1821. It languished in mediocrity through most of the nineteenth century. Under publisher Cyrus Curtis after 1897, the *Post* became the most successful general weekly magazine in U.S. history. Competition from television and rising costs led to its collapse in 1969.

The weekly *Saturday Evening Post* was founded in 1821 by Philadelphia printers Charles Alexander and Samuel Atkinson. The first Saturday issue in August looked like a newspaper, with four pages and five columns per page and no illustrations. The first editor, Thomas C. Clarke, wrote most of the original entries; he avoided political commentary and copied stories and poems from other papers to fill space. By 1822, attention was given to summaries of current drama productions, essays by outside contributors, and household advice. Circulation grew from 1,000 the first year to perhaps 4,000 by the third year. The owners made enough money from the *Post* to found a new monthly, later called *Graham's Magazine*, in 1825. By the late 1820s, woodcut illustrations appeared frequently in the *Post* and prizes were offered for essays.

In 1828, co-owner Alexander sold his share to Atkinson in order to establish a newspaper. Atkinson and new editor Benjamin Mathias moved the *Post* toward more literary offerings and added music coverage. Circulation continued to grow and reached 15,000 by 1832. George R. Graham was hired as editor in 1839 and soon entered into a partnership with new publisher John Du Solle, who in turn sold his share to Charles J. Peterson. Graham increased the size of the *Post* and substituted a superior quality paper. By 1846, the *Post* had survived five owners and six editors to become Philadelphia's only weekly.

Henry Peterson became editor of the *Post* in 1846 on the occasion of its separation from *Graham's Magazine*. The *Post* claimed to be a "family newspaper" devoted to a variety of information. Emma Southworth became a regular and popular contributor, along with a number of English serial entries. Circulation rose past the 80,000 figure in 1855. During the Civil War, the *Post* carried some news and illustrations of battles. Women writers became more numerous at the *Post* during the war, and the format was enlarged to eight pages. Novelist Bella Spencer became part owner and associate editor in 1865, and news accounts decreased once more. Peterson's era as editor ended in 1873, when he sold his majority shares in the *Post* to merchant J. C. Walker.

Several changes in management occurred over the next four years until Andrew Smythe became owner and editor in 1877. Over the next two decades, the quality of entries—serials, verse, and essays—declined, as did circulation. Cyrus H. K. Curtis, publisher of the profitable *Ladies' Home Journal*, offered to buy the bankrupt *Post* for $1,000 after Smythe's death in 1897. Curtis named William G. Jordan editor of his new journal, and the *Post* was soon refurbished. Curtis asserted that the *Post* had been founded in 1728 by Benjamin Franklin, and although the claim was spurious, it allowed Curtis to set a goal of quality for the *Post* that it had not achieved during its prior ownership.

Former Boston newspaperman George H. Lorimer became editor in 1899 and was given a free hand to begin a major overhaul. Lorimer started by obtaining competent writers to cover interesting subjects, including Arctic expeditions and personalities such as Theodore Roosevelt and Queen Victoria. Illustrations soon became a fixture in the *Saturday Evening Post*, adding to its flavor. Most importantly, however, Lorimer decided to shift the ideological focus from the family to men. He did so by concentrating on business, public affairs, and romantic adventures, all of which emphasized personalities. Articles about robber barons such as John D. Rockefeller and pieces written by successful businessmen such as James J. Hill became regular features. Short stories by Rudyard Kipling, Stephen Crane, and Joel Chandler Harris appeared. Political essays by former President Grover Cleveland and Albert Beveridge were complemented by a column

from the nation's capital. Circulation grew dramatically and reached 300,000 by 1901.

When circulation passed 600,000 in 1903, the *Saturday Evening Post* had established a solid reputation for quality writing. The trend continued from 1904 to 1908 with serialized novels by Jack London, Joseph Conrad, James Branch Cabell, and David Graham Phillips. Short stories from O. Henry and Booth Tarkington and nonfiction by William Allen White added more flavor. At the end of 1908, the *Post* boasted 1 million readers. After 1909, the successful male-oriented formula was amended to include topics for women and humor, which required lengthening the journal to 100 pages. These changes only enhanced circulation further; it reached 2 million in late 1913, making the *Post* the largest-circulation magazine in history. The new automobile industry took up one-fourth of the advertising space in the *Post* by 1915. New writers appearing for the first time included Ring Lardner, P. G. Wodehouse, and Sinclair Lewis.

During World War I, the *Post* sent four correspondents to follow events on the battlefields of France. William Allen White reported the postwar peace conference in Paris. The war caused a slight decline in circulation, but it moved back to just under 2.5 million afterwards and remained steady throughout the 1920s. Will Rogers contributed a regular feature on his travels around the United States, James J. Corbett penned an essay on boxing, and Amos Alonzo Stagg wrote another on football, all of which demonstrated the versatility of the *Post*. Murder mysteries appeared regularly, including Earl Derr Biggers's "Charlie Chan" series and Rex Stout's "Mr. Moto" escapades. By the late 1920s, the *Post* printed 200-page issues, about 60 percent advertising. *Post* covers after 1912 featured elements of Americana from rural to urban settings.

The depression of the 1930s caused a loss of advertising, but circulation did not decline. In fact, the *Post* hit the 3 million mark in circulation in 1937. Advertising revenues reached a low point in 1933 but recovered by 1936. The *Post* continued to include quality writers such as Agatha Christie, Gertrude Stein, Dorothy Thompson, Rex Stout, and Stephen Vincent Benét. Publisher Cyrus Curtis died in 1933, and president George Lorimer retired in 1936. Upon Lorimer's death in 1937, the *New York Times* called him the "Henry Ford of American Literature."

Lorimer's successor was longtime staffer Walter D. Fuller as president; 14-year veteran Wesley Stout became editor. Stout recruited excellent writers to contribute fiction, detective stories, short stories, and humor. He also maintained Lorimer's editorial position, which criticized Roosevelt's New Deal. Improved type and layout techniques added to the *Post*'s aesthetics. Circulation continued to grow, and in 1942, the price of the *Post* was raised for the first time in its history from a nickel to a dime.

After a disagreement with management, Stout resigned in 1942 and was replaced by Ben Hibbs, an experienced magazine editor. Hibbs quickly began making changes: a modernized layout, shorter articles, less fiction and more verse, cartoons, and reader surveys. A majority of stories during World War II dealt directly with the conflict as reported by eight war correspondents. The *Post* remained Republican in its politics during the postwar era. The price was raised to 15 cents in 1947, but it did not detract from circulation, which hit the 4 million mark in 1949. During the 1950s, advertising declined gradually, but the revenue slack was made up with increased sales, which topped 7 million by the end of the decade.

Hibbs retired as editor in 1961 and Robert Fuoss took over. Fuoss altered traditions in the cover, design, and editorial content but was dismissed within months. Several more editors followed in short order before Clay Blair took over, reversed earlier modifications, and plunged the *Post* into exposés that led to expensive libel suits totaling $27 million in losses in 1963. Even though circulation remained high at 6.7 million in 1968 with William A. Emerson as editor, the *Saturday Evening Post* was sold in 1969 by the Curtis Publishing Company to Bert SerVaas of Indianapolis. Packaged in a

new format, the *Post* became a monthly, then a quarterly, and finally appeared six times a year. Circulation declined from 650,000 in 1973 to 520,000 in 1992.

References Friedrich, Otto, *Decline and Fall* (1970); Tebbel, John W., *George Horace Lorimer and the* Saturday Evening Post (1948).

Scribner's Magazine

Book publisher Charles Scribner began an attractive, illustrated general-interest magazine, *Scribner's*, in 1886 as a successor to an earlier monthly journal. *Scribner's* quickly established a reputation as a leading literary journal, publishing the work of writers such as Stephen Crane, Thomas Wolfe, Ernest Hemingway, Edith Wharton, and Robert Louis Stevenson. Unfortunately, competition and cost factors forced the magazine out of business in 1939.

Charles Scribner launched a monthly magazine in 1870 to publicize his book publishing operation. It merged into the *Century* monthly in 1881, and Scribner agreed not to attach his name to another journal for five years. At the end of the moratorium in 1886, Scribner planned a new illustrated literary monthly. *Scribner's Magazine* published its first 128-page issue in January 1887 to compete directly with *Century*, *Atlantic*, and *Harper's* in a heated but limited market. Edward G. Burlingame was editor of *Scribner's* from 1887 to 1914. He had received a Ph.D. at Heidelberg after an undergraduate degree at Harvard and was experienced in both newspapers and book publishing. *Scribner's* gained an immediate advantage over its 35-cent competitors by selling for 25 cents. Circulation reached 100,000, third behind *Century* and *Harper's*, within two years.

Scribner's specialized in variety; it had serial novels, sonnets, short stories, and essays on the fine arts and public affairs, all of which were handsomely illustrated. There were also some special projects, such as the publication of letters by William Makepeace Thackeray, a specially illustrated edition on the occasion of the 1893 World's Fair, and Robert Louis Stevenson's novel *The Master of Ballantrae* in serial form. Well-known authors who contributed to *Scribner's* in its early years included William Dean Howells, Thomas Nelson Page, Henry James, Henry Cabot Lodge, and Alfred Thayer Mahan. There were frequent articles about modern technology's impact on modern life and work.

During the Spanish-American War (1898), the magazine carried accounts of battles by its own correspondents—headed by Richard Harding Davis—and by participants such as Theodore Roosevelt. There were often accounts of travel to distant places such as France and Japan. Art and literary criticism became a regular feature in the 1890s. Advertising space grew to 100 pages in the decade, demonstrating the growth of profits. Competition from the new ten-cent illustrated magazines caused a temporary decline in circulation in the mid-1890s, but by 1900, it rose again to 165,000 and hit 200,000 in 1910. Novels by Edith Wharton and John Galsworthy were major attractions during the first decade of the twentieth century.

Although *Scribner's* sometimes included articles on business and labor, it did not indulge in muckraking, which was both popular and profitable for other journals. Rather, *Scribner's* kept its original formula of fiction, poetry, biography, literary criticism, and essays on art, travel, and wildlife. Autobiographies and articles on automobiles proved popular in the years before World War I. Full-color illustrations were commonplace in *Scribner's* during the early twentieth century. When Burlingame retired as editor in 1914 and was succeeded by associate editor Robert Bridges, circulation and advertising sales had begun to slip.

The outbreak of World War I allowed *Scribner's* to feature special patriotic articles related to the conflict and to send reporters such as Davis to report the fighting again. Each issue averaged four to six major items about the war, and there were even some war-related paintings and poems. Once the war ended, *Scribner's* returned to its traditional format. Illustrations and full-color plates became less frequent, the magazine

was printed on inferior quality paper, and subscription prices were raised to bolster sagging finances. The quality of writing remained high even with new and younger contributors. By the mid-1920s, *Scribner's* increased its space devoted to public affairs, assailing big unions. Circulation fell again after the war, hitting a low of 70,000 in 1924 and still trailing that of *Atlantic* and *Harper's*.

In 1930, young, Princeton-educated Alfred Dashiell became editor of *Scribner's*. A new group of contributors was recruited, including Sherwood Anderson, D. H. Lawrence, Erskine Caldwell, F. Scott Fitzgerald, Marjorie Kinnan Rawlings, William Saroyan, and William Faulkner. Columns on religion, education, and business complemented frequent articles on politics that debated the merits of the New Deal. The shifts in authors and topics drove many longtime subscribers away from *Scribner's*, and there were few new readers. When circulation dropped to 40,000 in 1936, Dashiell left *Scribner's* for *Reader's Digest*.

The new editor, Harlan Logan, rolled the price back to 25 cents, revamped the format, added color plates again, and replaced the dull paper with a quality stock. Logan hired established critics to write reviews: John Chamberlain for books, Gilbert Seldes for movies, and George Jean Nathan for plays. Circulation climbed back to 100,000, and financial losses were trimmed but not eliminated. Nevertheless, the firm faced bankruptcy in mid-1939. *Scribner's* subscribers were offered *Esquire* as a replacement, and the name was bought by *Commentator*.

Reference Allen, Frederick L., "Fifty Years of *Scribner's Magazine*," *Scribner's* (1937).

Scripps-Howard Company

The string of newspaper acquisitions by E. W. Scripps in the 1880s was one of the earliest examples of media chain ownership. Scripps started with five dailies and formed a partnership with M. A. McRae, which led to further acquisitions. By 1922 when the Scripps-Howard Company was formed, the chain owned 22 newspapers. Roy Howard became the driving force behind further expansion of the company. By 1990, the $1.5 billion company ranked ninth in daily newspaper circulation with 23 dailies and almost 1.7 million readers. About one-third of company holdings is in broadcasting, video, cable, and book publishing ventures.

James E. Scripps worked on newspapers in Chicago and Detroit before founding the evening *Detroit News* in 1873. He sought assistance from his brother George and his young half brother Edward Willis Scripps to make the *News* a success. The Scripps brothers tried to start two other one-cent evening papers in Buffalo and St. Louis, but they failed. The *Cleveland Press* and *Cincinnati Post* begun by Edward Scripps did succeed, however. The penny *Cleveland Press*, founded in 1878, forced all but one of its evening competitors out of business by 1905. The penny *Cincinnati Post*, launched in 1880, faced stiff opposition from the Taft-owned evening dailies but also became a circulation leader.

Edward Scripps geared his papers toward the working classes in medium-sized cities. The format featured clearly written news and human-interest stories complemented by editorial backing for reform programs. Approaching his task much like a schoolmaster, Scripps encouraged the working classes to organize labor unions that would promote their rights against egregious capitalists. Scripps editorials protested the undemocratic and corrupt system of government, the co-optation of power and influence by the wealthy and educated, and the lack of opportunity for the common people. Scripps recruited editors such as the *Cleveland Press*'s Robert Paine, who shared his views.

In 1889, Edward Scripps and his business manager at the *Cincinnati Post*, Milton McRae, formed a partnership called the Scripps-McRae League of Newspapers. Using a market niche strategy, the partners researched growing industrial cities that lacked working-class newspapers as locations to start dailies. The partners would underwrite the launching of a paper, and if it obtained a 15 percent profit, Scripps-

McRae would finance up to half of the stock in the company. Profits over 15 percent would be reinvested in the local paper. If the new paper failed to show a profit after ten years, it would be sold. Their system presumed a considerable local investment but was also geared toward the company's own profit margins. Scripps-McRae set the format standards, prescribing modest headlines and short news summaries to economize on size and thus production costs.

By 1911, the Scripps-McRae League consisted of 18 newspapers from Ohio to Tennessee to Colorado. Independent of the league, Scripps also bought the *San Diego Sun* in 1893 and ten other West Coast papers over the next 15 years. Although the *San Francisco News* proved profitable, most of the other papers did not survive. Scripps also experimented with the no-advertising *Chicago Day Book* in 1911, edited by N. D. Cochran with Carl Sandburg as primary reporter. The *Day Book* circulation grew to 25,000 and was on the verge of breaking even when World War I drove newsprint prices up and forced its closing. A similar experiment in Philadelphia begun in 1912 also fell through. Editorially, Scripps papers favored the Progressive reforms of President Theodore Roosevelt and fought boss rule in cities where the papers were published.

Meanwhile, the Scripps-McRae League faced a dilemma when the United Press wire service failed in the 1890s. Scripps allowed McRae to apply for a full partnership with Associated Press, but the request was rejected. Scripps then organized regional wire services for league papers on the East and West Coasts and in the Midwest. These regional organizations were merged into the United Press Associations in 1907, which offered rival Associated Press serious competition.

Sales, purchases, and consolidations occurred fast and furious in the industry after World War I. The Scripps-McRae League was transformed into the Scripps-Howard Company in 1922, linking Edward Scripps the veteran with Roy Howard the novice. The company started three new dailies: the *Washington, D.C., Daily News, Fort Worth*

Press, and *Birmingham Post*. New purchases included the *Indianapolis Times, Youngstown Telegram, Albuquerque State Tribune, Buffalo Times, Pittsburgh Press, Rocky Mountain News* in Denver, and *Memphis Commercial Appeal*. The chain's *Akron Press* bought its local competitor in 1925. The company sold papers in Des Moines, Sacramento, and Baltimore. By 1930, the Scripps-Howard chain owned 25 dailies. Roy Howard took more direct control of the company after Edward Scripps's death in 1926, and was not as sensitive to working-class issues as Scripps.

Mergers continued to dominate the period after 1930. When the Scripps-Howard Company bought Pulitzer's *New York World* in 1931, it was merged into the *Telegram* to produce the *World-Telegram*. When another famous New York daily, the *Sun*, was bought in 1950, it was merged into the *World-Telegram*, which died in 1967 after crippling strikes and the death of Roy Howard in 1964. The *Washington News* merged with the *Star* in 1972, and the once-profitable *Cleveland Press* was sold in 1980. Scripps-Howard papers in Houston, Fort Worth, and San Francisco ended publication in the 1960s and 1970s. The money-losing United Press International was put up for sale in the late 1970s and finally sold in 1982 at a considerable loss. Still concentrated in daily newspapers, the Scripps-Howard Company owned 23 dailies in 1988 with a circulation of just under 1.7 million; it had ten Sunday papers as well. Editorial guidance was provided by Edward W. Scripps II, grandson of the chain's founder, until his premature death in 1987. A 1988 decision to sell common stock raised $130 million while allowing the company to retain majority control. An E. W. Scripps School of Journalism at Ohio University was endowed by the Scripps-Howard Foundation for $1.5 million in 1983. The foundation also provided 300 journalism scholarships to students across the nation.

See also Chain Newspapers; United Press.

Reference Trimble, Vance H., *The Astonishing Mr. Scripps: The Turbulent Life of America's Penny Press Lord* (1992).

Sedition Act (1798)

The Sedition Act of 1798 was part of a package of legislation known as the Alien and Sedition Acts passed by the Federalist-dominated Congress. The measures were designed to restrict Democratic-Republican opposition to the Federalist administration of John Adams and an undeclared war with France. The Sedition Act clearly violated the protections of free speech and press included in the First Amendment to the Constitution.

The dispute with France began with the so-called XYZ Affair. While attempting to settle an affront to the U.S. ambassador by France, American diplomats were told that they must pay a bribe to France before the matter would be discussed. The Federalist-controlled Congress was incensed at the French government's treatment of the United States and pressured President Adams to declare war. Although there was some naval warfare between 1798 and 1800, Adams never asked for a declaration of war. In addition, Congress became alarmed at the pro-French Democratic-Republican press criticism of administration foreign policy. The result was the passage of the Alien and Sedition Acts, four separate pieces of legislation designed to curtail Democratic-Republican opposition.

Congressional Federalists used the English common-law definition of "seditious libel" in the Sedition Act. Among other things, the Sedition Act forbade the printing of "false, scandalous or malicious writing" against the government of the United States, its representatives, or symbols. Punishments included fines up to $2,000, imprisonment up to two years, or both. Several Democratic-Republican–oriented publications became targets of prosecution under the Sedition Act. The best-known antiadministration publication was the *Philadelphia Aurora*, published by Benjamin Franklin Bache—grandson of Benjamin Franklin—and edited by William Duane. Bache was influenced by the first major Democratic-Republican paper, the *National Gazette* edited by Philip Freneau, but the *Aurora* was more violently partisan. There was a total of 14 indictments under the Sedition Act, 11 trials, and ten convictions—eight involving newspapers. Bache died of yellow fever during his prosecution, but his wife and Duane continued publication of the *Aurora*.

Technically, the Sedition Act did not prevent a publication from criticizing the government; it permitted truth as a defense and provided for jury trials. Nonetheless, its passage and enforcement under partisan conditions created serious questions about freedom of the press. The act was all the more controversial because a congressional declaration of war, anticipated by the legislation's Federalist authors, never occurred. Yet the administration's use of the act to muzzle opposition critics did not raise constitutional questions before the partisan Federalist judges who enforced it. Democratic-Republican leaders Thomas Jefferson and James Madison claimed that the Alien and Sedition Acts were unconstitutional in the Kentucky and Virginia Resolutions of 1798 and 1799. Many of those who were prosecuted were unusually caustic in their criticism of President Adams and the Federalists, and after the law lapsed in 1801, most opposition editors tended to be more restrained in their published statements. The Sedition Act's passage and enforcement had helped clarify the extent of free expression as provided in the First Amendment. The Sedition Act also demonstrated that public opinion as well as the Constitution would establish the boundaries for actions by government and its officials.

References Smith, James Morton, *Freedom's Fetters: The Alien and Sedition Laws and American Civil Liberties* (1956); Stevens, John D., "Congressional History of the 1798 Sedition Law," *Journalism Quarterly* (1966).

South-Carolina Gazette

Begun by an associate of Benjamin Franklin in 1732, the *South-Carolina Gazette* in Charles Town (Charleston after 1783) was the first newspaper published south of Maryland. Edited and published in its early years by Lewis Timothy, his wife, and their son Pe-

ter, the *Gazette* had a more literary flavor than most colonial newspapers, printing the work of many English authors.

In 1731, South Carolina's legislature needed someone to print its documents and advertised for a printer in northern papers. Benjamin Franklin, owner of the *Pennsylvania Gazette*, noticed the ad and sent Thomas Whitemarsh to Charles Town. The *South-Carolina Gazette* began publication in 1732, with Franklin offering to provide one-third of the financial funding until 1737. When Whitemarsh died of yellow fever the same year, the paper was in limbo. Franklin obliged the colony by dispatching another associate, Lewis Timothy. An Anglicized French Protestant immigrant from the Netherlands, Timothy had edited the colonies' first foreign language paper, the Franklin-owned *Philadelphia Zeitung*, in 1732. Timothy's wife Elizabeth became the first woman newspaper publisher after her husband died in 1738. She was succeeded by her son Peter in 1746 when he turned 21.

Printed on a half-sheet with four columns per page, the *South-Carolina Gazette* included local news, printed government documents, reprinted items from English newspapers, literary works of English writers such as Alexander Pope and Jonathan Swift, and items from the *Spectator* magazine. The *Gazette* invited local residents to contribute essays and poetry for publication. The paper adopted an impartial editorial position regarding politics, but this did not prevent Peter Timothy from criticizing a governor's enforcement of the Sunday "blue laws" in 1746. Timothy assisted in founding the Library Society of Charles Town in 1748. Like his father before him, he also served as postmaster for Charles Town. Although the city's status as a major port meant that the *Gazette* got considerable advertising from commercial interests, that did not prevent occasional financial difficulties for the owners. Peter Timothy sent subscription agents as far north as North Carolina and as far west as Mobile.

During the years before the Revolutionary War, the *Gazette*'s position as official government printer and Peter Timothy's sympathy with the patriot cause clashed. Timothy suspended the *Gazette* in 1764 to reorganize its finances and repeated the action in 1765 so that he would not have to comply with the Stamp Act tax. Timothy's brother-in-law Charles Crouch, backed by some local politicians, agreed to start the *South-Carolina Gazette and Country Journal*, which supported the colonial government and continued to publish up to 1775.

After resuming publication of the *Gazette* when the Stamp Act was repealed in 1766, Timothy became more openly patriotic. The *Gazette* favored the nonimportation agreement, which boycotted British goods listed in the Townshend Duties (1767). Yet Timothy allowed commercial opponents space in the *Gazette* to express their disfavor. The *Gazette* was the only southern newspaper to mourn the violence of the Boston Massacre in 1770. In 1772, Timothy attempted to leave the printing business by hiring Thomas Powell and Edward Hughes as partners to run the *Gazette*. Shortly thereafter, Hughes died and Powell was arrested, forcing Timothy to resume control in 1773.

Peter Timothy became a member of the patriotic Committee of Correspondence in 1774. To show support for the colony's becoming a state, the paper's title was changed to the *Gazette of the State of South Carolina* in 1777. When Charles Town was captured by the British in 1780, Timothy was taken prisoner of war but was released the next year. He drowned at sea in 1782 while traveling to Antigua to live with his daughter. Peter Timothy's widow, Ann, managed the *Gazette* until her death in 1792. The couple's son, Benjamin Franklin Timothy, educated at Princeton, continued to publish the *Gazette* until 1802, when it was closed.

References Baker, Ira L., "Elizabeth Timothy: America's First Woman Editor," *Journalism Quarterly* (1977); Cohen, Hennig, *The* South Carolina Gazette, *1732–1775* (1953).

Space Program

Because it coincided with the rapid expansion of television, the superpower space race that began in 1957 was ideally suited to media coverage. With the launching of the Soviet *Sputnik* satellite in 1957, the United States began a crash program for peacetime development of space technology, climaxing with astronauts landing on the moon in 1969. News about the activities of the National Aeronautics and Space Administration (NASA) continued to feature spectacular scenes of rocket launches and space shuttle landings.

By the twentieth century, the specialization of the U.S. media had led to the hiring of science writers by several newspapers and journals. Yet nothing could have matched the magnitude of media coverage caused by the so-called space race. When the Soviet Union announced the successful orbiting of an unmanned satellite called *Sputnik* in October 1957, it set the U.S. government and media into a frenzy of activity. The first goal was to get a U.S. satellite into orbit quickly. The media followed the early failures of the U.S. Navy rockets from Cape Canaveral, Florida, and announced the success of the army's Jupiter rocket when it launched the *Explorer* satellite into orbit in January 1958. A few months later, Congress created NASA to assume responsibility for peaceful space research. Billions of dollars began pouring into NASA projects, including rocket development and manned space launches.

Cape Canaveral became a regular scene for media pictures of NASA space shots in the early 1960s. The public was drawn into following these events and marveling at the technological improvements and the daring of astronauts. The first manned space shots from 1961 to 1963, called the Mercury program, involved single astronauts—including Alan Shepard, Virgil Grissom, and John Glenn—orbiting the globe and returning via "splashdowns" in the ocean. The two-man Gemini program began in 1965 with Grissom and John Young, and the first space walk occurred in 1966.

In 1968, the three-man Apollo program was developed, with the goal of landing astronauts on the moon. The first Apollo flight made 163 orbits around earth; television

This Advanced Communications Technology Satellite was launched by NASA in 1993 and allowed President Clinton to participate in video conferences with Haiti-based U.S. military commanders in October 1994.

cameras showed the astronauts working inside and provided views of the earth below. In December 1968, Apollo astronauts James Lovell, William Anders, and Frank Borman flew around the moon and back. The moon landing on the Sea of Tranquility occurred in 1969; it was covered from the scene by an RCA-built television camera. Pictures of Neil Armstrong's famous first steps on the moon were sent back to earth via video in 1.3 seconds. Armstrong and Edwin Aldrin set up a camera to follow their exploratory surface activities and the planting of the American flag. The astronauts then carried on a live conversation with President Richard Nixon. Several months after the first successful moon landing, a second group of astronauts landed near the original site and spent over 31 hours exploring the moon's surface. Millions of awed television viewers around the world watched the adventures on the moon through live coverage.

Following the moon landings, NASA focused its efforts on the space shuttle program, which was to precede an orbiting space station project. During the space shuttle flights beginning in 1981, television cameras regularly recorded astronauts' activities from within the space capsule. Of course, the cameras also recorded NASA's fatal disasters, including the death of three Apollo astronauts in 1967 on the launch pad and the disintegration of the space shuttle *Challenger* seconds after liftoff from Cape Canaveral in 1986.

NASA facilitated the advent of the satellite broadcast age by launching the *Telstar* satellite in 1962. Satellite relays were a particularly vital by-product of space research and technology for the electronic media. NASA's interplanetary probes also explored the solar system. The *Ranger* and *Surveyor* moon probes mapped locations for the later manned landings in the 1960s. The *Mariner* probe orbited Mars on several occasions between 1962 and 1973, and *Viking* landed on the planet in 1975. NASA's *Pioneer* and *Voyager* probes to Jupiter, Saturn, and Venus in the 1970s were followed by more recent photographic efforts. Although NASA's budget has been slashed from its

1960s heyday and Americans are now more accustomed to space exploits, media attention to space issues remains significant.

See also Satellites.

Sports Reporting

As the United States became more urbanized and attained more leisure time in the nineteenth century, sports and recreational activities became an integral part of society. The reporting of sports events in the media grew more slowly than the spectator interest at first. Although the weekly *Sporting News* was founded in 1886, it was not until the 1890s that newspapers unveiled the sports page. Following World War II, general sports magazines such as *Sports Illustrated* competed with specialized journals focusing on golf and tennis as well as baseball, football, and basketball. With the advent of broadcasting in the 1920s, sports events were integrated into radio and later television programming. The televised Olympic Games beginning in the 1950s acquired worldwide audiences. By the end of the twentieth century, sports programming and reporting had become a multibillion-dollar industry for media companies as well as participants.

The first sports publications in the United States dealt mainly with horse racing and boxing. The *American Turf Register and Sporting Magazine*, founded in 1829 by Baltimore's John S. Skinner, provided coverage for horse-racing enthusiasts. William T. Porter edited the *Spirit of the Times* (1831–1902), which provided racing news and some other sports coverage from New York City. By the 1850s, prizefighting attracted a large following, and match results were published in some papers. *Frank Leslie's Illustrated Newspaper* carried a series of illustrations portraying a match featuring U.S. champion John Heenan's 1860 fight in Great Britain. *New York Herald* reporter Henry Chadwick wrote an account of the new sport of baseball in 1862, and papers reported the popular walk races in the 1870s.

Joseph Pulitzer created the first "sports department" with a "sporting editor" at the *New York World* in the mid-1880s. At about the same time, *The Sporting News* was launched in St. Louis as a general sports weekly. During the 1890s, when boxing was made so popular by the reign of heavyweight champion "Gentleman Jim" Corbett, the "sports page" became a regular feature of the "yellow" dailies committed to the exploitation of sensational news. At the turn of the century, baseball gradually rose to prominence. The so-called Black Sox scandal in the World Series of 1919, in which Chicago White Sox players were accused of throwing a game, brought more than ordinary attention to the sports pages. In the 1920s and 1930s, boxing remained at the top in spectator interest during the reigns of heavyweight champions Jack Dempsey and Joe Louis. Yet sports pages also began to feature stories about golfer Bobby Jones and football stars such as "Red" Grange. In 1954, Henry Luce took a gamble with *Sports Illustrated* magazine, hoping that a specialized journal could be profitable. It took ten years before *Sports Illustrated* eliminated its red ink, but it set the course for others. The Times Mirror Company includes several sports magazines among its holdings: *The Sporting News*, concentrating on football, baseball, and basketball, and *Golf* and *Ski* magazines.

After the turn of the century, sports reporters began to gain recognition for their special skills, especially in New York City. Writing for various New York dailies, Joe Vila, Damon Runyon, and W. O. McGeehan developed their craft into a popular form. Grantland Rice took his first sportswriting job with the *Cleveland News* in 1905 but was best known for his column "The Sportlight" in the *New York Herald Tribune* from 1914 to 1930. The column was syndicated to over 100 papers. William Taylor became the first sportswriter to win a Pulitzer Prize in 1934 for reports of the America's Cup yacht races. Walter "Red" Smith began his sportswriting career at the *Philadelphia Record* (1936–1945), where he penned a widely read column. He became

the most widely syndicated columnist in the United States with his "Views of Sports" in the *New York Herald Tribune* (1945–1966) and wrote for the *New York Times* in the 1970s.

Radio broadcasting offered a great boost to sports enthusiasts and grew rapidly to cover all types of events. Radio Corporation of America (RCA) broadcast a Dempsey boxing match in 1920 that was heard by 300,000 listeners. That event spurred the growth of radio as much as any other single broadcast. KDKA in Pittsburgh followed in 1921 with the broadcast of another boxing match. WJZ in New York broadcast a baseball World Series game between the Giants and Yankees later in 1921. WWJ in Detroit and WEAF in New York City began airing football games in 1922. NBC's 1927 broadcast of Graham McNamee's description of a Jack Dempsey heavyweight boxing match in Chicago's Soldiers' Field was carried by 73 stations and reached 50 million listeners. By the end of the 1920s, sports broadcasting had assumed a regular place in programming. Armed Forces Radio broadcast baseball games to soldiers overseas during World War II through shortwave relays. A new era had begun, and the potential could not have been fathomed by the early participants.

The next phase of sports broadcasting involved the development of television. The first sports telecast occurred in 1939 when a college baseball game was broadcast locally in New York City using a single camera. A second camera was added to broadcast a professional game in Brooklyn shortly thereafter. NBC televised a boxing match featuring Joe Louis in 1946, and boxing was an immediate hit with television viewers. When 70 correspondents converged on Helsinki to cover the 1952 summer Olympics, television was there, as it was during the 1956 summer Olympics in Melbourne. Thus, in 1960, CBS paid $50,000 for the privilege of broadcasting the winter Olympics from Squaw Valley, California. When the 1964 games arrived, competition was heated, with ABC outbidding its rivals and paying $500,000 to telecast the winter Olympics from Innsbruck. CBS reentered the Olympic competition in 1992 with a successful bid of $243 million to telecast the winter games from France.

The same bidding wars that preceded Olympics telecasts occurred in other sports as well. CBS contracted with the National Football League for $28 million to televise games in 1964 and 1965 but recouped its investment in just two huge advertising contracts with Ford Motor Company and Philip Morris. In 1988, ABC paid $17 million for a single telecast of the Super Bowl, which brought high advertising revenues because of its ratings. Sports broadcasting benefited from improvements in videotaping, which allowed the "instant replay." Local television newscasts included sports segments as part of their regular formats beginning in the 1950s.

The media have made sports big business, as reflected in the salaries of broadcasters, players, and coaches. In 1988, the three television networks sold $2.3 billion worth of sports program advertising. In the 1960s, ABC's Roone Arledge took the lead in diversifying and expanding television sports coverage. The Saturday "Wide World of Sports" program began in the summer of 1961 and was hosted by Jim McKay. It eventually presented 120 different events, including track and field, figure skating, tennis, and boxing, telecast from six continents. ABC followed with another blockbuster in 1970 with the creation of "NFL Monday Night Football." Both professional and college sports programs benefited from the enormous monies derived through telecasts, especially end-of-the-season finales such as the World Series, Super Bowl, college bowl games, and Final Four college basketball, not to mention major golf and tennis tournaments. The ESPN all-sports network debuted in the 1970s on cable television systems and began successfully bidding against the three networks for live programming. Salaries soared for professional players and college coaches in particular, mainly because of broadcast revenues. A star system developed among broadcasters; sports commentators such as Howard Cosell, Curt Gowdy, and Pat Summerall

received their share of the largess in multimillion-dollar salaries.

Reference Rader, Benjamin G., *In Its Own Image: How Television Has Transformed Sports* (1984).

Stanley, Henry Morton (1841–1904)

Unquestionably, one of the most romantic figures of U.S. journalism was Henry M. Stanley, who searched Africa for missionary David Livingstone on behalf of the *New York Herald*. Stanley was a first-rate reporter who also covered Indian wars, European rebellions, and other explorations of Africa.

Born in Wales and orphaned at age two, John Rowlands left England when he was 18 to become a cabin boy and eventually ended up in New Orleans. There he was supported by a merchant named Henry Hope Stanley, whose name Rowlands assumed at Stanley's death. Stanley joined the Confederate army and was taken prisoner at the Battle of Shiloh (1862). He was allowed to join a Union army regiment in Illinois but received a medical discharge. After a trip to England, Stanley returned to the United States and joined the Union navy in 1864 before deserting in early 1865.

After the war, Stanley traveled in the West and also went to Turkey. While doing some freelance reporting of the Indian wars along the Platte River for the *St. Louis Globe-Democrat* in 1867, Stanley became acquainted with General William T. Sherman, Bill Hickock, and George A. Custer. Stanley sent some of his Indian war accounts to the *New York Herald*, which led to a job offer by publisher James Gordon Bennett Jr. in 1868. He was assigned to be a war correspondent, traveling with British General Sir Robert Napier to rescue British and other European prisoners held by King Theodore of Abyssinia (Ethiopia). He also covered the 1868 revolt against the Turks on Crete and an internal rebellion in Spain. Stanley's accounts brought him plaudits and secured his position as the *Herald*'s chief foreign correspondent.

James Gordon Bennett Jr. had taken over the management of the *Herald* from his father by 1866. He was fascinated by reports of the exploits of Scottish medical missionary Dr. David Livingstone in Africa. Thus, he was determined to locate Livingstone after his apparent disappearance. Bennett traveled to Paris in late 1869 to convince Stanley to undertake a search for Livingstone in East Africa. Two years later, Stanley's expedition left Zanzibar and moved into the interior. Stanley found Livingstone at a village on Lake Tanganyika in 1872. The account carried in Bennett's *Herald* also secured notice in European papers and made Stanley a legendary reporter thereafter. It was the kind of drama that newspaper publishers loved, simply because it sold papers.

Stanley had become an experienced African explorer in addition to his reporting skills. After Livingstone's death in 1874, Stanley arranged a joint venture financed by the *Herald* and the London *Daily Telegraph* to explore central Africa. Stanley traveled across Africa from the east coast up the Congo River to its mouth on the Atlantic coast in 1877. Because of Stanley's familiarity with central Africa, he was engaged by King Leopold II of Belgium to undertake a five-year expedition to explore the interior of central Africa along the Congo River basin and claim the territory for Belgium. Stanley retired to England, where he was knighted and elected to Parliament.

Reference McLynn, Frank, *Stanley: The Making of an African Explorer* (1989).

Stars and Stripes
See World War II.

Steffens, Lincoln
See Muckrakers.

Stone, Isidor Feinstein (1907–1989)
Avant-garde New Left editor and moralist I. F. Stone was at the forefront of New Journalism, which critiqued government and society during the 1950s and 1960s. *I. F. Stone's Weekly* began in 1952 with a focus on the Korean War and McCarthyism. After

the Hungarian crisis of 1956, Stone began criticizing Soviet communism. Early in the Vietnam War, Stone attacked U.S. policy and was revered by the New Left.

Son of Russian Jewish immigrants, Isidor Feinstein Stone began publishing a newspaper called *The Progress* while attending high school in New Jersey. *The Progress* condemned William Randolph Hearst's lack of ethics and praised Gandhi's Indian nationalist movement. Stone's father made him give up the project because it detracted from his studies. The Romantic poets headed Stone's reading list. Stone gave up attending the University of Pennsylvania in 1927 because he would not put his class assignments ahead of his eclectic reading. While working as a reporter for the *Camden (New Jersey) Courier-Post*, Stone had an opportunity to cover the Sacco-Vanzetti trial. When his editor refused to give him the assignment, Stone quit. He also wrote briefly for the *Philadelphia Inquirer*. In his youth, Stone was inspired by the writing of George Seldes, publisher of the no-advertising paper *In Fact*, who vigorously defended freedom of the press and advocated a self-policing ethical code for journalists.

After a six-year stint as an editorial writer for the *New York Post* (1933–1938), Stone moved to the liberal journal of opinion *The Nation* (1938–1946), which suited his tastes better. Then he worked for the unique New York newspaper *PM* for the last two years of its existence (1946–1948). In 1946, he traveled with Jewish émigrés sailing from Europe to Palestine and wrote gripping accounts of Holocaust survivors for *PM*. From *PM*, Stone went to the *New York Compass*, which collapsed in 1952. During his time at the *Compass*, Stone wrote *The Hidden History of the Korean War*, criticizing the anticommunist crusade that was central to the Cold War policy of the United States. Because of his outspoken attacks on the government, Stone found himself without a professional opportunity in 1952 when *The Nation* would not rehire him.

On a bare-bones budget with only his wife to assist him, Stone began the four-page *I. F. Stone's Weekly* in Washington,

D.C., in 1953 so that his political opinions could not be stifled. Stone started with 5,300 subscribers recruited from his old publications. The *Weekly* targeted Senator Joseph McCarthy and his communist witch-hunt as the major symbol of wrong-headed U.S. leadership. Stone's infatuation with Soviet communism was dealt a blow, however, by the brutal suppression of Hungarian freedom fighters by Soviet armed forces in 1956. Shortly after the Hungarian episode, Stone traveled through the Soviet Union and returned to bluntly criticize the repressive society he had seen. Some of Stone's left-wing readers were not pleased by what he said about the bastion of communism, and the *Weekly* lost some readers. Stone's *Weekly* also took favorable note of the civil rights campaign in the late 1950s.

At a low point in popularity in the early 1960s, Stone's *Weekly* questioned U.S. policy in Vietnam. His reputation and following among the New Left revived during the 1960s, and Stone became almost a cult figure among the hard-core Left intellectuals. Yet Stone's independence often frustrated his followers, such as his condemnation of random violence by student radicals in the 1960s. He also advocated equal treatment for Palestinian Arabs who desired a homeland like the Jews. Stone consistently upheld the true virtues of U.S. society as he saw them—freedoms of speech and press. Stone's wife, Esther, held much more conservative views, but she dutifully handled the financial management of the *Weekly* during its existence. Ill health caused Stone to publish biweekly after 1968 and to give up his *Weekly* altogether in 1971, at the peak of its circulation—70,000. In his valedictory essay, Stone expressed gratitude for being able to freely express himself over the years. He was an occasional contributor to the *New York Review of Books* during the 1970s.

Reference Cottrell, Robert C., *Izzy: A Biography of I. F. Stone* (1992).

Tabloids

Among the many innovations introduced in the 1920s was the tabloid newspaper, known more for its sensational content than for the compact format from which its name derived. The first tabloids originated in England but came onto the U.S. scene after World War I.

Sensational journalism itself was not new in the 1920s; it had been preceded by the penny press of the 1830s and the yellow press of the 1890s. Moreover, tabloid publishers were not so much seeking to take readers away from the daily newspapers as to capitalize on the indecorous interests of popular culture. Newspapers that pioneered the tabloid size included the *New York Daily Graphic* in the 1870s and 1880s and Frank Munsey's *Daily Continent* in the early 1890s, but other than their inclusion of numerous illustrations, they did not correspond to the post–World War I genre of tabloid products.

The first major English tabloid oriented toward sensational content was the *Daily Mirror*, published in London after 1903 by Alfred Harmsworth, later Lord Northcliffe. During World War I, it was Northcliffe who introduced the tabloid idea to an American soldier, James Medill Patterson, copublisher of the *Chicago Tribune* with Robert R. McCormick. Patterson commenced publishing the *New York Illustrated Daily News* in 1919, featuring extensive photographs and sensational stories. Within five years, the paper had achieved a circulation of 750,000; by the end of the decade, it surpassed 1.3 million.

The era of the 1920s was characterized by a political "return to normalcy," which diverted the public from political and foreign affairs to sex, violence, and Jazz Age entertainment. Prohibition led to the emergence of colorful gangsters such as Al Capone and Legs Diamond. Hollywood movie stars flaunted their glamour, and the public was infatuated with celebrities—ranging from airplane pioneer Charles Lindbergh to heavyweight boxing champ Jack Dempsey. The primary readers of the tabloids were not traditional subscribers of the major dailies but the immigrant and poorer urban classes that were so prominent in New York City.

The success of the *Daily News* led to a competitor in 1924, William Randolph Hearst's *Daily Mirror*. Bernarr McFadden's *Daily Graphic*—similar to his *True Story* magazine—also debuted in 1924 and lasted almost a decade. The *Daily Graphic* tested the limits of sensationalism; its confessional stories, outrageous contests, and romantic fiction—accompanied by revealing photos—made it the most controversial of the tabloids. The tabloids stirred interest in murder trials involving romantic triangles. In one case involving Ruth Snyder, who had conspired with her lover to murder her husband, the *Daily News* surreptitiously obtained a photograph of Mrs. Snyder's execution and plastered it on the front page. The event stimulated an extra 250,000 sales of that issue. With the advent of the Great Depression following the stock market crash of 1929, the tabloids added stories about the effects of the depression on a variety of people.

Patterson's *Daily News* was an early supporter of Franklin Roosevelt's New Deal programs, but it broke with the president over involvement in World War II. By the time of Patterson's death in 1946, the *Daily News*'s circulation was almost 2.5 million daily subscribers and 4.5 million Sunday subscribers. Although television and other broadcast media expansion after the war led to a gradual decline in *Daily News* circulation, it still remained the largest daily through the late 1970s.

Meanwhile, the competition was also facing adjustments. Tabloids always found it difficult to attract traditional advertisers, who were unsure of the effect of their association with sensational topics. The Hearst family sold and then repurchased the *Daily Mirror* in the late 1920s. It was given a second chance in the 1930s with the hiring of gossip columnist Walter Winchell and editor Arthur Brisbane, but the *Daily Mirror* was always a money-losing proposition because of a lack of advertising, and it was terminated in 1963. McFadden's *Daily Graphic* also failed to secure sufficient advertising, lost huge sums, and was closed in 1932.

Besides New York City, the tabloids found success in Boston, Chicago, Los Angeles, New Orleans, Philadelphia, and Washington, D.C. In 1936, there were 47 tabloids operating in cities outside of New York with a circulation of 1.7 million—about the equal of New York's tabloids. The imitators included a chain established by Cornelius Vanderbilt during the 1920s and Marshall Field's *Chicago Sun-Times*, begun in the 1940s. Even more traditional papers such as *Newsday* used the tabloid format, although they were more restrained in their treatment of news items. Even today, racy supermarket tabloids such as the *National Enquirer* and the *Star* appeal to a certain segment of the public obsessed with celebrity scandal, gossip, and science fiction.

References Bessie, Simon M., *Jazz Journalism: The Story of the Tabloid Newspapers* (1938); Covert, Catherine L., and John D. Stevens, *Mass Media between the Wars* (1984).

Talk Media

Although not a new phenomenon, talk shows became the rage of both radio and television during the late 1980s, based on the idea of allowing the audience to become participants. Talk shows have become an integral part of the popular culture and have proved to be economically attractive to stations and networks.

The spoken word has fascinated the U.S. public since colonial times. Talented speech makers were able to mesmerize audiences with polished or colloquial rhetoric. The advent of electronic media in the twentieth century gave much greater currency to such oral traditions. Talk radio and television, even computer talk via bulletin boards and electronic mail, involved diverse elements that reflected changes in U.S. society. Electronic communications have made it possible to transmit news almost instantaneously to audiences around the globe. The amount of information—whether substantive or trivial—that is available to the average person is mind-boggling. Greater leisure time allowed Americans more opportunities to partake of media offerings.

During the late 1920s, when only NBC and CBS operated radio networks, there were almost two dozen talk shows devoted to subjects such as public affairs, religion, and home economics. By the late 1940s, the number of such shows had grown to 55, which sometimes amounted to as much as one-fourth of the schedule. Some of the early hosts included Victor Lindlahr talking health issues on Mutual radio, Marion Taylor providing various social advice on CBS, and Nell Vinick on beauty. The interview talk show dealing with educational or public affairs topics also began very early in radio. CBS's "The People's Platform" (1938–1952), hosted by Lyman Bryson, featured a four-person panel that included an expert as well as laypeople (always a man and a woman). Similar programs were offered by NBC ("America's Town Meeting") and Mutual ("American Forum of the Air") during the 1930s and 1940s. "Vox Pop" began as a local Houston interview show in 1932 and was later carried at various times by NBC, CBS, and ABC.

Almost all the early radio talk shows were one-dimensional, with no audience participation. However, host Art Baker used listener interaction in several radio shows, such as "Paging John Doe," during the 1930s and 1940s. NBC radio's "Breakfast Club" variety program (1933) accepted listener requests. Finally, game shows such as "The Answer Man" (1937) and "Truth or Consequences" (1940) involved a form of interaction, since people in the audience became participants. Variety shows also engaged audience members as contestants, including "Arthur Godfrey's Talent Scouts" and "The Amateur Hour," both of which began on radio in the 1930s and made the transition to television in the 1950s. Godfrey's risqué commentary seemed to portend the more modern techniques of talk-show hosts. Art Linkletter's "People Are Funny" on both radio and television combined elements of talk and game shows before both a live and a broadcast audience.

As television displaced network radio programming in the 1950s, radio moved to a music and news format. However, local radio disc jockeys interspersed talk with recorded music. They also invited "call-in" requests from listeners, which were often taken on the air. During the mid-1950s, several local radio stations recognized the listener interest in call-in shows and devoted late-night programming to the format. By the mid-1960s, 80 percent of local radio stations had some form of talk show. KABC in Los Angeles was the first station to convert its entire programming to talk in 1961, followed by KMOX in St. Louis. Talk programming involved greater costs to cover more personnel and telephone charges, but sponsors were anxious to buy time on such programs because of the high ratings.

A corollary to the all-talk format was the all-news format of some radio stations, which also appeared in the 1960s. The all-news format, which included call-ins and interviews, projected an image of public service and appealed to some of the same older audience that was attracted to talk radio. All-news stations also saw their costs increase with added staff. Although conversion costs and added expenses deterred some stations, those that made the change saw their ratings increase from 25 to 250 percent. Advertisers liked the authoritative ambience produced by the show's host reading their scripts. Despite the example of many urban stations that successfully converted to talk formats, other stations viewed the associated expenses and risks as too great.

It was only a matter of time before talk shows came to television. The interview format was introduced in the 1950s on the "Today" and "Tonight" shows on NBC. The "Tonight" show even involved limited audience participation. Edward R. Murrow's "Person to Person" interview show on CBS in the 1950s focused on celebrities, as did the daytime shows hosted by David Frost, Merv Griffin, Mike Douglas, and Dinah Shore in the 1960s. "The Phil Donahue Show" airing in 1967 from Dayton, Ohio,

became the real pioneer of the new genre of interactive audience participation. Donahue tapped the public thirst for interpersonal experiences beyond banal "expert" authorities and broached taboo social topics. The show also appealed to a narcissistic generation obsessed with improving its self-image. Audience participation blurred the gap between expert or celebrity guests and the public at large—between insider and outsider.

Of course, as "Donahue" proved its economic worth to station and network executives, imitators appeared—slowly at first, but rapidly by the 1980s. The list of shows grows longer each year: Oprah Winfrey, Geraldo Rivera, Maury Povich, Ricki Lake, Jenny Jones, Montel Williams, Sally Jesse Raphael, Jerry Springer. All these shows rely on subject matter and guests that exhibit the sensational, taboo, bizarre, bombastic, and provocative. There is almost no concern about factual accuracy, and few boundaries remain to limit discussions or audience questions. The outer limits of this genre were reached by shock artists Morton Downey Jr. and Howard Stern. By 1992, the talk show was the best money-making bet for television—meaning that the form was driven by economics as well as public interest.

Another form of talk and audience participation show is the news–public affairs commentary format. David Susskind's program from 1960 to 1986 featured sometimes controversial guests such as Nikita Khrushchev. Joe Pyne's 1960s show, syndicated to 85 stations from Los Angeles, focused more on the host's personal prejudices and audience interaction than substantive topics. CBS's "Town Meeting of the World" hosted by Charles Collingwood in the early 1960s took advantage of satellite technology to stage a cross-Atlantic debate on specific issues. William F. Buckley's syndicated "Firing Line" interview program first aired in 1966 and featured a debate format; it was noted in its early years for rhetorical bombast. The Cable News Network's "Crossfire" program in the 1980s sought to imitate "Firing Line." "Agronsky and Company," begun in 1969, was a half-hour roundtable discussion of current events by journalists. This format has been replicated often and successfully by the networks, chiefly on Sundays. In the 1990s, NBC's cable financial network CNBC converted from financial news during the day to talk programming in prime time, including information topics such as consumer affairs, public affairs and policy, and sex, as well as celebrity interviews.

Meanwhile, radio talk shows continued to grow in popularity and numbers. By 1974, 113 radio stations carried at least some syndicated talk programs, and many others featured local morning talk and call-in shows. In 1987, the number of stations carrying talk shows rose to 238; by 1993, the total reached 875. The subjects and formats of the talk shows further expanded to include celebrity chats, sports, pop psychology, self-help services, and the traditional public affairs and news commentary. The National Association of Radio Talk Show Hosts was founded in 1989 with 25 members; by 1992, its membership had grown to 250. A newsletter for radio talk-show hosts, *Talkers*, became a guide for program preparation. Some of the more successful syndications, such as "Rush Limbaugh," were duplicated on television.

Whether the talk-show phenomenon is merely a phase in media history or not, it has raised many questions about the role of talk programming in U.S. society. Certainly, talk shows seemed suited to the public desire to disturb the United States' plastic, image-conscious culture. Interpersonal formats allow the blurring of lines between spectators and participants and make the public-private realms seem interchangeable. Talk media may also be simply the means to reestablish the oral culture that, since colonial times, has been subsumed by the written medium.

Reference Munson, Wayne, *All Talk: The Talk-show in Media Culture* (1993).

Tarbell, Ida
See Muckrakers.

Telecommunications
The development of telecommunications technology—from the telegraph to satellites—has revolutionized the media, especially its ability to gather and disseminate news. The telegraph and the telephone, invented in the nineteenth century, allowed the rapid transmission of news to publishing centers. As a result, the public could receive news within a matter of a day or two rather than a week or more. Computer and satellite telecommunications developments of the twentieth century not only enhanced the speed of transmission of news but also expanded coverage from local or national areas to worldwide access.

Samuel F. B. Morse invented the telegraph and issued the first wired communication in 1844. The telegraph depended on the extension of power lines across the length and breadth of the nation, so its initial expansion was slow and gradual. It was not until 1861 that the East Coast was connected with the West Coast in the first transcontinental circuit. In turn, the East Coast of the United States was connected by trans-Atlantic cable to the British Isles in 1858. The Harbor News Association was established in 1848, and eventually seven New York newspapers founded the Telegraph and General News Association in 1851, later known as the Associated Press. The association negotiated a reduced rate from telegraph companies for use of their service. The pioneering Magnetic Telegraph Company was founded in 1844 by Morse, Philadelphia publisher William M. Swain, and journalist Amos Kendall; soon, several other companies competed for telegraph business. By the end of the Civil War, however, Western Union had established a virtual monopoly.

During the Mexican War of the 1840s, several metropolitan newspapers used the telegraph through collective pool services to speed news of the war to their readers. The Civil War accelerated telegraphic use by newspapers even more. The major problem of the early telegraphs was that the lines were often down and service was interrupted frequently. By the standards of the day, telegraphic access was expensive, requiring reporters to be as concise as possible in dispatching reports to their papers. Sometimes reporters who were anxious to beat the competition would dispatch a story about the outcome of a battle before the actual results could be confirmed. Clearly, such tactics led to embarrassment for some editors when the actual results did not coincide with the newspaper account.

In 1875, Alexander Graham Bell invented the telephone; within two years, transmissions were expanding beyond his laboratory in Massachusetts. The spread of telephone use among major daily newspapers was rapid during the 1880s, even though the number of phones was limited. The American Telephone and Telegraph Company's founding in 1885 spurred the rapid expansion of telephone service. Just as with other new technology, the practitioners of news gathering were slow to implement the full possibilities of the new telephone technology. Like the telegraph, the telephone was limited by the extent of power lines, so access within large cities was better than links between cities. By 1900, there was one telephone per 100 population, and telephone service was nationwide. Guglielmo Marconi's wireless experiments in Europe culminated with the transatlantic cable in 1902. Marconi incorporated his wireless telegraph company in the United States in 1899; it was the forerunner of the Radio Corporation of America.

By the 1960s and 1970s, telecommunications were absorbing new technological innovations. The development of satellites allowed not only instant verbal communication worldwide but also the transmission of video pictures. The emergence of on-line services to interconnect personal computer users with one another as well as with other computer databases was a novel aspect of modern telecommunications. The newest technology to affect telecommunications was the emergence of fiber optics, successfully demonstrated in 1977. The system uses ultra-thin glass fibers to transmit a much greater volume of signals than traditional coaxial wiring, with static-free clarity. The technology actually changes the electrical impulse into a light impulse during the transmission across the fibers and returns the impulse back to an electrical one at the point of distribution. A trans-Pacific fiber-optic cable completed in 1989 between the West Coast of the United States and Japan allowed 40,000 telephone connections simultaneously. Fiber optics are also used to transmit television signals—in competition with satellites—and to connect interactive telecomputer systems.

All these developments have led to varying degrees of government regulation, principally through the Federal Communications Commission (FCC), founded in 1934. The FCC's primary focus has been on supervising and licensing radio and television broadcasting, but it has also maintained control over telephonic communications, including the most recent phenomenon of cellular telephones. The issue of telephone companies competing with broadcast media companies has become a factor requiring government involvement.

Reference McLuhan, Marshall, and B. R. Powers, *The Global Village: Transformations in the World Life and Media in the 21st Century* (1989).

Television

Although television technology was demonstrated as early as the 1920s, it was not until the 1940s that regular programming and widespread broadcasting were implemented by the networks. Since that time, television has had the most profound impact of all media technology in the twentieth century. Canadian broadcasting savant Marshall McLuhan warned that modern society's infatuation with television demonstrated that "the medium is the message." British journalist Malcolm Muggeridge opined that television nurtured illusions because of its limited perspective through the camera lens. The emergence of satellite broadcasts and cable systems offered instantaneous coverage of worldwide events and a greater variety of programs for consumers.

The technology of television was obviously related to earlier developments of electricity, photography, wired communications, and radio broadcasting. The 1923 invention of the iconoscope, an electric video tube, by Westinghouse scientist Vladimir Zworykin paved the way for the new medium. Radio Corporation of America (RCA) hired Zworykin to continue his work, and he developed the kinescope film recording process. Meanwhile, by 1926, science teacher Philo Farnsworth had invented an electronic television camera using electric light relays and magnetic imagers. Farnsworth agreed to license RCA to use his technology. During the 1930s, Allen DuMont perfected home receiving sets with screens measuring eight by ten inches. American Telephone and Telegraph (AT&T) scientist H. E. Ives successfully transmitted a closed-circuit picture from Washington to New York City in 1927. General Electric's broadcasting station WGY began experiments with telecasting in 1928. RCA's National Broadcasting Company (NBC) launched its television station W2XBS in New York City in 1930 for local broadcasts on a limited basis, which led to regular programs by 1939. RCA touted its new technology at the 1939 World's Fair in New York. By 1941, six television stations—including one each for NBC and the Columbia Broadcasting System (CBS)—had received licenses from the Federal Communications Commission (FCC) to broadcast, but the development stalled because of World War II.

NBC's morning "Today" show set in 1961. "Today" popularized a TV magazine format that featured both news briefs and "magazine" variety-interview segments.

During the lull created by the war, RCA produced the image-orthicon tube, which replaced Zworykin's iconoscope in cameras. AT&T began extending the coaxial cables for transmission during the 1940s. NBC and CBS were joined by the American Broadcasting Company (ABC) in offering regular programs in 1948. By that year, the number of television broadcasting stations had expanded to 41 in 23 cities, and almost 500,000 television sets had been sold. The networks televised coverage of the 1948 presidential nominating conventions to major East Coast cities, and NBC televised the baseball World Series in 1951. However, the FCC issued a freeze on new television station licensing between 1948 and 1952, which frustrated television's further expansion. Microwave relay technology spread across the continent during the FCC freeze, allowing most areas of the country to receive broadcasts for the first time. In 1950, Eastman Kodak helped perfect the magnetic recording tape first demonstrated in 1927 by John Baird. A videotape recorder was developed the next year.

The FCC rules issued in 1952 provided for 2,000 television channels to about 1,300 cities in the nation by expanding the broadcast frequencies from VHF (very high frequency) channels 2 through 13 to UHF (ultrahigh frequency) channels 14 to 83. However, the FCC did not require television set manufacturers to provide for UHF tuning until 1964, so VHF stations held an advantage for many years. Educational broadcast stations were given 242 channels by the FCC. Color broadcasting technology also emerged in the late 1940s. The color technology developed by CBS was incompatible with the older black-and-white sets, but RCA's system was compatible; RCA got FCC approval in 1947. The Mutual Broadcasting System decided not to pursue television broadcasting; the DuMont Network, started in 1939, lacked the resources to compete with the big three and ended its effort in 1955. By 1960, 533 television stations broadcast to 55 million homes. Television advertising income surpassed the combined revenues of radio and

magazines by 1955. In 1987, 1,000 commercial and almost 300 noncommercial television stations were broadcasting to 98 percent of U.S. homes.

Television's dual purpose of entertaining and informing led to separate network production departments. Some programs such as NBC's "Today" show, started in 1952, blended news with entertainment. Edward R. Murrow's CBS program "See It Now" in 1951 showed that news could be entertaining as well. Television news broadcasts developed as slowly as radio news and consisted mostly of newsreels, which were formerly reserved for movie theaters. As mobile technology for cameras and magnetic tape for recording developed, networks could offer live coverage of news events. The networks began regular early evening newscasts in the 1940s. NBC's "Camel News Caravan" was anchored by John Cameron Swayze, and CBS's 15-minute "Evening News" was hosted by Douglas Edwards. By the 1960s, the networks produced 30-minute evening newscasts, and anchors such as David Brinkley and Chet Huntley on NBC and Murrow and Walter Cronkite on CBS became familiar to millions of Americans. Television news caused the most severe crisis ever for daily newspapers, which succumbed in droves during the 1960s.

Documentary and public affairs programs complemented the news shows. NBC's "Meet the Press" was begun in 1945 on radio in an interview format and later moved to television. Murrow's CBS program "Person to Person" featured interviews with notable celebrities. Documentaries re-creating historical events and personalities showed the positive potential of television. Network coverage of presidential nominating conventions and election campaigns expanded rapidly from 1952. Citizens depended increasingly on television as their primary source of information about public affairs. The first televised coverage of Congress came in 1951 with the Kefauver Senate committee hearings on organized crime, followed by the 1954 McCarthy hearings on purported communist infiltration of the government. Television brought the reality of national tragedy into millions of homes following the assassination of President John Kennedy in 1963. Television revealed the horrors of war in Vietnam and transmitted pictures of the first moon landing in 1969.

The entertainment side of television followed a path similar to that of the motion picture phenomenon, except that it ultimately reached a far larger audience. Network programming first featured former radio stars making the transition to television, including Milton Berle and Jack Benny, as well as former radio shows such as "Gunsmoke." Ed Sullivan's variety show on CBS was a ratings leader from the outset. Adult westerns, murder mysteries, and situation comedies became popular formats. NBC pioneered the late-night talk show "Tonight" in the mid-1950s. Daytime programs featuring game shows and soap operas developed more slowly than prime-time programming. The quiz show became enormously popular in the late 1950s with programs such as CBS's "$64,000 Question" and NBC's "Twenty-One." Perhaps the first indication of the video illusions that Muggeridge alluded to was revealed when a contestant confessed in 1957 that "Twenty-One" was rigged. Despite such setbacks, television reached 90 percent of U.S. homes in 1958, and the thirst for a greater and better variety of programs gave the network producers a welcome challenge.

The creation of satellite technology in the 1960s allowed television to show events from halfway around the globe as they occurred. Cable technology created the possibility of virtually unlimited programming choices through dozens of channels. Cable companies received transmissions from both broadcast stations and satellites and then sent them through wires into homes. Cable television offered a serious challenge to the supremacy of the three major networks, which saw their share of viewers decline for both news and entertainment programming from over 90 percent to about 60 percent. High-definition television (HDTV) and direct broadcast satellite

(DBS) reception in the 1990s promise more options for future viewers.

See also American Broadcasting Company; Columbia Broadcasting System; National Broadcasting Company.

Reference Barnouw, Erik, *Tube of Plenty: The Evolution of American Television* (1975).

Thomas, Isaiah (1749–1831)

An editor of the *Massachusetts Spy* during the colonial period, Isaiah Thomas is remembered even more for his history of early American publishing. Thomas founded the American Antiquarian Society, which houses one of the most important collections of early colonial research material.

Isaiah Thomas

Because Isaiah Thomas's father abandoned him and his mother, Thomas was apprenticed at age six to a Boston printer named Zechariah Fowle. Having no formal education, Thomas learned to spell by setting type, and he read from galley proofs to broaden his knowledge. Thomas left Fowle's employ in 1765 and traveled to Halifax, Nova Scotia, where he was soon managing the official government (and only) newspaper in Nova Scotia, the *Ga-*

zette. Thomas lost his job by protesting the recently passed Stamp Act and traveled widely over the next four years, including a tour through several southern colonies. He returned in 1770 to Fowle's printing establishment in Boston and took a wife.

Thomas and Fowle began the triweekly nonpartisan *Massachusetts Spy*, but three months later, with financial backing from John Hancock and others, Thomas purchased control of the paper. The *Spy* changed to a weekly issue, and within a few years, its circulation rose to 3,500. By this time, Thomas had become adept at weaving news events into lively commentary. He had also learned to be concise so as to attract more readers from the common social stratum. Thomas started a monthly periodical, the *Royal American Magazine*, in 1774 but gave it to another *Spy* investor and columnist, Joseph Greenleaf, after only a few issues. Paul Revere engraved some cartoons for the journal.

Following the Boston Massacre in 1770 and the loss of most Tory readers, the *Massachusetts Spy* increasingly took the patriot position in quarrels with Great Britain. Thomas used his newspaper to support the activities of the Sons of Liberty and gained a reputation as an incendiary. Using post riders, Thomas dispatched copies of the *Spy* to other cities, including New York and Baltimore. Invariably, Thomas's *Spy* ran afoul of Massachusetts Governor Thomas Hutchinson, who attempted without success to indict Thomas. Sparring with the authorities helped establish Thomas's reputation as an independent editor. Just before fighting broke out between British and colonial forces in April 1775, Thomas moved his press into the interior at Worcester so that the *Spy* could continue being distributed. It was Thomas who dispatched Paul Revere on his famous ride to warn the militia about British plans to march toward Concord. Indeed, Thomas was present at Lexington to report firsthand the "shot heard round the world" that initiated the American Revolution.

Thomas served as postmaster in Worcester and expanded his print shop to seven

presses and 150 employees. The *Spy*'s profits allowed Thomas to establish a major book publishing firm that produced 400 books dealing with farming, science, education, and the law. Thomas's publishing house produced the first American dictionary by William Perry. Thomas trained many printers, including Benjamin Russell, founder of the *Columbian Centinel*, and Thomas Greenleaf, editor of the *New York Journal*. Thomas also helped establish the *New-Hampshire Journal* (later *Farmer's Weekly Museum*) at Walpole, New Hampshire, in 1793.

After his retirement in 1802, Thomas began writing his comprehensive two-volume *The History of Printing in America, with a Biography of Printers and an Account of Newspapers*, first published at Worcester in 1810. Thomas sought to demonstrate the press's instrumental role in the early development of the United States, especially its direction of the patriot cause against Great Britain. He also founded the American Antiquarian Society at Worcester in 1812, which housed one of the most important collections of materials relating to the American Revolution. In addition to 8,000 volumes from his own collection, Thomas purchased the massive Mather family library and included it in the Antiquarian Society archive. Thomas composed the first listing of American publications from the colonial era as part of his research for *The History of Printing*.

Reference Shipton, Clifford K., *Isaiah Thomas: Printer, Patriot, and Philanthropist* (1948).

Thomas Hearings

The confirmation hearings for Supreme Court nominee Clarence Thomas before the Senate Judiciary Committee in 1991 produced a media event. The televised hearings dealt with two of the most explosive issues in the contemporary United States—race and gender. The fact that Judge Thomas was only the second black nominated to the high court was overshadowed by the sexual harassment charges of a professional colleague, Anita Hill. The hearings caused feminists to criticize the mostly male Senate for insensitivity toward women, and the event divided the black community.

Supreme Court Justice Thurgood Marshall, the first African American to serve on the high court, announced his retirement in 1991. As the search for a replacement began, a White House source told *Newsweek* that a list of several black candidates had been compiled. A few days later, President George Bush nominated a federal appeals court judge, Clarence Thomas, to succeed Marshall. The liberal *Washington Post* viewed Thomas's nomination favorably. However, Thomas's conservative ideology stirred liberal groups, including feminists and some civil rights advocates, into opposition—despite the fact that Thomas, like Marshall, was an African American. Staff members of liberal Democrats on the Judiciary Committee learned secondhand of Thomas's alleged sexual harassment of a coworker, Anita Hill, at the Equal Employment Opportunity Commission, where Thomas had been Hill's supervisor. Meanwhile, the Judiciary Committee hearings proceeded over a ten-day period, during which Judge Thomas and other witnesses testified about his qualifications. The committee vote was split evenly on whether to recommend Thomas's nomination to the full Senate (six Republicans and one Democrat voted for recommendation; seven Democrats voted against). A few days later, the Senate began debate on Thomas's confirmation.

Although Anita Hill's written allegations had been seen by members of the Judiciary Committee before their vote, the nation was unaware of them until National Public Radio and *Newsday* broke the news. The Senate vote was delayed to allow the Judiciary Committee to investigate Hill's charges, which Thomas categorically denied. A week after the news story broke, the Judiciary Committee reconvened before a live nationwide television audience. Thomas appeared first, denying the charges and claiming that he had been wrongfully defamed by Hill. Hill's testimony followed, including graphic details of Thomas's alleged sexual

misconduct. Thomas then returned to rebut the allegations again and to criticize the committee's conduct of the hearings. After three days of televised hearings, the Senate resumed deliberation and voted 52 to 48 to confirm Thomas to the Supreme Court.

The debate about the Thomas hearings did not end with his confirmation, however. In the aftermath, special-interest groups assailed one another over the issues, personalities, and nature of the charges. First, the case caused division in the black community. Both Thomas and Hill were graduates of Yale Law School. Many African Americans—including intellectuals such as economist Thomas Sowell and poet Maya Angelou—admired Thomas, who had been born into southern poverty and worked diligently to achieve a solid record of accomplishments. Some civil rights activists vilified Thomas as an "Uncle Tom" who went along to get along in the white establishment system. Some thought that Anita Hill showed jealousy and vindictiveness in trying to sabotage Thomas as a role model for blacks. Hill's defenders tried to exploit racial stereotypes about black males to cast doubts on Thomas.

A second area of conflict involved the gender issue, which created as much tension and posturing as the racial element. Feminists painted Hill as the quintessential female victim of male sexual harassment, although their primary concern was Thomas's antiabortion views. They vented anger toward the all-male Judiciary Committee. The committee's members were torn ideologically; the Democrats found themselves on the horns of a political dilemma because of intraracial and gender issues with regard to job relations, and the Republicans felt compelled to attack Hill's credibility to defend their conservative nominee.

Both the racial and the gender issues were explored and debated elaborately in the media during and after the Thomas hearings. The National Association for the Advancement of Colored People (NAACP) voted to oppose Judge Thomas's nomination; the Southern Christian Leadership

Conference and the National Urban League supported Thomas. Books published since the confirmation of Justice Thomas have focused on the veracity of Anita Hill. One major work questioned Hill's ability to be truthful, and another advanced purported corroboration of some of Hill's charges.

Reference Phelps, Timothy M., and Helen Winternitz, *Capitol Games: Clarence Thomas, Anita Hill, and the Story of a Supreme Court Nomination* (1992).

Thompson, Dorothy (1893–1961)

Dorothy Thompson was a prize-winning columnist for the *Philadelphia Public Ledger* and the *New York Post*. She served as a European correspondent for both papers during the 1920s and 1930s. Later she wrote a column on international affairs for the *New York Herald Tribune*. Her column "On the Record" was syndicated in 1936 and widely quoted. Thompson created controversy throughout much of her career and was perhaps the most written-about columnist of the twentieth century.

Dorothy Thompson was born in New York to an English Methodist preacher who had married an American woman. An avid reader with a keen memory, Dorothy was sent to a Chicago high school after her mother's death. Thompson attended Syracuse University, where she became involved in the suffragist movement. Working for a philanthropic group after graduation, Thompson sold several articles to newspapers and magazines. She decided to travel to Europe with a friend in 1920 to begin her writing career.

Thompson sold some articles about Europe to the *New York Post* and the *Christian Science Monitor*. The *Chicago Daily News*'s European bureau chief Paul Scott Mowrer suggested that Thompson go to Vienna. She persuaded the *Philadelphia Public Ledger* to make her its Austrian correspondent. Working with Marcel Fodor of the *Manchester Guardian*, Thompson covered the opera and interviewed a Habsburg prince, Sigmund Freud, and the president of Czechoslovakia. She was transferred to Berlin in 1922 to cover the horrendous inflation

in Germany, and by 1925, she represented the *New York Post* as well as the *Public Ledger*.

In 1927, Thompson traveled to the Soviet Union to report activities on the tenth anniversary of the Bolshevik Revolution. She wrote a series of articles for the *New York Post*, later published in book form as *The New Russia* (1928). Dorothy Thompson met novelist Sinclair Lewis in 1927; the two married (the second for both) the next year in London and returned to a Vermont home. After giving birth to a son in 1930, Thompson returned to Europe with Lewis, where she resumed writing for the *Saturday Evening Post*. Thompson turned down an offer from Oswald Villard to be managing editor of *The Nation* in order to remain in Europe. During 1931, Thompson interviewed Adolf Hitler for *Cosmopolitan* magazine and later published a book based on the encounter, *I Saw Hitler*. After the Nazis gained power in 1933, her critical pieces caused Thompson to be expelled from Germany in 1934.

Upon returning to the United States, Thompson interviewed Louisiana's controversial Huey Long and future Republican presidential nominee Alfred Landon. Thompson signed an agreement in 1936 to write a column of political commentary, "On the Record," for the *New York Herald Tribune*. Her column would appear three times a week, alternating with one by Walter Lippmann. Thompson's self-described philosophy of "liberal conservatism" led her to critique the New Deal economic policies and endorse Republican Landon in the 1936 election. After one year, Thompson's column appeared in 130 dailies, leading to another monthly column for *Ladies' Home Journal* beginning in 1937. Entitled *Let the Record Speak*, a collection of her *Herald Tribune* columns was published in 1939. Dorothy Thompson also added another audience when she became a regular on the General Electric radio program on Mondays. Thompson was awarded an honorary degree from her alma mater Syracuse University in 1937, the same year that her marriage to Lewis ended.

Dorothy Thompson could not keep her

attention away from events in Europe. She wrote a stirring article in *Foreign Affairs* in 1938 calling for international assistance to the victims of Nazi repression. After covering the presidential nominating conventions of 1940 and endorsing Roosevelt's bid for a third term, Thompson lost her position with the *Herald Tribune* in 1941. Her syndicated column was taken up by the Bell Syndicate, and Thompson returned to the *New York Post*. She also wrote columns for the *Chronicle* (London) during trips to Europe in 1940 and again in 1941 to observe firsthand the course of the war. Thompson delivered shortwave broadcasts in German in 1942 for CBS, encouraging the resistance inside the Third Reich.

After World War II, Thompson's expressions of sympathy for non-Nazi Germans, her attacks on Zionists, and her opposition to the Nuremberg war crimes trials led the *New York Post* to cancel her column in 1947. Thompson's anti-Zionism led her to question the creation of a Jewish religious state, Israel. She became president of the American Friends of the Middle East, a pro-Arab group, in 1956. Her position caused many papers to drop her syndicated column, which was finally ended by Bell in 1958. Her nonpolitical articles in *Ladies' Home Journal* continued to appear and were collectively published by Houghton Mifflin in 1957, entitled *The Courage To Be Happy*.

Reference Sanders, Marion K., *Dorothy Thompson: A Legend in Her Time* (1973).

Time

Founded by Henry Luce as a weekly newsmagazine in 1923, *Time* quickly became the benchmark for a new genre of periodicals. The purpose of *Time* was to organize the presentation of the news in categories and provide accurate but concise summaries for readers to assimilate. *Time* pioneered what today is known as "interpretive reporting." Despite its commitment to covering the news, *Time*, like other newsmagazines, found that sensational stories sell best. By 1987, *Time*'s advertising revenues were the second highest in the industry, and its circu-

lation was the twelfth highest nationally.

When Henry R. Luce and partner Briton Hadden conceived of *Time* in 1923, they were concerned about the diffuse nature of news coverage by the current media, especially the superficial international coverage. They also recognized that most readers with a desire to be informed—especially college graduates and professionals—had precious little time to spend acquiring such information. *Time* would contain concise summaries, print only necessary information, and explain events for readers. The struggle to make the new magazine successful was a difficult one, from the 28-page inaugural issue in 1923. One problem was that Hadden and Luce often alienated potential advertisers with their brash accounts of business activities. It took five years for *Time*, with Hadden as editor and Luce as business manager, to make a profit. Circulation rose over the first five years from 9,000 to 200,000 by 1928; thereafter, *Time* was a fixture on the U.S. media scene.

Time stories characteristically provided historical background to the current events it covered. The editors also coalesced the work of several reporters to produce a story. Such collective efforts required patient organization, but *Time* showed pride in its group writing. *Time* also boldly expressed an opinion about the stories it included so that readers could not mistake the magazine's editorial positions. *Time*'s novel approach required a large staff of editors, reporters, and researchers, although all articles were unsigned. Eventually, the cover of the magazine was used to introduce the lead story, which was often thematic. "*Time*-style" described the magazine's often eccentric use of words, phrases, and stylistic techniques. Many of the terms used by *Time* have become familiar words in the American vocabulary: tycoon (from a Japanese word), pundit (from the Hindu), and kudos (from the Greek).

One of *Time*'s most noteworthy innovations was the "Man of the Year" feature, started in 1927. A full portrait on the cover honored the individual selected. The first recipient was Charles Lindbergh; others included Franklin D. Roosevelt, Mohandas Gandhi, Chiang Kai-shek, Adolph Hitler, Joseph Stalin, Winston Churchill, Dwight Eisenhower, Charles de Gaulle, Martin Luther King, and Nikita Khrushchev. Indeed, *Time* focused on the role of personality in the news throughout its history.

By the 1930s, *Time* began to rely on its own correspondents and bureaus to collect the news. It also developed regular departments such as national affairs, with subheadings on the presidency, cabinet, Congress, and politics. The second most popular department was foreign news, followed by books. Other departments included art, theater, music, education, religion, medicine, law, and finance. *Time*'s iconoclasm in its use of language soon spread to other media. Certainly, competing newsmagazines openly copied *Time*'s techniques, proving that imitation is the sincerest form of flattery. *Time*'s success also enabled it to purchase a major competitor in 1938, the *Literary Digest*. *Time*'s profits allowed Luce to pursue other interests during the 1930s—*Fortune* and *Life*. Hadden's death in 1929 was a great loss to the editorial leadership, but once the techniques had been established, it was easy to find editors to continue them, especially since Luce retained oversight as editor in chief.

Time sent its first foreign correspondents overseas to cover World War II in 1941 and published its first foreign edition (Latin America) the same year. Soon, five international editions were being published. Circulation grew by 86 percent during the 1940s (1 million in 1942), due in large part to extensive coverage of the war. Net income grew from $2.7 million in 1936 to $9.3 million in 1960. By the 1960s, *Time* published nine regional editions supported by 12 domestic bureaus in order to facilitate local advertisers. *Time* also had four bureaus in Canada and 14 other foreign bureaus. Signed essays by writers such as Charles Krauthammer marked a departure from the traditional anonymous entries in *Time*. A profitable book-publishing division, Time-Life, was launched in 1961.

When managing editor Otto Fuerbinger ordered that an article be written criticizing the press corps covering the Vietnam War in the 1960s, *Time* reporters Charles Mohr and Mert Perry resigned in protest. After Henry Luce's death in 1967, many of his prejudices, such as a staunch U.S. nationalism and political conservatism, were modified. New publisher Hedley Donovan changed *Time*'s editorial support of the Johnson administration and criticized Vietnam policies, to the great displeasure of the president.

Time's reputation for accuracy has been tainted since Luce's death. A jury awarded the wife of Russell Firestone III $100,000 in a 1976 libel suit for incorrect reporting about a divorce. Although *Time* was absolved of guilt in a case brought by Israeli politician Ariel Sharon in 1986, the jury chastened the magazine for its sloppy research. Already noted for its "Letters" department, which sometimes included retractions or corrections by the editors, *Time* later admitted its errors in the Sharon articles.

Despite the damage done by such reporting errors, a Gallup survey for the Times Mirror Company in the mid-1980s ranked *Time* fifth among media institutions for believability. Such public opinions were reflected in 1987 statistics that showed *Time* still leading in weekly newsmagazine circulation with over 4.6 million, including subscriptions and single-copy sales, which produced $612 million in revenue. *Time* published 37 editions in Europe alone, where circulation totaled 400,000. Altogether, over 1.5 million copies of *Time* were sold abroad. *Time* has been able to hold its niche in a category of publications that is sorely tested by television competition.

See also Luce, Henry Robinson.

Reference Elson, Robert T., *Time, Inc.* (1968–1973).

TV Guide

Taking advantage of the burgeoning television audiences of the 1950s, Walter Annenberg launched the weekly *TV Guide* in 1953. *TV Guide* passed the 1 million mark in circulation its first year and has become the largest domestic circulation magazine in the United States. In 1988, *TV Guide* was sold to Rupert Murdoch in a blockbuster deal. In recent years, it has been forced to make adjustments brought about by the growth of cable television.

Walter Annenberg was heir of the profitable publishing enterprise Triangle Publications, begun by his father, Moses. Annenberg recognized reader demand for printed television schedules and became curious about the circulation success of a Philadelphia weekly called *TV Digest*. He soon envisioned a similar magazine on a national scale. Annenberg obtained information about a similar magazine, *TV Guide*, published locally in New York City since 1948 by Lee Wagner. During 1952, Triangle Publications methodically purchased the major metropolitan television publications: *TV Guide* in New York City, *TV Digest* in Philadelphia, and *TV Forecast* in Chicago. Annenberg assigned former television station manager Roger Clipp to head *TV Guide*'s operations because of his connections among broadcasters. Other production executives were borrowed from the family's *Philadelphia Inquirer*.

The first issue of *TV Guide* appeared in April 1953 in ten metropolitan markets. Its sales reached 1.5 million at the end of the first year, although advertising did not keep pace at first. Annenberg's plan for the magazine was simple, but it took intuitive genius to recognize the idea's potential. Critics did not believe that a magazine could be both local and national. The Hearst chain launched an imitator, *TV Week*, in 1955, but it lasted only a few issues. Soon published in dozens of local editions, *TV Guide* doubled its circulation in the 1960s, reaching 14 million in 1968. Such rapid growth was unprecedented for the post–World War II era. Publishing operations were moved from Triangle's Philadelphia headquarters to nearby Radnor, Pennsylvania, in 1957.

In addition to weekly network and local television schedules, the magazine featured articles on television programs and personalities. Movie critic Judith Crist offered reviews of television movies, and Cleveland Amory examined the quality of network programs. *TV Guide* shied away from serious examinations of the internal machinations in the television industry, however. *TV Guide* writers were held to a strict ethics code that forbade accepting gratuities from television companies.

By the 1960s, when *TV Guide*'s influence could not be ignored by either advertisers or television executives and stars, the magazine began publishing more serious articles and recruited notable authors such as Arthur Miller and Alistair Cooke. Some *TV Guide* staffers such as Edith Efron eventually made reputations for themselves as media critics. During the 1970s, *TV Guide*'s circulation surpassed magazine industry leader *Reader's Digest* to garner first place in the nation. By the late 1980s, circulation totaled 17 million, almost half of which was from single-copy newsstand sales. Advertising revenues of $331 million also led the magazine industry. In 1988, Triangle Publications, which included *TV Guide* and *Seventeen* magazine, was purchased by media mogul Rupert Murdoch's News Corporation for $3 billion in the nation's largest media deal ever.

Reference Cooney, John, *The Annenbergs* (1982).

United Press

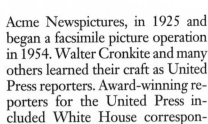

The Scripps-Howard Company began the United Press Associations in 1907 as a rival to the powerful Associated Press. United Press grew to become a major force in news gathering before its decline and merger with International News Service in 1958 to form United Press International.

Because of the Associated Press's closed membership policy, several chain newspaper owners operating in different markets decided to launch a press association of their own. The original United Press founded in 1882 by publishers in Boston, Philadelphia, Chicago, Detroit, and New York City never fully developed. Associated Press secretly agreed in 1885 to share news accounts, so United Press was not truly independent. United Press folded in 1897 during a time of transition for Associated Press. When some publishers such as Edward W. Scripps were denied contracts with the new Associated Press, they decided to establish their own news service.

Between 1897 and 1907, Scripps ran regional news services in the Midwest and West. In 1907, he merged his own services with an independent eastern service to form the United Press Associations, which had over 300 afternoon papers as subscribers. Roy W. Howard, a veteran editor on several Scripps papers, became the head of United Press in 1908. Howard immediately established bureaus in Europe and negotiated cooperative agreements with major European papers not affiliated with Associated Press. During World War I, United Press established several South American bureaus because Associated Press was absent from the region. Howard permitted United Press reporters to write interpretive essays, and some, such as Westbrook Pegler, became widely read columnists after the war.

By 1920, when Howard left United Press, the service had 780 subscribers and showed profits of $200,000. United Press was the first news service to provide news to radio stations in the 1920s and to television stations beginning in 1951. United Press started its own photographic news service, Acme Newspictures, in 1925 and began a facsimile picture operation in 1954. Walter Cronkite and many others learned their craft as United Press reporters. Award-winning reporters for the United Press included White House correspondents Merriman Smith and Helen Thomas, Vietnam War reporter Neil Sheehan, and foreign news editor Harrison Salisbury. Six United Press reporters and photographers have won Pulitzer Prizes. A 1945 Supreme Court decision ended Associated Press's exclusionary policy and allowed many papers to subscribe to both Associated Press and United Press, but the decision also required expensive outlays for United Press to cover state and local news.

In 1958, the merger of United Press Associations (95 percent of stock) and the Hearst International News Service (founded in 1909) produced United Press International (UPI), Associated Press's only serious remaining rival. The last year UPI showed a profit was 1961. By the 1970s, only about one-fourth of the daily newspapers subscribed to UPI alone, compared with just under half that subscribed only to Associated Press. Chain-owned newspapers especially viewed two wire service subscriptions as too expensive. Moreover, several major conglomerates launched bargain press services, which placed UPI at a further disadvantage. However, UPI had slightly more radio and television subscribers than Associated Press.

In 1982, the Scripps Company sold UPI with its 800 daily newspaper subscribers to Nashville television partners Douglas Ruhe and William Geissler. The new owners' lack of experience led to ill-conceived proj-ects such as a polling service, which drove the company deeper into debt. The owners' quarrels with president Louis Nogales and management over policy and financing resulted in UPI staffers absorbing a 25 percent wage cut in 1984 to keep the company solvent. By 1985, UPI's primary creditor threatened to withdraw support unless Ruhe and Geissler yielded control to Nogales. The owners refused, resulting in

Chapter 11 bankruptcy and a forced sale of UPI in 1986. The purchaser, Mexican media mogul Mario Vazquez-Rana, began major staff reductions and administrative shake-ups. At the time of the sale, UPI had 2,800 radio and television and 550 newspaper subscribers. The losses—more than $12 million a year by 1988—continued under Vazquez until he sold UPI to Earl Brian's cable television Financial News Network in 1988 for $55 million. UPI was but a shadow of its former self, facing an uncertain future, yet still operating in 1994.

References Gordon, Gregory, and Ronald E. Cohen, *Down to the Wire: UPI's Fight for Survival* (1990); Morris, Joe Alex, *Deadline Every Minute: The Story of the United Press* (1957).

U.S. News & World Report

From the *United States Daily* (1926), the weekly *U.S. News* (1933), and the *World Report* (1946), David Lawrence produced the third national newsmagazine after *Time* and *Newsweek*. Lawrence's product included distinctions that have kept *U.S. News & World Report* in a competitive albeit third-place position throughout the century. Mortimer Zuckerman revived the weekly after his purchase of it in 1984.

David Lawrence gained his first journalism experience by working for Associated Press while he was a student at Princeton. After graduation, he became Associated Press's Washington correspondent and had frequent access to President Woodrow Wilson. In 1916, he took a position with the *New York Post*, where he started a syndicated column based in Washington. Lawrence covered the Paris peace conference in 1919 for the *Post*. He launched the *United States Daily* in Washington in 1926 with the determination to publish complete and unbiased accounts of government affairs in the nation's capital. A forerunner of the *Federal Register* (1935), the newspaper printed texts of federal government documents, policies and programs, and federal court decisions. Because the *United States Daily* was mostly a compendium of dry facts, it never attracted a large readership.

Lawrence decided to transform his newspaper into a weekly newsmagazine in 1933. *U.S. News* was born at the same time as another newsmagazine, *Newsweek*, which imitated the successful *Time*. Lawrence wanted to report, analyze, and even predict news events, but the magazine did not include extraneous material such as the fine arts found in *Time* and *Newsweek*. *U.S. News* trailed its rivals in circulation throughout the 1930s and early 1940s. After World War II, Lawrence decided to expand coverage to world affairs and started *World Report* in 1946. Two years later, the national and international magazines were merged to become *U.S. News & World Report*.

The format for *U.S. News & World Report* did not include front-page photographs like *Time* and *Newsweek* but had a listing of contents within. The journal continued to quote extensively from official documents, speeches, and so forth, but it also included unsigned analytical pieces. News categories included national and international summaries, people making news, capital gossip, labor, and financial news. The sparse photographs normally appeared in black and white. The editorial tone remained conservative under Lawrence. *U.S. News & World Report* stood for law and order and against social permissiveness; it was mindful of government waste and the threat of inflation.

During the 1950s, in an era of rapid growth of magazine readership nationally, *U.S. News & World Report* grew at a greater rate than its two more successful competitors. Circulation reached 1.2 million by the early 1960s and added another 500,000 readers over the next decade. After the death of founder David Lawrence in 1973, the magazine seemed to languish without direction for the next decade. In 1984, former real estate tycoon Mortimer Zuckerman entered the media industry by purchasing the employee-owned *U.S. News & World Report* for more than $160 million; he also bought the monthly *Atlantic* at the same time.

Although Zuckerman wanted to make *U.S. News & World Report* distinct from its competition, he did not change its original mission to be a specialized source of information and sophisticated comment on the news. The journal increased its circulation above the 2 million mark and ranked fifteenth in magazine advertising revenues within a few years under Zuckerman. Former Reagan White House communications director David Gergen and former *Time* writer Roger Rosenblatt became editors. Experienced advertising and marketing executives began to target number-two *Newsweek* as vulnerable to *U.S. News* sales and ad enhancement. *U.S. News* gained new respectability for accuracy, in-depth reporting, and analyses. The covers were redesigned and more color added, along with new departments oriented toward con-sumer needs. *U.S. News* remained aggressive in covering foreign events and even had to defend one of its reporters who was unfairly accused of espionage by the Soviet Union in 1986. Translated editions of *U.S. News & World Report* began to be distributed to 18 foreign countries in 1986. In 1988, *U.S. News* circulation totaled 2.3 million, compared with *Time*'s 4.6 million and *Newsweek*'s 3.3 million. Its advertising revenue of $106 million was less than half of *Newsweek*'s and only one-third of *Time*'s.

USA Today
See Gannett Company.

Videocassette Recorders (VCRs)

With the invention of magnetic videotaping in the 1950s, television news gathering became portable. The development of commercially formatted videocassette recorders (VCRs) in the 1960s allowed individuals to tape-record programs from television broadcasts as well as play back prerecorded cassettes for purposes of entertainment, business, or education.

Early in the television era, engineers attempted to create a system for recording televised images on magnetic recording tape that could then be replayed. The technology of video recording was similar to audio recording, but a television picture contained a much greater volume of electronic data than audio, so the tape had to move more rapidly. Another early problem was that recording heads tended to break down after a short time because of extensive friction generated by the tape. The larger electronic companies such as Radio Corporation of America (RCA) experimented with a video recorder, but it was the small Ampex Corporation that perfected the system in 1956. Ampex demonstrated its system at the Columbia Broadcasting System (CBS) television affiliates' meeting in Chicago. The Ampex system recorded on the tape vertically rather than horizontally, so the amount of tape required was comparable to that for a 16-mm film. RCA produced its version of the videotape recorder in 1957, which allowed color reproduction.

The original Ampex recording machine was very heavy and bulky—about the size of a refrigerator. However, thanks to the emerging technology of transistors and semiconductors, the size of the tape hardware was gradually reduced over the next decade. Machtronics electronic company produced a portable videotape camera utilizing three-quarter-inch tape in 1962. By the 1960s, television networks and stations were using videotape instead of film on a regular basis to record news events and play them back within hours on broadcasts.

The development of home recorders occurred in the mid-1970s. The Japanese Sony Corporation produced its Betamax system using a one-inch tape in a cassette in 1969. Shortly thereafter, U.S. manufacturers utilized a three-quarter-inch tape known as VHS for their machines and cassettes. Despite the quality of Japanese electronics, Americans opted overwhelmingly for the VHS over the Betamax system, in part because it was more compact. The commercial VCRs could be programmed to record programs at any time even if the television set was not playing. VCRs have a variety of features such as freeze-frame and slow motion, which make them even more useful for educational purposes. The prerecorded videotape rental industry mushroomed in the 1980s, with some companies such as Blockbuster becoming national in reach. Customers could also purchase cassette movies for their personal libraries. By 1988, customers spent more money ($4.5 billion) renting home videos than they paid to attend movie theaters. Another popular use of VCRs was to produce home recordings with a video camera. Advertisers have begun to offer videocassettes to potential customers as a marketing tool. They also attach commercials to the rented video movies.

Some legal questions invariably arose about the use of taped programs. Sony claimed that under the "fair use" provisions of the 1976 Copyright Act, private users could not profit from the recording of commercial products. The federal courts agreed that "fair use" included personal use of recorded programs in the home short of resale for profit. However, permission (and thereby payment of fees) must be obtained to use recorded material in classrooms, for example.

See also Television.

Reference Levy, Mark R., *The VCR Age: Home Video and Mass Communication* (1989).

Vietnam War

The war in Vietnam during the 1960s and 1970s broke the tradition of generally cooperative media-government relations in

A couple watch as the television brings the Vietnam War closer to home. For the first time in American history, television displaces newspapers as the primary source of news for most Americans.

previous wars. The reasons for the shift were varied: the absence of traditional censorship, the muddled political objectives and related military directives, and the role of television. Conflict began at the outset between the reporters on the scene and the civilian and military authorities. Media executives in the United States tended to be on friendly terms with Presidents Kennedy and Johnson, so critical reporting was muted and limited until 1968, when media moguls shifted from supporting the war to questioning the purpose and conduct of the conflict. The clash between the government and the *New York Times* in 1971 over the

publication of the Pentagon Papers epitomized the tense relations between media and government. Whatever the intentions of the media, the conflict demonstrated how potently the media influenced public opinion.

Because the Vietnam War occurred in a distant, unrecognizable political geography to most Americans, young reporters who ventured to the war zone initially relied on maps to explain their stories. Unlike reporters in the Korean War who had also covered World War II, almost none of the Vietnam-era reporters were experienced war correspondents. The print media dominated early coverage of the Vietnamese insurrection during the Kennedy administration. The American people had been committed to the containment of communism since the beginning of the Cold War, but readers had difficulty following the relationships in Southeast Asia, especially because of the dramatic social and political differences compared with Western culture. Prior to the landing of U.S. ground troops in 1965, there were only five U.S. media organizations covering the Vietnam War directly: Associated Press, United Press International, the *New York Times*, *Time*, and *Newsweek*. From 1961 to 1963, reporters noted the frustration of the American officers who were trying to train the South Vietnamese military, as well as the political corruption in the South Vietnamese government. Yet the government attempted to convince the reporters that political and military progress was being made. Tensions began in 1963 when President Kennedy pressured the *New York Times* (which had approved his policy) to remove its Saigon correspondent David Halberstam, who had been accused of obstructing U.S. policy. Even veteran journalists such as Joseph Alsop and Marguerite Higgins, along with *Time* magazine editors, believed that reporters were trying to undermine U.S. credibility.

The presidents during the Vietnam era were obviously uncomfortable with the notion of explaining their policies to the public, since they themselves did not fully understand the nature of the conflict. Although the Johnson administration consistently blamed the communist Chinese as the force behind the aggression in South Vietnam, the actual external factor was the Soviet Union rather than China. Moreover, North Vietnamese leader Ho Chi Minh's motives were confusing because of his anticolonial nationalism mingling with Soviet-taught revolutionary communism.

Despite assiduous efforts by the Johnson administration to convince the media that U.S. policy was both appropriate and successful, doubts began to multiply in press reports. *New York Times* columnists James Reston, Max Frankel, and Tom Wicker be-

gan questioning the need for further escalation in 1965. *Times* editor Harrison Salisbury traveled to Vietnam in 1966 and reported that U.S. bombing damaged civilian centers as well as military targets. In 1967, both *Time* and *Life*, directed by Hedley Donovan, questioned the importance of U.S. involvement in Vietnam. Editorials in Knight-Ridder newspapers warned Johnson about further escalations of the war in 1967.

It was during the Vietnam era that television displaced newspapers as the primary source of news for most Americans, and polls showed that CBS news anchor Walter Cronkite was "the most trusted man in America." The television networks had already begun to give Americans a nightly dose of the horrors of the war—from reporters such as CBS's Morley Safer—when the North Vietnamese Tet offensive began in February 1968. At that point, the tide had turned against the Johnson administration, despite the defeat of the North Vietnamese incursion. Network news anchors such as Cronkite, broadcasting from Saigon, cited the difficulty and complexity of the military strategy. Johnson was successfully challenged for the presidential nomination by Senator Eugene McCarthy of Minnesota in the New Hampshire primary. The president withdrew from the nomination process and announced a restriction on the bombing in North Vietnam.

The Vietnam War had a direct bearing on the presidential election of 1968, especially after police and antiwar demonstrators clashed violently before television cameras at the Democratic convention in Chicago. During President Richard Nixon's "Vietnamization" process of gradual U.S. withdrawal, the press coverage slackened somewhat but occasionally revived, such as after the bombing of Cambodia in 1969 and 1970. Antiwar activity continued to plague the Nixon administration, including the publication of the so-called Pentagon Papers in 1971 by the *New York Times*, *Washington Post*, and *St. Louis Post-Dispatch*. The Justice Department attempted to use prior restraint to stop the publication, but the courts found that U.S.

security would not be compromised and allowed the publication to go forward.

There was less censorship of the press by the military during the Vietnam War than during any other twentieth-century conflict. However, the press had to deal with frequent restrictions applied by the South Vietnamese government. The military did censor its newspaper *Stars and Stripes* and the Armed Forces Radio Network, mostly involving stories that would have embarrassed the South Vietnamese government or military.

Many journalists won awards for covering the Vietnam War. Halberstam and Associated Press's Malcolm Browne were awarded Pulitzer Prizes in 1964, and Associated Press reporter Peter Arnett won in 1966. Freelance reporter Seymour Hirsch uncovered the facts behind the civilian My Lai massacre in 1969, which won him a Pulitzer Prize in 1970. William Tuohy won a Pulitzer for reports on the war for the *Los Angeles Times* in 1969. Photographers who won Pulitzers included Host Faas (1965) and Edward Adams (1969) of Associated Press and Kyoichi Sawada (1966) and Toshio Sakai (1968) of United Press International. The *Akron Beacon Journal* received a 1971 Pulitzer for covering the shooting of students at Kent State University by National Guardsmen during an antiwar demonstration. Eight journalists were killed covering the Vietnam War.

Reference Hallin, Daniel C., The *"Uncensored War": The Media and Vietnam* (1986).

Virtual Reality

Virtual reality is a three-dimensional simulation created by computers; it is used to allow the semblance of user interaction in present time. Virtual reality is also referred to by the terms "total immersion environment," "cyberspace," or "artificial reality." The interactive nature of virtual reality allows the user to make choices and change directions without regard to predetermined patterns. The removal of the user from the existing environment into the virtual reality is accomplished by a head-mounted display mechanism that appears to be bulky gog-

gles. In a sense, computers simply enhance humans' historical desire to let their imaginations run free.

Artist-scientist Myron Krueger coined the term "virtual reality" in 1974 and is considered by most to be the founder of the technology. With National Endowment for the Arts funding in 1976, Krueger designed VIDEOPLACE at the Milwaukee Art Museum as part of the Bicentennial celebration. As a person entered VIDEOPLACE, his or her life-sized silhouette was projected on a screen and introduced to a simulated creature that could be engaged in some form of interaction. Krueger believed that simulated play environments even for adults would produce interesting educational feedback.

An early explorer of virtual reality, Jaron Lanier, suggested that virtual reality was effectively the culmination of culture. In other words, the world of imagination has been part of human development since the beginning of history. Simulation of reality had existed before virtual reality arrived, in the form of arcade games and airplane flight simulators. Computer applications increased the speed and environmental duplications of previous simulations. Flight and automobile simulators using purely mechanical devices provided the framework for later computer applications. Three-dimensional computer systems were initially used by automobile manufacturing engineers to create vehicle simulations for design purposes. Architects used the systems to explore possible building designs. Medical uses of x-rays and lasers can create three-dimensional simulations for examining human anatomy.

The prospects of using virtual reality for more than just whimsical explorations are numerous. The Oz Project at Carnegie-Mellon University used a text-based narrative environment to teach literary forms. Filmmaker George Lucas of the *Star Wars* saga established Habitat as a virtual world entertainment laboratory for application in films. Scientific and educational applications have been numerous, including ExploreNet, which was used in elementary schools. It

This unidentified man tries out virtual reality at a 1993 convention. By wearing a pair of 3-D glasses and manipulating a joystick, the user can explore numerous simulated environments.

offered students a three-dimensional simulated world of caves, jungles, deserts, rivers, and mountains with which they interacted. College-level students may utilize a historical model such as Leonardo da Vinci's flying machine to imagine how it would have actually worked. Virtual reality models can even include musical instruments. Virtual reality allows engineering, molecular, and architectural design modeling that goes beyond the two-dimensional computer-aided design (CAD). Teleconferencing enables engineers to work together to develop design possibilities from different locales—an extension of video conferencing.

Of course, Hollywood was among the first to recognize the potential of virtual reality for its motion pictures. In films such as *Terminator 2* and *Lawnmower Man,* virtual realities became the central attraction of the film, almost obscuring plots and characters. It was natural for Hollywood to offer simplistic solutions to a complicated world by allowing cyborgs in cyberspace the opportunity to fix society's ills, since human beings are deemed incapable of overcoming evil.

See also Computers.

Reference Loeffler, Carl E., and Tim Anderson, eds., *The Virtual Reality Casebook* (1994).

Wall Street Journal

The *Wall Street Journal* began as a local specialized financial sheet in the 1880s in New York City. A century later, it retained its financial bent but expanded to general national news and reached an international as well as national reading audience. Today, it is the largest-circulation daily newspaper published in the United States.

After learning the financial news business with the Kiernan News Agency, Charles Henry Dow, Edward Davis Jones, and Charles Bergstresser decided to form their own financial agency, Dow, Jones and Company, in 1882. The firm was committed to providing current financial news to customers on Wall Street. Jones gathered street gossip at a local hotel catering to brokers, Bergstresser collected news accounts from domestic papers and the London financial markets, and Dow analyzed companies and industries. A year after the company was formed, it issued an afternoon newsletter to its clients that was soon breaking important stories about major companies' fortunes.

The afternoon newsletter was transformed into the *Wall Street Journal* in 1889; it was a four-page, six-day-a-week paper costing two cents a copy. The first issue featured a story on the price averages of 12 key stocks over the previous five years. Charles Dow had introduced his stock averages in the 1884 newsletter and expanded them to 30 by 1887. The *Journal* stationed correspondents in Boston, Philadelphia, and Chicago and received reports from London as well. The major advertisers in the *Journal* were New York banks and brokerage firms. In short, except for the absence of editorials, the basic ingredients that have made the *Journal* so distinctive and widely known were there from the outset.

Soon after the passage of the Sherman Silver Purchase Act in 1890, the *Journal* began to take editorial positions opposing the legislation because of its effect on the gold reserve. The *Journal* proudly announced the repeal of the measure after the Panic of 1893 proved its disastrous consequences. In 1897, Dow, Jones and Company installed its first telegraph ticker service for customers, which was sold in a package with the *Journal*. A morning edition of the paper began in 1898, just before Edward Jones announced his retirement and withdrawal from the company in January 1899. Charles Dow died at the end of 1902. By that time, the *Journal*'s price had increased to three cents, the size was up to eight pages, and the advertising became more diverse.

Just before Dow's death in 1902, the company was sold to Clarence W. Barron, who published a Boston newsletter and the *Philadelphia Financial Journal*. Barron's wife, Jessie, actually took direct charge of the *Wall Street Journal*'s management while her husband remained in Boston. The daily circulation remained modest at about 12,000 under the Barrons. The paper was a strong editorial supporter of Theodore Roosevelt's antitrust reforms even during the Panic of 1907. In the aftermath, the *Journal* called for a revived central banking system. When the paper's circulation declined to 7,500 in 1912, Clarence Barron moved from Boston to New York City to assume direct control of the *Journal*.

Barron backed the Federal Reserve Act of 1913 and showed keen insight into future economic issues, including inflation, energy, agriculture, and the role of the automobile. He spent much time in Europe during World War I, reporting news directly from the scene. In 1921, Barron launched a weekly financial paper, *Barron's*, published on Mondays and promoted in the *Wall Street Journal*. Meanwhile, the *Journal* prospered with new advertisers led by automobile manufacturers, and circulation grew to over 22,000 by 1924. Barron increasingly spent time in Florida following the land boom and allowed editor K. C. Hogate to establish editorial policy independent of any Wall Street influences.

At the death of Clarence Barron in 1928, Hugh Bancroft became president of Dow, Jones and Company and promised to continue to let editor Hogate have a free hand at the *Journal.* In December 1928, the *Journal* issued a warning about the stock market frenzy and continued urging an end to speculative stock buying and selling. The *Journal* began publishing a West Coast edition a week before the stock market crash of October 1929. Surprisingly, during the early depression, the *Journal*'s circulation actually increased—to 52,000 by 1930. Its physical plant was expanded, and Dow, Jones and Company stock paid handsome dividends in 1929 and 1930. By 1932, however, circulation had been cut in half, and advertising suffered as well.

In 1933, company president Bancroft died and editor Hogate succeeded to the position. Hogate modernized the company's telegraph ticker services, made William Grimes managing editor, sent chief writer Bernard Kilgore to head the Washington bureau, and recruited new correspondents. The *Journal* remained skeptical and critical of New Deal programs. By 1938, the financial fortunes of the paper began a slow revival from a circulation low of 28,000. In 1941, when circulation rose to 32,000, Grimes took over the editorial page and Kilgore returned from Washington to be managing editor. Kilgore organized the front page into various categories of business news with a brief summary of key points. Circulation continued to grow from 35,000 in 1942 to 64,000 in 1946, above the predepression high. The West Coast edition brought in 11,000 subscribers.

Meanwhile, Kilgore had become general manager of the firm and, upon Hogate's death in 1947, became president. Grimes's editorials won the *Journal* its first Pulitzer Prize in 1947, and circulation reached 76,000. A Dallas edition joined the New York and California editions in 1947. When the *Journal* purchased the *Journal of Commerce* in 1950, Chicago became the fourth location for its publication. Total circulation grew from 130,000 in 1948 to 148,000 by 1950. Technological advancements paved the way for more efficiency. J. J. Ackell's electronic typesetter, perfected in 1954, enabled stock quotations and editorials to be set at all four printing sites simultaneously.

Warren Phillips became managing editor in 1957, and Vermont Royster succeeded Grimes as editor in 1958. Circulation exploded past 784,000 in 1961, and the nation's media recognized the *Wall Street Journal* as the only national newspaper. Dow, Jones and Company moved into the new Wall Street Journal Building, a 47-story structure, in 1965. Bernard Kilgore stepped down in 1966 as chief officer and was replaced by William F. Kerby. Under Kilgore's management, Dow, Jones and Company earnings grew from $211,000 in 1945 to over $13 million in 1966. Dow, Jones and Company negotiated an agreement with Associated Press to report foreign financial news in 1968, beginning with seven nations.

Robert Bartley became editor of the *Journal* and Warren Phillips was elected president of the company in 1972. The new management began an Asian edition of the *Journal* from Hong Kong in 1976. The *Wall Street Journal*'s circulation passed that of the *New York Daily News* to become the nation's largest daily—with 1,768,000 readers—in 1979. The *Journal* launched a cable television news program in 1981 on the USA network. *Journal* circulation passed the 1.9 million mark in 1992.

Reference Wendt, Lloyd, *The* Wall Street Journal (1982).

Walters, Barbara (1929–)

Perhaps no other woman has had a greater impact on commercial broadcasting than Barbara Walters. Although she may appear to be merely a television celebrity, Walters demonstrated skill as an interviewer and journalist for the NBC and ABC networks. Undoubtedly, her success paved the way for other women journalists to reach the top levels of the industry.

Barbara Walters was born in Boston to Louis Edward Walters, an English-born vaudeville agent and later nightclub operator, and Dena Seletsky, daughter of Russian Jewish immigrants. Walters's relationship with her parents was affected by the death of their firstborn, a son who died of pneumonia when he was less than two years old, and the birth of another daughter who was retarded and received undue attention from the parents. Walters was educated at private preparatory schools in New York City as well as at a Miami Beach, Florida, public school. She matriculated in 1947 at Sarah Lawrence, an elite women's college outside New York City. Walters's notion of becoming an actress was not advanced by her few uninspiring parts in college plays. She was unaffected by campus controversies, including an investigation of communist influence at Sarah Lawrence by the House Un-American Activities Committee and a scathing satire of the school by novelist Mary McCarthy. In fact, Walters's political naivete showed in her friendship with Roy Cohn, chief counsel for the infamous communist hunter Senator Joseph McCarthy.

After graduation from Sarah Lawrence, Walters obtained a promotional position with NBC-owned television station WBNT. In her first exclusive interview, Walters talked with a union official about New York City's taxi strike. Within a year she was producing a local children's program, which led to a feature in *TV Guide*. Walters left her first position after she married businessman Robert Henry Katz in 1955.

When she decided to return to broadcasting, Walters first inquired at NBC's "Today" show. Rebuffed by NBC, she was offered an assistant producer's position with CBS television's "Morning Show." She convinced the producers to air fashion segments and even modeled some of the outfits on the air. When the "Morning Show" was replaced by the "Good Morning" program in 1956, Walters remained on the staff. By 1957, Walters was out of work again and suffered through two traumas in 1958: her divorce from Katz and the collapse of her father's nightclub business.

Barbara Walters reentered the business world in 1958 as head of the radio and television department at a New York public-relations firm. Walters's supervisor at the firm was William Safire, with whom she formed a lasting friendship. Her tenure at the New York firm ended in 1960, and she obtained a position as a writer for NBC's "Today" show in 1961. Walters was soon producing a regular segment on the show featuring "Today girl" Anita Colby. Soon after host Dave Garroway resigned in mid-1961, Barbara Walters made her first on-air appearance.

In 1962, Walters was assigned by "Today" to accompany First Lady Jacqueline Kennedy on a goodwill visit to India. Although she was unable to interview Mrs. Kennedy, Walters interviewed the one journalist who had free access to the First Lady, Joan Braden. Another shake-up at "Today" occurred in 1962, when Hugh Downs replaced John Chancellor as anchor. Walters was in charge of producing one show a week for "Today," and she was able to obtain more airtime for herself by introducing film stories. During the aftermath of the assassination of President Kennedy in 1963, Walters received on-air assignments to cover the tragedy for "Today."

When the show sought a new "Today girl" in 1964, Walters tried to convince the producer to name her. Instead, NBC hired former screen actress Maureen O'Sullivan, much to Walters's disappointment. Unhappy with her role on the show, O'Sullivan was removed within a few months. Walters again applied for the on-air slot and got it in October 1964, thanks to support from Downs. She hired a publicist, who succeeded in getting her story into *TV Guide*, New York newspapers, and, most importantly, a spread in *Life*, which irritated "Today" brass. In addition to promoting herself, Walters worked diligently to obtain interviews with President Johnson's daughters, Truman Capote, and Princess Grace of Monaco. She also did pieces on Paris fashions, nuns, women in reform school, and high school dropouts.

The subjects for Barbara Walters's interviews became increasingly high profile. In 1968, she did a rare interview with Fred Astaire for "Today" and a five-part interview with former Secretary of State Dean Rusk in 1969. She covered the investiture of Britain's Prince Charles in 1969. In 1970,

Walters signed a contract with Doubleday for a book, *How To Talk with Practically Anybody about Practically Anything*, which was ghostwritten for Walters. Also in 1970, Walters became the moderator of a morning talk show, "For Women Only"—later changed to "Not for Women Only"—on WNBC-TV. It was the prototype talk show and was imitated often in following years.

Walters became a celebrity, using her friendship with major figures such as Henry Kissinger to promote her career. She obtained an exclusive one-on-one interview with President Richard Nixon in 1971 and was invited to accompany the president on his historic trip to China in 1972. Upon her return from China, Walters wrote a summary for *Ladies' Home Journal* and was invited to address the East Asian Institute at Harvard and the Woodrow Wilson International Affairs School at Princeton. Walters's on-air relationship with "Today" host Hugh Downs ended with his retirement in 1971. Downs's replacement, Frank McGee, maintained an openly hostile attitude toward Walters. After McGee's death in 1974, NBC announced that Walters would become the cohost of "Today" with McGee's replacement, Jim Hartz. Actually, Walters's new contract had specified that if McGee left "Today," she would become cohost.

Walters did not allow her new title to slow her quest for interviews with notables. When she accompanied Senator George McGovern to Cuba in 1975, she wangled an interview with Fidel Castro. It was during 1975 that Walters launched the first of many "specials" that focused on the rich and famous. She was named "Broadcaster of the Year" in 1975 by the International Radio and Television Society. Her talent and celebrity allowed Walters to shop around as her contract with NBC neared an end. Anxious to improve its sagging evening news ratings, ABC offered Walters a $1 million contract in 1976 to become the first network anchorwoman, teaming with Harry Reasoner. The agreement also allowed her to continue the specials she had begun at NBC.

Media professionals were aghast at ABC's deal with Walters because they did not view her as a true journalist. Reasoner himself was uneasy at the prospect of working with Walters. The duo's first show in October 1976 included a Walters interview with Egyptian President Anwar Sadat. Walters's only respite from the continued media criticism and tension with Reasoner in the months that followed was positive publicity by columnist Liz Smith. The end of the coanchor scheme came in 1978 when Reasoner went back to CBS. The new format featured three anchors and Walters as chief reporter-interviewer—an arrangement that was acceptable to Walters. Her time on the evening news gradually declined as she undertook other assignments.

Her contract with ABC allowed her to do four prime-time specials each year. Walters continued the pattern started at NBC of featuring the rich and famous—the first special included interviews with Barbra Streisand and President-elect Jimmy Carter. The specials were successful because they allowed Barbara Walters to use her interviewing talent to the fullest. In 1988, Walters celebrated her fiftieth special for ABC. When Walters renewed her contract with ABC in 1981, she agreed to rejoin Hugh Downs on the ABC newsmagazine "20/20" as an occasional reporter and in 1985 as cohost. Walters's interviews with high-profile news figures helped raise the show's ratings.

Reference Oppenheimer, Jerry, *Barbara Walters: An Unauthorized Biography* (1990).

War Correspondents
See individual wars.

War of 1812
Press partisanship had become a way of life for newspapers from the drafting of the Constitution in 1787 to the outbreak of War of 1812. The pressure of western interests craving more territorial expansion led the press and the nation into the most curious war in its history. The press helped

create a patriotic veneer to cover the naked aggression of the "War Hawks." More patriotic slogans emerged from this conflict than from any other in U.S. history. The war also revealed sectional differences among the vigorous antiwar elements centered in New England.

The background of the War of 1812 can be traced to a lengthy war between Great Britain and France that began in 1792. The United States assumed a neutral position toward the combatants but wanted to trade with both countries. Predictably, both France and Britain tried to stop trade from the United States to the other country. Political and public opinion had almost resulted in a declaration of war against France under Federalist President John Adams in 1798 because of trade depredations. Similar interference by Great Britain resulted in an abortive trade embargo under Democratic-Republican President Thomas Jefferson in 1808, which was very unpopular in New England. Indeed, Federalist-dominated New England showed the most concern about resolving the trade issues, but it was Democratic-Republicans in western states and territories, led by congressional "War Hawks," who promoted war with Britain in order to acquire Canada and Florida as well as to end Indian uprisings in the West.

The presidential election of 1812 became a virtual referendum on war or peace. Congress had voted in favor of a declaration of war, but British peace proposals received later seemed to resolve the issues, making war unnecessary. Virtually every newspaper in the commercial Northeast favored peace and endorsed DeWitt Clinton of New York, who proposed negotiating a settlement. However, newspapers in the South and West largely favored prosecuting the war and endorsed President Madison for reelection. Madison won the election and the war proceeded. Government attempts to muzzle the opposition press during the war were noteworthy.

Press divisions during the War of 1812 were the most notable in U.S. history. Whereas nationalist papers such as the *National Intelligencer* in Washington offered

strong support for Madison and the war effort, Boston's *Columbian Centinel* and *Repertory* decried the conflict. Publishers Jacob Wagner and Alexander Hanson of the *Baltimore Federal Republican* incited furious attacks by their pointed criticism of the government's war aims. Even though Wagner and Hanson's caustic remarks were inflammatory, suggestions of repression were opposed by former military leaders such as Generals James Lingan and Henry Lee. A mob pulled a cannon to the front door of the *Republican*'s offices before negotiations allowed the printers to leave. Nonetheless, the *Republican*'s building was torn down, General Lingan was killed, and other newspaper staffers were beaten.

Newspaper accounts of battles during the War of 1812 were uneven, in part because victories received much greater attention than defeats. The *National Intelligencer*'s offices were abandoned and subsequently destroyed by British troops occupying the capital in 1814. A few correspondents near the fighting provided reports, but most of the war news came through official government channels. James M. Bradford enlisted with Andrew Jackson's army in New Orleans and sent reports that were published in his Louisiana newspaper. Merchants in port cities clamored for news that might affect their businesses. New England newspapers reported the Hartford Convention meeting in 1814, which threatened secession if the Constitution were not amended to prevent a recurrence of a similar war. Yet once the news of peace arrived in New England, most residents and editors seemed content to look to the future "era of good feelings" rather than the past.

Washington Post

Founded in 1877 as a Democratic morning daily, the *Washington Post* gained a national reputation that was second only to the *New York Times*'s in the twentieth century under the Meyer-Graham family. Unlike other Washington, D.C., papers, the *Post* took a national perspective, which set it apart.

The *Post* garnered respect for its accurate, in-depth reporting as well as its strong editorial stands.

During the Civil War, New England native Stilson Hutchins edited the *Dubuque (Iowa) Herald*, which maintained an antiwar, "Copperhead," Democratic editorial policy, with open sympathy for the Confederate cause. After the war, Hutchins moved to St. Louis and bought the *Dispatch*, which led to the hiring of lifelong friend Joseph Pulitzer. When Hutchins arrived in Washington in 1877 to fulfill a dream by launching the four-page morning *Post*, the city already had five dailies, although only the emerging evening *Star* was noteworthy. Hutchins was determined to make the *Post* an influence among political leaders in the executive and legislative branches. In addition to its partisan Democratic stance, the *Post* became a great news-gathering operation.

The first editor of the *Post* was John A. Cockerill, former editor of the *Cincinnati Enquirer* and later Pulitzer's editor in St. Louis and New York. In less than two years, Cockerill set the standard for thorough reporting and taut editorials. Hutchins's son Walter served as editor for the remainder of his ownership. Future *Chicago Daily News* columnist Eugene Field also worked briefly for the *Post*. After one year, the *Post*'s circulation rose to just under 12,000 but continued to trail the evening *Star*'s. In 1888, the *Post* was strong enough to buy two competitors. Under Hutchins, the paper continued to align itself with white southern positions, including racial segregation, but it showed concern about the increased number of race-related lynchings. Although critical of industrial robber barons, the *Post* showed little empathy for labor unions.

After the Democratic defeat in the 1888 elections, Hutchins put the *Post* up for sale. It was bought in 1889 for $210,000 by former Republican Postmaster General Frank Hatton and Ohio banker and Democratic Congressman Beriah Wilkins. The new publishers promised to maintain Hutchins's reporting tradition and to have an independent editorial policy. The *Post* began using illustrations frequently, and political cartoonist Clifford Berryman established a national reputation. Although the *Post* opposed talk of further continental territorial expansion, it clamored for overseas imperialism. During the Spanish-American War (1898), the *Post* sent a reporter to Cuba and generally paid greater attention to international affairs. The *Post* remained editorially neutral in the presidential elections of 1896 and 1900.

Soon after the deaths of Hatton and Wilkins, John Roll McLean bought the controlling interest in the *Post* in 1905. As publisher of the *Cincinnati Enquirer*, McLean had been a leader in Ohio Democratic circles. In 1895, McLean briefly owned the *New York Journal* before selling to William Randolph Hearst. McLean had started a Washington business interest in 1892 and had become a civic-minded resident by the time of the *Post* investment. As editor, McLean gave the *Post* more diversity, establishing sports, women's, and art departments. In short, McLean applied some of the techniques of the "new journalism" without the worst elements of sensationalism. Because fierce competition kept the *Post* third among the city dailies, McLean lowered the price to two cents in 1911, which brought circulation from about 20,000 to 30,000. The *Post* backed President's Wilson policy of neutrality in 1914 but also urged strong preparedness for possible U.S. intervention in World War I.

Upon John McLean's death in 1916, the family debated the future of the *Post*. Editorial page editor Ira Bennett maintained the previous editorial policies, and Edward B. McLean, John's son, took over management. Although it remained supportive of the Wilson administration, the *Post* fought U.S. membership in the League of Nations, endorsed the women's suffrage amendment without enthusiasm, and opposed the Prohibition amendment as foolishness. Prosperity reached historical proportions for the *Post* after the war; ad linage increases of over 100 percent since 1914 meant that there was not enough space for all the advertising. The *Post* strongly backed Republican Warren G. Harding in the 1920 election, and

George R. Brown's widely quoted political column during the 1920s reflected the *Post*'s conservative and isolationist stances. Edward McLean hired former U.S. ambassador to England George Harvey as editor of the *Post* in 1924, but disagreements quickly led to his replacement again by Bennett.

When Edward McLean was forced to retire because of alcoholism, the family sold the *Washington Post* to Eugene Meyer, multimillionaire chief executive of Allied Chemical Company, in 1933 for $825,000. The *Post* was in dire need of renewal, with circulation down to about 50,000, but it took Meyer a few years to obtain the personnel to accomplish the feat. Chief editorial leader became Felix Morley, former journalist working at the Brookings Institution. The *Post* critiqued President Roosevelt's New Deal formula of reform. By 1938, circulation had doubled to 100,000 from its 1933 level, even though deficits continued to be significant. In 1938, the *Post* began carrying the widely read syndicated columns of Walter Lippmann, Dorothy Thompson, and Mark Sullivan.

When World War II began in 1939, publisher Meyer and editor Morley differed over U.S. policy. Meyer advocated intervention to aid Britain, whereas Morley remained an isolationist. Morley resigned in 1940, and Meyer appointed Herbert Elliston the new editor. Elliston was an experienced foreign correspondent who had worked for ten years at the *Christian Science Monitor*. Circulation was at 125,000 in 1940—still trailing the evening *Star* by 25,000—but advertising revenue showed steady gains. At the end of 1945, Meyer hired two veteran GIs—his son-in-law Philip Leslie Graham as associate publisher, and Herbert L. Block as editorial cartoonist. Within a few months, Meyer retired to allow Graham to become publisher.

After making profits for the first time in more than a decade, the *Post* bought the competing *Times-Herald* in 1954, leaving the *Post* as Washington's only morning daily. Editor Elliston won an editorial Pulitzer Prize in 1949, but ill health forced his retirement in 1952. Graham offered the

editor's post to James Reston of the *New York Times*, but Reston refused. Graham then selected young editorial writer Robert Estabrook as editor. The *Post* was among media stalwarts assailing Senator Joseph McCarthy's anticommunist campaign, and Block won a 1954 Pulitzer Prize for an editorial cartoon directed at McCarthy. The *Post* did not directly endorse but showed support for the presidential campaigns of Republicans Thomas Dewey in 1948 and Dwight Eisenhower in 1952 and 1956, as well as Democrat John F. Kennedy in 1960.

When Philip Graham committed suicide in 1963, his wife Katherine took over the publishing responsibilities. Despite her inexperience, Katherine Graham showed an ability to learn the business. She became the first woman elected president of the American Newspaper Publishers Association. The Washington Post Company had purchased *Newsweek* magazine in 1961, and it reflected the *Post*'s editorial positions. Graham moved Benjamin Bradlee from *Newsweek* to become the *Post*'s managing editor in 1966; he was later promoted to executive editor. Editor-reporter Alfred Friendly won a Pulitzer Prize for covering the Arab-Israeli War in 1967. The *Post* continued to back Democratic presidential candidates Lyndon Johnson in 1964 and Hubert Humphrey in 1968.

The *Washington Post* gained the greatest national recognition in its history through its coverage of the Nixon administration's Watergate crisis from 1972 to 1974. Reporters Carl Bernstein and Robert Woodward spearheaded an investigation, which brought the *Post* another Pulitzer Prize. Columnist David Broder won a Pulitzer in 1973 for commentary about the Watergate issue. By the mid-1970s, the *Post*'s circulation was over 500,000, putting it far ahead of the evening *Star*. Katherine Graham's son Donald gradually assumed publishing responsibilities at the *Post* in the late 1970s. The paper suffered embarrassment in 1981 when it was revealed that reporter Janet Cooke had fabricated the story that won her the Pulitzer Prize. The *Post* returned the prize. In 1989, the *Washington Post* ranked sixth nationally in daily circulation, with 812,000.

Reference Roberts, Chalmers M., *The* Washington Post: *The First 100 Years* (1977).

Washington Star

For more than a decade after its founding in 1852, the evening *Washington Star* was an independent local paper. The Noyes and Kauffmann families purchased the *Star* in 1867 and held it until 1974, when Joe All-britton bought the paper. Crosby Noyes and later Frank Noyes gave the paper quality editorial leadership. Time, Inc., acquired the *Star* in 1978 but could not stop its decline. The paper was terminated in 1981.

Thomas Conolly began the *American Daily Telegraph* in 1851 as a nonpartisan two-cent, four-page daily, joining seven other Washington dailies. The *Telegraph* was sold in 1852 to Joseph Tate, who changed the name to the *Washington Evening Star* and lowered the price to a penny. The *Evening Star* struggled to find readers and editorial quality. In 1853, Tate sold the paper to W. D. Wallach, who conceived of the *Star* as basically a local paper with little notice that the District of Columbia also happened to be the nation's capital.

In 1856, Wallach hired Crosby S. Noyes as a roving reporter. Born in Maine to a family steeped in New England history, Noyes had served as a congressional reporter for the *Washington News* from 1848 to 1855 and knew something about his territory. Within two years, Noyes was promoted to assistant editor but continued to report events such as John Brown's trial in Virginia. Noyes served a term as alderman in the District of Columbia, allowing him to become acquainted with many government figures. He had perhaps the closest relationship of any reporter to Secretary of War Edwin Stanton during the Civil War. President Abraham Lincoln gave Noyes his notes from the 1861 inaugural address, allowing the *Star* to scoop all other papers in printing it first.

Although the paper had thrived during the Civil War, it seem to languish again afterwards, and Wallach offered Noyes a chance to buy the *Star* for the huge sum of $100,000 in 1867. Noyes obtained four partners to raise the money, including Samuel H. Kauffmann, an Ohio newspaper publisher who became president of the company, and former *New York World* correspondent George W. Adams. In a few years, these three each owned a one-third portion of the *Star*. Noyes became editor of the *Star* and held that post until his death in 1908. The vision that Noyes had was for the *Star* to become an advocate for the residents of the District of Columbia rather than any wider audience. The *Star* consistently championed improvements in parks, roads, bridges, and hospitals. Politically, the *Star* remained independent and preferred to focus on issues rather than parties.

A paperboy sells a Washington Star *in 1916. The headline reads "U.S. at War with Germany."*

Both of Noyes's sons became involved in the *Star* as they grew to maturity. Frank B. Noyes became business manager in 1886 and stayed until 1901, when Victor Lawson persuaded him to become editor and publisher of the crusading *Chicago Record Herald*, the morning counterpart to Lawson's *Chicago Daily News*. Noyes returned to the *Star* in 1910 and served as president until his death in 1948. Frank Noyes had been a founding director of the Associated Press in the 1890s and was elected president in 1900, a post he held for 38 years.

Crosby Noyes's second son, Theodore, graduated from what is now George Washington University and became associate editor at the *Star* in 1886. Theodore Noyes followed his father as editor, guiding the *Star* until his death in 1946. Theodore exhibited the same civic concerns of his father. He promoted the expansion of Rock Creek and Potomac Parks, criticized railroads for safety hazards at their crossings, and influenced the building of Union Station. He also urged Congress to assume responsibility for partial financing of district projects. Noyes showed concern for his employees by paying them a fair wage as well as a range of benefits. Theodore Noyes insisted on accurate, objective reporting and concentrated on logic in his editorial campaigns. Circulation of the *Star* grew dramatically under the Noyes brothers, from 48,000 in 1910 to 211,000 in 1948, making it not only the largest paper in Washington but also the paper with the most advertising linage in the United States.

Samuel Hay Kauffmann, grandson of the company's first president, followed Frank Noyes as president of the *Star* in 1948. Kauffmann had begun as an assistant advertising manager in 1926. John Kauffmann succeeded his father as president in 1963. Benjamin M. McKelway served as editor from 1946 until 1963, when Frank Noyes's grandson Newbold Noyes Jr. became editor. *Star* reporter George Beveridge won a local reporting Pulitzer in 1958, and Miriam Ottenberg won a Pulitzer in 1960 for a story about a used-car swindle. Haynes Johnson won another Pulitzer in 1966 for reporting the violent 1965 Selma to Montgomery, Alabama, civil rights march.

Despite circulation growth from 258,000 in 1963 to 309,000 in 1968, rising production costs plagued the *Star*, along with many other dailies. Financial troubles forced the sale in 1974 to Texan Joe Allbritton, who gave the editorial reins to former *New York Herald-Tribune* editor James Bellows. Bel-

lows, in turn, hired three Pulitzer Prize winners: columnist Mary McGrory, reporter James Polk (who won at the *Star* for his Watergate coverage), and former *Denver Post* cartoonist Patrick Oliphant. Their efforts could not save the continued erosion, however, and Time, Inc., bought the *Star* in 1978. The paper finally succumbed in 1981 after further circulation and advertising losses.

Watergate Hearings

The so-called Watergate affair that ended Richard Nixon's presidency came right on the heels of the antiwar furor over Vietnam and the growing mistrust of government. The media were directly involved, providing televised coverage of congressional hearings in 1974. The incident that initiated the hearings occurred during the 1972 presidential campaign, so the story moved slowly before reaching the 1974 climax. The media were revered by some and reviled by others for their role in Watergate.

Several reporters, including Bob Woodward and Carl Bernstein of the *Washington Post*, followed the story of the burglary at Democratic campaign headquarters in Washington's Watergate complex in the summer of 1972. As the investigation was pursued, reporters discovered that the burglars were connected with the Committee to Reelect the President, an ad hoc group that raised money and campaigned for Richard Nixon's reelection. The committee was headed by Nixon's former attorney general John Mitchell; its staff included other former White House employees. Bernstein and Woodward tied one arrested accomplice, James McCord, to the Central Intelligence Agency. President Nixon publicly condemned the activities of the committee members, but his own staff, headed by John Ehrlichman and H. R. Haldeman, began a cover-up to prevent the burglars' being linked to the White House. Those actions would ultimately doom Nixon's presidency.

Prior to the election in November 1972, few media organizations pursued the Watergate story. Only 15 reporters were assigned to cover the story, and fewer than two dozen political columns out of 500 focused on the story before the election. Although CBS news devoted almost twice as much time as NBC and ABC to the story, it had only 71 minutes of coverage in the seven weeks before the election. *Washington Post* reporters Bernstein and Woodward revealed in October that the Watergate break-in was part of a campaign of "dirty tricks" carried on by the Committee to Re-elect, which included spying on the president's enemies. Meanwhile, Nixon won the election by a landslide, the Vietnam War ended in early 1973, and the president's popularity reached an all-time high. A Gallup poll in mid-1973 showed that 83 percent of Americans knew about Watergate, but half thought that the furor was mostly partisan politics.

McCord testified during his burglary trial in federal court that the reelection committee's activities, including the Watergate burglary, were directed from the White House. Gradually, a variety of additional testimony from various sources revealed a more serious problem than most had been willing to recognize. Resignations of several White House aides, including Haldeman and Ehrlichman, seemed to confirm the testimony, but Nixon continued to deny complicity.

Congress had begun investigations in 1973, and a witness before a Senate select committee controlled by Democrats testified as to the existence of a White House audiotaping system. The Senate committee sought to obtain the tapes from the White House to seek corroboration of the testimony. Initially, President Nixon refused to yield the 64 tapes, claiming executive privilege, but late in 1973, he agreed to turn over edited transcripts of the tapes. Eventually, the Supreme Court ordered Nixon to release the tapes themselves. When Nixon ordered a special prosecutor in the Justice Department dismissed, the House Judiciary Committee, which also contained a majority of opposition Democrats, began impeachment proceedings in 1974. Both the

Senate and House committee hearings were televised extensively by the networks. Staunch Republican media voices such as *Time, National Review,* and the *Chicago Tribune* called for Nixon's resignation in the spring of 1974. When it appeared that the Judiciary Committee was poised to vote impeachment charges, Nixon submitted his resignation in August 1974. He became the first president to resign from office.

Although the press did not bring down Nixon's presidency, it played a vital role in the process of its collapse. The *Washington Post* won a public service Pulitzer Prize largely because of Bernstein and Woodward's efforts; the *Post*'s David Broder won a Pulitzer for commentary. Despite a long tradition of press scrutiny of government, many in the public grew more skeptical of media motives because of Watergate. The media responded with a flurry of activity seeking to buttress media credibility, including an emphasis on ethics and the creation of the watchdog National News Council in 1973.

Reference White, Theodore H., *Breach of Faith—The Fall of Richard Nixon* (1975).

Watterson, Henry
See Louisville Courier-Journal.

Webb, James Watson (1802–1884)
As the colorful publisher of the *New York Courier and Enquirer* from 1829 to 1861, James Watson Webb had notable contests with rival New York publishers James Gordon Bennett, Benjamin Day, and Horace Greeley. Webb's *Courier and Enquirer* was the leading New York paper for two decades after its merger, despite its concentration on commercial news. Webb broke with Democrat Andrew Jackson, and the *Courier and Enquirer* became the leading Whig Party paper before converting to the Republicans in 1857.

James Watson Webb was born in New York, the son of a Revolutionary War general. Both his parents died by the time Webb was five years old. After working for a while in his brother's Cooperstown general store, Webb fancied that he would become a soldier. He persuaded Secretary of War John C. Calhoun to grant him an army commission in 1819. Webb was assigned to a fort in the Illinois territory, where he fought in some Indian wars. Webb also participated in two duels with fellow officers. After a quarrel with his commanding officer, Colonel Webb resigned in 1827 to become editor and publisher of the *New York Morning Courier*, which he bought for $6,000.

The *Courier* was a typical New York mercantile daily concentrating on business news, ship schedules, commodity prices, and stock and bond quotes. There was little original reporting or writing. After one year's ownership, the *Courier*'s circulation rose above 2,000, taking third place among New York dailies. Webb organized a newsboat harbor association with two other papers in 1828 to enhance the *Courier*'s newsgathering capabilities. The association sent small boats to collect foreign papers from transatlantic ships in the harbor before the mailbags were delivered to the city.

Webb's *Courier* backed the young Democratic Party and its standard-bearer Andrew Jackson. Not only did the *Courier* support Jackson's presidential candidacy against John Quincy Adams in 1828, but it also opposed the protective tariff recently passed by Congress. During Jackson's first term as president, Webb split with the administration over the future of the national bank. Although Webb did not want the existing charter renewed, he favored a reformed national bank. Thus, when Jackson turned against the bank in 1832, Webb broke with the president. Webb's new motto for the paper was "principles, not men."

Meanwhile, the *Courier* had merged with Mordecai Noah's *Enquirer* in 1829 to become the *Courier and Enquirer*. Daily circulation improved to 4,000; advertising also increased after the merger, allowing Webb to purchase a high-speed Napier press with his profits. The *Enquirer*'s Washington correspondent James Gordon Bennett continued in that position for Webb's paper until he left in 1835 to start the *New York Herald*.

Because of Webb's acquaintance with Louis Napoleon Bonaparte and a couple of trips to England in the late 1830s, the *Courier and Enquirer* carried more international news than other papers and soon had a European correspondent. When abolitionist groups opposed the annexation of Texas after 1837, which Webb favored, he became critical of their movement. Webb eventually supported nativist policies that showed prejudice against Catholics and immigrants. Although most papers promoted civic pride, Webb was a steady champion of making New York safer and cleaner and of improving transportation facilities.

Since Webb had parted ways with Jackson, it was perhaps natural for him to become a Whig supporter. But the Whig Party's main attraction for Webb became its nationalistic economic principles, which called for an activist government to develop the United States' economic potential. Webb blamed the Panic of 1837 on ill-conceived Jacksonian fiscal policies. The depression was a boon to Whig candidates in the elections of 1838 and 1840. The *Courier and Enquirer* worked tirelessly for the Whig ticket of William Henry Harrison and John Tyler in the 1830 presidential campaign.

Meanwhile, the advent of the "penny press" in the 1830s produced two new papers, Benjamin Day's *Sun* (1833) and James Gordon Bennett's *Herald* (1835). The circulation of both soon eclipsed the leadership position of the *Courier and Enquirer*. The *Herald*'s circulation alone was 17,000 by 1840. The penny press papers appealed to a different class of people than the older commercial papers like Webb's. Webb relied on speedy news gathering to compete with his cheaper rivals. The *Courier and Enquirer* often published news from Washington a day ahead of the other New York dailies. Frequent trips kept Webb away from management of the paper, whereas Bennett worked 18-hour days to make the *Herald* a success. Webb raised advertising rates at an inauspicious time in 1836, on the eve of the panic.

Webb became notorious for raucous, often violent personal clashes with his critics.

William Leggett, an associate editor at the *New York Post*, assaulted Webb on the street, only to be severely caned by Webb. Bennett himself was the object of two physical batterings by Webb on Wall Street. Webb's fierce critique of a Kentucky congressman who had labeled the *Courier and Enquirer* a "hireling press" in 1842 led to Webb's wounding in a duel in Delaware. He was prosecuted in New York for illegal dueling and sentenced to two years in prison but was pardoned by the Whig governor. Webb's criticisms of novelist James Fenimore Cooper resulted in a less violent episode—a libel suit, in which Webb was acquitted.

Henry J. Raymond, the future founder of the *New York Times*, became associate editor of the *Courier and Enquirer* in 1843 and helped maintain the paper's vitality. The publishers of all the major New York papers, including Webb, met in 1848 to organize the New York Associated Press. Although Webb initially welcomed Horace Greeley's *Tribune* in 1841 because it was Whig, he was soon trading barbs with the vigorous new competition. Despite the 1848 Whig victory and Webb's early backing of presidential candidate Zachary Taylor, both Whig and Webb fortunes waned as the slavery issue heated up. Disappointed that he was not named ambassador to Germany, Webb accepted the post of chargé d'affaires at Vienna in 1849. After arriving in Vienna in 1850, however, Webb learned that the Senate had defeated his nomination.

Upon his resumption of editorial control from Raymond in 1850, Webb backed the Compromise of 1850. Raymond had become an ardent antislavery man and resigned in 1851 to begin the *New York Times*. The *Courier and Enquirer* never recovered from its loss. Webb eventually moderated his position on the slavery issue, and the breakup of the Whig Party led him to the new Republican Party by 1857. Inexorably, Webb's paper was drawn away from its traditional concerns about economic and foreign issues to the slavery question. After Abraham Lincoln's election in 1860, Webb lobbied for an ambassadorship to England but received instead an appointment to Brazil in 1861. In order to extinguish debts, Webb sold the *Courier and Enquirer* to the *New York World*. After two terms as ambassador to Brazil, Webb returned to the United States in 1869.

Reference Crouthamel, James L., *James Watson Webb: A Biography* (1969).

Webster, Noah (1758–1843)

Although best known for his dictionary and textbooks, Noah Webster was also an important editor of the *American Minerva* newspaper. He edited the *American Magazine* for a brief time in 1787 before starting his newspaper. Webster was a staunch supporter of the Federalist Party in an era of an extremely partisan press. Obviously, Webster brought considerable literary qualities to his editing.

Noah Webster was born in Hartford, Connecticut, the descendant of a former governor. His father was a farmer and justice of the peace. Webster's education at Yale (1774–1778) was interrupted briefly to serve in the Continental army during the Revolution. He studied law after graduating from Yale and was admitted to the bar in 1781, the same year he completed a master's degree at Yale. Webster chose to teach school rather than practice law, however. While teaching in New York, he published an enormously popular three-part textbook, *Grammatical Institute of the English Language* (1783–1785), consisting of sections on spelling, grammar, and reading.

Webster was editor and publisher of the monthly *American Magazine* for a year beginning in 1787. Primarily a literary journal, the *American Magazine* also gave strong support to the ratification of the Constitution, though it opposed the Bill of Rights as unnecessary. Webster also expounded at length on what a formal education should include, arguing that mastery of the English language was most important. He believed that education should be offered to girls as well as boys. Webster included poetry and fiction in the magazine, especially the type to attract female readers. Seeking a national distribution for the *American Magazine*, Webster recruited part owner/correspondents in cities such as Boston, Philadelphia, and Charleston. These efforts ultimately failed, however, and the *American Magazine* never sold more than 500 subscriptions. After canceling the magazine in December 1788, Webster returned to Connecticut to practice law. He wrote 28 anonymous essays on morals for the *Hartford Courant* in 1791.

Noah Webster

As a supporter of the Federalist Party and especially New York's Alexander Hamilton in the 1790s, Webster was urged by John Jay and Rufus King to become editor of the *American Minerva* newspaper. Webster agreed and made the paper an ardent Federalist organ. He penned numerous articles signed "Curtius" that embraced Hamilton's financial program and Jay's treaty with Great Britain. Webster self-righteously defended Washington's administration from attacks by editors such as Philip Freneau in the Democratic-Republican *National Gazette*. Webster produced the first column labeled an "editorial" in the *American Min-*

erva; his editorials appeared irregularly in 1793 and then in every issue after 1796. Concentrating on his main themes of keeping the United States out of foreign disputes and promoting nationalism, Webster also found time to editorialize against slavery and in favor of medical research, improved sanitation, and forest conservation.

In addition to the daily *American Minerva*, Webster edited a semiweekly edition published as the *Herald*, aimed at rural residents around New York. The *Herald* reprinted items from the *American Minerva* and proved to be very profitable. The circulation peak of the daily and semiweekly editions was 1,700. In 1797, the names of the two papers were changed; the *American Minerva* became the *Commercial Advertiser*, and the *Herald* was renamed the *Spectator*. In 1798, Webster grew tired of politics and retired as active editor to return to his work with the English language. He retained control of the *Commercial Advertiser* and *Spectator* until they were sold in 1803. Webster's dictionary was published in its preliminary format in 1806 and completed in 1828.

Reference Coll, Gary, "Noah Webster, Journalist: 1783–1803," in *Colonial Newsletters to Newspapers*, ed. Donovan H. Bond and W. Reynolds McCleod (1977).

Weed, Thurlow (1797–1882)

Thurlow Weed founded the *Albany Evening Journal* in 1830 as an anti-Mason paper, but it soon embraced the new Whig Party. The *Evening Journal* had a larger circulation than the New York City papers until the *Tribune* was established in the 1840s. Weed served in the state legislature and worked closely with Whig leaders on the national and state levels, becoming the effective boss of the New York Whig Party. After the Civil War, Weed briefly edited the *New York Commercial Advertiser*, started by Noah Webster.

A native of upstate New York, Thurlow Weed apprenticed as a printer in 1808 and set his mind on editing as a career. He obtained a foreman's job at the *Albany Register* in 1817 and saved enough money to start the weekly *Republican Agriculturalist* at Norwich in 1818. The paper was not well received, and Weed launched another weekly, the *Manlius Republican*, in 1821. Unable to make financial ends meet, Weed solicited and received a post as editorial writer at the *Rochester Telegraph* in 1822. Weed sincerely liked people; he was attracted to politics and was elected to the state assembly in 1824. With his new position, Weed was able to purchase the *Telegraph* in 1825 but sold it the next year.

Thurlow Weed

Freemasonry became a serious issue for politicians in the 1820s. Many, like Weed, argued that political leaders should not ask for voter support if they subscribed to secret tenets as members of the Freemasons. After becoming a leader of the anti-Masons in the state assembly, Weed decided to establish the *Anti-Masonic Enquirer* in 1828. Editor Weed became noted for his highly inflammatory rhetoric against political Masons. His tenure with the *Enquirer* caused Albany political elites to take notice. They persuaded Weed to help them launch a political paper in the capital. The four-page *Albany Evening Journal* appeared in March 1830, with Weed as editor, reporter, and

typesetter. After formation of the Whig Party in 1832, Weed joined most anti-Masons as a Whig.

Weed formed two important alliances as a leader in the New York Whig Party: William Seward, who was elected governor in 1838, and journalist Horace Greeley, who owned the *New York Tribune*. Weed, Seward, and Greeley all played major roles in promoting Whig presidential candidate William Henry Harrison in the 1840 election. Because of the *Evening Journal*'s location in the state capital, it had a greater circulation than the New York City dailies. Whenever the Whigs controlled state government, Weed's paper got the state printing contracts, which proved lucrative.

Weed was unable to bring off Seward's reelection for governor in 1842 but later got him elected to the U.S. Senate. The *Evening Journal* was instrumental in leading Whig presidential candidate Zachary Taylor to victory in the 1848 election. Because the Free-Soil vote for favorite son Martin Van Buren split the Democratic vote in New York, the Whigs were able to carry the state for Taylor, which provided the margin of victory in the electoral college. Weed tried to sell the *Evening Journal* to George Jones and Henry J. Raymond in 1848, but one of the stockholders refused to give up some *Journal* stock and the deal fell through. Raymond and Jones founded the *New York Times* in 1851. The 1850s saw the collapse of the Whig Party due to divisions over slavery, and the *Evening Journal* threw its support behind the Republican Party.

At the Republicans' Chicago convention in 1860, Weed backed his old ally William Seward for the presidential nomination, which was won by Abraham Lincoln. Weed then used the *Evening Journal* to campaign for Lincoln's election. When Seward became secretary of state, he asked Weed to lobby England and France for support in the Civil War. Like Seward, Weed favored a conciliatory policy toward the South and promoted all peace efforts in the *Evening Journal*. Weed tired of the war and decided to give up his paper in 1863. After the war, he tried to make a comeback in 1867 as editor of the *New York Commercial Advertiser*, a four-page mercantile daily that had criticized the conduct of the war at times. Weed remained only a year as editor before retiring again due to ill health.

Reference Van Deusen, Glyndon, *Thurlow Weed: Wizard of the Lobby* (1947).

Welles, Orson
See Radio.

White, William Allen (1868–1944)
Embodying the peculiar qualities of the small-town editor, William Allen White gained national recognition for quality writing and outspoken editorials. White's paper, the *Emporia (Kansas) Gazette*, became the most quoted country paper in big-city dailies, and his essays in leading magazines gave him a national audience. Initially skeptical of reform movements such as Populism, White became an advocate for Progressive reforms after 1901. He also embraced unpopular positions such as opposing neutrality in the 1930s.

William Allen White was born in Emporia, Kansas, to a physician father and schoolteacher mother who had opposite political views. The Whites moved when William was one year old to an even smaller frontier town, El Dorado. White's father died just before he finished high school. After his first year at the College of Emporia, White worked as a printer's devil at a small weekly paper and then part-time with the *Emporia Daily News* upon returning to college. In 1886, White enrolled at the University of Kansas in Lawrence and worked for the local paper. White left school before receiving a degree to accept the post of assistant editor of his hometown paper, the *El Dorado Republican*, in 1890. White tried to rally traditional Republicans against the Populist Party emerging from the farmers' alliance movement.

White was offered positions with both the *Kansas City Journal* and William Rockhill Nelson's *Kansas City Star* in 1891. He stayed less than a year with the *Journal* before moving to the *Star*. While working in Kansas City, White nurtured a dream of editing his own paper. When he learned that the *Emporia Gazette* was for sale in 1895, White bought the daily for $3,000. In White's inaugural editorial, he promised that the *Gazette* would support the community and limit political positions to the editorial page. White's *Gazette* proved to be successful enough to force its daily competitor, the *Republican*, out of business within ten years.

During the 1896 presidential campaign, which featured Populist William Jennings Bryan running as the Democratic presidential nominee, White wrote a scathing editorial—"What's the Matter with Kansas?"—about the Populists. It was widely reprinted in major dailies around the nation. White's fame led to many opportunities, including Samuel McClure's invitation to write stories for *McClure's Magazine*. On a trip to Washington, D.C., in 1897 to visit Republican dignitaries, White met his hero Theodore Roosevelt. White wrote articles about Kansas society during 1897 for *Atlantic* and *Scribner's* magazines and soon became a regular contributor to *Collier's* and the *Saturday Evening Post*.

During the Spanish-American War of 1898, White exhibited a patriotic nationalism that resisted the jingoism of the yellow press. When the political fortunes of Theodore Roosevelt rose as a result of his notoriety in the war, White himself shifted his political conservatism toward a Progressive stance. White defended Roosevelt's trust-busting policy in a *Saturday Evening Post* article in 1902. White may have encouraged *McClure's* writers Lincoln Steffens and Ida Tarbell to launch their muckraking essays in 1903. The *Emporia Gazette* editorialized in favor of various Progressive reform measures, including railroad regulation. A series of sketches about small-town perspectives that had been published in the *Saturday Evening Post* was issued in book form as *In Our Town* in 1906. White stuck with Roosevelt even when he formed his splinter Bull Moose Party in 1912.

White's international perspective unfolded rapidly after World War I began. The *Emporia Gazette* supported President

Woodrow Wilson's deliberate preparations for war. White went to France just after the U.S. declaration of war and worked as a volunteer for the Red Cross. He returned to Europe several times and covered the peace conference in 1919 for the Wheeler Syndicate. White supported U.S. participation in the League of Nations as an important method of preserving the peace. When the Treaty of Versailles floundered in the Senate, White was troubled, as he was by the attitude of "return to normalcy." White's editorial in the *Gazette* defending railroad workers' right to free speech against a gubernatorial order won a Pulitzer Prize in 1922. White also attacked the Ku Klux Klan revival as early as 1921. He analyzed Calvin Coolidge as the epitome of the national spirit in a series of articles for *Collier's* in 1925, which also appeared in book form.

White and the *Gazette* backed Republican Herbert Hoover in the 1928 presidential election. Critical of Coolidge's "dollar diplomacy" in Latin America, White helped Hoover shape a new "good neighbor" policy, which recommended the withdrawal of U.S. troops from Haiti. Although critical of Republican policies during the depression, White backed Hoover against Franklin Roosevelt in the 1932 election. White offered support for early New Deal measures and was even consulted by some New Deal brain trusters. Still, White remained loyal to the Republicans when they nominated Progressive Kansan Alfred Landon for president in 1936. White retained his interest in international affairs. He took a trip to Europe in 1933 to cover an economic conference and a tour through the Far East in 1935 and 1936 with Rockefeller Foundation trustees.

White showed alarm at the continued isolationist tendencies in the United States in the face of totalitarian dictators such as Hitler. The *Gazette* opposed the Neutrality Acts passed by Congress to keep the United States from becoming involved in European conflicts. White chaired a lobbying committee to revise the acts in 1939. After the Nazis began conquering Europe in 1939 and 1940, White organized and chaired the Committee to Defend America by Aiding the Allies during 1940 and 1941. The committee favored more aggressive U.S. aid to Great Britain and France to stop the Nazi drive. When the United States entered World War II following the Japanese bombing of Pearl Harbor in December 1941, White felt justified in his previous campaigns. Just after his death in 1944, White's autobiography was published, for which he was awarded another Pulitzer Prize posthumously in 1947.

Reference McKee, John DeWitt, *William Allen White: Maverick on Main Street* (1975).

Woman's Home Companion

One of the earliest magazines to feature subjects of interest to women, *Woman's Home Companion* became a huge success in the twentieth century, especially during the editorship of Gertrude Battles Lane. As part of the Crowell publishing firm after 1885, the *Companion* reached a peak of circulation in the mid-1950s just before its termination because of financial losses.

Brothers S. L. and Frederick Thorpe began publication of the monthly magazine called *The Home* in Cleveland in January 1874. It was eight folio pages and cost 50 cents a year. The material in *The Home* included various aspects of homemaking and fiction by unknown authors. *The Home* actually sold fairly well until Frederick Thorpe's death in 1877. S. L. Thorpe purchased another Cleveland monthly in 1878 and merged it with *The Home* to become *Home Companion: A Monthly for Young People*. The price was lowered to 35 cents, and the circulation grew to 88,000 by 1879. *Home Companion* became a semimonthly in 1880 at 60 cents a year before being sold by Thorpe to E. B. Harvey and Frank Finn in 1881. After Harvey and Finn launched a different juvenile monthly, they sold *Home Companion* in 1883 to a Springfield, Ohio, publishing firm headed by Phineas Mast and John Crowell.

Mast and Crowell also bought another Cleveland juvenile paper and merged it with *Home Companion*, boasting a circulation of

30,000. After they bought yet another magazine in 1884 and absorbed it into *Home Companion* in 1886, the name was changed to *Ladies' Home Companion*. The magazine was enlarged to 32 quarto pages and was published semimonthly; a yearly subscription cost 50 cents. Editor T. J. Kirkpatrick improved the quality of fiction entries and added several new departments and reprints from other magazines. By 1888, more emphasis on subjects such as food and fashion was complemented with frequent illustrations and serialized fiction. In 1890, the magazine passed the 100,000 circulation figure. Most of the authors in *Ladies' Home Companion* were women. Halftone photographs were introduced in 1894.

Increasingly conscious of its more successful rival, *Ladies' Home Journal* (started in 1883), the *Companion* reverted to a monthly publication schedule in 1896. Soon after becoming editor in 1896, Joseph F. Henderson changed the name again to *Woman's Home Companion* and recruited more women to write on subjects such as education, art, travel, and women's clubs. Even the advertising layouts improved. Circulation climbed to 300,000 in 1898—still only half of the *Journal*'s readership. When Arthur Vance succeeded Henderson as editor in 1900, the magazine became tailored to appeal to all members of the family. Public affairs topics appeared for the first time, especially reform-oriented essays about child labor and sweatshops. Short stories by authors such as Sarah Orne Jewett, Bret Harte, and Jack London found space in the *Companion*.

By 1901, Crowell was the sole owner of the *Companion*, and the editorial offices were removed to New York City. Joseph Palmer Knapp bought the majority stock in the Crowell company in 1906 for $750,000. Frederick Collins replaced Vance as editor during 1906 and added prominent names to the list of contributors, including Edward Everett Hale and Margaret Sanger. Special editions of the *Companion* appeared on Valentine's Day and Easter as well as one for the spring fashion review.

Gertrude Battles Lane joined the staff of the *Companion* in 1903 as the household editor. Publisher Knapp promoted Lane to editor in 1911, replacing Collins. Lane held that position for the next 29 years. Circulation in 1911 totaled a healthy 727,000, but by the end of Lane's tenure in 1940, it had grown to 3.5 million. At that point, the *Companion* edged ahead of competition such as *Ladies' Home Journal* and *McCall's*. Lane visualized the American woman as industrious, intelligent, curious, and anxious to acquire more leisure time. Editor Lane recruited female fiction writers such as Edna Ferber, Dorothy Canfield Fisher, Willa Cather, Ellen Glasgow, Pearl Buck, and Kathleen Norris to contribute to the *Companion*. The magazine's regular features included sections on fashion and beauty, homemaking, food, gardening, marriage and romance, teens and children, and public affairs. Lane's Better Baby Bureau promoted improved health care for children. In 1935, Lane established a panel of 2,000 subscribers to render opinions on contemporary issues. The editors tapped the interests of women from these polls, and the identified issues became the basis for many articles in the magazine.

Veteran *Companion* staffer Willa Roberts succeeded Lane as editor in 1941. During World War II, the *Companion* sent Doris Fleeson to Europe as a war correspondent. Edward Anthony became publisher of the *Companion* in 1943 and began changing the format to include editorials and articles on current events, social issues such as juvenile delinquency and racial strife, and international relations. Managing editor William Birnie became editor in 1943 and started employing former newspaper reporters to pursue exposés about social issues such as crime and divorce. The shift to nonfiction was complemented with regular opinion polls.

In 1953, Birnie became publisher at the height of the *Companion*'s success, and Woodrow Wirsig moved to editor. The new emphasis was on colorful articles dealing with technological advances for the home, and fiction and nonfiction essays shrank in number. Circulation climbed from 3.7 million in 1946 to 4.3 million in 1953, and advertising revenues brought in just under $12 million in 1953.

The impressive figures could not be maintained due to rising expenses and mismanagement. In 1956, the *Companion* fell from second to third place after *Ladies' Home Journal* and *McCall's*, and revenues dropped to $9 million. A major advertiser canceled $1 million worth of ads after seeing the poor financial condition of the *Companion*. Editor Wirsig was replaced in 1956 by Theodore Strauss, but no shake-up could revive the magazine. Television in the mid-1950s dealt a heavy blow to many specialized publications such as the *Companion*. The last issue of *Woman's Home Companion* appeared in January 1957, when it met the same end as other Crowell publications, including *Collier's*. The Securities and Exchange Commission investigated Crowell stock trading and imposed penalties on three Wall Street firms. Some observers blamed management at Crowell for siphoning profits from the magazines without making appropriate capital improvements. Others thought that the lack of editorial independence was the key to the failure, but everyone agreed that rising costs had contributed.

World War I

The media initially showed less enthusiasm and interest in World War I than any previous conflict. Few newspapers challenged the official neutrality of the United States before 1917, yet virtually all showed patriotic support for the war effort after United States entry in 1917. Press censorship through the Committee on Public Information and the Sedition Act raised fewer complaints than censorship in any other twentieth-century war. War correspondents covering the fighting for American newspapers performed admirably.

The Progressive Era preceding World War I spurred by the muckraker journalists engaged the public in reform enthusiasm and political action far more than any previous event in American history. The outbreak of what most Americans considered a European conflict in 1914 brought immediate distractions to the domestic agenda. Newspaper publishers assumed predictable positions based upon their heritage—British progeny sympathized with the allied side while German Americans accepted the Central Power versions of the war's origins. Hence, William Randolph Hearst's open Anglophobia made his papers critical of the allied cause while Henry Watterson's *Louisville Courier-Journal* was pro-allied from the outset. Some editors, such as the *New Republic*'s Walter Lippmann, switched from an antiwar position to interventionism after 1917. Yet, most American newspapers, including the *Los Angeles Times, Washington Post, San Francisco Chronicle*, and *Cincinnati Enquirer*, backed President Woodrow Wilson's declaration of neutrality.

Nonetheless, America was drawn inexorably into the conflict. Unlike the Spanish-American War where the yellow press was directly responsible for war agitation, after 1914 large corporations and banks profiting from business with the allied side influenced the political leadership to compromise American neutrality. The New York *Times*, which editorially backed the allied cause, reprinted European belligerent "white papers" giving their explanations for the outbreak of war and justifying their national interests. President Wilson's reelection campaign in 1916 was based in large part upon the phrase "He kept us out of war." Yet the unrestricted German submarine warfare endangering American civilians in the Atlantic became the ultimate reason given by Wilson for a declaration of war against Germany in April 1917.

Just one week after the declaration of war, President Wilson created by executive order the Committee on Public Information to act as a clearinghouse for government news about the war. Experienced journalist George Creel chaired the Committee and was determined to rigorously control media access to war news. Within a month the Committee began issuing its weekly "Official Bulletin," which consisted of summaries of war news and statistics. The Committee also published monographs educating the American people about the issues in the European conflict. There were also periodic press releases for special information from the Committee. The Committee on Public Information worked effectively because the war was brief, most of the media were patriotic, and antiwar sentiments were viewed suspiciously by average Americans. Although incomplete, the Committee's information was accurate.

Concern about enemy espionage and sabotage led Congress to pass the Espionage Act in 1917 to facilitate suppression of such efforts. The Act allowed the Post Office to remove printed material it deemed harmful to the security of the nation. Most of the postal interdictions concerned pacifist or German-American publications such as the *American Socialist* and the Socialist-anarchist journal *The Masses*. Altogether led by Postmaster General Albert Burleson, the Post Office took some action against 75 papers, though only four were suspended. Victor Berger's Socialist Milwaukee *Leader* lost its mailing privileges and Berger was prosecuted for violating the Espionage Act in his antiwar editorials. Publications such as Oswald Villard's New York *Post* and *The Nation* had serious circulation declines because of opposition to the war.

The Sedition Act of 1918 enacted even more stringent restrictions upon free expression by criminalizing language—verbal or written—against the flag, Constitution, government or military. Socialist Party presidential candidate Eugene Debs was convicted of violating the Sedition Act by criticizing allied motives. The author of a letter published in the Kansas City *Star* charging the government used the war to enhance capitalist profits was jailed also. Most officials and media voices defended the harsh measures as necessary during wartime.

American war correspondents were already dispatching reports about the fighting long before the United States declaration of war. Approximately 500 American journalists were in Europe in 1915 and at least 40 directly covered the American forces after 1917. Allied governments such as Britain and France cleverly manipulated American

reporters to favor their war efforts and thereby influence American opinion. Richard Harding Davis sent firsthand reports of major battles in 1914 to the *New York Tribune*. Will Irwin documented the German use of poison gas writing for *Collier's*. Sigrid Schultz of the *Chicago Tribune* and the *New York Times*'s Cyril Brown sent reports from Berlin. Paul Scott Mowrer, working from Paris for the *Chicago Daily News*, became one of the best-known correspondents with Davis. The *New York World*'s Herbert Bayard Swope explored various aspects of military operations. American Expeditionary Forces commander General John Pershing permitted American reporters to visit the front lines rather freely.

General Pershing also allowed the American Expeditionary Forces to establish their own newspaper, *Stars and Stripes*, in February 1918. The eight-page paper was published in Paris and edited by Harold Ross, later editor of *New Yorker*. Ross was assisted by Grantland Rice, later a famous sportswriter, and Alexander Woollcott, soon to make a name in radio broadcasting. *Stars and Stripes* continued publishing for 16 months and included news accounts, editorials, cartoons, and advertising. The *Chicago Tribune* published a military edition in Paris during 1917–1918 for American soldiers. The *Baltimore Sun* produced a military news tabloid printed in the United States and mailed to Maryland GIs in France. The Young Men's Christian Association sponsored military camp newspapers in 38 locations in the United States. *Richmond News-Leader* publisher John S. Bryan coordinated the camp papers.

Reference Crozier, Emmet, *American Reporters on the Western Front, 1914–1918* (1959).

World War II

World War II received the greatest media coverage of any U.S. conflict. The number of overseas correspondents—print and broadcast—grew from about 300 before the war to 2,600 covering the fighting in Europe and the Pacific. The war also gave celebrity status to many journalists, including Margaret Bourke-White, Edward R. Murrow, and Ernie Pyle. Cartoons, photography, and motion pictures played a prominent role in showing the war's impact to Americans. Press censorship by the government was managed effectively through the Federal Communications Commission (FCC), Office of Censorship, and Office of War Information as well as battlefield commanders.

The United States had been in an isolationist mood for almost two decades when World War II began in 1939. Further, the nation's attention had been concentrated for years on the impact of the depression rather than ominous foreign developments. The media's distraction from foreign difficulties roughly paralleled the public's, although many media organizations had full-time correspondents covering European capitals before the war. A minority of the press led by the McCormick-Patterson–owned *Chicago Tribune* and *New York Daily News* continued to advocate U.S. neutrality and isolation until the Japanese attack on Pearl Harbor in December 1941.

Even before the United States entered into the war in 1941, Associated Press and United Press as well as major dailies and radio networks had begun on-the-scene coverage, mostly from London. In 1939, Associated Press had 2,500 stringers to complement seven European bureaus with two dozen correspondents. The *New York Times* also operated seven European bureaus; the *New York Herald Tribune, Chicago Daily News, Chicago Tribune,* and *Christian Science Monitor* each had five European bureaus. Otto Tolischus of the *New York Times*'s Berlin bureau won a Pulitzer in 1940 for covering events during 1939. Associated Press reporter Laurence E. Allen won a Pulitzer for firsthand reports of naval warfare in the Mediterranean during 1941.

At one time or another, about 2,600 correspondents covered the war in Europe, Africa, and the Pacific. Radio broadcasting—a new element in media coverage of the war—featured correspondents such as Columbia Broadcasting System's (CBS's) Charles Collingwood, William L. Shirer in Berlin,

and Edward R. Murrow in London; National Broadcasting Company's (NBC's) Hans Van Kaltenborn; and later in the war, American Broadcasting Company's (ABC's) George Hicks. CBS and Mutual Broadcasting System radio also had broadcasters at the front lines using tape recordings.

Marguerite Higgins of the New York Herald Tribune *was one of the first women to work as a war correspondent.*

Marguerite Higgins, who arrived in Europe during 1944 to cover the end of the war for the *New York Herald Tribune*, represented the new breed of women war correspondents. United Press and Associated Press used women reporters, as did the *Chicago Daily News, Cleveland Plain Dealer,* and *Boston Globe*. Famed photographer-reporter Margaret Bourke-White sent numerous war accounts to *Time* and *Life* magazines. Thirteen Pulitzer Prizes were won by war correspondents and photographers. Among them were Carlos Romulo of the *Herald Tribune*, who reported General MacArthur's retreat from the Philippines in 1942, and

Mark Watson of the *Baltimore Sun*, who won in 1945 for accounts of the 1944 Normandy invasion. Thirty-seven journalists were killed while covering the war.

Ernie Pyle, employed by the Scripps-Howard chain, may have been the best-known U.S. war correspondent. Already an experienced foreign reporter when the war began, Pyle reported the German bombing of London during 1940's Battle of Britain. When U.S. troops arrived in 1942, Pyle traveled with them to battlefields in North Africa, Italy, and France. His realistic writing was especially popular among soldiers. He won a Pulitzer Prize even before he left Europe for the Pacific in late 1944. Pyle was killed covering the Allied invasion of Okinawa in the last weeks of the war.

The official military newspaper *Stars and Stripes*, begun during World War I, became even more important during World War II, publishing European and Pacific editions. Cartoonists gave perhaps the most realistic expression of the difficulties faced by GIs. Pulitzer Prize–winner Bill Mauldin's "Willie and Joe" cartoon characters expertly represented the enlisted man's perspective, along with George Baker's "Sad Sack" and Milton Caniff's "Male Call." The cartoons appeared in the widely read magazine *Yank* as well as in *Stars and Stripes*.

Although levels of cooperation between the media and government were high during World War II, censorship methods were more elaborate than in previous conflicts. For example, since radio broadcasting was a new facet of media coverage, the FCC monitored radio reports in the United States. Immediately after the declaration of war in December 1941, the government created the Office of Censorship headed by former Associated Press editor Byron Price.

The office set standards for voluntary censorship by the press, monitored news accounts both entering and leaving the United States, and supervised all foreign correspondents working in the United States. The annual budget for the Office of Censorship with its 15 regional offices rose above $25 million by 1943, but because the office returned approved material to media organizations fairly quickly, there were few complaints. The office also dispatched thousands of official reprimands to news organizations, however. Battlefield commanders tended to be freer with the information they gave to reporters because they knew that government censors would excise any sensitive material.

The primary task of the Office of War Information created in mid-1942, with operations in the United States as well as overseas, was to coordinate government propaganda, much as the Creel Committee had done during World War I. Former *New York Times* executive Elmer Davis chaired the policy-making committee with three editor-publishers. The Office of War Information's budget slightly exceeded that of the Office of Censorship—$132.5 million over three years, spent mostly in its overseas offices. Broadcasting regulation became a major area of responsibility for the office, and it sponsored the Voice of America radio network. The Office of War Information also maintained a motion picture division that worked with the army to produce patriotic films. Newsreels played in movie theaters became an important source of information about the war for Americans as well as an effective government propaganda technique.

Reference Desmond, Robert, *Tides of War: World News Reporting, 1931–1945* (1984).

Yellow Journalism

Beginning with the advent of the penny press in the 1830s, sensationalism has been a periodic element in U.S. media history. Undoubtedly the most publicized era of sensationalism was the 1890s, when the so-called yellow press used sensational headlines and stories to sell newspapers. Joseph Pulitzer and William Randolph Hearst are most often associated with the yellow press age. The influence of the yellow press was most evident in its ability to lead the United States into the Spanish-American War in 1898.

By the 1890s, technological developments in printing allowed newspapers to gather news and be produced faster and with better-quality print and photographic illustrations. In short, newspapers had become attractive and widely read by all classes of Americans. Newspapers still sold at a very cheap price, meaning that competition for sales was intense in major markets that had several dailies. Yellow journalism, in essence, made sales the priority—ahead of accurate and fair news accounts. Unlike the earlier penny press, the yellow press sometimes resorted to outright fraud and often to unnecessary scare tactics. Moreover, sales focused on street vendors and newsstands rather than on traditional subscribers. Since most of the potential new buyers represented the lower socioeconomic classes, the yellow press gave them entertaining news—crime, violence, and sex.

When William Randolph Hearst purchased the *New York Journal* in 1895, he was determined to challenge the circulation dominance of Joseph Pulitzer's *World*. In 1893, the new five-color presses had been used by Pulitzer's *Sunday World* color supplement, which featured comic strips. The most closely followed comic strip was Richard Outcault's "Hogan's Alley"; it brought working-class tenements to life, especially through the principal character known as the "Yellow Kid." Outcault was one of several *World* staffers hired away by Hearst. Thus, both the *Journal* and the *World* used the "Yellow Kid" as an advertising gimmick; hence the name the yellow press. Pulitzer was forced to cut the *World*'s price to a penny to compete with the *Journal*.

Hearst was particularly adept at using headlines to grab potential readers' attention. Thus, headlines featured exaggerations, half-truths, and innuendo to entice the man on the street to make a purchase. Both the *World* and the *Journal* also engaged in crusades against corruption, emphasizing the powerful establishments—government and business—that exploited the taxpayer-consumer. By 1897, the Sunday editions of the *World* and the *Journal* each sold 600,000 copies.

In 1896, the yellow press seized upon its most popular issue—territorial expansion. The same issue had fueled both the War of 1812 and the Mexican War in the 1840s. In the 1890s, the issue focused on territories outside the bounds of the continental United States, especially in the Pacific and the Caribbean. Beginning with the business and military aims in the Samoan and Hawaiian Islands in the late 1870s, U.S. attention was drawn to the possibility of an overseas empire. U.S. foreign policy before the 1870s had been staunchly isolationist. Increased overseas trade and growth of a modern navy helped change that position.

The convergence of U.S. imperialism and the yellow press occurred in Cuba, starting with an 1895 revolution that aimed for independence from Spain. Cuban-American influence favoring independence was felt in major cities from New York to Miami, led by a Cuban newspaper in New York City. Cubans helped fan the flames of anti-Spanish sentiment by providing U.S. reporters with biased accounts of events in Cuba. When the Spanish government decided on a policy of repression through General Valeriano Weyler in 1896, the stage was set for a unique era in U.S. foreign policy and journalism.

Both the *World* and the *Journal* led U.S. media outlets to cover the Cuban revolt through their own correspondents. Other New York papers with reporters in Cuba were the *Sun* and the *Herald*. Chicago papers that sent reporters to Cuba included the *Tribune, Daily Times*, and *Times-Herald*. The *Boston Herald, San Francisco Chronicle, Milwaukee Sentinel, New Orleans Times-Democrat, Atlanta Constitution*, and *Indianapolis Journal* also provided close coverage. General Weyler gave the U.S. press plenty of material through his arbitrary arrests, torture, and concentration camps. Even the Spanish government recognized the public-relations nightmare, and Weyler was recalled. The *New York Journal* successfully concentrated pressure on Spain to release Evangelina Cisneros, daughter of the Cuban rebel leader, from jail in 1897. A letter from Spain's ambassador to the United States to a diplomat friend in Havana was stolen from the mails and appeared in Hearst's *Journal* in February 1898. The letter made disparaging remarks about the United States and President McKinley, which led to the ambassador's discharge. U.S. public opinion was inflamed against Spain by the yellow press. Finally, the yellow press unduly stimulated U.S. public opinion through charges of Spanish complicity in the 1898 sinking of the United States battleship *Maine* in Havana harbor. "Remember the *Maine*" became the resounding cry heard across the nation as the drumbeat of war accelerated in 1898.

Not all reporters stirred war fever. Early accounts of the Cuban insurrection by the *Herald*'s George Rea and the *World*'s William Shaw Bowen showed skepticism about charges of Spanish repression. However, later reporters such as James Creelman, who worked for both the *World* and the *Journal* in Cuba, and well-known war correspondent Richard Harding Davis provided

fuel for the yellow press fire. Once the fighting began, the 500 reporters, artists, and photographers became war correspondents, following the campaigns with the U.S. military. Hence, war heroes such as Colonel Theodore Roosevelt and Commodore George Dewey gained added luster because reporters and photographers were present to record their exploits for U.S. public consumption. Press coverage and pressures translated directly to the leaders of government—from the president to Congress—throughout the Cuban events. The carryover from the Spanish-American War was the full blossoming of U.S. imperialism with the acquisition of Puerto Rico and the Philippines from Spain, along with the annexation of Hawaii and the subjugation of Cuba itself. The Spanish-American War had proved how powerful the press's influence could become, especially when it resorted to sensationalism for profits.

The Spanish-American War helped sweep other major dailies into the yellow press syndrome. About one-third of the major dailies in 1900 reflected yellow journalism—from Boston to Philadelphia on the East Coast, to Cincinnati and St. Louis in the Midwest, to Denver and San Francisco out West. As Hearst began to build a chain of major city dailies, yellow journalism spread more rapidly. After 1901, the *New York World* began toning down its headlines, leading the yellow press into a decline. It was soon eclipsed by the sensational documentaries of the muckrakers.

See also Hearst, William Randolph; Pulitzer, Joseph.

Reference Wilkerson, Marcus M., *Public Opinion and the Spanish-American War* (1932).

Zenger, John Peter
See Freedom of the Press.

Chronology

1662　Licensing Act passed by English Parliament allows government censorship of printing.

1690　*Publick Occurrences* becomes the first American newspaper, published in Boston by Benjamin Harris, but the colonial government shuts the paper down after one issue.

1694　Parliament refuses to renew the Licensing Act, allowing it to lapse in 1694. Printers could thereafter publish without government authority, and the foundations for freedom of the press were laid.

1704　John Campbell begins publication of the *Boston News-Letter*, America's first continuous newspaper, which ended publication in 1776.

1735　John Peter Zenger of the *New York Weekly Journal* is prosecuted for "seditious libel" but acquitted by a jury, establishing another milestone toward freedom of the press.

1741　Benjamin Franklin publishes America's first magazine, the *General Magazine and Historical Chronicle*, but it fails after six months.

1767　John Dickinson's 14 "Letters from a Farmer in Pennsylvania" are published in the *Pennsylvania Chronicle*, opposing British colonial policies and demonstrating the significance of the media in the revolutionary era.

1770　Isaiah Thomas founds the *Massachusetts Spy*, which becomes the most widely read patriot paper during the Revolutionary War.

1776　Thomas Paine publishes the extremely popular pamphlet *Common Sense*, which influences Congress to issue the Declaration of Independence.

1788　James Madison, Alexander Hamilton, and John Jay author the "Federalist Papers," which are published in New York papers and become the most persuasive arguments for ratifying the Constitution.

1789　Alexander Hamilton founds the *Gazette of the United States*, edited by John Fenno. It is the first of many partisan newspapers in the nation.

1791　The First Amendment to the Constitution protecting freedom of the press and speech is ratified as part of the Bill of Rights.

1798　Federalist Sedition Act violated First Amendment right of freedom of the press, but lapsed in 1801.

Chronology

1811 A steam-driven cylinder printing press is invented in England by Frederick Koenig and improved by David Napier. The first Napier press began operating in New York City in 1825.

1821 The *Saturday Evening Post* begins publication in Philadelphia and becomes the most successful magazine in U.S. history.

1827 John B. Russwurm and Samuel Cornish publish *Freedom's Journal*, the first African-American newspaper.

1831 William Lloyd Garrison founds *The Liberator*, the leading abolitionist newspaper before the Civil War.

1832 Richard Hoe's double-cylinder printing press gives printers twice the capacity of the old Napier press.

1833 Benjamin Day's *New York Sun* launches the mass-audience "penny press" era for daily newspapers.

1835 James Gordon Bennett founds the *New York Herald* and employs more efficient news-gathering techniques.

1839 Frenchman Louis Daguerre invents photography, which eventually revolutionizes U.S. media.

1841 Horace Greeley founds the *New York Tribune* and becomes the best-known journalist in the nation.

1844 Samuel F. B. Morse perfects the telegraph, which allows the rapid transmission of news across the continent.

1848 The Harbour News Association is formed in New York City as forerunner of the Associated Press.

1851 Henry J. Raymond founds the *New York Times*, which soon becomes the most influential national daily.

1855 *Frank Leslie's Illustrated Newspaper* pioneers the application of photographs with woodcut engravings for illustration.

1865 E. L. Godkin founds *The Nation* magazine, which inaugurates the modern news-commentary journal.

1873 *New York Daily Graphic* becomes the first fully illustrated newspaper.

1877 Thomas A. Edison invents the phonograph, which eventually revolutionizes the radio, music, and motion picture industries.

1879 The U.S. Post Office allows magazines to be mailed via inexpensive second-class postage, thereby stimulating mass-audience magazine publication.

1886 Ottmar Mergenthaler's linotype machine casts the first type for the *New York Tribune*.

1888 Thomas A. Edison demonstrates the motion picture camera, which paves the way for the birth of motion pictures beginning in 1896.

1889 Charles Dow and Edward Jones start the *Wall Street Journal*, which eclipses all competition as the premier financial newspaper. In the twentieth century, it will have the largest circulation in the nation.

1895 William Randolph Hearst purchases the *New York Journal* and, in competition with Joseph Pulitzer's *New York World*, launches the era of yellow journalism.

1903 *The Great Train Robbery* by Edwin S. Porter is the first motion picture with a story line.

1906 Pure Food and Drug Act requires "truth in advertising."

1917 The first Pulitzer Prizes in journalism and letters are awarded by Columbia University from a grant provided by Joseph Pulitzer.

The Commission on Public Information headed by George Creel is established to control war information.

American Association of Advertising Agencies founded.

1919 Radio Corporation of America (RCA) is founded and becomes a leader in the development of both radio and television under the guidance of David Sarnoff.

James Medill Patterson founds the *New York Daily News*, beginning the era of "tabloid" journalism in the 1920s.

1920 Detroit's WWJ (owned by the *Detroit News*) and Pittsburgh's KDKA become the first radio broadcasting stations with regular programming.

1922 Motion Picture Producers and Distributors of America founded to establish guidelines for motion picture content.

1923 The American Society of Newspaper Editors issues its "Canons of Journalism" as a code of ethics.

Walt Disney Productions is established and becomes a leader in the production of animated films.

Henry Luce begins publication of *Time*, a new-generation weekly newsmagazine.

1926 The National Broadcasting Company (NBC) is created as the broadcast subsidiary of RCA and establishes the first radio network.

1927 The Columbia Broadcasting System (CBS) is established as a second radio network and becomes competitive under William Paley.

Congress creates the Federal Radio Commission, with authority to license broadcasting stations and set standards.

Al Jolson stars in *The Jazz Singer*, the first motion picture utilizing sound.

1930 A frequency modulation (FM) radio patent is obtained by Edwin Armstrong, but FM radio does not catch on until after World War II.

NBC's station W2XBS begins limited television broadcasts in New York City.

1933 The American Newspaper Guild becomes the first labor organization for professional journalists.

1934 Congress creates the Federal Communications Commission (FCC) to replace the Radio Commission as the government's broadcast licensing and regulatory agency.

1936 Henry Luce begins his pictorial newsmagazine *Life*, which becomes popular immediately.

A. C. Nielsen begins audience ratings system for network broadcast programs.

1943 Edward Noble founds the American Broadcasting Company (ABC) when the government forces the sale of NBC's "blue" radio network.

1945 John Mauchly and John Eckert invent the electronic computer at the University of Pennsylvania.

1947 William Shockley and associates at Bell Laboratories invent the transistor, which replaces vacuum tubes in radios, televisions, and computers.

1948 The three major broadcast networks begin regular television programming.

The first cable television system is started in Astoria, Oregon.

1950 Photographic offset printing technology is invented to replace the old "hot type" produced by linotypes.

1951 The Kefauver Senate hearings on organized crime are televised live with huge local audiences in New York City.

1952 The FCC sets television broadcasting standards, including the new ultrahigh frequency (UHF) channels.

Chronology

1953 Walter Annenberg launches *TV Guide*, which becomes the largest-circulation magazine in the United States by 1974.

1956 Ampex Corporation demonstrates magnetic videotape recording.

1960 The Kennedy-Nixon presidential debates are televised live by the three networks, inaugurating a tradition of broadcasting presidential debates.

1962 The National Aeronautics and Space Administration (NASA) launches the AT&T satellite *Telstar* into orbit, beginning the era of satellite communications as permitted by the Communications Satellite Act.

1964 New York Times *v. Sullivan* limits libel suits involving public officials.

1966 Freedom of Information Act allows media access to government documents.

1969 Television pictures of U.S. astronauts landing on the moon are transmitted to a global audience.

1970 Associated Press becomes the first major media company to use computerized typesetting.

Newspaper Preservation Act allows "joint operating agreements" exemption from the antitrust laws.

1974 The Watergate hearings are televised live by the networks, contributing to the collapse of Richard Nixon's presidency.

Artist-scientist Myron Krueger initiates virtual reality technology at Milwaukee's VIDEOPLACE.

1979 Cable Satellite Public Affairs Network (C-SPAN) and Cable News Network (CNN) begin broadcasting.

CompuServe becomes first public online computer service.

1982 The Gannett Company begins publication of *USA Today*, a national weekday paper using satellite and computer technology.

Steven Spielberg's motion picture *E.T.: The Extra-Terrestrial* grosses $228 million, the largest profits in the history of movies.

1986 Capital Cities media company acquires ABC to form the largest multimedia conglomerate in the United States.

General Electric buys RCA and NBC for $6.6 billion.

1987 Iran-Contra Congressional Hearings televised live.

1991 The Persian Gulf War becomes the most extensively televised conflict in history.

1992 Congress passes the Cable Television Consumer Protection and Competition Act, giving the FCC the right to review cable rate charges.

1995 The O. J. Simpson murder trial in Los Angeles drives the media into the greatest frenzy of sensationalism ever.

Bibliography

Aldridge, Alfred O. *Man of Reason: The Life of Thomas Paine* (Philadelphia: Lippincott, 1959).

Alexander, John K. *The Selling of the Constitutional Convention: A History of News Coverage.* (Madison, WI: Madison House, 1990).

Allen, Frederick L. "Fifty Years of *Scribner's Magazine.*" *Scribner's* 101 (January 1937): 19–24.

Allen, Frederick L. *Harper's Magazine, 1850–1950* (New York: Newcomen Society, 1950).

Ames, William E. *A History of the National Intelligencer* (Chapel Hill: University of North Carolina Press, 1972).

Anderson, Robin. "Oliver North and the News." In Peter Dahlgren and Colin Sparks, eds. *Journalism and Popular Culture* (London: Sage Publications, 1992).

Andrews, J. Cutler. *The North Reports the Civil War.* (Pittsburgh: University of Pittsburgh Press, 1955).

———. *The South Reports the War.* (Princeton: Princeton University Press, 1970).

Ashley, Perry T., ed. *Dictionary of Literary Biography: American Newspaper Journalists, 1690–1872* (New York: Gale, 1985).

Ashley, Perry T., ed. *Dictionary of Literary Biography: American Newspaper Journalists, 1926–1950* (Detroit: Gale, 1984).

Axelrad, Jacob. *Philip Freneau: Champion of Democracy* (Austin: University of Texas Press, 1967).

Bainbridge, John. *Little Wonder, or Reader's Digest and How It Grew* (New York: Reynal and Hitchcock, 1946).

Baker, Ira L. "Elizabeth Timothy: America's First Woman Editor." *Journalism Quarterly* 54 (1977): 280–285.

Baker, Thomas Harrison. *The Memphis Commercial Appeal* (Baton Rouge: Louisiana State University Press, 1971).

Barnouw, Erik. *A History of Broadcasting in the United States.* 3 vols. (New York: Oxford University Press, 1966–1970).

Barnouw, Erik. *Tube of Plenty: The Evolution of American Television* (New York: Oxford University Press, 1975).

Barrow, Lionel C. "'Our Own Cause': *Freedom's Journal* and the Beginnings of the Black Press." *Journalism History* 4 (1977): 118–122.

Bauer, Jack K. *The Mexican War, 1846–48* (New York: Macmillan, 1974).

Baughman, James L. *Henry R. Luce and the Rise of the American News Media* (Boston: G. K. Hall, 1987).

Bayley, Edwin R. *Joe McCarthy and the Press* (Madison: University of Wisconsin Press, 1981).

Bibliography

Becker, Stephen. *Comic Art in America: A Social History of the Funnies, the Political Cartoons, Magazine Humor, Sporting Cartoons, and Animated Cartoons* (New York: Simon and Schuster, 1959).

Becker, Stephen. *Marshall Field III: A Biography* (New York: Simon and Schuster, 1964).

Belville, H. M. *Audience Ratings: Radio, Television, Cable* (Hillsdale, NJ: L. Erlbaum Associates, 1988).

Bennett, W. Lance, and David L. Paletz, eds. *Taken by Storm: The Media, Public Opinion and U.S. Foreign Policy in the Gulf War* (Chicago: University of Chicago Press, 1994).

Berger, Meyer. *The Story of the New York Times, 1851–1951* (New York: Simon and Schuster, 1951).

Berges, Marshall. *The Life and Times of Los Angeles: A Newspaper, a Family and a City* (New York: Atheneum, 1984).

Bessie, Simon M. *Jazz Journalism: The Story of the Tabloid Newspapers* (New York: Dutton, 1938).

Bode, Carl. *Mencken* (Carbondale: Southern Illinois University Press, 1969).

Bok, Edward W. *The Americanization of Edward Bok* (New York: Charles Scribner's Sons, 1920).

Bond, Donovan H., and W. Reynolds McCleod, eds. *Colonial Newsletters to Newspapers* (Morgantown: West Virginia University School of Journalism, 1977).

Britt, George. *Forty Years—Forty Millions, the Career of Frank A. Munsey* (New York: Holt, Rinehart and Winston, 1935).

Brogan, Patrick. *Spiked: The Short Life and Death of the National News Council* (New York: Priority Press, 1985).

Brown, Charles H. *William Cullen Bryant* (New York: Charles Scribner's Sons, 1971).

Bryan, Carter R. "Negro Journalism in American before Emancipation." *Journalism Monographs* 12 (September 1969).

Bumgardner, Georgia, ed. *American Broadsides, 1680–1800* (Barre, MA: Imprint Society, 1971).

Canham, Erwin D. *Commitment to Freedom: The Story of the Christian Science Monitor* (Boston: Houghton Mifflin, 1958).

Carlebach, Michael L. *The Origins of Photojournalism in America* (Washington: Smithsonian Institution Press, 1992).

Carlson, Oliver. *The Man Who Made News* (New York: Duell, Sloan and Pearce, 1942).

Cebula, James E. *James M. Cox: Journalist and Politician* (New York: Garland, 1985).

Chafee, Zechariah Jr. *Government and Mass Communications.* 2 vols. (Chicago: University of Chicago Press, 1947).

Chalmers, David M. *The Social and Political Ideas of the Muckrakers* (New York: Citadel Press, 1964).

Clayton, Bruce. *W. J. Cash: A Life* (Baton Rouge: Louisiana State University Press, 1991).

Cohen, Hennig. *The South Carolina Gazette, 1732–1775* (Columbia: University of South Carolina Press, 1953).

Cooney, John. *The Annenbergs* (New York: Simon and Schuster, 1982).

Cottrell, Robert C. *Izzy: A Biography of I. F. Stone* (New Brunswick, NJ: Rutgers University Press, 1992).

Covert, Catherine L., and John D. Stevens. *Mass Media between the Wars* (Syracuse, NY: Syracuse University Press, 1984).

Crouthamel, James L. *James Watson Webb: A Biography* (Middletown, CT: Wesleyan University Press, 1969).

Dabney, Thomas Ewing. *One Hundred Great Years: The Story of the Times-Picayune from Its Founding to 1940* (Baton Rouge: Louisiana State University Press, 1944).

Dabney, Virginius. *Richmond: The Story of a City* (Charlottesville: University of Virginia Press, 1990).

DeArmond, Anna J. *Andrew Bradford: Colonial Journalist* (Newark: University of Delaware Press, 1949).

Dennis, Everette E., and William L. Rivers. *Other Voices: The New Journalism in America* (San Francisco: Canfield, 1974).

Desmond, Robert. *Tides of War: World News Reporting, 1931–1945* (Iowa City: University of Iowa Press, 1984).

Dillon, Merton L. *The Abolitionists: The Growth of a Dissenting Minority* (DeKalb: Northern Illinois University Press, 1974).

Douglas, Sara. *Labor's New Voice: Unions and Mass Media* (Norwood, NJ: Ablex, 1986).

Ellis, L. Ethan. *Newsprint: Producers, Publishers, Political Pressures* (New Brunswick, NJ: Rutgers University Press, 1960).

Elson, Robert T. *Time, Inc.* 2 vols. (New York: Atheneum, 1968–1973).

Emery, Edwin. *History of the American Newspaper Publishers Association* (Minneapolis: University of Minnesota Press, 1949).

Field, Harry, and Paul F. Lazarsfeld. *The People Look at Radio* (Chapel Hill: University of North Carolina Press, 1946).

Foner, Eric. *Tom Paine and Revolutionary America* (New York: Oxford University Press, 1976).

Foner, Philip S. *Frederick Douglass: A Biography* (New York: Citadel Press, 1963).

Fox, Stephen. *The Mirror Makers: A History of American Advertising and Its Creators* (New York: Morrow, 1984).

French, Blaire Atherton. *The Presidential Press Conference: Its History and Role in the American Political System* (Washington, DC: University Press of America, 1982).

Friedrich, Otto. *Decline and Fall* (New York: Harper and Row, 1970).

Gale, Stephen H., ed. *Encyclopedia of American Humorists* (New York: Garland, 1988).

Gelatt, Roland. *The Fabulous Phonograph, 1877–1977*. 2d ed. (New York: Macmillan, 1977).

Ghiglione, Loren, ed. *The Buying and Selling of America's Newspapers* (Indianapolis: Berg, 1984).

Goldberg, Vicki. *Margaret Bourke-White: A Biography* (New York: Harper and Row, 1986).

Gordon, Gregory, and Ronald E. Cohen. *Down to the Wire: UPI's Fight for Survival* (New York: McGraw-Hill, 1990).

Gramling, Oliver. *AP: The Story of News* (New York: Holt, Rinehart and Winston, 1940).

Grunig, James E., and Todd Hunt. *Managing Public Relations* (New York: CBS College Publishing, 1984).

Gutierrez, Felix. "Spanish-Language Media." *Journalism History* 4 (1977).

Hallin, Daniel C. *The "Uncensored War": The Media and Vietnam* (New York: Oxford University Press, 1986).

Harlan, Robert D. "David Hall and the Stamp Act." *Papers of the Bibliographical Society of America* 61 (1967): 13–37.

Harpole, Charles, ed. *History of the American Cinema*. 3 vols. (New York: Charles Scribner's Sons, 1990).

Hart, Jim Alle. *A History of the St. Louis Globe-Democrat* (Columbia: University of Missouri Press, 1961).

Hatchen, William A., ed. *The Supreme Court on Freedom of the Press: Decisions and Dissents* (Ames: Iowa State University Press, 1968).

Hess, Stephen, and Milton Kaplan. *The Ungentlemanly Art: A History of American Political Cartoons*. Rev. ed. (New York: Macmillan, 1975).

Hill, George H. *Airwaves to the Soul: The Influence and Growth of Religious Broadcasting in America* (Saratoga, CA: R. and E. Publishers, 1983).

Hitchings, Sinclair. "A Broadside View of America." *Lithopinion* 5, no. 1 (Spring 1970): 65–71.

Hoffer, Thomas W. *Animation: A Reference Guide* (Westport, CT: Greenwood, 1981).

Hohenberg, John. *The Pulitzer Prizes* (New York: Columbia University Press, 1974).

Howe, M. A. D. *The Atlantic Monthly and Its Makers* (Boston: Atlantic Monthly Press, 1919).

Bibliography

Jamieson, Kathleen Hall, and David S. Birdsell. *Presidential Debates: The Challenge of Creating an Informed Electorate* (New York: Oxford University Press, 1988).

Johnson, Gerald W., et al. *The Sunpapers of Baltimore* (New York: Alfred A. Knopf, 1937).

Johnson, Icie F. *William Rockhill Nelson and the Kansas City Star* (Kansas City: Burton, 1935).

Johnson, Michael L. *The New Journalism* (Lawrence: University of Kansas Press, 1971).

Judis, John B. *William F. Buckley, Jr.: Patron Saint of the Conservatives.* (New York: Simon and Schuster, 1988).

Juergens, George. *Joseph Pulitzer and the New York World* (Princeton, NJ: Princeton University Press, 1966).

Keeler, Robert F. *Newsday: A Candid History of the Respectable Tabloid* (New York: William Morrow, 1990).

Keller, Morton. *The Art and Politics of Thomas Nast* (New York: Oxford University Press, 1968).

Kenny, Herbert A. *Newspaper Row: Journalism in the Pre-Television Era.* (Chester, CT: The Globe Pequot Press, 1987).

Kerns, Robert L. *Photojournalism: Photography with a Purpose* (Englewood Cliffs, NJ: Prentice Hall, 1980).

Kluger, Richard. *The Paper: The Life and Death of the New York Herald Tribune* (New York: Alfred A. Knopf, 1986).

Kobre, Sidney. "The First American Newspaper: A Product of Environment." *Journalism Quarterly* 17 (1940): 335–345.

Kramer, Dale. *Ross and the New Yorker* (Garden City, NY: Doubleday, 1951).

Kreig, Andrew. *Spiked: How Chain Management Corrupted America's Oldest Newspaper* (Old Saybrook, CT: Peregrine Press, 1987).

Lacy, Stephen, and Todd F. Simon. *The Economics and Regulation of United States Newspapers* (Norwood, NJ: Ablex, 1993).

Leab, Daniel J. *A Union of Individuals: The Formation of the American Newspaper Guild, 1933–1936* (New York: Columbia University Press, 1970).

Leapman, Michael. *Arrogant Aussie: The Rupert Murdoch Story* (Secaucus, NJ: Lyle Stuart, 1984).

Lemay, J. A. Leo, ed. *The Oldest Revolutionary: Essays on Benjamin Franklin* (Philadelphia: University of Pennsylvania Press, 1976).

Lent, John A. *Newhouse, Newspapers, Nuisances: Highlights in the Growth of a Communication Empire* (New York: Exposition Press, 1966).

Levy, David W. *Herbert Croly of the New Republic* (Princeton, NJ: Princeton University Press, 1985).

Levy, Mark R. *The VCR Age: Home Video and Mass Communication* (Newbury Park, CA: Sage, 1989).

Lewis, Anthony. *Portrait of a Decade: The Second American Revolution.* (New York: Bantam Books, 1965).

Lichty, Lawrence W., and Malachi C. Topping, eds. *American Broadcasting: A Sourcebook on the History of Radio and Television* (New York: Hastings House, 1975).

Lindley, William R. *Journalism and Higher Education* (Stillwater: Journalistic Services, 1976).

Loeffler, Carl E., and Tim Anderson, eds. *The Virtual Reality Casebook* (New York: Van Nostrand Reinhold, 1994).

Lutz, William W. *The News of Detroit* (Boston: Little, Brown and Company, 1973).

Luxon, Norval Neil. *Niles' Weekly Register* (Baton Rouge: Louisiana State University Press, 1947).

Lyon, Peter. *Success Story: The Life and Times of S. S. McClure* (New York: Charles Scribner's Sons, 1963).

Lyons, Eugene. *David Sarnoff: A Biography* (New York: Harper and Row, 1966).

Lyons, Louis M. *Newspaper Story: One Hundred Years of the Boston Globe.* (Cambridge: Harvard University Press, 1971).

McKee, John DeWitt. *William Allen White: Maverick on Main Street* (Westport, CT: Greenwood Press, 1975).

McLuhan, Marshall, and B. R. Powers. *The Global Village: Transformations in the World Life and Media in the 21st Century* (New York: Oxford University Press, 1989).

McLynn, Frank. *Stanley: The Making of an African Explorer* (London: Constable, 1989).

Marks, Leonard H. "Communication Satellites: New Horizons for Broadcasters." *Journal of Broadcasting* 9 (1965): 97–101.

Meek, Phillip J. *Fort Worth Star-Telegram* (New York: Newcomen Society, 1981).

Meggs, Philip. *A History of Graphic Design* (New York: Van Nostrand Reinhold, 1983).

Miller, William D. *A Harsh and Dreadful Love: Dorothy Day and the Catholic Worker Movement* (New York: Liveright, 1973).

Mills, George. *Harvey Ingham and Gardner Cowles, Sr.: Things Don't Just Happen.* (Ames, IA: Iowa State University Press, 1977).

Moore, William Howard. *The Kefauver Committee and the Politics of Crime* (Columbia: University of Missouri Press, 1974).

Moran, James. *Printing Presses* (Berkeley: University of California Press, 1973).

Morris, Joe Alex. *Deadline Every Minute: The Story of the United Press* (New York: Doubleday, 1957).

Morrison, Joseph L. *Josephus Daniels: The Small-d Democrat* (Chapel Hill: University of North Carolina Press, 1966).

Munson, Wayne. *All Talk: The Talkshow in Media Culture* (Philadelphia: Temple University Press, 1993).

"NBC: 50th Anniversary; Spearhead of Broadcast Industry Marks Beginning." *Television/Radio Age* 24 (21 June 1976).

Nerone, John C. "The Mythology of the Penny Press." *Critical Studies in Mass Communications* 4 (1987): 376–404.

Nevins, Allen. *The Evening Post: A Century of Journalism* (New York: Boni and Liveright, 1922).

Notson, Robert C. *Making the Day Begin: A Story of* The Oregonian (Portland: Oregonian, 1976).

O'Brien, Frank M. *The Story of the Sun.* Rev. ed. (New York: Appleton-Century-Crofts, 1928).

O'Connor, Richard. *Heywood Broun: A Biography* (New York: G. P. Putnam's Sons, 1975).

Ogden, Rollo. *Life and Letters of Edwin Lawrence Godkin* (New York: Macmillan, 1907).

Oppenheimer, Jerry. *Barbara Walters: An Unauthorized Biography* (New York: St. Martin's Press, 1990).

Paltsits, Victor H. "New Light on 'Publick Occurrences.'" *American Antiquarian Society Proceedings* 5 (1949): 75–88.

Parsons, Patrick. *Cable Television and the First Amendment* (Lexington, MA: Lexington Books, 1987).

Perkin, Robert L. *The First Hundred Years: An Informal History of Denver and the* Rocky Mountain News (Garden City, NY: Doubleday, 1959).

Pfaff, Daniel W. "Race, Libel and the Supreme Court." *Columbia Journalism Review* 8 (Summer 1969): 23–26.

Phelps, Timothy M., and Helen Winternitz. *Capitol Games: Clarence Thomas, Anita Hill, and the Story of a Supreme Court Nomination* (New York: Hyperion Press, 1992).

Pickett, Calder M. *Ed Howe: Country Town Philosopher* (Lawrence: University of Kansas Press, 1968).

Pilat, Oliver. *Drew Pearson: An Unauthorized Biography* (New York: Harper and Row, 1973).

Pitts, Alice Fox. *Read All About It—Fifty Years of the ASNE* (Reston, VA: American Society of Newspaper Editors, 1974).

Powell, Hickman. "Collier's." *Scribner's Magazine* (May 1939): 19–23.

Quinlan, Sterling. *Inside ABC: American Broadcasting Company's Rise to Power* (New York: Hastings House, 1979).

Rader, Benjamin G. *In Its Own Image: How Television Has Transformed Sports* (New York: The Free Press, 1984).

Ray, W. B. *FCC: The Ups and Downs of Radio-TV Regulation* (Ames: Iowa State University Press, 1990).

Rees, David W. E. *Satellite Communications: The First Quarter Century of Service* (New York: Wiley, 1990).

Reisig, Robin. "The Feminine Plastique." *Ramparts* (March 1973): 25–29, 55–59.

Roberts, Chalmers M. *The Washington Post: The First 100 Years* (Boston: Houghton Mifflin, 1977).

Robinson, Phyllis C. *Willa: The Life of Willa Cather* (Garden City, NY: Doubleday, 1983).

Saalberg, Harvey. "The Canons of Journalism: A 50-Year Perspective." *Journalism Quarterly* 50 (1973): 731–734.

Sanders, Marion K. *Dorothy Thompson: A Legend in Her Time* (Boston: Houghton Mifflin, 1973).

Sass, Herbert R. *Outspoken: 150 Years of the News and Courier* (Columbia: University of South Carolina Press, 1953).

Schultze, Quentin J. *Televangelism and American Culture: The Business of Popular Religion* (Grand Rapids, MI: Baker Book House, 1991).

Schuneman, R. Smith. "Art or Photography: A Question for Newspaper Editors in the 1890s." *Journalism Quarterly* 42 (1965): 43–52.

Schwarzlose, Richard A. "Early Telegraphic News Dispatches: Forerunner of the AP." *Journalism Quarterly* 51 (1974): 595–601.

Sharpe, Ernest. *G. B. Dealey of the Dallas News* (New York: Henry Holt, 1955).

Shaw, Archer H. *The Plain Dealer* (New York: Alfred A. Knopf, 1942).

Shipton, Clifford K. *Isaiah Thomas: Printer, Patriot, and Philanthropist* (Rochester, NY: Leo Hart, 1948).

Simmons, Steven J. *The Fairness Doctrine and the Media* (Berkeley: University of California Press, 1978).

Singleton, L. A. *Telecommunications in the Information Age.* 2d ed. (Cambridge, MA: Ballinger, 1986).

Smiley, Nixon. *Knights of the Fourth Estate: The Story of the Miami Herald* (Miami: E. A. Seeman, 1974).

Smith, Anthony. *Goodbye Gutenberg: The Newspaper Revolution of the 1980s* (New York: Oxford University Press, 1980).

Smith, James Eugene. *One Hundred Years of Hartford's Courant* (New Haven: Yale University Press, 1949).

Smith, James Morton. *Freedom's Fetters: The Alien and Sedition Laws and American Civil Liberties* (Ithaca, NY: Cornell University Press, 1956).

Smith, Sally Bedell. *In All His Glory: The Life of William S. Paley* (New York: Simon and Schuster, 1990).

Smith, William E. "Francis P. Blair, Pen-Executive of Andrew Jackson." *Mississippi Valley Historical Review* 17 (1931): 543–556.

Smyth, Albert Henry. *The Philadelphia Magazines and Their Contributors, 1741–1850* (Philadelphia: R. M. Lindsay, 1892).

Sobel, Robert. *RCA* (New York: Stein and Day, 1986).

Sperber, Ann M. *Murrow: His Life and Times* (New York: Freundlich Books, 1986).

Steel, Ronald. *Walter Lippmann and the American Century* (Boston: Little, Brown and Company, 1980).

Steele, Janet E. *The Sun Shines for All: Journalism and Ideology in the Life of Charles A. Dana* (Syracuse, NY: Syracuse University Press, 1993).

Stephens, Mitchell. *A History of News: From the Drum to Satellite* (New York: Viking Press, 1988).

Sterling, Christopher H. "Trends in Daily Newspaper and Broadcast Ownership, 1922–70." *Journalism Quarterly* 52 (1975): 247–256, 320.

Stevens, John D. "Congressional History of the 1798 Sedition Law." *Journalism Quarterly* 43 (1966): 247–256.

Stickney, William, ed. *Autobiography of Amos Kendall* (Boston: Lee and Shepard, 1872).

Stone, Melville E. *Fifty Years as a Journalist.* (Garden City, NY: Doubleday Books, 1921).

Stonecipher, Harry W. *Editorial and Persuasive Writing: Opinion Functions of the News Media.* (New York: Hastings House, 1979).

Swanberg, W. A. *Citizen Hearst* (New York: Charles Scribner's Sons, 1961).

Swanberg, W. A. *Pulitzer* (New York: Charles Scribner's Sons, 1967).

Talese, Gay. *The Kingdom and the Power* (New York: New American Library, 1969).

Tebbel, John W. *George Horace Lorimer and The Saturday Evening Post* (Garden City, NY: Doubleday, 1948).

Thomas, John L. *The Liberator: William Lloyd Garrison* (Boston: Little, Brown and Company, 1963).

Trimble, Vance H. *The Astonishing Mr. Scripps: The Turbulent Life of America's Penny Press Lord* (Ames: Iowa State University Press, 1992).

Van Deusen, Glyndon. *Thurlow Weed: Wizard of the Lobby* (Boston: Little, Brown and Company, 1947).

Wainwright, Loudon. *The Great American Magazine: An Inside History of Life* (New York: Alfred A. Knopf, 1986).

Wall, Joseph F. *Henry Watterson: Reconstructed Rebel* (New York: Oxford University Press, 1956).

Wells, Robert W. The Milwaukee Journal: *An Informal Chronicle of Its First 100 Years* (Milwaukee: Milwaukee Journal, 1981).

Wendt, Lloyd. *Chicago Tribune: The Rise of a Great Newspaper* (Chicago: Rand McNally, 1979).

Wendt, Lloyd. *The Wall Street Journal* (Chicago: Rand McNally, 1982).

White, Theodore H. *Breach of Faith—The Fall of Richard Nixon* (New York: Atheneum, 1975).

Whited, Charles. *Knight: A Publisher in the Tumultuous Century* (New York: Dutton, 1988).

Wilensky, Harry. *The Story of the* St. Louis Post-Dispatch (St. Louis: St. Louis Post-Dispatch, 1981).

Wilkerson, Marcus M. *Public Opinion and the Spanish-American War* (Baton Rouge: Louisiana State University Press, 1932).

Williamson, Samuel T. *Imprint of a Publisher: The Story of Frank Gannett and His Newspapers* (New York: R. M. McBride, 1948).

Wilson, Harold S. McClure's Magazine *and the Muckrakers* (Princeton, NJ: Princeton University Press, 1970).

Wittke, Carl. *The German Language Press in America* (Lexington: University of Kentucky Press, 1957).

Wolseley, Roland E. *The Black Press, U.S.A.* (Ames, IA: Iowa State University Press, 1971).

Yoakam, Richard D., and Charles F. Cremer. *ENG: Television News and the New Technology.* 2d ed. (Hightstown, NJ: McGraw-Hill, 1989).

Index

Index

Index

Index

Index

Index

Voice of America, 317
Wade, Harry V., 73
Wagner, Jacob, 301
Wagner, Lee, 286
Walker, David, 3, 94
Walker, John B., 63
Wall Street Journal, 33, 42, 167, 258, 297–298
Wallace, DeWitt, 241–242
Wallace, Tom, 10
Wallach, W. D., 304
Walson, John, 35
Walter, Basil, 44
Walters, Barbara, 8, 298–300
Waples, Paul, 88
War of 1812, 42, 92, 166, 196, 300–301
Ward, Artemus (Charles F. Browne), 53, 138
Waring, Thomas R., 43
Warner, Charles D., 61
Warner Brothers, 8, 12, 149, 151, 212
Washington Daily News, 262–263
Washington Globe, 19–20, 115
Washington Journalism Review, 171
Washington Post, xii, 37, 58, 126, 135, 167, 194, 203, 227, 282, 293, 301–304, 305–306, 314
Washington Star, 50, 85, 166, 263, 302–303, 304–305
Washington Times/Times-Herald, 153–154, 203, 303
Washington Union, 145
Watergate Hearings, 305–306
Watson, Ebenezer, 61
Watson, Mark, 317
Watterson, Henry, 76, 129–130, 234, 314
Waymack, W. W., 72
Weaver, Sylvester L., 163
Webb, James Watson, 19, 306–308
Webster, Noah, 76, 308–309
Wechsler, James, 177
Weed, Thurlow, 309–311
Weeks, Edward, 16
Welles, Orson, 57, 150, 237
Western Union, 13, 25, 257, 276
Westinghouse Electric Company, 162, 212, 228, 235, 239, 278
Westwood One, 162, 163
Weyl, Walter, 173–174
Wheeler, John, 46
White, E. B., 140
White, Horace, 47, 175–176
White, Paul, 57
White, Robert M., 183
White, Theodore H., 128

White, William Allen, 85, 136, 259, 311–312
Whitechapel Club, 221
Whitehead, Don, 118
Whitemarsh, Thomas, 264
Whitney, John Hay, 183
Whittemore, George, 42
Whittier, John Greenleaf, 16
Wicker, Tom, 179, 293
Wilcox, Grafton, 183
Williams, John L., 246
Williams, Montel, 275
Williams, Nick, 129
Willington, Aaron S., 42, 188
Wilson, Edmund, 174
Wilson, Richard, 72
Winchell, Walter, 146, 273
Winfrey, Oprah, 275
Winship, Laurence, 22
Winship, Tom, 23
Winslow, E. D., 24
Winston-Salem Journal-Sentinel, 247
Winter, William, 182
Wirsig, Woodrow, 313–314
Wisner, George, 205
Wolfe, Tom, 171
Woman's Home Companion, 56, 85, 312–314
Women's National Press Club, 85
Woo, William F., 254
Wood, J. Howard, 48
Woods, William S., 127
Woodward, Robert, 303
Woollcott, Alexander, 57, 185, 315
Working Man's Advocate, 121
World War I, 29–30, 44, 92, 193, 259, 314–315
World War II, 26, 37, 44, 57, 70, 193, 315–317
Wortham, Louis J., 88
Wright, Henry J., 10
Yank, 317
Yeardon, Richard, 42
Yellow journalism, 22, 37, 105–107, 233, 268, 319–320
Yost, Casper S., 10, 252
Young, Chic, 38
Young, Lafayette, 72
Young, Owen D., 162, 235, 238
Zenger, John Peter, 91–92
Ziegler, Ron, 223
Zuckerman, Mortimer, 16, 288–289
Zukor, Albert, 149
Zworykin, Vladimir, 278